APPLYING KARNATIC RHYTHMICAL TECHNIQUES TO WESTERN MUSIC

This important study provides a comprehensive view of one of the richest rhythmic traditions in the world. Built on sustained experiential learning, Karnatic rhythm provides an almost scientific investigation of rhythmic possibility, something which, through dedication and long study, Rafael Reina is especially able to convey and invoke. His is a study from a Western musician, and the double benefit of this book is that he is then able to demonstrate the efficacy and inspiration that a Karnatic approach to rhythm and rhythmic structure can bring to Western music, showing both how it can enhance performance and learning techniques, and also be a source for the composer of intriguing and reframing compositional devices.

Peter Wiegold, Brunel University, UK

Applying Karnatic Rhythmical Techniques to Western Music

RAFAEL REINA
Amsterdam Conservatoire, The Netherlands

Routledge
Taylor & Francis Group
LONDON AND NEW YORK

First published 2015 by Ashgate Publishing

Published 2016 by Routledge
2 Park Square, Milton Park, Abingdon, Oxon OX14 4RN
711 Third Avenue, New York, NY 10017, USA

Routledge is an imprint of the Taylor & Francis Group, an informa business

British Library Cataloguing in Publication Data
A catalogue record for this book is available from the British Library

The Library of Congress has cataloged the printed edition as follows:
Reina, Rafael, 1961-
Applying Karnatic rhythmical techniques to Western music / by Rafael Reina.
pages cm
Includes index.
ISBN 978-1-4724-5149-1 (hardcover) -- ISBN 978-1-4724-5150-7 (pbk) 1. Carnatic music--Theory. 2. Tala. 3. Music--Indic influences. I. Title.
MT6.R333A67 2015
780.954'091821--dc23

2014033492

ISBN 9781472451491 (hbk)
ISBN 9781472451507 (pbk)

Bach musicological font developed by © Yo Tomita

Contents

Instructions to Access Online Material *vii*
Acknowledgements *ix*
Glossary of Karnatic Terms *xi*

Introduction 1

PART I DESCRIPTION OF KARNATIC CONCEPTS AND TECHNIQUES

A: Foundations 11

1 The Tala System 13

2 Gatis 21

3 Jathis 35

4 Gati Bhedam 45

5 Rhythmical Sangatis 61

6 Jathi Bhedam 69

7 Introduction to Anuloma-Pratiloma 81

B: Exclusively Creative Techniques 91

8 Mukthays 93

9 Yati Phrases 105

10 Yati Mukthays 113

11 Tirmanas 123

12 Compound Mukthays 129

13 Yatis Prastara 135

14 Double and Triple Mukthays 141

15 Mukthay Combinations 147

16 Poruttam A 161

17 Moharas 173

C: Motta Kannakku 181

18 Nadai Bhedam 183

19 Mixed Jathi Nadai Bhedam 205

20 Combinations Anuloma-Pratiloma 213

21 Derived Creative Techniques 245

D: Recent Developments 253

22 Tala Prastara 255

23 Further Development of the Mukhy System 271

24 Latest Developments of Gatis 289

PART II PEDAGOGICAL AND CREATIVE APPLICATIONS TO WESTERN MUSIC

25 Application of Karnatic Techniques to Existing Western Pieces 321

26 Analysis of Students' Pieces 365

Conclusion *443*

Appendix: Sources of Information *451*

Index *457*

Instructions to Access Online Material

Audio tracks

While reading the book, open the website which has links to all audio tracks:

http://www.rafaelreina.org/book-online-material.html

Right click on the relevant track to open it in a new browser tab or window. The track will play automatically.

Pedagogical and Curricular Applications

http://www.rafaelreina.org/pedagogical-weekly-schedule.html

This document has a dual purpose:

- It proposes a five-year weekly schedule that can be of great help to musicians wishing to establish a regular practice routine.
- It can provide a solid architecture to anyone qualified to teach this material, in terms of how much time each topic needs to be practised and the step-by-step process required.

Karnatic Metronome

http://www.rafaelreina.org/karnatic-metronome.html

This metronome, created by Jos Zwaanenburg at the Amsterdam Conservatoire, can also be of great help when practising the techniques and concepts described in this book.

Acknowledgements

This book is the result of over 20 years of research, teaching, composing and experimenting with the material. Trying to thank everyone who has somehow supported me throughout these years would be an impossible task. Therefore I would like to acknowledge those who have actively participated in one way or another to finalise this text.

On the western front, firstly I would like to thank Michiel Schuijer for fighting to get me some (much-needed) financial support to do the research and writing, and Peter Wiegold for helping me with his deep and constructive tips. My deepest gratitude goes to Jos Zwaanenburg for his immense patience; for his help with many of the recordings and audio editing; for resolving many doubts about Sibelius; and for providing a huge number of examples of contemporary music for analysis (and for advising me to watch more *Monty Python* when things looked a bit dark over all those years). I wish to show my deep appreciation to David de Marez Oyens for providing numerous jazz pieces (and corresponding audio files). Thanks also to both for proof-reading the whole book (not an easy task).

My gratitude to Luis Nesvara for also proof-reading this text without knowing anything about karnatic music! Thanks so much to Ere Lievone for his invaluable help with many transcriptions (and making the corresponding Sibelius files) as well as to Robbert van Hulzen for his transcription of the N.G. Ravi solo. My gratitude also goes to Andys Skordis, Hans Leeuw and Louis Aguirre for writing for this project, and to all the students who performed their pieces so enthusiastically and willingly. Also my deepest gratitude goes to the Ashgate Publishing team who believed in this project from the very beginning, and guided me through every step in the journey to publication: Heidi Bishop (publisher), Emma Gallon (assistant editor) and Kevin Selmes (production editor). Last but not least, I thank my wife, Vanessa Goad, for her infinite patience with my exuberance regarding anything karnatic and/or South Indian, for her editing work to improve my non-native English and for her constant support, regardless of circumstances.

On the Indian front, I want to thank B.C. Manjunath for his teaching, inspiration and recordings (many of them in very uninspiring circumstances); N.G. Ravi and A.R.A.K. Sharma for transmitting so much knowledge; and so many amazing karnatic musicians and non-musicians who have, directly or indirectly, helped me learn so much about their culture. They include T.N. Seshagopalan, Mysore Brothers, Karaikkuddi Mani, Dr. Balamuralikrishna, Rajakeishari, Hari, Kalavathy, Jayaprakash, Bhanu and Shri Mataji Nirmala Devi, just to mention a few.

This book is dedicated to the memory of Jahnavi Jayaprakash, my main teacher between 1993 and 2002, for her knowledge; for accepting me as part of her family; for her willingness to go the extra mile in every demand I made; and for respecting what I wanted to do with karnatic music. Meeting her changed my life and the life of many others.

The research that took place between 2010 and 2013 was made possible with financial support from the Amsterdamse Hogeschool voor de Kunsten (AHK) and the Conservatorium van Amsterdam.

The composition by Louis Aguirre was funded by the Danish Statens Kunstfond and the Danish Composers' Society.

Glossary of Karnatic Terms

The use of many karnatic terms is inevitable considering the nature of this book. I have tried to use English terms wherever feasible to make the text as understandable as possible. However, either certain terms lack a clear translation or the translation falls short of the many implications or ramifications of the term.

Many terms are confined to a specific chapter: these do not form part of this glossary since they can be understood by reading that chapter. However, many other terms appear quite often and in different chapters. This glossary thus presents a concise definition of those terms to help the reader remember their meanings without having to refer back and forth.

Angas: Construction blocks of different sizes with which a *tala* is structured.

Anudrutam: One of the *angas* of a *tala.* One beat long. It is shortened to 'A'.

Anuloma: When the number of *matras* in a beat are doubled, tripled or quadrupled.

Balamuralikrishna: Great singer and composer from South India who revolutionised many concepts of karnatic music from the 1960s onwards.

Bhedam: Literally 'change through destruction'; when applied to music, it implies that a concept is modified in some way.

Combinations anuloma-pratiloma: Whenever an *anuloma* speed is inserted within any *pratiloma* speed or frame; also, when a frame is not expressed in quarter notes.

Compound mukthay: A ready-made *mukthay* that uses two *gatis* and different types of augmentation on a 'seed' phrase.

Chapu tala: Folkloric type of *tala*; fast tempo and odd number of beats.

Chatusra: One of the *gatis*; the same as a duplet in western music.

Damaruyati: One of the six types of *yati phrases.*

Drutam: One of the *angas* of a *tala.* Two beats long. It is shortened to 'D'.

Gati: Subdivision of the beat into an equal number of units called *matras*. Four are frequently used, with three being of recent usage.

Gati bhedam: When the phrase is constructed around the *jathi* applied on a *gati*.

Gopuchayati: One of the six types of *yati phrase*.

Jathi: A systematic accent applied to a *gati*. In a wider sense, it is essentially any accent, and in specific contexts can also be understood as a phrase.

Jathi bhedam: Sequence of irregularly distributed accents whose goal is to provide the illusion of a continuous change of metres within the *tala*.

Jati laghu: The number of beats that this *anga* (*laghu*) takes in a *tala*. It could be 3, 4, 5, 7 or 9.

Kala: Literally means beat; it is also a system of counting *shadanga talas*.

Khanda: One of the *gatis*; the same as a quintuplet in western music.

Konnakkol: see *Solkattu*.

Krama: The original exposition of any musical object.

Kriya: Conducting pattern made up of a combination of hand gestures and finger-counts.

Laghu: One of the *angas* of a *tala*. It could be 3, 4, 5, 7 or 9. It is shortened to 'L'.

Laya: It refers to tempo, but can also be pulse or the underlying *gati* over which different techniques can be used.

Matra: Every unit of a *gati*.

Misra: One of the *gatis*; the same as a septuplet in western music.

Mixed jathi nadai bhedam: It is a technique whereby two different accents alternate systematically whilst a constant *nadai* is superimposed on each frame (this frame is provided by the alternating accents).

Mohara: A creative technique where every conceivable parameter is based on, or has as the most important element, the number 4 or 8.

Mohara (mixed gati): A very intricate variation on a regular *mohara* in which two gatis are alternating throughout the eight cycles that the sequence usually lasts.

Motta kannakku: Any kind of superimposition or any 'irregular grouping' that is smaller or bigger than a beat.

Mridangamyati: One of the six types of *yati phrase.*

Mukhy system: System designed by Dr *Balamuralikrishna* in order to reintroduce the *shadanga tala*. It also refers to the regroupings of the inner structure of one of these *talas*.

Mukthay: One of the largest chapters in karnatic music theory; essentially, it is a phrase that is repeated three times, usually separated by a gap, that resolves on *tala sam*. However, there are quite a few variations on this basic definition.

Mukthay combination: In a very strict sense this is a sequence that takes as its starting point a double or triple *mukthay* and 'repeats' it three times.

Nadai: The superimposed *gati* on the frame provided by a *gati/jathi* combination.

Nadai bhedam: A technique that embodies the concept of polypulse par excellence by superimposing a *gati* on the frame provided by a *gati/jathi* combination. It should always have a preparation, development and resolution.

Pala: Name given to any phrase of a *mukthay* or *yati phrase.*

Poruttam: A simple definition would be a sequence of at least 3 cycles of a *tala*, in which fragments of the theme are interwoven with different rhythmical techniques.

Pratiloma: When the number of *matras* in a *gati* is spread throughout 2, 3, 4, 5, 6 or 7 beats.

Purandaradasa: First-known karnatic theoretician, who in the sixteenth century systematised the *suladi talas* and the *janaka ragas.*

Purvanga: First part of a *tirmana* sequence.

Rhythmical sangati: Refers to when a phrase that has previously been performed in one *gati* is realised or 'transformed' into a different *gati*.

Sam: The first beat of every *anga.*

Sama mukthay: A phrase (*pala*) that is repeated three times, usually separated by a gap, that starts and finishes on *tala sam.*

Samayati: One of the six types of *yati phrase.*

Sankirna: One of the *gatis*; the same as a nonuplet in western music.

Shadanga tala: The old *tala* system that was employed for many centuries before *Purandaradasa* elaborated and implemented the *suladi tala* around the sixteenth century. Since the 1960s it has been the system that has inspired musicians to produce more 'experimental' music.

Solkattu: Also called *konnakkol*, this is the name given to the syllables used to 'sing' a rhythmical phrase. Every karnatic musician 'sings' a phrase using a combination of syllables that would feel suitable for the given phrase before setting any melody to it.

Srotovahayati: One of the six types of *yati phrase.*

Sub-mukthay: A phrase that is fragmented into two cells and follows the specific pattern of **AB** (gap) **AB** (gap) **B** (gap) **B**|*tala sam.*

Suladi tala: The system of *talas* that *Purandaradasa* elaborated in the sixteenth century.

Tala: The metric container, the framework wherein all the rhythmical concepts and techniques explained in this book are utilised.

Three-fold mukthay: A phrase conceived in two or (mostly) three different *gatis*, usually separated by a gap.

Tirmana: A phrase of 3, 4, 5, 6 or 7 notes in which each note is separated from another by the same number of *matras*.

Tisra: One of the *gatis*; the same as a triplet in western music.

Uttaranga: Second part of a *tirmana* sequence.

Vakra: Random permutation of a previous sequence, as long as the derived sequence is comprised of clearly differentiated steps or phrases.

Viloma: Reverse order of any previous phrase or of a sequence with several steps.

Yati phrase: Sequence of phrases in which the first phrase (*pala*) forms the nucleus of the sequence. Every subsequent *pala* takes the previous one as a starting point, applying a systematic increase or decrease to the number of *matras*.

Yati mukthay: In this sort of *mukthay* the number 3 is intertwined with the *yati* concept of systematic increase or decrease of a musical parameter.

Yatis prastara: A technique whereby two different *yati phrases* intermingle. Each *pala* of one *yati phrase* alternates with another *pala* of a different *yati phrase*.

Introduction

Summary

My research addresses ways in which the karnatic rhythmical system can enhance, improve or even radically change the teaching of rhythmical solfege at a higher-education level and how this learning can influence the creation and interpretation of complex contemporary classical and jazz music.

Since 1995 I have taught a programme at the Amsterdam Conservatoire based on extended research I conducted between 1993 and 1997 in all aspects of karnatic music. The present book is the result of re-examining and deepening the material learnt throughout that initial period and, further, during various trips to South India made in 2010–12.

One of the main goals of the research and subsequent explanation of the different techniques is to use the architecture and skeleton of this musical culture not only to improve, modify, enhance or even replace the current rhythmical solfege system imparted in music centres all over the West, but also to increase the array of tools, awareness and accuracy among musicians to perform western complex composed or improvised music. I have developed these ideas into a book that aims to:

- Systematise those rhythmical karnatic devices which can be considered sufficiently universal to be integrated with western classical and jazz aesthetics, so there is finally a comprehensive and complete text providing access to many rhythmical elements used in karnatic music;
- Provide a methodology for how these devices can be practised and taught within a western framework in order to enhance enormously the current western solfege rhythmical system;
- Explain how these techniques can be used as a source of creative ideas for composers and improvisers;
- Demonstrate every step of every technique, with the aid of recordings made especially for this purpose;
- Analyse sections of existing contemporary repertoire (both classical and jazz) where karnatic techniques can be used to perform passages with more accuracy and understanding, or where parallels with karnatic concepts can be established.
- Provide analyses and audio recordings of scored and improvised pieces created by three composition students.[1]

[1] All performers and composers are or have been students of my programme at the Conservatoire.

Research Topic

The expansion of rhythmical possibilities has been one of the cornerstones of musical development in the last 100 years, whether through western development or borrowings from non-western traditions. Most classical performers, whether in orchestral or ensemble situations, will at some stage have to face a piece by Ligeti, Messiaen, Varèse or Xenakis, to mention just a few well-known composers, while improvisers face music influenced by Dave Holland, Steve Coleman, Aka Moon, Weather Report or elements from the Balkans, India, Africa or Cuba. Furthermore, many creators, whether from the classical or jazz world, are currently organising their music not only in terms of pitch content but also by rhythmical structure, and are eager to obtain information that would structure and classify rhythmical possibilities in coherent and practicable ways.

One of the triggers that led me to embark upon creating the present text was an interview with Pierre Boulez that I came across a few years ago. I felt I had acquired a knowledge that could eventually lead to bridge what he mentions as one of the main obstacles to communication between composers and the public. In that interview Boulez said:

> For me, what still has to be acquired is the degree of precision you need from an orchestra. This is not only because I am obsessed by precision, but also because the orchestral sonority changes completely. The clarity is suddenly there; you can really hear the score as it is written. Sometimes with a piece of Stockhausen, Berio or myself, the precision is not in the performer's head before playing. As a conductor I have to be demanding. If you have sixteen violins playing a quintuplet (which is, by the way, something quite easy compared to a lot of music composed after 1950), they have to really be thinking a quintuplet. The kind of tempo modulation you have in Elliot Carter's music – well, it has to be very precise or otherwise is not effective. This type of precision is still not really a musician's habit, shall we say [...] .
>
> If the rhythms and phrasing that are peculiar to contemporary music would be taught in the best conservatories in an intensive way, the future of contemporary music would certainly change and performers and [the] general public would really start enjoying pieces by Berio, Xenakis or myself. The lack of accuracy in orchestras is the biggest obstacle for communication between composers and [the] public.[2]

I will argue that today's music demands a new approach to rhythmical training, a training that will provide musicians with the necessary tools to face with accuracy

[2] 'Pierre Boulez the Composer and Musician's Musician', interview by Jed Distler in August 2000 with composer/conductor Pierre Boulez. http://www.andante.com/article/article.cfm?id=12737.

more varied and complex rhythmical concepts, while keeping the emotional content.

The incredible wealth of rhythmical techniques, devices and concepts; the different types of *tala* construction; the use of rhythm as a structural and developmental element; the use of mathematics to sometimes very sophisticated levels in South India. All these enable the western musician to improve and enhance their accuracy and/or their creative process, and make the study of karnatic rhythm a fascinating adventure of far-reaching consequences. The large variety of rhythmical devices used in karnatic music is, in the West, one of the least known and least documented elements, yet potentially the most universal.

After many years teaching and experimenting with these concepts in my own music, I have refined my knowledge into what can be divided into 'local' and 'universal' techniques. The former implies, for example, ways of using rhythm to accompany the melody within a tala, or phrases that are a means and an end in themselves and that are very 'aesthetically charged'. They are, however, of no relevance to the aim of this book. Universal techniques, on the other hand, are those concepts which have a clear set of rules that enable musicians to elaborate their own phrases and combinations, stripped of any cultural context. They can also be used to establish a methodology for studying and approaching rhythm and rhythmical complexities. The latter forms the cornerstone of this book, since a system as complete, compact, consistent and far-reaching as the one used in South India has no equivalent in western musical cultures.

Through my research and through collaboration with Jahnavi Jayaprakash (who came to the Amsterdam Conservatoire to give seminars between 1998 and 2002) and B.C Manjunath (between 2003 and 2011), I have been able to assemble a body of practical devices, all of which can, on the basis of my experience and research, greatly influence the thinking and development of western music. This has involved a sifting of techniques: there are many devices used quite often in South Indian music which are not relevant to my project; similarly, there are concepts used by only a handful of extremely good musicians in South India which can have enormous potential within a western context.

The reader may wonder why karnatic rhythmical structures, rather than any other non-western culture, can have this enormous potential (or not to the same extent). Reflecting on my previous studies of Flamenco, Berber, African, Turkish and Maghreb music cultures in the light of my knowledge of karnatic music, I have come to the conclusion that any rhythmical technique in these cultures can be studied using names and applications within karnatic music. While many karnatic music principles are unique to South Indian culture, many are susceptible to use in completely different contexts. The three main differences at a rhythmical level between karnatic music and other non-western music are as follows.

- The role of the percussion in karnatic music is generally very active, providing layers of polyrhythms and polypulses rather than providing a sort of 'mattress' for the melody or outlining the *tala* or metre. The most plausible explanation for this difference is the fact that in every concert of karnatic music there is always someone 'conducting' (keeping *tala*) and thus providing the musicians with a visual reference of the metre.

- While accompanying or soloing, the percussionist can elaborate phrases and frames of a high rhythmical complexity, always keeping in mind that any development needs to have a common denominator. This point will be a very important issue in the book, as it is probably the element that enables the karnatic musician to study highly complex material and, simultaneously, to relate rhythmic relationships (3:5, 15:16 etc.) to a wide array of specific concepts for how these can be developed and combined.
- All musicians undergo strict rhythmical training, with instrumentalists reciting each phrase many times with the so-called *solkattu* (set of rhythmical syllables) before they add a melody to it.

An account of this strict and deep rhythmical training forms the basis of the book. During my musical studies in South India, I concluded that musicians' methodology could be divided into the way lessons are imparted and the methodology of the content. The former is diametrically opposed to the western way of teaching,[3] although the stereotype in the West of the 'old guru teaching a disciple', for example, while still part of the learning process in India, now exists alongside university studies.

A study of the methodology of the content is at the very heart of my research: how karnatic musicians practise the elements, how these elements are interwoven and how one technique is the basis for a more advanced technique.

Publications and Written Material

A majority of the books available on Indian music are dedicated to North Indian music, a very different musical culture to that of South India: in particular concerning form, raga development and, foremost, rhythmical devices and their development. Most publications produced in the West are more raga or melody-oriented, and the few books that try to offer an overview of rhythm cover only a small part of the four-year programme, 'Contemporary Music through Non-Western Techniques', which I teach at the Amsterdam Conservatoire. In a prolonged and intense search for written material covering what I was taught, I have found nothing that properly describes, elaborates and analyses the variety of rhythmical concepts used by karnatic musicians and, more importantly, how these techniques could be the basis for a fundamental change in the way we can teach and conceive rhythm in the West.

There are three main types of written source material.

[3] A more elaborate explanation of the difficulties of obtaining the right information from Indians will be presented later in this introduction.

- Books written in vernacular languages (Tamil, Kannada etc.). These tend to be very practical but inaccessible to the western musician, since there are no translations into English.
- Books written by Indians in English. These tend to be very specific, focusing on one particular aspect, and are basically for musicians who already know the background information regarding the particular subject. Two considerable obstacles for most western musicians are the fact that they do not posses this information and that Indian writers use exclusively Indian terms for every musical and emotional concept. In order to read any of these books, I had to learn at least 2,000 words, compared to the 150–200 Indian terms I teach my students.
- Books written by westerners. The few books trying to offer an overview of rhythm usually provide rather superficial explanations of one or two types of tala construction, giving only the very basics. Importantly, they omit any explanation about the most complex concepts that, though more rarely used in South India, are of great interest for westerners as tools enabling them to approach complex composed or improvised contemporary music.

There is no book in the West that would explain all these devices used in karnatic music. No text provides a complete explanation of the techniques and their construction, developmental rules etc. The goal of this book is thus to create such a text, presenting systematically in one document the results of almost two decades of research, along with over 20 years' experience of teaching and composing with these elements. This text will include:

- all the main rhythmical techniques, concepts and devices in karnatic music that are suitable to be used within a western contemporary composed or improvised framework;
- an explanation of each technique, describing it and distinguishing it from other similar devices;
- written examples in western notation, together with an explanation of how to express the karnatic principles within a notation that tries to fuse the best of both worlds;
- an account of how these techniques, stripped of any cultural or aesthetic element, can be practised by and taught to western musicians;
- a link to 262 audio tracks and to a 'karnatic metronome'.

My intention has been to explore the subject as comprehensively as possible, since this work is the first step in bringing the rich possibilities of karnatic rhythmical structures to the attention of western musicians. In India many of the techniques are taught orally, and although no written information is available, most musicians know the techniques through their professional practice. In the West all these techniques need to be compiled and explained so that musicians can have at their disposal a clear, complete and comprehensive summary of techniques, a clear and complete guide that will enable classical performers, improvisers, composers, future solfege teachers and students to use these techniques and their methodology to greatly improve their rhythmical skills.

However, *it cannot be stressed enough*: the way the concepts and techniques are explained in this book differ greatly from the way karnatic music is taught in South India, whether to Indians or westerners.

As mentioned previously, the main source of information for any student is lessons with their 'guru'. The lessons are always addressed at performers, and all techniques are imparted by first teaching phrases that the student will practise without knowing the theoretical backbone that enables their creation. Only in an ulterior stage *may* the student learn this theory (and not always), but with many aesthetic connotations and, I would daresay, conditionings.

In my case, as a composer, I was not willing to go through the extremely lengthy process of learning how to sing or how to play a percussion instrument (all of them requiring great technical complexity). This made the process for my teachers and for myself quite problematic and laborious, since there is no methodology to explain only concepts, and certainly not in the way the reader will find in this book. Therefore, alongside my studies I had to resort to listening to many recordings, reading numerous books and asking the same question many times and in many different ways in order to conclude something concrete. The bottom line is that, despite the amazing mathematical and logical Indian mind, many social and cultural differences have formed a way of explaining not only music but essentially anything that is diametrically opposed to the general western way. It was only during my third visit to India that I began to fully realise this difference and understand what to ask and how to phrase questions in order to receive an answer I could understand.

Consequently, what is set out here is by no means the way I received the information. *Rather, it is the distillation of a long-lasting process of analysis and comparison of karnatic material, along with a translation of these concepts for a western mind.*

The Book's Structure

My decision was to separate as far as possible the description of karnatic techniques and concepts from their possible application to western music, both pedagogically and creatively. Thus, the book is divided into two parts. The first presents a description of karnatic concepts and techniques, subdivided into four sections that share a common denominator: 'Foundations', 'Exclusively Creative Techniques'[4], 'Motta Kannakku' and 'Recent Developments'. The second part is

---

[4] Musicians who are only interested in improving their rhythmical skills but not interested in creating with this material can omit this second section.

similarly divided across two large chapters: 'Applications to Western Pieces' and 'Analysis of Students' Creations'.

Notwithstanding the above, a neat and complete separation of both 'worlds' has not been entirely possible. Often it was necessary to resort to certain comparisons between karnatic and western music for a better understanding of a particular point. The most extreme case can be found in Chapter 4, *Gati Bhedam*, where I needed to devote more than half of the chapter to explain the alternative notation that permeates techniques where crossing accents is the core concept. Without this explanation at that particular point, the presentation of many subsequent transcriptions would have been impossible.

An important recommendation needs to be made: the 262 recorded tracks provide the 'flesh and bones' of the text. Reading the book without listening to the tracks can result in a drier experience, more theoretical in nature. However, by listening to the examples, the reader's experience will undoubtedly be a completely different one.

Practice Method

Many chapters contain a practice method section which provides a practical and analytical methodology for western musicians to master karnatic concepts and techniques. Each practice method provides a step-by-step explanation of how to approach the daily practice of the main techniques, along with recordings and examples for almost every step. Musicians should take into consideration that, depending on intensity of practice and musical background, each technique could take a few weeks to several months to master.

The goal of these techniques is to develop a higher degree of accuracy and awareness of rhythmical complexities (without losing feeling) in order to perform music of the twentieth and twenty-first centuries that use these complexities in any shape or form.

The use of a metronome at all times is of utmost importance in order to achieve the desired level of performance as well as to improve the sense of *inner pulse*. The latter is essential if the musician wishes to achieve the level of independence required to perform all the concepts that go against the beat, as well as for playing in an ensemble or orchestral situation where different tempi/metres, or the illusion of them, work together. In addition, computer aid can be of great help for most techniques as an intermediate step to achieving this aim, especially for topics using superimposition (see the karnatic metronome).[5]

A practice methodology for techniques covered in Part I Section B ('Exclusively Creative Techniques') such as yati phrases or mukthays is not explained because they are creative concepts that branch out of the fundamental rhythmical

[5] This karnatic metronome can be found along with the audio files, and can be downloaded for practice purposes.

techniques. For instance, in order to perform a yati phrase the required technique would be jathi bhedam (see Chapter 6), and anyone wishing to perform a 3-fold mukthay will need to master gati bhedam.

PART I
Description of Karnatic Concepts and Techniques

A: Foundations

The following seven chapters expound the main concepts, the primary building blocks from which every other technique, principle or concept – whether pedagogical or creative – is derived or drawn. Together these concepts constitute the essential pedagogical tools that every karnatic musician has to master before facing any ulterior technique or concept.

At the same time, each concept can already be used creatively, since a separation between pedagogical techniques and creative techniques is unimaginable to a karnatic musician; they are simply two sides of the same coin.

Chapter 1
The Tala System

Tala is the metric container, the framework wherein all the rhythmical concepts and techniques that will be explained in this book are utilised, and the common reference point for all music layers employed in karnatic music.

Simply put, tala can be translated as metre. The main (and far-reaching) difference with western metre is that karnatic talas are constructed following specific and strict rules, and that the inner construction derived from these rules really do have a decisive effect on many musical decisions as to where phrases or techniques should start or finish.

The main role of the tala is to provide regularity to all performers so that the continuous illusion of tempo and metre changes that the many techniques provide has a constant common denominator throughout a piece of music.[1] Indeed, except for a form called *talamalika* and operas or dance programmes, the tala and tempo in karnatic music never changes in a piece. This allows the proliferation of a multitude of techniques that work against the beat or tempo, many times in different layers. Therefore, karnatic musicians prefer this regularity and common reference that the tala provides rather than changing metres and tempos during a composition or improvisation.

There are several types of tala in karnatic music, each with its own set of construction rules:

Suladi	Chapu	Shadanga	Shoshadanga
Janaka	Dhruvarupaka		

The most common construction used for the last six centuries in South India is suladi, and shadanga is the one employed quite often by innovative musicians. Chapu talas are taken from folk music (they will be described at the end of this chapter). Shoshadanga, janaka and dhruvarupaka are 'branches' of shadanga and will be discussed in Chapter 22 on *tala prastara*.

Suladi Talas

The construction of suladi talas responds to combinations of three *angas*. A ready-made English translation for the word *anga* does not exist, 'construction blocks of

[1] See the 'Concept of Cycle' later in the chapter for a deeper explanation of the concept of 'regularity'.

different size' being the closest one can get to its actual meaning. The conventions pertaining to every anga are as follows:

- *Anudrutam*: 1 beat long. It can be used once or not at all. It has to be preceded or followed by a *drutam*, and it can never be the first or last anga of a tala.
- *Drutam*: 2 beats long. It can be used once, twice or not at all. In order to use it, at least one *laghu* has to be used in the construction of the tala.
- *Laghu*: This can be 3, 4, 5, 7 or 9 beats long. It can be used once, twice or three times. Once a number of beats has been chosen for a laghu, this number has to remain for every laghu of the tala (this is called *jati laghu*). Therefore, a laghu of 4 beats cannot coexist with a laghu of 3, 5, 7 or 9 beats. Each jati laghu has a specific name:

# Beats per laghu	Jati laghu name
Three	Tisra jati
Four	Chatusra jati
Five	Khanda jati
Seven	Misra jati
Nine	Sankirna jati

From these explanations it can be deduced that, hypothetically, the shortest tala would be 3 beats long (using only one laghu of 3 beats) and the longest would utilise 3 laghus of 9 beats each, 2 drutams and 1 anudrutam. This would produce a tala of 32 beats. For instance, a tala of 7 beats could be constructed in the following ways:[2]

L3 D D   L4 A D   L5 D   L7

However, it could not be constructed following these patterns:

L3 A L3, because there is no drutam to precede or follow the anudrutam;
L5 A A, because there are 2 anudrutams (1 is the maximum allowed), and one of them is the last anga;
D A D D, because there are 3 drutams (2 is the maximum) and no laghu;
L4 L3, because there are two different jati laghus.

However, just by following the rules scrupulously hundreds of talas could mathematically be constructed by combining these three angas. Yet, this is not the case in karnatic music.

---

[2] From now on, the following abbreviations will be used: Laghu: L, Drutam: D, Anudrutam: A These abbreviations differ from those used in South Indian books which, personally, I find it too cumbersome.

Categories

In the sixteenth century a composer and performer named Purandaradasa (1484–1564) organised into concrete systems talas and ragas that at the time existed in rather confused ways and varied, sometimes radically, almost from village to village.

During his time the shadanga talas were the ones used commonly but, according to various sources, developments took place in such a way that made these talas unmanageable.[3] Purandaradasa decided to unify the extreme differences into one system that could be known to all musicians, and invented seven categories or combinations out of the myriad possibilities that the theory explained above could provide. These seven combinations or categories of suladi talas are:

Dhruva:	L D L L
Matya:	L D L
Rupaka:	D L
Jhampa:	L A D
Triputa:	L D D
Ata:	L L D D
Eka:	L

Because laghu varies its number of beats through its five jatis, five separate talas are derived from each of the seven categories. Table 1.1 shows the 35 talas that Purandaradasa invented and which became the system that is now used in no less than 70 per cent of music created in South India.

Table 1.1 Chart of 35 Suladi Talas

	Category	**Jati**	**Angas**	**Name**	**# Beats**
1	Dhruva__________	Tisra	L3 D L3 L3	Mani	11
2	-----	Chatusra	L4 D L4 L4	Srikara	14
3	-----	Khanda	L5 D L5 L5	Pramana	17
4	-----	Misra	L7 D L7 L7	Purna	23
5	-----	Sankirna	L9 D L9 L9	Bhuvana	29
6	Matya__________	Tisra	L3 D L3	Sara	8
7	-----	Chatusra	L4 D L4	Sama	10
8	-----	Khanda	L5 D L5	Udaya	12
9	-----	Misra	L7 D L7	Urdina	16
10	-----	Sankirna	L9 D L9	Rava	20
11	Rupaka__________	Tisra	D L3	Chakra	5
12	-----	Chatusra	D L4	Patti	6
13	-----	Khanda	D L5	Raja	7
14	-----	Misra	D L7	Kula	9
15	-----	Sankirna	D L9	Bindu	11

[3] A historical background and some reasons why the talas became 'unmanageable' will be given in Chapter 22, dedicated to this type of tala.

Table 1.1 *Concluded*

	Category	Jati	Angas	Name	# Beats
16	Jhampa	Tisra	L3 A D	Kadamba	6
17	-----	Chatusra	L4 A D	Madhura	7
18	-----	Khanda	L5 A D	Chana	8
19	-----	Misra	L7 A D	Sura	10
20	-----	Sankirna	L9 A D	Kara	12
21	Triputa	Tisra	L3 D D	Sankha	7
22	-----	Chatusra	L4 D D	Adi	8
3	-----	Khanda	L5 D D	Dushkara	9
24	-----	Misra	L7 D D	Lila	11
25	-----	Sankirna	L9 D D	Bhoga	13
26	Ata	Tisra	L3 L3 D D	Gupta	10
27	-----	Chatusra	L4 L4 D D	Lekha	12
28	-----	Khanda	L5 L5 D D	Vidala	14
29	-----	Misra	L7 L7 D D	Loya	18
30	-----	Sankirna	L9 L9 D D	Dhira	22
31	Eka	Tisra	L3	Sudha	3
32	-----	Chatusra	L4	Mana	4
33	-----	Khanda	L5	Rata	5
34	-----	Misra	L7	Raga	7
35	-----	Sankirna	L9	Vasu	9

A tala of 15, 19, 21, 24, 25, 26, 27, 28 or longer than 29 beats could never be used according to the conventions of suladi tala organisation. Nevertheless, when other tala types are described these and many other talas will come under its scope.

Influence of Talas on Musical Development

There are many techniques that serve the purpose of articulating the tala. Phrasing around the strong points of the tala is the one most often used. The strong points of a tala are:

- the downbeat of the tala: tala *sam*
- the downbeat of an anga: anga sam, usually adding the name of the anga (drutam sam, laghu sam etc.).

However – and possibly due to the fact that in karnatic music there is always a 'conductor' (someone *keeping tala*) – this type of music has developed much more in the way western music has from the end of nineteenth century onwards. The metre is a framework that does not need to be articulated by means of patterns, vamps or repetitive melodies or phrases in any instrument. A wide range of music cultures shape a metre or tala in these ways. But the fact that karnatic music is always conducted (including solos) enables the musicians to develop ideas in a much more abstract way, frequently producing polyrhythms and polypulses between the melodic layer and the percussion layer. But, despite this fact, there are ways to create material that works around the inner division of the tala.

- The main melody or the commencing cycles of the percussion are usually built around or articulating the tala.
- In the development of a piece, whenever a polyrhythm or polypulse of any kind is used between two layers, the resolving points should always be a tala or anga sam.
- A phrase cannot stop in the middle of an anga. Once a phrase starts, it needs to continue until at least the next sam of the tala.

At this point it would be futile to give all the techniques that are influenced by the inner construction of a tala. Suffice to say for now that there is a constant tension–relaxation in the development of a piece: the tension is provided by techniques that go against the pulse whilst the relaxation is provided by phrasing around the tala and all layers along the pulse.[4] Karnatic musicians do not feel the need for the tala to be continuously 'recognisable' by a listener.

Tempo

The concept of tempo – called *laya* in karnatic music – is very straightforward. Tempo indications are never written, the sole indications being:

- vilamba laya: slow tempo (usually ♩=20–ca. 46)
- madhya laya: medium tempo (usually ♩=ca. 48–ca. 66)
- druta laya: fast tempo (anything above 70 but rarely going above 130, the exception being with chapu talas).

Notwithstanding this, laya has also two other meanings: pulse and underlying gati over which different techniques are used.[5] In the suladi tala system, tempos ranging from ♩=30 to 54 are the most commonly used, but it is not rare to hear pieces set in ♩=20.

The Concept of Cycle

The real meaning of tala is not metre but cycle (*avartana*). The whole socio-cultural Hindu background inherited in the music created a concept that separates itself from our (i.e. western) concept of metre – although, in fact, the concept of

---

[4] When relevant and necessary it will be explained how certain techniques need this inner division in order to create musical events or organise material.

[5] For the concept of gati, see Chapter 2.

cycle is common to all eastern musical cultures, from Morocco to Vietnam, in very similar ways. In the West the closest notion to a cycle can be found in the 12-measure round of blues, the 32 bars (with the A A B A shape) of the swing era and, ultimately, in many of the canons and fugues of Bach and his contemporaries.

Where then is the line that separates cycle from metre? I do not think that a concrete set of rules can be given in Aristotelian fashion, as opposed to most of the concepts and techniques that will be described in this book. A cycle is, somehow, a recurring frame that is born, develops and dies. There is a certain 'narrative' quality to it, a quality that generally lacks the western construction of metres. The length of the tala and tempo are two important parameters that help create the impression of 'larger and recurrent segments of music'.

1. Short talas tend to group in larger groups in which an idea is explored and resolved. Long talas (usually from 10 beats upwards) tend to resolve any musical event every one, two or, at maximum, three cycles. Any technique is always thought of within the boundaries of a cycle or number of cycles, even if this technique may give the impression (until its resolution) that the tempo and/or the metre have been changed.
2. Tempo is possibly the element that enables the musician or listener to create or hear the feeling of a larger and recurrent fragment of music; but this never implies that the musical content is repeated to convey a feeling of cycle. It is the fact that any musical idea or development will always be resolved at regular intervals in time. A cycle will always possess this aspect of regularity.

However, it is my perception that the concept of cycle is not a technical one that can be dissected and regulated; it somehow belongs to the realm of 'feeling' or 'intuition'. There is a Vedantic concept that, I believe, can illustrate to a large extent this 'realm of intuition'. The concept is called *pragnya* and could be summarised as follows:

> Pragnya is the flash of intuition that comes from clarity of mind. An enlightened person comes to know things he never thought he knew. As soon as the question flashes the answer is there, coming from a deeper field of intuitive wisdom where the ordinary mind cannot reach.

I do not mean to infer that only an 'enlightened person' can understand and feel what a cycle is. Many artists, scientists and so on experience this 'flash of intuition'. My sole intention is to give a 'philosophical' framework to illustrate the fact that the concept of cycle goes beyond any rationale and is, ultimately, a personal experience.

For a long time I (and many of my students) thought we understood this concept and we were using it. However, it was not until a few years after incorporating karnatic techniques into my music that this 'flash of intuition' allowed me to 'feel' the concept and start using it in a completely different way. Therefore, since the intuitive understanding of the concept of cycle is an empirical process, in my view and experience analysing or dissecting the concept of cycle in a Cartesian manner will always fall short of the complexity, extent and nuances of this concept, which is closer to a philosophical notion than to a musical technique.

Tala Conducting

In karnatic parlance conducting is called *keeping tala*, and the way to be reckoned or conducted is called *kriya*. Musicians always keep tala by beating their hands and fingers against their lap or knee, sometimes producing some noise. These are the different ways to keep tala, depending on the type of anga:

- Anudrutam: hand down;
- Drutam: hand down followed by hand up, except if the drutam is the last anga of the tala, in which case the hand will create a wave to its right as to signal the last beat of the tala;
- Laghu: hand down followed by *finger counts*. Fingers hit the thumb, the lap or knee, replacing the movement of the whole hand. Most musicians start counting from the pinkie (little) finger, going towards the right.
  - 3 beats: hand down followed by 2 finger counts
  - 4 beats: hand down followed by 3 finger counts
  - 5 beats: hand down followed by 4 finger counts
  - 7 beats: hand down followed by the pinkie, moving towards the right and using the thumb to signal the 6th beat of the laghu; the pinkie is used again for the 7th beat
  - 9 beats: follow the same way of counting as with 7, adding the ring and index fingers for the 8th and 9th beats respectively

Chapu Talas

These are talas borrowed from folk music. They are fast in tempo and reckoned with clapping on the lap on the divisions shown below. No angas are used, the tala sam being the only resolving point for all devices and phrasing. There are four varieties:

- Tisra chapu: 1+2
- Khanda chapu: 2+1+2
- Misra chapu: 3+2+2 (sometimes vice versa)
- Sankirna chapu: 2+2+3+2

For instance, a khanda chapu would have 3 claps while conducting (on the 1st, 3rd and 4th beats), and the 2nd and 5th beats will be silenced. Depending on the tempo a khanda chapu tala, for instance, could be notated in western music as 5/8 or 5/16.

Chapter 2
Gatis

Gati is the name given to the subdivision of the beat into an equal number of units called *matras*. The beat can be divided into five different gatis:

Tisra (triplets):	3 matras
Chatusra (duplets):	4 matras
Khanda (quintuplets):	5 matras
Misra (septuplets):	7 matras
Sankirna (nonuplet):	9 matras, always divided 4+5 or vice versa.[1]

For exercise purposes, every gati has an assigned set of syllables (called *solkattu* or *konnakkol*), used to help the musician better internalise the gatis. The syllables assigned to every gati are:

Tisra:

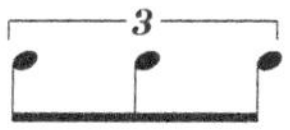

ta - ki - da

Chatusra:

ta - ke - di - mi

When 2 beats of chatusra are sung consecutively, it is customary to use the syllables

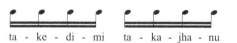

ta - ke - di - mi ta - ka - jha - nu

Khanda:

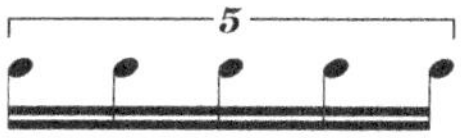

ta - di - ghi - na - to

Misra:

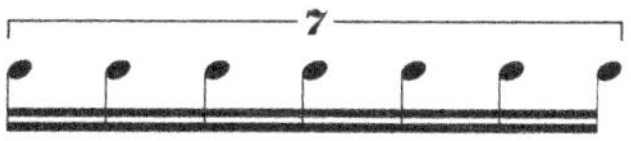

ta - ki - da - ta - ke - di - mi

or *ta–ke-di-mi-ta-ki-da* can also be used.

[1] Sankirna will be covered in a separate chapter due to its special characteristics. For the purposes of explaining and describing the various rhythmical devices of karnatic music, only four gatis will be used.

The four gatis look like this:

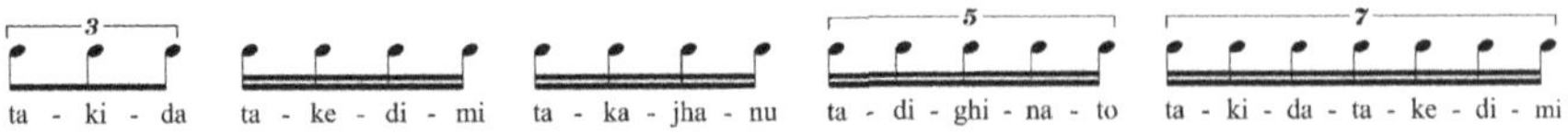

Solkattu Syllables

Solkattu (or konnakkol) is the name given to the syllables used to 'sing' a rhythmical phrase. In karnatic music every musician can 'sing' a phrase using a combination of syllables that feels suitable for the given phrase before setting any melody to it.

As long as simple common sense is used for the choice – for example, using strong sounds for accents, soft sounds and different parts of the tongue and mouth for faster passages – musicians have complete freedom to apply different syllables to the same phrase.

The following syllables are supposed to be the phonetisation of all the sounds employed by the main karnatic percussion instrument, the *mridangam.*

List of syllables *(track 1)*

TA	KI	DA	MI	DI	GHI	NA
TO(N)	KA	JHA	NU	NAM	RI	GU
LAAN	GA	NU	KU			

The following sounds are essentially peculiar to the Sanskrit language and seldom appear in any western European language.

NA	N is pronounced with a nasal quality and with the tongue back from the teeth.
THA	TH is pronounced as the th in si**t-h**ere.
DHI	DH is pronounced as the dh in re**d-h**ead.
THOM	TH is pronounced as a combination of si**t-h**ere and ca**th**ode.
DHEEM	DH is pronounced as re**d-h**ead and the EE as the long E in s**ee**.

Phrasing with Gatis

The approach in karnatic music to learning how to phrase with gatis is far removed from the way western solfege approaches this issue. It is not solely the fact that from the beginning any music student will work on four gatis without giving more importance to any particular one; the thinking behind it is also radically different.

The very first step is to systematically study all the possible cells that can be created in each gati and internalise the feeling for these cells through the mathematical proportions that the note values provide. This internalisation of every cell as an independent entity – without the use of rests, tie-overs or 𝅘𝅥𝅯 notes – is one of the factors that enable any karnatic musician to create phrases of great complexity.

Every note value has an associated number; for instance a ♪ note will have the number 2 associated with it, since it will always be 2 matras long. Musicians think in terms of numerical relationships between the note values, something of great benefit when it comes to start using rests and tie-overs to construct phrases.

The number of possible cells in every gati is as follows:[2]

Chatusra: 7 *(track 2)*

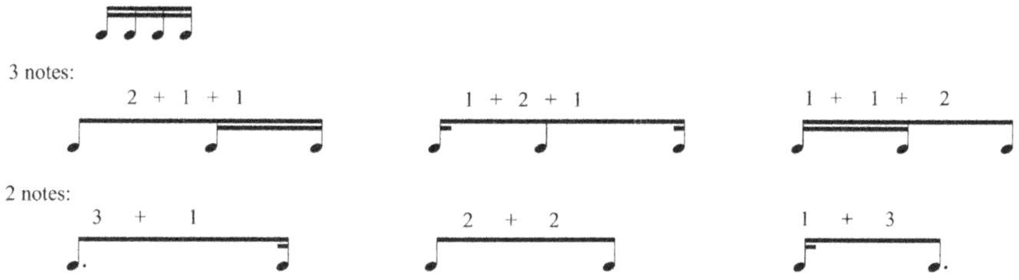

Khanda: 15 *(track 3)*

[2] On the audio files, every cell is repeated twice.

Tisra: 31 (taken as sextuplets for phrasing purposes) *(track 4)*

Misra: 60 *(track 5)*

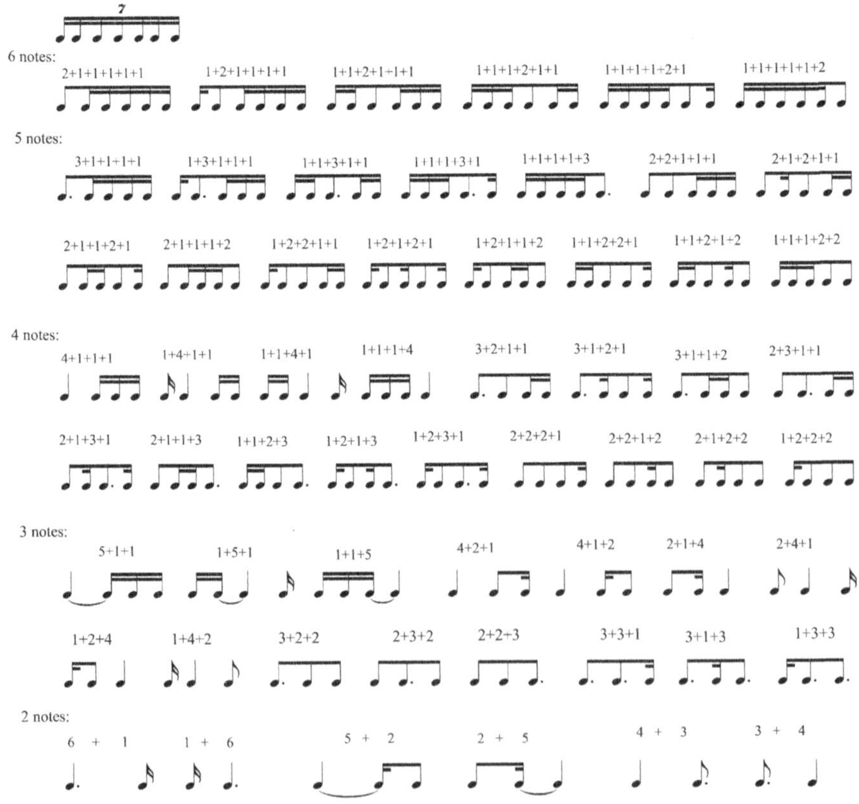

Development of Phrasing with Gatis

The approach of learning only a certain number of cells and looking at any phrase simply as a combination of these cells whilst, simultaneously, treating the rests and tie-overs as 'non-attacked' notes of a particular cell provides the musician with a high sense of security and accuracy without losing the feeling of the gati.

- *Rests*: Needless to say, when a note is silenced this will produce a different phrase; and when a number of rests are used the phrase can change entirely. However, a karnatic musician's thinking while performing a phrase with rests does not differ from when doing the phrase without them. What changes in his or her mind is that, instead of attacking the note, this one is silenced. But he or she never departs from thinking in cells, regardless of how many rests are used in a phrase. This avoids plunging into trying to 'understand' a myriad of phrases.
- *Tie-overs*: These are treated as rests, with the difference that a tie-over is an elongation of a note from one beat into the next.
- 𝅘𝅥𝅯 will be explained in the chapter on anuloma-pratiloma.

From the creative standpoint, any given phrase constructed by combining cells can produce an almost infinite number of derived phrases by applying rests and tie-overs. Depending on how many rests/tie-overs are used and where they are placed, a listener can recognise more or less proximity to the original phrase. This system is widely used in South India to develop phrasing. There is always an underlying consistency and coherence, regardless of how far-fetched the new phrase may be.

The following examples will serve to illustrate what it has just been expounded. The use of rests/tie-overs on a phrase constructed by combining a few cells will make necessary the use of a completely different set of solkattu syllables and the phrase will sound different.[3]

Original phrase in khanda

First development

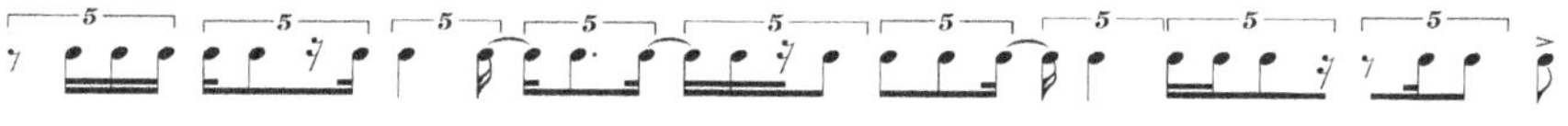

[3] Syllables are not provided because the phrases could take many different sets of syllables. The audio example should not be considered as the best choice of syllables, but rather one of many possibilities.

Second development

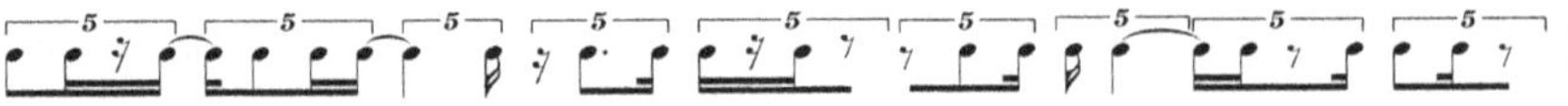

The three phrases in a row *(track 6)*

Original phrase in misra

First development

Second development

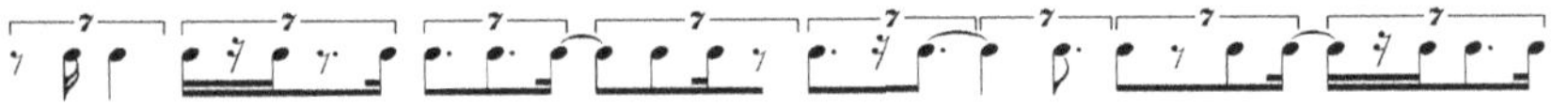

The three phrases in a row *(track 7)*

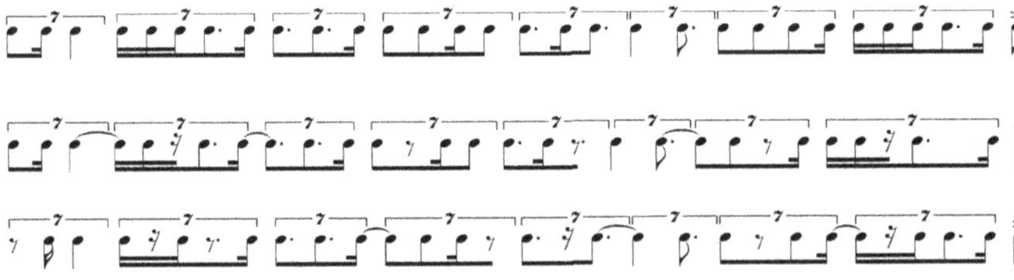

Relationship of Gati to Tala

As opposed to western music where, in any metre, a beat in khanda can be followed by another beat in tisra and then by, for instance, a 7:6♩. in karnatic music a change of gati can occur only on tala sam. A gati has to be used for at least one whole cycle of the tala. Many techniques will be explained that will contradict this principle, but they will always follow a coherence that departs from a random change of gatis.

This seemingly restricting factor has in fact enabled karnatic music to reach the high level of complexity and include the vast number of creative techniques that characterise it nowadays. This will become clear as more concepts and techniques are described later on in the book.

Practice Method

Use of Solkattu

Any technique should always be practised with solkattu (as karnatic musicians do) before proceeding to add melodies to the phrases. This working process is of great importance and one of the keys to the accuracy demonstrated by karnatic musicians. A phrase could have an almost infinite set of syllable combinations.

It would be convenient to start by using just a few syllables with any given phrase and slowly incorporate more syllables. The most commonly used, besides those given as the characteristic syllables of specific gatis, are:

TA or THA for accents
DHEEM for longer notes and sometimes also for accents
KI, KA, DA, KE, DI, MI, GHI, NA TO(N) for the rest of notes.

At an early stage syllables like MI would mostly be used when a group of four 𝅘𝅥𝅯 notes (in any gati) appears in a phrase. Similarly, GHI, NA and TO(N) are essentially used when a 5-note grouping appears in a phrase (again, regardless of the gati).

Numerous combinations are possible with these syllables alone. The musician can begin by relying on a few syllables, to prevent the range of available possibilities from becoming an obstacle rather than a helpful tool. It is also possible to write the syllables underneath a phrase in order to sing it. The most important thing is to first internalise these few syllables and use them in all contexts until they really become an intuitive part of one's musical vocabulary. Afterwards, other syllables can be added gradually, preferably one or two at a time.

A) Gatis

In order to familiarise themselves with the four gatis and to internalise the feeling and relationships among them, performers should practise them in three ways:

1. By repeating a gati for 4 or 5 minutes, making sure that every matra has the same length and that the matra that falls on the beat never falls slightly

before or after it. In this way the musician starts developing not only a sense of the specific gati but also a steady feeling of pulse.

2. Going through all the gatis in order, from tisra to misra and back, to become aware of their relationship and underlying proportionality. Exercise doing 4 beats per gati, then 3 etc. until changes occur every beat. Make sure that the speed of one gati does not carry on into the next gati. *(tracks 8 and 9)*
3. Once a good feeling for the relationship between gatis is achieved, a musician should practise them randomly in both number of repetitions of a gati and order. *(track 10)*

B) Phrasing with gatis

1. The most important element to incorporate into one's musical vocabulary is the internalisation of all cells for each gati shown previously in the chapter.
2. Having learnt all the cells and being able to really feel the difference between, for example, a ♪. and a ♩ in khanda or misra, the next step is to start combining them in phrases where all beats are attacked and no rests or tie-overs are used.
3. Take any previous phrase and apply a variety of rests within the cells and tie-overs between the last note of a cell and the first note of another cell (still without 𝅘𝅥𝅯 notes).

What follows is a very detailed account of a systematic process for classical and jazz musicians, introducing rests and tie-overs in a gradual fashion. These exercises are examples for musicians to create their own phrases following the increasing degree of complexity of every set of exercises.

Classical Musicians[4]

weeks 1-2

khanda (6 beats)

tisra (6 beats)

weeks 3-4

khanda (9 beats)

tisra (9 beats)

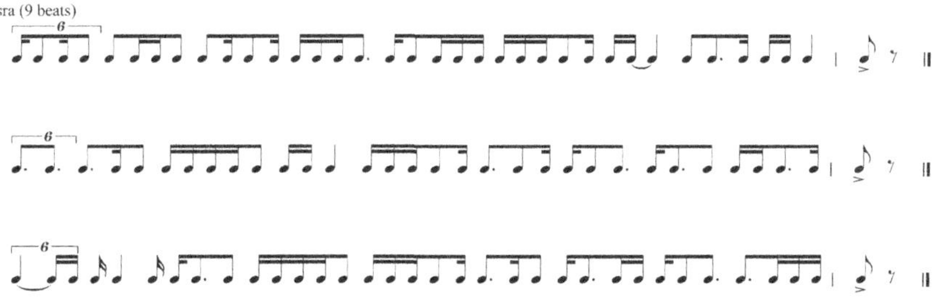

4 The week number shown before every set of exercises corresponds to my experience as a teacher of the programme at the Amsterdam Conservatoire, and is the average time that students need to reach a good level with the proposed material.

2 misra (6 beats)

weeks 5-6

khanda (9 beats)

tisra (9 beats)

misra (8 beats)

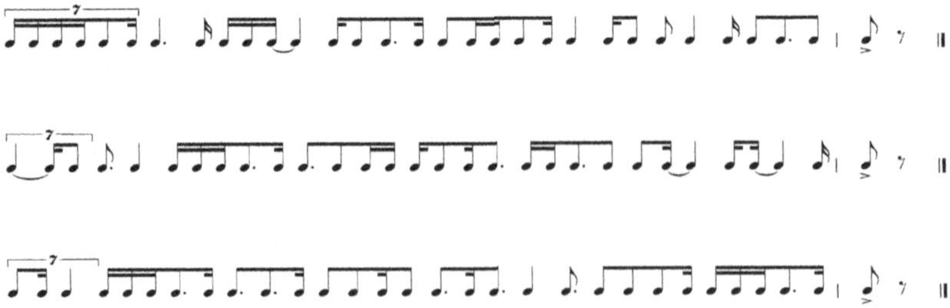

3

weeks 7-8

khanda (12 beats)

tisra (12 beats)

misra (8 beats)

weeks 9-10

khanda (16 beats)

misra (14 beats)

Improvisers

Improvisers

Weeks 1-2

-Practice with accuracy all cells in khanda and tisra

-Improvise in duos with instruments in khanda. One person keeps a groove with the following supporting cells (in any order) while the other improvises melodically, choosing 2, 3 or 4 cells from "Gatis cells chart".

Possible groove cells:

Weeks 3-4

khanda (6 beats)

tisra (6 beats)

-Improvise in duos with instruments in khanda. Same procedure as previous exercises

Weeks 5-6

khanda (9 beats)

tisra (9 beats)

-Improvise in duos with instruments in misra. Same procedure as previous exercises.

Possible groove cells:

-Improvise in duos in khanda. Free phrasing (with tie-overs, rests etc.)

3

Weeks 7-8

khanda (6 beats)

tisra (6 beats)

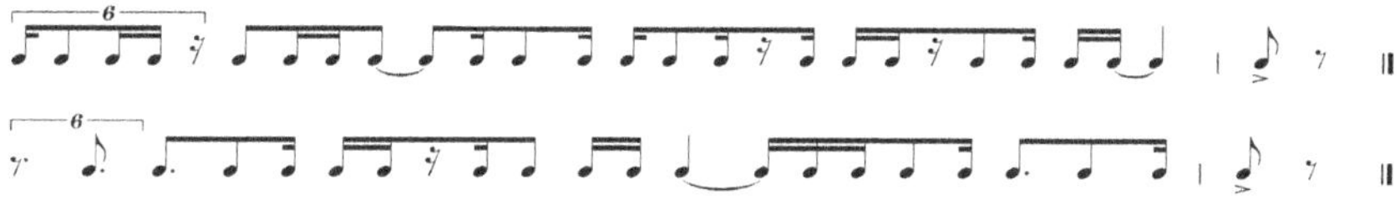

misra (6 beats)

khanda (9 beats)

-Improvise in duos with instruments in misra and khanda. Same procedure as previous lessons; improviser can use tie-overs, rests etc, (free phrasing).

Weeks 9-10

tisra (9 beats)

misra (8 beats)

-Free improvisation. Same procedure as previous lessons. Misra and khanda only

Chapter 3
Jathis

A jathi can be defined as a systematic accent applied to a gati,[1] producing as a result crossing accents over the beat. A jathi takes a number of matras that is always different to the number of the gati.[2] There are four jathis: 3, 4, 5, and 7; consequently, every gati can use three jathis.

One of the first and most important things to know in order to use the concepts derived from the notion of jathi is how to keep track of how many beats and accents are necessary for a gati/jathi combination to resolve.[3] This information is provided as follows:

- The number of the *gati* establishes the number of *accents* necessary for this device to meet with a beat.
- The number of the *jathi* will provide the number of *beats* required to fall on a beat (for example, chatusra jathi 3=4 accents in 3 beats).

Having both elements very clear in one's mind (gati=number of accents and jathi=number of beats) will save a lot of time when working with more complex material that, in one way or another, is derived from this concept.

Analysis of the chart below will show that chatusra, regardless of the jathi applied to it, will always use 4 accents to resolve on a beat. Similarly, any gati that would use jathi 4 will need 4 beats to resolve on a beat. This device is taught in South India even before a student learns how to phrase with gatis, due to the tremendous importance it has for their system. This importance will become clear as more techniques are explained.[4]

---

[1] Jathi is a name applied to what might apparently be divergent concepts, although the need for these different concepts to have the same name will later become clear.

[2] There would be no such thing as chatusra jathi 4 or khanda jathi 5, since these accents will always fall on a beat.

[3] As hinted at in the first chapter, all structures that provoke some form of rhythmical tension need to resolve.

[4] In the audio file every gati is preceded by 2 beats, and every example is performed twice.

(track 11)

tisra jathi 4

tisra jathi 5

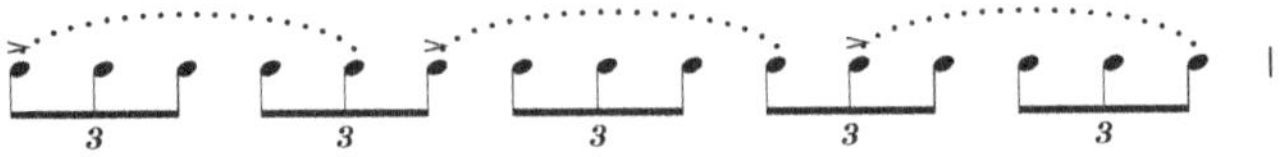

tisra jathi 7

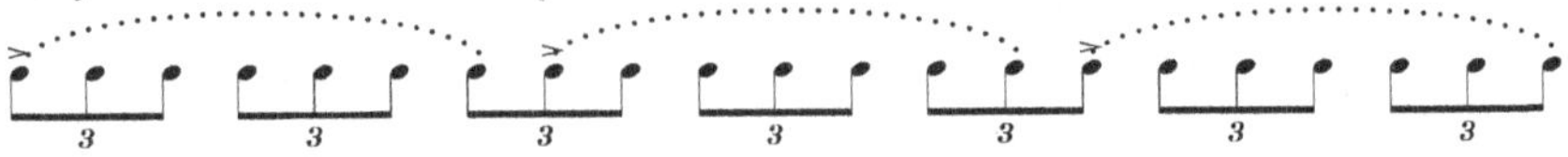

(track 12)

chatusra jathi 3

chatusra jathi 5

chatusra jathi 7

(track 13)

khanda jathi 3

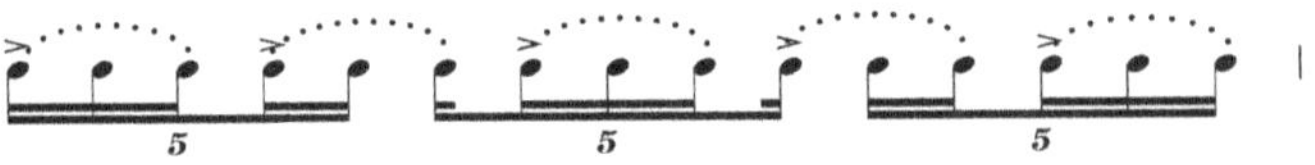

khanda jathi 4

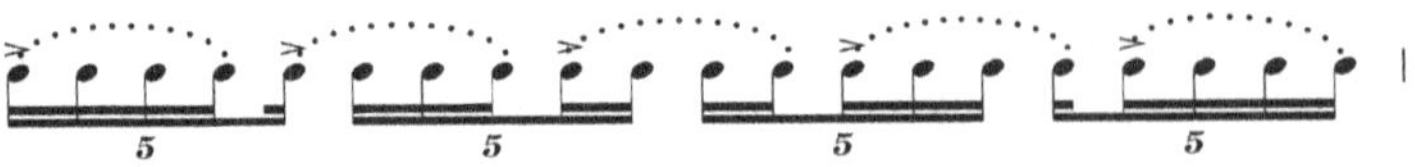

khanda jathi 7

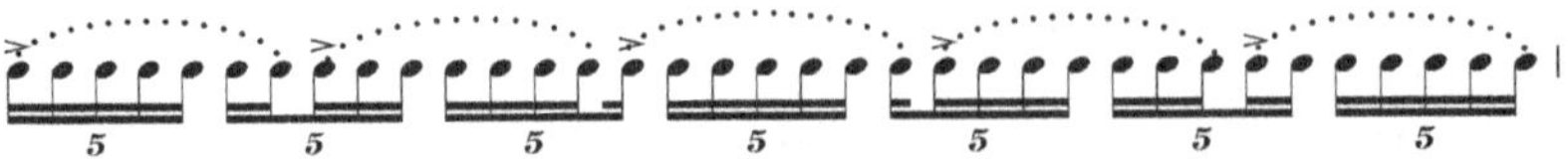

(track 14)

misra jathi 3

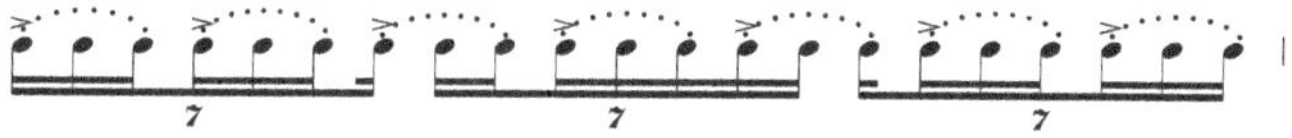

misra jathi 4

misra jathi 5

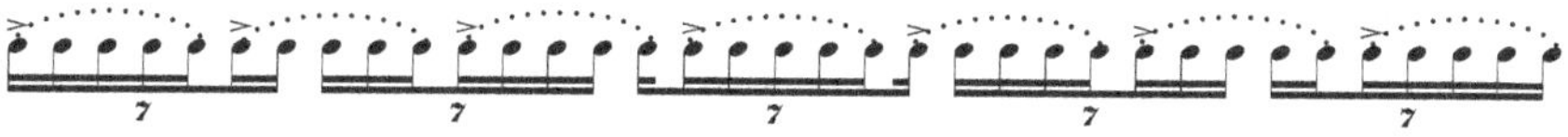

(track 15)

tisra 2nd speed jathi 4

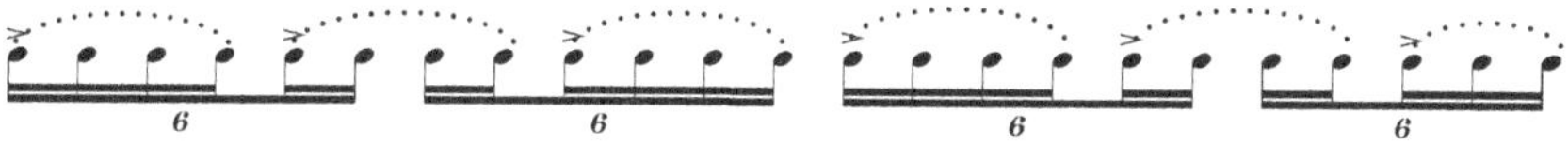

tisra 2nd speed jathi 5

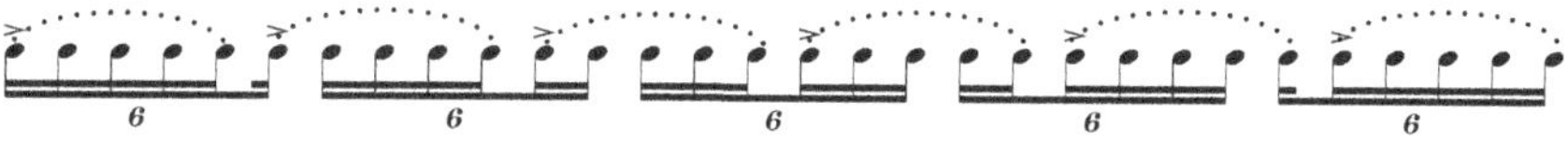

tisra 2nd speed jathi 7

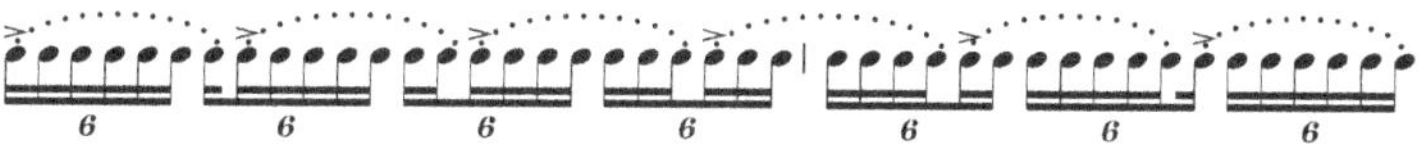

Solkattu Syllables

The syllables assigned to every gati have been seen in the gati section. The syllables assigned to a jathi will always correspond to the chosen number and will never take the syllables assigned to the gati. In other words, a jathi 3 will utilise TA-KI-DA in any gati and will never use the original syllables of the gati while emphasising the syllable corresponding with an accent. The latter would not only make it very difficult for the gati/jathi combination to be internalised, but also would never capture the actual feeling that is pursued by applying a jathi to a gati. For instance, if the following syllables are applied to tisra jathi 4:

It will never convey the feeling of 4. Consequently, feeling the flow of tisra (the *laya* of tisra) while using the syllables of chatusra will obtain the result sought:

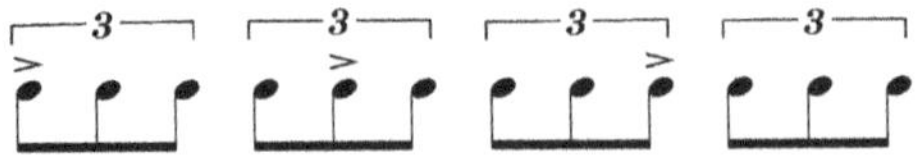

TA - ke - di mi - TA ke - di - mi - TA - ke - di - mi

The only exception to this usage of solkattu syllables is while using jathi 7. This jathi changes its syllables depending on the gati in the following way:

- Tisra: TA-KI-DA-TA-KE-DI-MI
- Chatusra: TA-KE-DI-MI-TA-KI-DA
- Khanda: TA-DI-GHI-NA-TO-TA-KA

Vertical Possibilities with Gati/Jathi Combinations

1) Both Layers Keep the Same Gati but Use Different Jathis

In this option, both performers or layers have the common denominator of sharing the same gati; but, as a result of using different jathis, they produce different 'metres' or structures. For instance, if chatusra jathi 3 is used in one layer and chatusra jathi 5 in the other layer, they will effectively be producing a 3/4 working against a 5/4. Both layers will not only produce crossing accents individually, but they will indeed also bring forth a polymetre or polyrhythm that will need a longer interval to meet. Table 3.1 provides all possible combinations and their resulting durations.

Table 3.1 Same Gati, Different Jathis

1) Chatusra jathi 3 vs. Chatusra jathi 5=15 beats	**2)** Chatusra jathi 3 vs. Chatusra jathi 7=21 beats
3) Chatusra jathi 5 vs. Chatusra jathi 7=35 beats	**4)** Tisra jathi 4 vs. Tisra jathi 5=20 beats
5) Tisra jathi 4 vs. Tisra jathi 7=28 beats	**6)** Tisra jathi 5 vs. Tisra jathi 7=35 beats
7) Khanda jathi 3 vs. Khanda jathi 4=12 beats	**8)** Khanda jathi 3 vs. Khanda jathi 7=21 beats
9) Khanda jathi 4 vs. Khanda jathi 7=28 beats	**10)** Misra jathi 3 vs. Misra jathi 4=12 beats
11) Misra jathi 3 vs. Misra jathi 5=15 beats	**12)** Misra jathi 4 vs. Misra jathi 5=20 beats

Audio examples

Chatusra jathi 5 vs. chatusra jathi 7=35 beats *(track 16)*

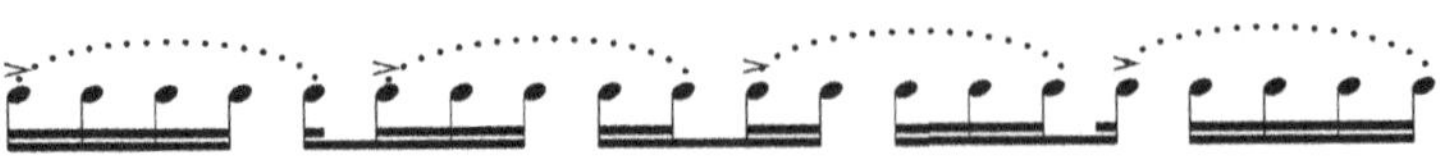

× 7 times

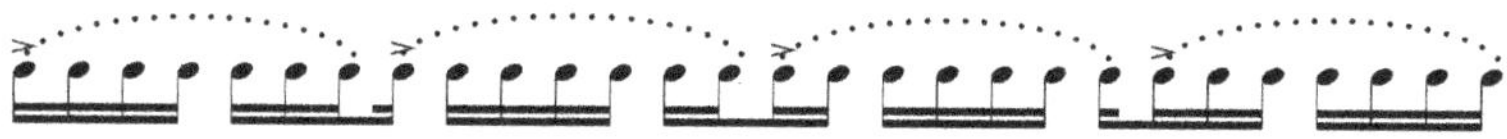

Khanda jathi 3 vs. khanda jathi 4=12 beats *(track 17)*

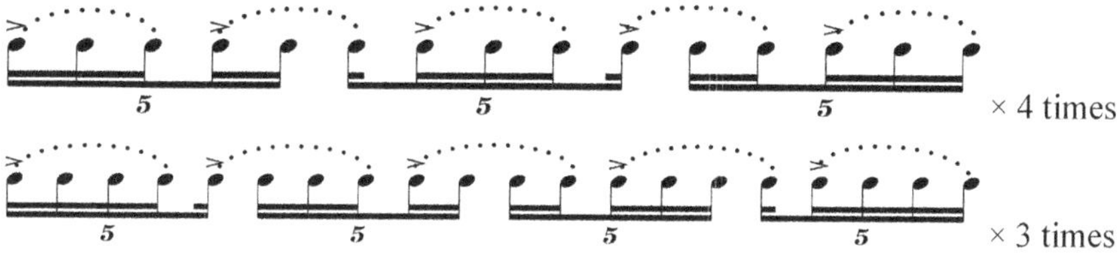

2) Both Layers Keep the Same Jathi but Use Different Gatis

In this option both performers or layers play the same jathi but, due to the fact that the jathi is performed in two different gatis, the listener perceives two different pulses or tempi played simultaneously.

As has already been explained, jathi will indicate the number of beats that the gati/jathi combination needs to resolve. Therefore, if both gatis use the same jathi they will meet after 3, 4, 5 or 7 beats (Table 3.2); in this case there will be no polyrhythm, but the sounding result will be a polypulse.

Table 3.2 Same Jathi, Different Gatis

1) Chatusra jathi 3 vs. Khanda jathi 3	**2)** Chatusra jathi 3 vs. Misra jathi 3
3) Khanda jathi 3 vs. Misra jathi 3	**4)** Tisra jathi 4 vs. Khanda jathi 4
5) Tisra jathi 4 vs. Misra jathi 4	**6)** Khanda jathi 4 vs. Misra jathi 4
7) Chatusra jathi 5 vs. Tisra jathi 5	**8)** Chatusra jathi 5 vs. Misra jathi 5
9) Tisra jathi 5 vs. Misra jathi 5	**10)** Chatusra jathi 7 vs. Khanda jathi 7
11) Chatusra jathi 7 vs. Tisra jathi 7	**12)** Tisra jathi 7 vs. Khanda jathi 7

Audio examples
Chatusra jathi 5 vs. tisra jathi 5 *(track 18)*

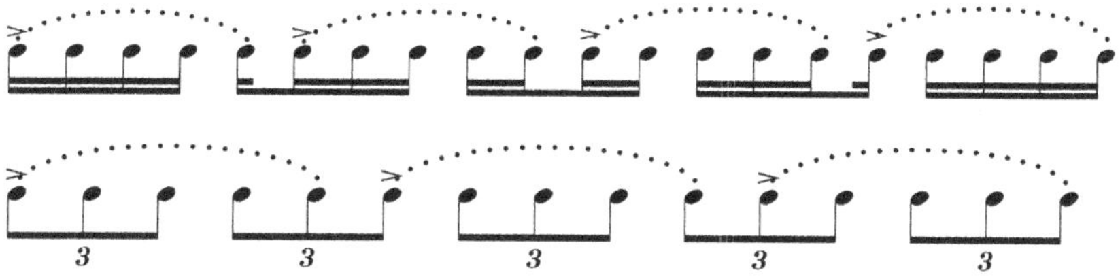

Khanda jathi 4 vs. misra jathi 4 *(track 19)*

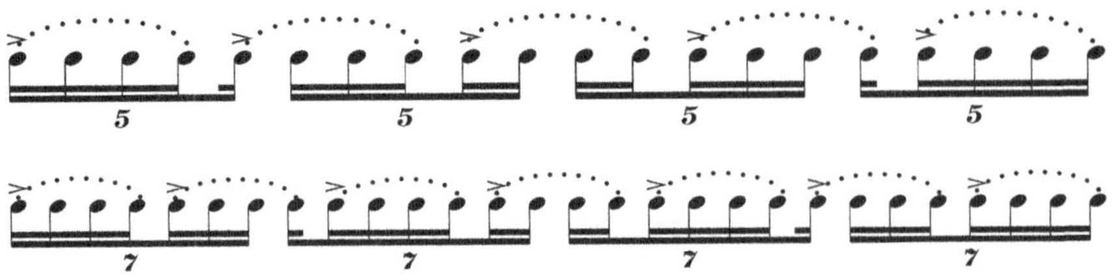

3) Both Layers Use Different Gatis and Jathis

This option is a combination of the two previous concepts: longer structures of polyrhythms mixed with the perception of both layers having two different tempi (Table 3.3).

Table 3.3 Different Gati, Different Jathi

1) Chatusra jathi 3 vs. Tisra jathi 4 = 12 b.	**2)** Chatusra jathi 3 vs. Tisra jathi 5 = 15 b.
3) Chatusra jathi 3 vs. Khanda jathi 4 = 12 b.	**4)** Chatusra jathi 5 vs. Tisra jathi 4 = 20 b.
5) Chatusra jathi 5 vs. Khanda jathi 3 = 15 b.	**6)** Chatusra jathi 5 vs. Khanda jathi 4 = 20 b.
7) Tisra jathi 4 vs. Khanda jathi 3 = 12 b.	**8)** Tisra jathi 5 vs. Khanda jathi 3 = 15 b.
9) Tisra jathi 5 vs. Khanda jathi 4 = 20 b.	**10)** Chatusra jathi 3 vs. Tisra jathi 7 = 21 b.
11) Chatusra jathi 3 vs Khanda jathi 7 = 21 b.	**12)** Chatusra jathi 3 vs. Misra jathi 4 = 12 b.
13) Chatusra jathi 3 vs Misra jathi 5 = 15 b.	**14)** Chatusra jathi 5 vs Tisra jathi 7 = 35 b.
15) Chatusra jathi 5 vs Khanda jathi 7 = 35 b.	**16)** Chatusra jathi 5 vs. Misra jathi 3 = 15 b.
17) Chatusra jathi 5 vs. Misra jathi 4 = 20 b.	**18)** Chatusra jathi 7 vs Tisra jathi 4 = 28 b.
19) Chatusra jathi 7 vs. Tisra jathi 5 = 35 b.	**20)** Chatusra jathi 7 vs. Khanda jathi 3 = 21 b.
21) Chatusra jathi 7 vs Khanda jathi 4 = 28 b.	**22)** Chatusra jathi 7 vs. Misra jathi 3 = 21 b.
23) Chatusra jathi 7 vs Misra jathi 4 = 28 b.	**24)** Chatusra jathi 7 vs Misra jathi 5 = 35 b.
25) Tisra jathi 4 vs Khanda jathi 7 = 28 b.	**26)** Tisra jathi 5 vs Khanda jathi 7 = 35 b.
27) Tisra jathi 4 vs. Misra jathi 3 = 12 b.	**28)** Tisra jathi 4 vs. Misra jathi 5 = 20 b.
29) Tisra jathi 5 vs Misra jathi 3 = 15 b.	**30)** Tisra jathi 5 vs. Misra jathi 4 = 20 b.
31) Tisra jathi 7 vs Khanda jathi 3 = 21 b.	**32)** Tisra jathi 7 vs. Khanda jathi 4 = 28 b.
33) Tisra jathi 7 vs. Misra jathi 3 = 21 b.	**34)** Tisra jathi 7 vs. Misra jathi 4 = 28 b.
35) Tisra jathi 7 vs. Misra jathi 5 = 35 b.	**36)** Khanda jathi 3 vs Misra jathi 4 = 12 b.
37) Khanda jathi 3 vs. Misra jathi 5 = 15 b.	**38)** Khanda jathi 4 vs. Misra jathi 3 = 12 b.
39) Khanda jathi 4 vs Misra jathi 5 = 20 b.	**40)** Khanda jathi 7 vs. Misra jathi 3 = 21 b.
41) Khanda jathi 7 vs. Misra jathi 4 = 28 b.	**42)** Khanda jathi 7 vs. Misra jathi 5 = 35 b.

Audio examples

1) Tisra jathi 4 vs. khanda jathi 3=12 beats *(track 20)*

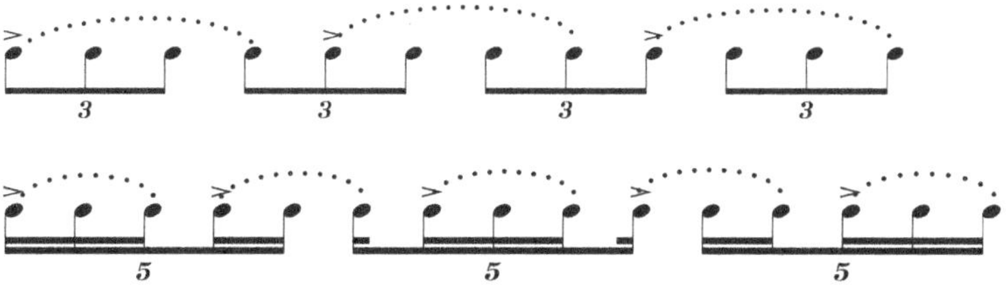

× 3 times

× 4 times

2) Chatusra jathi 3 vs. misra jathi 5=15 beats *(track 21)*

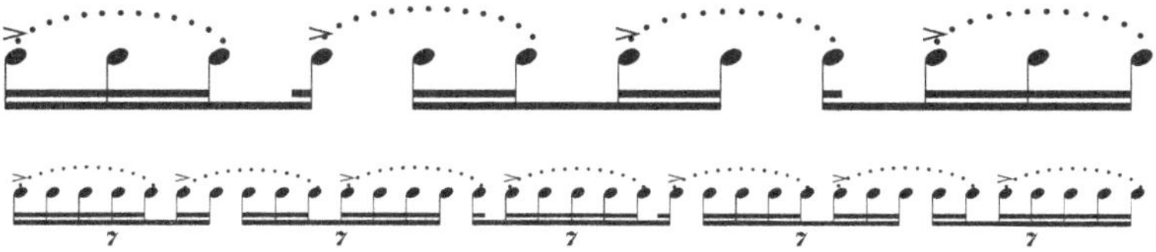

× 5 times

× 3 times

Relationship of Gati/Jathi Combinations to the Tala

Any of the three vertical possibilities seen above always has to resolve on tala or anga sam, and never on any other beat of the tala. The longer the two-layered gati/jathi combination is, the more it needs to resolve on tala sam.

If chatusra jathi 3 against chatusra jathi 5 (15 beats long) is to be performed and the chosen tala is 7 beats (with the construction of tisra triputa – L3 D D), calculations are needed to establish the starting point of the polyrhythm.[5]

1. In order to resolve on tala sam, the device should commence on the last beat of the tala and go through 2 cycles of tala 7. This is 1+7+7=15 beats.
2. If the resolution is on the first drutam sam, the starting point would be 3 beats later, because the 1st anga (L3) is 3 beats long. Consequently, the starting point would be the 3rd beat of the tala. Since the tala is 7 beats long, one must count how many beats remain to finish that specific cycle, go through a complete cycle and add the first 3 beats of the tala to resolve on the 1st drutam sam. This is 5+7+3=15 beats.
3. If the device is to finish on the 2nd drutam sam, one should simply add 2 beats to the previous starting point, since the length of the previous anga (first drutam) is 2 beats. Therefore, the starting point will be the 5th beat. Using the calculation method explained above, one should count the

[5] See Chapter 1 for tisra triputa. Karnatic musicians seem to have a built-in calculator in their brains because they are likely to instantly know the starting point for every polyrhythm in any given tala.

remaining number of beats to complete the cycle, go through one entire cycle of 7 beats and add the first 5 beats of the tala to resolve onto the 2nd drutam sam. This is then 3+7+5=15 beats.

Individual Structures of Polyrhythms

In practice, these long structures of polyrhythms are rarely used in karnatic music, not only because much of it is improvised but, more importantly, because karnatic musicians consider these long chunks of crossing structures tedious and repetitious. Karnatic musicians prize more a constant change of techniques and variety over a long segment of music with crossing accents, regardless of how much tension this could create in the music. For all practical purposes, all of the above has a more pedagogical value in order to develop the principles of:

a. internalising every gati/jathi combination in order to increase a better sense of pulse and the gatis per se;
b. gaining independence while playing different gatis and/or devices;
c. building a clear understanding as to where accents fall within the beat so that this system can be the foundation for other concepts or techniques that use the gati/jathi combinations as a reference frame or starting point.

Karnatic musicians tend to use the concepts expounded in this chapter by having *both layers start in different places and resolve together*. This provides much more freedom for using different gati/jathi combinations against one another.

In all the examples explained above, if one layer performs a jathi 3 and another a jathi 5, both starting on the same beat, they would have to complete a whole fragment of music of 15 beats in order to meet or resolve together.

But if the two layers start at different points they would have many more options as to how many times a particular gati/jathi combination could be used. If jathi 3 against jathi 5 are taken, the layer in jathi 3 could, for instance, simply perform it twice (6 beats) while the 2nd layer could perform it only once (5 beats), starting a beat later than the 1st layer and resolving together on a tala or anga sam.

This occurs many a time in the improvised sections of karnatic music.[6] As said before, every musician seems to be aware of every finishing point of any number of repetitions of any gati/jathi combination in any tala. So, once the performer of the 2nd layer hears the first musician starting a gati/jathi at a given point of the tala, this 2nd-layer performer will immediately know how many times the 1st layer will repeat the polyrhythm and where it will resolve. Subsequently, the 2nd-

[6] The fact that this technique is used in improvised parts of their music does not imply that it can be used exclusively by improvisers. The important element here is the concept of two individualised gati/jathi combinations starting separately, but finishing together.

layer performer is free to choose any of the three vertical options, to choose the number of times that the gati/jathi combination will be performed (and depending on this choice, the beat in the tala he should start) and make sure that both layers finish together.

This idea expands the concept of polyrhythms and polypulses to a higher dimension, since the number of options becomes almost infinite, as opposed to the very few structural combinations seen above. Variety indeed can be increased, and the possible tediousness or predictability that a fragment of 21 or 35 beats could give the music can be avoided. Furthermore, the fact that both layers start at different points in the tala provides a surprise factor to the listener – especially when, after a very short passage, they resolve together.

Practice Method

1) Practise every single gati/jathi combination presented on pages 36–37 until you acquire a high level of precision and a good feeling for whether you are speeding up or slowing down. *Visualising and memorising where the accents fall in relationship to the beat* are essential parts of the training and of great importance for techniques that use gati/jathi combinations as their reference frame or starting point.

Before starting any gati/jathi combination, it is useful to perform all the matras of the gati for a few beats in order to get a feeling for the beat and gati. Subsequently, proceed to the jathi, making sure that the only matras accented are those corresponding to the jathi – and never emphasise any matra falling on a beat. For instance, if you practise chatusra jathi 3, it should simply sound as though you are performing tisra, while being in the laya of chatusra.

As opposed to what one might think, starting to practise this chart before the gatis have been completely internalised does actually help perfect the feeling of the gati itself.[7]

2) Staying in the same gati, go from one jathi to another: first, in an increasing and decreasing way and then, after some time, changing jathis randomly.

Example: chatusra jathi 3 going to jathi 5 and jathi 7 *(track 22)*

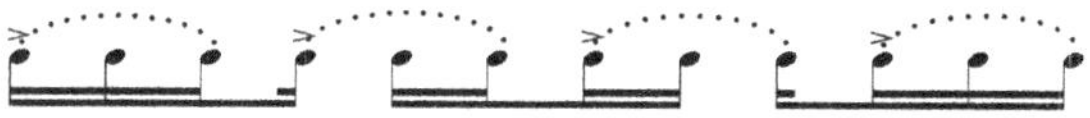

[7] It is my experience that many students who could not do khanda or misra at an adequate level after a few weeks acquired a much higher level of feeling for the mentioned gatis by practising these particular gatis with all their possible jathis.

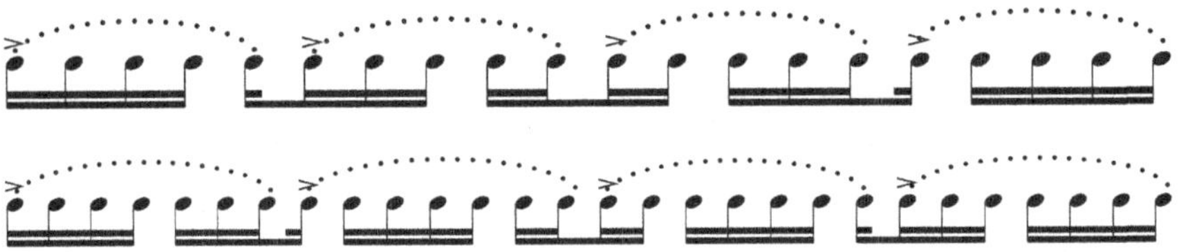

3) Keeping the same jathi, go from gati to gati. As in the exercise suggested above, first proceed in an orderly fashion, and then change randomly.

Example: tisra jathi 5 going to chatusra jathi 5 and then misra jathi 5 *(track 23)*

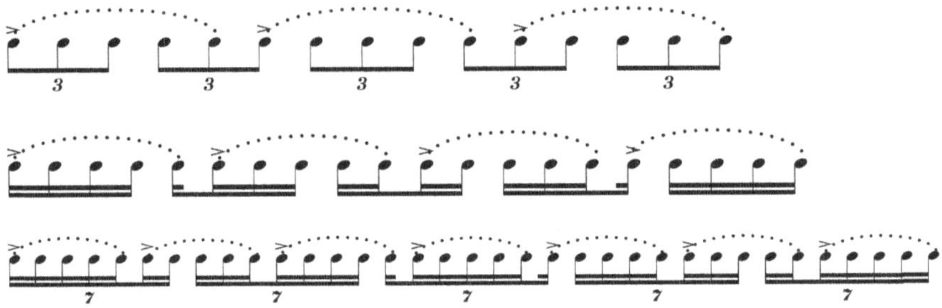

4) Practise the *three vertical techniques* explained earlier in the chapter. If you cannot meet up with anyone to practise together, a computer aid or similar device would be of great help. As mentioned previously, these vertical possibilities enable the performer to:

a. internalise every option more deeply;
b. gain independence, not only in relation to the beat but, moreover, to another player or group of players who may be performing a different gati or gati/jathi combination (or, ultimately, any other technique);
c. build a clear understanding as to where accents fall within the beat.

Chapter 4
Gati Bhedam

The Sanskrit term *bhedam* roughly translates as 'change through destruction'. (It has clear spiritual/religious connotations, referring to the destruction of inner energies, attitudes or negativities in order to change.) When used in combination with any other musical term, it will *always* affect the concept that precedes it in one way or another.

Gati bhedam is a technique by which the *phrasing in a gati/jathi combination is constructed around the jathi rather than the gati.* When the phrase is structured on the jathi it creates the illusion that the phrase is in a different gati and tempo than the laya (here laya means both pulse and gati going along the pulse). Hence a phrase in, for example, khanda jathi 3 should sound as if the performer is playing a phrase in tisra. The listener should not only perceive that the performer is playing a phrase in tisra; but simultaneously, because the underlying pulse (laya) is khanda, it should also appear that the phrase is being performed in a different tempo.

This concept of phrasing according to the jathi, and not the gati, is so ingrained in karnatic music that in khanda jathi 3 one would never conceive of phrasing in khanda and giving accents every 3 matras to provide some sort of 'colouring' of tisra.

In fact, the term 'khanda jathi 3' is one I have coined myself for clarity's sake in order to make the concept and terminology of the gati/jathi combination more clear and understandable to western musicians starting to study this material. A karnatic musician would never say khanda jathi 3, but rather *tisra in khanda*, which denotes quite emphatically the notion behind it: to give the impression of being in tisra while the underlying gati is khanda.[1]

Notation

Western notation was born and developed because of specific musical parameters. However, it can fall short when concepts like gati bhedam and other related techniques are to be conveyed. Hence, in order to be able to incorporate this concept into our (western) musical system, a notation should be devised that would convey the aforementioned feeling. Therefore, it is necessary to explain here how, based on my own study and experience, I arrived at creating an alternative notation,

[1] For the purposes of this book the term 'khanda jathi 3' will be kept – to the detriment of the real karnatic term – to avoid confusion.

since this will become a key issue in order to show many of the concepts of this book.

After years of composing using the traditional western notation – where the phrase is always 'divided' according to an imaginary 'beat-line' notion, and experimenting with all sort of accents, double accents, slurs, dotted slurs etc. – I realised that this traditional notation could never convey to the performer the feeling of being in a different gati than the laya (trying to convey a feeling of tisra whilst being in khanda). Rather, what I obtained from the performer was the feeling of the gati with a dynamic accent on specific notes, but failing to be felt as a cyclic accent that should provide the feeling of being in a different gati and tempo.

If the following phrase in khanda jathi 3 were written according to the notation rules of traditional solfege, I do not think a western player without knowledge of the concept of gati bhedam and its ulterior practice could perform the phrase with the feeling of tisra as a karnatic musician would.

After reviewing scores by Ives, Bartók, Messiaen and Xenakis, I realised that there have already been attempts in western contemporary music to notate the phrase according to the phrase , and not breaking it in order to adapt it to the 'beat-line' division of traditional solfege. Therefore, I decided to experiment with the way karnatic musicians notate their phrases.

When using gati bhedam, phrases are always notated every 3, 4, 5 or 7 matras within any given gati. Ignoring the beat-line that characterises the western notation system, each phrase is separated by the sign - . For instance, the first three beats of the previous phrase would be written as follows:

Khanda[2]

Tha gadadina- ka di gu- dheem. ga- taka di mi- tadheem. gu-//

Explanation of symbols

- One syllable (Tha) = A 𝅘𝅥𝅯
- One syllable followed by a dot: the note value is doubled
  - dheem. = 𝅘𝅥𝅮
- One note followed by two dots: the note value is tripled
  - dheem.. = 𝅘𝅥𝅮.
- A syllable or group of syllables underlined: the note value is halved
  - gadadina = 𝅘𝅥𝅰
  - dheem. = 𝅘𝅥𝅯

[2] Karnatic musicians always write the name of the gati instead of a sign or bracket like the western quintuplet.

- tadheem. = 𝅘𝅥𝅯 followed by 𝅘𝅥𝅯.
- The sign ▬ signifies the end of the phrase, while the sign // signifies a bar line.

In karnatic notation, no symbol for accent is employed. The sign ▬ that signifies the end of a phrase also implies that the first note of the next grouping is to be *emphasised* (which is, in essence, what the concept of accent is all about) and, very importantly, *performed with a downbeat feeling*. (Possibly herein lies the Gordian knot of how accents – or their concept – are approached in both western and karnatic music.)

As we shall see throughout the book, an accent in karnatic music is always to be performed with a down-to-earth feeling, and with the intentionality of being the first note of a phrase (similar to the intentionality we may have in western music with the downbeat of a metre), whereas in western music accents are related to the level of dynamic expressions or to provide a feeling of syncopation or anticipation.

Accordingly, I decided to find or create a notational device that would enable me to convey the feeling of the jathi. I found that, in most cases, by

a. **beaming** the phrase together every 3, 4, 5 or 7 matras; and
b. **using an accent** on the first note of a grouping of jathi 3, 4, 5 or 7

most western musicians received a clear visual impression that made them understand and try to convey what was meant by beaming the notes together. Therefore, the phrase in khanda jathi 3 written above

became *(track 24)*

Khanda jathi 3

Something that I found quite surprising was the fact that gati bhedam phrases in khanda, tisra or misra (with any jathi) were performed with more accuracy than phrases in chatusra. I attributed the problem to a simple fact: when beaming a phrase in a way that does not correspond to the traditional beat-line, the usage of brackets – as normally employed in tisra, khanda and misra – enabled the performer to know how every note related to the beat. On the other hand, when the bracket was absent (as it was the case in chatusra), the performer had more problems in relating to the beat.

Subsequently, I concluded that when using the concept of gati bhedam the best way was to be coherent and use brackets on all gatis. I started placing a bracket with the number 4 when using chatusra – something that has proven very helpful with gati bhedam as well as with many other techniques that call for the beaming of phrases in this 'unorthodox' manner.

At approximately the same time, I encountered the second problem. This one occurred when, for instance, a note in the phrase did not fall entirely within one beat, but rather fell on either side of the beat – for instance, a ♪ before the beat and another ♪ after the beat. I decided then to compromise between the karnatic and western notations for the sake of clarity, and proceeded as follows:

- I divided the note value into two notes at either side of the beat and brackets.
- I used a tie-over linking both notes.
- I kept both notes under the same beaming.

Another element I started using to increase the clarity of the phrase was dotted slurs. I used this articulation technique in two cases:

a. when notes longer than ♪. are part of the phrase and, therefore, no beaming can be applied; and
b. when phrases are longer than nine matras.

Reading phrases longer than nine matras in one beaming seems to be visually too cumbersome for the performer. Most of these phrases longer than 9 matras are the result of applying specific techniques (not yet explained), and I found that the best way of notating them was to 'break' them according to the technique's construction logic while a *dotted slur* embraced all the smaller groupings.

The following example in chatusra jathi 7 shows the use of the bracket on chatusra, which makes the reading of the phrase and the relationship of every note to the beat much clearer. Also, the above-mentioned problem of splitting one note into two (between 5th and 6th beats, 13th and 14th beats and 15th and 16th beats) can be observed. *(track 25)*

Chatusra jathi 7

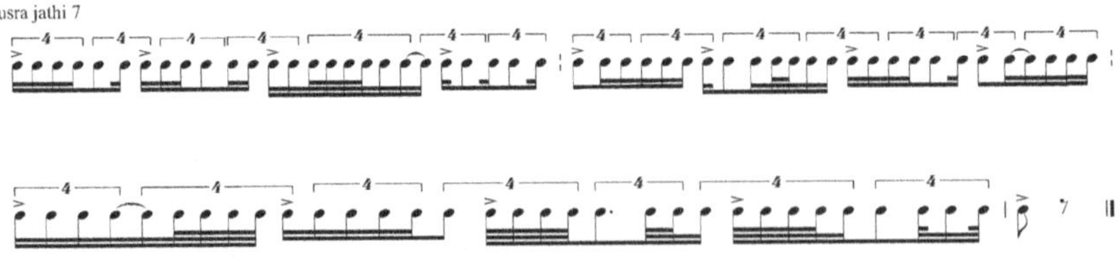

In order to get a glimpse of each gati and each jathi, two more examples are given below. *(track 26)*

Tisra jathi 5

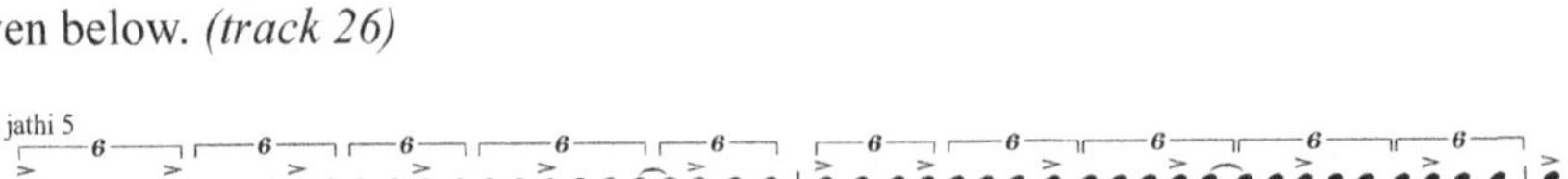

(track 27)

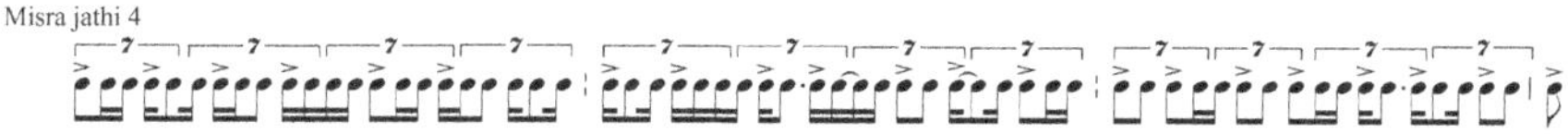

Creative Applications

From a creative standpoint, when using the vertical possibilities shown in Chapter 3 in conjunction with the gati bhedam concept, karnatic musicians emphasise the need to construct phrases that would work well against each other, in order to avoid blurry passages when clarity in the polypulses is desired.

In order to create music with this device it is important to keep in mind that its essential purpose is to create an illusion of polypulses or polytempi. The phrase is *always* created around the accent provided by the jathi. A possible danger is to start skipping accents. When accents are skipped, the feeling of being in a different gati vanishes; therefore, using the notation proposed for gati bhedam does not make any sense. If a gati bhedam phrase in combination with skipping accents is desired, using the regular, traditional notation would probably be more sensible.

Karnatic musicians clearly state that gati bhedam exists only when all the accents are attacked and the phrase is created around the jathi. Having said this, something that occurs in karnatic music is that once the feeling of the polytempi has been established, a few accents can be skipped now and again, provided that the feeling of the jathi is still kept intact. There are only two simple rules to avoid losing the feeling of the jathi:

1. Never skip two accents in a row.
2. Never skip the accent that falls on the beat.

The point at which a feeling of polytempi is established is a very subjective issue, and possibly one can establish a feeling more easily with chatusra jathi 3 than with khanda jathi 7. Nevertheless, one should remember that, as with any other technique presented in this book, gati bhedam calls for specific 'rules' in order to be what it is. Departing from the basic principle of gati bhedam too often and/ or too soon simply cancels the technique as such and the possibility of creating illusions of polytempi that it offers.

Below is a transcription of part of a piece in 5/8, or khanda chapu, in which the singer is continuously making phrases with jathi 2, 3, 4 and 6. *(track 28)*

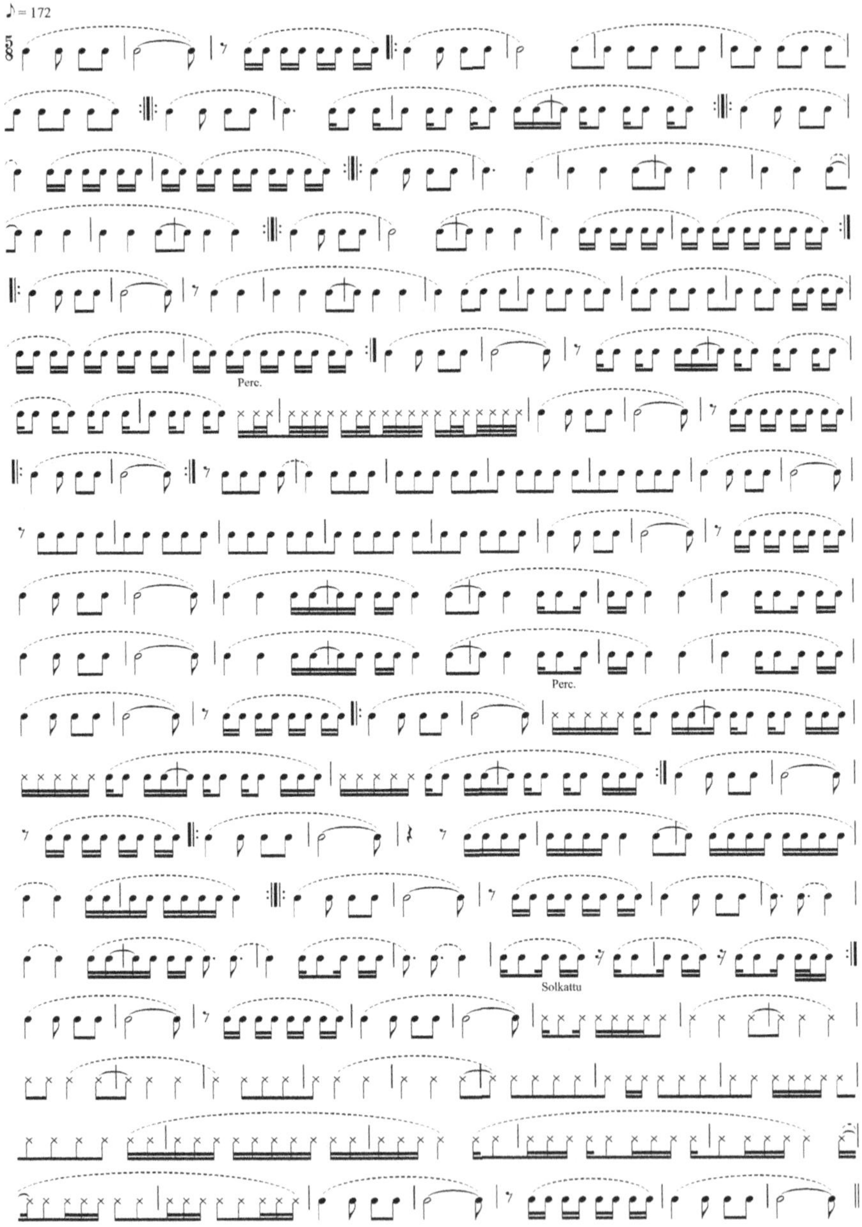
♪ = 172
Perc.
Perc.
Solkattu

Tree of Gati Bhedam (*Gati Vruksha)*

A tree of gati bhedam is essentially the development of ideas by connecting two musical objects via a *common denominator*, or an element that links these two musical events in a highly logical manner. Many techniques that will be seen later on can be used as part of a tree, but the elements explained thus far are sufficient to start working with this creative tool.

A tree of gati bhedam is a concept that can be applied to a short section, longer segments or even a whole piece of music. In the latter it can be used to map out key changes throughout the piece, whether composed or improvised. When used as a sequence in a short time-span, the rules explained below are the only ones to be observed for its construction. If utilised in a longer segment or for a whole piece, it is simply thought of in a conceptual fashion as a way of connecting ideas at specific points of a segment or a piece.

Before the tree of gati bhedam as such is explained, it is first necessary to explain the possibilities for connecting two musical objects. So far, the only material seen – besides the suladi tala system – is phrasing in gatis, gati/jathi combinations and gati bhedam phrasing. These elements, which are ultimately the main ones required to construct a tree, can obviously be used in many different contexts as well.

1) Gati/jathi Combination as Starting Point

If, for example, chatusra jathi 3 is taken as the starting point, from this gati/jathi combination one could go to any of these four options:

a. regular chatusra phrasing (without jathi)
b. chatusra jathi 5 or 7
c. tisra
d. khanda or misra jathi 3.

Two of these options are connected by having the gati element as common denominator: it is possible for chatusra jathi 3 to either go to chatusra without any jathi or to any other jathi within chatusra. The other two options are connected through the jathi element: jathi 3 can become a gati (tisra) or the jathi of the other two remaining gatis. Therefore, from this particular case, the following general rule can be established: any given gati/jathi combination could only go to four musical objects, two of them providing two options:

a. regular phrasing of the chosen gati
b. any other jathi within the chosen gati (two possibilities)
c. the jathi becomes a gati
d. the number of the jathi remains the same in any other gati (two possibilities).

Hence, from chatusra jathi 3 one cannot go freely to, for instance, khanda or misra unless the music first passes through khanda or misra jathi 3. Similarly, it could not go to tisra jathi 4, 5 or 7, unless it passes through regular tisra first.

2) Regular Gati as Starting Point

If chatusra is taken as the starting point, this gati could go to:

a. chatusra jathi 3, 5 or 7
b. tisra, khanda or misra jathi 4
c. regular tisra, khanda or misra.

In this context, since the starting point contains only one element, everything has to be connected using either chatusra or the number four. Consequently, either the gati remains, using any of its possible jathis, or it becomes the jathi in any other gati. Finally (which within this context seems to be the most far-fetched option), the gati goes to any other gati.

From this example a general rule can be concluded: when the musical object is a regular gati, it can go to any of the three following concepts, resulting in nine possibilities:

a. The regular gati can stay in the gati, using any of its jathis (three possibilities).
b. The gati becomes the jathi in any other gati (three possibilities).
c. The gati goes to another gati without any jathi (three possibilities).

With this logic of connecting steps, chatusra would therefore never go to any other gati using a jathi, other than jathi 4: for instance, chatusra could never go to tisra or misra jathi 5 since there is no common denominator between the two of them.

The following is a tree of gati bhedam (still without any relationship to any tala) in which the connections are chosen with the goal of using all the linking options provided above. The explanation given for the first three connections will serve to illustrate the selection process.

Chatusra jathi 3 could go to:

Regular chatusra	Chatusra jathi 5 or 7	Regular tisra	Khanda or misra jathi 3

Chatusra jathi 7 is chosen. After performing chatusra jathi 7 a number of times, this musical object could go to:

Regular chatusra	Chatusra jathi 3 or 5	Regular misra	Khanda or tisra jathi 7

Khanda jathi 7 is the chosen object. After performing it a number of times, this musical object could go to:

Regular khanda   Khanda jathi 3 or 4   Regular misra   Chatusra or tisra jathi 7

This tree is just one possible outcome, designed to incorporate all the given possibilities rather than thinking musically. *(track 29)*

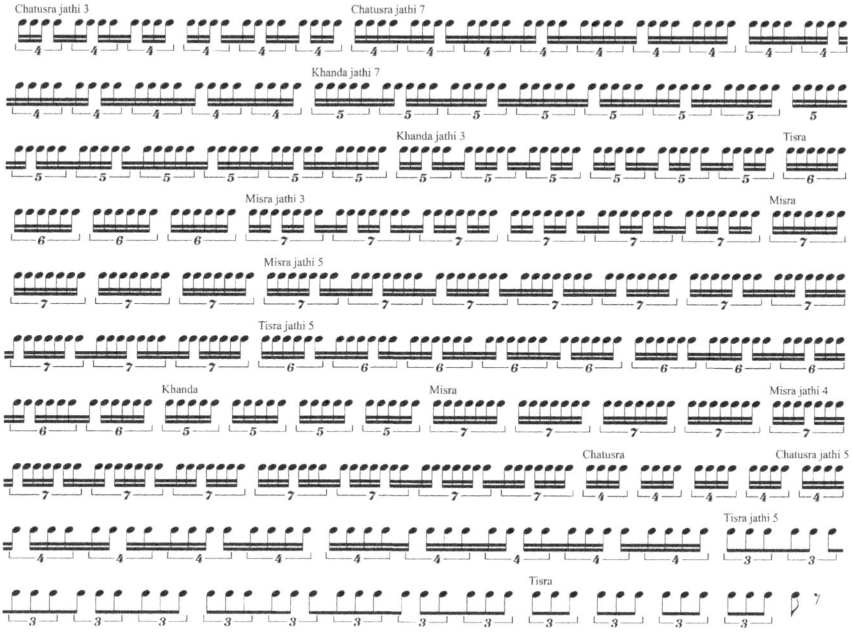

Relationship to the Tala

Connections between two musical elements, the number of repetitions of a gati/jathi combination and the choice of the number of beats for a regular phrase will never happen randomly in a tree of gati bhedam. They need to be related and adjusted to the tala or anga sams of a tala, and some calculations are required. There are three basic rules as to where changes can take place.

1. While staying in the same gati and moving between any of its jathis or regular phrasing without jathis, changes can happen anywhere in the tala. For instance, chatusra can go to chatusra jathi 3, 5 or 7; and any of these jathis can go to another jathi (while staying in chatusra) or go to regular chatusra at any point of the tala.

An exception to this rule occurs when, at a particular moment, a gati/jathi combination creates a polyrhythm or polypulse with another layer. In this case the rules seen in previous chapters apply and the gati/jathi combination should resolve on a tala or anga sam.

2. A gati/jathi combination can go to any other gati/jathi combination (provided the same jathi is preserved) or go from any gati without jathi to another gati without jathi *exclusively* on tala sam. For instance, khanda jathi 4 can go to misra or tisra jathi 4 (and never to any other gati with a different jathi than 4); or any gati can go to any other gati provided that this change occurs on tala sam.
3. When a gati becomes a jathi (chatusra going to any other gati with jathi 4) or a jathi becomes a gati (any gati with jathi 4 going to chatusra), the change can also happen on an anga sam.

As mentioned at the beginning of the chapter, a tree can be used in three different ways: as a short sequence or as a tool to map out key changes in a bigger segment of music, or even a whole piece.

With the elements seen so far in this and previous chapters, the most feasible option is to create a short sequence. Taking the sequence written above, almost infinite musical and structural variations could be created. The following example shows how the sequence and the tala can interrelate (Table 4.1). It is the transcription of a tree of gati bhedam by B.C. Manjunath.

Table 4.1 Tree of Gati Bhedam in Tala 7 (L3 D D)

1) Chatusra × 8 beats	2) Chatusra jathi 3 × 4=12 beats	3) Chatusra jathi 5 × 3=15 beats
These first three steps resolve on tala sam after 5 cycles of tala 7 (8+12+15=35 beats)		
4) Khanda × 5 beats	5) Khanda jathi 3 × 3=9 beats	
These two steps resolve on tala sam after 2 cycles (5+9=14 beats)		
6) Khanda jathi 4 × 2=8 beats	7) Khanda × 6 beats	
These two steps resolve on tala sam after 2 cycles (8+6=14 beats)		
8) Tisra jathi 5 × 3=15 beats	9) Tisra × 6 beats	
These two steps resolve on tala sam after 3 cycles (15+6=21 beats)		
10) Misra × 7 beats	*(1 cycle)*	
11) Misra jathi 3 × 4=12 beats	12) Misra jathi 4 × 4=16 beats	
These two steps resolve on tala sam after 4 cycles (12+16=28 beats)		
13) Chat × 7 beats	*(1 cycle)*	

The transcription shows that the number of times a particular gati/jathi combination is performed has an effect on the way the phrases are constructed. If jathi 5 is chosen and the number of repetitions of the gati/jathi combination is 3, the phrase is constructed around three cells of jathi 5, which adds another subtle layer of polyrhythm to the existing feeling provided by the gati/jathi combination. The dotted slur in the notated transcription clarifies these cells. However, this phrasing choice is just one of the multiple possibilities to create phrasing in a tree of gati bhedam.[3] *(track 30)*

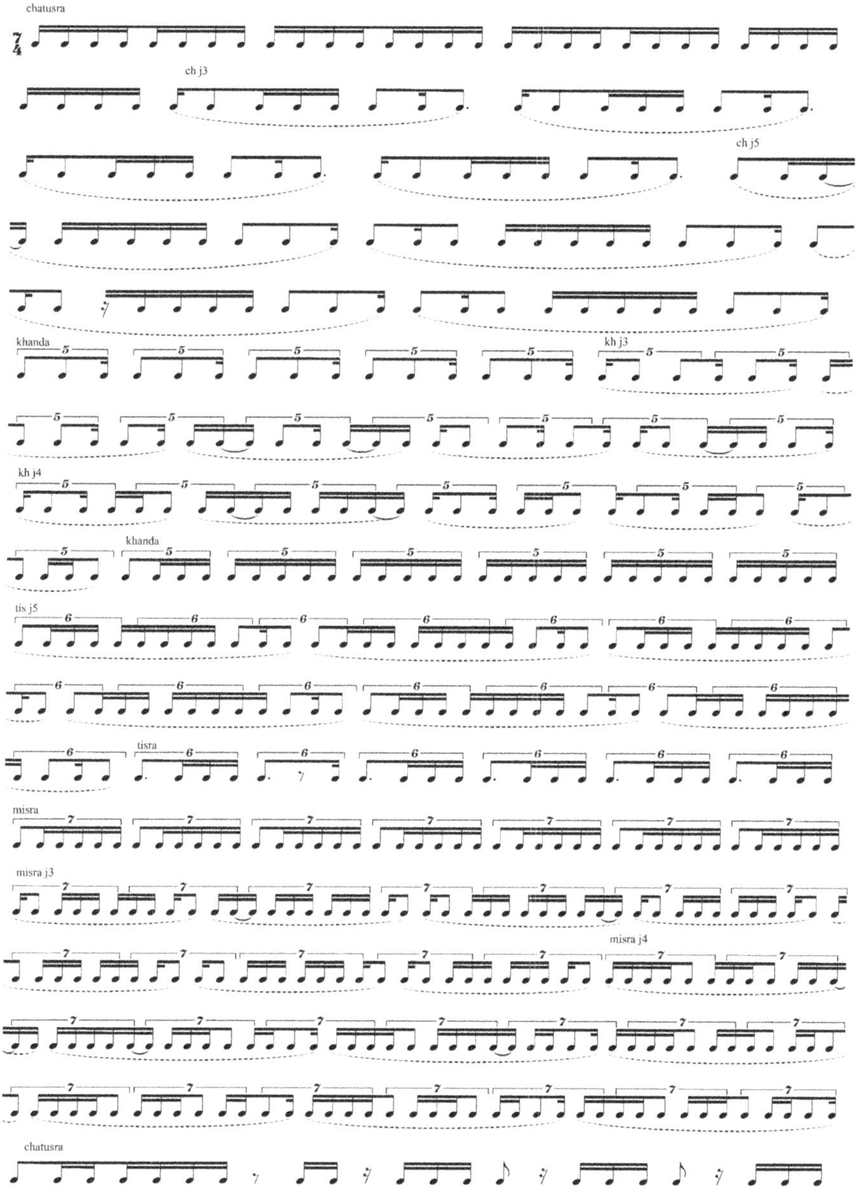

[3] Chapter 5 on rhythmical sangatis will give more options as to the various sorts of phrasing and development that can be used in a tree.

At the very end of the example, in the misra jathi 4 phrase, the listener can hear a subdivision of 6+5+5 rather than a jathi 4. This 'exception' will be understood when jathi bhedam is explained in Chapter 6.

Practice Method

It is very important at this point to have acquired a very clear understanding and command of all the gati/jathi combinations, and to be well aware of where all the accents fall in relation to the beat.

1. Start practising the phrases as if they were a gati, and sing them along the pulse. For example, for a phrase in chatusra jathi 5, sing it first as a phrase in khanda on the pulse. In this way you can familiarise yourself with the phrase more easily and give it a better feeling when performed as a jathi in any other gati.

Chatusra jathi 5

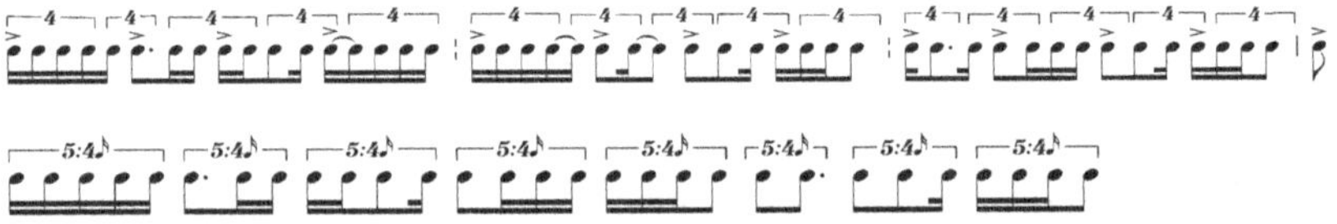

2. Avoid emphasising notes that fall on beats or performing an accent in a syncopated manner. Every accent has to be felt as the down beat of a 3/16, 4/16, 5/16 or 7/16 metre. Subsequently, always make sure that the feeling of the original gati is avoided. It should at all times sound as if the jathi is actually a gati with its own pulse (the pulse to lean on is the accents of the gati/jathi combination).
3. Once phrases using all gati/jathi combinations have been perfected, practise them as follows:
   a) Staying in the same gati, go from jathi to jathi – first in an increasing and decreasing fashion, and afterwards randomly. *Example*: chatusra jathi 3 going to jathi 5 and jathi 7

Chatusra jathi 3

Chatusra jathi 5

Chatusra jathi 7

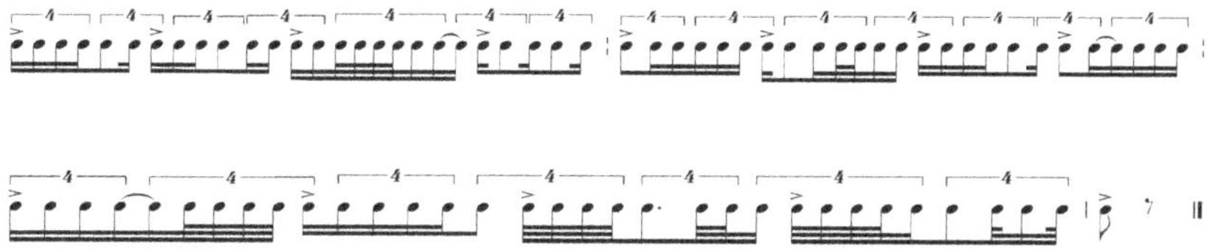

b) Keeping the same jathi, go from gati to gati. First proceed in an orderly fashion to then change randomly. *Example*: jathi 3 in chatusra going into khanda and misra

Chatusra jathi 3

Khanda jathi 3

Misra jathi 3

3. Perform all the vertical possibilities explained in Chapter 3 (jathis), but replacing the use of only matras by gati bhedam phrases. Although the phrases presented at the end of this chapter are thought to be used in linear fashion, performing them with all the possibilities already practised can enhance the internalisation of the gati/jathi combinations as well as the phrasing of gati bhedam.
4. Eventually, construct trees of gati bhedam as sources to deepen the understanding and proficiency of the gati bhedam phrasing. It is important to adhere to the construction rules in relation to the common denominator concept.

One example per gati/jathi combination is shown below; every option is represented as a guide that could help musicians create their own phrases. It is worth noting that, while phrasing with the gati bhedam principle in misra jathi 3, and in order to be able to do phrases with some variety, the 7 accents every 3 matras become 3 accents of 6 matras and 1 of 3 matras.

Gati Bhedam Phrases

Chatusra jathi 3

Chatusra jathi 5

Chatusra jathi 7

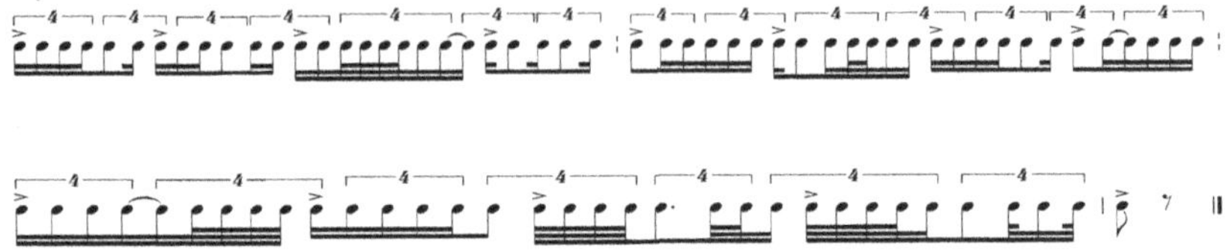

Tisra jathi 4

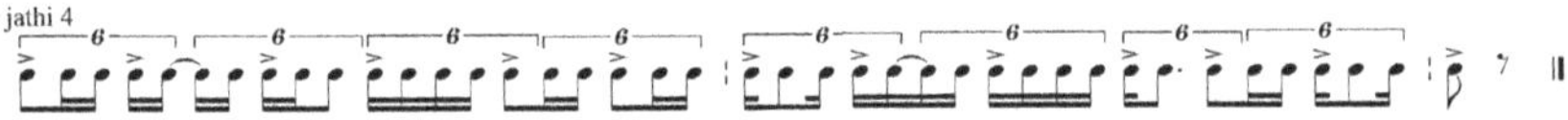

Tisra jathi 5

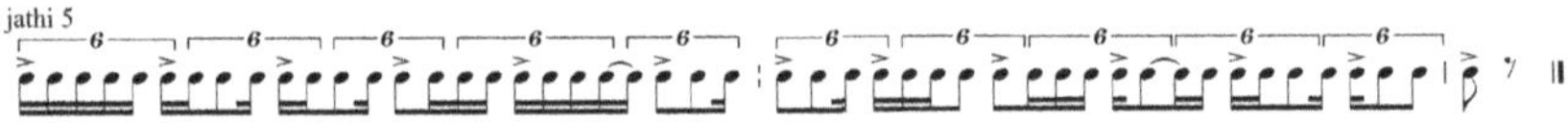

Tisra jathi 7

Khanda jathi 3

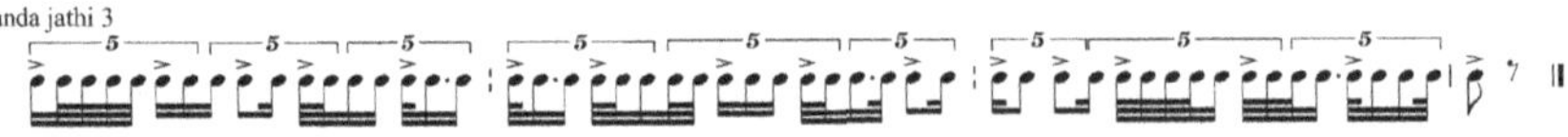

Khanda jathi 4

Khanda jathi 7

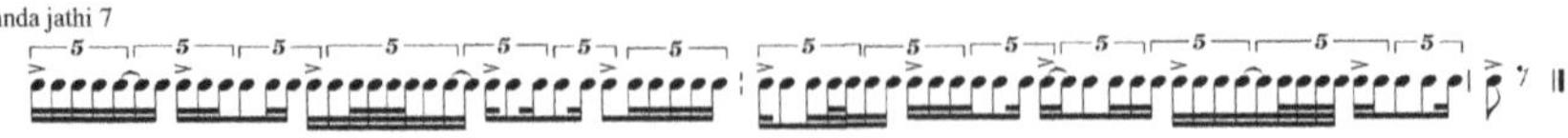

2

Misra jathi 3

Misra jathi 4

Misra jathi 5

Chapter 5

Rhythmical Sangatis

A rhythmical sangati occurs when a phrase that has previously been performed in one gati is realised or 'transformed' into a different gati. There are three possible ways to make this change of gati.

1) The Original Gati becomes the Jathi in the New Gati

If, for instance, a 5-beat phrase in chatusra is taken as starting point and 'transferred' to khanda, jathi 4 will be applied and the phrase will simply sound like the original, but in a faster tempo.

The original phrase in chatusra, *(track 31)*

when transferred to khanda jathi 4, will look like this: *(track 32)*

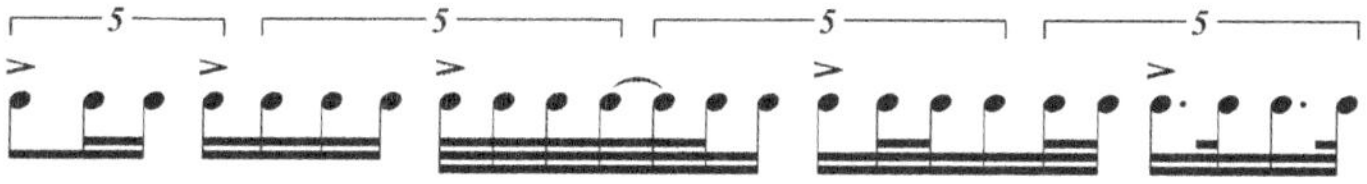

2) Keeping the Flow of the New Gati

In this option, what remain of the original are the note values and their order; but the flavour of the original phrase and gati will disappear, while the feeling of the new gati (khanda in this example) should be present. What was grouped every 4 matras is now grouped and beamed every 5 matras. Nonetheless, the listener can perceive a relationship with the original phrase.

Taking the previous phrase in chatusra, the new phrase looks like this *(track 33)*

3) Using a Different Jathi

With this option, the original phrase is further modified, since two elements are applied to it: the change of gati and the use of a jathi different to 4 (if we take the chatusra example). There will then be two possible jathis to choose from (in this example it could be jathi 3 or 7).

However, this option encounters a 'problem'. In the two previous examples the number of beats and accents was complete: in khanda jathi 4 there were 5 accents in 4 beats; and in the second example the phrase was 4 beats long.

When a different jathi is used, the number of accents that the new jathi requires to resolve on a beat cannot be completed with the original length of the phrase (in this case 5 beats of chatusra or 20 matras). If the phrase is to be performed in, for instance, khanda jathi 3, the 20 matras of the original phrase will provide 6 accents of 3 matras, and there will still be 2 matras left that, obviously, could not take a jathi 3. There are three solutions to this dilemma:

a. Start the phrase on the beat, and after the six accents of jathi 3 conclude the last two matras of the phrase as a jathi 2. *(track 34)*

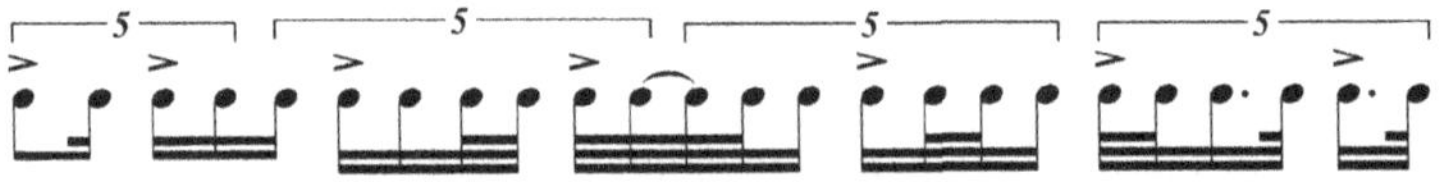

The main problem with this option is that it could eventually sound as though the last grouping of 2 matras is in reality a mistake committed by the performer in order to meet the beat or the conductor. Karnatic musicians seldom use this option.

b. Start the phrase with the jathi 2 at the beginning and proceed with the jathi 3 right afterwards. In this way the tension created by the jathi 3 will be resolved on a beat.[1] *(track 35)*

c. This is the most common option that, simultaneously, opens up a wide range of developmental possibilities. Jathi 3 is used from the beat (and not off-beat as in the previous example); and, on arriving at the problematic point of the 2 matras, extend the phrase using jathi 3 until it resolves on a beat. *(track 36)*

[1] This possibility has very interesting ramifications when using polyrhythms and while developing phrases in a tree. These will be explained later.

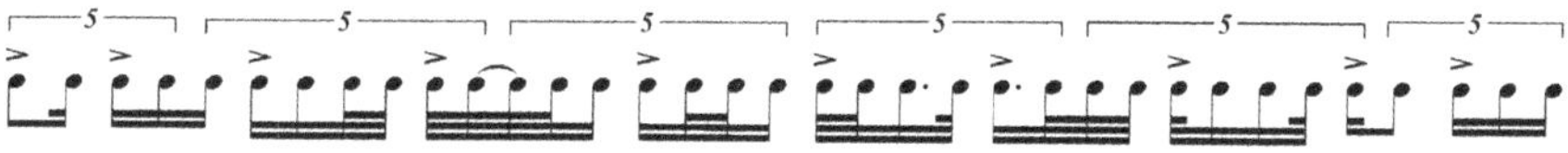

The first 2 matras of the 7th accent (where the original phrase finished previously in the example 'A'), by virtue of the addition of two 𝅘𝅥𝅯 are now part of a jathi 3 phrase. Further, the phrase has been extended by adding three groups of jathi 3 to ensure that it finally resolves on a beat.

When using this third option it is often impossible to apply the chosen jathi in a 'clean' way, generally because of the length of note values of the original phrase. If there were two ♪and jathi 3 were to be applied to them, this would obviously be impossible, since they are two notes of 2 matras. What karnatic musicians may do in this situation is divide the second ♪ into two different notes (two 𝅘𝅥𝅯) with separate attacks: the first one would become the 3rd matra of a grouping of jathi 3, and the second one would be the 1st matra of the next grouping of jathi 3.

While this does occur and is 'allowed' in karnatic music, musicians are somewhat reticent to use this possibility. This is because the underlying relationships established by the note values and the mathematical proportionalities that any phrase creates is broken if a note is divided into two. Hence, using it more than a couple of times in a phrase (the number will depend on the length of the phrase) is strongly discouraged.

Developmental Ramifications

While the first two techniques of rhythmical sangatis are quite self-explanatory and do not open many possibilities beyond the technique in itself, the third option of applying a different jathi has opened up a wide array of questions and possibilities that can also be applied to the first two adapting options.

The solutions to the problem created in a khanda jathi 3 version of a 5-beat long phrase in chatusra can be taken further into other contexts.

The example given here (5 beats in chatusra taken into khanda) enabled the khanda phrase to be 4 'neat', complete beats long. But what happens when a creator wants to take, for instance, a 4-beat phrase in chatusra (16 matras) into tisra, or a 7-beat phrase in khanda (35 matras) into chatusra?

Any phrase in any gati, regardless of its length, can be taken into any other gati, and any of the possibilities explained above can be applied – keeping the flow of the original phrase, keeping the flow of the new gati or using a different jathi besides the new gati. Now in a different context these options can be defined as follows:

The rhythmical sangati concept is not an end in itself, but a developmental notion to bind gati and/or jathi changes and to try to provide cohesion to these changes.

Starting Point of a Rhythmical Sangati

Any rhythmical sangati phrase can have two starting points.

1. Start on a beat and finish wherever in the beat the length of the original phrase permits. Taking the two examples mentioned above – 16 matras in chatusra taken into tisra and 35 matras of khanda taken into chatusra – would simply imply that the first phrase will finish on the 1st matra of the 6th beat. Further, the 35 matras of khanda will result in a phrase in chatusra that will finish on the 3rd matra of the 9th beat.

Not finishing neatly on a beat does not mean that phrasing in the new gati has to come to a stop. Consequently, the rhythmical sangati serves the purpose of commencing a phrase in a new gati, connecting it to a new idea while binding the gati change. Once the rhythmical sangati phrase has finished, regardless of its position in the beat, the creator can simply incorporate new rhythmical phrases or ideas afterwards. This is basically the notion explained in the above example of khanda jathi 3 that extended the phrase until the jathi 3 resolved on a beat (although without necessarily having to resort to using this way of adapting a phrase).

Subsequently, the phrase in tisra of 5 beats and 1 matra can use any of the adapting techniques: keeping the flow of the original phrase, therefore using jathi 4 in this case; keeping the flow of the new gati – tisra in this case; or applying a different jathi to tisra – jathi 5 or 7 in this case. Although the musical result of the chosen adapting technique will be different in each case, the resulting phrase can connect with any other musical idea within tisra immediately afterwards.

2. Start off the beat and finish on a beat. For this possibility, some calculations are required:
   - If 16 matras in tisra: leave 2 matras off the beat and start on the 3rd matra. The phrase will resolve on a beat.
   - If 35 matras in chatusra: leave 1 matra off the beat and start on the 2nd matra.

'Leaving' matras off the beat does not mean there has to be a silence of that length before the rhythmical sangati starts; any phrase can precede the rhythmical sangati phrase without any disruption. This notion can be found in the example of khanda jathi 3 when the 2 remaining matras were used to start the phrase.

A complete classification of options would be excessively long, and possibly futile; but as long as the following points are clear, it is up to the creator to explore the many possibilities opened up by this concept – with its many options and ramifications:

- the main idea of what constitutes a rhythmical sangati
- the three ways of adapting a phrase into a new gati
- the developmental purpose of rhythmical sangati as binding element.

'Incomplete' Gati/Jathi Combinations

Until now, any gati/jathi combination was thought of in terms of how many times the whole combination would be performed: a chatusra jathi 3 was always characterised by 4 accents in 3 beats, and the calculations were based on these numbers of beats. Consequently, this combination could result in 3 beats or any multiple thereof. However, as was also seen with the polyrhythms starting on different beats, a gati/jathi combination does not necessarily have to start on a beat.

In a tree of gati bhedam, when linking regular phrasing with any jathi of that gati, the regular phrasing can be followed by a jathi that starts on any of the accents of that particular combination. For example, if a chatusra phrase is to be followed by chatusra jathi 5, this device could start on any of the other three accents of this gati/jathi combination.

Needless to say, the original structure of where every accent falls within the beat should be kept intact. Starting off the beat does not imply starting anywhere in the beat, but starting on any of the possible accents of a particular gati/jathi combination. For example, a chatusra jathi 5 structure could also start on the:

- 2nd matra after the 2nd beat
- 3rd matra after the 3rd beat
- 4th matra after the 4th beat.

In the following example there are 7 beats of regular chatusra followed by chatusra jathi 5. The phrase of this gati/jathi combination starts on its 3rd accent, the one that would fall on the 3rd matra after the 3rd beat. Therefore, the chatusra jathi 5 combination contains 6 accents and lasts for 7+½ beats. *(track 37)*

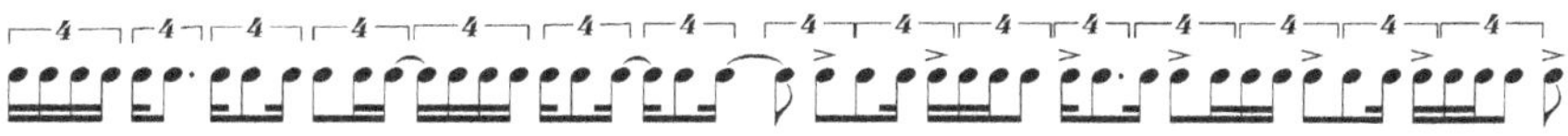

In this fashion, gati/jathi combinations become a much more flexible tool that do not need to be counted in terms of complete number of beats, or even number of blocks, but can appear fragmented and mixed with regular phrasing. Simultaneously, they provide more freedom while using rhythmical sangatis within any musical context but, more significantly, within a tree of gati bhedam where gati bhedam is possibly used more abundantly than anywhere else within karnatic music.

Summarising, rhythmical sangatis can be used as a developmental technique:

- in any context, anywhere in the creation of a piece, or in an improvised solo;
- with specific creative techniques that will be explained further on in the book;
- as the main source of ideas within a tree of gati bhedam.

Although not exclusively the only technique used to develop phrases in a tree, rhythmical sangati is indeed the 'trade mark' of a tree. Below is a short example of a tree of gati bhedam using primarily rhythmical sangatis.

Commencing with a short phrase of usually 4–6 beats, the various ways of adapting phrases characteristic of rhythmical sangatis and the connection of any rhythmical sangati to any other phrase enables the creator to shape a spider's web of interrelated ideas that can be further modified, distorted etc.

Depending on the creator's taste for 'closeness' to or 'distance' from the raw material, during the development of a tree one can find recurring phrases in different gatis, or phrases that hold similarities and subliminal cohesion with one another, while the musical result is a continuous exploration of ideas. *(track 38)*

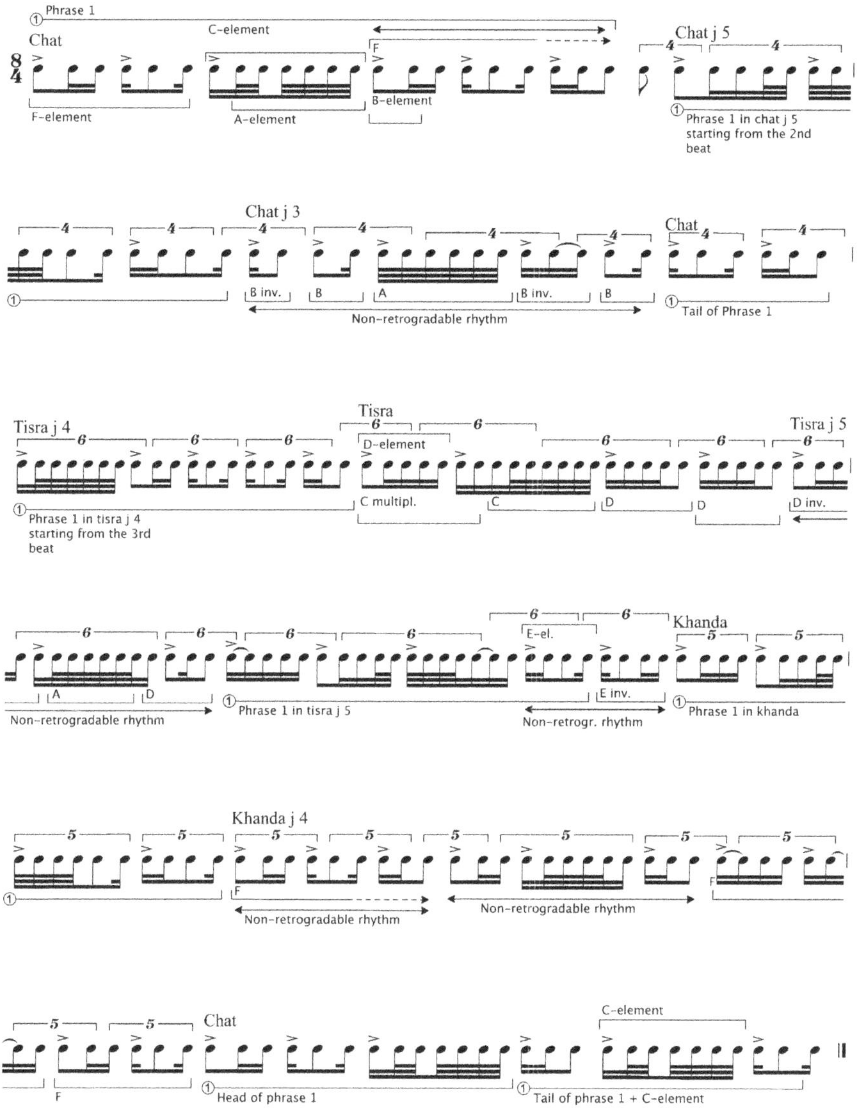

Phrase 1
Chat
C-element
F
F-element
A-element
B-element
Chat j 5
Phrase 1 in chat j 5 starting from the 2nd beat
Chat j 3
B inv.
B
A
B inv.
B
Non-retrogradable rhythm
Chat
Tail of Phrase 1
Tisra j 4
Tisra
D-element
Tisra j 5
Phrase 1 in tisra j 4 starting from the 3rd beat
C multipl.
C
D
D
D inv.
A
D
Non-retrogradable rhythm
E-el.
Khanda
Phrase 1 in tisra j 5
E inv.
Non-retrogr. rhythm
Phrase 1 in khanda
Khanda j 4
F
Non-retrogradable rhythm
Non-retrogradable rhythm
F
F
Chat
C-element
Head of phrase 1
Tail of phrase 1 + C-element

Chapter 6
Jathi Bhedam

This technique is the karnatic equivalent of the western concept of continuous metre changes or, as some musicians prefer to call it, *amalgamation* (of which Stravinsky's *Le Sacre du Printemps* is possibly the first and best-known example).

Jathi bhedam is a concept whereby accents embracing groups of matras of different length succeed one another. It could be defined as a sequence of irregularly distributed accents whose aim is to provide the impression or illusion of an *inner amalgamation* or continuous change of metre within the tala. Simultaneously, it is also a very important creative device in karnatic music from which many other creative techniques are derived.

As opposed to the western version of amalgamation, where the metre changes usually apply to all instruments (exceptions to this generality can be found in pieces by Charles Ives, among others), in karnatic music a jathi bhedam sequence can be performed in 1 layer only while another layer could be doing something entirely different. Furthermore, the calculations for a jathi bhedam sequence will always be thought of within the boundaries of the tala, whether 1, 2 or more cycles long.

As with gati bhedam – where the feeling of the jathi prevailed over the gati and the phrases needed to be felt and performed as 3/16, 4/16 etc – in jathi bhedam the chosen numbers must also be felt as though they were a metre of 5/16, 7/16, 3/8 etc. Consequently, a jathi bhedam sequence could eventually be structured in such a way that an accent may never fall on a beat, except when resolving on tala sam.

Construction of a Sequence

In order to construct a jathi bhedam sequence, more accent possibilities are available than in gati bhedam. Accents may occur every 1, 2, 3, 4, 5, 6, 7, 8 or 9 matras.[1]

Method of Construction

1. Decide on the gati and number of cycles to be used for the sequence, and calculate the number of resulting matras. In the example below the tala is 9 beats long and the gati is chatusra, which results in 36 matras.

[1] When using 6 or 8 matras the phrase has to be felt as such, and never as 2 times 3 or 4.

2. Choose numbers which, when added together, would equal the resulting number of matras.[2] The choice of these numbers and, more importantly, their ordering to construct the sequence needs careful thought for reasons that will become more apparent later in the chapter. In the following example the numbers are:
   - 3 × 4 times 5 × 2 times 1 × 1 time 2 × 1 time
     4 × 1 time 7 × 1 time
3. Establish an order with the chosen numbers. To do so, all karnatic musicians should observe a series of rules. However, of the many possible rules in karnatic music to construct the sequence, I consider only the following as relevant for laying the foundations of a jathi bhedam sequence in a western context:
   a. No accent should fall on a beat until at least the 4th accent of the sequence has been reached (the importance of the number 3 in karnatic music will become clear later).
   b. Never accent two consecutive beats; consequently, avoid the number 4 in chatusra where the previous accent falls on the beat (5 if khanda etc).
   c. Do not place the same number more than 3 times in a row, in order to avoid any feeling of regularity or gati bhedam.
   d. If 2 or more cycles have been chosen for the sequence, never accent any of the intermediate tala sams until the resolving tala sam.

In the example below, a few potential problems need to be taken into consideration.

- The number 3 has been chosen 4 times: repeating this number 4 times in a row should be avoided if the third rule (avoiding the same number more than 3 times in a row) is to be respected.
- The sequence starts with the number 7: subsequently, if the first rule (no accent should fall on a beat until at least the 4th accent of the sequence has been reached) is to be respected, the numbers 1 or 5 should be avoided as the 2nd accent in the sequence (7+1=8 matras// 7+5=12 matras).
- The 4th and 8th accents fall on the 5th and 8th beats respectively: accordingly, the number 4 should not be used at those points.

The final sequence (7 4 5 3 3 1 5 2 3 3) and a phrase that articulates this sequence is thus *(track 39)*

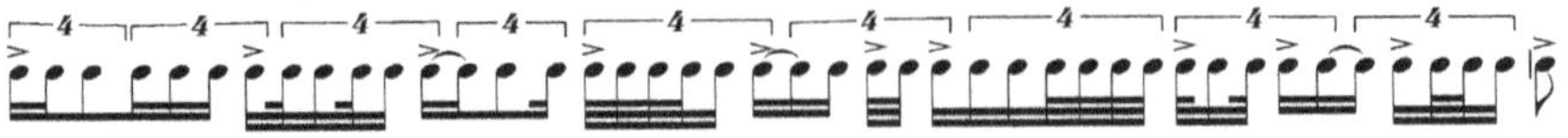

2 Numbers and accents mean exactly the same in the context of jathi bhedam.

It is important to emphasise that jathi bhedam phrasing always revolves around the accent. In fact, the phrase *is a result of* the chosen numbers, and no accent should be skipped or silenced. Doing the latter would simply result in a different sequence to the one worked out in advance.

It is also necessary to comment on the notational aspect: it can be observed that the notation devised for gati bhedam – beaming the phrase across the beat-line and placing brackets over 4, 5, 6 or 7 matras (depending on the gati) – is also applied here. If traditional notation is utilised it would be very difficult to transmit the idea of inner amalgamation in a context of continuous accent changes. In fact, the 'style' proposed in Chapter 4 and employed above has become one of the notational cornerstones in my music and in that of many of my students in order to translate karnatic techniques into a readable western notation that conveys the desired feeling behind this and derived creative techniques.

Phrasing Possibilities

There are two ways to create phrases in a jathi bhedam sequence.

1) *Apply the same number of notes per accent*: In this particular case every accent is taken as a 'cell' against which the same number of notes is utilised. The choice is usually 2, 3 or 4 notes per cell. In the following example, 2 cycles of tala 7 are used for the sequence. The first option is solely performing the accent without any other added note (therefore, 1 note per cell). *(track 40)*

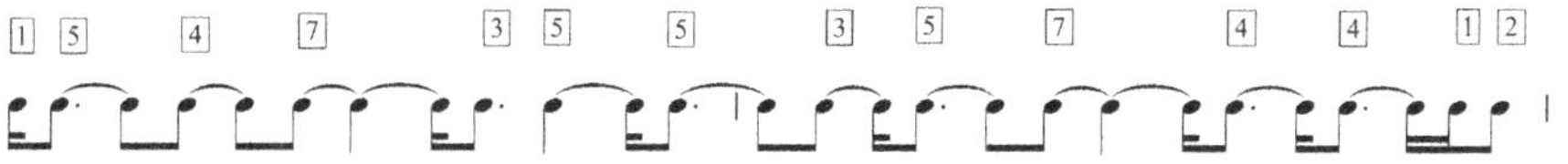

In the second option the choice is 2 notes per cell. Although in this example every accent of 3, 5 or 7 uses the same phrase, this does not have to be the case. When using this phrasing possibility, every 'repetition' of a number can take a completely different phrase as long as the same number of notes is respected. *(track 41)*

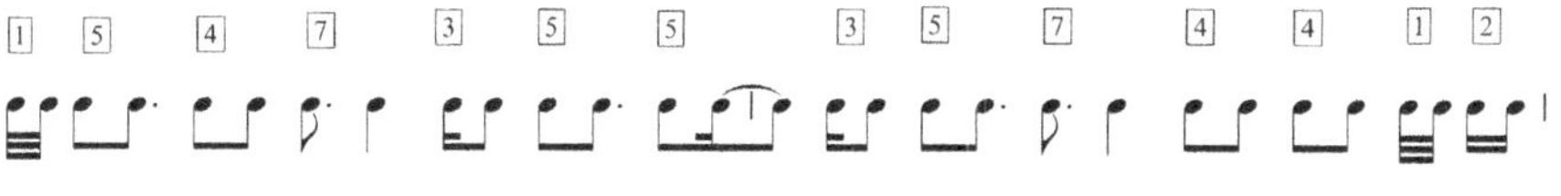

In the third option the choice is of 3 notes per cell. It can be observed that the gati used on the cells of 1 and 2 matras is not chatusra but tisra (against 1 and 2 matras respectively). This, in principle, contradicts what it has been said so far about not mixing 2 or more gatis in one cycle.

However, this gati mixing is just a glimpse of a far-reaching and complex approach to what in the West is generally called 'irregular groupings', and will be further explored and explained in Chapter 20 on combinations *anuloma-pratiloma.* Suffice it to say that, when using this phrasing possibility – and due to the systematic choice of the number of notes per cell (3 in this case) – a triplet could eventually be used against each cell (and not only against 1 or 2 matras). *(track 42)*

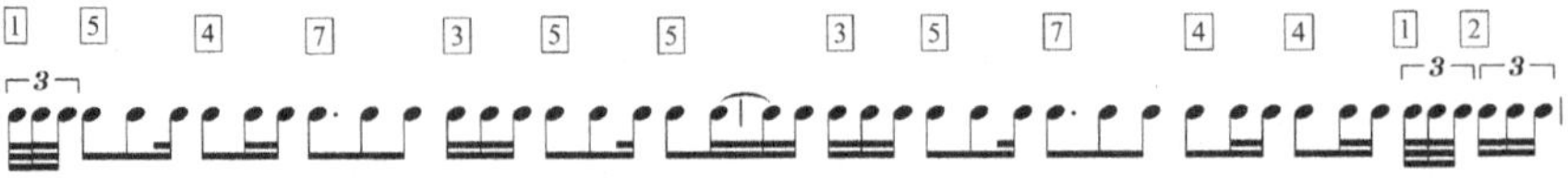

2) *Free phrasing*: This concept is quite self-explanatory: as long as the phrase is created around the accents, the phrase can be done with any number of notes per cell. *(track 43)*

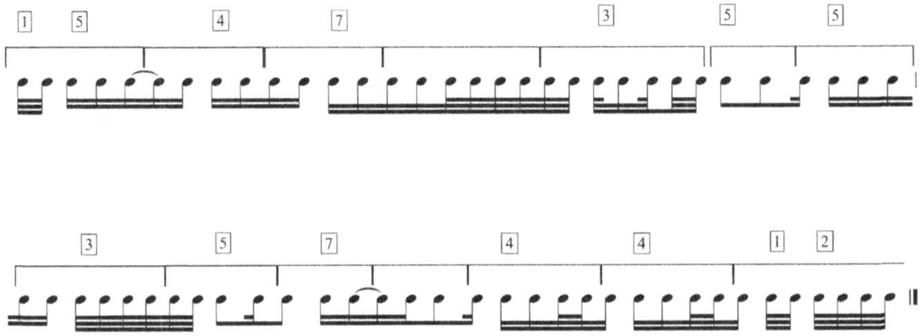

For the purposes of acquiring a bigger picture of phrasing possibilities, the following two examples are provided with the audio tracks. *(track 44)*

tisra 12 beats [7 4 5 3 3 1 5 3 3 2 4 3 5 1 3 4 5 4 7]

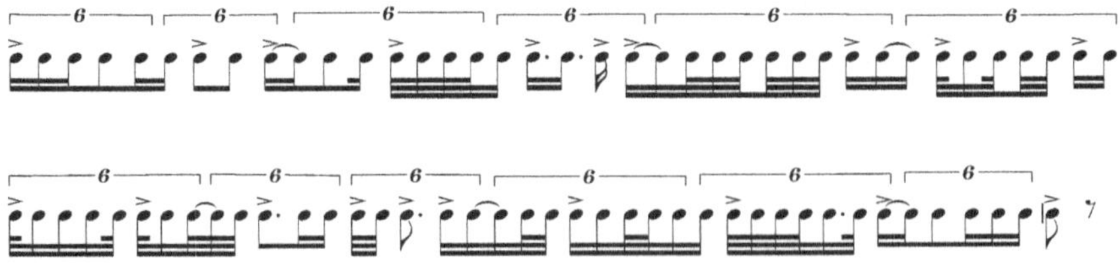

(track 45)

khanda 9 beats [7 7 5 6 4 4 5 1 3 3]

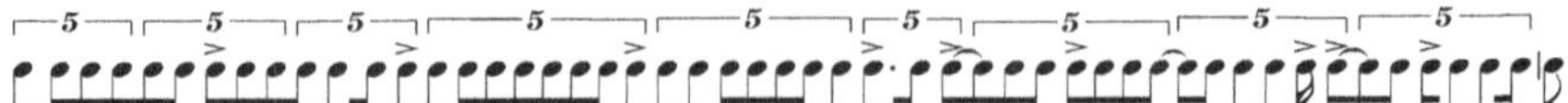

If the two previous examples are translated into western outer amalgamation, the time signatures would be similar to or the same as the ones created by Brian Ferneyhough, in which the denominator denotes ♪ or 𝅘𝅥𝅯 of triplets or quintuplets – such as 7/24, 2/12, 5/24 (as the first three numbers of the example in tisra would suggest) – or 7/20, 3/10 and 4/20 (as the 1st, 4th and 5th cells of khanda would imply).

Developmental Possibilities of a Sequence

A sequence of jathi bhedam in karnatic music is almost as important as the motivic material could be in be-bop or much nineteenth-century classical composition. However, any development on the sequence would be based exclusively on numerical relationships within the sequence and will never have a 'phrase-development' character. Consequently, in order to create phrases, a karnatic musician will take into consideration the two phrasing techniques described previously and, more importantly, the musical context where the sequence is utilised.

The first step (the step that is actually thought out while creating the original sequence) is to split the sequence into 2, 3 or a maximum 4 fragments that will become *independent units*. The parameters to determine which number can or should be the first or last of a fragment, or how many cells should be part of every fragment, might seem rather subjective. The only element found systematically is the avoidance of the accent of 1 matra as the last accent of a fragment, possibly due to the 'pushing forward' character of this accent. Another element is that fragments of similar length are rarely employed.

However, the establishment of a certain feeling for numerical patterns and a clear logic behind decisions is of utmost importance. It is my conviction that the highly mathematical nature of karnatic music enables its practitioners to see relationships that might easily escape the western eye or mind frame, so that what is 'clear' logic to Indian musicians may be quite obscure to westerners.

If the first sequence in chatusra is taken and 2 fragments are chosen

7 4 5 3 3 1 5 2 3 3
the division into 7 4 5 3 3 (A) 1 5 2 3 3 (B)

seems like the most logical choice. This is because of the repetition of 3 3 at the end of each fragment, and because 1 starts the second fragment – something that usually gives character or 'push' to the numerical sequence.

Dividing this particular sequence into 3 fragments would probably result in very few developmental options due to the fact that making fragments of 3 cells diminishes the number of possible variations within the fragments. In addition, karnatic musicians would probably find them too random and not sufficiently logical. For example:

7 4 5	3 3 1 5	2 3 3
7 4 5 3	3 1 5	2 3 3

If the second numerical sequence in chatusra is taken (2 cycles of tala 7)

1 5 4 7 3 5 5 3 5 7 4 4 1 2

a clear logical numerical pattern may not be easy to find at first sight, but a few options could be:

1 5 4 7 3	5 5 3 5 7	4 4 1 2
1 5 4 7	3 5 5 3 5	7 4 4 1 2
1 5 4 7 3 5	5 3 5 7	4 4 1 2

The last option seems to contain more logic due to the relationship of the last 3 5 of the first fragment with its retrograde 5 3 of the second fragment, and the 7s being placed at similar points in relation to the 3s and 5s in the first and second fragments.

On the other hand, the second option accumulates all the 3s and 5s in the second fragment, while using 7 to finish and start the first and third fragments respectively.

As mentioned before, the reasoning behind these choices can become extremely subjective. However, after the description below of one of the possible developments, it will become clearer why the third option is a better one.[3]

Techniques

A) When the Development Occurs in the Same Gati as the Original

1) Keeping the original order of the fragments.
Keeping the fragments A, B and C in the same order enables the 'inner content' or sequence of numbers to be retrograded; but, more interestingly, it enables two consecutive numbers to exchange their position in the sequence. Both concepts can be used in the same development but applied to different fragments. All the possibilities are thus:

Original	1 5 4 7 3 5	5 3 5 7	4 4 1 2
Exchange two consecutive numbers	5 1 4 7 3 5	3 5 5 7	4 1 4 2
	1 4 5 7 3 5	5 5 3 7	4 4 2 1
	1 5 7 4 3 5	5 3 7 5	
	1 5 4 3 7 5		
	1 5 4 7 5 3		
Retrograded version	5 3 7 4 5 1	7 5 3 5	2 1 4 4

[3] From now on, the fragments will be called A, B and C.

2) Keeping the original order of the cells
If the 'inner content' or original sequence of the numbers remains intact, one can:

- reorganise the order of the fragments
- repeat and/or omit fragments.

Through these options, and since the three possibilities can coexist in any development, the number of variations would go beyond any classification. Here there are just a few examples:

B B A C A   A C A B   A B A B   C A   C B C A B

Repetition and/or omission of a fragment will result in lengthening or shortening the original sequence; therefore, the developed sequence would not fit into the original number of cycles of the tala. In this case it is customary to finish the sequence on tala sam by adding what is called a *short mukthay*.

Mukthays are one of the longest, most varied and most fascinating subjects in karnatic music, and short mukthays are just their simplest form. However, for the purposes of completing the information needed for this chapter suffice it to say that a short mukthay is a phrase repeated three times – every repetition usually separated by a 'gap'.[4]

If the third example above is taken (A B A B), since A is 25 matras long and B is 20, the total length would be 90 matras. This number of matras would not fit into any multiple of tala 7. Therefore, one should establish how many cycles of the chosen tala would be closest to the resulting number: 90 matras in chatusra equals 22 beats plus 2 matras. One, two or three cycles of tala 7 would fall short of this number of beats. Four cycles thus seems to be the most logical choice, since it would be 28 beats or 112 matras long.

In order to decide the length of the short mukthay, one must subtract 90 matras (the length of sequence A B A B) from 112 matras (4 cycles of tala 7), which will give 22 matras.

These 22 matras will be the total length of the short mukthay. Since a mukthay is a phrase repeated three times, 22 matras must be divided by 3. This would give 3 phrases of 7 matras each, plus 1 matra left over for the gap. Given that there are 2 gaps (between 1st and 2nd phrase and 2nd and 3rd) and *every gap has to be the same length*, every gap would be ½ matra long (or a ♪). The phrase to be used can be as close to or as contrasting with the previous material as the creator would like it to be.

[4] 'Gap' is a literal translation of the word kaarvai, used to describe the separation between phrases. The reason karnatic musicians call it a gap and not a silence or rest will become clearer in Chapter 8.

So the whole sequence would look like this:

A (25 matras) B (20 matras) A B+short mukthay (7, ½, 7, ½, 7)|tala sam

Summarising: There are two elements that can be used for developing a jathi bhedam sequence – the 'inner content' of the fragments (or sequence of numbers) and the order of the fragments itself. *Only one of them can be changed.* If one decides to make any alteration to the original order of the fragments in the sequence, the order of the numbers must be left intact and vice versa; if one wants to change the order of the cells, the original order of fragments must be kept intact.

B) When the Development Occurs in A Different Gati to the Original

1) The number representing the new gati becomes an important element for resolving the sequence on tala sam

If the original sequence of 2 cycles of tala 7 is performed in, for instance khanda, the result will be that the 56 matras in chatusra of the original sequence become 11 beats plus 1 matra in khanda. Consequently, 2 beats and 4 matras are 'missing' in order to resolve the whole sequence onto tala sam. These 2 beats need to represent the choice of the new gati, therefore the number 5 should be chosen twice (as a general rule, the number representing the gati should be used as many times as the number of beats remaining to complete the tala).

Eventually, as is the case in this example, there could be a number of matras left that do not complete a beat. This number will be used as such for the completion of the sequence and never split into further cells. Thus the sequence of 56 matras will require of a cell of 5 matras × 2 times, plus a cell of 4 matras. This can be done in any of the following ways:

5 5 4 5 4 5 4 5 5[5]

Placement of added cells:

a. at the beginning of the tala followed by the sequence 5 5 4 A B C
b. after the sequence ends A B C 5 5 4

In these two cases the cells inside every fragment can be developed as explained previously, as long as the order of the fragments is kept intact. Fragments are always kept in the original order – although, eventually, a simple exchange between A and B or B and C can be found in karnatic music. No repetition or omission of fragments is ever done when the sequence is taken into another gati.

[5] For the examples 5 5 4 is chosen, but either of the other two options could have been taken.

a. Inserting the added cells between the fragments.

This option is possibly the most interesting and far-reaching, since all the new cells do not appear as a block and the number of options increases. Some examples could be:

A 5 B 4 5 C   4 A 5 B 5 C   5 A B 5 C 4

However, with this option none of the possibilities regarding the development of the inner content or order of fragments is ever applied.

2) Using a Short Mukthay

The last option to resolve the sequence onto tala sam, quite surprisingly, destroys all the care put into showing the new gati by means of repeating its number as many times as beats are left over. This option is simply to work out a short mukthay to be played after the sequence is finished. In this example the 14 matras would be divided by 3 to give a phrase of 4 matras repeated 3 times and 2 gaps of 1 matra each.

Practice Method

- Prior to trying any phrase, practise the sequence of numbers by singing all the matras of every cell. Try to clearly feel the accents with a 'downbeat' feeling regardless of their position in the beat. Therefore, for the following jathi bhedam phrase it is useful to do all matras without the phrase.

chatusra 9 beats [7 4 5 3 3 1 5 2 3 3]

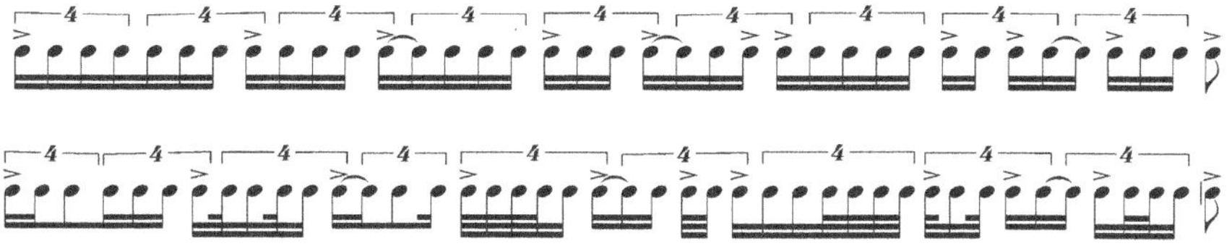

- Exaggerate the dynamic level and intentionality given to the accent, since each accent has to be performed with a downbeat feeling, as though the metres were changing continuously, and never as dynamic accents or syncopations to a phrase. Furthermore, avoid giving any downbeat feeling to any note that is not accented. Obviously, this does not mean that phrases have to sound 'flat' or emotionless. However, the westerner would certainly have a tendency to emphasise either notes falling on a beat or longer notes inside a phrase. Musicians should always be aware of this tendency.

- Once the sequence of numbers and accents is internalised, proceed to play every phrase separately so that the phrase begins to grow as such. Here, two approaches can be used:
  - Perform every cell of the phrase within a beat by turning the number of matras of each cell into a gati. For example, if a cell of the phrase is written around a jathi 5, play the phrase in khanda (as proposed in Chapter 4 for gati bhedam).
  - Perform the cell as if the number of matras of the accent were a metre. If jathi 5 in chatusra, play it as though a 5/16 metre; if tisra, 5/24 and so forth. Eventually, combining the two methods can help you acquire more accuracy and a better feeling for the phrase.

Below are two examples per gati, some of which are recorded and can be found elsewhere in the chapter.

chatusra 9 beats [7 4 5 3 3 1 5 2 3 3]

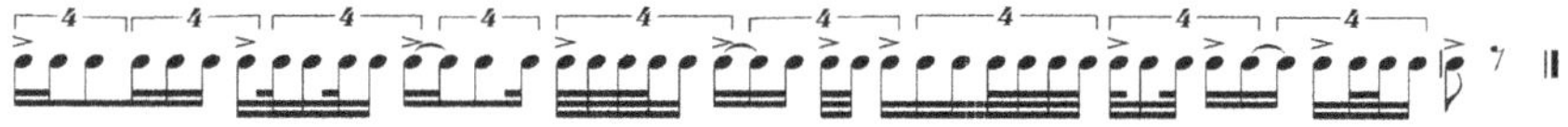

chatusra 12 beats [1 4 5 3 7 7 5 6 4 1 5]

tisra 9 beats [4 5 7 5 4 3 4 1 6 7 3 5]

tisra 12 beats [7 4 5 3 3 1 5 3 3 2 4 3 5 1 3 4 5 4 7]

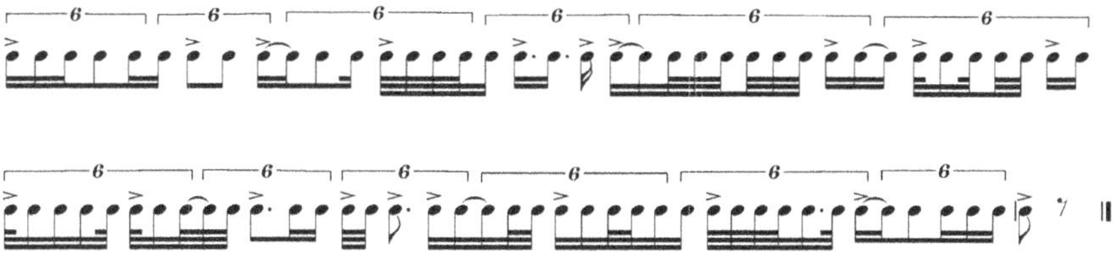

khanda 9 beats [7 7 5 6 4 4 5 1 3 3]

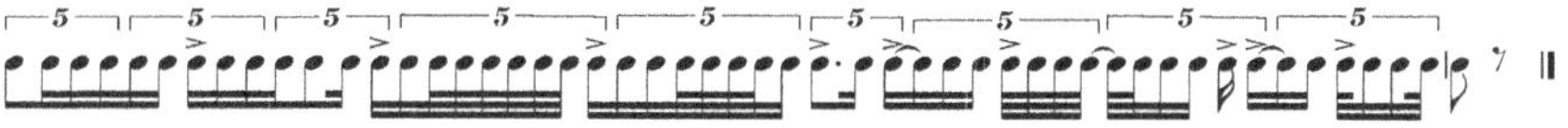

khanda 12 beats [3 5 4 4 5 1 6 7 2 7 6 3 4 3]

Chapter 7
Introduction to Anuloma-Pratiloma

Due to its multiple possibilities, complexity and ramifications, I find it necessary to introduce or offer a glimpse of this technique at this point (already of great depth in itself) and leave the more substantial part for later in the book. This technique is possibly one of the most complex in terms of performance, and far-reaching in terms of the creative possibilities of the whole constellation of concepts found in karnatic music. It could be said that, rather than a technique, it is an entire theoretical corpus that can be used to organise (both pedagogically and creatively) one of the rhythmical cornerstones of the last 80 years or so in western contemporary music: the use of 'numbers against numbers' or 'numbers against frames' – like 15:16, 5:6, 14:12 and so forth.

So far in this book, all techniques have been worked out using the so-called 'regular' or 'neutral' speed of every gati (except for tisra, which has been shown with triplets as well as sextuplets). Here the possibilities of 'speeds' in each gati will be increased by nine. Table 7.1 charts the entire range of anuloma-pratiloma.

Table 7.1 Chart of Anuloma-Pratiloma

		Anuloma		
	Tisra	Chatusra	Khanda	Misra
4th speed	12	16	20	28
3rd speed	9	12	15	21
2nd speed	6	8	10	14
		Neutral or Regular		
1st speed	3	4	5	7
		Pratiloma		
2nd speed	3:2	4:2	5:2	7:2
3rd speed	xx	4:3	5:3	7:3
4th speed	3:4	xx	5:4	7:4
5th speed	3:5	4:5	xx	7:5
6th speed	xx	4:6	5:6	7:6
7th speed	3:7	4:7	5:7	xx

Anuloma could be defined as *when the number of matras in a beat is doubled, tripled or quadrupled.* This constitutes a new notion when compared to the way western solfege has developed, where every new 'speed' or note value is twice as fast as the previous one. As it can be seen in Table 7.1, the 3rd speed anuloma of every gati is triple the regular speed. Therefore, karnatic musicians think of a regular triplet and superimpose the gati on every ♪ of the triplet.

It can also be found that the number (12) is repeated in two different gatis. When it is the 4th speed of tisra it is felt as 4 times tisra, and when it is the 3rd speed of chatusra it is felt as 3 times chatusra. *(track 46)*

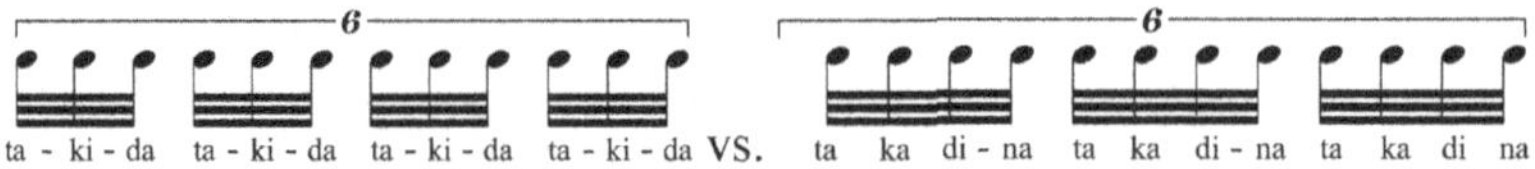

For all practical purposes, the 4th speed is used exclusively in the context of *combinations anuloma-pratiloma* that constitute the aforementioned large corpus of theory.[1]

Regarding the 3rd speed, this seems to be used as such solely by percussionists. However, other musicians may use it if the tempo is extremely slow. Otherwise, it also belongs to the realm of combination anuloma-pratiloma.

The 2nd speed – the equivalent of the western 𝅘𝅥𝅯 (except for tisra, where it would equal the western sextuplet) – is used quite frequently, with the exception of the 2nd speed misra, which tends to be used mostly by percussionists.

Pratiloma could be defined as *when the number of matras in a gati is spread throughout 2, 3, 4, 5, 6 or 7 beats.*

The 2nd, 3rd and 4th pratiloma speeds are also used quite often, whereas the 5th, 6th and 7th –, though practised and perfected by students and most professionals nowadays (who, consequently, are all capable of performing them) –, are seldom performed as such, belonging more to the realm of combinations anuloma-pratiloma.

In order to gain accuracy gradually as well as to start using this concept creatively with a certain degree of restriction, this chapter will only use the following speeds: *(track 47, with the two possibilities for 3rd speed pratiloma)*

	Tisra	Chatusra	Khanda	Misra
		Anuloma		
2nd speed	6	8	10	XX
		Neutral or Regular		
1st speed	3	4	5	7
		Pratiloma		
2nd speed	3:2	4:2	5:2	7:2
3rd speed	XX	4:3	5:3	7:3

[1] Combinations anuloma-pratiloma will be explained in Chapter 20.

A few irregular groupings have been used quite frequently in western contemporary music as well as jazz, from the 1960s onwards, namely 5:6𝅘𝅥𝅯, 7:6𝅘𝅥𝅯 and 4:3♪. These can be practised using a glimpse of combinations anuloma-pratiloma that can be added to the selected speeds for this chapter.

By introducing the principle of using the 2nd speed anuloma (8, 10 and 14 matras) within a 3rd speed pratiloma (that is, 8:3♩, 10:3♩ and 14:3♩), these three speeds can be added for purposes of this chapter, and the 3rd speed pratiloma will have two different options to work with:

3rd speed	xx	4:3	5:3	7:3
3rd speed	xx	8:3	10:3	14:3

Notation

Before proceeding further, it might be useful to have a completely clear picture of what could be considered the 'proper' notation for these karnatic speeds. Fortunately, this notation is readily available in western music – although, in my experience, few musicians are entirely clear about it.

The numbers used in Table 7.1 respond to karnatic notation. However, the first problem here is that currently no notation programme can recognise 14:3♩ as 14𝅘𝅥𝅯 in the time span of 3♩ – or even 5:3♩ for that matter. Nevertheless, despite this 'technical' impediment, the existing western notation can convey these karnatic concepts without any problem.

Tisra

- There is no discrepancy between the karnatic and western ways of notating the chosen speeds. The same is the case with

Chatusra

- Except for 8:3♩, which should be written 4:3♪ (or 8:6𝅘𝅥𝅯) × 2 times.
- 4:2♩ is simply 4♪

Khanda

- 5 and 10 should use the customary bracket of a quintuplet. The sole difference is that when the 2nd-speed anuloma is used, 𝅘𝅥𝅯 tends to be the majority of employed notes and, more importantly, the feeling behind its conception and performance will vary.[2]

[2] A fuller explanation of the implications of choosing a speed will be provided later in this chapter.

- 5:2♩ = 5:4♪
- 5:3♩ = 5:6♪
- 10:3♩ = 5:6𝅘𝅥𝅯 × 2 times

Misra

- 7 and 14 should use the customary bracket of a septuplet.
- 7:2♩ = 7:4♪
- 7:3♩ = 7:6♪
- 14:3♩ = 7:6𝅘𝅥𝅯 × 2 times

Developmental Concepts

In order to develop ideas with anuloma-pratiloma speeds it is necessary to fully understand the concept of speed, according to the karnatic tradition. In western music a phrase written in, for instance, 5:4♪, may include 𝅘𝅥𝅯 and even 𝅘𝅥𝅯. Ultimately, the only difference in western music regarding the issue of 'speeds' boils down to a difference between binary and ternary frames (taking into consideration only the possibilities given in this chapter).

In karnatic music every speed will use *its matra as the fastest note of that speed* so the difference between speeds can be appreciated. Therefore, 5:4♪ will have ♪ as its fastest note. Similarly, 5:6♪ will have ♪ as its fastest note and 14:3♩ (or 7:6𝅘𝅥𝅯 × 2) will have 𝅘𝅥𝅯 as the fastest possible note.[3] In this manner, besides the difference that binary and ternary frames can provide, the difference between regular 2nd anuloma and 2nd pratiloma speeds can be established, helping to add another dimension to the perception of tempo change while actually staying in the same laya.

With the whole theoretical corpus of combinations anuloma-pratiloma there are six developmental techniques, which are reduced to only two with the material explained in this chapter.

1) Choosing One Speed

A musician can take any of the speed possibilities presented in Table 7.1 and develop phrasing within that particular speed (the only phrasing seen so far was in the regular speed of every gati with some 𝅘𝅥𝅯 added). Now the possibility of phrasing is increased five-fold.

Depending on how long one decides to stay in a particular speed, more or fewer 'incursions' into faster speeds can be utilised, provided that the feeling of the chosen speed remains clear and constant throughout the whole passage.

[3] See 'phrases in different speeds' under point 6) of the practice method for a clear understanding of this notion.

The following phrase is written in 14:3♩. using the correct notation of 7:6𝅘𝅥𝅯. × 2. In such a short phrase, according to karnatic musicians, the use of 𝅘𝅥𝅰 (a faster note value than the fastest 'permitted' in 14:3♩.) would blur the feeling of 14:3♩. sought for. *(track 48)*

2) Mixing Speeds Linearly

In this concept a gati is chosen and all speeds pertaining to that gati can be used one after the other if desired. How frequently speed changes occur and/or if all possible speeds are utilised depends on what the creator wants to achieve. In this technique every speed has to limit itself to its own characteristics and avoid 'incursions' into any other speed. In the examples below, changes occur rather fast and all speeds are used in a very short time span – although I have heard passages with as many speed changes at a number of concerts.[4] *(track 49)*

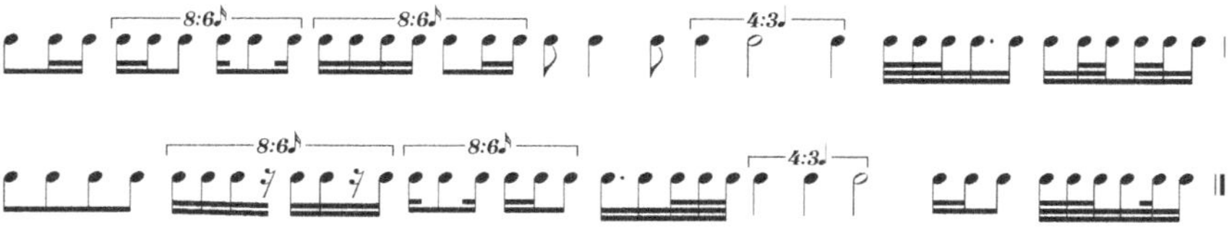

(track 50)

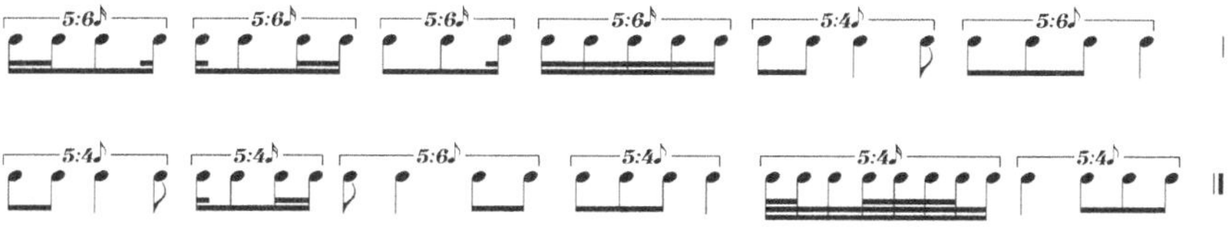

(track 51)

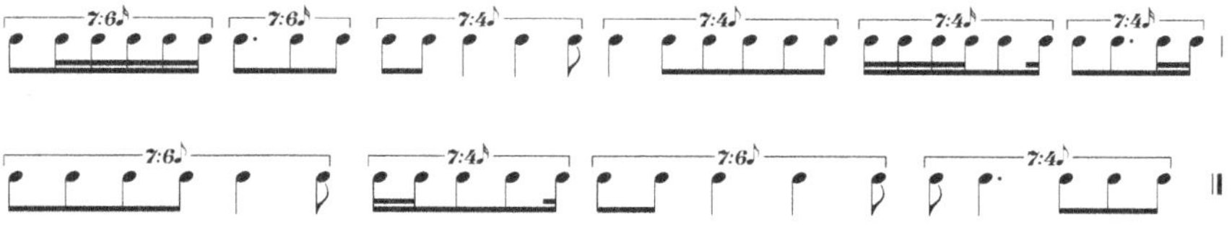

4 In the audio files the phrases are preceded by the speed changes performing all the matras.

- Both techniques must always resolve on a tala sam and last for at least one cycle of the tala.
- Rests can be used in both techniques, as seen in Chapter 2 on gatis. Tie-overs tend to happen much more often in the first than in the second technique, and to an even lesser extent when the tie-over is used between two different speeds.
- Anuloma-pratiloma speeds belong to the category of 'regular phrasing' in the tree of gati bhedam. This has a double effect on the tree:
  - 'Regular phrasing' possibilities are increased five-fold.
  - The changes between regular phrasing and gati bhedam phrasing can become more sporadic; and, as indicated in Chapter 4, the tree can also be used as an instrument to map out changes in a section or a whole composition.
- Gati bhedam, jathi bhedam and rhythmical sangatis can be applied to any speed as they were used on the regular speed.

Phrasing in 2nd speed anuloma

Phrasing possibilities with ♪. in chatusra and khanda go beyond the subdivision of 4+4 or 5+5. A few phrases which avoid this subdivision are given below. *(track 52)*

(track 53)

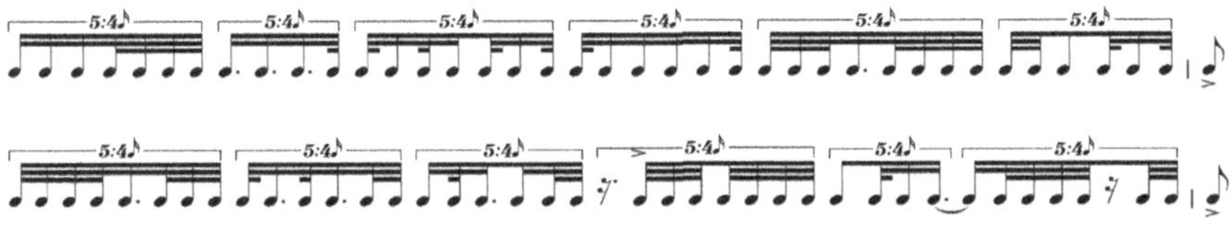

The following example is a transcription of a short solo by B.C. Manjunath, where he explores some of these ideas combined with rhythmical sangatis. *(track 54)*

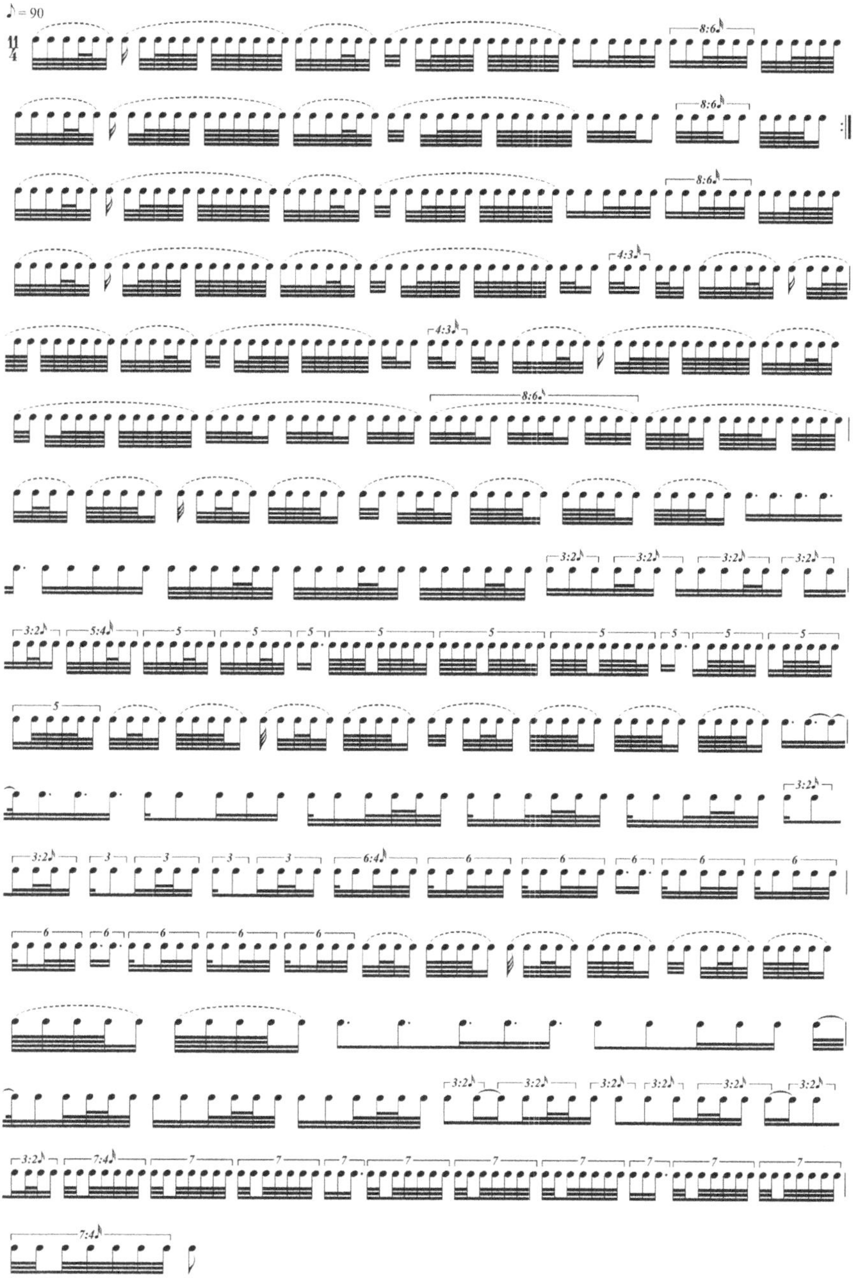
♪ = 90

Practice Method

1) As far as pratiloma is concerned, the starting point (as in gati bhedam) is to have a very clear idea of where the accents of a gati/jathi combination fall in relation to the beat, and then to practise every pratiloma speed separately until the latter is internalised.

a) In order to practise the 3rd speed pratiloma one should feel jathi 3 and isolate the accents; these accents would provide 4:3♩, 5:3♩ and 7:3♩ *(track 55)*[5]

b) 2nd speed pratiloma has an implicit jathi 2 on tisra, khanda and misra. Practising every gati at the regular speed – taking 2 beats as a frame while using the syllables TA-KI – can help visualise where every note of a 3:2♩, 5:2♩ and 7:2♩ would fall in relation to the beat. *(track 56)*

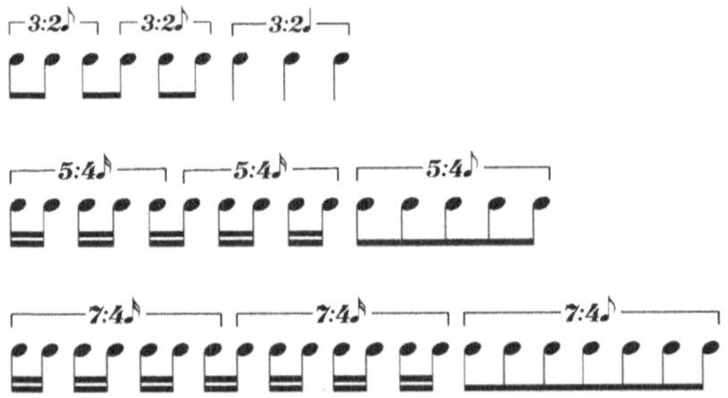

c) The jathi 2 can also be used while practising 8:3♩, 10:3♩ and 14:3♩. The musician should take the original 3rd speed pratiloma and double every accent – that is, sing 2 matras for every accent. Once this step is internalised, proceed to make two groups of 4, 5 and 7 respectively. *(track 57)*

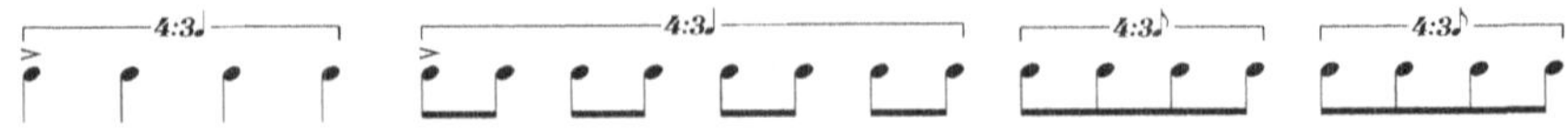

[5] Each step in the examples is recorded twice in the audio tracks.

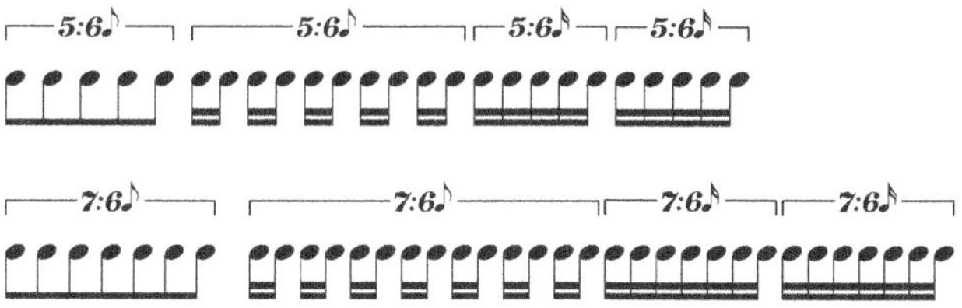

d) As for anuloma, since only the speeds of 8 and 10 are newly introduced, work on doubling the regular speed while doing two groups of 4 and 5 ♪. per beat.

2) Once every speed is internalised separately the first obstacle anyone would find is going between 2nd and 3rd speed pratiloma with accuracy. Consequently, practising these speeds in a loop would be beneficial.

3) Proceed to practise every gati with the following pattern:

regular speed	2nd anuloma	back to regular speed	2nd pratiloma
3rd pratiloma	2nd anuloma within 3rd pratiloma		reverse the order

4) Change speeds at random.

5) Practise changes of gatis while keeping the same speed as common denominator. For example, in 2nd speed pratiloma proceed as follows:

3:2 4:2 5:2 7:2 reverse order

Once the feeling for the proportionality between gatis is achieved, one can proceed to change gatis randomly.

6) Write simple phrases in every gati and perform the same phrase in the different speeds. In this manner, the phrase is felt in the regular speed, so playing it in the different speeds becomes less problematic than trying to perform a phrase in 5:2 or 7:3 in an isolated way. In fact, if a musician encounters a phrase in any of the speeds seen so far, it is quite advisable to practise the phrase by taking it to the regular speed so that the feeling for the phrase itself will become easier.

Below there are two examples – one in khanda and one in misra – using the correct notation and the karnatic terminology alongside. They also show that the notation for the phrases in 5:4♪. and 5:6♪. is the same. This is because in 5:4♪. and 5:6♪. there are 5 ♪. against 4 and 6 respectively. The time span for these 5 notes is different, but both examples use ♪. as their matra unit. *(track 58)*

Khanda

2nd speed anuloma

2nd speed pratiloma

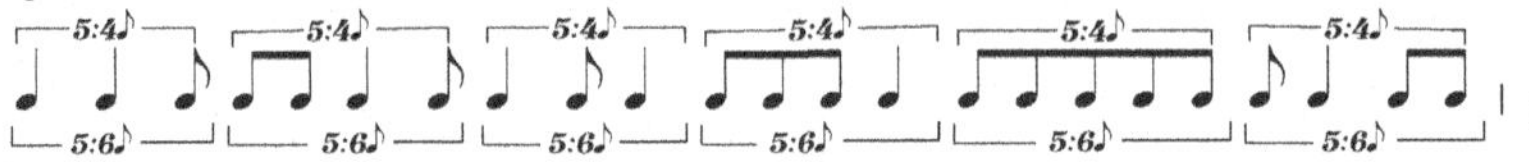

3rd speed pratiloma

(track 59)

Misra

2nd speed pratiloma

3rd speed pratiloma

7) Write phrases using the two developmental techniques explained above. As far as the 2nd developmental technique is concerned, you should first practise the speed changes by doing all the matras and, once the speed changes are internalised, proceed to perform the phrases. The phrases presented in the developmental techniques section can serve as an example for students to create their own phrases.

B: Exclusively Creative Techniques

Drawing on the foundations, the next 10 chapters are essentially of use to creators: they show the main creative ramifications derived from the concepts presented in Section A.

As a general way to explain their main red-thread while developing ideas, Indian musicians frequently use the image of a 'branch on a branch on a branch': 'every idea can be utilised only once but never only once'. In other words, every musical event is and should be susceptible to further development but never repeated without any sort of alteration. Beginning with a very strict set of rules, every device adds paths to gradually make techniques more flexible, and also shows how all concepts are ultimately interconnected.

Chapter 8
Mukthays

As mentioned in the chapter on jathi bhedam (Chapter 6), mukthays are one of the longest, most varied and most fascinating subjects in karnatic music. Musicians are continually exploring new paths and expanding the seemingly endless creative possibilities that this concept can bring forth.

This chapter will explain the most common (and possibly important) type of mukthay – sama mukthay – along with another type used less frequently (3-fold mukthay). However, their common denominator is that they are creative techniques derived from two concepts already seen: while jathi bhedam is the root technique for sama mukthays, gati bhedam is the base for 3-fold mukthays.

Sama Mukthays

This is the only type of mukthay that has concrete techniques for development throughout a piece, as opposed to most mukthays that tend to be a one-time occurrence. The principle is essentially the same as in short mukthays: a phrase is repeated three times, usually separated by a gap, that resolves on tala sam.

The main differences are that, while short mukthays are a tool to bridge the end of any technique or phrase and tala sam (but can start anywhere in the tala), sama mukthays must start and finish on tala sam. Further, any karnatic musician constructing a sama mukthay will always choose a possibility that will allow every repetition of the phrase to start in a different place within the beat, therefore provoking a displacement of the first phrase, while always making it sound as if it starts on the beat.

Each phrase of a mukthay is called a *pala*, an important term to avoid confusion when talking about the mukthay as a phrase, as opposed to a phrase of the mukthay (the latter called pala).

Construction of a Sama Mukthay

1) Choose the gati on which the original sama mukthay will be constructed and calculate the number of matras in one or two cycles of the tala.[1] In the example below, the chosen tala is 14 beats, the gati is chatusra and the number of cycles is 1. This will result in a mukthay of 56 matras (14×4).

---

[1] The original sama mukthay does not have to be constructed on chatusra, although the vast majority of them are indeed constructed in this gati.

2) Divide the number of matras by 3, since this is the number of palas of a sama mukthay. This division will provide the longest possible pala in the tala, and most of the time results in 1 or 2 matras left over that will be used for the gaps. In this example, 56:3=18 matras per pala, plus 2 remainder matras. These 2 matras will be divided by 2, since this is the number of gaps, and the length of the gaps must always be the same.

18 (1) 18 (1) 18|T.S.

3) Make a short list of possible pala and gap lengths so that the most suitable mukthay can be constructed. The first option does not necessarily have to be the one chosen (in fact, this rarely happens). To find these different options, subtract 1 matra per pala that will be added to the remainder matras to work out the length of the gaps.

If one matra per pala is subtracted, the length of every pala will be 17 matras. This 'releases' 3 matras that, together with the 2 remainder matras of the first calculation, would give 5 matras for the gaps. This number 5 will then be divided by 2 and will give two gaps of 2+½ matras.

17 (2+½) 17 (2+½) 17|T.S.

However, these 'fractional matra' gaps (the term used by karnatic musicians) are usually avoided. In order to avoid them, ½ matra is added to every gap, and the last matra of the last pala will resolve on tala sam. In order to make this possible, the last matra of the pala needs to be a ♪ and must always be attacked. The previous construction would then look like this:

17 (3) 17 (3) 16+|1 *(the 1 is the last matra of the 3rd pala and falls on tala sam)*

If two matras per pala are subtracted, the result will be:

16 (4) 16 (4) 16|T.S.

If three matras are subtracted:

15 (5+½) 15 (5+½) 15|T.S.

In this case, the addition of the ½ matra to each gap is necessary and the construction will result in

15 (6) 15 (6) 14+|1

One can go as far as one would like. However, under karnatic 'aesthetics' a sama mukthay with a gap longer than 5 or 6 matras is usually discarded.

4) Once the different options have been constructed, decide which one is the most suitable for the piece. In the decision-taking, factors other than the primary construction are observed: usually the developmental possibilities and whether the number of the pala gives scope for displacement within the beat or not are taken into account. These are the four valid constructions to choose from, once the options with 'fractional matra' gaps have been discarded:

18 (1) 18 (1) 18|T.S. 17 (3) 17 (3) 16+|1 16 (4) 16 (4) 16|T.S.
15 (6) 15 (6) 14+|1

Out of these four options, the second and third possibilities would automatically be discarded because in both cases all the palas will start on the beat; also, as mentioned before, the longest pala is not necessarily the best option. Subsequently, the fourth option will serve the purpose of illustrating this technique and its developmental possibilities.

5) Construct a short jathi bhedam sequence on the *length of 1 pala.* This sequence tends to have 2–4 cells (eventually 5) and it always bears a close relationship to the jathi bhedam sequence of the piece. A choice with 15 matras could be 6 4 5. This sequence will always be repeated in every pala and never permutated, because that is the essence of a sama mukthay: the repetition of a phrase three times.

6) Write a phrase on the chosen sequence. As will be seen in the developmental possibilities, the primary phrase, as well as the primary short jathi bhedam sequence worked out for the pala, has an important influence on the development. Therefore, this phrase needs to be thought of quite carefully.

With all the elements seen so far, the example below is a possible phrase, resulting from all previous numerical choices. It shows that because the last matra of the third pala falls on tala sam, this has been taken into consideration in writing the phrase. *(track 60)*

Developmental Possibilities

Staying in the Same Gati

Within this context, one of two elements can be used for developing a sama mukthay, each excluding the other: original jathi bhedam sequence on the pala, and original phrase.

1) If the latter is chosen, the phrase can be re-grouped (therefore creating a different jathi bhedam sequence), provided that all the note values and original order of notes are kept intact. Obviously, every accent has to attack a pre-existing note. Depending on the re-grouping, the new phrase can sometimes sound quite different to the original, for reasons given in the gati and jathi bhedam chapters: all accents have to be felt and performed with a downbeat feeling. Two examples are given using this option.[2]

a. The resulting jathi bhedam sequence through this re-grouping is 3 4 5 3. *(track 61)*

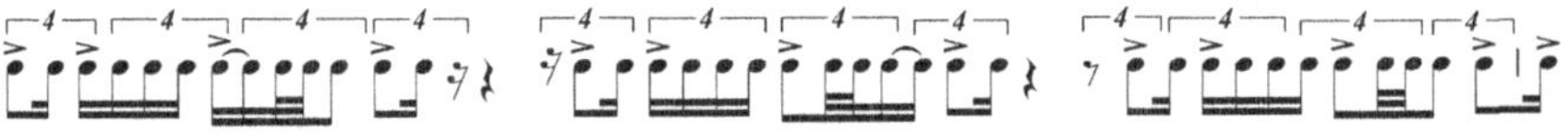

b. The resulting jathi bhedam sequence through this re-grouping is 5 7 3. *(track 62)*

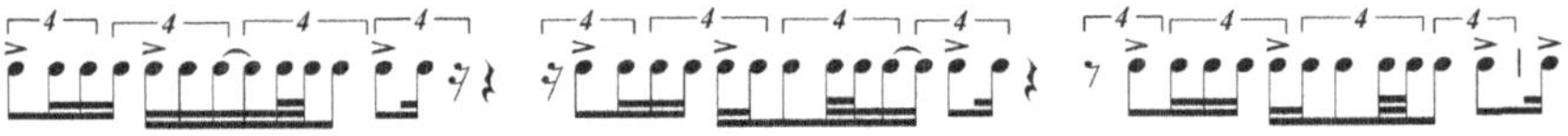

2) If the original jathi bhedam sequence is preserved, the number of different phrases that can be created is almost infinite. The phrase will depend on the musical context of the moment. The following two examples are extremely contrasting, in order to demonstrate that the jathi bhedam sequence can produce a variety of phrases with any kind of activity and atmosphere. *(track 63)*

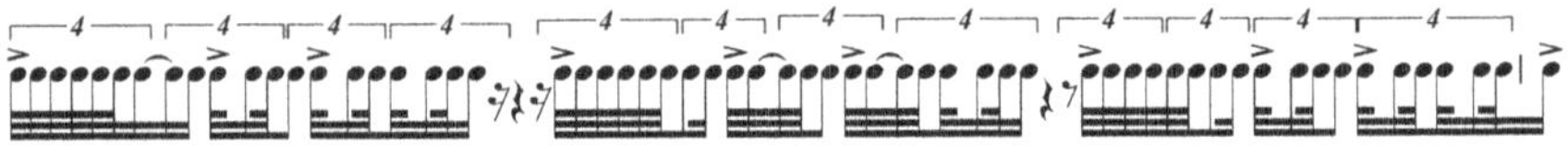

(track 64)

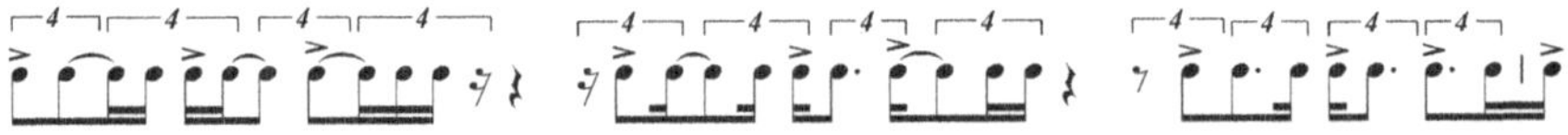

Taking the Mukthay into Another Gati (Rhythmical Sangati)

When this option is chosen, the original phrase, as well as the original jathi bhedam sequence, must remain intact.

Needless to say, when a mukthay is taken into another gati, it will not fit within the tala: it will either be shorter (if a faster gati is chosen) or longer (if a slower gati

2 Both examples show that every note perfectly matches the original phrase in terms of note value and order within the phrase.

is chosen) than the original number of beats of the tala. Adjustments to the phrase or gaps are not possible.

In this case it is customary to add a mini-mukthay at the end of the original sama mukthay (a mukthay within the mukthay, a microstructure within the macrostructure).[3] Certain calculations are required:

- The number of beats and matras of the tala that the new gati will use. In the example below, khanda is chosen for the rhythmical sangati. Considering that the original length of the mukthay is actually 57 matras and not 56, due to the fact that the last matra of the 3rd pala is used to resolve on tala sam, 57 matras should be divided by 5 (number of khanda):

  57:5=11 beats and 2 matras

- Subtract the number of beats in the tala from the length of the mukthay in the new gati. The resulting number will be used for creating the mini-mukthay:

  14 beats-11 beats and 2 matras=2 beats and 3 matras of khanda (or 13 matras of khanda)

The original jathi bhedam sequence was 6 4 5. The number of matras remaining with which to construct the mini-mukthay is 13. A choice of 3 (2) 3 (2) 3|T.S. could seem quite logical. However, the number 3 was not used in the original jathi bhedam sequence, and so should not be contemplated for the mini-mukthay.

The next option is to consider the number 4, which was included in the original sequence. This will result in:

4 (½) 4 (½) 4|T.S.

To avoid the 'fractional matra' gap, ½ matra can be added to every gap and, consequently, the last matra of the 3rd pala of the mini-mukthay will fall on the tala sam:

4 (1) 4 (1) 3 +|1

[3] It is important to note the difference between short and mini-mukthays: for the purposes of construction, a short mukthay does not need to take into consideration any of the numerical or even the phrasing/musical contexts that precedes it. A mini-mukthay is used exclusively to finish a sama mukthay transferred to a different gati, and it must always use 1 cell, or a combination of 2, of the original jathi bhedam sequence as a starting point. In terms of phrasing, the mini-mukthay has more freedom, as it can be used as a climactic factor or as a phrase that slows down the potential climax reached with the sama mukthay.

The mukthay would then look as follows: *(track 65)*

Two Alternatives for Mini-Mukthay Construction
In the above example, the mini-mukthay started immediately after the sama mukthay had concluded and stayed in the same gati. Eventually, one or even both elements can differ.

c. *Overlapping*: The last matra of the sama mukthay can simultaneously be the first matra of the mini-mukthay. If this is applied to the example, the number 5 can be employed, since the mini-mukthay 'steals' 1 matra of the sama mukthay; and, simultaneously, the last matra of the 3rd pala can fall on tala sam. This would result in the construction

   5 (0) 5 (0) 4 +|1 *(track 66)*

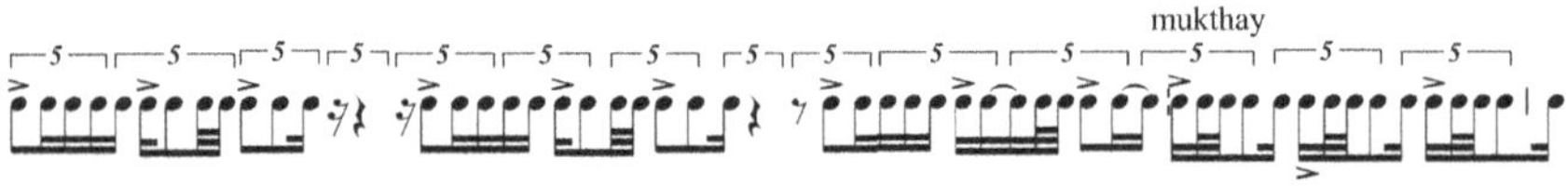

d. *Different gati*: Mini-mukthays can be structured in a different gati from the sama mukthay. However, this is only possible if the last matra of the sama mukthay finishes on the last matra of the beat; or, by combining it with the overlapping option, if it finishes on the beat and is taken as the 1st matra of the mini-mukthay by means of overlapping.

In the case of tala 14, if the choice of pala was 18 (1) 18 (1) 18|T.S. this would result in 56 matras, the original length used for the first calculations. This number of matras in khanda would result in 11 beats plus 1 matra. If this last matra is overlapped, the remaining 3 beats to complete the tala could take another gati for the mini-mukthay, as long as the rules regarding which cells can be employed for its construction are observed. The choice of gati depends on the desired musical effect.

In any event, there should never be any separation between the conclusion of the sama mukthay and the beginning of the mini-mukthay, regardless of which option is chosen for the latter.

Concept of Gap

As mentioned previously, 'gap' is the literal translation of the word *kaarvai*, which does not mean silence. Gap is the term that all karnatic musicians use when speaking English, but the word 'separation' possibly better conveys the meaning. A gap can be a silence (as all examples presented in this chapter) or it could be attacked, normally producing a note of the same length as the gap itself.

- It will always be a silence when the longest note of the phrase is as long as or longer than the gap.
- It can be attacked (optional) when the longest note of the phrase is shorter than the length of the gap.

3-Fold Mukthays

The 3-fold mukthays take regular phrasing and gati bhedam as a source for construction and phrasing. The section on sama mukthays mentioned that this is the only type of mukthay with a clear set of rules enabling the creator to develop an initial idea. Other mukthays tend to ignore any possible development in the piece, and are subject only to the context and how close to or contrasting with this context the creator would like the mukthay to be: 3-fold mukthays are a clear representation of this notion.

Construction Method

Depending on a few variables, there are three construction methods for this type of mukthay. Firstly, the steps common to all of them will be explained.

1. A number of matras common to 2 gatis in any of their speeds must be chosen, with complete independence from the tala. Usually, the numbers taken for every gati are 3, 6, 4, 8, 5, 10 and 7. Therefore, the number chosen will be the result of multiplying any given speed of two different gatis.[4] In the first example below, the number of matras is 35 – the result of multiplying 5 (regular khanda) by 7 (regular misra).
2. One of the gatis is chosen as the main pala and a phrase is constructed that *always* attacks the beat. In the example below, the chosen gati is khanda. Since the length is 35 matras, it will result in a phrase of 7 beats.

[4] 3×6, 4×8 or 5×10 would never be used as they are two speeds of the same gati.

3. The other chosen gati (misra) performs the same phrase, applying the gati bhedam concept. Consequently, if the original phrase is constructed in khanda, the other gati will use a jathi 5.

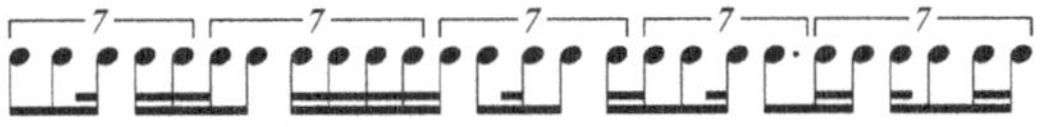

4. Since the essence of mukthays is that a phrase, in one way or another, is repeated three times, the choice of features for the remaining pala is what will determine the type of 3-fold mukthay. The choice of the 3rd pala and its influence on the order of the sequence of gatis within the tala will be further explained later in this chapter.
5. Once the three palas have been chosen and their order determined, the 3-fold mukthay is organised within the tala. Unlike sama mukthays, 3-fold mukthays do not need to start on tala sam; consequently, the first pala could start anywhere in the tala, as long as the last pala of the mukthay resolves on tala sam.

Due to the nature of this type of mukthay in which at least two different gatis are used, if gaps are chosen they will always be expressed in number of beats rather than number of matras, as is always the case in short and sama mukthays.

Type A

In this type the gati on which the original phrase is constructed is repeated twice, followed by the other chosen gati.

In the example below, the tala is of 11 beats. The phrase in khanda is 7 beats long, therefore when played twice will result in 14 beats. The misra jathi 5 pala is 5 beats long. Added up, the length of the 3 palas is 19 beats. Obviously, at least 2 cycles of the tala 11 will be needed to perform the 3-fold mukthay: 22 beats of the tala minus 19 beats of the 3-fold mukthay leaves 3 beats to work out length of gaps and starting point of the mukthay in the tala. In the first example below, the choice made is 1 beat per gap and starting the mukthay 1 beat off tala sam. It is customary in this sort of mukthay to always attack the gap for its entire duration (because the length of the gap will most likely be longer than the longest note of the phrase). *(track 67)*

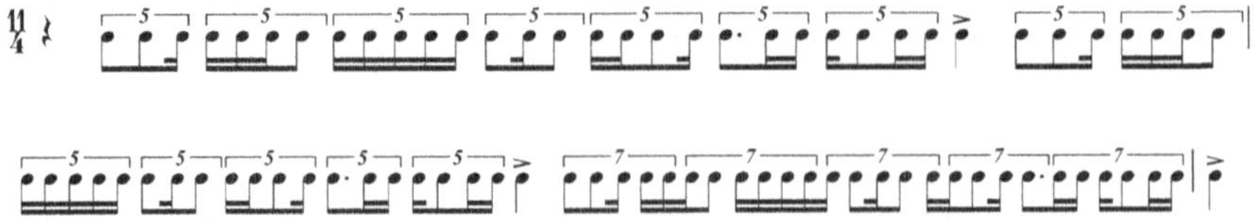

In the next example, the first tala starts on the 4th beat and is followed by the 3 palas with no gap in between.

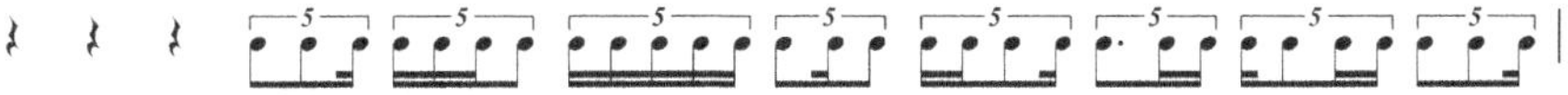

Whether in the first or second example, the gap at the beginning of the tala does not imply that it has to be a silence, as in the examples. It simply means that the mukthay commences at that precise spot but it can be preceded by any other technique or regular phrasing.

Type B

In this second type, the 3rd pala to complete the mukthay is the 2nd speed anuloma version of the gati on which the phrase was constructed (see Chapter 7 for the concept of anuloma).

In the following example, the number of matras chosen is 30, which is the result of multiplying 5 (regular khanda) by 6 (tisra 2nd speed anuloma). The main phrase is constructed on khanda.

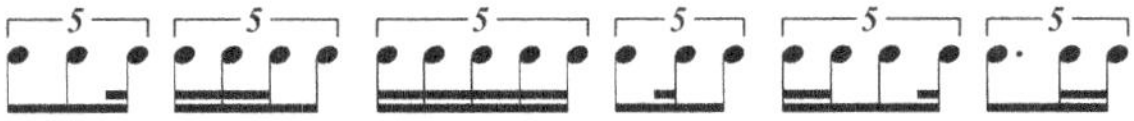

The other gati will thus use jathi 5. The second pala will be set in tisra 2nd speed anuloma jathi 5.

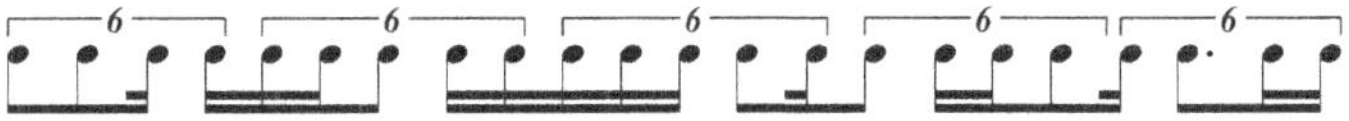

The third pala will be performed in khanda 2nd speed anuloma.

As opposed to Type A, in which the order is regulated by the formula of repeating the main phrase twice followed by the 2nd gati, in Type B the order of the gatis is left entirely up to the musician.

The order chosen within a tala of 8 beats is the khanda 2nd speed anuloma version of the phrase, followed by the original phrase and finishing with the tisra jathi 5 as 3rd pala. The gaps are of 1 beat each. *(track 68)*

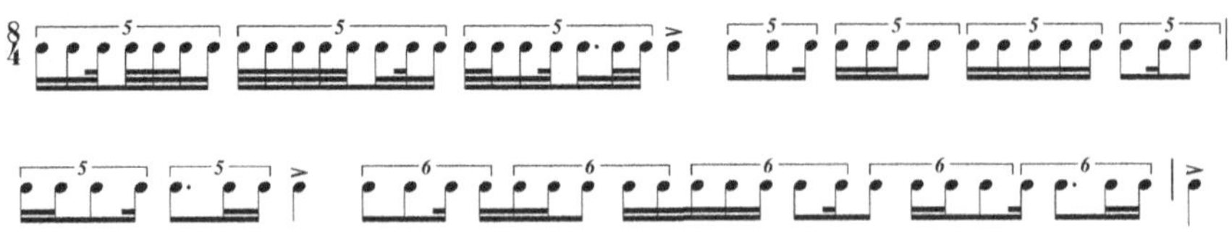

There is, though, an exception to what just has been explained: if the main phrase has an odd number of beats, this will automatically produce a 2nd speed anuloma version with *x* number of beats plus ½ beat. For instance, if the same phrase as in Type A is taken,

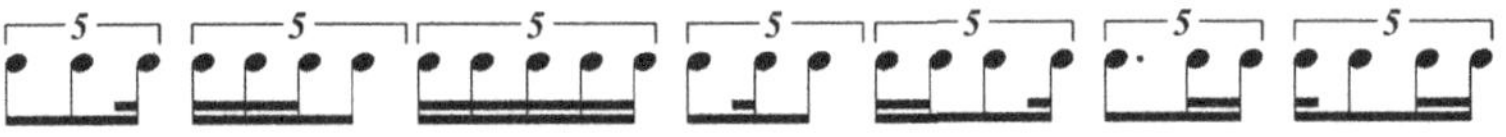

the 7 beats of the original phrase in khanda – when taken into its 2nd speed anuloma – will produce a phrase of 3 + ½ beats.

It has previously been explained that the duration of gaps between palas must always be the same. If a phrase of 3+½ beats is used as a 2nd or 3rd pala, this will inevitably produce one gap longer than the other. In order to avoid this, the 2nd speed anuloma phrase needs to be the 1st pala of the mukthay; the musician can then choose the order of the other 2 palas. The version in 2nd speed anuloma will start on the second half of the beat so that the phrase does not finish in the middle of the beat. The silence preceding the start of the phrase could be a rest or the end of a previous device/phrasing. *(track 69)*

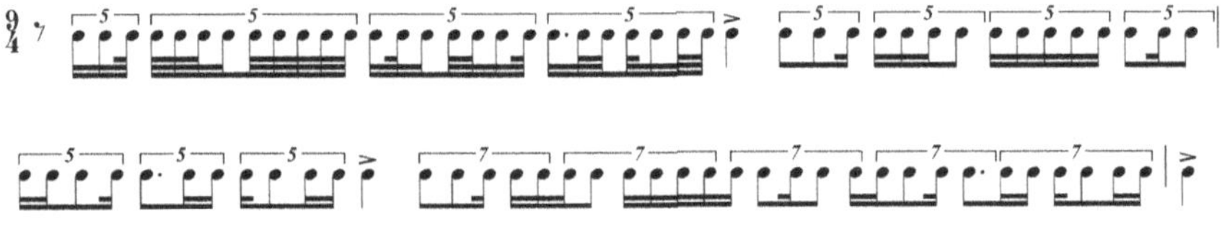

Type C

This is the type used most frequently by karnatic musicians. It involves using a third gati that inevitably will produce a phrase in which one beat will be incomplete.

Taking the first example (35 matras, with a pala in khanda and another in misra jathi 5), chatusra or tisra can be chosen. Choosing chatusra will produce a phrase of 8 beats and 3 matras; if tisra 2nd speed anuloma, the resulting phrase will be 5 beats and 5 matras long. In either case, this 3rd gati has to use jathi 5, because the original phrase was constructed in khanda, and it will always be the 1st pala of the mukthay in order to avoid one gap being longer than the other.

In the example below the choice of tisra 2nd speed anuloma jathi 5 is taken, and the gaps are of 1 beat each.

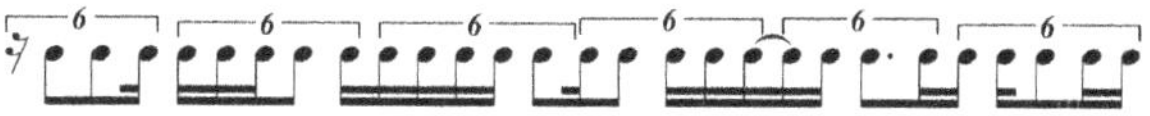

The order of the 2nd and 3rd palas is again left to the musician to decide. *(track 70)*

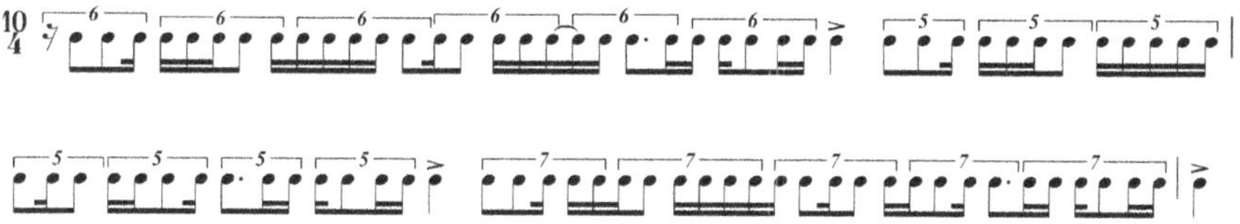

Chapter 9
Yati Phrases

The generally accepted 'definition' of yati phrases is phrases that use some form of 'geometric' shape to develop. However, for the purposes of this book, this definition will be avoided, since in reality one should rather talk of a sequence of phrases in which the first phrase (or, better, *pala)* forms the nucleus of the sequence, every subsequent pala taking the previous one as a starting point with a systematic increase or decrease in its number of matras. This is the essence of yati phrases. However, due to the fact that there are six different types, each one with its own set of rules and features, it seems more appropriate to explain the characteristics of each of them individually.

1) Samayati

This is a phrase repeated at least three times (usually no less than four times, to distinguish it from a sama mukthay). Samayatis are usually short phrases that are always repeated with a different melody (unlike sama mukthays, where the melody tends to be the same or very similar in its three palas). Samayatis can start anywhere in the tala; may or may not have gaps between repetitions; and generally resolve on tala sam.

Due to the proliferation and diversity of mukthays, samayatis are seldom used. However, when they are used, displacement within the beat is the main priority. The tendency is to utilise them in the context of *yatis prastara*, which will be explained in Chapter 13.

2) Srotovahayati

Srotovahayati is a sequence of at least three palas in which the initial one is the shortest. Each successive pala is an increased version of the previous one, this increase being calculated systematically by adding the same number of matras to every pala. Consequently, if the first pala is 4 matras long and the second pala is 7 matras long, it implies that the third pala must also be increased by 3 matras – and thus its length would be 10 matras. A fourth pala would be of 13 matras, a fifth one 16 matras etc.

The phrases can be increased by adding matras in three different places. Once the position is chosen, every added cell then has to respond to the chosen pattern.

a) Adding Matras at the End of the Phrase

This yati sequence is constructed as follows:[1]

4 (2) 7 (2) 10 (2) 13|T.S. *(track 71)*

The pala of 7 matras uses the cell  after the initial phrase has been repeated. The pala of 10 matras adds the cell  at the end of the repetition of the 7 matras, whereas the pala of 13 matras utilises the cell  at the very end of the cycle.

b) Adding Matras from the Beginning of the Phrase

In this option, every new cell has to precede the repetition of the previous pala – again, in systematic fashion. Consequently, the initial pala is heard as the last cell of every new phrase, and the new cell precedes the repetition of the previous one. *(track 72)*

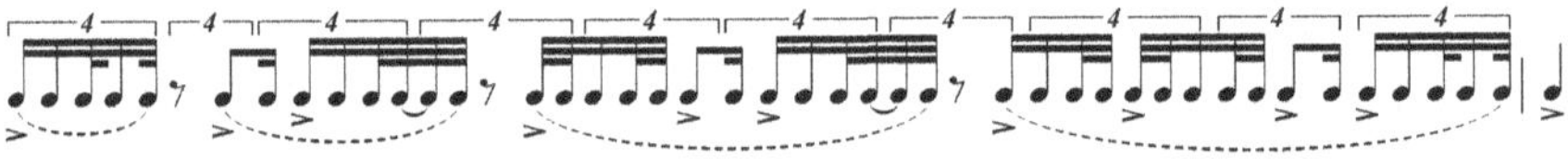

c) Adding Matras in the Middle of the Phrase

In this option the only rule that must be followed is that the first note(s) of the original pala must always be the first note(s) of every pala, and the same applies to the last note or recognisable fragment. The added cells can be organised in any order the performer finds suitable. *(track 73)*

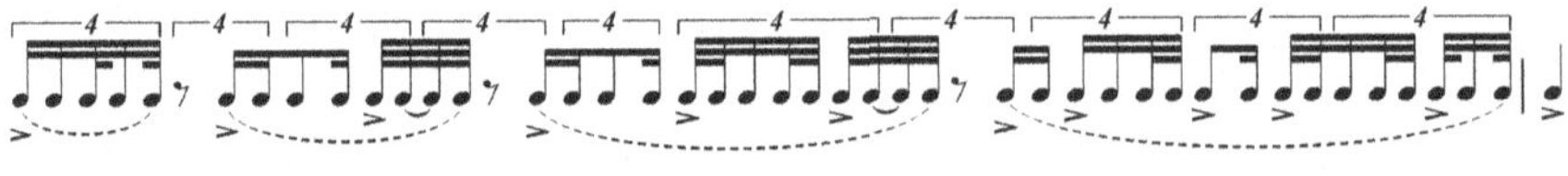

In the example above, the first 4 matras motif is split between  and  in the pala of 7 matras by inserting the cell  in between. In the pala of 10 matras, the cell  is again inserted between the new phrase created by combining  and , and the last fragment of the original phrase . In the very last pala of 13 matras, the cell 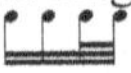 separates the cell that initiated palas 2 and 3.

This example is almost 'conservative', since it keeps intact every cell that has been played previously. Many karnatic musicians prefer a more 'sophisticated'

[1] All the gaps, as was the case for mukthays, must always be the same length.

development, achieved by inserting a new cell in a position that would break any of the previous cells. For instance, in the 10 matras phrase, the cell could have been split into a 'sub-cell' of a and another of a and the phrase could have resulted in

In short, it can be said that when choosing to add cells in the middle, except for the split cells of the original pala that need to remain as the first and last cells of all palas, any new cell can be inserted anywhere in the phrase, including breaking existing cells into sub-cells.

Srotovahayatis can start and finish on tala sam (as is the case in all previous examples). They can also finish anywhere in the tala, if followed without any break by a short mukthay. Also, as sometimes happens because of difficulties with the calculations or because the musician so desires, they can start off tala sam provided that the 'gap' before the start of the yati sequence is always shorter than a beat.[2] Also, as was the case in sama and short mukthays, the last matra of the last phrase can fall on tala sam.

3) Gopuchayati

Gopuchayati is the exact reverse of a srotovahayati, with the first phrase being the longest. Each successive pala is a decreased version, always omitting the same number of matras. The three options regarding where to omit notes are the same as explained above for srotovahayati: from the end, the beginning or the middle of the phrase. Since these options have already been explained, one example should suffice to illustrate gopuchayatis: the option that omits from the end. *(track 74)*

4) Mridangamyati

In its simplest possible definition, a mridangamyati is a srotovahayati followed by a gopuchayati. However, there are various elements to take into consideration that can, in many cases, turn this simple notion into a more elaborate technique. These elements are:

[2] The length of the gap before the beginning of the sequence does not have to correspond with the length of the gap used between the palas.

a. *Placement of added and omitted matras*: Since there are three possible ways to add or omit notes, every segment can choose a completely different way. For instance, the srotovahayati fragment (first part) could add notes at the end of the phrase, while the gopuchayati (second part) could omit them from either the beginning or the middle.
b. *Use of different gatis*: Every fragment can be performed in different gatis, regardless of where the gati change takes place within the tala.
c. *Gaps*: Each fragment can have a different number of matras in its gaps, as long as every fragment keeps the same number of matras for all its gaps.
d. *Short mukthays*: The length of every fragment does not have to equal to an exact number of cycles, regardless of whether performed in the same gati or not. A mridangamyati can be followed, without any break, by a short mukthay.

All these elements can also be combined while constructing a mridangamyati. In addition to these, there are two structural methods of developing the whole sequence.

A) First Structural Method: Viloma

Viloma means 'retrograde'. There are several ways of retrograding a melody and a rhythm (and their combinations) in karnatic music. What it is quite interesting is how karnatic music makes use of the retrograde concept in a 'structural' way, retrograding not only the rhythm or the melody but also steps of a sequence or various other parameters. To avoid confusion with the western term (which basically refers to the retrograde of pitch content or of a particular rhythm), I prefer to use the karnatic term viloma.

When viloma is applied to the construction of a mridangamyati, it means that the numbers used for the length of palas for the first segment are applied to the second segment in reverse order. How palas omit matras, and whether the second fragment uses a different gati or different number of matras in its gap, is an ulterior consideration.

If the srotovahayati sequence exposed above is taken once again

4 (2) 7 (2) 10 (2) 13

the viloma version will be

13 (*x*)[3] 10 (*x*) 7 (*x*) 4

[3] x denotes the fact that the gap could be of a different length from the one used for the first fragment.

Needless to say that when the longest phrase is performed twice in a row, there is no possibility of creating any change to that phrase (phrases are not to be changed or ornamented arbitrarily in a mridangamyati, or in any yati for that matter). Although the development of the second fragment could result in an entirely different phrase from the first fragment, the fact remains that the pala of 13 matras is repeated twice in a row. Although this can be done in the same gati, it is customary that, in order to give some 'spice' to this repetition, the second fragment is performed in a different gati. This provides room for the possibility of using a different number of matras for the gap and/or the use of a short mukthay at the end of the second fragment.

In the example below, the chatusra version is 4 (2) 7 (2) 10 (2) 13, and it is followed immediately by the reversed version expounded above, but in khanda. Counting only the number of matras that the 4 palas of the srotovahayati sequence provide, there are 34 matras. A whole cycle of tala 10 in khanda is 50 matras long: therefore, the sequence is short by 16 matras to resolve on tala sam. In the following example, the gap has been varied (only a 1 matra gap between phrases of the gopuchayati) and a short mukthay added. The calculations for the gopuchayati segment are

13 (1) 10 (1) 7 (1) 4

which gives 37 matras: therefore the sequence is still 13 matras short to resolve on tala sam. The short mukthay that follows the second fragment is 3 (2) 3 (2) 3|T.S. *(track 75)*

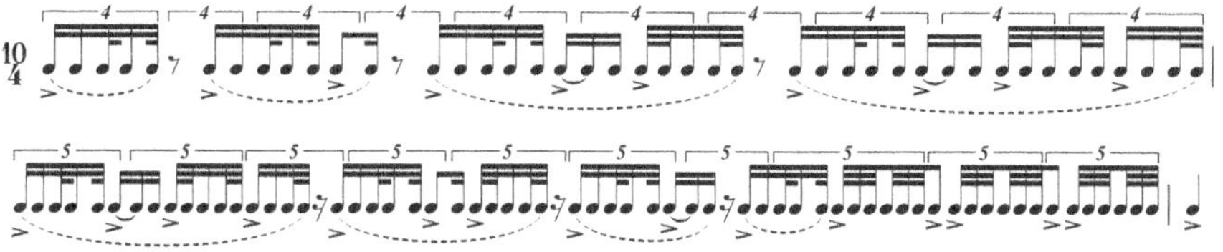

In this specific mridangamyati, the increased and decreased palas have followed the same pattern (adding and omitting from the end). But, as indicated previously, the second fragment – besides the change of gati and number of matras in the gap – could have omitted from the beginning or the middle.

B) Second Structural Method: Palindrome

The concept of palindrome, as with viloma, is used abundantly to develop melodies and rhythms in karnatic music. But, as in the case of viloma, it can also be utilised for structural purposes. The main difference between the two concepts is that, in a retrograded version of a musical object, the whole object is reversed, whereas in the palindrome version the very last element (be it a pitch, a note of a rhythm, a step etc.) is never repeated, creating a sort of 'axis' point.

When applied to a mridangamyati, this implies that the longest phrase is not repeated in the second fragment. Consequently, the phrase sequence would be as follows (*without gaps*):

4 7 10 13 -- 10 7 4

Again, this second segment could omit matras from a different place in the phrase; go to another gati; use a different gap from the first segment; and be followed by a short mukthay. In the example below, except for the gati change, all other possibilities are present. The calculations are:

4 (2) 7 (2) 10 (2) 13---10 (1) 7 (1) 4, followed by the short mukthay 5 (1) 5 (1) 5|T.S. *(track 76)*

The first fragment adds matras at the end of the pala, while the second fragment omits matras from the middle. The very first pala of the second fragment (10 matras long) removes the cell , which was the second cell of the srotovahayati sequence. Similarly, the second pala of the gopuchayati (7 matras long) removes the cell  that was the third cell of the original phrase.

In fact, the palindrome option is used more often than the viloma option because it avoids the repetition of the longest pala, which matches the aversion to potential 'repetitiousness' that most karnatic musicians tend to have (as already mentioned a few times).

5) Damaruyati

This technique is the opposite of a mridangamyati: it is a gopuchayati followed by a srotovahayati.

All the elements used in the mridangamyati to add variation or modify the second segment are used here as well. Similarly, the viloma and palindrome structural options are also used, although in the case of a damaruyati the viloma option is used more often than in the mridangamyati, due to the fact that the last pala of the first fragment is the shortest pala of the whole sequence. Consequently there is, a priori, no risk of 'repetitiousness'. Furthermore, the fact that the last phrase of the sequence is the shortest one results in the addition of another technique to the viloma and palindrome options.

Corresponding to the 'taste' of karnatic musicians to use the number 3 in any possible way (derived from cultural and religious elements), the last phrase of the first fragment could be repeated three times to then be followed by the reversed version of the rest of the srotovahayati. The sequence below is structured as follows (*without gaps*): 13 10 7 4 4 4 7 10 13

In this option, a gati change *should* take place in the second fragment (this is not given as a fixed rule, but is common practice in karnatic music). This gati change can be applied to the second or third time the shortest pala is repeated, depending on calculations or musical purposes. In this case, the gati change takes place the second time the shortest pala is performed. The first fragment has a gap of 2 matras, while the second fragment uses a 3 matras gap. The placement for adding and omitting matras is the same (from the end). This placement for omitting matras in the second fragment could also have been constructed differently. Further, the whole sequence could have finished anywhere in the tala and be followed by a short mukthay.

This option of repeating the shortest phrase three times, surprisingly enough, does not have a name in karnatic music. The most common answer I have heard from teachers and musicians is 'like a mukthay'. Therefore, I have coined this possibility the 'mukthay-like' option, for lack of a better or more 'sophisticated' term. *(track 77)*

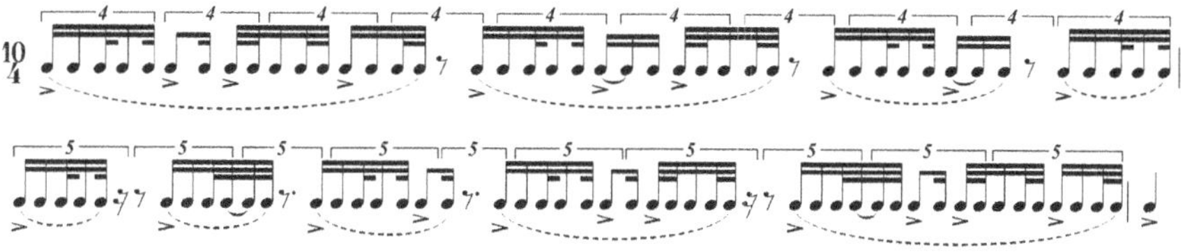

6) Visamayati

This type of yati is the least clear of all. The general definition found in various books is that it 'does not follow any order' or descriptions along this line. Asking musicians what characterises a visamayati results in enormously varying explanations and turns this technique into a theoretical concept that karnatic musicians barely, if ever, use.

Chapter 10
Yati Mukthays

This form of mukthay is the first to depart from the generic idea that a mukthay is a phrase repeated three times. The number 3 is undoubtedly present, but not in the transparent manner encountered so far. Instead, the number 3 is intertwined with the yati concept of systematic increase or decrease of a musical parameter; and, in addition to the increase or decrease of matras in phrases, this concept is also applied to other parameters. Yati mukthays are divided into three different types.

1) Type A

The format of this type follows the pattern **AAA** (gap) **BBB** (gap) **CCC**

'A' is a shortened or elongated version of 'B', and 'C' will be shortened if 'A' is elongated (and vice versa) by the same number of matras. This in itself would not be different from a regular sequence of yati phrases. In order to turn it into a mukthay, every pala is repeated three times and is structured into a specific pattern (unlike a yati sequence that could have any number of palas).

Calculations

This type, for developmental reasons explained later, exclusively starts and finishes on tala sam; therefore, the option of using the last matra of the last pala falling on the tala sam is discarded. These are the steps to construct a yati mukthay of type A:

1. Decide on which gati the mukthay will be constructed. In the example below, the tala is 14 beats and the gati is chatusra. If the mukthay is constructed on one cycle of the tala, the number of matras will be 56.
2. Divide 56 matras by 9 (because this is the number of palas in the mukthay). This division will result in every pala being of 6 matras with 2 remainder matras that will be used for the gaps.
3. The resulting number of 6 matras will actually be applied to the 'B' phrases of the mukthay. 'A' phrases will add or omit x number of matras and, whether the 'A' phrases are increased or decreased, the 'C' phrases will omit or add the same number of matras. Here there are some possibilities.

555 666 777   444 666 888   999 666 333

4. The number of remainder matras will be used for the gaps. Since there are 2 remainder matras and both gaps must have the same length, every gap will be 1 matra long. Therefore, if the first example above is taken, the mukthay will be 555 (1) 666 (1) 777

As opposed to sama mukthays, where a list of potential pala durations for the mukthay constituted the initial step, in type A yati mukthays this step is discarded. If the longest possible pala of the example is 6 matras, and 1 matra is subtracted from every pala (as was the case in sama mukthays), not only will the gap be rather long (something that could be quite effective but is usually avoided by karnatic musicians), but it will also invariably give fractional matras. Consequently, unless a long gap and/or a 𝅘𝅥𝅯 displacement of the phrase is sought, the result of the first division will always give the number of matras for the 'B' phrases and the remainder number will be used for the gaps.

Phrase Construction

Besides the fact that, unlike yati phrases, all types of yati mukthays follow a specific pattern, a major difference between yati phrases and yati mukthays lies in how the phrases are increased or decreased. Whereas in a yati phrase sequence the palas are increased or decreased by adding or omitting notes, in yati mukthays *the palas are increased or decreased by shortening or elongating note values while the number of notes of the first pala remains the same.*

However, this shortening or elongation of note values is never random and must follow some form of protocol, a logic and coherence which can sometimes be very clear (and almost predictable), while at other times it may be more intricate and difficult to follow.[1] There are two main principles that rule the increase of note values:

- increase on already increased notes
- increase on new notes, usually those that follow or precede already increased notes. *(track 78)*

The first phrase ('A') is 5 matras long and uses 5 notes. Therefore 'B' and 'C' should keep 5 notes and increase the value of one or two notes. The logic behind this is that the second note becomes a ♪ in the 'B' phrase and the same happens with the first note of the 'C' phrase.

[1] As long as the creator finds some form of logic or coherence as to which notes can be increased or decreased and the musical result does not sound like a random or obscure choice of increased or decreased notes, the developmental possibilities are quite rich.

The example below would follow a more transparent logic, by which the note that has been increased by one matra in the 'B' phrases is again increased by another matra in the 'C' phrases. *(track 79)*

Another possibility with the same calculations would be to have a 4-note phrase in 'A', in which the last note is a ♪ and turn successively every previous 𝅘𝅥𝅯 in the 'B' and 'C' phrases into a ♪ leaving only the very first note intact in all three phrases. *(track 80)*

Development of Yati Mukthay Type A

It was seen that sama mukthays have a large corpus of developmental possibilities, whereas 3-fold mukthays were a one-time occurrence. Type A yati mukthays are developed in a very specific manner.

The exposition of the pattern **AAA** (gap) **BBB** (gap) **CCC** is called *krama* (in reality, any exposition of any material is named krama, which means 'in order'). This is followed in the next cycle by the viloma form of the *groups*, but the rhythm is never retrograded. Therefore, the phrase would follow the pattern **CCC** (gap) **BBB** (gap) **AAA**. If the first example is taken, the viloma version would look like this

Finally, the groups are 'de-constructed' and every 'A', 'B' or 'C' phrase can be mingled without following a specific pattern. This is called *vakra* – or, as karnatic musicians would translate it into English, a 'zigzag' phrase. The only requisite is that every group must be constructed with 3 palas and be separated by the gap. Although this may seem to open the door to 'chaos', the actual mathematical possibilities to make the 9 phrases fit into one cycle of the tala are ultimately only two:

a. Every 'A', 'B' and 'C' is played 3 times, in any order.
b. 'A' and 'C' phrases are performed twice, while 'B' is done five times, also in any order.

Here there are just a few options covering the two possibilities:

CCB (gap) **BBC** (gap) **AAA**
ABC (gap) **BBB** (gap) **CBA**

CAC (gap) **BAB** (gap) **BBB**
ABC (gap) **CBA** (gap) **BBB**

If the last option is chosen, the vakra version of the yati mukthay would be[2]

Consequently, this mukthay would be performed in 3 cycles of tala 14. The fact, mentioned previously, that this type of mukthay should be enclosed within the cycle and never have the last matra of the last pala attacking tala sam derives from this developmental notion – otherwise, the viloma version would start on the 2nd matra, the vakra on the 3rd matra and the final note will be played on the 4th matra of the beat.

In reality, the entire previous explanation in tala 14, using ♪ and ♪., is a simplification of a mukthay by Jahnavi Jayaprakash performed in a tala of 7 beats with 𝅘𝅥𝅯 and 𝅘𝅥𝅯. with a gap of ½ matra. *(track 81)*

The melody impedes any feeling of repetitiousness or predictability; on the contrary, it becomes rather difficult to follow the rhythmical pattern with the same ease as when the rhythm is heard only with solkattu.

Another yati mukthay in tisra in tala 12 is presented below. The number of matras in 1 cycle is 72; when divided by 9 this gives 8, with 0 left over. This

[2] This option is the most 'conservative' because it maintains 18 matras per group. But this does not necessarily mean it is the one preferred or most frequently performed.

implies that the 'B' phrases will be 8 matras long and the mukthay will have no gaps.

The 'A' phrases are 6 matras long, but they contain only 5 notes. This number of notes must be kept in the 'B' and 'C' phrases. 'B' phrases are 8 matras long and, in order to keep the same number of notes as 'A', the third and fourth notes are elongated from 𝅘𝅥𝅯 to 𝅘𝅥𝅮; 'C' phrases are 10 matras long and the musician decided to elongate the first and fifth notes into a 𝅘𝅥𝅮 as well. It can be observed that the vakra version takes the pattern **AAC** (gap) **BBC** (gap) **BBB**. *(track 82)*

This krama–viloma–vakra concept, besides being used in the manner just explained (essentially as a block or sequence), can also be separated within a piece of music with the viloma and vakra versions appearing at different places in the music. Generally, when this is done it follows certain patterns of specific sections of karnatic forms, or is used as a way to develop mixing techniques (explained later).

2) Type B

This type of yati mukthay would follow one of the following patterns:

A (gap) **AB** (gap) **ABC** **ABC** (gap) **AB** (gap) **A**

Calculations for Increasing the Length of Palas

As can be deduced from the patterns, there are 6 palas in this type of yati mukthay: 'A' is performed 3 times, 'B' is played twice and 'C' only once. The number of matras of the 'A' phrase is increased by x number of matras in the 'B' phrase, and the 'C' phrase is increased by the same number of matras in relation to the 'B' phrase.

There are specific formulas for type B yati mukthays. The decision as to which of the patterns shown above should be taken does not affect the calculations. The formula used for increasing the palas is

$$T=(6\times P)+(4\times I)+(2\times G)$$

- where **T** is the number of matras of the whole mukthay. This number is the result of multiplying the chosen gati by the number of beats of the tala, eventually multiplied by more than 1 cycle. This number has to equal
- **6×P** (which means that the core number of matras, the one of phrase 'A', is to be performed 6 times) plus
- **4×I** (this is the number of matras to increase the core phrase multiplied by 4) plus
- **2×G** (number of matras in the gap multiplied by 2)

In the example below, the tala is of 12 beats and the gati is tisra, which results in 72 matras. This is the **T** of the formula that has to match the following calculations:

- The core phrase ('A') is 9 matras long, but these 9 matras are also the first building block of the other two phrases. Therefore, these 9 matras are to be performed 6 times and result in 54 matras.
- The increase applied to 'B' is of 3 matras. Since 'B' is played twice, there are 6 more matras to match **T**. The 'C' phrase is increased by 3 matras over the 'B' phrase, and so is consequently 6 matras longer than the 'A' phrase. The increase of 3 matras multiplied by 4 gives 12 matras, which, added to 54, equals 66 matras. This number is still 6 matras short of completing the number of matras required by **T**. These 6 matras will be distributed equally between the two gaps and then the two parts of the equation will finally match.
- T (72 matras)=6×P (54 matras)+ 4×I (12 matras)+2×G (6 matras)

So, with the pattern **A** (gap) **AB** (gap) **ABC** becomes 9 (3) 9 12 (3) 9 12 15
As with type A, the phrases are increased by elongating certain notes while maintaining the same number of notes of the 'A' phrase. The 3 matras for the increase applied to the 'B' phrase are distributed by adding 1 matra to every ♪ and turning the second ♪ into ♪; in this way, the original seven notes are preserved.

The 'C' phrase is similarly increased by 3 matras. These are used in a similar fashion to the 'B' phrase: the first two notes are increased by 1 matra, becoming ♩, and the fourth ♪ of the original phrase is turned into ♪ *(track 83)*

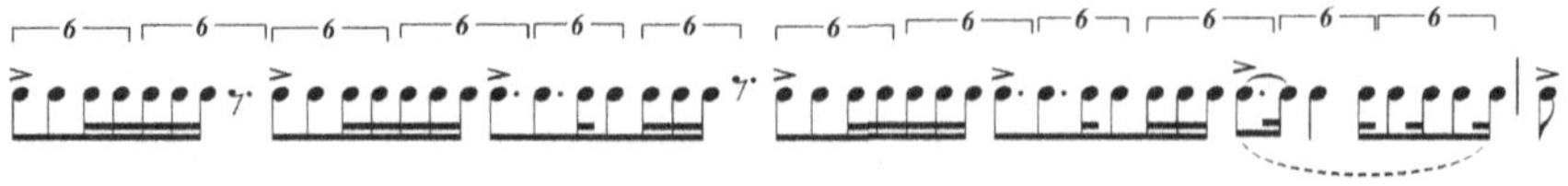

In the second example, based on the same calculations and 'A' phrase, the development is similar in the 'B' phrase (adding 1 matra to every ♪ and turning this time the last ♪ into ♪). However, the manner in which the 'C' phrase is increased differs more drastically than in the first example. The first two notes remain the same, the first and second ♪ are turned into ♪, while the very last note (already increased by one matra in the 'B' phrase) is once again increased by one matra. *(track 84)*

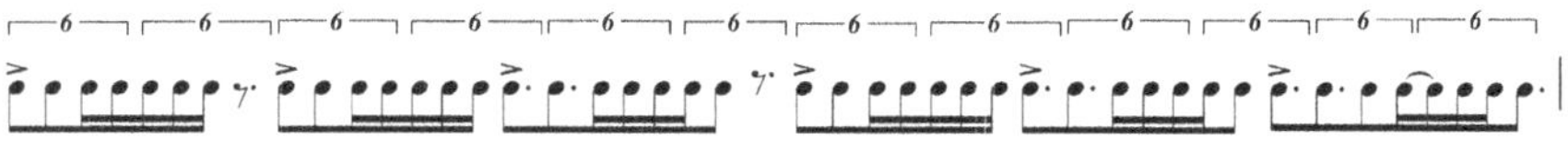

The first example represents a more 'transparent' and almost straightforward notion of increasing logically, whereas the second example juggles more with the two main principles that rule the increase of note values, mentioned at the beginning of the chapter:

- increase on already increased notes
- increase on new notes, usually those that follow or precede already increased notes.

Both notions can be mixed, which most of the time produces a more varied musical result. In the 'C' phrase of the second example, the notion of increasing on increased notes is applied to the last note. The new notes that are increased are the first and second ♪ (following the karnatic logic of transforming notes next to the ones that were already increased). In this context, since the last ♪ was increased in the 'B' phrase, the third and fourth ♪ could have been increased as well because they are next to the last note. However, increasing the first and third, or second and fourth ♪ would be considered illogical.

Calculations for Decreasing the Length of Palas

The formula for a decreased version of the patterns **A** (gap) **AB** (gap) **ABC** or **ABC** (gap) **AB** (gap) **A** is as follows:

$$T=(6\times P)-(4\times D)+(2\times G)$$

In this context, the **4×D** signifies the four times that the core phrase is decreased. The resulting number is to be subtracted from the multiplication of the number of matras in the core phrase by 6. Therefore, the latter must always be larger than the number of matras in the tala (**T**).

In the next example, the tala and gati are the same (72 matras long). Since the 'A' phrase is 14 matras long, this number multiplied by 6 results in 84 matras, a number sufficiently bigger than **T** so that there would be more room to use a variety of choices for the decreased 'B' and 'C' phrases.

The 'B' phrase is 10 matras long and the 'C' phrase is, necessarily, 6 matras. This implies that **4×D** is 4 matras multiplied by 4, resulting in 16 matras.

Subtracting the number of matras in **6×P** (84 matras) from **4×D** (16 matras) gives 68 matras, 4 matras short of **T**. Therefore, every gap has to be 2 matras long.

T (72 matras)= 6×P (84 matras)-4×D (16 matras)+2×G (4 matras)

So the pattern **A** (gap) **AB** (gap) **ABC** becomes 14 (2) 14 10 (2) 14 10 6 *(track 85)*

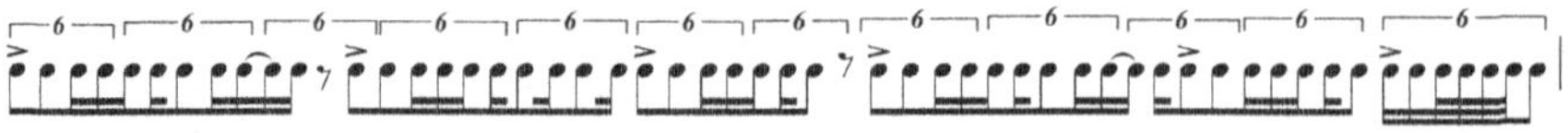

Phrase Development

One of the possible variations regarding phrasing in type B can be observed in this mukthay. Unlike type A, which rigorously follows the notion of exclusively increasing or decreasing note values, in Type B a combination of adding/omitting notes with increasing or decreasing note values is not an unusual occurrence. There are four possibilities:

a) Increasing length of phrases

- The 'B' phrase increases the note value of some notes while the 'C' phrase adds notes in any manner seen in the previous chapter on yati phrases. In the example below, the 3 added matras in the 'C' phrase split the 'B' phrase into two parts, and 3 ♪ become inserted in between. *(track 86)*

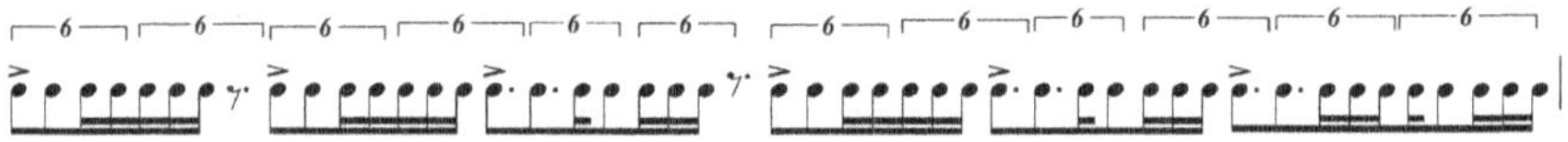

- The 'B' phrase increases by adding notes: in this case, the 'C' phrase has to increase the note values of some of its notes. In the example below, 3 ♪ have been added at the beginning of the 'B' phrase, which produces a 10-note phrase. Therefore, the 'C' phrase has to increase, maintaining 10 notes instead of 7. The 2 ♪ increase by 1 matra each, whereas the second ♪ of the group of 5 ♪ is increased by 1 matra. *(track 87)*

b) Decreasing length of phrases

- Omitting notes in the 'B' phrase is the most common framework, possibly in order for the 'C' phrase to be more playable. The same two options and rules explained above are applicable here.
- The example for the explanation of the calculations of the decreased type B yati mukthay shows that the 'B' phrase is shortened by omitting its last 4 matras. This produces a phrase of 7 notes. Consequently the 'C' phrase has

to keep this number of notes while reducing the note value of every note by half, except for the very last ♪ that is kept intact.

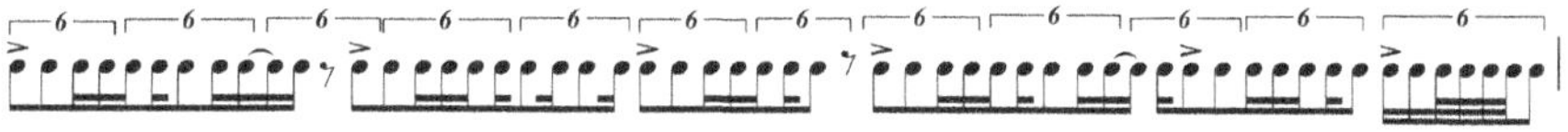

The option of omitting notes of the 'C' phrase, although theoretically possible, is considered rather 'sloppy' and never used by karnatic musicians. The first option is essentially the only one utilised.

Consequently, it can be concluded that only one phrase ('B' or 'C') can be increased or decreased by adding or omitting notes, and never both of them. If 'B' is increased or decreased, 'C' must use the same number of notes as 'B' and increase or decrease note values.

Ornamentation

Although a not uncommon occurrence in sama mukthays and yati phrases, this element is quite present in type B yati mukthays. However, unlike ornamentation in other techniques, a concise explanation is needed since this sort of mukthay bases its shortening or elongation of phrases on the number of notes of a previous phrase.

If, for instance, the second time that an 'A' phrase is played the performer decides to ornament the phrase, the 'B' phrase will be constructed exclusively on the number of notes of the first 'A' and never on the ornamented version performed the second time. The same holds true for the 'C' phrase in relation to 'B'.

3) Type C

This type follows the pattern

A (gap) **AA** (gap) **AAA**

Unlike types A and B that needed to start on tala sam, type C yati mukthays can start anywhere in the tala. In fact, this mukthay is used also as a 'short mukthay'. Less commonly used than the short mukthay in its sama version (repetition of a phrase three times), this type can be used as a short mukthay with any technique that could call for it, such as jathi bhedam sequences or yati phrases. Usually the phrase is quite concise.

Calculations

Divide the remaining number of matras before tala sam by 6 instead of 3; the remainder will be used for the gaps. Thus, if there are 20 matras before tala sam, divide 20 by 6 and every 'A' phrase will be 3 matras long; the 2 matras remainder will be distributed between the two gaps.

Phrase Construction

Since all the phrases share the same length, there is a variety of options, for example:

- Repetition of the same phrase: This is generally realised only when the phrase is quite short (between 3 and 5 matras). The example below follows the above calculations. *(track 88)*

- Variation on the initial phrase: These are simple ornamentations – one or two notes shortened or elongated, or a note added, but without following any pattern or specific rules. *(track 89)*

- Permutation of note values within the same sort of cell: The example below is a typical yati mukthay using this notion. The ♪ is placed differently among the two ♪ *(track 90)*

Chapter 11
Tirmanas

Tirmanas are sequences made up of the following elements:

- A phrase of 3, 4, 5, 6 or 7 notes in which each note is separated from another by the same number of matras.
- A section called *purvanga* in which the phrase is repeated at least two more times, although the separation between notes is decreased systematically. This section ends when the last phrase has reached a separation between notes of 2 matras (eventually 3, depending on the system applied to decrease the separation between notes).
- A section called *uttaranga* in which the only requisite is that every repetition of the phrase is constructed in a shorter time-span than the previous step. As a result of this flexible concept, several uttarangas can be structured for one purvanga.

Tirmanas start and resolve on tala sam. They can be constructed in any number of cycles and have two unique features:

a. Unlike any other technique seen thus far, they are exclusively constructed in chatusra.
b. Once the sequence has reached the uttaranga, the number of notes chosen gives the possibility of going to another gati, and the change can occur anywhere in the tala. If, for instance, a phrase of 5 notes is chosen, in the uttaranga these 5 notes can be used as khanda against any frame.

Construction of the Sequence

The first step is to choose the number of cycles of the tala for the whole tirmana, and how many notes will be used for the phrase. There are no formulas or short cuts to construct tirmanas. Karnatic musicians have learnt many tirmanas for all talas, but when faced with different situations I have observed that they need to make calculations and a sort of trial and error process ensues.

In the example below, two cycles of tala 9 have been chosen along with a 5-note phrase. Therefore, the tirmana has to be set to 72 matras (18 beats × 4 matras=72 matras). All notes in the first phrase are separated by 6 matras, resulting in

5 notes × 6 matras of separation=30 matras

In the second step the separation between notes has been reduced to 4 matras. Therefore,

5 notes × 4 matras of separation=20 matras

In the third step, every note must necessarily be separated by 2 matras to continue with the systematic decrease among notes by 2 matras. This will imply

5 notes × 2 matras of separation=10 matras

These three steps will constitute the purvanga, since the third step has reached the 'threshold' of 2 matras of separation. Adding up the three steps leads to 60 matras, 12 matras short of 72 matras. *(track 91)*

The remaining 12 matras need to be completed by the uttaranga. A first option could be

5 notes × 1 matra of separation	=5 matras
5:4♪	=4 matras
5:3♪	=3 matras

which will result in the 12 matras sought. It can be observed that when the phrase goes into khanda, it is the *number of matras of the frame* that counts for the calculations and *never* the number of matras of the gati. *(track 92 with the four uttaranga options)*

A second option for the uttaranga could be to use one of the rules of tirmanas: the very last step in a tirmana can be repeated twice or three times. If a 5:4♪ is repeated 3 times, the necessary 12 matras are obtained.

If 5:6♪ is repeated twice, the frame of 6♪ twice would again give the 12 matras needed.

A fourth possibility could be to use a 5:7 followed by 5

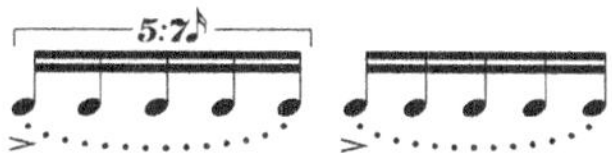

If the first uttaranga option is chosen, the whole tirmana will look as follows *(track 93)*

Purvanga

Development of Tirmanas

A tirmana can be performed a number of times, merely changing the uttaranga each time, or be developed in a similar fashion to type A yati mukthays utilising the concept of krama, viloma and vakra. The concept can be applied to constructing a long sequence of tirmana with krama-viloma-vakra or the viloma and vakra segments can be used in different parts of the piece.

KRAMA

Once more, the concept of viloma is applied exclusively to the order of the steps and not to the rhythm.

VILOMA

In the vakra segment, the steps are permutated at the creator's will. As with many other techniques, one of the goals is to produce some form of displacement of steps without creating any feeling of syncopation; all phrases should sound as in the krama version, regardless of their position in the beat. The example below is just one possibility.

VAKRA

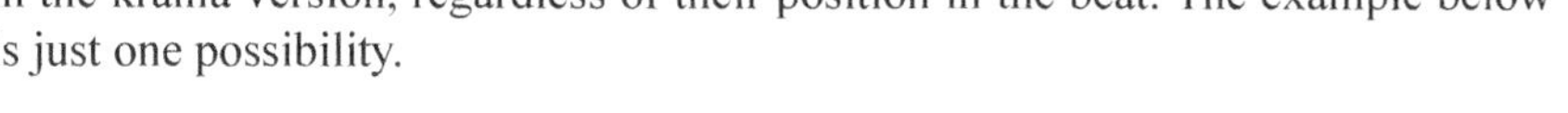

If the three segments are to be performed as a sequence, the result will be *(track 94)*

Duration of Notes

All examples thus far have been written with the full duration of the notes, a fact that may lead the reader to ask why tirmanas are explained as a 'separation' between notes rather than a phrase of 3, 4, 5, 6 or 7 notes with specific lengths that are systematically shortened.

The reason is that every note is like a 'space' of a determined length, but the note itself does not have to last for the whole duration that separates it from the next note. As long as each note is attacked in its proper place, the duration of the note could be as short as a 𝅘𝅥𝅰 followed by a silence that would complete the number of matras that separates it from the next note.

In the example below, many notes have been shortened to simply give an impression of the concept of duration of notes in the tirmana. The dotted line helps one see the original phrase. Obviously, this concept is more applicable to the purvanga than the uttaranga sections.

Tirmana-Mukthays

A tirmana can be turned into a mukthay when the krama-viloma-vakra development is calculated as a whole within a number of cycles of the tala, and the viloma and vakra will be separated from the previous fragment by a gap. In a regular tirmana the calculations are thought of for the krama, and the viloma and vakra will always start on tala sam and will never be separated by a gap.

However, a tirmana with the development krama-viloma-vakra is frequently conceived as a mukthay when the total number of matras provided by the chosen number of cycles of the tala is divided by 3 and the calculations for the tirmana as explained above are realised on one pala. Each fragment resulted of this division will take the krama, viloma and vakra versions. Moreover, a tirmana-mukthay will never be constructed on three cycles of the tala (or any multiple of 3), to ensure that every pala is displaced within the tala. In the following example, the tirmana-mukthay is constructed on 4 cycles of tala 11.

11 beats × 4 cycles × 4 matras per beat=176 matras

These 176 matras are divided by 3. The division brings forth 58 matras per pala with 2 remainder matras to be used in the gaps.

The phrase is of 6 notes and the calculations are

6 notes × 5 matras of separation	=30 matras
6 notes × 3 matras of separation	=18 matras
6 notes × 1 matra of separation	=6 matras
6:4𝅘𝅥𝅯	=4 matras

The total is 58 matras per pala, with 1 matra per gap. It can be observed, for instance, that the 6:4𝅘𝅥𝅯 after the first gap will start on the 4th matra of the beat. *(track 95)*

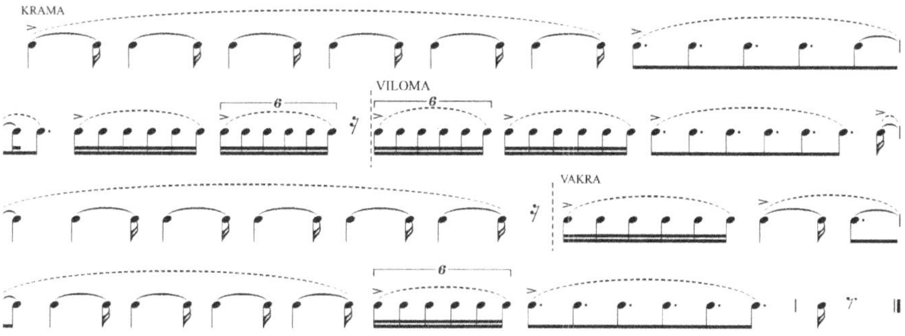

In the next example, constructed on 4 cycles of tala 9 (144 matras), the number of matras per pala after dividing 144 by 3 is 48 with no remainder; therefore, every pala would start on a beat. When this occurs, a karnatic musician would make calculations so that the number of matras of all the steps together will always be shorter than the length provided by the division in order to create gaps and displacement of palas within the beat.

Here the number of notes in the phrase is 5, so the calculations give 46 matras instead of 48.

5 notes × 5 matras of separation	=25 matras
5 notes × 3 matras of separation	=15 matras
5:4𝅘𝅥𝅯	=4 matras
5:4𝅘𝅥𝅰	=2 matras

These 2 matras of difference between the original division and the actual length of the four steps of the tirmana multiplied by 3 palas gives 6 matras. Distributed between the two gaps, each one will be of 3 matras, which provokes displacement of the original pala. For instance, the 5:4𝅘𝅥𝅯. will start on the 2nd matra of the beat in the 2nd pala, whereas it should start on the 4th matra of the beat in the 3rd pala. *(track 96)*

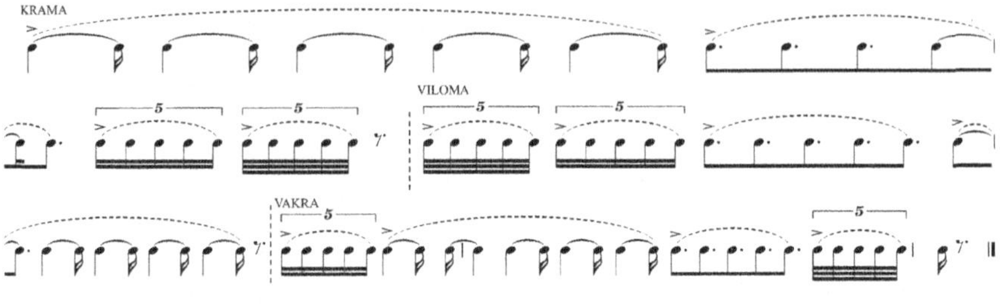

Chapter 12
Compound Mukthays

A compound mukthay is constructed around the following elements:

- The number of matras for the *beeja sangati* (literally 'seed phrase', the original phrase from which other phrases sprout in order to construct the compound mukthay) will always be the same as, half of or double the number of beats in the tala. Therefore, if the tala is 6 beats long, the number of matras in the seed phrase could be 6, 3 or 12. If the number of matras is 6, it will produce a mukthay of 2 cycles; if half the number of matras it will be 1 cycle long; and if double it will be 4 cycles.
- The seed phrase will be developed or modified in different ways so that all the resulting phrases will fit into the aforementioned number of cycles. The elements utilised to construct a compound mukthay are:
  - repetition of the seed phrase three times;
  - multiplication of every note value of the seed phrase by three matras;
  - rhythmical sangati of the seed phrase that will be taken into tisra 1st speed and tisra 2nd speed.

If a tala of 6 beats and a seed phrase of 6 matras are chosen, the mukthay will be 2 cycles long. If the seed phrase is  the developed version of the phrase will be:

1. The seed phrase repeated 3 times.

2. Every note value of the seed phrase is multiplied by 3 matras.

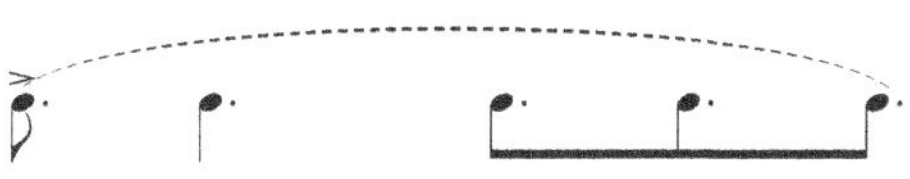

3. The seed phrase is taken into tisra 1st speed.

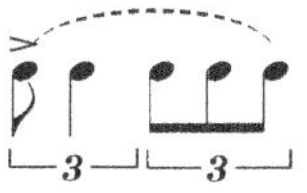

4. The seed phrase is taken into tisra 2nd speed.

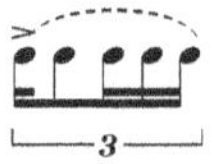

The entire phrase will then be *(track 97)*

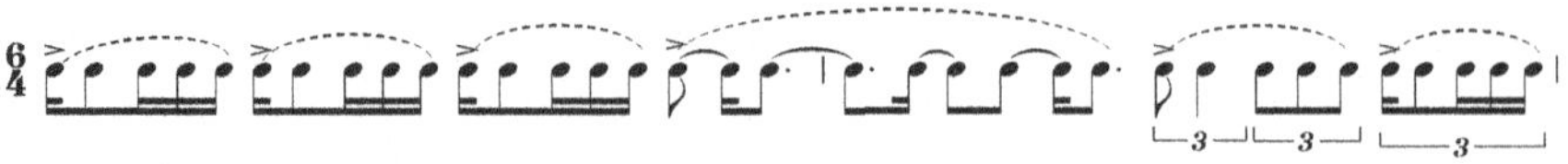

There is no other way of constructing a compound mukthay. No other gatis would provide the result that this construction delivers. It is a very clear pattern and the musician's choice lies solely in determining what the seed phrase can be within the number of matras chosen. Afterwards, one must adhere to the steps described. Although any permutation of these elements would theoretically be possible, no permutation is ever used in karnatic music.

A compound mukthay is relatively easy to perform when created in even number talas. It becomes slightly more difficult when performed in odd number talas, since the tisra 1st speed version will invariably start on the second half of the beat, although the phrase should be performed with a feeling of downbeat and never with a feeling of syncopation.

Notation

In terms of notation for the tisra phrases, the following conveys to the musician the placement of every note within the beat, although it does not convey the phrase with the downbeat feeling as performed by karnatic musicians. Visually, it gives a clear sense of syncopation. *(track 98)*

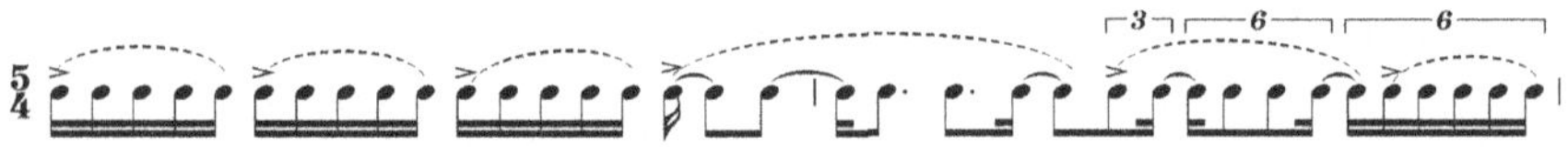

In the following example in tala 7, the triplet over a ♪ is written at the end to provide a clearer sense of the phrase. In order to enhance the clarity of the phrase, the first triplet is against 2 beats, the second against 1 beat and against a ♪ at the end. However, in this way the problem the performer would encounter is not knowing where the notes fall within the beat, since the tisra phrase starts on the second half of the beat. *(track 99)*

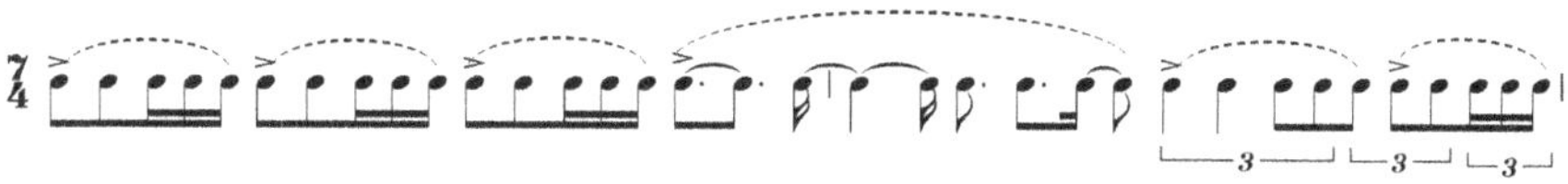

The only possible rewriting of the previous phrase will look like a mukthay in tala 5, so the notational problem remains – unless the notation of the mukthay in 7 beats is considered as the most beneficial for phrasing purposes and the one in 5 beats is written as an *ossia*, so that information as to where every note falls within the beat is provided.

Variation on the Structure

Another set of elements exists to create a compound mukthay, which quite closely resembles the concept of tirmana (in fact, both concepts co-exist, creating various mukthays that will be explained later in this chapter).

- every note of the seed phrase multiplied by three matras;
- every note of the seed phrase multiplied by two matras;
- the seed phrase, only once;
- the seed phrase taken into tisra 1st speed and tisra 2nd speed.

If the seed phrase  in tala 7 is taken, the compound mukthay will result in *(track 100)*

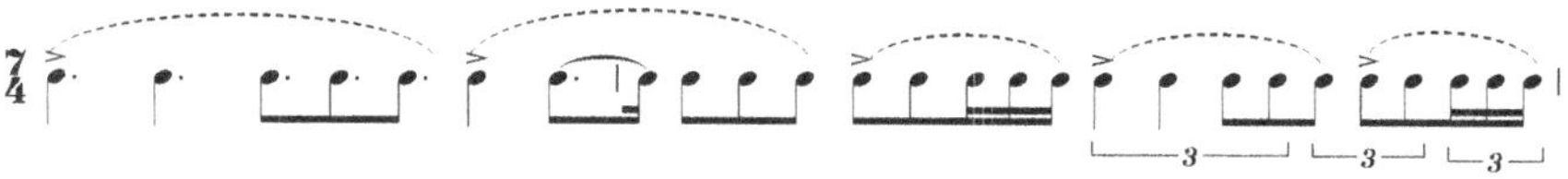

Tirmana-Compound Mukthays

As mentioned above, both concepts intertwine, so other types of mukthays that could not be ascribed to one or the other type are born. None of these seem to have any specific name, so I have coined the term 'tirmana-compound mukthays' for mukthays that somehow fall between the definitions of both concepts. There are two basic types.

1. In the first option, the tirmana-compound mukthay is similar to the variation on the compound structure explained above. It basically involves taking any regular tirmana or tirmana-mukthay, and instead of having a phrase that is constantly separated by the same number of matras, uses the concept of multiplying every note value by the same number of matras, as in a compound mukthay.

The next example could actually be the first three steps of a compound mukthay of the second type. But, as opposed to tirmanas, where any number of steps would be possible, in these mukthays there would only be three steps. The way to construct it would always be by thinking of a seed phrase and multiplying every note value by *x* number of matras. The systematic reduction seen in tirmanas remains, but the 'threshold line' is reached when every note value is multiplied by 1 or 2 matras.

The seed phrase is . The first step, or (better in this context) pala, multiplies every note value by 3 matras; the second pala multiplies it by 2 matras; and the last pala is the original seed phrase. The mukthay fits in a cycle of tala 9. *(track 101)*

A variation on the first type occurs when the seed phrase is not played but, instead, the number of matras used for the seed phrase becomes a gati. In the following example, in 1 cycle of tala 10 the seed phrase is . This phrase serves as starting point to create the mukthay, but does not appear in it. In the first pala every note value is multiplied by 3 matras, in the second pala by 2 matras, but in the third pala the phrase of 7 matras goes into misra. *(track 102)*

As opposed to tirmanas, this sort of tirmana-compound mukthay can be created in any gati. The following example is in khanda, in 1 cycle of tala 11. The seed phrase is

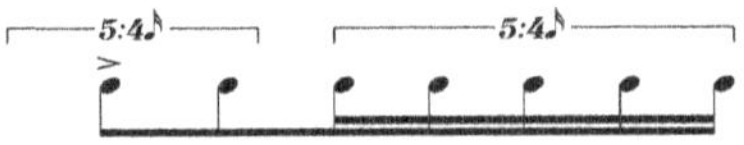

The first pala is multiplied by 3 matras, the 2nd pala by 2 matras and the third one is the seed phrase *(track 103)*

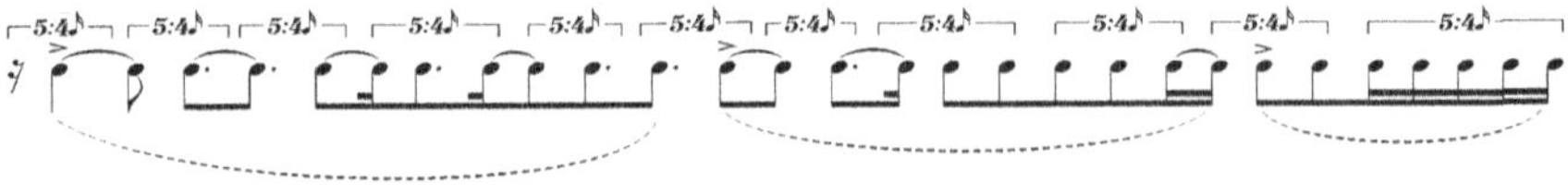

2. In this second possibility, the notion of multiplying every note value by *x* number of matras, and systematically reducing it while creating 3 palas, intertwines with the yati mukthay pattern of A, AA, AAA, but without gaps.

The pattern of this sort of mukthay is as follows:

- First pala, multiplied by the largest number of matras, performed once;
- Second pala, multiplied by a shorter number of matras, performed twice;
- Third pala, whether the seed phrase as such or in another gati, performed three times. *(track 104)*

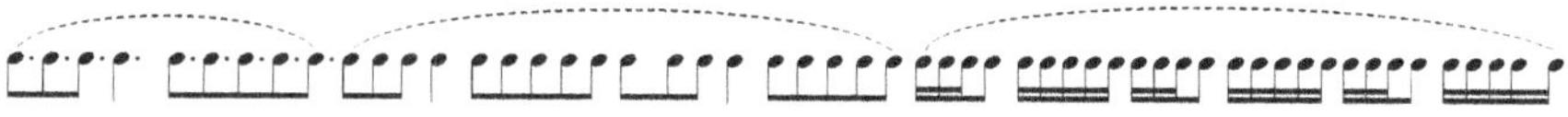

The other two options elucidated for the previous mukthay apply similarly in this possibility:

- The seed phrase would not appear in the mukthay and the last pala would go into another gati.
- The mukthay can be created in any gati.

Other Mukthays

There is a myriad of other mukthay constructions – formudaisi, 'magic number', palindromic, sub-mukthays, to name just a few – and augmenting these is a large variety with unknown designated names. I have explained thus far the most important and most frequently occurring types of mukthay which share the common denominator that all of them can be combined, mixed, modified and altered within the context of double and triple mukthays, or serve as starting points for the highly creative and imaginative concept of mukthay combinations (all of these will be explained in different chapters).

As opposed to the mukthays explained so far, the very many not included are really one-time occurrences in the strictest sense, and they seldom or never mix or combine with any other type of mukthay. Therefore, I feel compelled to end the explanation of mukthays at this point, with one exception: sub-mukthays.

Sub-Mukthays

This sort of mukthay has a double use: as a third option for short mukthays[1] as well as being utilised within the context of double, triple and mukthay combinations. A sub-mukthay is a phrase that is fragmented into two cells and follows the specific pattern of

AB (gap) AB (gap) B (gap) B|T.S.

[1] Wherever the book says that a short mukthay could follow a specific technique to complete the tala, a sub-mukthay could be used.

If the pattern is analysed, it can be observed that from the second **B** onwards the phrase could be interpreted as a short mukthay of the sama type. But it is simultaneously part of a phrase that has previously been played; therefore, it is not yet another sama mukthay. Again, it somehow falls between definitions, since the whole phrase is performed only twice (therefore, it does not qualify as a mukthay), but the second cell is performed four times altogether. In addition, there are three gaps, something that occurs exclusively in this kind of mukthay.

In the example below, the 'A' phrase is 7 matras, the 'B' phrase is 4 matras and the gap is of 3 matras. The whole mukthay is 39 matras long, and it can be placed in any tala and used in any gati. *(track 105)*

Chapter 13
Yatis Prastara

Yatis Prastara is a technique whereby two different yati phrases intermingle. Each pala of one yati phrase alternates with another pala of a different yati phrase. The sequence can eventually commence off tala sam (provided that the rest is always shorter than one beat), but it ought to resolve on tala sam. One of the yati phrases can use one more pala than the other one.

An important difference with yati phrases is that there are no gaps between palas. Calculations are always made so that the total sum of matras of both yati phrases would complete a chosen number of cycles of the tala. A simple short cut would be to calculate two different yati phrases of the same length and proceed to mix the palas. However, this is never done in karnatic music. The aim is always to ensure that the duration of every yati phrase is different.

For the purposes of yatis prastara only the sama, gopucha and srotovaha yatis are considered. The possible combinations are:

Sama-sama	Gopucha-gopucha	Srotovaha-srotovaha
Sama-gopucha	Sama-srotovaha	Gopucha-srotovaha[1]

One important feature in yatis prastara is that the two different ways of increasing or decreasing explained for yati phrases and yati mukthays are used together in this context. In some cases, a phrase can even be elongated or shortened by simultaneously applying the two notions.

Analysis of Examples

1) The first example to be analysed is a gopuchayati intermingled with a srotovahayati. The gopuchayati decreases by leaving out the first 3 matras of the previous pala

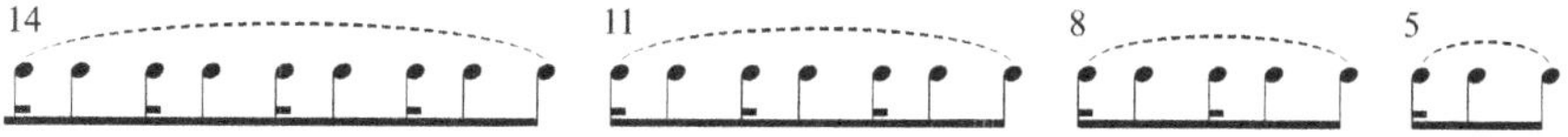

whereas the srotovahayati increases by adding 1 matra to the first 2 notes in every pala, keeping the last 3 ♪ intact as a recognisable feature of the development:

[1] In the last three options the order can be reversed.

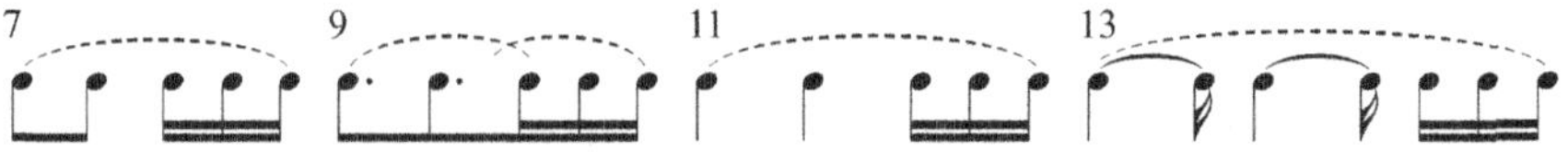

The two intermingled phrases fit in 2 cycles of tala 10, starting 2 matras off tala sam. *(track 106)*

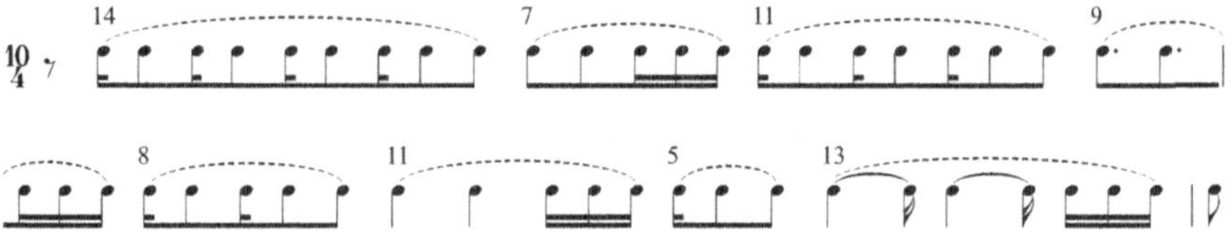

2) The second example features a gopuchayati (14 11 8 5) intermingled with a samayati (14 14 14). The manner of decreasing in this gopuchayati is by shortening the second, third and fourth notes by 1 matra at a time whilst keeping the first ♪ intact throughout. Samayatis do not have any variation, but it is interesting to observe the sort of sama mukthay thinking behind its construction. *(track 107)*

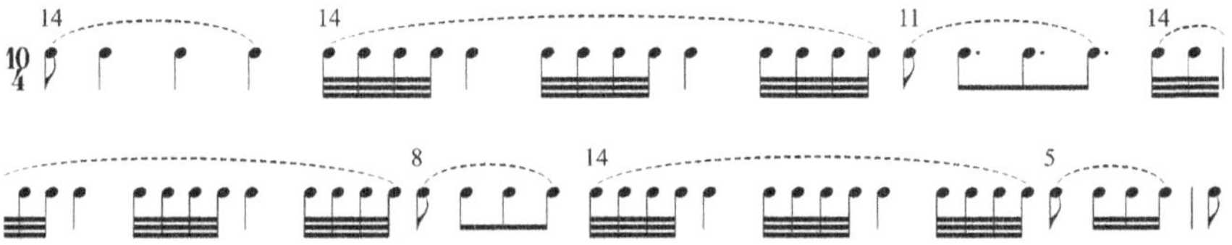

3) In this third example two samayatis are intermingled. This sort of yatis prastara is possibly the most predictable or repetitive of all the options. I have chosen it because I find it quite interesting that, although of different length, both samayatis use the same number of notes and somehow create a feeling of continuous tempo change. *(track 108)*

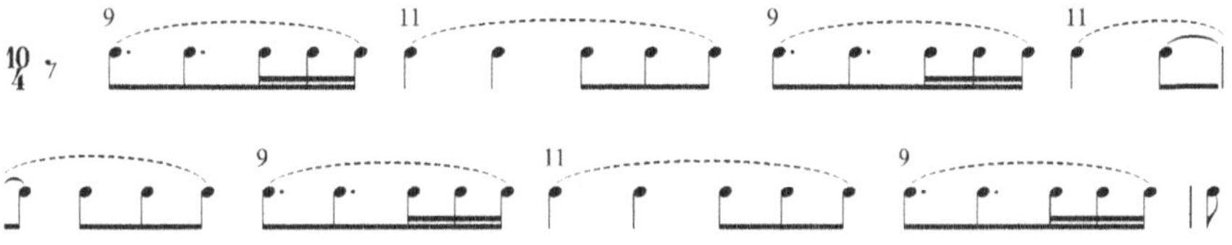

Usage of Superimposed Gatis on Samayati Frames

Whenever a yatis prastara containing a samayati has previously been played and is repeated elsewhere in a piece, the number of matras of the samayati can be used as a frame over which different gatis can be superimposed. However, this superimposition does not occur randomly: it also follows the notion of logical increase or decrease of a musical element. In this context the superimposed gatis follow a pattern regarding the number of matras by which every new gati increases or decreases.

In the example below, the musician has chosen to use a length of 14 matras as the frame for superimposing gatis. Since there are 3 palas of 14 matras, 3 different gatis need to be used. The 14 matras are divided into 2 equal frames of 7 ♪ and the gatis are increased by 2 matras, giving the following outcome:

5:7♪ twice   7:7♪ twice   9:7♪ twice

The reader could think that a 7:7♪ is not a superimposed gati, but rather chatusra jathi 7: this would be completely correct. But, as will be explained further in Chapter 19 on *mixed jathi nadai bhedam*, this is essentially due to the fact that misra (or any gati with jathi 7) are simply different ways to work with the number 7. *(track 109)*

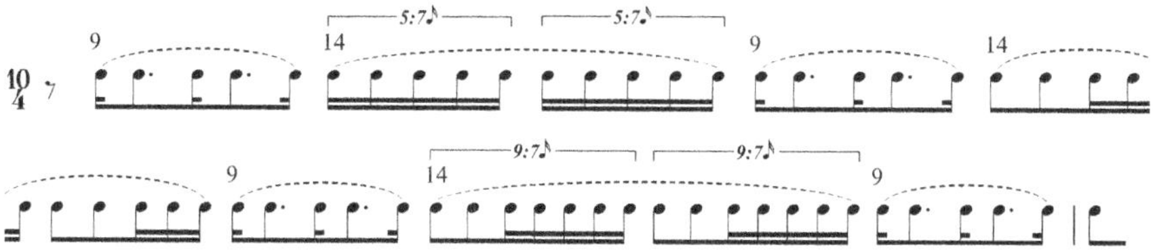

Development of Yatis Prastara

In a similar fashion to tirmanas or type A yati mukthays (among others), a yatis prastara sequence can be developed by using the possibility of repeating it three times in one of the following options:

- krama-krama-viloma
- krama-viloma-krama

The vakra option is completely discarded here, since the intermingling of two different yati phrases contains in itself the seed of the concept of vakra. In order to develop yatis prastara, the sequence has to start on tala sam and never off tala sam.

In the next example, the second phrase analysed previously (gopuchayati mixed with samayati) serves as the starting point for the development. The krama (lasting 2 cycles of tala 10) is followed by the viloma (once again, of the numerical sequence and not of the phrase itself) to finally conclude the whole development with a repetition of the krama version. (track 110)

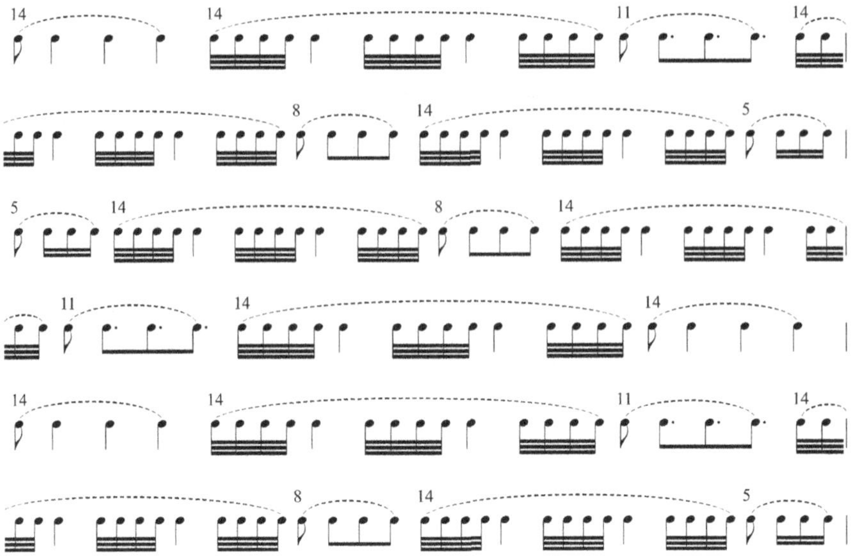

However, this option is not the one that karnatic musicians would favour the most. Many a time the development of krama-viloma-krama is purely numerical, and every segment can create a completely different phrase while keeping the same numbers or phrase durations. It is in this context that the technique of superimposing gatis can be found more frequently than as isolated occurrences (although this can also be the case). The superimpositions tend to be used in the repetition of the krama.

In the example below, which takes as starting point the same yatis prastara calculations as the previous example, the cells of the gopuchayati of the krama version are permutated in the second krama, whilst the samayati calculations serve as the frame to superimpose 5:7♪, 7:7♪ and 9:7♪ twice each. In this case the number of notes for the three superimposed gatis remains the same.

The viloma version is the same yatis prastara as in the previous example. *(track 111)*

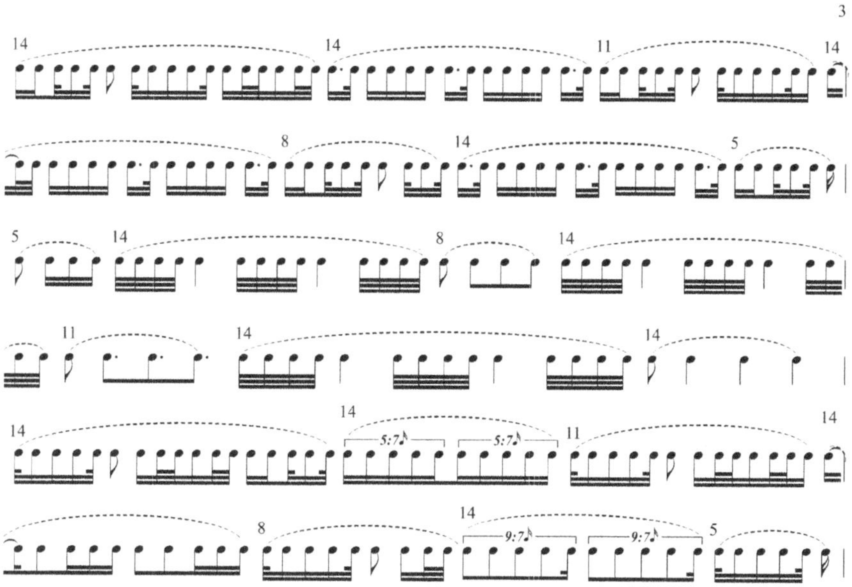

Eventually (but not exceptionally), a long sequence of krama-viloma-krama can be thought of in advance as a unit. When this is the case, the total number of matras of the chosen number of cycles of the tala is divided by 3 and the yatis prastara is constructed within these boundaries.

The example overleaf is constructed on a *shadanga* tala of 27 beats (this type of tala will be explained in Chapter 22). This tala is written as a 27/8.

The complete sequence is set to 4 cycles of the tala, giving 216 matras. When divided by 3 it gives a framework of 72 matras on which the krama of the yatis prastara is to be constructed.

The combination of yatis is samayati with gopuchayati. The number of matras for the samayati is 7 and the palas of the gopuchayati are 14, 17 and 20 matras long.

In the first krama, the gopuchayati increases by adding notes in the middle. As a viloma, it actually functions as a srotovahayati. The phrase is different to the krama phrase and omits notes from the middle as well. When the sequence of numbers is repeated in the second krama, the number 7 prevails in both yatis. In the gopuchayati palas, 7 is the number of notes that is increased by elongating different notes in the different palas, and the 7 serves as a frame to superimpose gatis in the samayati. On this occasion the gati decreases by 1 matra at a time, with the following result: 6:7𝅘𝅥𝅯.; 5:7♪. and 4:7𝅘𝅥𝅯. *(track 112)*

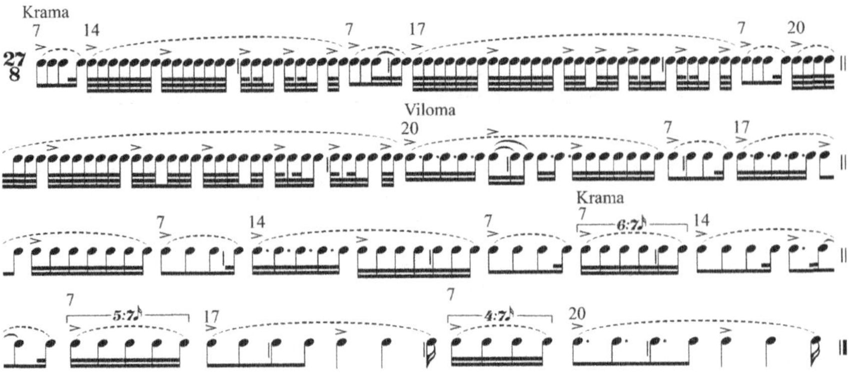
Krama
7
14
7
17
7
20
27
8
Viloma
20
7
17
7
14
7
Krama
7
6:7
14
7
5:7
17
7
4:7
20

Chapter 14
Double and Triple Mukthays

These mukthays have been referred to several times in previous chapters. In essence, they are musical objects made up of two or three mukthays performed one after the other (not intermingled, as was the case with yatis prastara) and without any gap separating the different mukthays. However, the possibilities are somewhat more ample and less straightforward than this concise definition infers.

Of the myriad mukthays explained and left out, the following are the ones that can potentially be used in double or triple mukthays:

- sama
- three types of yati
- three types of 3-fold
- two types of compound
- two types of tirmana-compound
- sub-mukthays.

In a similar way to yatis prastara, the construction of mukthays in this context avoids the structural aspect that forms the blueprint of some mukthays (sama, type A and B yati and compound). Any of these mukthays can be constructed on any number of beats, preferably longer or shorter than the number of beats of the tala. In compound mukthays any number of matras can be chosen for the seed phrase. In addition to these possibilities, two more options can be added to create double and triple mukthays:

- tirmanas (provided there are only three steps)
- yati phrases (provided there are only three palas).

As was the case for yatis prastara, both concepts of increasing or decreasing palas in yati phrases and yati mukthays can be mixed, as long as they keep their characteristic patterns. Consequently, a yati phrase could increase or decrease by elongating or shortening note values, and vice versa – a yati mukthay could be increased or decreased by adding or omitting notes (in both cases, a creative combination of both notions is possible in this context).

Double Mukthays

Double mukthays tend to conform more to the concise definition given at the beginning of the chapter. In terms of theoretical information there is essentially nothing else to add. However, the analysis of a few examples can help clarify how these mukthays are worked out.

Analysis of Examples

1) The first double mukthay takes 3 cycles of tala 8, consequently 96 matras long, and is made up of three steps of a tirmana, constructed in the following fashion

5 notes × 4 matras of separation:	20 matras
5 notes × 3 matras of separation:	15 matras
5 notes × 2 matras of separation:	10 matras

that gives a total of 45 matras, followed by a sama mukthay structured

15 (3) 15 (3) 15 that gives a total of 51 matras.

It is interesting to note the inner division of the sama mukthay in three short phrases of 5 matras each, which could be considered a sama mukthay in itself. The musician plays with the idea of a short mukthay that is repeated three times. *(track 113)*

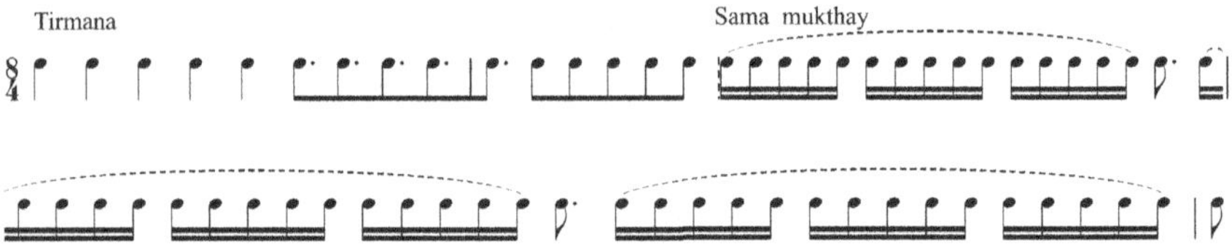

2) The second double mukthay is constructed on 4 cycles of tala 8 (128 matras) and consists of a sama mukthay structured

21 (0) 21 (0) 21

followed by a yati mukthay of type A (aaa, bbb, ccc) with the following length per pala

9 9 9 (1) 7 7 7 (1) 5 5 5

In the 'B' phrases two ♪ have been omitted, whilst the number of notes of these 'B' phrases (5) is preserved in the 'C' phrases. *(track 114)*

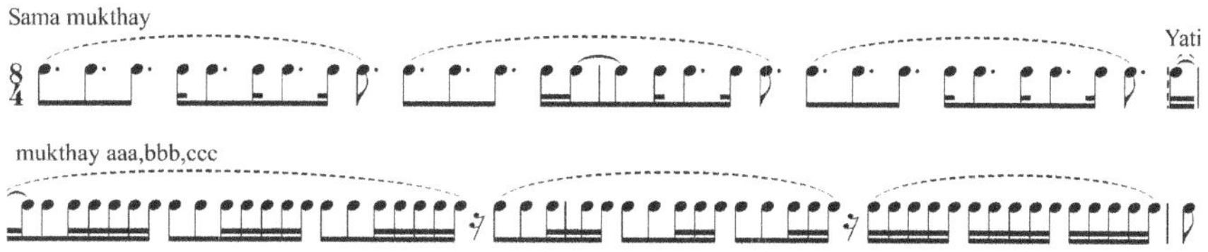

3) The third example, also in 4 cycles of tala 8 (128 matras), is made up of three steps of a srotovahayati, increased by adding in the middle of the phrase, with the following structure

14 (0) 19 (0) 24

The second mukthay is once more a yati mukthay of type A (aaa, bbb, ccc) with the following durations per pala

8 8 8 (4) 7 7 7 (4) 6 6 6

In the reduction of matras of the 'B' phrases, the omission of notes is intermingled with the elongation of note values: the last two 𝅘𝅥𝅯 of the original 'A' phrases are omitted, while the first note becomes a ♪ *(track 115)*

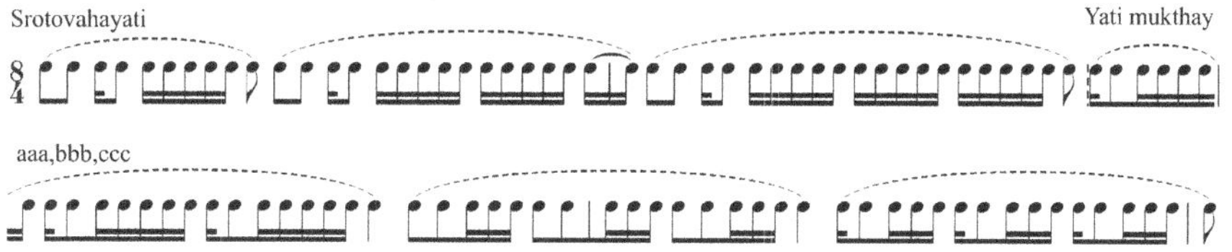

Triple Mukthays

An important feature in triple mukthays is that the transparent succession of mukthays seen in double mukthays becomes more blurred and less straightforward, as if anticipating the rather imaginative concept of mukthay combinations.[1]

Also, besides all the possible mukthays described previously for the double mukthays, a yatis prastara can be considered yet another mukthay, as long as it is not developed with the krama-viloma-krama option.

Karnatic musicians create triple mukthays with the objective of constructing a musical object that would defy a clear analysis or definition of the different parts, although there is not a single vestige of randomness in their development. All the mukthays can be analysed as such, but the construction and, moreover, the manner in which they are entangled with each other, are the elements that prevent

1 These will be explained thoroughly in the next chapter.

triple mukthays from being considered a simple sequence of three consecutive mukthays.

Analysis of Examples

1) The first triple mukthay, constructed on 4 cycles of tala 9, uses the following elements:

- 3-fold mukthay based on a 20 matras long pala (which is common to khanda and chatusra) using the type B possibility. The phrase is created on khanda (4 beats) and, following the pattern of type B, the original phrase is also performed in khanda 2nd speed anuloma (2 beats) and chatusra jathi 5 (5 beats). Since there are no gaps, the total length of this 3-fold mukthay is 11 beats.
- Yati mukthay of type B (a, ab, abc) with the following duration of palas

  7 (1) 7 10 (1) 7 10 13

The development of this mukthay exclusively uses the elongation of certain note values. The three 𝅘𝅥𝅯 of phrase 'A' are turned into ♪ and ♪. in phrases 'B' and 'C' respectively. It can be observed that the third time the 'A' phrase is repeated, the three 𝅘𝅥𝅯 are ornamented and turned into two groups of three 𝅘𝅥𝅯

- The third mukthay is a yatis prastara, intermingling two gopuchayatis. The first one is 12 9 6 3 and the other is 8 5 2.

The last of the 3 matras pala falls on tala sam. *(track 116)*

2) The second example responds more to the aforementioned concept of 'blaring' mukthays by different means. It is constructed on 6 cycles of tala 11.[2] *(track 117)*

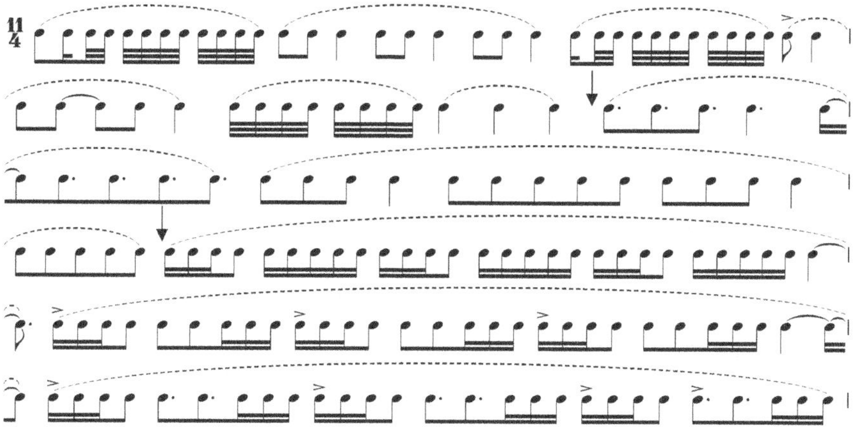

- The first mukthay is a gopuchayati with the construction 32 24 16. However, the musician has fragmented the phrase into two parts and the omission takes place in a rather unorthodox way. In the first pala, the first fragment is 8 matras long, whereas the second fragment is 24 matras.

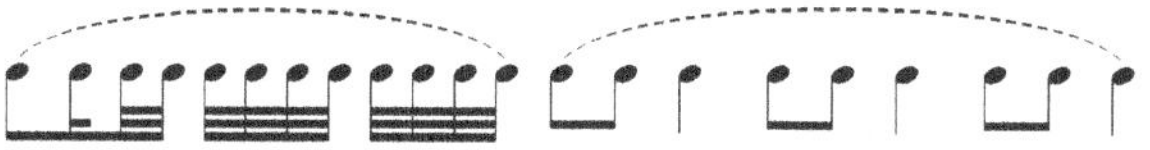

In the second pala, the first fragment is 6 matras long, whereas the second fragment is 18 matras long. Consequently, the omission of notes in the first fragment has been of only 2 matras whilst in the second fragment the first ♪ of the cell , which is repeated three times, is systematically left out.

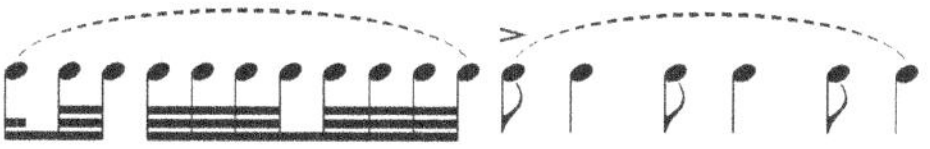

In the third pala, the first fragment is 4 matras long, whereas the second fragment is, logically, 12 matras long.

- The second mukthay of the sequence is one of the unnamed mukthays that I termed tirmana-compound mukthays.

[2] Arrows in the transcription indicate the beginning of each new mukthay.

This type is based on the repetition of the second pala two times and the third pala three times; the separation between notes is reduced in tirmana fashion, but with the compound mukthay notion of multiplying every note value by the same number of matras.

In the first pala, the seed phrase (10 matras long) is multiplied by 3 matras; in the second pala (performed twice), it is multiplied by 2 matras; and in the third pala (performed three times), it is multiplied by 1 matra.

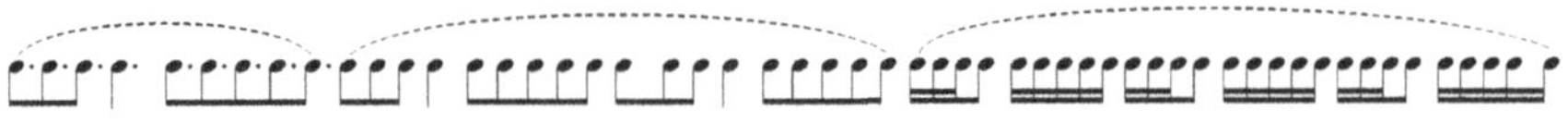

It is at this point that the lack of clarity as to where one mukthay ends and another one starts appears for the first time.

- The third mukthay is a yati mukthay type A (aaa, bbb, ccc) with the following structure

10 10 10 (7) 12 12 12 (7) 14 14 14

The original 10 matras of the seed phrase are divided into two small cells of 5 matras each, and the increase is applied exclusively to the second cell. The first two 𝅘𝅥𝅯 of the second cell are turned into ♪ and ♪. in the 'B' and 'C' phrases respectively. However the phrase that served as the third pala of the second mukthay

is simultaneously the AAA phrase of the previous yati mukthay. This overlapping is one of the techniques most often used by karnatic musicians to create triple mukthays. It is, however, by no means the only 'trick' to blur the structure of triple mukthays. The next chapter (mukthay combinations) will present more possibilities for blurring or disguising the inner structure of a triple mukthay.

Chapter 15

Mukthay Combinations

Due the nature of the technique and the almost limitless creative possibilities they encompass, not only are mukthay combinations almost impossible to define, but any attempt to define them also simply goes against their very essence.

In a very strict sense, a mukthay combination is a sequence that takes as its starting point a double or triple mukthay which is then 'repeated' three times. In every repetition there should be a development using, on a larger scale, a mukthay concept different to the ones employed to construct the double or triple mukthay. It thus becomes an entanglement of different mukthay concepts applied to the construction and development of this musical object.

In light of the fact that there is no a theoretical backbone beyond what has already been expounded – and that mukthay combinations really defy any possible definition, description or encapsulation – the best way to get acquainted with them is by trying to dissect a few examples as far as possible.

Analysis of Examples

1) The first example takes a double mukthay as starting point, with elements of tirmana (3 steps) and sama mukthay as the 'building blocks' for the development of the overall sequence. It is constructed on 9 cycles of tala 6. The whole sequence is *(track 118)*

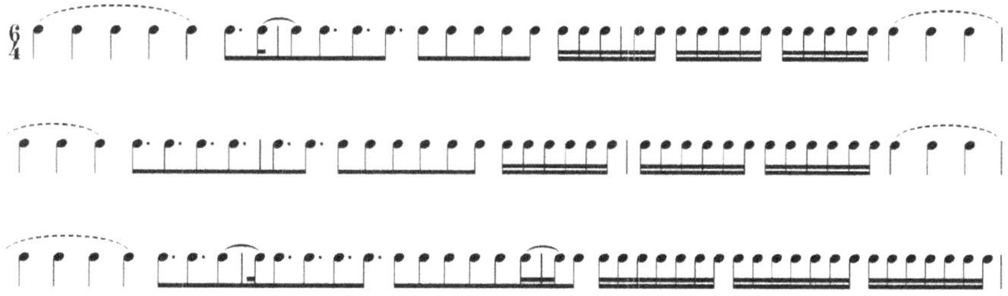

The first time the double mukthay is performed is based on a 5-note phrase throughout

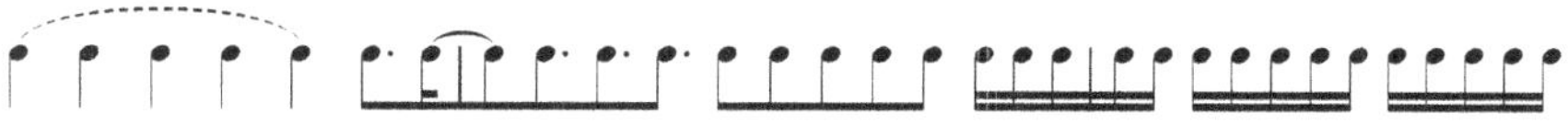

where the three steps of a tirmana are followed by a simple sama mukthay. The tirmana's calculations are

5 notes × 4 matras of separation:	20 matras
5 notes × 3 matras of separation:	15 matras
5 notes × 2 matras of separation:	10 matras

and the sama mukthay is 5 (0) 5 (0) 5

The second time the double mukthay is based on a 6-note phrase throughout

The calculations are

6 notes × 4 matras of separation:	24 matras
6 notes × 3 matras of separation:	18 matras
6 notes × 2 matras of separation:	12 matras

and the sama mukthay is 6 (0) 6 (0) 6

The third time the double mukthay is based on a 7-note phrase throughout

The calculations are

7 notes × 4 matras of separation:	28 matras
7 notes × 3 matras of separation:	21 matras
7 notes × 2 matras of separation:	14 matras

and the sama mukthay is 7 (0) 7 (0) 7

It can easily be inferred that the way the tirmana has been developed through the different repetitions is by applying a yati phrase concept to the overall sequence of tirmanas: every block takes one more note than the previous one. Similarly, all sama mukthays obey the same logic by adding one note per pala.

The thinking behind the construction of this mukthay combination is basically the same applied to a yati mukthay type A (aaa, bbb, ccc) . The middle 'phrase' (or 2nd block of the double mukthay in this case) is where all calculations are realised in order to complete 3 cycles of the tala. In this particular case it is the 6-note phrase that makes it possible to fit the double mukthay into 3 cycles of the tala.

Afterwards, a simple calculation and thinking lies behind matters: in order to make it coherent, it has to obey some form of mukthay concept applied to a larger format. In this mukthay combination the overall idea is that of a yati phrase, increasing by one extra note. Therefore, one note of the tirmana as well as the sama mukthay are 'omitted' in the 1st block, and this note is added to the 3rd block. When the mukthay is heard, the original construction based on the 6-note phrase is displaced within the tala and, consequently the only resolving point of the whole sequence appears on the 10th tala sam.

2) This second example is also based on a double mukthay made up of a sama mukthay and a sub-mukthay and performed within 3 cycles of tala 10. *(track 119)*

The development of the sama mukthay in the three blocks follows the concept of a gopuchayati phrase. In the 1st block, the length of the palas is 8 (0) 8 (0) 8

In the 2nd block, the length of the palas is 7 (0) 7 (0) 7

In the 3rd block, the length of the palas is 6 (0) 6 (0) 6

Similarly, the development of the sub-mukthay follows srotovahayati logic. In every block the whole phrase is increased by 1 matra. However, instead of adding this matra at any point in the phrase, every cell of the sub-mukthay is increased by ½ matra. This is the way the first cell of the sub-mukthay is developed

Block A: 6 𝅘𝅥𝅯 Block B: 7 𝅘𝅥𝅯 Block C: 8 𝅘𝅥𝅯

And this is the second cell of the sub-mukthay

Block A: 5 𝅘𝅥𝅯 Block B: 6 𝅘𝅥𝅯 Block C: 7 𝅘𝅥𝅯

The two cells of the sub-mukthay following each other are thus

Block A

Block B

Block C

Every double mukthay would then look like this

Block A

Block B

Block C

As opposed to the first example, this mukthay combination is not constructed on the middle block. It is structured around the idea of having the same number of matras in every block and each double mukthay, but deleting 1 matra from the first mukthay in blocks B and C and adding it to the second mukthay.

3) The third example responds more clearly to a stereotypical mukthay combination, where the boundaries of a phrase belonging to some mukthay not only overlap but also even become unrecognisable. The only clue the musician gives the listener is a simple sama mukthay at the beginning of every block. The rest is a continuous spider's web of phrases that can, somehow, even be analysed as two different mukthays simultaneously.

The large-scale idea behind the mukthay combination is a mixture of a 3-fold mukthay notion with a srotovahayati. The essential and basic idea at a micro-structural level is the seed phrases (of 5, 6, and 7 matras respectively) that are developed alongside the notion of transforming these phrases into khanda, tisra and misra at some point in the development. The seed phrases are

5 matras

6 matras

7 matras

The whole mukthay is developed in 12 cycles of tala 8. *(track 120)*

Mukthay combination in Tala 8 (L4 D D)

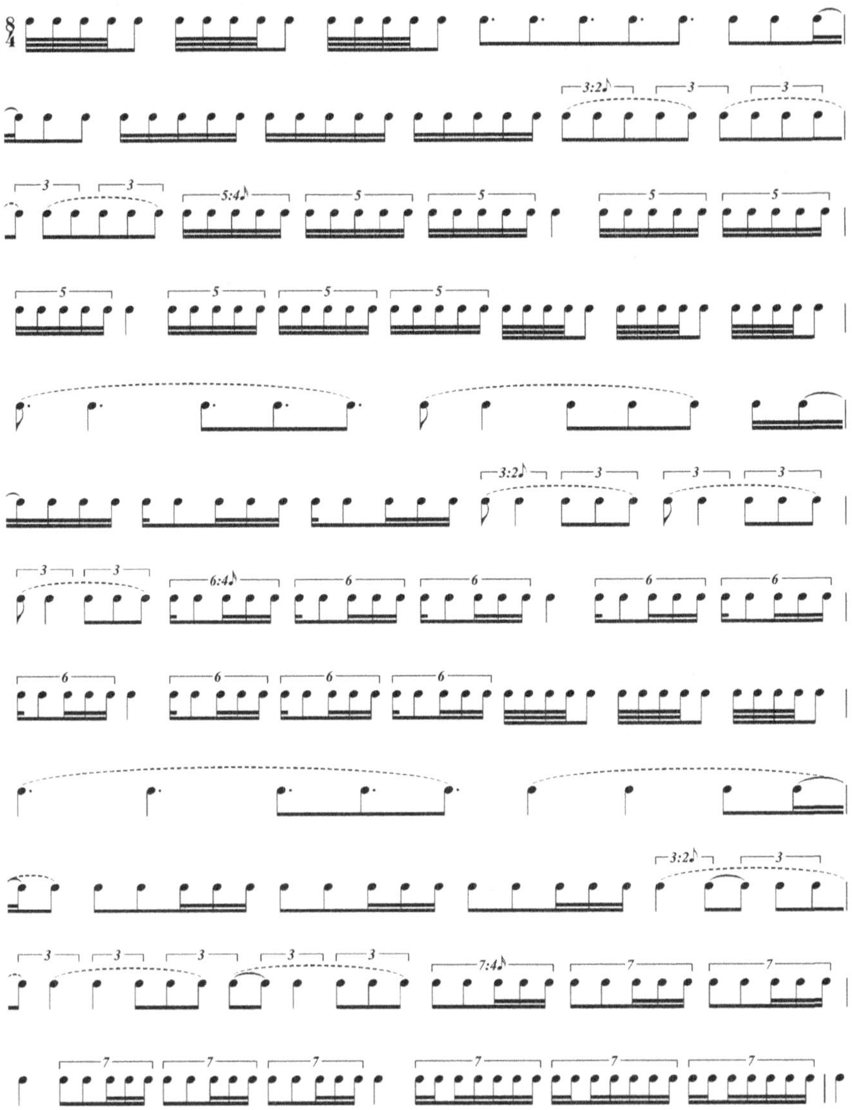

The first element, as mentioned before, is a simple sama mukthay of 3 beats that does not develop at all. This can be heard three times, marking the beginning of every block.

The second element is a tirmana-compound mukthay based on the 5 matras seed phrase. In the first pala the phrase is multiplied by 3 matras and in the second pala by 2 matras.

This is the point at which the overlapping of mukthays begins: the seed phrase of 5 matras – that is, the last pala of the tirmana-compound mukthay – is repeated three times, which turns it into a sama mukthay. Simultaneously, on a larger scale it becomes the first pala of a 3-fold mukthay of a 15 matras phrase (the common number between tisra and khanda). The phrase is actually constructed on khanda while the palas in chatusra and tisra use jathi 5.

Therefore, the seed phrase of 5 matras accomplishes three functions: the last pala of a tirmana-compound; by repeating it three times it becomes a sama mukthay; and it is the first pala of a 3-fold mukthay.

The phrase in tisra jathi 5

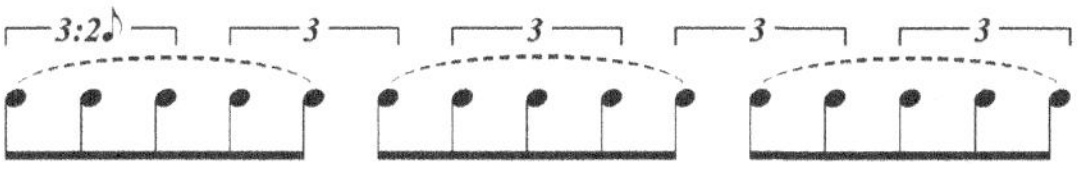

And, finally, the phrase in khanda as the last pala. However, this is not the end of the block: the phrase in khanda, the last pala of the 3-fold mukthay, is repeated three times, turning it into a sama mukthay of 15 matras per pala with a gap of 4 matras. Consequently, the idea of the 5 matras seed phrase becoming khanda gati responds to two different mukthay criteria: it is the last pala of a 3-fold mukthay and, simultaneously, the first pala of a sama mukthay.

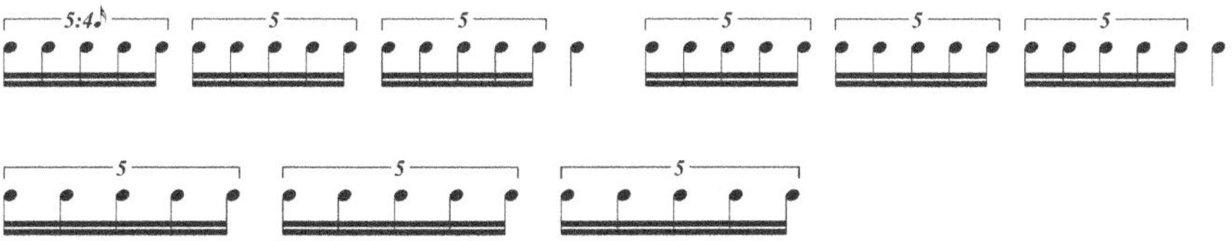

The whole 1st block, leaving out the short mukthay of 3 beats, looks as follows

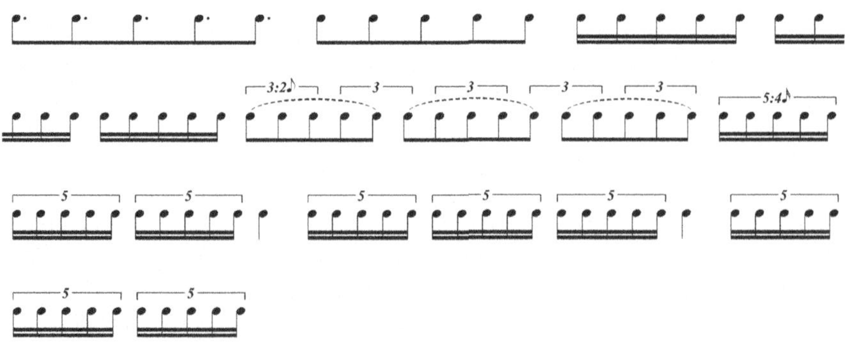

The 2nd block begins with the short mukthay of 3 beats, and the whole construction explained for the 5 matras seed phrase is used now for the 6 matras seed phrase. First, the tirmana-compound mukthay in which every note value of the seed phrase is multiplied by 3 and 2 matras respectively in the first two palas:

This is followed by the seed phrase that functions as the last pala of the tirmana-compound mukthay, as a sama mukthay by repeating it three times and as the first pala of a 3-fold mukthay of 18 matras. Therefore, jathi 6 is utilised.

The second pala is in tisra 1st speed.

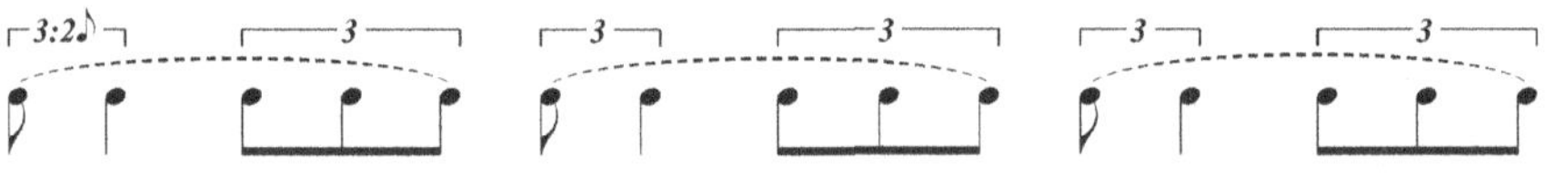

The last pala is in tisra 2nd speed that, as was the case with the khanda phrase of the 1st block, is repeated three times to become a sama mukthay:

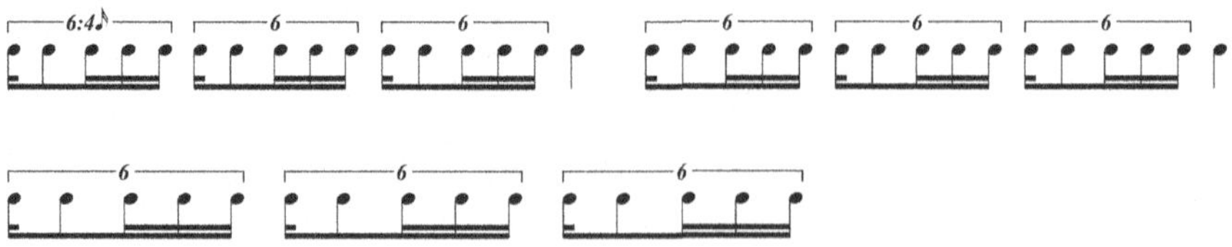

The whole 2nd block, without the initial sama mukthay of 3 beats, looks as follows:

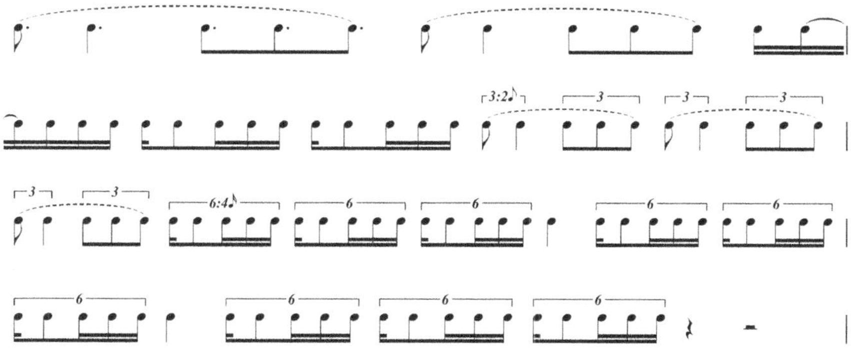

I deliberately left the 3 beats rest at the end of the block to show that this was actually the initial calculation and that the musician decided to add the simple 3-beat sama mukthay at the beginning in order to complete the 4 cycles of the tala. As with the very first example analysed, the middle block is where the calculations for the 'triple mukthay' take place. One note is deleted from the seed phrase of the 1st block that is then added to the seed phrase of the 3rd block.

The development in the 3rd block should be more transparent at this point. After the short sama mukthay comes the tirmana-compound, with the same multiplications of every note value as in the previous two blocks: 3 matras for the first pala and 2 matras for the second pala

followed by the last pala, which once again functions as three different mukthays. That is, by repeating the last pala of the tirmana-compound mukthay three times this becomes a sama mukthay; and it is the first pala of a 3-fold mukthay of 21 matras, which is the common number of tisra 1st speed and misra. Therefore, the chatusra and tisra palas utilise jathi 7.

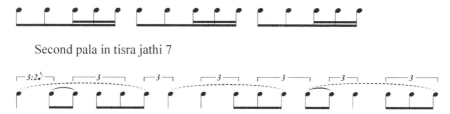

Second pala in tisra jathi 7

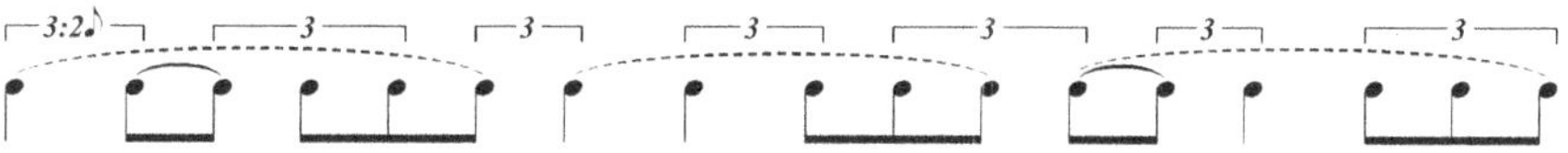

The last pala is in misra that, as in the two previous blocks, is repeated three times, becoming a sama mukthay:

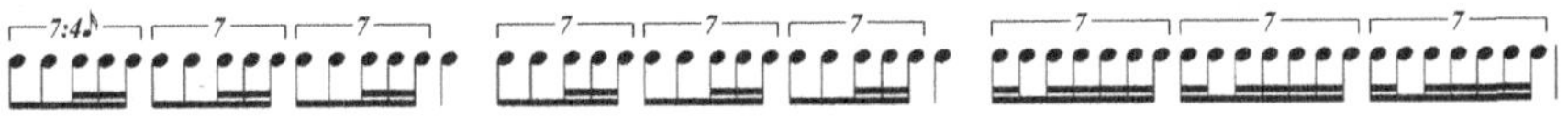

The whole 3rd block, without the short sama mukthay, looks as follows:

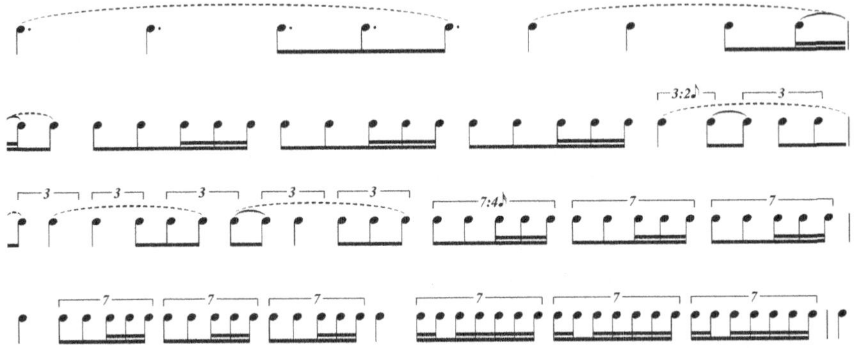

4) The last example is constructed in 11 cycles of tala 10 and, for the first time, a gap of 1 beat is inserted between blocks. The very basic idea behind its construction is quite similar to the previous mukthay: a 5 matras phrase that becomes khanda; a 6 matras phrase that becomes tisra 2nd speed; and a 7 matras phrase that becomes misra.[1] *(track 121)*

[1] The thin arrows indicate the beginning of each mukthay, and the thick arrows show the gap and the beginning of each block.

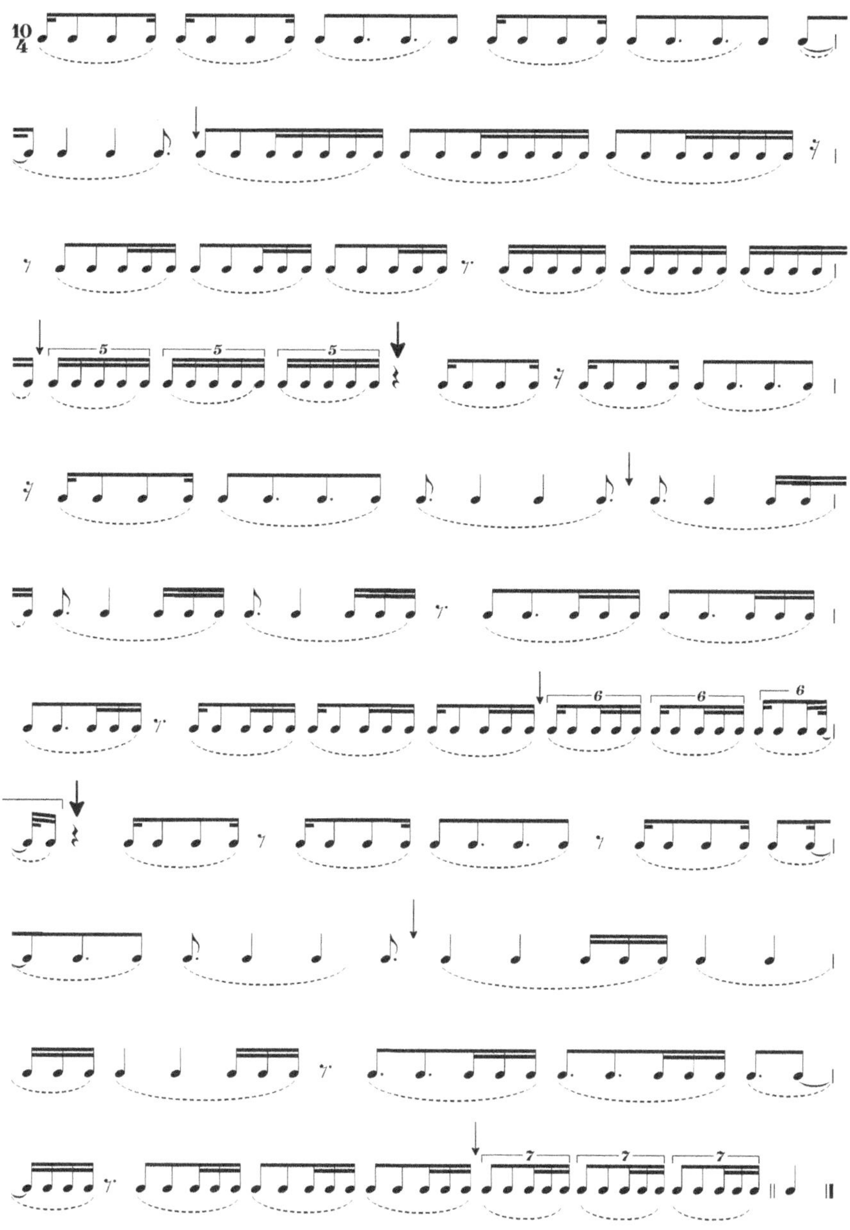

In order to link the core idea, the 5, 6 and 7 matras phrases are the last palas of a type A yati mukthay (aaa bbb ccc). The yati mukthay is developed on a large scale as if it were a srotovahayati.

- The structure of the 1st block of the yati mukthay is 9 9 9 (3) 7 7 7 (3) 5 5 5

The 'B' phrases use the concept of yati phrases of omitting notes in relation to the 'A' phrases, whilst the 'C' phrases keep the same number of notes as the 'B' phrases.

- The structure of the 2nd block is 10 10 10 (3) 8 8 8 (3) 6 6 6

In this yati mukthay, 'B' and 'C' phrases rigorously follow the principle of maintaining the same number of notes in all phrases and decrease the note values of the first two notes.

- The structure of the 3rd block is 11 11 11 (3) 9 9 9 (3) 7 7 7

It can be observed not only that the 'B' and 'C' phrases keep the same number of notes as the 'A' phrases, but also that this mukthay is somehow a continuation of the one in the 2nd block as it also maintains the number of notes in five.

With this construction, the link of each 'C' phrase to khanda, tisra and misra respectively is logical from a structural viewpoint. Every gati becomes the 3rd mukthay of each block by repeating every beat three times. Every mukthay is 3 beats long, but in different gatis that are increased following the pattern of a srotovahayati. The phrase in each gati is a repetition of the previous 'C' phrase of the yati mukthay, maintaining 5 notes in each gati:

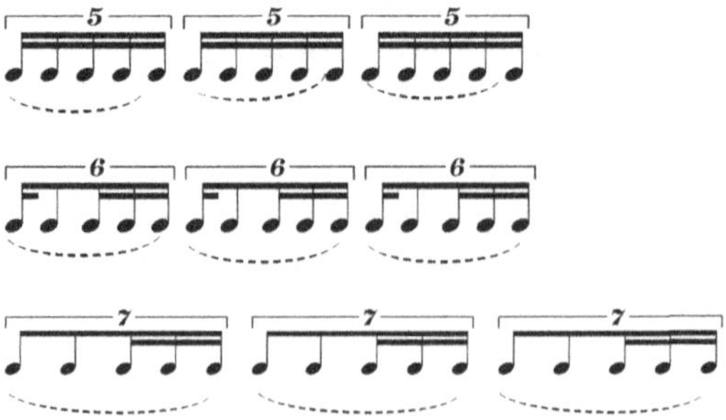

The total length of the three blocks of yati mukthays is 234 matras or 58 +1/2 beats. The sama mukthays in the three different gatis add up to 9 beats; consequently, both mukthays add up to 67+½ beats, still far short of the 110 beats that are required to complete 11 cycles of tala 10: 42+½ beats need to be created.

As the first mukthay of the triple mukthay, a yati mukthay of type B is chosen (a, ab, abc). The idea of using it as a first mukthay is possibly to somehow make less clear to a listener the mindset used to construct the second and third mukthays.

A first objective in this first mukthay is to construct it in such a way that it would add up to x number of beats plus the ½ beat. In the construction of this mukthay the length of all phrases remain intact, whereas the number of matras in the gap is the changing element. Each note in the 'B' phrase is elongated by 1 matra; the same procedure is applied to each note of the 'C' phrase.

In the 1st block there are no gaps between palas. The length of palas is

6 (0) 6 10 (0) 6 10 14

In the 2nd block the gap is of 1 matra: 6 (1) 6 10 (1) 6 10 14

And in the 3rd block the gap is of 2 matras: 6 (2) 6 10 (2) 6 10 14

Obviously, the calculations have been made on the 2nd block so that, when multiplied by 3, they will result in sufficient beats to either complete the 110 beats of the whole sequence or to leave some matras over to be used as gap between the blocks. But, *if a gap is used in between blocks, it needs to be longer than any gap used to separate palas of the different mukthays.*

Consequently, the length of the mukthay in the 2nd block is 54 matras, which, when multiplied by 3 gives 162 matras or 40+½ beats. The two remaining beats to complete the 11 cycles of tala 10 are used as gaps of 1 beat each, separating the three blocks.

Chapter 16
Poruttam A

A simple definition of *poruttam* would be a sequence of at least 3 cycles of a tala in which fragments of the theme are interwoven with different rhythmical techniques. Some of these techniques have already been covered, and others will be explained later. However, there are more parameters and ramifications that turn this definition into a more elaborate concept.

There are two ways of constructing a poruttam, as well as an entirely different set of techniques associated with each of these methods. Perhaps because the basic concept remains the same, karnatic music does not seem to have two different names for the different ways of constructing and developing the concept of poruttam. Notwithstanding this, in order to explain the two different ways of constructing and developing poruttam, I simply decided to divide the whole poruttam concept into two separate chapters and call the first construction 'A' and the second 'B'.

There are only two points common to both types of poruttam: the choice of theme fragments (and subsequent deletion of notes in every fragment); and the concept of filling the empty space provided by the omission of these notes with concrete techniques.

- *Theme fragments*: In karnatic music, every theme is split into two, three or sometimes even four segments or cells. This fragmentation has multiple consequences, particularly in the development of melodic material but also in the development of some rhythmical elements. If a musician decides to use poruttam in a piece, the theme will usually be fragmented into three cells; alternatively, a theme will be constructed where the musical flow can be easily subjected to this fragmentation into three cells.

Once the three cells have been established, the musician then proceeds to omit the number of notes considered appropriate. The general idea is to leave just the *first* 3 to 5 notes of every fragment (essentially enough musical material to make these few notes recognisable) and delete the rest. For calculation purposes the last note of each fragment can be shortened as much as the musician likes.

- *Filling the empty space*: The first note of every fragment of the theme serves as a sort of resolving point. Between the last note of one cell and the first note of the following cell, the omission of notes creates a space that is filled with different sets of techniques, depending on the choice of construction. Each technique will resolve on the first note of the following cell, as it would on a tala or anga sam.

Structure of Poruttam A

The explanation of this whole subject is based on a 12-cycle sequence of poruttam A created on a theme in tala 11. The theme is

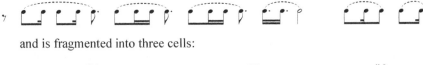

and is fragmented into three cells:

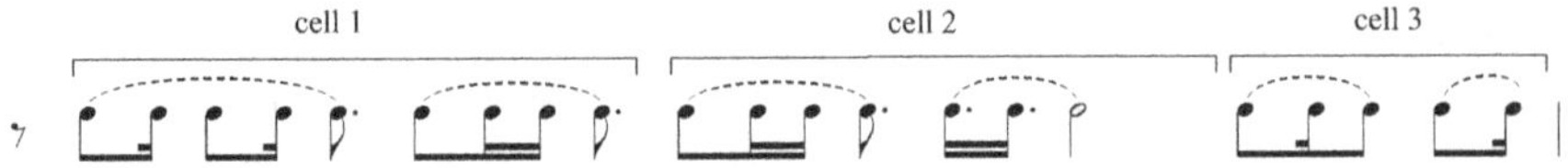

Thus, the cells of the theme are subjected to the deletion of a number of notes and the shortening by one 𝅘𝅥𝅯 of the last note of cells 1 and 2.

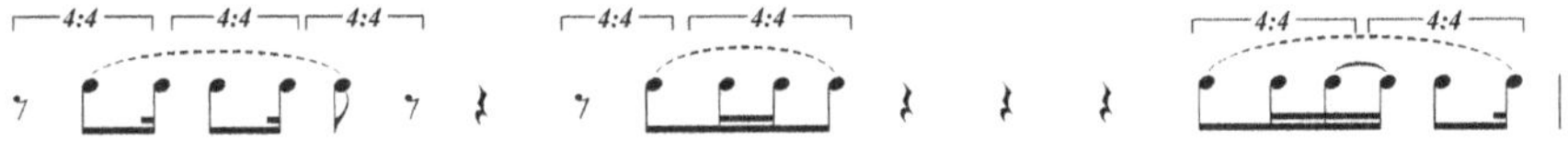

Actually, up until this point all the steps are common to both types of poruttam. The first element that differentiates poruttam A from its B counterpart is the way the cells are distributed within the tala and how much space is created between them.

In poruttam A, every cell, while *always staying in its original position within the tala* according to the original theme, is performed in different cycles of the tala (as shown in the example below). Usually this way of spacing the cells into different cycles of the tala produces a sequence of 4 cycles. The rests represent the empty space that will be filled by different techniques.

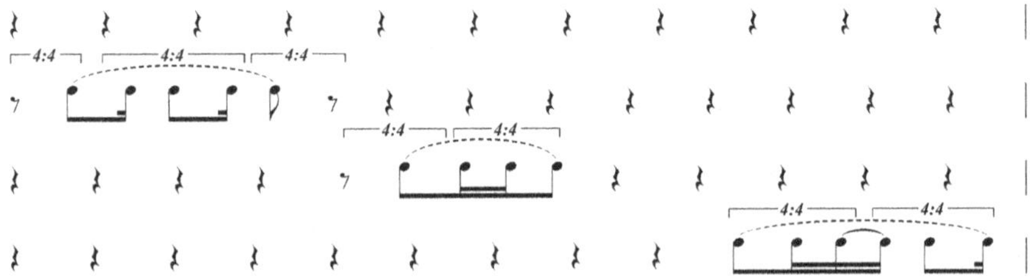

It can be observed that the first cell is preceded by a whole cycle with rests. This implies that a sequence of poruttam A never starts with the first cell followed by a technique; it always starts by first using a technique that resolves on the first note of the first cell. This is due to the fact that a sequence of poruttam A will last 8 or 12 cycles (eventually, although rarely, 16 cycles). Therefore, the construction of 4 cycles shown above will be repeated twice or three times.

Since each cell of the theme needs to be separated by at least a whole cycle (consequently, *the last cell cannot be followed immediately by the first cell*), this first technique preceding the first cell ultimately forms part of the techniques used in the cycle separating the last and first cells.

This construction produces segments of different durations to be filled. The first technique always has the duration of 1 cycle plus the *eduppu* (beginning point of a theme within the tala). The fact that there are 3 cells will invariably produce three different techniques per block:

- The first technique starts 1 cycle before and leads to the first cell.
- The second technique occurs between the end of the first cell and the beginning of the second cell.
- The third technique occurs between the second and third cells.[1]

Construction and Development of Techniques

Before explaining the creative part, there are two important elements to take into consideration.

- *Durations between cells*: These distances need to be calculated beforehand. In the case of the example to be analysed, the durations between cells are as follows:
  - The cycle preceding the first cell plus the matras off tala sam before the eduppu: 11 beats plus 2 matras (46 matras in chatusra).
  - Between the end of the first cell and the beginning of the second cell: 13 beats (52 matras in chatusra). Note that, in this particular example, the second technique will always start on the second half of the beat, and will similarly resolve on the second half of the beat since the second cell begins on the third matra.
  - Between the end of the second cell and the beginning of the third cell: 14 beats (56 matras in chatusra).

These distances remain unaltered regardless of how many times the sequence of 4 cycles is repeated. No cell will ever be performed in a different place from its position in the original theme. Techniques must always fit into the framework of the given duration.

- *Potential techniques to be utilised*: Not all techniques seen so far are suitable for use in the context of a poruttam A sequence. The following techniques are the ones used most by karnatic musicians:
  - gati bhedam (followed by a short mukthay, or not)
  - jathi bhedam (followed by a short mukthay, or not)
  - combination of gati and jathi bhedam; poruttam A is the only rhythmical concept where both techniques can be interwoven or follow one another

[1] What happens when the last cell finishes before the end of the tala is explained later.

- six types of yati phrases (with a short mukthay, or not)
- three types of yati mukthays
- sama mukthays (followed by a mini-mukthay, or not)
- three types of 3-fold mukthays
- tirmanas and tirmana-mukthays (no restrictions on how many steps can be used)
- compound mukthays; the number of matras of the seed phrase will always be half the number of beats of the fragment to be filled, and will have *no* relationship to the number of beats of the tala
- compound-related mukthays
- sub-mukthays
- yatis prastara

There is a constellation of mukthays with no names that essentially constitute combinations of two or more different concepts of mukthay.[2] However, many of these unnamed and rare mukthays are used in poruttam A (as well as in double, triple and mukthay combinations). One example of an unnamed mukthay will be shown and explained in the analysis of the 12-cycle poruttam.[3]

- Relevant rules for creating and connecting techniques:
  a. Each block of 4 cycles should have three differentiated techniques (as listed above) that will last for the entire duration of the fragment between theme cells.
  b. Each technique used in the 1st block will be connected in the same place in subsequent blocks by using the same or similar technique. For instance, if the first technique in the 1st block is a srotovahayati with the palas 5 9 13 17, the first technique in the 2nd and 3rd blocks should hold a relationship with the srotovahayati (or with one or more of its numbers) in one way or another. This relationship could vary from a rather obvious one, almost a repetition of the technique, to a more far-fetched connection.
  c. Changes of gatis are allowed after each cell, since the cell is considered a sort of tala sam.

[2] There are a fair number of these mukthays and many a time they respond more to the creativity of a particular musician than to a specific set of rules of construction.

[3] Needless to say, western creators can equally try to construct mukthays that are outside the scope of this volume by combining two or more concepts, as karnatic musicians frequently do.

Analysis of Example

The best way to fully understand the poruttam A construction, the connections between techniques and phrasing development, is by analysing a very clear yet elaborate sequence of 12 cycles by B.C. Manjunath.[4] *(track 122)*

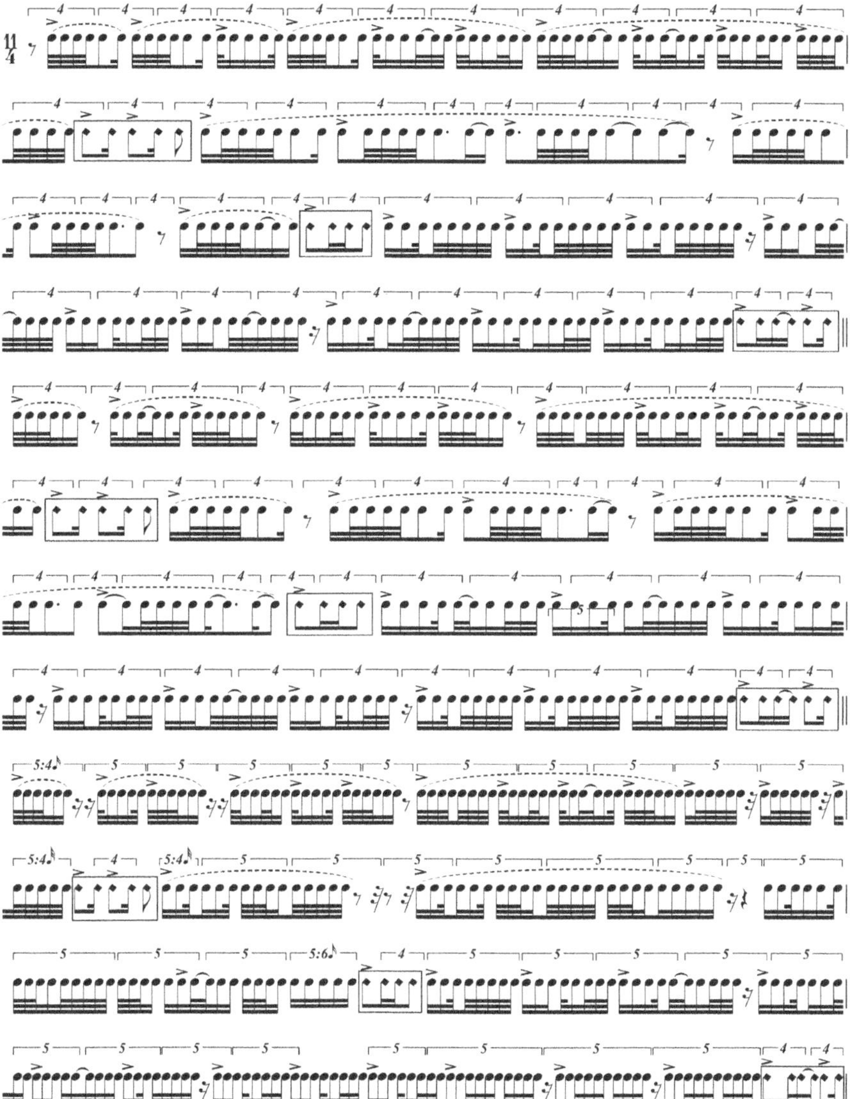

[4] The theme cells are boxed and with a diamond-shaped note-head.

Techniques used in the 1st block

1) 11 beats plus 2 matras (46 matras in chatusra): a srotovahayati structured (2) 5 (0) 9 (0) 13 (0) 17. It uses the option of adding matras at the end of every pala.

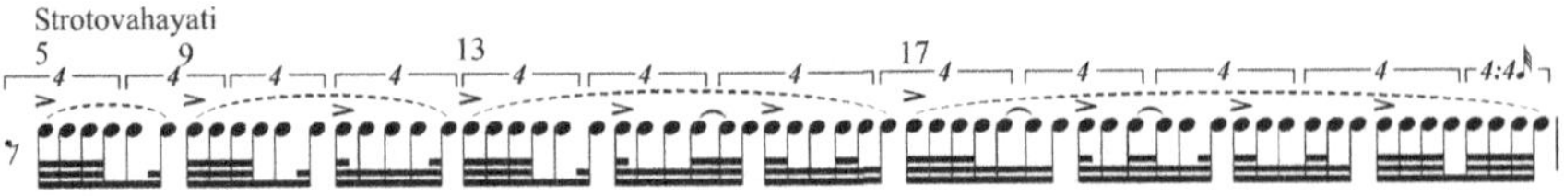

2) 13 beats (52 matras in chatusra): yati mukthay type B. It increases the number of matras using the pattern abc (gap) ab (gap) a . The length of the palas is[5] 6 9 12 (2) 6 9 (2) 6

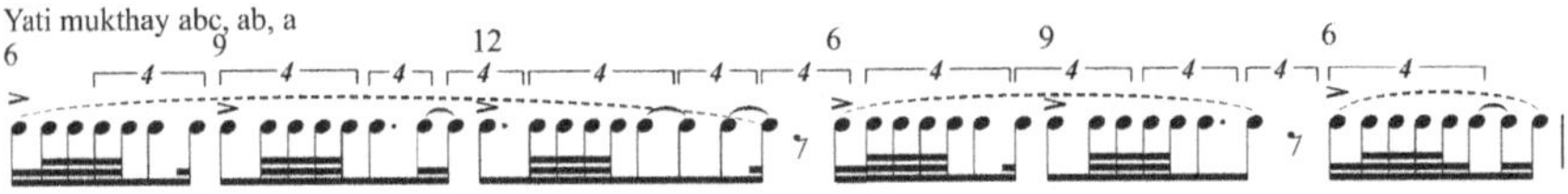

The 'B' and 'C' phrases use the same number of notes as the 'A' phrase. They increase by leaving the group of four ♪ intact while adding 1 matra per remaining note.

3) 14 beats (56 matras in chatusra): yati mukthay type A. This also uses the option of increasing the number of matras with its characteristic pattern aaa (gap) bbb (gap) ccc. Length of palas is 5 5 5 (1) 6 6 6 (1) 7 7 7

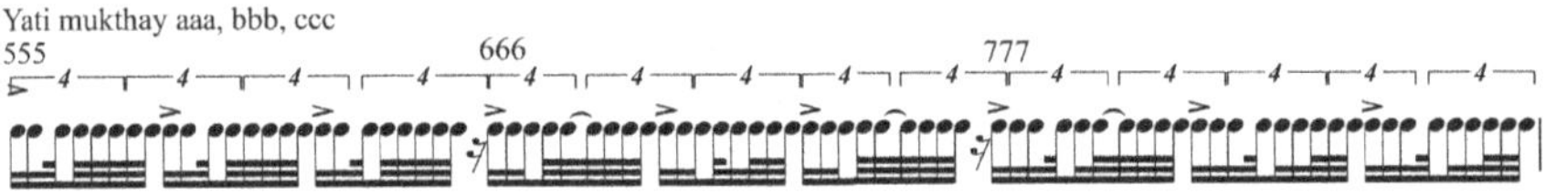

The seed phrase in the 1st pala of 5 matras is divided in two parts: the first part is increased by a ♪ in the first part of the 6-matra pala, whereas a ♪ is added in the 7-matra pala.

The second part consistently uses the increase of note values, following the pattern of increasing by a ♪ the second note in the 'B' phrases and the first one in the 'C' phrases.

The whole block, mixed with the theme cells, would look like

[5] It can be observed that the first and last 2 matras of the yati mukthay do not receive any bracket; this is due to the fact that those notes start and finish respectively in the second half of the beat.

Techniques used in the 2nd block
The three techniques exposed in the 1st block need to be developed or connected with the techniques to be used in the 2nd block.

1) 11 beats plus 2 matras (46 matras in chatusra): a srotovahayati with different calculations to the first one, but one that is clearly related because it uses the same number of matras to increase the palas and, more importantly, because the whole passage sounds almost identical. Instead of starting with the 2 matras gap, which in the context of the second block would most likely sound like a mistake rather than as an intentional gap, the musician takes 1 matra off every pala of the first block (thus releasing 4 matras) that, united with the 2 matras of the gap in the first block, provides 6 matras to distribute as a gap in between palas. The calculations are then

4 (2) 8 (2) 12 (2) 16

The only changes are that in the 1st pala the ♪ of the first cell 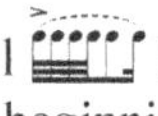 has been decreased to 𝅘𝅥𝅯  and that the choice of adding notes is from the beginning rather than the end.

Srotovahayati

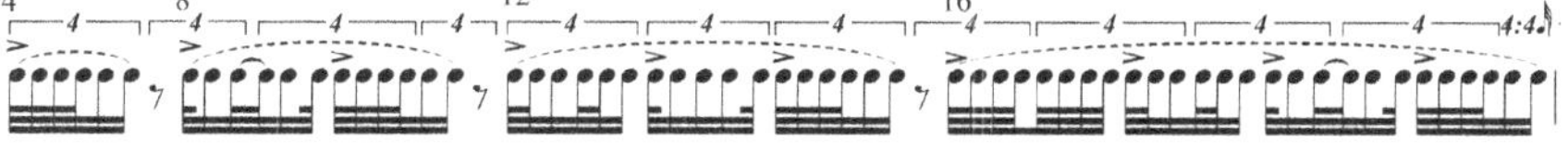

2) 13 beats (52 matras in chatusra): yati mukthay, type B. This also uses the option of increasing the number of matras but the pattern is reversed, thus a (gap) ab (gap) abc. Length of palas is 6 (2) 6 9 (2) 6 9 12

Yati mukthay a, ab, abc

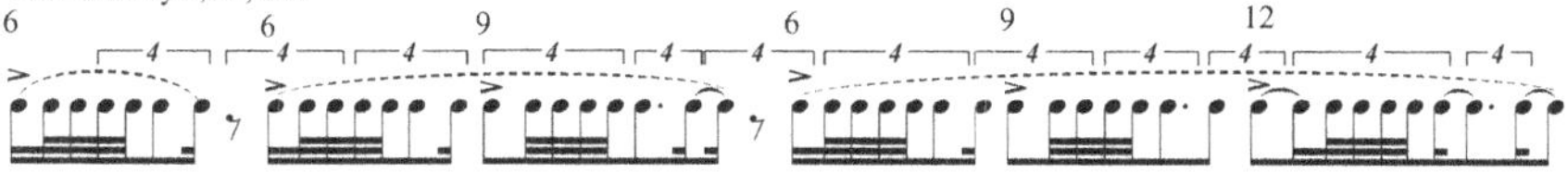

Each pala remains identical to the first block.

3) 14 beats (56 matras in chatusra): yati mukthay type A. It is the viloma version of the 1st block,[6] thus using the pattern ccc (gap) bbb (gap) aaa. The length of palas is 7 7 7 (1) 6 6 6 (1) 5 5 5

Yati mukthay ccc, bbb, aaa (Viloma)

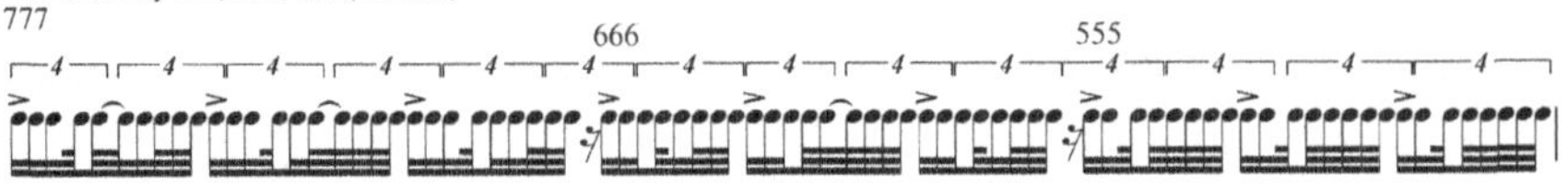

Thus, the whole second block looks like this:

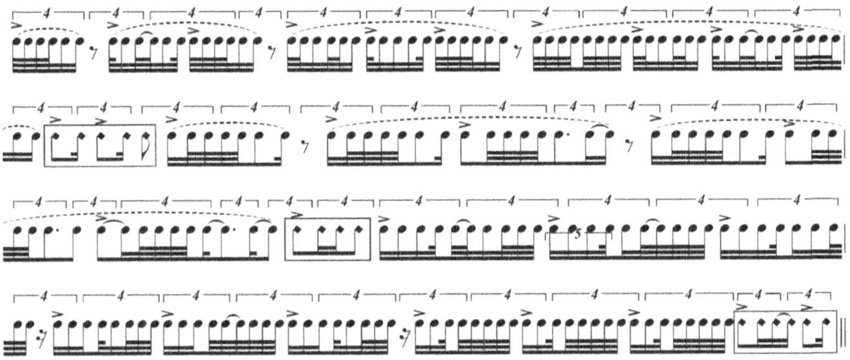

Techniques used in the 3rd block

In this third block, the development on the two previous blocks is realised entirely in khanda. This change of gati (an application of the rhythmical sangati concept) increases the number of possibilities, since the original length of phrases in chatusra when re-grouped in khanda is shorter than the duration of the fragments between cells.

1) 11 beats plus 2 matras (55 matras in regular khanda plus ½ beat; or 115 matras of khanda 2nd speed anuloma).

The original length of the srotovahayati was 46 matras. Bridging the difference between chatusra and khanda in order to complete the original length would require the use of one of the following options or a combination of them:[7]

[6] As explained in Chapter 10 (yati mukthays), the viloma and vakra versions of a type A yati mukthay do not need to happen as a sequence or block. They can be used in different parts of a piece or used as a developmental idea in mukthay combinations and poruttam A sequences.

[7] More imaginative options would also be possible, but the ones presented are those used most frequently.

- modification of the gaps on the srotovahayati constructed for the 1st or 2nd blocks;
- coherent change of the duration of palas that follows criteria similar to the one used for the creation of the srotovahayati in the 2nd block;
- short mukthay following the yati phrase and resolving the fragment onto the 2nd cell.

The musician has opted for the latter, but since the fragment has an extra ½ beat before attacking the first cell, the musician fills this ½ beat with 5 matras of khanda 2nd speed anuloma (thus a 5:4♪); and, instead of thinking in the number of matras in the regular speed, he thinks in the number of matras provided by using 2nd speed anuloma. The mukthay is then 7 (1) 7 (1) 7.

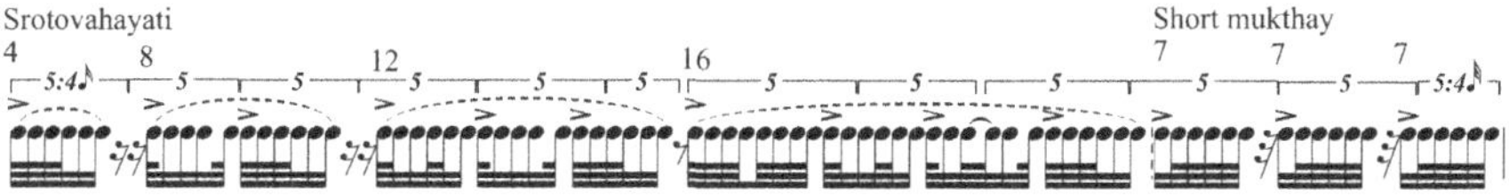

2) 13 beats (52 matras in chatusra): unnamed mukthay combining the concept of a yati mukthay type B with a compound-related mukthay, together with the notion of sub-mukthay.

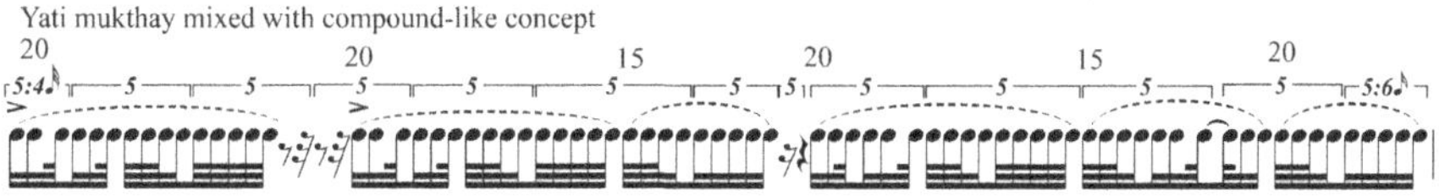

To begin with, the first phrase is not related to any of the palas of the yati mukthay type B. The seed phrase of the third technique (yati mukthay type A) is the source of the development (which constitutes another way of creating a more entangled development of ideas).

Secondly, the numbers do not relate to any of the mukthay concepts seen so far. Although the musician follows a large structure of a yati mukthay type B (a (gap) ab (gap) abc), the numbers do not follow what anyone at this point would expect from such a construction, namely:[8]

20 (10) 20 15 (10) 20 15 20

This numerical construction clearly defies any mukthay construction explained so far; but a dissection of the different concepts utilised will show the logic behind its creation.

[8] Once again, the musician thinks in number of matras of 2nd speed anuloma rather than in regular khanda.

The two cells of the seed phrase of the last technique (yati mukthay type A) form the core of the mukthay: is repeated twice and is the last group of the 1st pala and, as will be seen, the seed for the development of the entire mukthay.

The larger structure of a yati mukthay type B has already been established. But the 'A' phrase is divided into two cells in the same fashion as a sub-mukthay.

Cell 1  and Cell 2 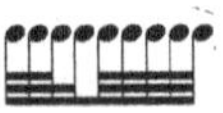

The 2nd pala ('B' phrase) takes only the 2nd cell, and once again splits it into the 1st and . The last 5 matras are developed in the 'B' phrase with the idea of a compound: each matra is multiplied by 2. This multiplication is applied only to the 2nd cell of the pala, following the notion of a sub-mukthay. The 'B' phrase thus looks like this

Lastly, the logic in the construction of the 'C' phrase does not follow the pattern of the yati mukthay type B, but the logic combines once again the ideas of compound mukthay with that of a sub-mukthay.

If in the 'B' phrase the seed cell was multiplied by 2, in the 'C' phrase it is multiplied by 3 matras: 5 notes multiplied by 3 matras is 15 matras of 2nd speed anuloma, which results in a 5:6♪ for all practical purposes. Added to the first 5 matras cell this results in the 20 matras that, at least initially, could confound the logic behind the mukthay's construction. The 'C' phrase thus looks like this:

3) 14 beats (70 matras in khanda): The final technique is the vakra version of the yati mukthay type A of the 1st block. The pattern of the mukthay is abc (gap) cba (gap) bbb. The length of palas is 5 6 7 (1) 7 6 5 (1) 6 6 6.

The fact that this vakra version is performed in khanda allows for a final mukthay that would give a clear climax to the whole section. The 16 matras of difference between the 14 beats in chatusra and khanda have been organised as a short and extremely active mukthay, with the calculations 4 (1) 4 (1) 4

This last technique thus looks like this

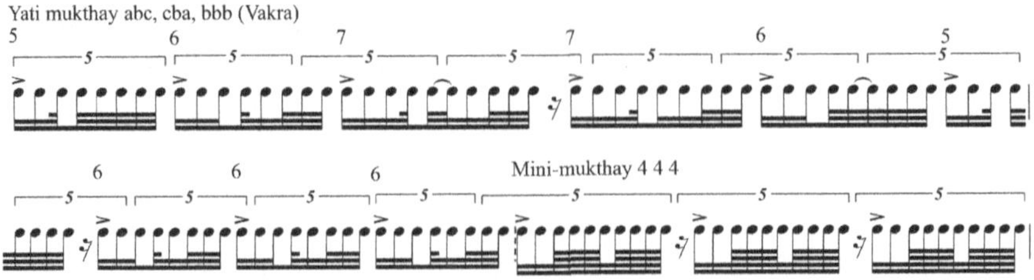

The whole 3rd block, mixed with the theme cells:

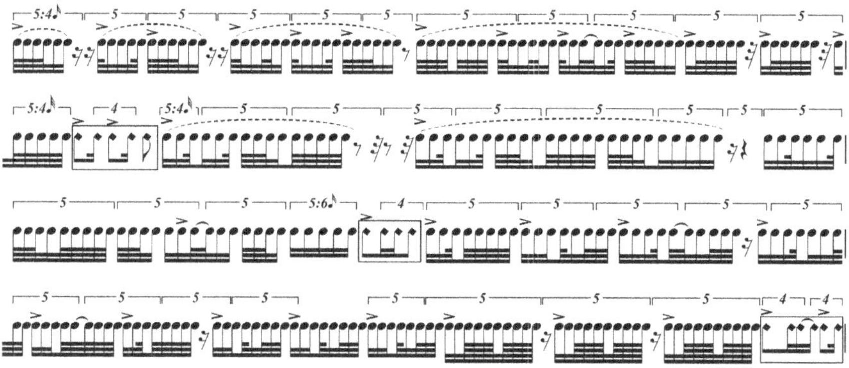

Procedure for a Last Cell that Does Not Resolve on Tala Sam

In the example presented in this chapter, the last cell lasted for the whole length of the phrase, which is rather unusual. Most poruttam A sequences will have a third cell that does not finish on tala sam. This fact has two consequences:

a. Every first technique of all blocks, except the very first one, should add the number of matras remaining to finish the cycle to the calculations made for the 1st block. Therefore, the first technique, the one leading from the last to the first cells, will always be longer in the second and subsequent blocks than in the first one.
b. An extra cycle at the end of the last cell should be added to finish the sequence. The duration of this last technique will be the result of adding the number of matras remaining to finish the cycle plus 1 entire cycle.

Since this is in reality a fourth technique, used only once, it tends to be quite contrasting with the rest of the sequence and very active and climactic in character (similar to the short mukthay of the analysed example, but on a larger scale).

Different Ways of Using the Blocks

1. *As a whole sequence*: This is the manner in which the poruttam A has been explained in this chapter.
2. *Spread across different parts of a piece*: In some forms of karnatic music, the poruttam A is a fully composed section and follows a concrete set of rules as to where in a piece it should be performed. Depending on the form, a division of the whole sequence is asked for, and then the different blocks are performed in different parts of a composed section of a piece. The completion of the 3 cells forming a block of 4 cycles is never split. The division of the sequence refers only to the blocks.

3. *As a question/answer improvised section between two performers*: Karnatic music includes a number of improvisational sections, each with its own set of rules – elements that must be used, could be used or should be avoided altogether. A common factor of most improvisations is the dialogue established by at least two instruments.

Chapter 17
Moharas

This creative technique is the only one in the whole constellation of karnatic rhythmical devices where every conceivable parameter is based on or has as the most important element the number 4 or 8. The parameters taken into consideration to create a mohara are:

a. *Number of cycles*: In a mohara, the number of cycles will always be either 4 or 8.
b. *Number of phrases*: This is always 4 and the process to determine their length is to take the number of matras of 1 cycle and divide it by 4; this will provide the duration for each phrase. However, not all talas and gati combinations can produce 4 equal phrases.

For instance, if a mohara uses khanda in tala 11, the 55 resulting matras cannot be divided by 4; therefore, this option would never be considered. Gaps are never used between phrases – that is, *a cycle must always be divided into 4 equal phrases without any gaps*. The phrases will be called A, B, C and D throughout this chapter.

c. *Inner construction of phrases*: Only a few options are possible, mostly revolving around the number 4 or 8. These are:
   - Divide the number of matras by 2 equal halves
   - 4+*x*
   - 8+*x*
   - 4+*x*+4

   where *x* refers to the number of matras remaining to complete the length of the phrase; the two digits could change their position.

If, for instance, tala 14 and chatusra are taken, each phrase would be 14 matras long and the possibilities for the inner construction of every phrase would be

7+7	4+10 or 10+4	8+6 or 6+8	4+6+4

'A', 'B' and 'C' phrases are constructed on the same inner division and are quite similar, usually variations on 'A'. The 'D' phrase has a contrasting feel to the other phrases and, whenever possible, it will utilise a different inner division to the other three phrases.

d. *Structure of sequence*: Every cycle will be divided as follows:

A		B	C	D	
A		B	C	D	
A		B	C	½ D	A
A *(continued)*	½ D	C	Mukthay		

'½ D' actually refers to the first cell of the 'D' phrase, whatever its length may be. In the 3rd cycle of the sequence, only the first cell of the 'D' phrase will be performed, followed by the 'A' phrase that will necessarily continue into the 4th cycle.

After the 'A' phrase is finished, the second '½ D' is performed. Although this is how karnatic musicians refer to it, in reality this '½ D' could be the first or second cell of the 'D' phrase, or, in case the phrase is divided into three cells, any combination of two of them as well. The 'C' phrase follows suit, often starting in a different place in the beat than the three previous times. Ultimately, the sequence concludes with a mukthay.

Analysis of Examples

1) The first example is a mohara constructed in adi tala (8 beats) with chatusra gati. Therefore, all possible parameters use number 4 or 8, and the 'D' phrase will have the same inner division as the others. Phrases are constructed with a 4+4 feeling and there are no displacements. The mukthay is a variation of a 3-fold mukthay, using the same phrase in three different speeds of chatusra, constructed 4 (2) 4 (2) 4|T.S. *(track 123)*

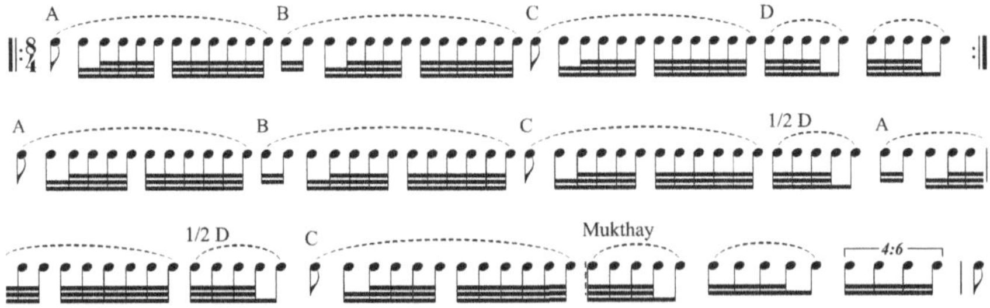

The 'A' phrase is 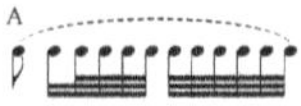 and the 'B' and 'C' phrases are basically a repetition of 'A'.

'D' is slightly contrasting 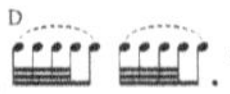. The '½ D' of the 3rd cycle is 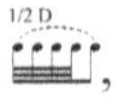, repeated in the 4th cycle. The mukthay is 

2) This example is also in a tala of 8 beats, but with khanda gati (10 matras per phrase). The ‘A’ phrase is divided 4+6 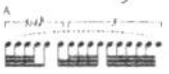 and the ‘D’ phrase is 5+5 . The ‘½ D’ in the 3rd and 4th cycles is  and the concluding mukthay is structured 4 (4) 4 (4) 4|T.S. 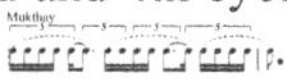. The whole mohara is thus *(track 124)*

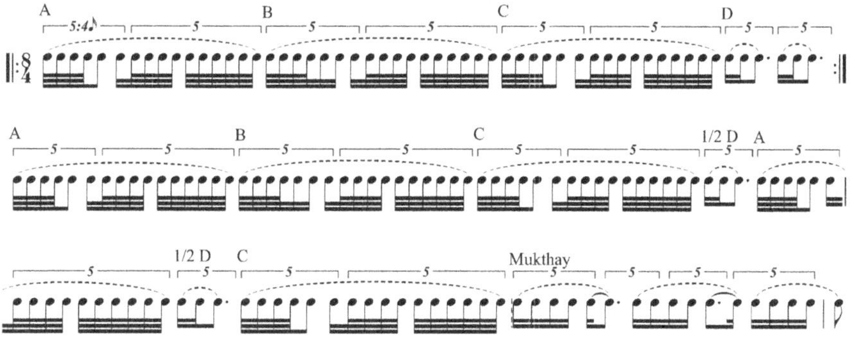

3) The last example is structured in tala 14, also in chatusra. ‘A’ phrase is divided 6+8  whereas the ‘D’ phrase is divided 7+7 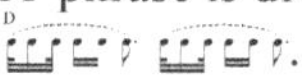.

‘½ D’ uses the first cell  and the final mukthay is structured on 10 (2) 10 (2) 10|T.S.

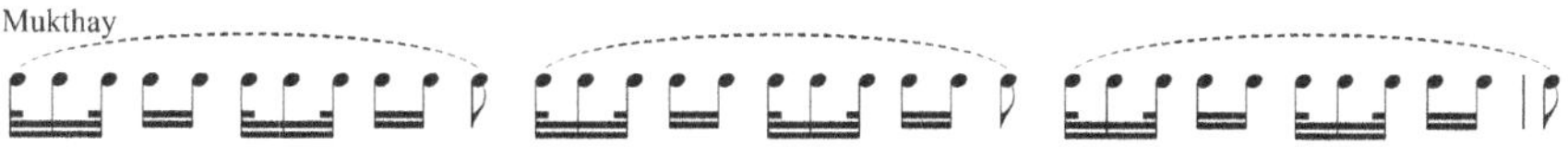

The whole sequence looks thus: *(track 125)*

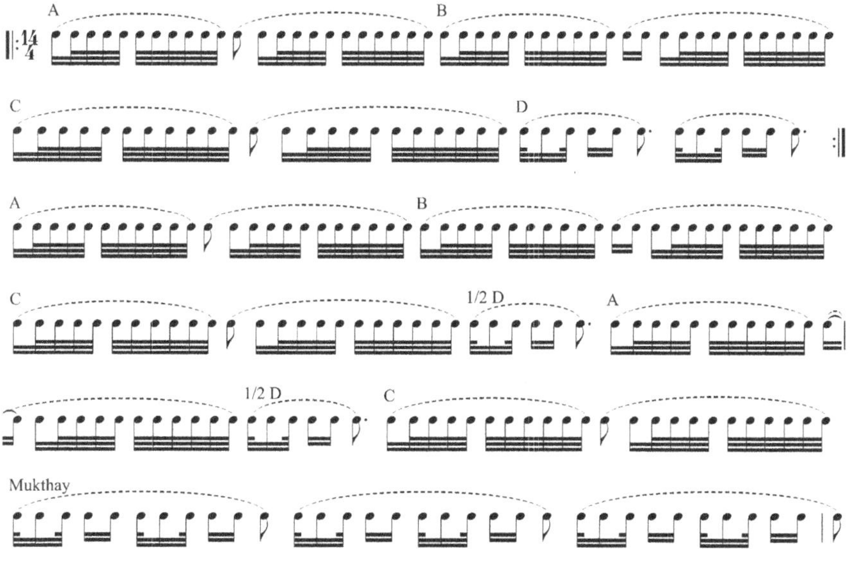

Mixed Gati Moharas

Mixed gati moharas are a very intricate variation in which two gatis alternate throughout the usually 8 cycles that the sequence lasts, and applies mainly the concept of rhythmical sangati in combination with phrasing through gati changes in the development.[1] The main differences from regular moharas lie in the following:

a. The tala is divided into 2 equal halves (even talas are used much more frequently than odd talas). Each half will *always* take a different gati (the choice of gatis for each half remains unaltered for the whole mohara), regardless of which phrases or displaced fragments of phrases are used in that particular half.
b. 'A' and 'C' phrases share the same inner division of the phrase and gati, while 'B' and 'D' phrases share the other gati – but not necessarily the same inner division.
c. Once the first '½ D' cell is used, phrases are displaced and proceed through the two different gatis. Also, final mukthays change gati at one or two points, depending on whether the second gati is slower or faster than the first one.
d. Since the sequence is structured in 8 cycles, phrases tend to be much longer than in regular moharas. This has several consequences:
   - Phrases with 3 or even 4 cells are used more frequently.
   - A phrase can be split into halves (which would respond to the first possibility of dividing a phrase) and then two different inner divisions can be applied to each half.
   - A sort of yati phrase idea can be used, provided that the number 4 or 8 is still the main core of the whole phrase and only 3 cells are used.

A general scheme of an 8-cycle mixed gati mohara with the second gati slower than the first is presented below.

Gati 1	Gati 2
A	B
C	D
A	B
C	D
A	B
C	½ D A
A *(continued)* ½ D	C
C *(continued)* Mukthay---------------	--------------------------------

[1] This concept will be explained in detailed in Chapter 24.

The following scheme responds to the second gati being faster than the first one:

Gati 1	**Gati 2**
A	B
C	D
A	B
C	D
A	B
C	½ D A
A *(continued)* ½ D C	C *(continued)* Mukthay
Mukthay *(continued)*------------------	--------------------------------------

Analysis of Examples

1) The first example uses gatis chatusra and tisra 1st speed in every half of a tala of 8 beats. *(track 126)*

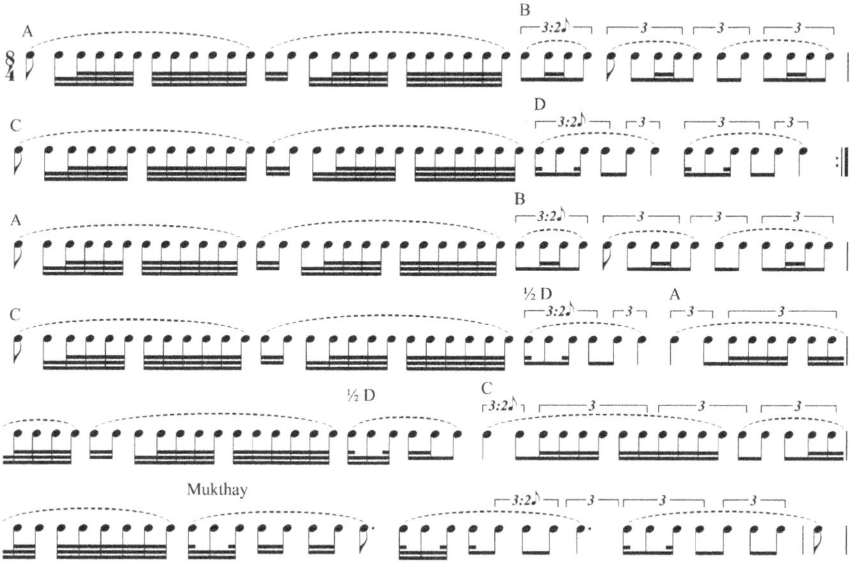

'A' and 'C' phrases are divided 8+8 . The 'B' phrase, in tisra, uses 3 cells, with a yati phrase idea, keeping the number 4 as the central phrase in a construction 3 4 5.

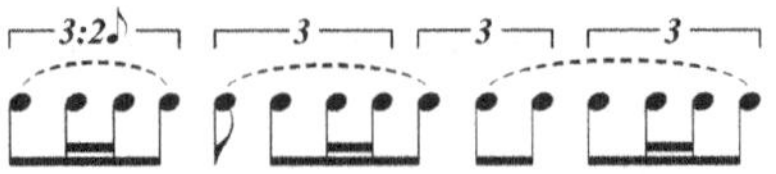

Finally, phrase ‘D’ is divided in 6+6.

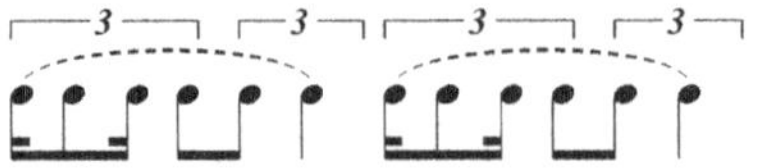

The first ‘½ D’ takes the first cell in tisra:

½ D

and the second one in chatusra:

½ D

Also, the first ‘½ D’ provokes a displacement of ‘A’ and ‘C’ phrases which are performed changing gati where this gati change takes place in the overall structure. This gati change does not imply a rupture in the phrasing; on the contrary, the phrase remains unaltered whilst the sensation for a listener is that of a tempo change. The same is true for the mukthay that also goes through a gati change in the middle of the phrase.

Mukthay

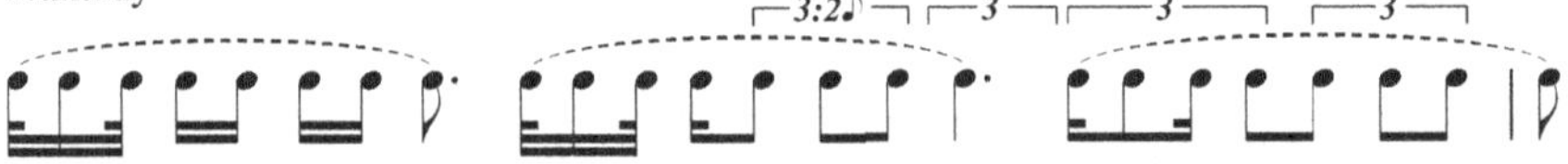

2) The last example is constructed in tala 10 using chatusra and khanda in each half of the tala. *(track 127)*

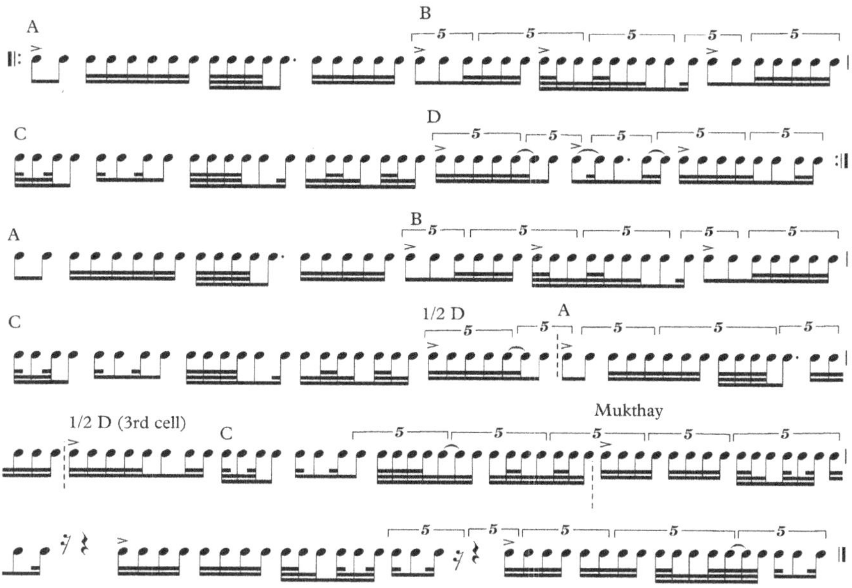

'A' and 'C' phrases are built around the division of their 20 matras in two fragments of 10 matras. Furthermore, the first fragment is divided 4+6, whilst the second one is 5+5.

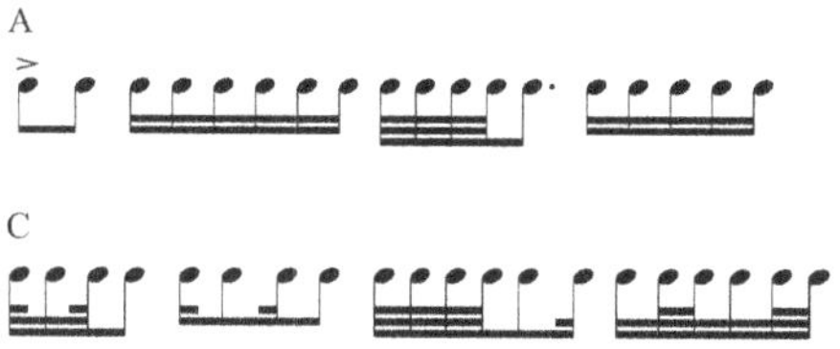

'B' and 'D' phrases, of 25 matras length, share the division as 8+8+9.

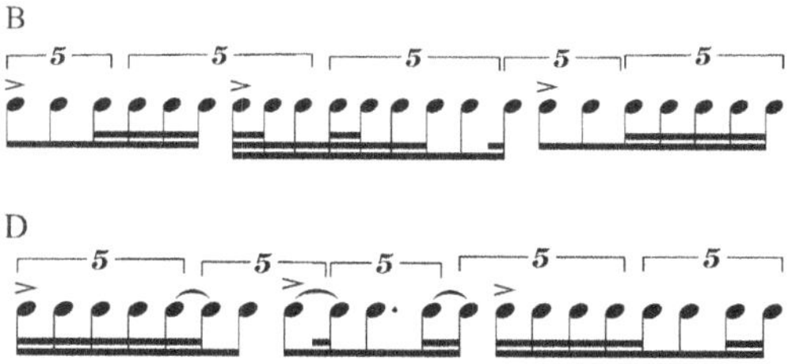

The first '½ D' is played in khanda:

1/2 D

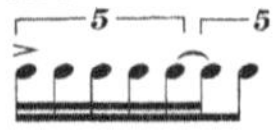

and the second, in the 7th cycle, in chatusra – although it takes the third cell of 9 matras:

1/2 D (3rd cell)

This choice of the third cell provokes more intricate displacements in the gati changes of 'A' and 'C' phrases.

Finally, the final mukthay starts in the 7th cycle. Subsequently, it goes through two gati changes.

C: Motta Kannakku

The English translation of this Tamil term is 'total calculations', which does not throw much light on its true nature. In essence, motta kannakku is a concept where either superimposition of gatis over given frames occurs, or where the frame is shorter or longer than one beat. This short and simple definition gives birth to two differentiated and, possibly along with mukthays, the largest bodies in the theory and practice of the rhythmical aspect of karnatic music: nadai bhedam and combinations anuloma-pratiloma.

Chapter 18
Nadai Bhedam

Nadai bhedam is a technique that embodies the concept of polypulse par excellence, as opposed to the concept of using vertically two different gatis with the same jathi (as seen in Chapter 3) that constitutes an 'illusion' of polypulse since the gati goes with the laya. Nadai bhedam also uses the gati/jathi combinations as a starting point, but with a completely different goal and result from gati bhedam or anuloma-pratiloma. In order to understand the essence of nadai bhedam, a step-by-step process of how to arrive at one will clarify the subject.

1) The first step is to go back to the very basics of karnatic rhythm and have a very clear picture of all gati/jathi combinations. For instance, if a 4:5♩ is wanted, chatusra jathi 5 will constitute this first step. *(track 128 with the first three steps)*

chatusra jathi 5

2) The second step is to isolate the accents, in a similar fashion to the procedure used to obtain pratiloma speeds.

chatusra jathi 5

3) Thirdly, convert every accent in a ♩; since the gati gives the number of accents and the jathi provides the number of beats, the result is indeed 4 accents or ♩ in the time span of 5 beats.

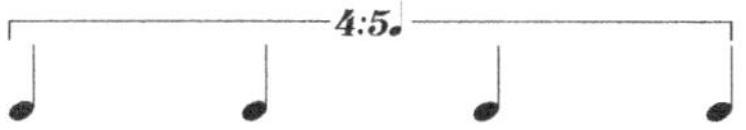

4) The next step is to superimpose any gati over every ♩ that has resulted from the isolation of the accents of chatusra jathi 5. This superimposed gati on the frame provided by the accents is called *nadai*. Therefore, on a 4:5♩ frame, chatusra, tisra or misra nadais can be superimposed. It is important to note that khanda will never be a nadai in a frame of 5 beats, since it would in fact be a gati bhedam.

In the example below, chatusra nadai has been chosen. *(track 129)*

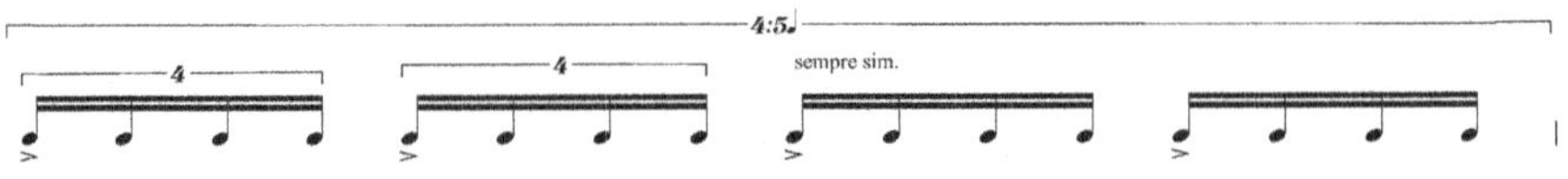

5) Finally, a phrase can be created on chatusra that will always attack every ♩ of the 4:5♩ frame.

Conceptually, nadai bhedam is *always used as a polypulse* and never as a continuous change of frame (the latter pertains to the 'territory' of anuloma-pratiloma combinations).

Relationship between Tempi

Although any nadai bhedam is felt and performed with a clear perception of polypulse in relation to the laya, no karnatic musician will try to find out the actual tempo that the nadai bhedam implies.

However, obtaining the tempo of a nadai bhedam frame within a western context can, eventually, be quite helpful to the performer and/or the creator. If the tempo of the nadai bhedam within the frame of 4:5♩ is sought, all one needs to do is to multiply the tempo by 4 and divide the result by 5. For instance, if ♩=60, the tempo that every accent of the frame of 4:5♩ will produce will be 60×4=240:5=**48**. Consequently, two tempi are effectively being used simultaneously: that of the laya (♩=60) and a second one provided by the nadai bhedam frame (♩=48).

The terminology used by karnatic musicians is quite helpful in clarifying which ♩ is being referred to, whether the one provided as a result of isolating the accents of a gati/jathi combination or the actual ♩ of the 'metronomic' tempo. In this context the following terms have a slightly different meaning to the way they have been used thus far:

- *gati*: number of accents of the frame (since this is the original gati used to produce the frame);
- *jathi*: number of beats needed to resolve the frame (the jathi always provides the number of beats);
- *nadai*: the gati superimposed on the created frame.

Notation

In terms of notating nadai bhedam in western music, two different systems could be employed. The first one below corresponds to the process employed to build nadai bhedam, and is probably easier to understand or trace back to how it originated. The second system is the result of multiplying the number of the gati by the nadai to obtain the total number of matras whilst finding a frame expressed in ♩, ♪, 𝅘𝅥𝅯 or 𝅘𝅥𝅰 that would be the closest to that number of matras. This is basically the system most globally accepted, especially since the notation of irregular groupings in early computer notation programs was conceived like this.

In spite of this, I personally think that the 'double bracket' notation, as shown in Table 18.1, is needed to convey the concept and use of nadai bhedam if the original gati/jathi combination is to be traced back and the nadai perceived as a gati in a different tempo (rather than as a complex irregular grouping). Therefore, it is not only essential musically but also possible nowadays with the evolution of notation programs. Table 18.1, which shows all the conceivable combinations of nadai bhedam, offers both notation systems.

Table 18.1 Nadai Bhedam Chart

Gati	Jathi	Nadai	Western Notation *(following karnatic logic)*	Existing Notation
Tisra	4	Tisra	┌──*3:4♩*──┐ ┌*3*┐┌*3*┐┌*3*┐	┌─ *9:8♪* ─┐
		Khanda	┌──*3:4♩*──┐ ┌*5*┐┌*5*┐┌*5*┐	┌─ *15:16𝅘𝅥𝅯* ─┐
		Misra	┌──*3:4♩*──┐ ┌*7*┐┌*7*┐┌*7*┐	┌─ *21:16𝅘𝅥𝅯*─┐
Tisra	5	Tisra	┌──*3:5♩*──┐ ┌*3*┐┌*3*┐┌*3*┐	┌─ *9:10♪* ─┐
		Chatusra	┌──*3:5♩*──┐ ┌*4*┐┌*4*┐┌*4*┐	┌─ *12:10♪* ─┐
		Misra	┌──*3:5♩*──┐ ┌*7*┐┌*7*┐┌*7*┐	┌─ *21:20♪* ─┐
Tisra	7	Tisra	┌──*3:7♩*──┐ ┌*3*┐┌*3*┐┌*3*┐	┌─ *9:7♩* ─┐
		Chatusra	┌──*3:7♩*──┐ ┌*4*┐┌*4*┐┌*4*┐	┌─ *12:14♪* ─┐

	Khanda	┌── *3:7*♩ ──┐ ┌*5*┐┌*5*┐┌*5*┐	┌─ *15:14*♪ ─┐
Chatusra 3	Chatusra	┌── *4:3*♩ ──┐ ┌*4*┐┌*4*┐┌*4*┐┌*4*┐	┌─ *16:12*𝅘𝅥𝅯 ─┐
	Khanda	┌── *4:3*♩ ──┐ ┌*5*┐┌*5*┐┌*5*┐┌*5*┐	┌─ *20:12*𝅘𝅥𝅯 ─┐
	Misra	┌── *4:3*♩ ──┐ ┌*7*┐┌*7*┐┌*7*┐┌*7*┐	┌─ *28:24*𝅘𝅥𝅰 ─┐
Chatusra 5	Tisra	┌── *4:5*♩ ──┐ ┌*3*┐┌*3*┐┌*3*┐┌*3*┐	┌─ *12:10*♪ ─┐
	Chatusra	┌── *4:5*♩ ──┐ ┌*4*┐┌*4*┐┌*4*┐┌*4*┐	┌─ *16:20*𝅘𝅥𝅯 ─┐
	Misra	┌── *4:5*♩ ──┐ ┌*7*┐┌*7*┐┌*7*┐┌*7*┐	┌─ *28:20*𝅘𝅥𝅯 ─┐
Chatusra 7	Tisra	┌── *4:7*♩ ──┐ ┌*3*┐┌*3*┐┌*3*┐┌*3*┐	┌─ *12:14*♪ ─┐
	Chatusra	┌── *4:7*♩ ──┐ ┌*4*┐┌*4*┐┌*4*┐┌*4*┐	┌─ *16:14*♪ ─┐
	Khanda	┌── *4:7*♩ ──┐ ┌*5*┐┌*5*┐┌*5*┐┌*5*┐	┌─ *20:28*𝅘𝅥𝅯 ─┐
Khanda 3	Chatusra	┌── *5:3*♩ ──┐ ┌*4*┐┌*4*┐┌*4*┐┌*4*┐┌*4*┐	┌─ *20:12*𝅘𝅥𝅯 ─┐
	Khanda	┌── *5:3*♩ ──┐ ┌*5*┐┌*5*┐┌*5*┐┌*5*┐┌*5*┐	┌─ *25:24*𝅘𝅥𝅰 ─┐
	Misra	┌── *5:3*♩ ──┐ ┌*7*┐┌*7*┐┌*7*┐┌*7*┐┌*7*┐	┌─ *35:24*𝅘𝅥𝅰 ─┐
Khanda 4	Tisra	┌── *5:4*♩ ──┐ ┌*3*┐┌*3*┐┌*3*┐┌*3*┐┌*3*┐	┌─ *15:16*𝅘𝅥𝅯 ─┐
	Khanda	┌── *5:4*♩ ──┐ ┌*5*┐┌*5*┐┌*5*┐┌*5*┐┌*5*┐	┌─ *25:32*𝅘𝅥𝅰 ─┐

		Misra	⌐—— *5:4♩.* ——¬ ⌐*7*¬⌐*7*¬⌐*7*¬⌐*7*¬⌐*7*¬	⌐— *35:32*𝅘𝅥𝅯 —¬
Khanda	7	Tisra	⌐—— *5:7♩.* ——¬ ⌐*3*¬⌐*3*¬⌐*3*¬⌐*3*¬⌐*3*¬	⌐— *15:14♪* —¬
		Chatusra	⌐—— *5:7♩.* ——¬ ⌐*4*¬⌐*4*¬⌐*4*¬⌐*4*¬⌐*4*¬	⌐— *20:28*𝅘𝅥𝅯 —¬
		Khanda	⌐—— *5:7♩.* ——¬ ⌐*5*¬⌐*5*¬⌐*5*¬⌐*5*¬⌐*5*¬	⌐— *25:28*𝅘𝅥𝅯 —¬
Misra	3	Chatusra	⌐—— *7:3♩.* ——¬ ⌐*4*¬⌐*4*¬⌐*4*¬⌐*4*¬⌐*4*¬⌐*4*¬⌐*4*¬	⌐— *28:24*𝅘𝅥𝅯 —¬
		Khanda	⌐—— *7:3♩.* ——¬ ⌐*5*¬⌐*5*¬⌐*5*¬⌐*5*¬⌐*5*¬⌐*5*¬⌐*5*¬	⌐— *35:24*𝅘𝅥𝅯 —¬
		Misra	⌐—— *7:3♩.* ——¬ ⌐*7*¬⌐*7*¬⌐*7*¬⌐*7*¬⌐*7*¬⌐*7*¬⌐*7*¬	⌐— *49:48*𝅘𝅥𝅯 —¬
Misra	4	Tisra	⌐—— *7:4♩.* ——¬ ⌐*3*¬⌐*3*¬⌐*3*¬⌐*3*¬⌐*3*¬⌐*3*¬⌐*3*¬	⌐— *21:16*𝅘𝅥𝅯 —¬
		Khanda	⌐—— *7:4♩.* ——¬ ⌐*5*¬⌐*5*¬⌐*5*¬⌐*5*¬⌐*5*¬⌐*5*¬⌐*5*¬	⌐— *35:32*𝅘𝅥𝅯 —¬
		Misra	⌐—— *7:4♩.* ——¬ ⌐*7*¬⌐*7*¬⌐*7*¬⌐*7*¬⌐*7*¬⌐*7*¬⌐*7*¬	⌐— *49:32*𝅘𝅥𝅯 —¬
Misra	5	Tisra	⌐—— *7:5♩.* ——¬ ⌐*3*¬⌐*3*¬⌐*3*¬⌐*3*¬⌐*3*¬⌐*3*¬⌐*3*¬	⌐— *21:20*𝅘𝅥𝅯 —¬
		Chatusra	⌐—— *7:5♩.* ——¬ ⌐*4*¬⌐*4*¬⌐*4*¬⌐*4*¬⌐*4*¬⌐*4*¬⌐*4*¬	⌐— *28:20*𝅘𝅥𝅯 —¬
		Misra	⌐—— *7:5♩.* ——¬ ⌐*7*¬⌐*7*¬⌐*7*¬⌐*7*¬⌐*7*¬⌐*7*¬⌐*7*¬	⌐— *49:40*𝅘𝅥𝅯 —¬

The Chart and Its Usage

1) Although karnatic musicians study misra gati as a base for a nadai bhedam frame, it is seldom performed – for two reasons:

a. Any number combination produced with misra gati already exists if tisra, chatusra or khanda gatis are chosen.

b. Having seven accents restricts the phrasing possibilities quite drastically. This is possibly the most important reason since, for a karnatic musician, *28:20♪.* (for example) means nothing at all. These numbers could be the result of

4:5♩.		7:5♩.
⌐7¬⌐7¬⌐7¬⌐7¬	or	⌐4¬⌐4¬⌐4¬⌐4¬⌐4¬⌐4¬⌐4¬

In both cases, there are 28 matras superimposed on 5♩. (or 20♪.).

In the first option the feeling would be of a misra gati within a slower tempo than the pulse (♩.=48 if the pulse is 60), whereas in the second case the feeling conveyed would be of chatusra in a faster tempo than the laya (♩.=84 if the pulse is 60). The disadvantage of the latter option is that the possibilities of creating elaborate chatusra nadai phrases on 7 accents within 5 beats, in a much faster tempo than the pulse, are far more limited than performing misra nadai in 4 accents over 5 beats in a much slower tempo.

2) Tisra gati (3 accents against a frame of 4, 5 or 7 beats) can sometimes be performed as tisra 2nd speed, subsequently providing 6 accents instead of 3.

3) A frame of 6 beats (or jathi 6) can eventually be employed, especially when using misra nadai within chatusra or khanda jathi 3.

Some examples in every gati, jathi and nadai are presented below.[1] *(tracks 130 and 131)*

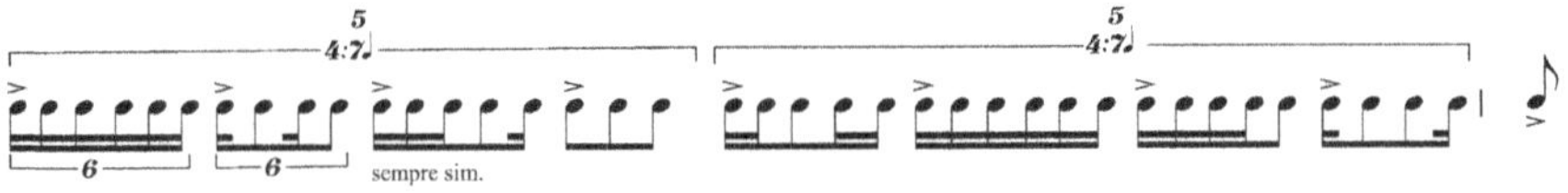

(tracks 132 and 133)

(tracks 134 and 135)

[1] In each example, the jathi or number of beats is multiple. This does not imply that the phrase is performed simultaneously over two different frames, but is simply to show that the same nadai can be part of all these frames. Every frame is recorded in a different track.

Sequence of Nadai Bhedam

Nadai bhedam is seldom used as a one-time occurrence. It is mainly conceived as a sequence that would rarely last less than 30 or 40 seconds, and it follows three stages – from preparation through development to resolution.

- *Preparation*: The easiest, but not necessarily the most widespread method, is the one seen in the explanation of how to arrive at a nadai bhedam. The frame provided by any given number of accents (gati) within any given number of beats (jathi) is preceded by the corresponding gati/jathi combination, either using all the matras of the combination or some gati bhedam phrasing. This gati/jathi combination becomes the frame and any nadai can be superimposed.[2]

The second manner is not so much preparing as 'jumping' from one element to another, usually of greater difficulty than the first option. A gati suddenly becomes the nadai of any of the possible frames where it would certainly be a nadai.

A chatusra gati could go to any of the following frames and become a nadai. *(track 136)*

┌——— *3:5♩.* ———┐
┌4┐┌4┐┌4┐

┌——— *3:7♩.* ———┐
┌4┐┌4┐┌4┐

┌——— *4:3♩.* ———┐
┌4┐┌4┐┌4┐┌4┐

┌——— *4:5♩.* ———┐
┌4┐┌4┐┌4┐┌4┐

┌——— *4:7♩.* ———┐
┌4┐┌4┐┌4┐┌4┐

┌——— *5:3♩.* ———┐
┌4┐┌4┐┌4┐┌4┐┌4┐

┌——— *5:7♩.* ———┐
┌4┐┌4┐┌4┐┌4┐┌4┐

- *Development*: This depends on whether all the parameters remain unaltered or if there is any change.

A) Development using the same three parameters

This notion is quite common in karnatic music, since nadai bhedam is used exclusively with the purpose of creating polypulses, and never as a source of rapidly changing irregular groupings.

Naturally, depending on which elements are chosen and the length of the development, the number of options can vary. For instance, if a 4:3♩. with chatusra nadai is being developed, karnatic musicians would probably perform some more elaborate techniques inside the frame than if a 5:7♩. with khanda or tisra nadai is chosen. The three options are:

---

[2] The explanation and music examples are shown at the beginning of the chapter.

1) Phrasing around the accents provided by the gati/jathi combination

In order to establish a feeling of polypulse, the 'downbeats' of the 'new' tempo need to be attacked and emphasised. The phrasing, as in gati and jathi bhedam, is always constructed around the accents of the frame.

2) Skipping accents

This option will be used only when the feeling of the nadai bhedam has truly been established. There are only two rules to follow in order to maintain the feeling of the nadai bhedam:

a. Never skip two accents in a row.
b. Never skip the accent that coincides with the beat (the accent that resolves the frame).

3) Applying a gati bhedam, jathi bhedam, yati phrase or mukthay to the nadai

These possibilities are used only when the whole sequence is of considerable length and as a one-time occurrence at a climactic point. One should not forget that all these techniques are constantly going against the beat (in this case, the beat of the nadai bhedam) and that the latter is already creating tension with the laya.

On the other hand, the phrasing applied to any of these techniques is quite simple, if used at all. (The general tendency is to play all the matras in gati and jathi bhedam while emphasising the accents derived from these techniques and, perhaps, use some ♪ in yati phrases and mukthays.)

1. Applying a gati bhedam: Except for a few exceptions, a gati bhedam will need to start off the first accent of the frame. In the example below, the first 4 matras of the frame are played in regular nadai bhedam fashion and a chatusra jathi 3 is applied from the second accent (chatusra jathi 3 needs 4 accents in 3 beats – in this case the 3 'beats' of the nadai bhedam frame). *(track 137)*

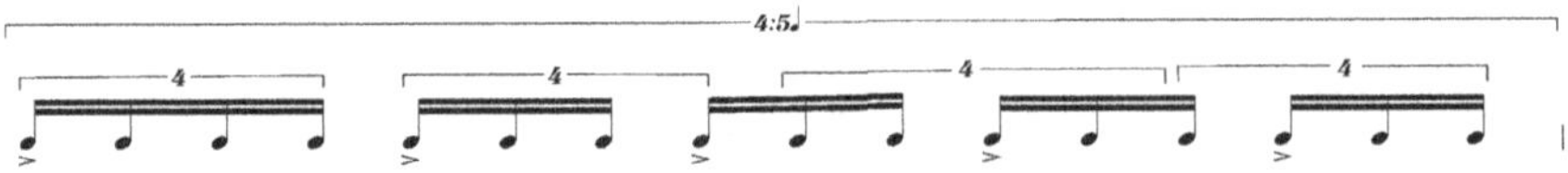

2. Applying jathi bhedam: Since the sequence needs to be short to fit into one frame, the jathi bhedam would necessarily start on the first accent. The numbers used in the example are 5 6 5. *(track 138)*

Eventually, a short sequence of two or three different jathi bhedam sequences can succeed one another, provided that they always start on the first accent. The following 3 frames take different numbers, but always 'resolve' at the end of the frame. *(track 139)*

3 4 2 4 3   5 6 5   7 3 4 2

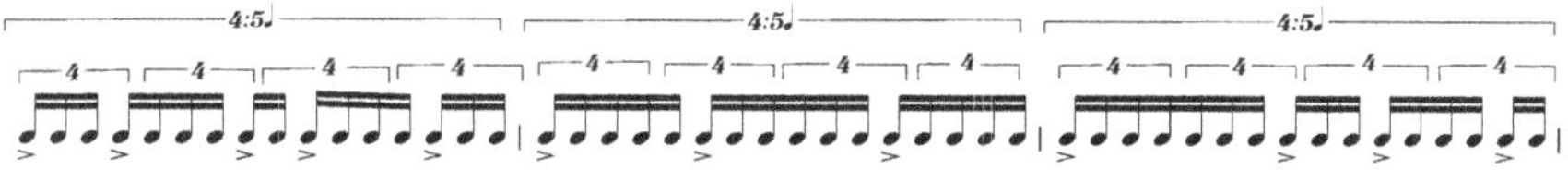

3. Applying a yati phrase: Simple phrasing, with some 𝅘𝅥𝅯 or ♪ to create a certain variety and a feeling of phrasing. In the example below the sequence starts with 1 matra and it is increased by 2 matras in every pala, without gaps: 1 3 5 7 *(track 140)*

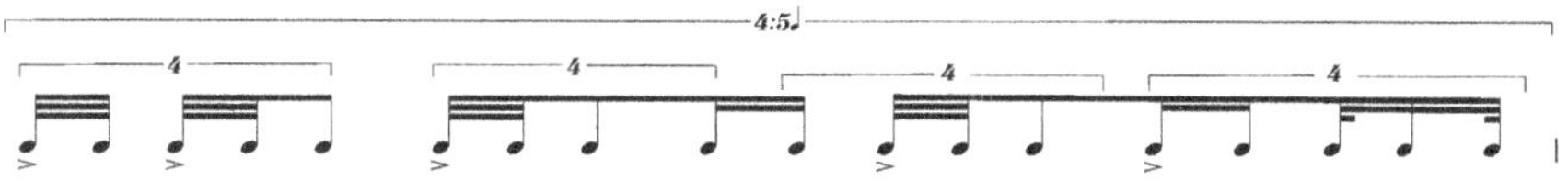

4. Applying short mukthays: As with yati phrases, some simple phrasing is created, in the case of the mukthay to create the perception of a phrase repeated three times. The structure is 4 (2) 4 (2) 4 . *(track 141)*

B) Development Changing One of the Parameters

Prior to explaining the three different options, an important observation should be made: before any change is applied to a parameter, *a minimum of three 'brackets' or frames with the same parameters have to be played.* This golden rule of nadai bhedam was created precisely to avoid rapid changes that would consequently decrease, or lose altogether, the feeling of polypulse.

1) Changing the nadai

This is the option used most frequently, since the 'tempo' provided by the frame remains intact; it would be the equivalent of a gati change within the pulse. There are no calculations required or any feeling of tempo change. The example below goes from

4:5♩. ⌐**4**¬⌐**4**¬⌐**4**¬⌐**4**¬ to **4:5♩.** ⌐*7*¬⌐*7*¬⌐*7*¬⌐*7*¬ *(track 142)*

2) Changing the number of beats (jathi)

In this option the feeling of a sort of 4/4 metre remains (if chatusra gati is used for the frame, 3/4 and 5/4 if tisra and khanda), but the inner tempo of the nadai bhedam changes. The gati and nadai remain, but the period over which the nadai is performed is modified. The elements used below are

4:3♩ / ⌐*5*¬⌐*5*¬⌐*5*¬⌐*5*¬ going to *4:7♩* / ⌐*5*¬⌐*5*¬⌐*5*¬⌐*5*¬ *(track 143)*

3) Changing the number of accents (gati)

This possibility is used more rarely, since the nadai and number of beats remain but the change in the number of accents produces a change in the tempo of the nadai bhedam and in the 'inner metre' resulting from the number of accents.

4:5♩ / ⌐*4*¬⌐*4*¬⌐*4*¬⌐*4*¬ goes to *6:5♩* / ⌐*4*¬⌐*4*¬⌐*4*¬⌐*4*¬⌐*4*¬⌐*4*¬ *(track 144)*

- *Resolution*: The sequence needs to have a clear ending. It would never resolve on a tala sam without one of the following three options:

1) Using Gati Bhedam in a Number of Accents of the Frame

Usually there is a shift in the last two or three accents of the frame from the nadai to the gati bhedam that created the frame. For instance, in a frame of

4:5♩
4 4 4 4

only the first and, perhaps, second accents will use the chatusra nadai to give way to a regular chatusra jathi 5 that would go along the pulse. The way to feel this shift would be as if changing from chatusra nadai to khanda nadai in the chosen accent. But, in reality, what happens is that the performer reverses the process that produced the frame: if in order to prepare a 4:5♩ frame chatusra jathi 5 was used to provide the number of accents within the 5 beats, in the resolution the chatusra jathi 5 is used to pave the way to return to the pulse. The position of accents does not change, but the performer must feel the 'khanda nadai' that is, in reality, the chatusra gati that goes with the laya, accented every 5 matras. If only one ♩ of the 4:5♩ frame uses the nadai, then three accents of chatusra jathi 5 would remain.

The best way to notate it would be by taking one frame of 4:5♪ if the nadai is superimposed on only one accent. Afterwards, the number of matras that do not complete one beat should be left without any bracket; and then the bracket of 4:4 should be used, as explained for gati and jathi bhedam concepts, for the remaining beats until the chatusra jathi 5 resolves on a beat (usually a tala sam). *(track 145)*

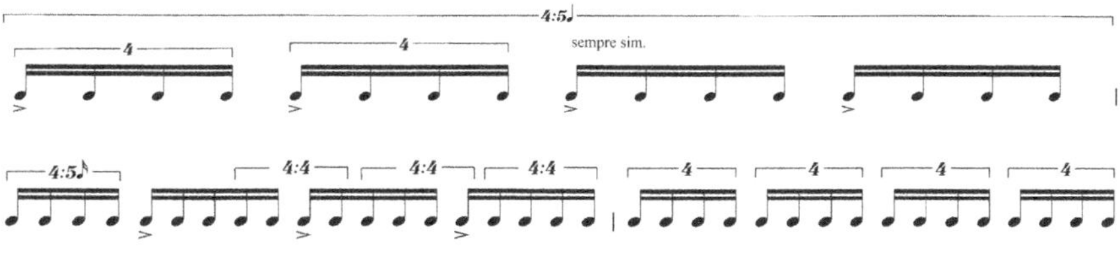

2) Using a Mukthay

As has been explained at various points throughout the book, karnatic musicians are fond of finishing most musical events with a mukthay. A nadai bhedam sequence is no exception. However, if musicians know in advance that they will end the sequence with a mukthay, they will rarely use this possibility while developing the sequence.[3]

3) Returning to the Pulse

In this option, whichever nadai has been used for the last frame becomes the gati of the laya. Once again, it is the sort of 'jumping' that was explained under preparation, but here the process is reversed and the musician 'jumps' from the tempo of the nadai bhedam to the metronomic tempo without any intermediate step. Therefore, nadai becomes gati. *(track 146)*

Relationship of Nadai Bhedam to Tala Structure

When karnatic musicians employ nadai bhedam and decide beforehand not to change the number of beats – changes of nadai or number of accents (gati) will not influence any calculations – they tend to use a number of beats (jathis) that will fit quite comfortably with the tala.

1. The first and most obvious choice is to take a number of beats for the nadai bhedam frame that is the same as or a multiple of the number of beats in the tala. In this manner, every two to four brackets the nadai bhedam meets the tala sam (eventually even every cycle). For instance, for tala 10 a frame of 5 beats could be chosen; for tala 7 or 14 a frame of 7 beats etc.
2. The second option is to choose a number of beats in the nadai bhedam frame that would create a simple numerical relationship with the tala. In this regard, even numbered talas are easier to work with if 4 or 5 beats are chosen for the frame (only a few repetitions are required to meet a tala sam). Three-beat frames do not function so well with many talas (except for talas that are a multiple of 3, and possibly tala 8). The choice of 7 beats, except when used with tala 7 or 14, implies very long fragments of the nadai bhedam frame before it meets any tala sam.
3. The third option is when there is a change in the number of beats. In this case calculations are required, although karnatic musicians have an amazing capacity to see the whole structural 'puzzle' in their minds while performing.

3 See the example above for calculations and framework.

The following transcription is an example of a sort of 'tree' of nadai bhedam in a tala of 14 beats in which phrasing within the nadai alternates with all the aforementioned possible parameter changes. The steps of the sequence are:

Khanda × 5 beats	Khanda jathi 4 × 2=8 beats
Khanda nadai in 5:4♩ × 4=16 beats	Khanda nadai in 5:3♩ × 5=15 beats
Chatusra nadai in 5:3♩ × 4=12 beats	Chatusra nadai in 5:7♩ × 4= 28 beats
Tisra nadai in 5:7♩ × 4=28 beats	Tisra nadai in 5:4♩ × 4=16 beats
Khanda nadai in 5:4♩ × 3=12 beats	Khanda × 14 beats

A few remarks about the notation and use of nadai bhedam in this transcribed sequence are necessary.

- The notation of the second step, khanda jathi 4, does not conform to the notation proposed in previous chapters. Here this notation has been chosen to show how the gati/jathi combination is the source of the frame of 5:4♩.
- No change of parameter occurs before the same elements have been performed at least four times.
- Finally, and as was the case in the tree of gati bhedam in Chapter 5, the number of repetitions of a frame has an influence on the 'cell construction' that is repeated as a sort of polyrhythm within the nadai bhedam frame. *(track 147)*

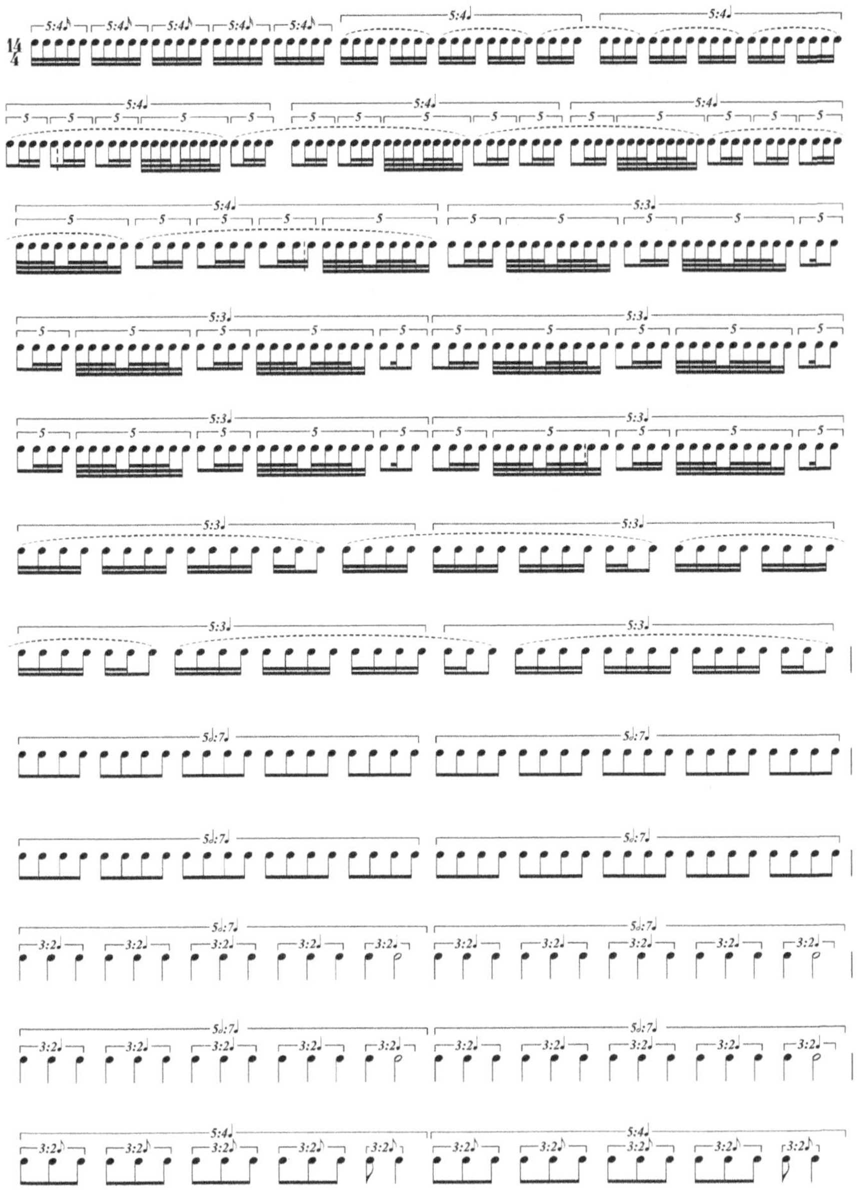

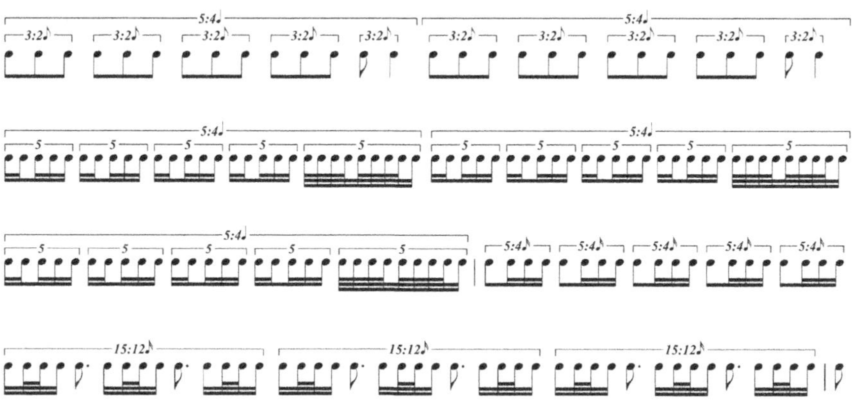

Consequently, it can be observed that when many changes occur in a sequence of nadai bhedam, there is no real 'concern' with, or need to know, how many times the first accent of a bracket will coincide with a tala sam. Usually, this meeting happens sporadically. However, this example is quite an exception in the use of nadai bhedam in karnatic music. The tendency is to stay as long as possible within the same parameters and, eventually, change the nadai – and, every once in a while, any of the other two parameters.

Relationship between Layers

In karnatic music, all the musicians can perform a nadai bhedam sequence in sort of 'structural' unison. (This unison does not necessarily mean that all the musicians play the same phrases but, rather, that the same frames will be used by all performers). This is the case in fully composed pieces (as in a form named *varnam*) or segments of pieces.

However, the most recurrent usage is when one layer (performed by one or several musicians) realises the nadai bhedam sequence and another layer plays along the pulse, trying to convey the feeling of this pulse, even if the pulse is also shown by the tala keeper. The phrasing of the layer creating the pulse necessarily goes with the beat; and, as was the case with the sequence of nadai bhedam itself, skipping beats or creating short sequences of gati/jathi bhedam or other techniques can occur, depending on the length of the sequence and only when both pulses have been clearly established.

There will always be a relationship (common denominator) between the choice of elements in the nadai bhedam and the laya. There are two reasons for this:

- Firstly, in order to avoid any feeling of randomness; if the nadai bhedam layer is performing

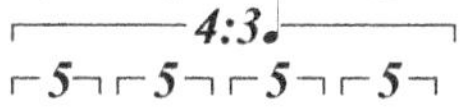

the other layer would never perform material in tisra or misra gati, since neither of these gatis holds any relationship to either the original gati that was used to create the frame or the nadai.

- Secondly, to avoid situations like the following one. If the previous frame/nadai is played, it will result in 20 matras within 3 beats. If misra is played along the beat, this layer will be using 21 matras in 3 beats. Even though one layer is conveying a feeling of khanda within a faster tempo and the other layer is playing with a feeling of misra within the pulse, the extreme proximity of both layers in terms of number of matras being performed can cause (quite) some confusion and the feeling of polypulse could easily vanish.

In the following short examples, the two options that the laya has to choose from are presented. These two options are the result of applying the following principles:

1. The laya utilises as a gati the *same number* as the nadai. Therefore, if the layer of nadai bhedam is performing
   ⌐——4:7♩——¬
   ⌐6¬⌐6¬⌐6¬⌐6¬

the other layer would perform tisra gati. *(track 148)*

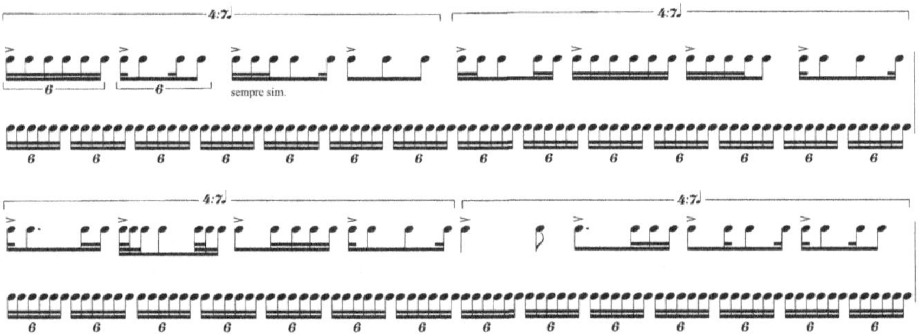

2. The laya stays in the *gati that originated the number of accents* for the frame. If the same case as above is taken, the layer performing along the pulse would employ chatusra gati. *(track 149)*

In the next two examples the laya first uses misra gati (same number as the nadai), and then tisra (the gati that originated the frame). *(track 150)*

(track 151)

Nadai Bhedam in 3-Fold Mukthays

One of the few contexts where a nadai bhedam frame would happen just once is as a fourth possibility within the 3-fold mukthays concept.

The choice of number of accents (gati) for the frame will depend of the number of beats used for the construction of the original phrase, and the nadai will be the same number as the gati employed for that phrase.

In the example below, the phrase has been constructed on 6 beats of khanda. Therefore, the number of accents could be 3 or 6 and the nadai would be khanda. The last parameter (the number of beats of the frame) would be chosen depending on how the whole calculation fits into the tala, as well as the desired musical effect. If 3:4♩ is taken, the result will be a phrase sounding slightly slower than the original phrase, whereas if 3:7♩ is taken, the phrase will sound much slower. *(track 152)*

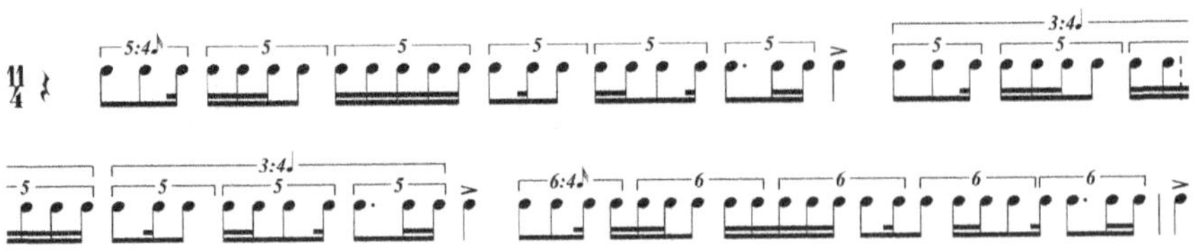

Practice Method

1) Anyone attempting to perform this technique must have previously mastered all the gati/jathi combinations and be able to visualise, as well as feel, where the accents of each one of them fall in relation to the beat. Indeed, this becomes *a sine qua non* to face the world of nadai bhedam, especially since mastering nadai bhedam is the key to practising combinations anuloma-pratiloma with greater understanding and confidence.[4]

2) Start isolating the accents and turn every accent into a ♩ within the frame provided by the combination as shown at the beginning of the chapter. To start with, the frames below seem to be more advisable because they are easier to internalise.

4:3♩   4:5♩   3:4♩   3:5♩   5:3♩   5:4♩   6:4♩

In an ulterior stage the remaining frames should be added.

4:7♩   3:7♩   5:7♩   6:5♩   6:7♩

Frames in misra gati (7:3♩, 7:4♩ and 7:5♩) are possibly best left aside for reasons already given in the chapter, although musicians could eventually dedicate some time to them at a later stage of the learning process.

3) Alas, there are no 'magic recipes' or short cuts to superimpose nadais onto the previous frames. In the same way all musicians learn how to fit 3, 4, 5 or 7 matras within a beat in the very early stages of rhythmical music education – that is, by intuition and repetition – they need simply to repeat the matras of all nadais in all of the frames until they intuitively feel the spacing between matras within a given frame. A great help could be to begin with a computer music program that would give the beat, the accents of the frame and all the matras of the superimposed nadais so that, by listening to them, one can become more familiarised with the

[4] This chain is probably one of the backbones of the whole book and its pedagogical applications: mastering gati/jathi combinations is key to performing nadai bhedam. Nadai bhedam is absolutely essential to gain control over combinations anuloma-pratiloma, while mastering the latter will enable any musician to perform complex rhythms with much clearer understanding and feeling.

different proportionalities that every frame/nadai combination provides and the relation of specific matras to the beat and the jathis.[5]

In the early stages of practising nadai bhedam, it is necessary to focus on achieving absolute precision with all the matras of the nadai and not to attempt to start performing phrases. It is of utmost importance that the feeling of every frame/nadai relationship is fully internalised.

4) Once all the frame/nadai relationships of the first seven frames suggested previously have been internalised, one can start creating phrases of great simplicity (some ♪ or two 𝅘𝅥𝅯 replacing a ♪ are possibly the best note values to start with) and then, step by step, add longer note values and syncopations of ♪ and 𝅘𝅥𝅯 combinations. Phrasing against the background of a computer that provides a 'mattress' for all the matras of the nadais is the safest way to avoid losing the feeling for the matra spacing within a frame. The following four examples present increasing levels of difficulty using the same frame and nadai.

5) The musician should alternate performing phrases with and without a computer aid (that is, using a metronome as the sole reference point). At some stage, they should eliminate the computer aid and perform all phrases exclusively with the metronome.

A number of phrases in every possible frame and nadai are presented below so that musicians can attempt these or similar phrases of their own.[6] Phrases in tisra should first be practised with 3 accents per frame before proceeding to practise them with 6.

---

[5] A 'karnatic metronome' providing these three elements can be found online (see 'Instructions to Access Online Material' at the beginning of the book).

[6] The use of two or three different numbers of beats per 'bracket' is to show that the phrase can be performed in the different frames.

4:5
sempre sim.
4:7
sempre sim.
4:7
sempre sim.
4:6
sempre sim.
6:5
sempre sim.
6:4
sempre sim.
6:4
sempre sim.
3:5
sempre sim.
5:3
sempre sim.
5:4
sempre sim.
5:4
sempre sim.
5:4
sempre sim.

6) Once these (or similar phrases) can be performed with complete confidence, the next step is to implement the three different options of parameter changes explained in the development of a nadai bhedam sequence. At a very early stage, the phrase should be preceded by performing all the matras of the nadai.[7]

a. Keeping the number of accents (gati) and number of beats (jathi), go through all the possible nadais without interruption (three options per frame).
b. Keeping the number of accents and nadai, go through all the possible number of beats where the nadai would stay as such and not as gati bhedam (usually two, sometimes three options per combination of number of accents/nadai).
c. Keeping the number of beats (jathi) and nadai, go through all the possible number of accents where the nadai would stay as such and not as gati bhedam (usually two, sometimes three options per combination of number of beats/nadai).

[7] For examples of every technique, refer to the examples given in that section of the chapter and proceed to work out more exercises with the same notions and with all the possibilities.

Chapter 19

Mixed Jathi Nadai Bhedam

Mixed jathi nadai bhedam is a technique whereby two different accents alternate systematically whilst a constant nadai is superimposed on each frame provided by the accents. These two accents (mixed jathi) could be any combination of the numbers 3, 4, 5, 6 and 7.[1]

Pedagogically and creatively, this device lays a bridge between the polytempi concept of nadai bhedam and the vast and complex world of anuloma-pratiloma combinations. By using two different accents, any feeling of creating a different pulse vanishes, because the nadai feels as though the tempo is changing continuously. However, by using only two accents (versus the wide range of possibilities that will be presented in anuloma-pratiloma combinations), this technique provides the musician with a clear anchor in order to perform the nadai in any position within the beat, something that will become essential when combinations anuloma-pratiloma are considered in the next chapter.

All the available combinations and the number of resulting beats are shown below:

Combination — Number of beats needed to resolve

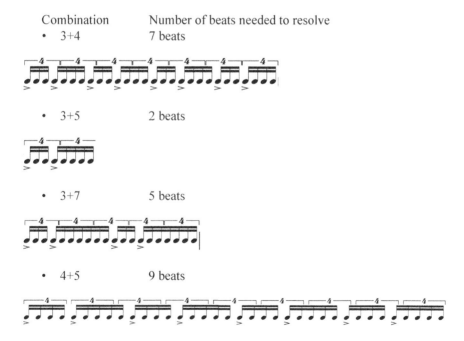

- 3+4 — 7 beats

- 3+5 — 2 beats

- 3+7 — 5 beats

- 4+5 — 9 beats

[1] Except for the combination 3+6 as the figures are multiples of one another.

- 4+6 5 beats

- 4+7 11 beats

- 5+6 11 beats

- 5+7 3 beats

- 6+7 13 beats

As can be seen, adding up the two accents does not necessarily result in the required number of beats. For instance, in the case of 3+5 the sum of these two numbers produces 8 matras, which in chatusra equals 2 beats.

In the chapter on nadai bhedam, tisra and khanda were used as the initial gati that produced a frame for a nadai bhedam. In the case of mixed jathi nadai bhedam, although theoretically possible (and in fact used sporadically by some very good musicians), this notion is rarely used. All frames take chatusra as the underlying gati over which the nadai is superimposed. Therefore, since the underlying gati is chatusra, all mixed jathi nadai bhedam segments will have four double accents, except for the exceptions seen above:

3+5=8 matras (one double accent in 2 beats)
3+7=10 matras × 2=20 matras (two double accents in 5 beats)
4+6=10 matras × 2=20 matras (two double accents in 5 beats)
5+7= 12 matras (one double accent in 3 beats)

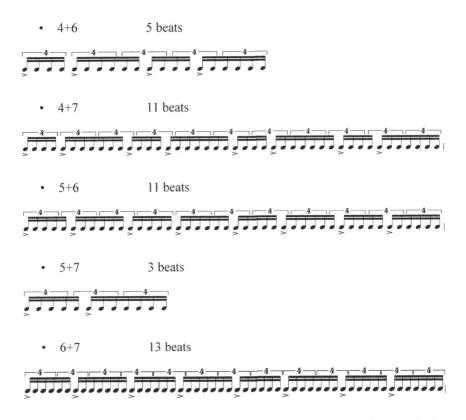

The following are two examples of several nadais superimposed on the frames of 3+4 and 5+7. The first line is the laya of chatusra with the double accent 3+4. The second line is tisra nadai superimposed. This implies that tisra is actually chatusra jathi 3 within the first frame and then a regular 3:4♪ within the second frame.[2]

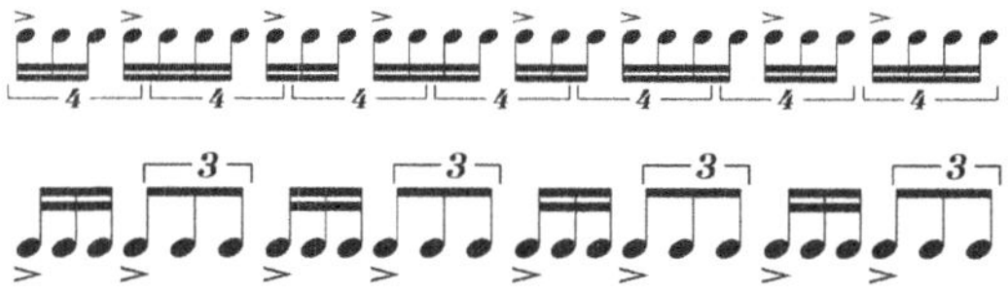

Two transcriptions follow on the double accent 3+4 and on 5+7 using several nadais. *(track 153)*

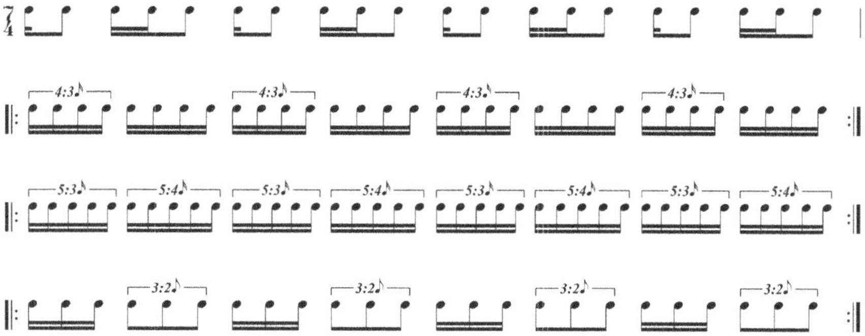

(track 154)

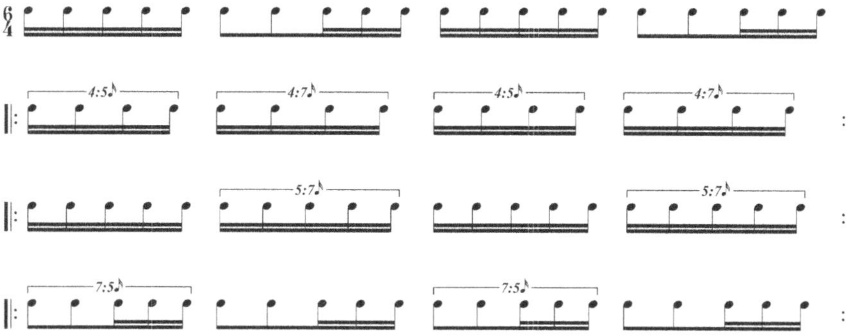

Once the mechanics of constructing a mixed jathi nadai bhedam are clear, the next logical step is to phrase with the chosen nadais. Here are four examples of phrasing, one per nadai.

---

[2] In every mixed jathi nadai bhedam there will always be two nadais that would actually be chatusra taking a jathi.

- The first one takes the double accent of 5+6 and chatusra nadai superimposed. *(track 155)*

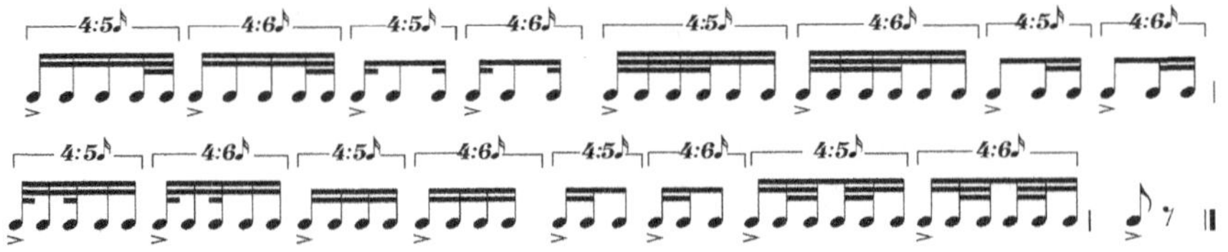

- The second example uses khanda nadai on the double accent of 3+5. As seen before, the nadai is actually a chatusra jathi 5 when used in a frame of 5 matras, while it is a 5:3♪ in the other frame. *(track 156)*

- In the third example, tisra nadai is superimposed on the double accent of 5+7. *(track 157)*

- And in the last example, misra nadai is used over the frames provided by the double accent 4+5. *(track 158)*

Many a time, the notation could make it difficult for performers to know where they are within the beat. A notational solution to this problem could be to provide a line above the phrase that indicates the length of the frame and its position within the beat, so that the performer knows the starting point of every frame within the beat. The following example uses the double accent 4+5 with tisra nadai.

Creative Use

Mixed jathi nadai bhedam tends to be a short passage in only one layer with no preparation or resolution. The main element in this device is that *every phrase is always repeated* (eventually ornamented) *in both frames.* There is never a continuous development of phrases through the alternating accents. Karnatic musicians think that a continuous development of phrasing would completely obscure the different frames and that the feeling to be achieved of a continuous change of tempo would be lost. However, at the same time, this continuous repetition of a phrase in both frames could easily become predictable or too repetitive; therefore, this device is used sporadically in a piece and is never a long segment of music.

The other important aspect to note is that, as was the case when the tree of gati bhedam was explained in Chapter 5 (rhythmical sangatis), a segment of mixed jathi nadai bhedam can start on a point other than a beat, as long as it resolves on a tala or anga sam. If the example below is taken

the starting point could also be the second matra of the third beat, the third matra of the fifth beat or the fourth matra of the seventh beat.

However, for a mixed jathi nadai bhedam to be considered as such, no less than three double accents are required. Subsequently, the last two starting options could exclusively be used if the whole segment were to have at least five or six double accents (those just explained plus an entire structure of 4+5).

Practice Method

1) Before starting to practise this device, musicians should have mastered the following elements:

a. the performance of all regular speeds of all gatis (that is, against one beat), but starting on every matra within a beat;

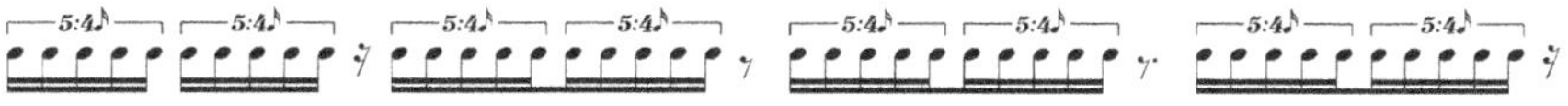

- the performance of chatusra jathi 3, 5, 6 and 7 – also starting on any matra of the beat;

- the frames of nadai bhedam of 4:3♩, 4:5♩, 4:6♩ and 4:7♩, and all the superimposed nadais.

2) Practise the mixed jathi chart, as shown at the beginning of the chapter, to achieve a good and clear picture as to where all the accents fall within the beat. Then practise solely the accents of the mixed jathi.

3) Start with easier frames, such as 4+6 or 3+5, and progressively incorporate all the mixed jathis. Spend time just working with all matras of the nadai with the alternating accents. This is essential to acquire a good feeling for the real change of proportionality and the sensation of tempo change that this device provides, and also to obtain a good sense of how to perform every frame/nadai starting anywhere in the beat.

4) With the aid of some device as was recommended for practising nadai bhedam, play all the matras of the nadai in the alternating accents and start phrasing against this backdrop. It is crucial to feel the differences in proportionality between the actual (real) length of, for instance, a ♪ in a 5:3♪ and 5:7♪ in the mixed jathi of 3+7.

5) Start combining performing the phrases with and without the aid until you feel confident enough to perform them only with the metronome.

Below four phrases are proposed, one per gati (the same phrases as the transcriptions shown elsewhere in this chapter). Each of these phrases can be performed with all possible combinations of mixed jathi. 'X' stands for one frame and 'Y' for the other. Similar phrases can be constructed on all gatis with all possible mixed jathis and all possible nadais.

6: x
6: y
sempre sim.

7: x
7: y
sempre sim.

Chapter 20

Combinations Anuloma-Pratiloma

This karnatic concept of creating and developing what in the West has come to be named 'complex irregular groupings' is possibly the closest to what could be thought of as 'new complexity'. As opposed to nadai bhedam, in combinations anuloma-pratiloma the changes occur with complete disregard for giving any feeling of a different tempo or metre. Through this technique, almost any conceivable numerical relationship can be found.

Before going any further, however, it is important to provide a short reminder of anuloma and pratiloma by repeating Table 7.1 (the anuloma-pratiloma chart).

- *Anuloma* could be defined as when the number of matras in a beat is doubled, tripled or quadrupled.
- *Pratiloma* could be defined as when the number of matras in a gati is spread throughout 2, 3, 4, 5, 6 or 7 beats.

Chart of Anuloma-Pratiloma

	Anuloma			
	Tisra	Chatusra	Khanda	Misra
4th speed	12	16	20	28
3rd speed	9	12	15	21
2nd speed	6	8	10	14
	Neutral or Regular			
1st speed	3	4	5	7
	Pratiloma			
2nd speed	3:2	4:2	5:2	7:2
3rd speed	xx	4:3	5:3	7:3
4th speed	3:4	xx	5:4	7:4
5th speed	3:5	4:5	xx	7:5
6th speed	xx	4:6	5:6	7:6
7th speed	3:7	4:7	5:7	xx

The introduction to this topic in Chapter 7 has already given a glimpse of the concept of anuloma-pratiloma combinations. The inclusion of the 2nd speed anuloma within the frame of the 3rd speed pratiloma provided the possibility of using 8:3♩, 10:3♩ and 14:3♩

There are two ways of creating a combination anuloma-pratiloma.

1) When Any of the Anuloma Speeds is Used Within the Frame Provided by Any of the Pratiloma Speeds

Within the karnatic tradition the chart above becomes the expanded chart shown below.[1] Every speed of anuloma (including the regular speed) can be used within any pratiloma speed or frame.

Tisra

1)	⌐3:2♩¬	⌐6:2♩¬	⌐9:2♩¬	⌐12:2♩¬
2)	⌐3:4♩¬	⌐6:4♩¬	⌐9:4♩¬	⌐12:4♩¬
3)	⌐3:5♩¬	⌐6:5♩¬	⌐9:5♩¬	⌐12:5♩¬
4)	⌐3:7♩¬	⌐6:7♩¬	⌐9:7♩¬	⌐12:7♩¬

Chatusra

1)	⌐4:2♩¬	⌐8:2♩¬	⌐12:2♩¬	⌐16:2♩¬
2)	⌐4:3♩¬	⌐8:3♩¬	⌐12:3♩¬	⌐16:3♩¬
3)	⌐4:5♩¬	⌐8:5♩¬	⌐12:5♩¬	⌐16:5♩¬
4)	⌐4:6♩¬	⌐8:6♩¬	⌐12:6♩¬	⌐16:6♩¬
5)	⌐4:7♩¬	⌐8:7♩¬	⌐12:7♩¬	⌐16:7♩¬

Khanda

1)	⌐5:2♩¬	⌐10:2♩¬	⌐15:2♩¬	⌐20:2♩¬
2)	⌐5:3♩¬	⌐10:3♩¬	⌐15:3♩¬	⌐20:3♩¬
3)	⌐5:4♩¬	⌐10:4♩¬	⌐15:4♩¬	⌐20:4♩¬
4)	⌐5:6♩¬	⌐10:6♩¬	⌐15:6♩¬	⌐20:6♩¬
5)	⌐5:7♩¬	⌐10:7♩¬	⌐15:7♩¬	⌐20:7♩¬

[1] A western alternative notation is provided later.

Misra

1)	⌐— *7:2♩* —¬	⌐— *14:2♩* —¬	⌐— *21:2♩* —¬	⌐— *28:2♩* —¬
2)	⌐— *7:3♩* —¬	⌐— *14:3♩* —¬	⌐— *21:3♩* —¬	⌐— *28:3♩* —¬
3)	⌐— *7:4♩* —¬	⌐— *14:4♩* —¬	⌐— *21:4♩* —¬	⌐— *28:4♩* —¬
4)	⌐— *7:5♩* —¬	⌐— *14:5♩* —¬	⌐— *21:5♩* —¬	⌐— *28:5♩* —¬
5)	⌐— *7:6♩* —¬	⌐— *14:6♩* —¬	⌐— *21:6♩* —¬	⌐— *28:6♩* —¬

2) When the Frame is Expressed in ♪, 𝅘𝅥𝅯 or, Eventually, 𝅘𝅥𝅰

Until now, all frames provided in superimposition of gatis have always been expressed in ♩, with the exception of mixed jathi nadai bhedam. Any frame of the new chart of anuloma-pratiloma combinations can be utilised replacing the ♩ by ♪, 𝅘𝅥𝅯 or 𝅘𝅥𝅰 which exponentially broadens the available options. Some combinations will inevitably produce frames that already exist or can be expressed in ♩, but many a time they will result in completely new material. In addition, as will be seen later in the chapter, combinations of all these different frame values can be realised, and produce rather complex displacements within the beat.

Notation

Having arrived at this degree of complexity, it is of the utmost importance to use clear and transparent notation. Although the karnatic notation is extremely clear, computer notation programs and western conventions in terms of how to notate irregular groupings constitute a major handicap to employing karnatic notation.

Below, notation is presented in the karnatic tradition of the previous chart, and written in parenthesis, one or even two different systems of western notation. As already stated in Chapter 7, I do not find any problem with using western notation with this particular technique, except when the 3rd and 4th anuloma speeds are involved. For these cases, the explanation given in the third and fourth points below present a preferred notation. There are four different systems to notate the frames, depending on whether the number superimposed on the pratiloma frame is a 1st, 2nd, 3rd or 4th speed anuloma.

1) Regular or 1st speed: Most of the time, there is no differentiation between the karnatic and the western way of thinking and notating. That said, possible differences between the karnatic and western notational systems have either been explained in Chapter 7 or are an obvious result of this explanation in the new frames of 4, 5, 6 or 7 beats.

2) 2nd speed: Similarly, the explanation provided in Chapter 7 should be sufficient to understand the notational adaptations that need to be implemented; all changes follow the same underlying pattern of thought.

3) 3rd speed: Further to showing the manner of notating that has already been provided in the chart of nadai bhedam as the notation that has been used more abundantly in western music since 1950s (see the right column of the nadai bhedam chart in Chapter 18), the alternative and possibly clearer notation to be used in this context is to borrow the notion of double brackets employed for nadai bhedam: a first bracket using 3:2, 4, 5 or 7 ♩ and a second line with three brackets of the given gati.

For example, two different notations can be used in a ***15:4♩*** (the karnatic way of expressing a 3rd speed anuloma within a 4th speed pratiloma): first the traditionally accepted ***15:16♪*** which, I would argue, makes it very difficult for performers to find a concrete system that would enable them to perform this irregular grouping. Second, and below this notation, the nadai bhedam approach is written. As already explained in Chapter 18, this notation has the advantage of facilitating the performer's task of finding a system that can be used for similar concepts, a clear clue to enable the performer to trace it back to a gati/jathi combination:

┌——— ***3:4♩*** ———┐
┌-***5***-┐┌-***5***-┐┌-***5***-┐

Indeed, a ***15:4♩*** or ***15:16♪*** is the result of the following steps:

a. tisra 1st speed
b. tisra jathi 4
c. isolation of accents to create the frame of 3:4♩
d. superimposition of khanda on every accent provided by the gati/jathi combination.[2]

The added advantage is that if a performer has already understood and practised nadai bhedam, this system will facilitate the task of performing all the frames resulting from the use of superimposing the 3rd speed anuloma over any of the pratiloma speeds.

Hence, the way to understand the different lines for one particular frame is: 1st line, the karnatic convention; 2nd line, the more accepted western notation; and 3rd and 4th lines, the two brackets needed for the nadai bhedam notation (which, in my view, better expresses the karnatic concept).

---

[2] A fuller explanation of how to practise and master all these groupings will be given in the 'Practice Method' section.

┌ 15:4♩ ┐
(┌ 15:16♪ ┐)
(┌── 3:4♩ ──┐)
┌5┐┌5┐┌5┐

4) 4th speed: Everything said about the 3rd speed is equally applicable here. The only difference lies in the fact that the nadai bhedam frame to keep in mind will always be a 4:3, 5, 6 or 7 ♩ with the corresponding gati repeated 4 times.

┌ 16:7♩ ┐
(┌ 16:14♪ ┐)
(┌── 4:7♩ ──┐)
┌4┐┌4┐┌4┐┌4┐

Tisra

1)	┌ 3:2♩ ┐	┌ 6:2♩ ┐ (┌3:2♪┐┌3:2♪┐)	┌ 9:2♩ ┐ (┌9:8♪┐)	┌ 12:2♩ ┐ (┌6┐┌6┐)
2)	┌ 3:4♩ ┐	┌ 6:4♩ ┐ (┌3:2♩┐┌3:2♩┐)	┌ 9:4♩ ┐ (┌9:8♪┐)	┌ 12:4♩ ┐ (┌3┐┌3┐┌3┐┌3┐)
3)	┌ 3:5♩ ┐ (┌3♩:5♩┐)	┌ 6:5♩ ┐	┌ 9:5♩ ┐ (┌9:10♪┐) (┌── 3:5 ──┐) ┌3┐┌3┐┌3┐	┌ 12:5♩ ┐ (┌12:10♪┐) (┌── 4:5 ──┐) ┌3┐┌3┐┌3┐┌3┐
4)	┌ 3:7♩ ┐ (┌3♩:7♩┐)	┌ 6:7♩ ┐	┌ 9:7♩ ┐ (┌── 3:7 ──┐) ┌3┐┌3┐┌3┐	┌ 12:7♩ ┐ (┌12:14♪┐) (┌── 4:7 ──┐) ┌3┐┌3┐┌3┐┌3┐

Chatusra

1)	┌ 4:3♩ ┐	┌ 8:3♩ ┐ (┌4:3♪┐┌4:3♪┐)	┌ 12:3♩ ┐ (┌4┐┌4┐┌4┐)	┌ 16:3♩ ┐ (┌16:12♪┐) (┌── 4:3 ──┐) ┌4┐┌4┐┌4┐┌4┐
2)	┌ 4:5♩ ┐	┌ 8:5♩ ┐ (┌4:5♪┐┌4:5♪┐)	┌ 12:5♩ ┐ (┌12:10♪┐) (┌── 3:5 ──┐) ┌4┐┌4┐┌4┐	┌ 16:5♩ ┐ (┌16:20♪┐) (┌── 4:5 ──┐) ┌4┐┌4┐┌4┐┌4┐

3)	⌐— *4:6*♩. —¬ (⌐ *2:3*♩. ¬ ⌐ *2:3*♩. ¬)	⌐— *8:6*♩. —¬ (⌐ *4:3*♩. ¬ ⌐ *4:3*♩. ¬)	⌐— *12:6*♩. —¬ (⌐*4*♪¬⌐*4*♪¬⌐*4*♪¬)	⌐— *16:6*♩. —¬ (⌐ *8:6*♪¬ ⌐ *8:6*♪¬)
4)	⌐— *4:7*♩. —¬ (⌐ *4*𝅗𝅥*:7*♩. ¬)	⌐— *8:7*♩. —¬ (⌐ *4:7*♪¬ ⌐ *4:7*♪¬)	⌐— *12:7*♩. —¬ (⌐ *12:14*♪¬) (⌐——— *3:7* ———¬) ⌐ *4* ¬ ⌐ *4* ¬ ⌐ *4* ¬	⌐— *16:7*♩. —¬ (⌐ *16:14*♪¬) (⌐——— *4:7* ———¬) ⌐ *4* ¬ ⌐ *4* ¬ ⌐ *4* ¬ ⌐ *4* ¬

Khanda

1)	⌐— *5:2*♩. —¬ (⌐ *5:4*♪¬)	⌐— *10:2*♩. —¬ (⌐ *5* ¬ ⌐ *5* ¬)	⌐— *15:2*♩. —¬ (⌐ *15:16*𝅘𝅥𝅯¬) (⌐——— *3:2* ———¬) ⌐ *5* ¬ ⌐ *5* ¬ ⌐ *5* ¬	⌐— *20:2*♩. —¬ (⌐*10:8*𝅘𝅥𝅯¬⌐*10:8*𝅘𝅥𝅯¬)
2)	⌐— *5:3*♩. —¬ (⌐ *5:6*♪¬)	⌐— *10:3*♩. —¬ (⌐ *5:6*𝅘𝅥𝅯¬ ⌐ *5:6*𝅘𝅥𝅯¬)	⌐— *15:3*♩. —¬ (⌐ *5* ¬ ⌐ *5* ¬ ⌐ *5* ¬)	⌐— *20:3*♩. —¬ (⌐ *20:24*𝅘𝅥𝅯¬) (⌐——— *4:3* ———¬) ⌐ *5* ¬ ⌐ *5* ¬ ⌐ *5* ¬ ⌐ *5* ¬
3)	⌐— *5:4*♩. —¬	⌐— *10:4*♩. —¬ (⌐ *5:4*♪¬ ⌐ *5:4*♪¬)	⌐— *15:4*♩. —¬ (⌐ *15:16*♪¬) (⌐——— *3:4* ———¬) ⌐ *5* ¬ ⌐ *5* ¬ ⌐ *5* ¬	⌐— *20:4*♩. —¬ (⌐*5*¬⌐*5*¬⌐*5*¬⌐*5*¬)
4)	⌐— *5:6*± —¬	⌐— *10:6*♩. —¬ (⌐ *5:6*♪¬ ⌐ *5:6*♪¬)	⌐—— *15:*♩ ——¬ (⌐*5:4*♪¬⌐*5:4*♪¬⌐*5:4*♪¬)	⌐— *20:6*♩. —¬ (⌐*10:12*𝅘𝅥𝅯¬⌐*10:12*♪¬) (⌐——— *4:6* ———¬) ⌐ *5* ¬ ⌐ *5* ¬ ⌐ *5* ¬ ⌐ *5* ¬
5)	⌐— *5:7*♩. —¬	⌐— *10:7*♩. —¬ (⌐ *5:7*♪¬ ⌐ *5:7*♪¬)	⌐— *15:7*♩. —¬ (⌐ *15:14*♪¬) (⌐——— *3:7* ———¬) ⌐ *5* ¬ ⌐ *5* ¬ ⌐ *5* ¬	⌐— *20:7*♩. —¬ (⌐ *20:14*♪¬) (⌐——— *4:7* ———¬) ⌐ *5* ¬ ⌐ *5* ¬ ⌐ *5* ¬ ⌐ *5* ¬

Misra

1)	⌐— *7:2*♩. —¬ (⌐ *7:4*♪¬)	⌐— *14:2*♩. —¬ (⌐ *7* ¬ ⌐ *7* ¬)	⌐— *21:2*♩. —¬ (⌐ *21:16*𝅘𝅥𝅯¬) (⌐——— *3:2* ———¬) ⌐ *7* ¬ ⌐ *7* ¬ ⌐ *7* ¬	⌐— *28:2*♩. —¬ (⌐ *14* ¬ ⌐ *14* ¬)
2)	⌐— *7:3*♩. —¬ (⌐ *7:6*♪¬)	⌐— *14:3*♩. —¬ (⌐ *7:6*𝅘𝅥𝅯¬ ⌐ *7:6*𝅘𝅥𝅯¬)	⌐— *21:3*♩. —¬ (⌐ *7* ¬ ⌐ *7* ¬ ⌐ *7* ¬)	⌐— *28:3*♩. —¬ (⌐ *28:24*𝅘𝅥𝅯¬) (⌐——— *4:3* ———¬) ⌐ *7* ¬ ⌐ *7* ¬ ⌐ *7* ¬ ⌐ *7* ¬

3)	┌ *7:4♩.* ┐ (┌ *7:8♪.* ┐)	┌ *14:4♩.* ┐ (┌ *7:4♪.* ┐┌ *7:4♪.* ┐)	┌ *21:4♩.* ┐ (┌ *21:16♪.* ┐) (┌—— *3:4* ——┐) ┌ 7 ┐┌ 7 ┐┌ 7 ┐	┌ *28:4♩.* ┐ (┌7┐┌7┐┌7┐┌7┐)
4)	┌ *7:5♩.* ┐	┌ *14:5♩.* ┐ (┌ *7:5♪.* ┐┌ *7:5♪.* ┐)	┌ *21:5♩.* ┐ (┌ *21:20♪.* ┐) (┌—— *3:5* ——┐) ┌ 7 ┐┌ 7 ┐┌ 7 ┐	┌ *28:5♩.* ┐ (┌ *28:20♪.* ┐) (┌—— *4:5* ——┐) ┌ 7 ┐┌ 7 ┐┌ 7 ┐┌ 7 ┐
5)	┌ *7:6♩.* ┐	┌ *14:6♩.* ┐ (┌ *7:6♪.* ┐┌ *7:6♪.* ┐)	┌ *21:6♩.* ┐ (┌ *7:4♪.* ┐┌ *7:4♪.* ┐┌ *7:4♪.* ┐)	┌ *28:6♩.* ┐ (┌ *14:12♪.* ┐┌ *14:12♪.* ┐) (┌—— *4:6* ——┐) ┌ 7 ┐┌ 7 ┐┌ 7 ┐┌ 7 ┐

Developmental Techniques

With the possibilities given in Chapter 7, only two developmental techniques were available. However, within the context of combinations anuloma-pratiloma, six options are at one's disposal.

1) Taking Just One Specific Gati, Speed and Frame

This is actually the first option given in Chapter 7, where an example of ***14:3♩.*** (written ┌ ***7:6♪.*** ┐┌ ***7:6♪.*** ┐) was shown. This new context presents multiple possibilities and, as mentioned before, any frame can also be expressed in smaller note values. Therefore, a sequence could be created using, for instance, a ***14:5♪.*** (written ┌ ***7:5♪.*** ┐┌ ***7:5♪.*** ┐). The rule would remain (as will be the case for the other five techniques) that *no change of technique can happen in the middle of a tala*; it would always have to occur on tala sam.

2) Keeping the Same Gati and Frame, Changing Speed

The same frame, be it 2, 3, 4, 5, 6 or 7 beats, should be kept throughout the whole passage, but different anuloma speeds of the same gati are superimposed on a particular pratiloma frame. In the example below, the performer uses the following speeds within khanda 3rd speed pratiloma:

10:3 15:3 5:3 20:3 15:3 *(track 159)*

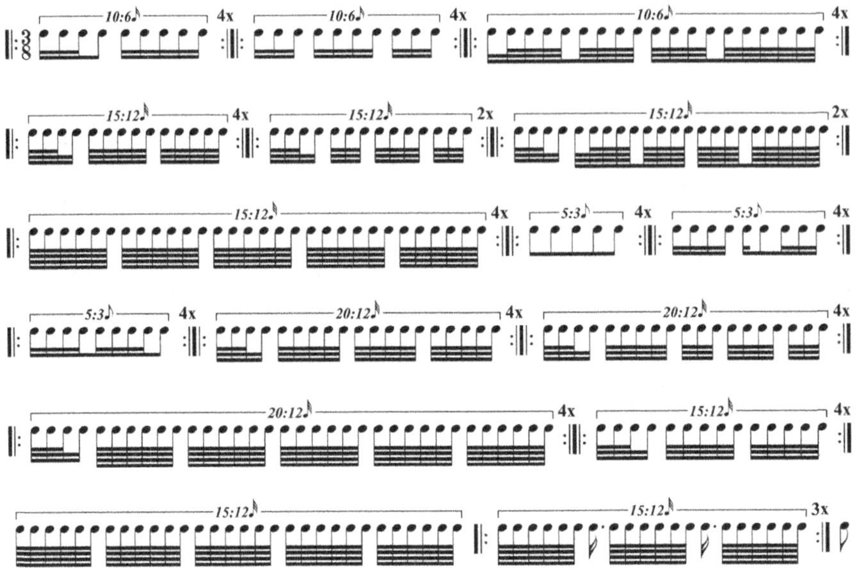

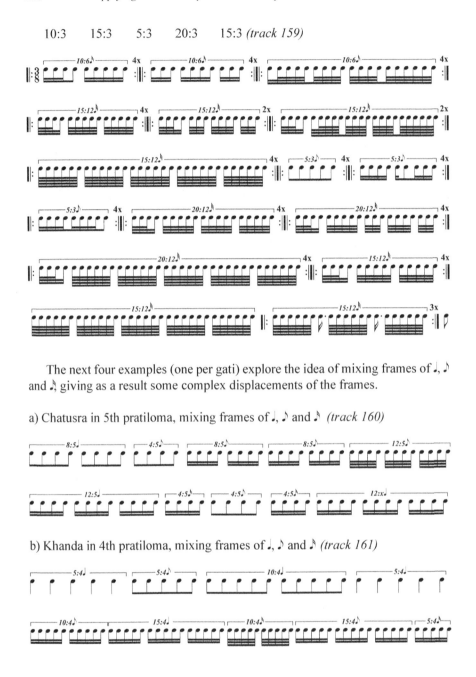

The next four examples (one per gati) explore the idea of mixing frames of ♩., ♪. and ♬. giving as a result some complex displacements of the frames.

a) Chatusra in 5th pratiloma, mixing frames of ♩., ♪. and ♬. *(track 160)*

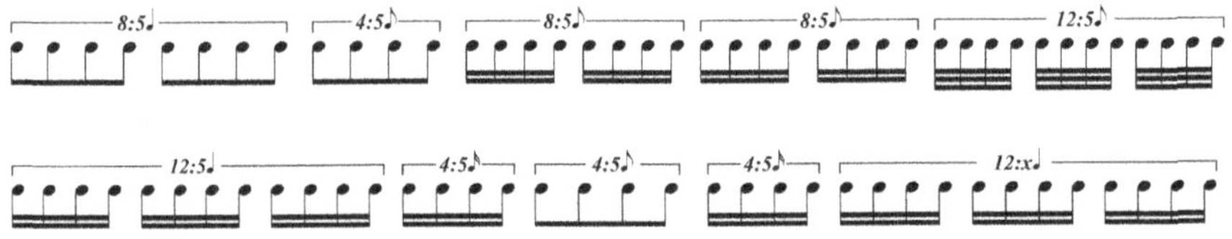

b) Khanda in 4th pratiloma, mixing frames of ♩., ♪. and ♬. *(track 161)*

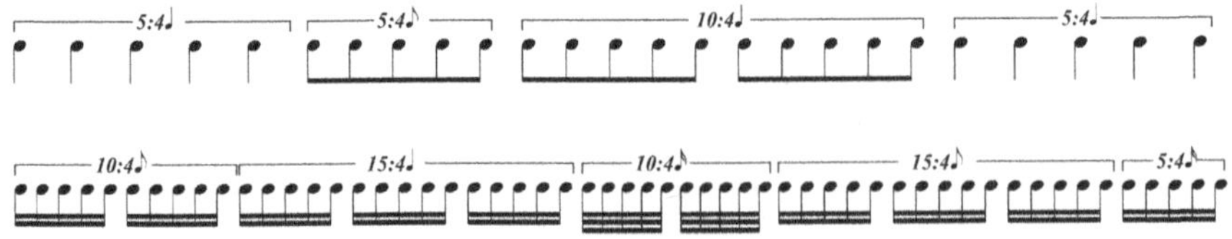

c) Tisra in 7th pratiloma, mixing frames of ♩ and ♪ *(track 162)*

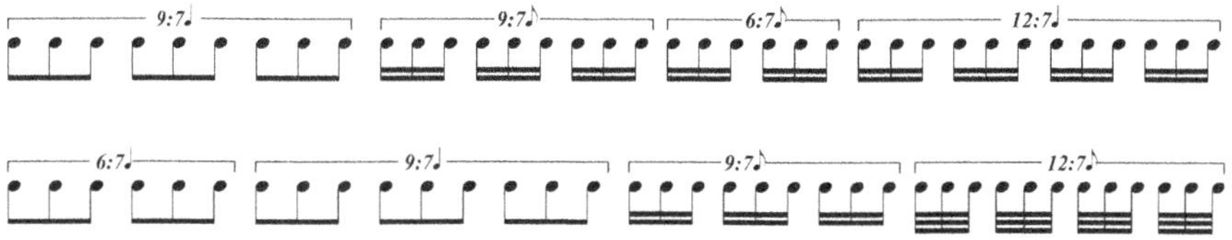

d) Misra in 3rd pratiloma, mixing frames of ♩., ♪ and 𝅘𝅥𝅯 *(track 163)*

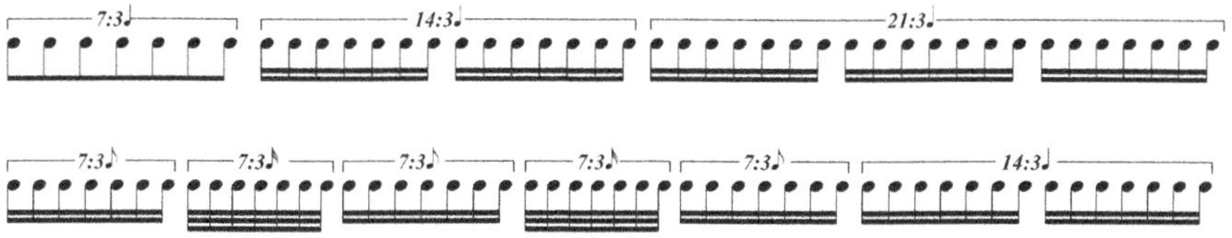

3) Keeping the Same Gati and Speed, Changing Frame

Here the musician has to stay in the same anuloma speed of a chosen gati, but can freely change the pratiloma frame.[3] The karnatic thinking behind this is:

10:3 10:4 10:2 10:7 10:6 *(track 164)*

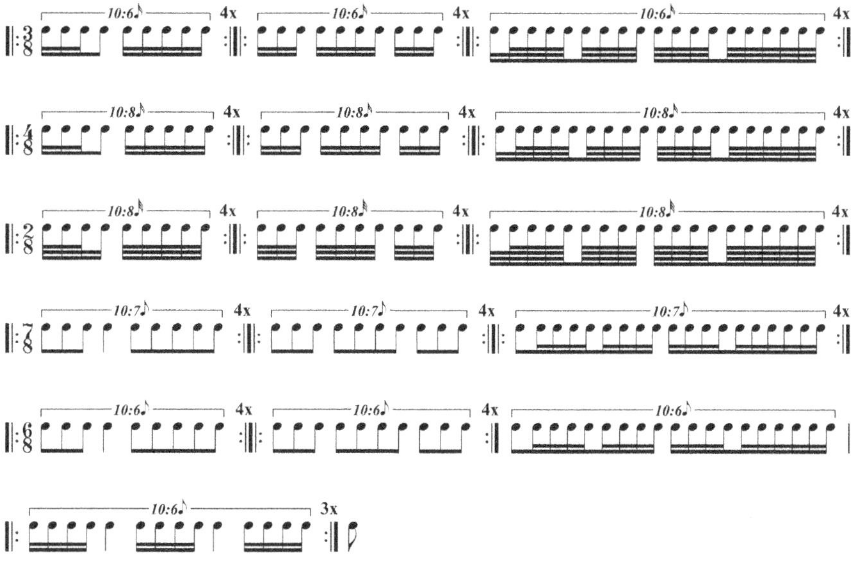

[3] Due to the changes of frames, I opted for using metre changes in the transcription notation as a way of showing the different frames.

The following four examples are based on exercises designed to perfect the frames of 5, 6 and 7 ♪ and 𝅘𝅥𝅯 and the displacement of these frames within the beat.[4]

a) Tisra 2nd speed in all frames *(track 165)*

┌— ***6:5♪***—┐ ┌— ***6:5𝅘𝅥𝅯*** —┐ ┌— ***6:5𝅘𝅥𝅯*** —┐ ┌— ***6:7𝅘𝅥𝅯*** —┐ ┌— ***6:7♪***—┐ ┌— ***6:7𝅘𝅥𝅯*** —┐

┌— ***6:5𝅘𝅥𝅯*** —┐ ┌— ***6:5♪***—┐ ┌— ***6:5𝅘𝅥𝅯*** —┐ ┌— ***6:7𝅘𝅥𝅯*** —┐ ┌— ***6:7𝅘𝅥𝅯***—┐ ┌— ***6:7♪***—┐

┌— ***6:5𝅘𝅥𝅯*** —┐ ┌— ***6:7𝅘𝅥𝅯*** —┐ ┌— ***6:7♪***—┐ ┌— ***6:5♪***—┐ ┌— ***6:5𝅘𝅥𝅯*** —┐ ┌— ***6:7𝅘𝅥𝅯*** —┐

b) Chatusra 2nd speed in all frames *(track 166)*

┌— ***8:5♪***—┐ ┌— ***8:5𝅘𝅥𝅯*** —┐ ┌— ***8:5𝅘𝅥𝅯*** —┐ ┌— ***8:7𝅘𝅥𝅯*** —┐ ┌— ***8:7♪***—┐ ┌— ***8:7𝅘𝅥𝅯*** —┐

┌— ***8:5𝅘𝅥𝅯*** —┐ ┌— ***8:5♪***—┐ ┌— ***8:5𝅘𝅥𝅯*** —┐ ┌— ***8:7𝅘𝅥𝅯*** —┐ ┌— ***8:7𝅘𝅥𝅯*** —┐ ┌— ***8:7♪***—┐

┌— ***8:5𝅘𝅥𝅯*** —┐ ┌— ***8:7𝅘𝅥𝅯*** —┐ ┌— ***8:7♪***—┐ ┌— ***8:5♪***—┐ ┌— ***8:5𝅘𝅥𝅯*** —┐ ┌— ***8:7𝅘𝅥𝅯*** —┐

c) Khanda 2nd speed in all frames *(track 167)*

┌—***10:6♪***—┐ ┌—***10:6𝅘𝅥𝅯*** —┐ ┌—***10:6𝅘𝅥𝅯*** —┐ ┌—***10:7𝅘𝅥𝅯*** —┐ ┌—***10:7♪***—┐ ┌—***10:7𝅘𝅥𝅯*** —┐

┌—***10:6𝅘𝅥𝅯*** —┐ ┌—***10:6♪***—┐ ┌—***10:6𝅘𝅥𝅯*** —┐ ┌—***10:7𝅘𝅥𝅯*** —┐ ┌—***10:7𝅘𝅥𝅯*** —┐ ┌—***10:7♪***—┐

┌—***10:6𝅘𝅥𝅯*** —┐ ┌—***10:7𝅘𝅥𝅯*** —┐ ┌—***10:6𝅘𝅥𝅯*** —┐ ┌—***10:5𝅘𝅥𝅯*** —┐ ┌—***10:6♪***—┐ ┌—***10:7♪***—┐

┌—***10:7𝅘𝅥𝅯*** —┐ ┌—***10:4𝅘𝅥𝅯*** —┐ ┌—***10:6𝅘𝅥𝅯*** —┐ ┌—***10:5𝅘𝅥𝅯*** —┐

This exercise introduces the notion of using gati bhedam in conjunction with anuloma-pratiloma. Subsequently, the 'missing speed' in all gatis (5:5 in the case of khanda) is actually chatusra using a jathi that would correspond numerically to the gati employed.

In the case of the previous example (c) in khanda, the chosen speed is 10 (2nd anuloma); therefore, the 10 notes would be 10 𝅘𝅥𝅯 in the frame of 5 ♪; this is, nonetheless, a clear chatusra jathi 5.

Hence, this possibility that was explored in the chapter of mixed jathi nadai bhedam is incorporated as well in the framework of combinations anuloma-pratiloma.

---

[4] Except for the example in misra, where a simple phrase is used to make a clear differentiation of the number 21, there is no phrasing in any of the other gatis. Therefore, I preferred not to use any notes, just using brackets as karnatic musicians would.

d) Misra 3rd speed in all frames *(track 168)*

21:6♩. 21:6♪. 21:6♪. 21:5♩. 21:5♩. 21:5♪. 21:5♪.
21:6♪. 21:6♩. 21:6♪. 21:5♪. 21:5♩. 21:5♪. 21:6♪.
21:5♪. 21:4♩. 21:6♪. 21:5♪. 21:6♩. 21:5♪.

4) Keeping the Same Gati, Changing Frame and Speed

This possibility was actually the second option explained in Chapter 7. The degree of difficulty increases due to the fact that only one parameter remains unaltered (thus far, whether in nadai bhedam or anuloma-pratiloma combinations, any change between two musical objects needed to have two common parameters).

Whereas in the first three techniques the use of frames in ♪. and 𝅘𝅥𝅯. is a common occurrence, all frames are expressed in ♩. in this technique. This obeys the notion that a phrase can move from any speed and frame to another speed and frame, a fact that greatly multiplies the number of options. The objective pursued in the first three techniques by mixing frames using ♪. and 𝅘𝅥𝅯. is almost automatically achieved in this technique because of the great variety of speeds and frames to choose from. However, I have heard examples where some ♪. or 𝅘𝅥𝅯. frames were used, although this is indeed rarer.

Here I have also opted for writing the frame as metre changes. The karnatic notational thinking for the following example is

10:3 15:4 5:2 20:7 20:3 15:2 *(track 169)*

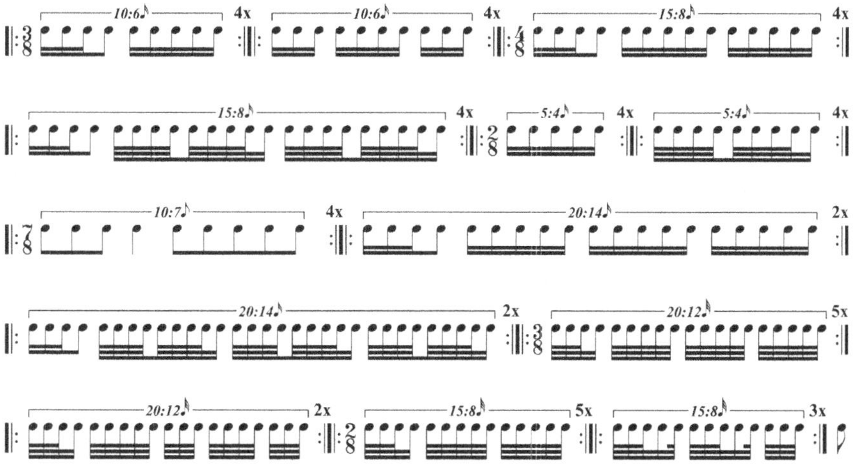

5) Keeping the Same Frame and Speed, Changing Gati

This technique chooses a common speed of anuloma in all gatis, along with a common number of beats (always expressed in ♩.), while the sequence can change gatis ‘randomly’. The karnatic frames are

10:3   14:3   8:3   18:3 *(track 170)*

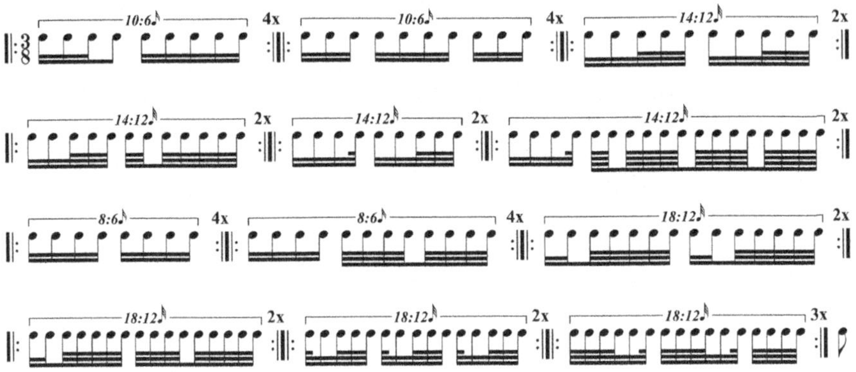

6) Keeping the Same Frame, Changing Gati and Speed

Of all the possibilities offered by anuloma-pratiloma combinations, this technique is possibly the most complex to perform. The only common denominator is the frame (always expressed in number of beats), while any gati and any speed can be chosen to succeed one another.

The first example uses the frame of 3 beats as a common denominator. The karnatic mindset is

10:3 7:3 27:3 16:3 5:3 8:3 14:3 *(track 171)*

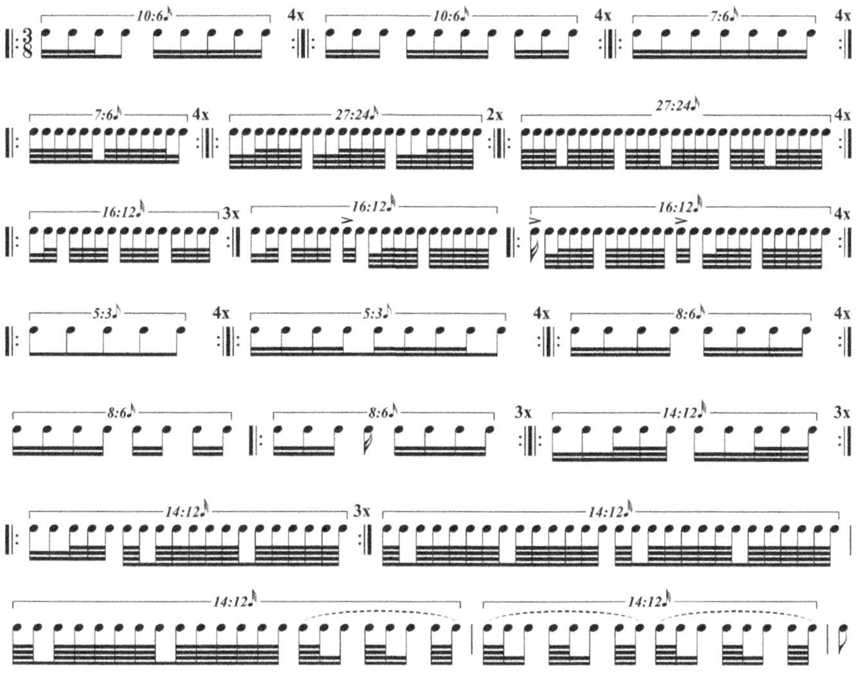

In the second example, the common denominator is a frame of 5 beats and the karnatic thinking would be

8:5 7:5 18:5 6:5 21:5 16:5 12:5 *(track 172)*

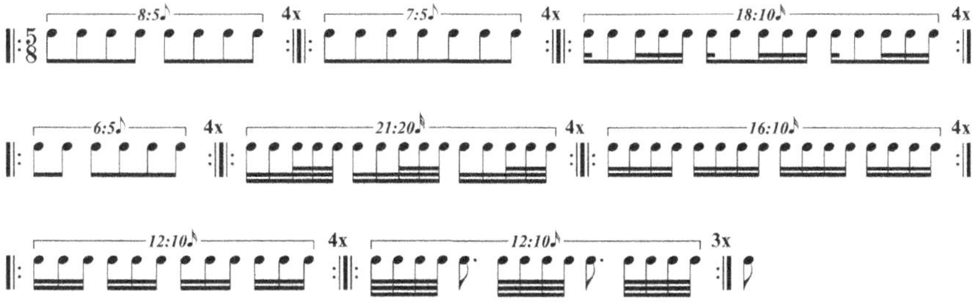

Use of Anuloma-Pratiloma Combinations in Jathi Bhedam Sequences

As was hinted at in the chapter on jathi bhedam to explain the two different approaches to creating phrases, when the chosen option is to have the same number of notes per cell, instead of having 3, 4 or 5 notes per cell with different note values while staying in a particular gati, the cells could use the superimposition of tisra, chatusra or khanda – as long as these gatis would utilise all the matras without any phrasing (since the phrasing must have precisely 3, 4 or 5 notes per cell).

Eventually, the concept of having the same number of notes could be broadened so that tisra 2nd speed or misra could be included in the number of options. The first example here is a jathi bhedam sequence with the numbers 5 4 7 6 5 6 7 3 4 4 5 in chatusra in a tala of 14 beats. The recorded examples are in tisra and chatusra. *(tracks 173 and 174)*

4♩ *6♩* *4♩*

⌐*x:5*𝅘𝅥𝅯¬ ⌐*x:4*𝅘𝅥𝅯¬ ⌐*x:7*𝅘𝅥𝅯¬ ⌐*x:6*𝅘𝅥𝅯¬ ⌐*x:5*𝅘𝅥𝅯¬ ⌐*x:6*𝅘𝅥𝅯¬ ⌐*x:7*𝅘𝅥𝅯¬ ⌐*x:3*𝅘𝅥𝅯¬ ⌐*x:4*𝅘𝅥𝅯¬ ⌐*x:4*𝅘𝅥𝅯¬ ⌐*x:5*𝅘𝅥𝅯¬

The second example shows a variation on the way a jathi bhedam sequence has been explained thus far; in this example the sequence starts after 3 beats and consists of the numbers 5 5 4 5 7 3 5 5. However, the first frame of 3 beats uses a speed of anuloma-pratiloma as well.

This sequence does not respond in the manner explained in Chapter 6 to organise or develop jathi bhedam, because it is purposely created to utilise anuloma-pratiloma over the different frames, as opposed to the previous one – that is, a jathi bhedam sequence created as such. Therefore, the possibility of mixing ♩, ♪ or 𝅘𝅥𝅯 is combined with the concept of jathi bhedam. The recorded examples are in khanda and misra. *(tracks 175 and 176)*

6♩ *8♩*

⌐*x:3*♩¬ ⌐*x:5*𝅘𝅥𝅯¬ ⌐*x:5*♪¬ ⌐*x:4*𝅘𝅥𝅯¬ ⌐*x:5*𝅘𝅥𝅯¬ ⌐*x:7*♪¬ ⌐*x:3*𝅘𝅥𝅯¬ ⌐*x:5*♪¬ ⌐*x:5*𝅘𝅥𝅯¬

Common Denominator Concept

Techniques 5 and 6 outlined above are seldom used, for reasons already seen and explained throughout the book: the change of gati in the middle of a tala does not happen unless it follows a very specific set of rules. At this point it may be worth reviewing in which techniques gati changes occur outside the change on tala sam, as a means to better understand the 'self-imposed limitations' of karnatic music regarding gati changes.

A change of gati that does not happen on tala sam occurs exclusively in the following techniques with the specified conditions:

- Tree of gati bhedam: when the gati became jathi (or vice versa) and only on anga sam.
- Development of a sama mukthay with rhythmical sangati: if the mini-mukthay started on a beat and always used a number pertaining to the original sequence for the creation of the pala.
- 3-fold mukthay: same phrase repeated in two or three different gatis.

- Mridangam and damaruyatis: in the second part of the yati phrase, provided that the main phrase and length of palas remains unaltered.
- Tirmanas: when the sequence reaches the uttaranga, the number of notes in the phrase can become a gati.
- Compound and related mukthays: as a result of the seed phrase.
- Yatis prastara: on the frame of a samayati, different gatis can be superimposed, always following the rule of systematic increase or decrease characteristic of all yati concepts.
- Mukthay combinations: while developing the large structure sequence, palas can change gati if the previous gati uses a jathi that links with the new gati (a similar concept to that of tree of gati bhedam).
- Poruttam A: similarly, in the overall development of the whole sequence there are gati changes while phrases or numbers are kept unchanged and, ultimately, because every target cell is considered a tala sam.
- Mixed gati mohara: following a very concrete set of rules and with a very specific goal. Rhythmical sangatis on the same phrases and taking a phrase through two different gatis are the basic notions behind this.

Hence, it can be concluded that in karnatic music gati changes *never* occur randomly; and, even when this change does not occur on tala sam (as shown in the techniques above), there is always a unifying factor, a common denominator that enables the gati to change inside a tala. This common denominator tends to be a phrase, a particular jathi or a clear and strong numerical relationship. Somehow, conceptually, the bottom line of any possible gati change is already exposed in the tree of gati bhedam, although in each of the techniques mentioned above limited small variations and 'exceptions' permit modifications to the notion of only changing gati on tala or anga sam.

So far in this chapter four developmental techniques have been explained in which the speed and/or frame can change, but the common denominator is always that the gati remains the same. Techniques 5 and 6 are the first exceptions to the rule of not changing gatis anywhere in the tala, permitting the change of gatis while keeping the common denominator in the number of beats.

Subsequently, if gati changes occur exclusively if and when there is a clear logic behind a particular technique, and always making use of a common denominator, why should anuloma-pratiloma be an exception? If we analyse the examples above, the conclusion is that if these changes happen because they share the same frame, using the regular speed of gatis would lead to the same notion: they all share the frame of one beat.

Karnatic musicians, especially those of what could be called the 'old school', are quite reluctant to use techniques 5 and 6 precisely because they find that the argument for keeping the same number of beats as the common denominator is weak; most musicians fear that exploring this path could dangerously lead to an 'anything goes' approach that they tend to associate with the way western culture produces music, be it pop or experimental.

> The essence is that it is precisely because of the common denominator concept that karnatic music has produced a pedagogical methodology that enables its musicians to create, and possibly even more importantly, perform music of great complexity with a very high degree of precision without excluding feelings or emotions.

However, younger generations of musicians, following in the wake of great artists like Dr Balamuralikrishna, Jahnavi Jayaprakash, Karaikkudi Mani or T.N. Seshagopalan, who tentatively started using techniques 5 and 6 in their compositions or improvisations, are starting to explore the musical possibilities of changing gatis while keeping the same frame throughout the sequence, *provided that these possibilities remain confined to the realm of combinations anuloma-pratiloma development and are never transferred to any other technique or phrasing concept seen so far*. In other words, only in the context of combinations anuloma-pratiloma are they willing to change gatis 'randomly', and provided that this does not affect their tradition and the vast possibilities that the concepts of common denominator and not changing gatis randomly have enabled them to create and elaborate.[5]

A transcription of a short improvisation by N.G. Ravi concludes this section of the chapter. This piece, utilising the misra chapu tala, places the emphasis on the division of the cycle into halves of 7𝅘𝅥𝅯. Over this division, he superimposes 6, 8 or 12 matras, therefore creating two 6:7𝅘𝅥𝅯, 8:7𝅘𝅥𝅯 or 12:7𝅘𝅥𝅯 per cycle, and a second layer of alternatively tisra and khanda is superimposed over the frame. In a few cycles, the percussionist also uses gati and jathi bhedam, including displacement of some figures. *(track 177)*

[5] See the Conclusion to this volume for reflections on the concept of common denominator, how it affects karnatic music pedagogically and creatively and how it similarly can affect our pedagogic and creative methodology and thinking.

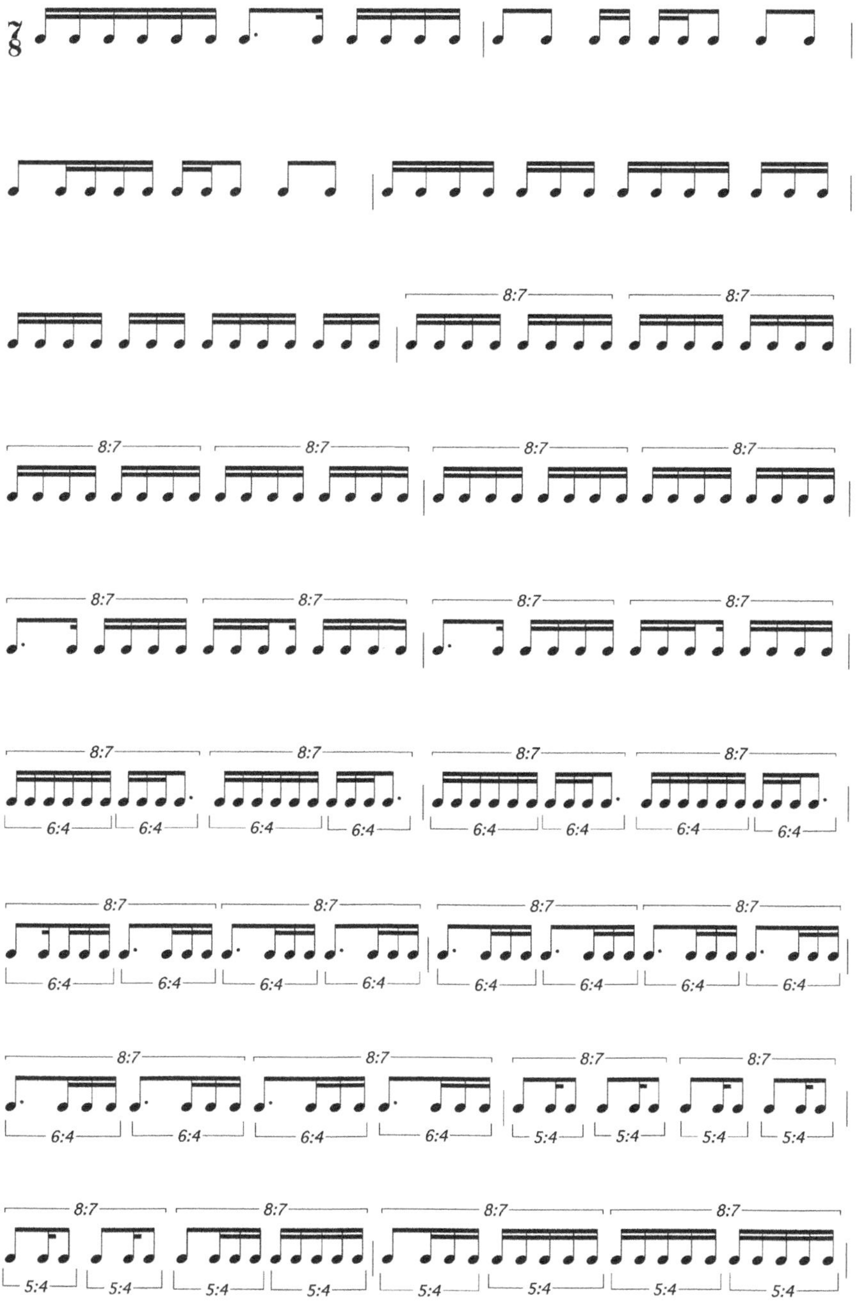
7/8
8:7 8:7
8:7 8:7 8:7 8:7
8:7 8:7 8:7 8:7
8:7 8:7 8:7 8:7
6:4 6:4 6:4 6:4 6:4 6:4 6:4 6:4
8:7 8:7 8:7 8:7
6:4 6:4 6:4 6:4 6:4 6:4 6:4 6:4
8:7 8:7 8:7 8:7
6:4 6:4 6:4 6:4 5:4 5:4 5:4 5:4
8:7 8:7 8:7 8:7
5:4 5:4 5:4 5:4 5:4 5:4 5:4 5:4

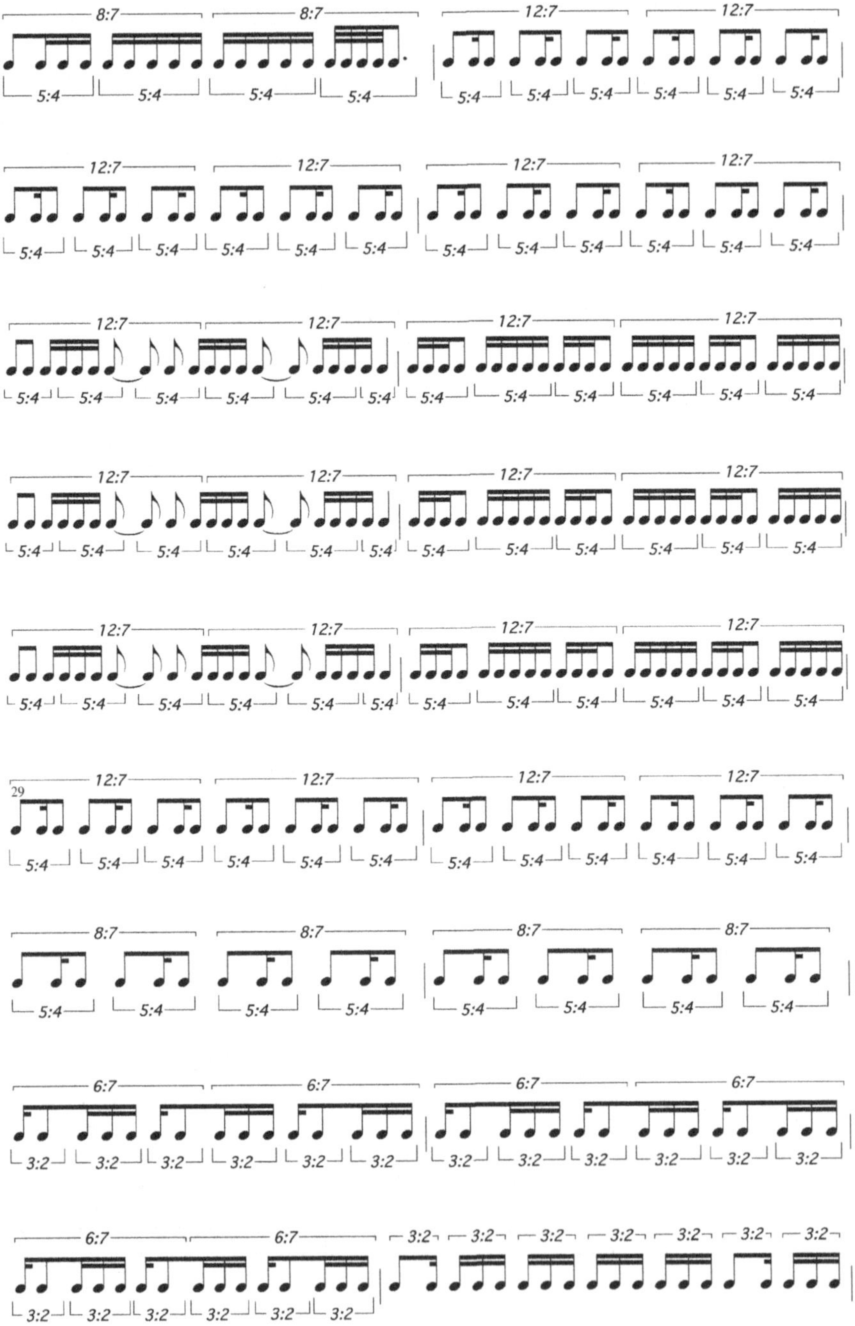
8:7 8:7 12:7 12:7
5:4 5:4 5:4 5:4 5:4 5:4 5:4 5:4 5:4 5:4
12:7 12:7 12:7 12:7
5:4 5:4 5:4 5:4 5:4 5:4 5:4 5:4 5:4 5:4 5:4 5:4
12:7 12:7 12:7 12:7
5:4 5:4 5:4 5:4 5:4 5:4 5:4 5:4 5:4 5:4 5:4 5:4
12:7 12:7 12:7 12:7
5:4 5:4 5:4 5:4 5:4 5:4 5:4 5:4 5:4 5:4 5:4 5:4
12:7 12:7 12:7 12:7
5:4 5:4 5:4 5:4 5:4 5:4 5:4 5:4 5:4 5:4 5:4 5:4
29
12:7 12:7 12:7 12:7
5:4 5:4 5:4 5:4 5:4 5:4 5:4 5:4 5:4 5:4 5:4 5:4
8:7 8:7 8:7 8:7
5:4 5:4 5:4 5:4 5:4 5:4 5:4 5:4
6:7 6:7 6:7 6:7
3:2 3:2 3:2 3:2 3:2 3:2 3:2 3:2 3:2 3:2 3:2 3:2
6:7 6:7 3:2 3:2 3:2 3:2 3:2 3:2 3:2
3:2 3:2 3:2 3:2 3:2 3:2

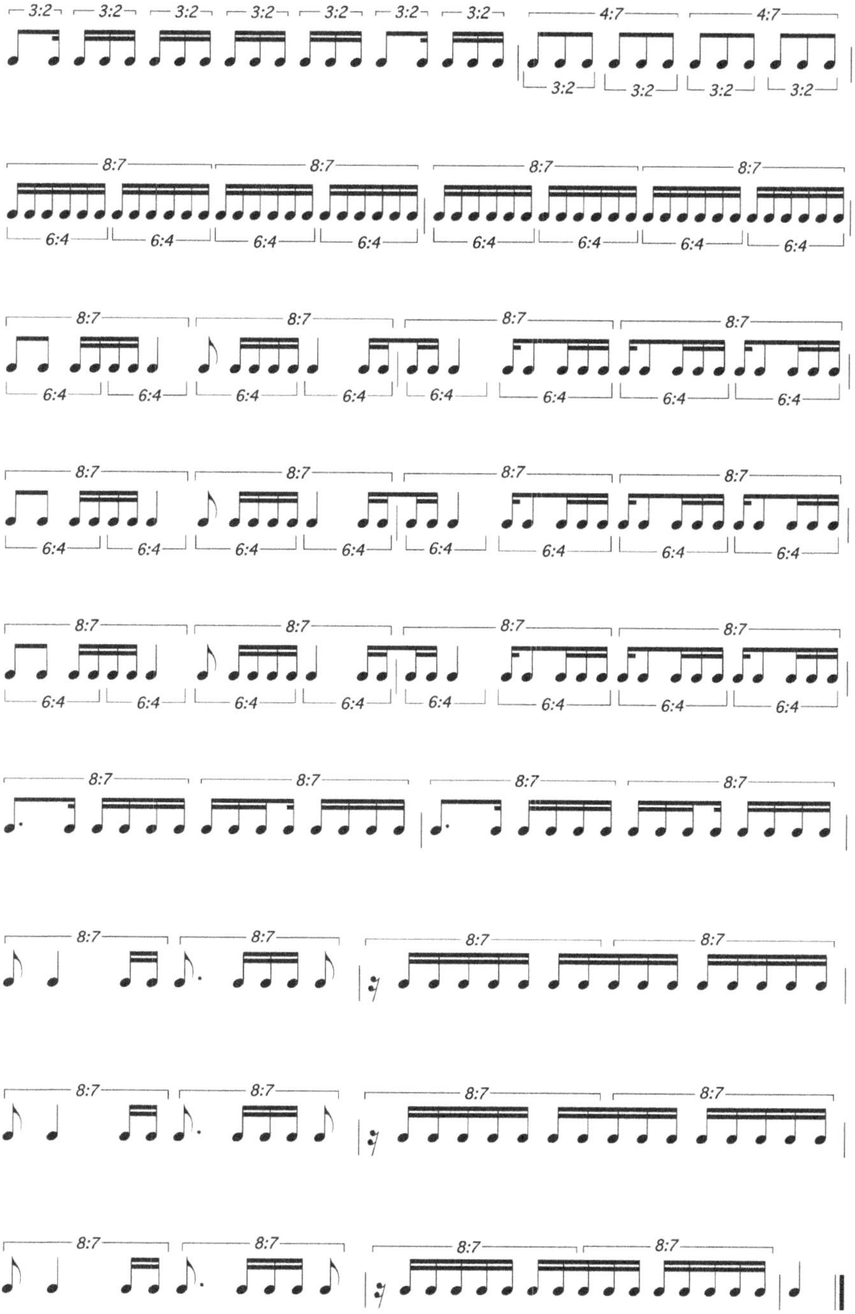
3:2 3:2 3:2 3:2 3:2 3:2 3:2 4:7 4:7
3:2 3:2 3:2 3:2
8:7 8:7 8:7 8:7
6:4 6:4 6:4 6:4 6:4 6:4 6:4 6:4
8:7 8:7 8:7 8:7
6:4 6:4 6:4 6:4 6:4 6:4 6:4 6:4
8:7 8:7 8:7 8:7
6:4 6:4 6:4 6:4 6:4 6:4 6:4 6:4
8:7 8:7 8:7 8:7
6:4 6:4 6:4 6:4 6:4 6:4 6:4 6:4
8:7 8:7 8:7 8:7
8:7 8:7 8:7 8:7
8:7 8:7 8:7 8:7
8:7 8:7 8:7 8:7

Practice Method

Combinations anuloma-pratiloma are possibly the most difficult technique to master as a performer, and without doubt the one that would require the longest time to master. This is due to the following:

- The number of frames of 'irregular groupings' that can be created far exceeds that of any other technique, including nadai bhedam.
- Changes can occur quite rapidly.
- Frequent use of frames in ♩, ♪ and 𝅘𝅥𝅯 with displacements within the beat.

There is a set of three differentiated exercises to practise this concept, the first of which addresses the different speeds within the same gati and frame.

The following chart has already appeared at the beginning of the chapter and was followed by a more elaborate one providing one or two alternative western notational possibilities for every karnatic speed. For practice purposes I prefer using the karnatic mindset for all the examples in this section.[6]

Exercises A

Tisra

1)	⌐— *3:2♩* —¬	⌐— *6:2♩* —¬	⌐— *9:2♩* —¬	⌐— *12:2♩* —¬
2)	⌐— *3:4♩* —¬	⌐— *6:4♩* —¬	⌐— *9:4♩* —¬	⌐— *12:4♩* —¬
3)	⌐— *3:5♩* —¬	⌐— *6:5♩* —¬	⌐— *9:5♩* —¬	⌐— *12:5♩* —¬
4)	⌐— *3:7♩* —¬	⌐— *6:7♩* —¬	⌐— *9:7♩* —¬	⌐— *12:7♩* —¬

Chatusra

1)	⌐— *4:2♩* —¬	⌐— *8:2♩* —¬	⌐— *12:2♩* —¬	⌐— *16:2♩* —¬
2)	⌐— *4:3♩* —¬	⌐— *8:3♩* —¬	⌐— *12:3♩* —¬	⌐— *16:3♩* —¬
3)	⌐— *4:5♩* —¬	⌐— *8:5♩* —¬	⌐— *12:5♩* —¬	⌐— *16:5♩* —¬
4)	⌐— *4:6♩* —¬	⌐— *8:6♩* —¬	⌐— *12:6♩* —¬	⌐— *16:6♩* —¬
5)	⌐— *4:7♩* —¬	⌐— *8:7♩* —¬	⌐— *12:7♩* —¬	⌐— *16:7♩* —¬

---

6 The western way of notating has been explained elsewhere in the chapter; memorising both the karnatic and the western way of notating should help relate the karnatic concepts and exercises to the western notation when working on contemporary pieces.

Khanda

1)	⌐– *5:2♩* –¬	⌐– *10:2♩* –¬	⌐– *15:2♩* –¬	⌐– *20:2♩* –¬
2)	⌐– *5:3♩* –¬	⌐– *10:3♩* –¬	⌐– *15:3♩* –¬	⌐– *20:3♩* –¬
3)	⌐– *5:4♩* –¬	⌐– *10:4♩* –¬	⌐– *15:4♩* –¬	⌐– *20:4♩* –¬
4)	⌐– *5:6♩* –¬	⌐– *10:6♩* –¬	⌐– *15:6♩* –¬	⌐– *20:6♩* –¬
5)	⌐– *5:7♩* –¬	⌐– *10:7♩* –¬	⌐– *15:7♩* –¬	⌐– *20:7♩* –¬

Misra

1)	⌐– *7:2♩* –¬	⌐– *14:2♩* –¬	⌐– *21:2♩* –¬	⌐– *28:2♩* –¬
2)	⌐– *7:3♩* –¬	⌐– *14:3♩* –¬	⌐– *21:3♩* –¬	⌐– *28:3♩* –¬
3)	⌐– *7:4♩* –¬	⌐– *14:4♩* –¬	⌐– *21:4♩* –¬	⌐– *28:4♩* –¬
4)	⌐– *7:5♩* –¬	⌐– *14:5♩* –¬	⌐– *21:5♩* –¬	⌐– *28:5♩* –¬
5)	⌐– *7:6♩* –¬	⌐– *14:6♩* –¬	⌐– *21:6♩* –¬	⌐– *28:6♩* –¬

Providing a practice method for every single speed and gati would probably take too much space and possibly be superfluous. A clear explanation of one option should suffice, and the performer should then be able to apply the principles to each possibility shown in the chart. I have chosen khanda in its 7th speed pratiloma because it is possibly one of the most difficult exercises.

⌐– *5:7♩* –¬ ⌐– *10:7♩* –¬ ⌐– *15:7♩* –¬ ⌐– *20:7♩* –¬

In the first part of anuloma-pratiloma seen in Chapter 7, the approach for pratiloma speeds was to have a very clear picture of where the accents of a gati/jathi combination fell within the beat and to isolate the accents. Afterwards, for a 10:3♩ or 14:3♩, every accent of a 5:3♩ or 7:3♩ was doubled (every accent or ♩ became 2 ♪). Although this thinking is still valid, in the context of combinations anuloma-pratiloma an entirely different approach will possibly speed up the learning process.

1) As explained in the notation section of this chapter, ***20:7♩*** is actually a frame already seen in nadai bhedam that could be written and felt as

⌐——— ***4:7♩*** ———¬
⌐-***5***-¬⌐-***5***-¬⌐-***5***-¬⌐-***5***-¬

regardless of what sort of phrasing was created for the 20 matras.

In order to work out a learning and performing system, borrowing the nadai bhedam feeling and notation provides the musician with an anchor point from where to approach this 4th speed anuloma within 7th speed pratiloma (and, by extension, all 4th speed anuloma within any pratiloma frame). Consequently, the 4th speed should be employed as the starting point for any exercise. The 3rd speed should be omitted for now and, subsequently, the 2nd speed should be the next step to practise.

2) In order to perform the 2nd speed (***10:7𝅗𝅥***) one should be feeling the 4th speed and attack every 2 matras of the ***20:7𝅗𝅥*** (track 178)

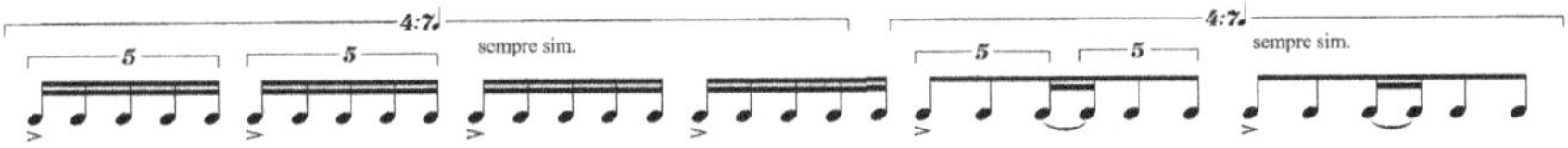

The line above is the way to *feel* the ***10:7𝅗𝅥***, as a sort of ramification of the ***20:7𝅗𝅥***, whereas the way to notate the ***10:7𝅗𝅥*** should be as the line below shows (2 times ***5:7♪***).

3) Practise going back and forth from the 4th speed to the 2nd speed to then add the 1st speed. The approach to perform the 1st speed could be, depending on the context, either to follow the same procedure of going from ***20:7𝅗𝅥*** to ***10:7𝅗𝅥*** or to apply a gati/jathi combination and isolate its accents (in this example, it should be khanda jathi 7). Therefore, the exercises should follow the next procedure – 20:7𝅗𝅥 10:7𝅗𝅥 5:7𝅗𝅥 – and, once this direction is mastered, proceed in reverse order: 5:7𝅗𝅥 10:7𝅗𝅥 20:7𝅗𝅥

4) The last step is to work on the 3rd speed, which departs from the way the previous elements interrelate. As explained earlier, the 3rd speed is the fruit of superimposing a gati on the frame provided by a gati/jathi combination based on tisra gati. Hence, ***15:7𝅗𝅥*** is the result of an already shown nadai bhedam frame, namely:

┌——*3:7𝅗𝅥*——┐
┌*5*┐┌*5*┐┌*5*┐

One of the exercises proposed in Chapter 18 for nadai bhedam (the one that was a direct result of one of the developmental techniques described there) was to go from one frame to another by keeping the nadai and the number of beats (jathi) intact and changing the number of accents (gati). If this step has already been internalised while practising nadai bhedam, going from ***20:7𝅗𝅥*** to ***15:7𝅗𝅥*** should not represent a major obstacle. The possible problem here is to obtain absolute accuracy and clarity while going from ***15:7♩*** to ***10:7♩*** or vice versa.

The frame ***10:7♩*** was obtained by attacking every two notes of the frame ***20:7♩***. However, with the incorporation of the 3rd speed, that reference point can easily fade and create imprecision in the ***10:7♩***. This is why it is so important to practise the previous step (that is, without throwing ***15:7♩*** into the equation) until an independent feeling for the 2nd speed is achieved without having to resort to coming from the 4th speed. Only in this fashion is the incorporation of the 3rd speed into the working process feasible.

5) Practise all four speeds going up and down in order. *(track 179)*

Repeat ***20:7♩*** ***15:7♩*** ***10:7♩*** ***5:7♩*** until the change from the 3rd speed to the 2nd speed is felt with complete accuracy. Then, the order should be reversed.

6) Once both orders have acquired a high level of accuracy, the performer should change speed randomly.

> Having followed all the steps just described, any performer should be able to apply these principles to all frames of all gatis in the set of Exercises A.

Exercises B

These focus on practising every anuloma speed in all its possible pratiloma frames. Intensive work on Exercises A should provide enough understanding to face this set. However, a few remarks may facilitate the practice of these exercises.

- Approach all 1st speeds with the system of isolating the accents of gati/jathi combinations.
- All 2nd speeds should be felt by doubling the number of matras in relation to the 1st speed (although, in some cases, applying the approach of the 1st speed can be equally fruitful).
- All 3rd speeds are based on the nadai bhedam frame of 3:*x*, superimposing the relevant gati 3 times.
- All 4th speeds are based on the nadai bhedam frame of 4:*x*, superimposing the relevant gati 4 times.

Therefore, the difficulty in these exercises lies in the fact that the same gati and speed remain while their number of beats change (these exercises bring forth the 3rd developmental technique).

Tisra

1)	┌ *3:2*♩ ┐	┌ *3:4*♩ ┐	┌ *3:5*♩ ┐	┌ *3:7*♩ ┐
2)	┌ *6:2*♩ ┐	┌ *6:4*♩ ┐	┌ *6:5*♩ ┐	┌ *6:7*♩ ┐
3)	┌ *9:2*♩ ┐	┌ *9:4*♩ ┐	┌ *9:5*♩ ┐	┌ *9:7*♩ ┐
4)	┌ *12:2*♩ ┐	┌ *12:4*♩ ┐	┌ *12:5*♩ ┐	┌ *12:7*♩ ┐

Chatusra

1)	┌ *4:2*♩ ┐	┌ *4:3*♩ ┐	┌ *4:5*♩ ┐	┌ *4:7*♩ ┐
2)	┌ *8:2*♩ ┐	┌ *8:3*♩ ┐	┌ *8:5*♩ ┐	┌ *8:7*♩ ┐
3)	┌ *12:2*♩ ┐	┌ *12:3*♩ ┐	┌ *12:5*♩ ┐	┌ *12:7*♩ ┐
4)	┌ *16:2*♩ ┐	┌ *16:3*♩ ┐	┌ *16:5*♩ ┐	┌ *16:7*♩ ┐

Khanda

1)	┌ *5:2*♩ ┐	┌ *5:3*♩ ┐	┌ *5:4*♩ ┐	┌ *5:6*♩ ┐	┌ *5:7*♩ ┐
2)	┌ *10:2*♩ ┐	┌ *10:3*♩ ┐	┌ *10:4*♩ ┐	┌ *10:6*♩ ┐	┌ *10:7*♩ ┐
3)	┌ *15:2*♩ ┐	┌ *15:3*♩ ┐	┌ *15:4*♩ ┐	┌ *15:6*♩ ┐	┌ *15:7*♩ ┐
4)	┌ *20:2*♩ ┐	┌ *20:3*♩ ┐	┌ *20:4*♩ ┐	┌ *20:6*♩ ┐	┌ *20:7*♩ ┐

Misra

1)	┌ *7:2*♩ ┐	┌ *7:3*♩ ┐	┌ *7:4*♩ ┐	┌ *7:5*♩ ┐	┌ *7:6*♩ ┐
2)	┌ *14:2*♩ ┐	┌ *14:3*♩ ┐	┌ *14:4*♩ ┐	┌ *14:5*♩ ┐	┌ *14:6*♩ ┐
3)	┌ *21:2*♩ ┐	┌ *21:3*♩ ┐	┌ *21:4*♩ ┐	┌ *21:5*♩ ┐	┌ *21:6*♩ ┐
4)	┌ *28:2*♩ ┐	┌ *28:3*♩ ┐	┌ *28:4*♩ ┐	┌ *28:5*♩ ┐	┌ *28:6*♩ ┐

Exercises C

These exercises are designed to combine frames in ♩, ♪ or 𝅘𝅥𝅯 and the displacements that the permutations of these different frames produce. The exercises are thought of in odd number frames because they are the ones that can effectively produce displacements at the beginning or the end of an irregular grouping within the beat. Exercises C are actually divided into two differentiated sets of exercises.

1) The first one is worked out in order to accomplish a double goal, namely to:

- enable the superimposition of any gati on any odd number frame, expressed in 𝅘𝅥𝅯 starting anywhere in the beat;
- enable the change from an irregular grouping to a pulse in chatusra gati and vice versa.

The practice procedure consists of the following elements:

a. Superimpose chatusra, tisra, khanda or misra over the underlined number of the exercises below, which is always expressed in 𝅘𝅥𝅯
b. The remaining numbers should be done performing all matras in regular chatusra, also expressed in 𝅘𝅥𝅯

Therefore, if we take the example 2+<u>**3**</u>+3, the first and last digits should be done performing all the matras in regular chatusra. The underlined <u>**3**</u> serves as the frame over which any other gati is superimposed. In the case of 3, chatusra, khanda and misra should be superimposed. *(track 180)*

3: 1 + <u>3</u> <u>3</u> + 1 2 + <u>3</u> + 3 3 + <u>3</u> + 2

Superimpose chatusra, tisra and misra on the underlined number. The rest of the numbers should be done in regular chatusra. (track 181)

5: <u>5</u> + 3 3 + <u>5</u> 1 + <u>5</u> + 2 2 + <u>5</u> + 1

Superimpose chatusra, khanda and tisra on the underlined number. The rest of the numbers should be done in regular chatusra. (track 182)

7: <u>7</u> + 1 1 + <u>7</u> 2 + <u>7</u> + 3 3 + <u>7</u> + 2

2) The second part of these is similarly structured around odd number frames, but combining frames of ♩, ♪ or 𝅘𝅥𝅯 that share the same number. In fact, every exercise is a multiple one because the frames in ♩, ♪ or 𝅘𝅥𝅯 exchange their positions so that every frame would start in a different place within the beat. The first approach would then be to practise the three possible permutations while the frame in ♩ is always the starting frame.

Using the exercise on ⌐*4:5*♩¬ ⌐*4:5*♪¬ ⌐*4:5*𝅘𝅥𝅯¬ as an example, the first thing to take into consideration is that the frame in 𝅘𝅥𝅯 needs to be performed twice so that the whole exercise can finish on a beat. The first three exercises would then be *(track 183)*

- ***4:5♩ 4:5♪ 4:5𝅘𝅥𝅯 4:5𝅘𝅥𝅯***

- ***4:5♩ 4:5𝅘𝅥𝅯 4:5𝅘𝅥𝅯 4:5♪***

- ***4:5♩ 4:5𝅘𝅥𝅯 4:5♪ 4:5𝅘𝅥𝅯***

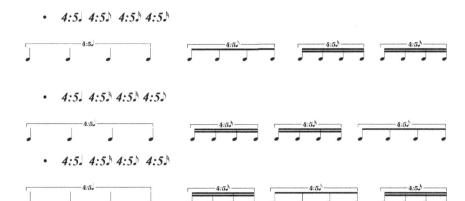

If a musician would like to delve deeper into all the permutations of ♩, ♪ and 𝅘𝅥𝅯, the remaining nine possibilities would be:

♩ 𝅘𝅥𝅯 𝅘𝅥𝅯 ♪	𝅘𝅥𝅯 𝅘𝅥𝅯 ♩ ♪	𝅘𝅥𝅯 ♩ 𝅘𝅥𝅯 ♪
𝅘𝅥𝅯 𝅘𝅥𝅯 ♪ ♩	𝅘𝅥𝅯 𝅘𝅥𝅯 ♩ ♪	𝅘𝅥𝅯 ♩ 𝅘𝅥𝅯 ♪
𝅘𝅥𝅯 ♪ ♩ 𝅘𝅥𝅯	𝅘𝅥𝅯 ♪ 𝅘𝅥𝅯 ♩	𝅘𝅥𝅯 ♩ ♪ 𝅘𝅥𝅯

Every exercise sown below can be practised exchanging its frames of ♩, ♪ and 𝅘𝅥𝅯 using all 12 possibilities. However, practising the first three permutations shown above should be sufficient.

In the following chart, the frame in 𝅘𝅥𝅯 is always followed by the reference ×2, meaning that this frame has to be realised twice in any permutation, whether played together or separately as shown above.

Tisra

1)	┌ *3:5♩* ┐	┌ *3:5♪* ┐	┌ *3:5𝅘𝅥𝅯* ┐ × 2
	┌ *3:7♩* ┐	┌ *3:7♪* ┐	┌ *3:7𝅘𝅥𝅯* ┐ × 2
2)	┌ *6:5♩* ┐	┌ *6:5♪* ┐	┌ *6:5𝅘𝅥𝅯* ┐ × 2
	┌ *6:7♩* ┐	┌ *6:7♪* ┐	┌ *6:7𝅘𝅥𝅯* ┐ × 2

Chatusra

1)	┌ *4:3♩* ┐	┌ *4:3♪* ┐	┌ *4:3𝅘𝅥𝅯* ┐ × 2
	┌ *4:5♩* ┐	┌ *4:5♪* ┐	┌ *4:5𝅘𝅥𝅯* ┐ × 2
	┌ *4:7♩* ┐	┌ *4:7♪* ┐	┌ *4:7𝅘𝅥𝅯* ┐ × 2

2) ┌─ ***8:3♩*** ─┐ ┌─ ***8:3♪*** ─┐ ┌─ ***8:3𝅘𝅥𝅯*** ─┐ × 2

┌─ ***8:5♩*** ─┐ ┌─ ***8:5♪*** ─┐ ┌─ ***8:5𝅘𝅥𝅯*** ─┐ × 2

┌─ ***8:7♩*** ─┐ ┌─ ***8:7♪*** ─┐ ┌─ ***8:7𝅘𝅥𝅯*** ─┐ × 2

Khanda

1) ┌─ ***5:3♩*** ─┐ ┌─ ***5:3♪*** ─┐ ┌─ ***5:3𝅘𝅥𝅯*** ─┐ × 2

┌─ ***5:7♩*** ─┐ ┌─ ***5:7♪*** ─┐ ┌─ ***5:7𝅘𝅥𝅯*** ─┐ × 2

2) ┌─ ***10:3♩*** ─┐ ┌─ ***10:3♪*** ─┐ ┌─ ***10:3𝅘𝅥𝅯*** ─┐ × 2 (only in very slow tempi)

┌─ ***10:7♩*** ─┐ ┌─ ***10:7♪*** ─┐ ┌─ ***10:7𝅘𝅥𝅯*** ─┐ × 2

Misra

1) ┌─ ***7:3♩*** ─┐ ┌─ ***7:3♪*** ─┐ ┌─ ***7:3𝅘𝅥𝅯*** ─┐ × 2

┌─ ***7:5♩*** ─┐ ┌─ ***7:5♪*** ─┐ ┌─ ***7:5𝅘𝅥𝅯*** ─┐ × 2

2) ┌─ ***14:5♩*** ─┐ ┌─ ***14:5♪*** ─┐ ┌─ ***14:5𝅘𝅥𝅯*** ─┐ × 2 (only in very slow tempi)

Exercises using Developmental Techniques as a Framework

Once Exercise sets A, B and C have been practised sufficiently, students should start combining the concepts of mixing frames of ♩, ♪ or 𝅘𝅥𝅯 through the four main developmental techniques (2nd, 3rd, 4th and 6th) explained earlier in the chapter. Practising phrases derived from these techniques helps crystallise the previous exercises into a more concrete format.

However, before starting to analyse and practise these exercises, it is useful to explain the possible sources that can be chosen in order to perform a particular passage; a performer will often have to play a given frame in a completely displaced position within the beat. Depending on the speed and whether the frame is expressed in ♩, ♪ or 𝅘𝅥𝅯, the performer will have to resort to one of the following sources.

a) *Nadai bhedam*: Any frame expressed in 𝅘𝅥𝅯 can be traced back to a nadai bhedam frame. If, for instance, a ***7:5𝅘𝅥𝅯*** starts on the second matra of the beat, all one needs to do is to 'remember' how this irregular grouping was played within a

┌──── ***4:5♩*** ────┐
┌─7─┐┌─7─┐┌─7─┐┌─7─┐

in the second bracket (which starts on the second 𝅘𝅥𝅯 of the beat, following the chatusra jathi 5 structure). If the same ***7:5*𝅘𝅥𝅯** is to be played starting on the second half of the beat, the performer should 'remember' how the third bracket was performed in the same nadai bhedam frame. Finally, if ***7:5*𝅘𝅥𝅯** is to be played starting on the fourth matra of the beat, the performer should resort to how the last bracket of the nadai bhedam frame was performed.

Therefore, for any frame *x*, provided that 1st, 2nd or 4th speed anuloma are used, the solution is to take the number of the frame (***5*𝅘𝅥𝅯** in this case) and use it as the number of beats of a nadai bhedam frame while always utilising 4 accents. (Subsequently, it will always be a result of using a ***4:3*♩**, ***4:5*♩**, ***4:6*♩** or ***4:7*♩** frame.) If the 3rd speed is used, then the nadai bhedam frame to be used is ***3:2*♩**, ***3:4*♩**, ***3:5*♩** or ***3:7*♩** (eventually ***6:4*♩**, ***6:5*♩** or ***6:7*♩**).

b) *Exercises C of anuloma-pratiloma combinations*: All the possible starting and ending positions of any possible irregular grouping (whether expressed in ♩, ♪ or 𝅘𝅥𝅯) can also be traced back to any of the possible permutations of these exercises. The performer needs to practise again the pertinent permutation and apply it to the specific point of the exercise (and, at a later stage, any piece of music). If, for instance, a 7:5♪ is to be played starting on the second matra of the beat, the musician should resort to practising the permutation ***7:5*𝅘𝅥𝅯** ***7:5*♪** ***7:5*𝅘𝅥𝅯** since the first frame of ***7:5*𝅘𝅥𝅯** ends on the second matra. Consequently, having previously internalised this exercise, the musician should be in a position to perform 7:5♪ starting on the second matra.

c) *Practice of even number frames starting in every matra of the beat*: All the frames against ***4*𝅘𝅥𝅯** or ***6*𝅘𝅥𝅯** should be practised starting on the 2nd, 3rd and 4th matras of the beat. It is of utmost importance that, for instance, a ***5:4*𝅘𝅥𝅯** or ***7:6*𝅘𝅥𝅯** should be performed with a downbeat feeling regardless of the starting point within the beat.

d) *Mixed jathi nadai bhedam*: Displaced frames can also be solved by 'remembering' the displacements of these frames within this concept; frames of 4 or 6 matras were combined with other numbers and, due to the alternating accents, a ***5:4*𝅘𝅥𝅯** or ***7:6*𝅘𝅥𝅯** was performed starting on every matra of the beat. In fact, this technique can also be applied to any odd or even number frame, since all of them were used in all combinations while practising this device. Therefore, any musician can resort to any of these four techniques (a–d) in order to manage any frame starting and finishing anywhere in the beat.

All exercises presented below will provide the student with the possibility of analysing all starting points and applying the best technique to perform the sequences with complete accuracy (also, listening to the examples recorded by B.C. Manjunath could help greatly). The examples below are to be practised without any phrasing, only with all the matras of the gati/speed.

Using Developmental Technique 2: Same Gati and Frames, Different Speeds

In the following exercises, the X on the right side of the bracket is to be replaced by 3, 4, 5, 6 or 7, since every example is to be practised with all the available pratiloma frames for each gati.

a) Chatusra: should be practised against 3rd, 5th, 6th and 7th pratiloma frames.

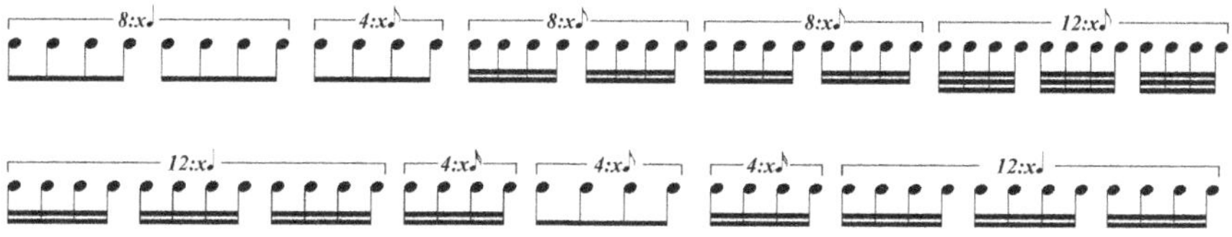

b) Khanda: should be practised against 3rd, 4th, 6th and 7th pratiloma frames.

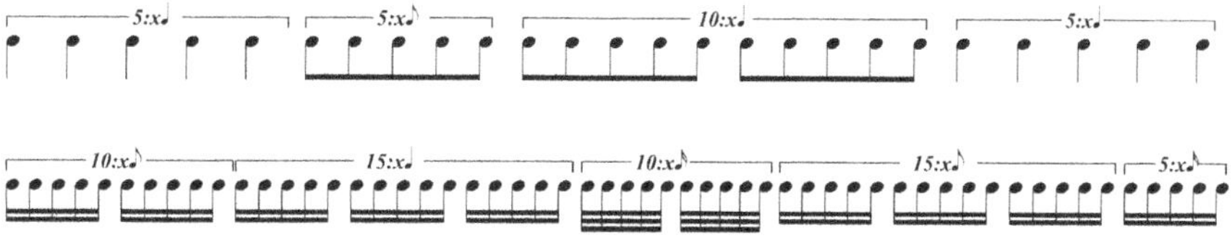

c) Tisra: should be practised against 2nd, 4th, 5th and 7th pratiloma frames.

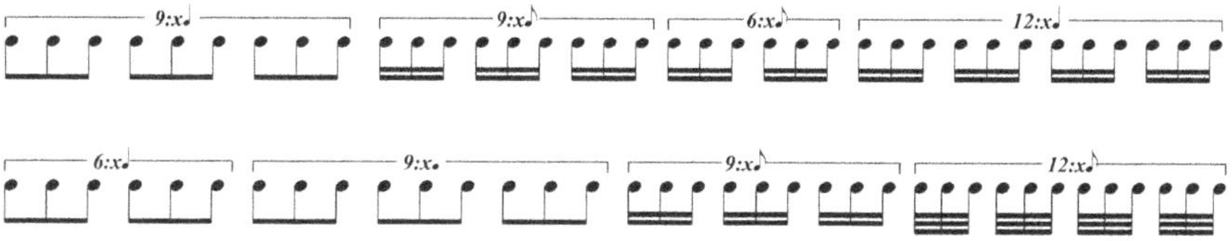

d) Misra: should be practised against 3rd, 4th, 5th and 6th pratiloma frames.

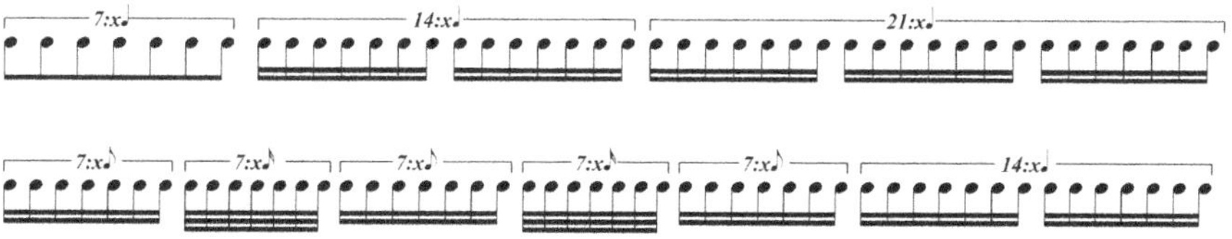

Using Developmental Technique 3: Same Gati and Speed, Different Frame

Every exercise should be practised with 1st and 2nd speeds.

a) Tisra

⌐x:5♪¬ ⌐x:5𝅘𝅥𝅯¬ ⌐x:5𝅘𝅥𝅯¬ ⌐x:7𝅘𝅥𝅯¬ ⌐x:7♪¬ ⌐x:7𝅘𝅥𝅯¬

⌐x:5𝅘𝅥𝅯¬ ⌐x:5♪¬ ⌐x:5𝅘𝅥𝅯¬ ⌐x:7𝅘𝅥𝅯¬ ⌐x:7𝅘𝅥𝅯¬ ⌐x:7♪¬

⌐x:5𝅘𝅥𝅯¬ ⌐x:7𝅘𝅥𝅯¬ ⌐x:7♪¬ ⌐x:5♪¬ ⌐x:5𝅘𝅥𝅯¬ ⌐x:7𝅘𝅥𝅯¬

b) Chatusra

⌐x:5♪¬ ⌐x:5𝅘𝅥𝅯¬ ⌐x:5𝅘𝅥𝅯¬ ⌐x:7𝅘𝅥𝅯¬ ⌐x:7♪¬ ⌐x:7𝅘𝅥𝅯¬

⌐x:5𝅘𝅥𝅯¬ ⌐x:5♪¬ ⌐x:5𝅘𝅥𝅯¬ ⌐x:7𝅘𝅥𝅯¬ ⌐x:7𝅘𝅥𝅯¬ ⌐x:7♪¬

⌐x:5𝅘𝅥𝅯¬ ⌐x:7𝅘𝅥𝅯¬ ⌐x:7♪¬ ⌐x:5♪¬ ⌐x:5𝅘𝅥𝅯¬ ⌐x:7𝅘𝅥𝅯¬

c) Khanda: two different exercises, one with 1st and 2nd speeds

⌐x:6♪¬ ⌐x:6𝅘𝅥𝅯¬ ⌐x:6𝅘𝅥𝅯¬ ⌐x:7𝅘𝅥𝅯¬ ⌐x:7♪¬ ⌐x:7𝅘𝅥𝅯¬

⌐x:6𝅘𝅥𝅯¬ ⌐x:6♪¬ ⌐x:6𝅘𝅥𝅯¬ ⌐x:7𝅘𝅥𝅯¬ ⌐x:7𝅘𝅥𝅯¬ ⌐x:7♪¬

⌐x:6𝅘𝅥𝅯¬ ⌐x:7𝅘𝅥𝅯¬ ⌐x:6𝅘𝅥𝅯¬ ⌐x:5𝅘𝅥𝅯¬ ⌐x:6♪¬ ⌐x:7♪¬

⌐x:7𝅘𝅥𝅯¬ ⌐x:4𝅘𝅥𝅯¬ ⌐x:6𝅘𝅥𝅯¬ ⌐x:5𝅘𝅥𝅯¬

Another exercise in khanda using 3rd and 4th speeds

⌐x:6♩¬ ⌐x:6♪¬ ⌐x:6♪¬ ⌐x:7♩¬ ⌐x:7♪¬ ⌐x:7♪¬

⌐x:6♪¬ ⌐x:6♩¬ ⌐x:6♪¬ ⌐x:7♪¬ ⌐x:7♩¬ ⌐x:7♪¬

⌐x:6♪¬ ⌐x:7♪¬ ⌐x:7♪¬ ⌐x:4♪¬ ⌐x:4♪¬ ⌐x:6♪¬ ⌐x:7♩¬

d) Misra: two different exercises, one with 1st and 2nd speeds

⌐x:5♪¬ ⌐x:5𝅘𝅥𝅯¬ ⌐x:5𝅘𝅥𝅯¬ ⌐x:6𝅘𝅥𝅯¬ ⌐x:6♪¬ ⌐x:6𝅘𝅥𝅯¬

⌐x:5𝅘𝅥𝅯¬ ⌐x:5♪¬ ⌐x:5𝅘𝅥𝅯¬ ⌐x:6𝅘𝅥𝅯¬ ⌐x:6𝅘𝅥𝅯¬ ⌐x:6♪¬

⌐x:5𝅘𝅥𝅯¬ ⌐x:6𝅘𝅥𝅯¬ ⌐x:5𝅘𝅥𝅯¬ ⌐x:4𝅘𝅥𝅯¬ ⌐x:5♪¬ ⌐x:6♪¬ ⌐x:5♪¬

Another exercise with 3rd and 4th speeds

⌐x:6♩¬ ⌐x:6♪¬ ⌐x:6♪¬ ⌐x:5♩¬ ⌐x:5♩¬ ⌐x:5♪¬ ⌐x:5♪¬

⌐x:6♪¬ ⌐x:6♩¬ ⌐x:6♪¬ ⌐x:5♪¬ ⌐x:5♩¬ ⌐x:5♪¬ ⌐x:6♪¬

⌐x:5♪¬ ⌐x:4♩¬ ⌐x:6♪¬ ⌐x:5♪¬ ⌐x:6♩¬ ⌐x:5♪¬

Using Developmental Technique 4: Same Gati, Different Speeds and Frames

a) Tisra with all speeds and frames

┌─ *3:4*♩ ─┐ ┌─ *9:2*♩ ─┐ ┌─ *3:5*♩ ─┐ ┌─ *9:4*♩ ─┐ ┌─ *6:2*♩ ─┐ ┌─ *9:5*♩ ─┐
┌─ *6:3*♩ ─┐ ┌─ *12:5*♩ ─┐ ┌─ *6:4*♩ ─┐ ┌─ *6:7*♩ ─┐ ┌─ *9:5*♩ ─┐ ┌─ *12:7*♩ ─┐
┌─ *6:4*♩ ─┐ ┌─ *9:2*♩ ─┐ ┌─ *12:3*♩ ─┐ ┌─ *12:5*♩ ─┐ ┌─ *6:4*♩ ─┐ ┌─ *9:7*♩ ─┐

b) Chatusra with all speeds and frames

┌─ *8:2*♩ ─┐ ┌─ *8:5*♩ ─┐ ┌─ *8:3*♩ ─┐ ┌─ *8:4*♩ ─┐ ┌─ *12:7*♩ ─┐ ┌─ *16:6*♩ ─┐
┌─ *8:5*♩ ─┐ ┌─ *12:4*♩ ─┐ ┌─ *12:5*♩ ─┐ ┌─ *8:6*♩ ─┐ ┌─ *16:5*♩ ─┐ ┌─ *8:7*♩ ─┐
┌─ *12:6*♩ ─┐ ┌─ *16:7*♩ ─┐ ┌─ *12:7*♩ ─┐ ┌─ *8:3*♩ ─┐ ┌─ *12:5*♩ ─┐ ┌─ *4:7*♩ ─┐
┌─ *4:3*♩ ─┐ ┌─ *8:7*♩ ─┐

c) Khanda with all speeds and frames

┌─ *10:3*♩ ─┐ ┌─ *15:4*♩ ─┐ ┌─ *5:7*♩ ─┐ ┌─ *15:5*♩ ─┐ ┌─ *20:6*♩ ─┐ ┌─ *20:7*♩ ─┐
┌─ *15:6*♩ ─┐ ┌─ *10:4*♩ ─┐ ┌─ *5:3*♩ ─┐ ┌─ *15:2*♩ ─┐ ┌─ *5:4*♩ ─┐ ┌─ *20:5*♩ ─┐
┌─ *5:6*♩ ─┐ ┌─ *20:3*♩ ─┐ ┌─ *10:7*♩ ─┐ ┌─ *10:6*♩ ─┐ ┌─ *15:4*♩ ─┐ ┌─ *10:3*♩ ─┐
┌─ *5:2*♩ ─┐ ┌─ *20:7*♩ ─┐ ┌─ *15:3*♩ ─┐ ┌─ *5:6*♩ ─┐

d) Misra with all speeds and frames

┌─ *7:3*♩ ─┐ ┌─ *14:2*♩ ─┐ ┌─ *21:7*♩ ─┐ ┌─ *28:6*♩ ─┐ ┌─ *14:5*♩ ─┐ ┌─ *7:2*♩ ─┐
┌─ *21:5*♩ ─┐ ┌─ *28:6*♩ ─┐ ┌─ *21:4*♩ ─┐ ┌─ *14:3*♩ ─┐ ┌─ *28:5*♩ ─┐ ┌─ *7:4*♩ ─┐
┌─ *21:6*♩ ─┐ ┌─ *28:6*♩ ─┐ ┌─ *28:3*♩ ─┐ ┌─ *21:4*♩ ─┐ ┌─ *7:6*♩ ─┐ ┌─ *21:5*♩ ─┐
┌─ *14:6*♩ ─┐ ┌─ *7:5*♩ ─┐

Using Developmental Technique 6: Same Frame, Different Gatis and Speeds

a) All gatis and speeds against 3 beats

┌─ *4:3*♩ ─┐ ┌─ *15:3*♩ ─┐ ┌─ *28:3*♩ ─┐ ┌─ *5:3*♩ ─┐ ┌─ *8:3*♩ ─┐ ┌─ *9:3*♩ ─┐
┌─ *10:3*♩ ─┐ ┌─ *14:3*♩ ─┐ ┌─ *7:3*♩ ─┐ ┌─ *16:3*♩ ─┐ ┌─ *20:3*♩ ─┐ ┌─ *21:3*♩ ─┐
┌─ *28:3*♩ ─┐ ┌─ *10:3*♩ ─┐ ┌─ *4:3*♩ ─┐ ┌─ *14:3*♩ ─┐ ┌─ *15:3*♩ ─┐ ┌─ *16:3*♩ ─┐

b) All gatis and speeds against 4 beats

⌐— ***3:4♩*** —¬ ⌐— ***10:4♩*** —¬ ⌐— ***21:4♩*** —¬ ⌐— ***7:4♩*** —¬ ⌐— ***12:4♩*** —¬ ⌐— ***15:4♩*** —¬

⌐— ***9:4♩*** —¬ ⌐— ***14:4♩*** —¬ ⌐— ***5:4♩*** —¬ ⌐— ***28:4♩*** —¬ ⌐— ***15:4♩*** —¬ ⌐— ***6:4♩*** —¬

⌐— ***21:4♩*** —¬ ⌐— ***10:4♩*** —¬ ⌐— ***7:4♩*** —¬ ⌐— ***9:4♩*** —¬ ⌐— ***5:4♩*** —¬ ⌐— ***8:4♩*** —¬

⌐— ***9:4♩*** —¬ ⌐— ***21:4♩*** —¬

c) All gatis and speeds against 5 beats

⌐— ***7:5♩*** —¬ ⌐— ***15:5♩*** —¬ ⌐— ***8:5♩*** —¬ ⌐— ***12:5♩*** —¬ ⌐— ***21:5♩*** —¬ ⌐— ***16:5♩*** —¬

⌐— ***15:5♩*** —¬ ⌐— ***4:5♩*** —¬ ⌐— ***9:5♩*** —¬ ⌐— ***28:5♩*** —¬ ⌐— ***6:5♩*** —¬ ⌐— ***20:5♩*** —¬

⌐— ***3:5♩*** —¬ ⌐— ***21:5♩*** —¬ ⌐— ***14:5♩*** —¬ ⌐— ***9:5♩*** —¬ ⌐— ***7:5♩*** —¬ ⌐— ***12:5♩*** —¬

⌐— ***21:5♩*** —¬ ⌐— ***16:5♩*** —¬ ⌐— ***7:5♩*** —¬ ⌐— ***6:5♩*** —¬

d) All gatis and speeds against 6 beats

⌐— ***4:6♩*** —¬ ⌐— ***15:6♩*** —¬ ⌐— ***28:6♩*** —¬ ⌐— ***5:6♩*** —¬ ⌐— ***8:6♩*** —¬ ⌐— ***9:6♩*** —¬

⌐— ***10:6♩*** —¬ ⌐— ***14:6♩*** —¬ ⌐— ***7:6♩*** —¬ ⌐— ***16:6♩*** —¬ ⌐— ***20:6♩*** —¬ ⌐— ***21:6♩*** —¬

⌐— ***28:6♩*** —¬ ⌐— ***10:6♩*** —¬ ⌐— ***4:6♩*** —¬ ⌐— ***14:6♩*** —¬ ⌐— ***15:6♩*** —¬ ⌐— ***16:6♩*** —¬

e) All gatis and speeds against 7 beats

⌐— ***6:7♩*** —¬ ⌐— ***15:7♩*** —¬ ⌐— ***21:7♩*** —¬ ⌐— ***20:7♩*** —¬ ⌐— ***4:7♩*** —¬ ⌐— ***9:7♩*** —¬

⌐— ***16:7♩*** —¬ ⌐— ***5:7♩*** —¬ ⌐— ***12:7♩*** —¬ ⌐— ***14:7♩*** —¬ ⌐— ***10:7♩*** —¬ ⌐— ***3:7♩*** —¬

⌐— ***15:7♩*** —¬ ⌐— ***8:7♩*** —¬ ⌐— ***20:7♩*** —¬ ⌐— ***6:7♩*** —¬ ⌐— ***16:7♩*** —¬ ⌐— ***5:7♩*** —¬

⌐— ***12:7♩*** —¬ ⌐— ***10:7♩*** —¬

Chapter 21

Derived Creative Techniques

Systematic Gati on Tirmanas

A tirmana is a phrase based on keeping the same distance between notes and decreasing this separation systematically. These distances can be turned into frames over which anuloma-pratiloma, in various forms, can be superimposed.

In this context, the difference in construction between the purvanga and uttaranga sections of a tirmana sequence allows for different approaches as to which developmental technique and gati can be chosen to superimpose over the frames. If one of the tirmanas analysed in Chapter 11 is taken as a first example, three different possibilities can be imposed on it. The tirmana is set to 2 cycles of a tala of 9 beats (72 matras). *(track 184)*

Purvanga

5 notes × 6 matras of separation =30 matras
5 notes × 4 matras of separation =20 matras
5 notes × 2 matras of separation =10 matras

Uttaranga

5 notes × 1 matra of separation =5 matras
5:4♪ =4 matras
5:3♪ =3 matras

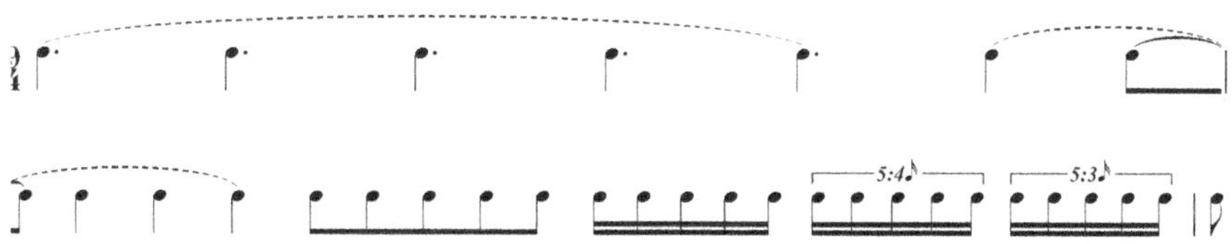

1) The Superimposition Occurs Only in the Purvanga Section

If this option is taken, the number of the superimposed gati must be the same as the number of notes of the phrase, so that when the uttaranga section is reached, the same gati is preserved. Consequently, the third developmental technique of anuloma-pratiloma combinations is the one to be applied (keeping the same gati and speed, changing the frame).

Therefore, if the number of notes of the tirmana phrase is 5, the gati to choose is khanda. The example below shows how khanda has been superimposed five times (the original number of notes) over the first three steps of the tirmana, the purvanga section:

1. Five times as a 5:3𝅘𝅥𝅮. (5 notes × 6 matras of separation)
2. Five times as a 5:4𝅘𝅥𝅯. (5 notes × 4 matras of separation)
3. Five times as a 5:4𝅘𝅥𝅰. (5 notes × 2 matras of separation)

This sequence is followed by the uttaranga that remains as in the original tirmana. *(track 185)*

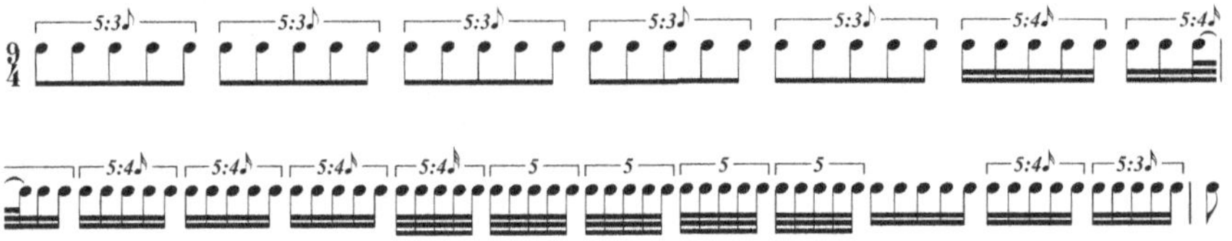

2) The Superimposition Occurs throughout the Whole Tirmana

This choice is, for obvious reasons, the most active and difficult to perform. Consequently, a slow gati is generally preferred. In the following example, tisra 1st speed has been chosen.

Although the first five frames can be seen as groupings of 3𝅘𝅥𝅮., in reality they conform to the possibility of using gati bhedam as one more speed of anuloma-pratiloma. Afterwards, every step takes tisra over the frame provided by the separation of matras in the original tirmana. Once the uttaranga is arrived at, every matra of the 5 notes × 1 matra of separation takes a triplet of 𝅘𝅥𝅯 and the last two steps (5:4𝅘𝅥𝅯. and 5:3𝅘𝅥𝅮.) take triplets of 𝅘𝅥𝅰 on every matra. *(track 186)*

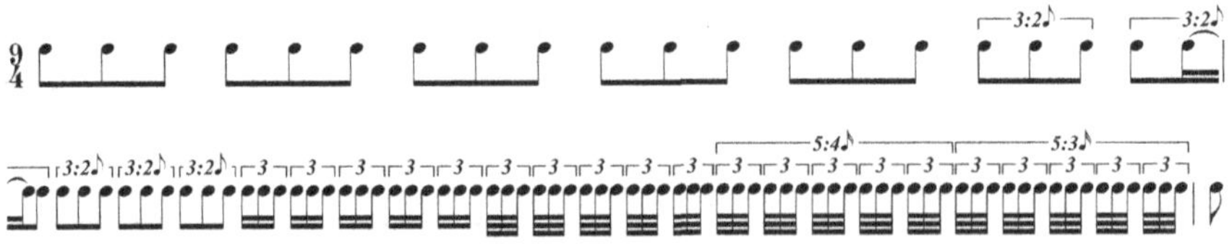

3) The Superimposition Occurs Only in the Purvanga Section, but the Gati Changes

This option is the only time in karnatic music where the *gati and frame change simultaneously*: as long as the gati change follows a concrete system, a gati change can occur whilst the frame is also changing.

The system is conceptually similar to a decreasing yati, in the sense that the number of the gatis will always decrease by the same number of matras. Consequently, a random choice of gatis is never applied to a tirmana sequence. The decrease in the example below is the same as the decrease in the number of matras of separation of the tirmana phrase (2 matras). This does not necessarily have to be the case, as long as:

- The decrease of gati or speed of gati responds to a clear system, always using the same number of matras.
- The number of notes in the first step of the uttaranga responds either to the pattern established by the previous gati changes, or is the same number as the last step of the purvanga.

A few examples are provided to illustrate the two different possibilities.

a. 11:6♪. 8:4♪. 5:2♪.

In example (a) above, the number of matras decreased in every gati is 3, and the last step uses the same gati as the number of notes of the first step of the uttaranga.

b. 11:6♪. 9:4♪. 7:2♪.

In example (b), the number of matras decreased per gati change is 2. The last step is misra, which leads into the uttaranga section that uses the number 5, thus responding to the pattern of decreasing the gati by 2 on every frame.

The recorded example responds to the first option: *(track 187)*

9:6♪. 7:4♪. 5:2♪.

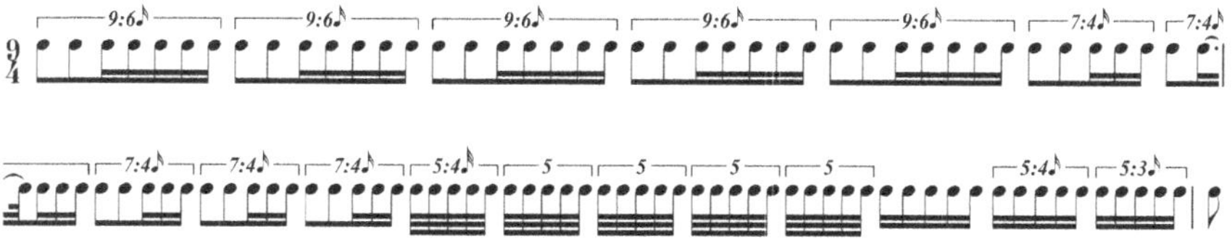

Three more examples are presented in a tirmana of tala 10. Each of them responds to one of the three techniques just explained, although the last one offers a slight variation. The tirmana is set to 2 cycles of tala 10 (80 matras), with the following structure: *(track 188)*

Purvanga

5 notes × 7 matras of separation=35 matras
5 notes × 5 matras of separation=25 matras
5 notes × 3 matras of separation=15 matras

Uttaranga

5 notes × 1 matra of separation=5 matras

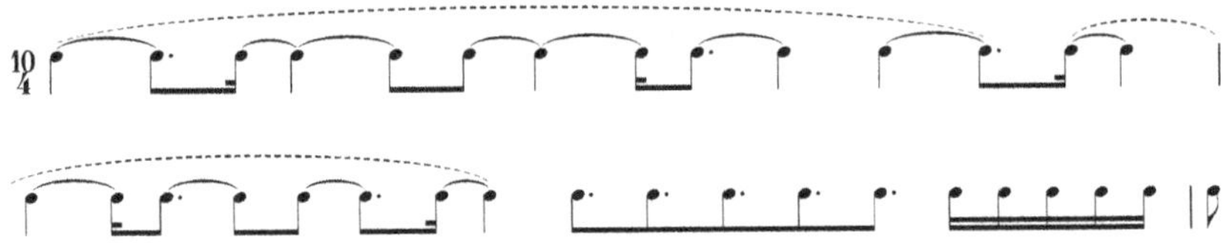

1) The Superimposition Occurs Only in the Purvanga Section

Since the number of notes in this tirmana is once again 5, the chosen gati needs to be khanda.

Five times as a 5:7♪	(5 notes × 7 matras of separation)
Five times as a 5:5♪	(5 notes × 5 matras of separation, using gati bhedam)
Five times as a 5:3♪	(5 notes × 3 matras of separation)

This sequence is followed by the uttaranga that remains as the original. *(track 189)*

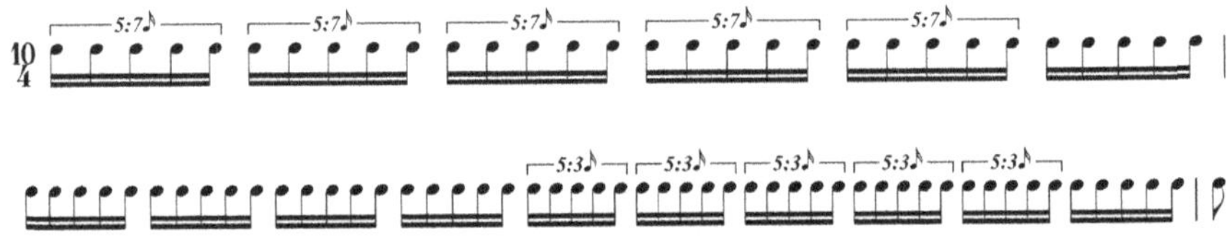

2) The Superimposition Occurs throughout the Whole Tirmana

The choice of tisra is taken again for this possibility, in order for the last step to be performed with relative ease. The third step of the purvanga uses gati bhedam (chatusra jathi 3). *(track 190)*

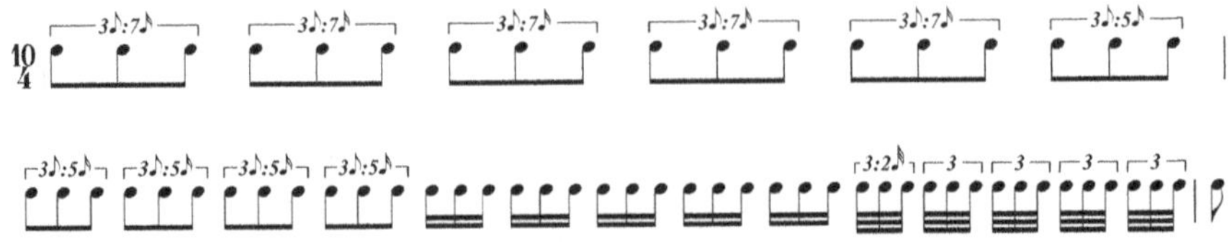

3) The Superimposition Occurs throughout the Whole Tirmana, but the Gati Changes

This is the variation on the third technique referred to above. All the steps of the tirmana, including the step of the uttaranga, respond to the systematic decrease of matras in the gati change. This possibly occurs because the uttaranga is relatively slow and has only one step. *(track 191)*

9:7♪ 7:5♪ 5:3♪ 3:1♪

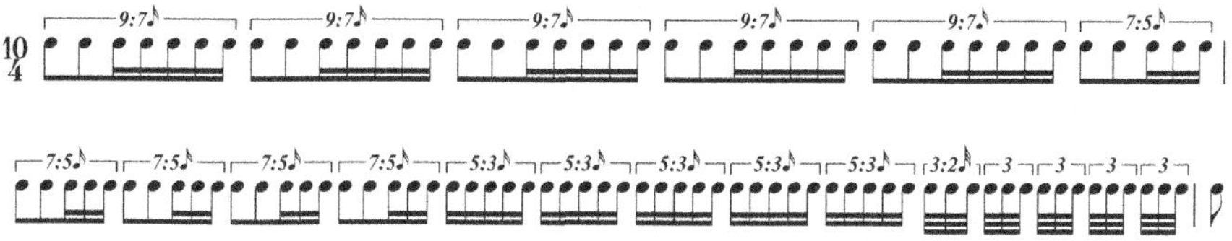

I think it is important to reiterate that this change of gati and frame occurs *exclusively* in this context and when utilising this particular technique. Karnatic musicians will never extrapolate this possibility to any other context, for the reasons explained in previous chapters regarding gati changes.

Poruttam B

The concept of poruttam has already been explained in Chapter 16. However, the difference between what I have coined poruttam 'A' and 'B' lies in the following:

- All the theme fragments and spaces created by deleting parts of the theme are spread throughout one cycle in poruttam 'B', as opposed to four in poruttam 'A'.
- Rather than employing and developing specific techniques, a short and single cell is developed per cycle by subjecting it to compression and expansion using combinations anuloma-pratiloma and gati bhedam principles exclusively; no phrasing modification is used on the cell at all.
- A sequence of poruttam 'B' needs to last for at least 3 cycles. However, the chosen cells are not developed throughout the sequence: only in the particular cycle where the cell is used does development take place, disregarding any relationship with any previous or subsequent cells.
- The number of notes chosen for the theme fragments tends to be shorter than in poruttam 'A': two or three notes are usually sufficient.

Poruttam 'B' ultimately consists of short passages of highly intricate and complex material, due to the exclusive use of anuloma-pratiloma and the almost continuous displacement of irregular groupings within the beat.

A 6-cycle example will suffice to illustrate this technique. This example is set to a tala of 27 beats, written 27/8 with an inner subdivision of 7 6 7 7.[1] The original theme is

and the fragmentation and subsequent empty spaces created through deletion of notes of the theme are

It can be observed that every theme fragment indeed uses only two or three notes, and that the last note of the second fragment is shortened by 5 matras.

The duration of the spaces is of 10, 9 and 8 matras respectively. These durations, as well as the position of the theme fragments within the tala, must remain unaltered; calculations must always fit into the aforementioned durations.

1) The first cycle uses a cell of 5 matras  subjected to the following development.

2) The second cycle uses a cell of 10 matras  that is actually split 6+4 for developmental purposes.

3) The third cycle again uses a cell of 5 matras , which leads to the following passage:

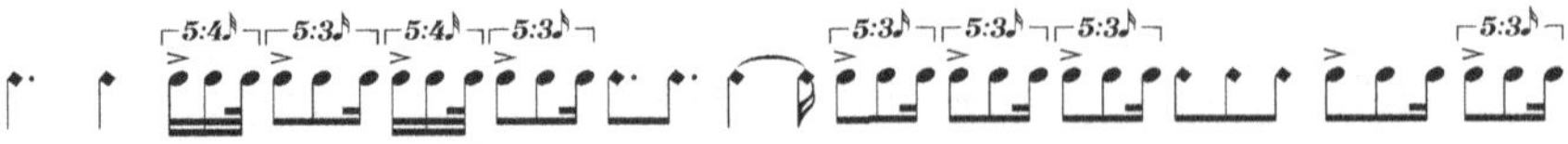

4) The fourth cycle uses a cell of 9 matras  against 10 and 8 matras in 1st and 3rd spaces.

1 This sort of tala will be explained in Chapter 22.

5) The fifth cycle once again uses a cell of 5 matras  subjected to different anuloma speeds.

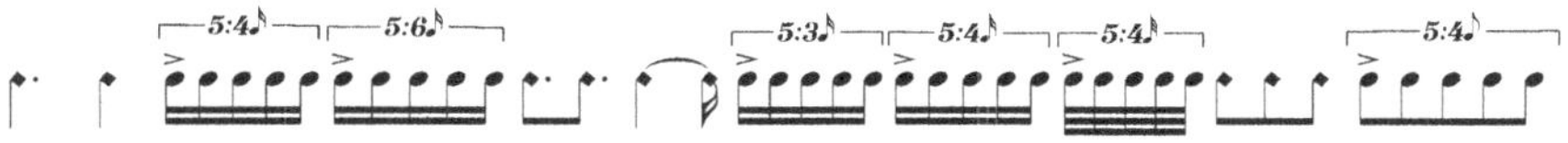

6) The final cycle uses a short cell of 3 matras .

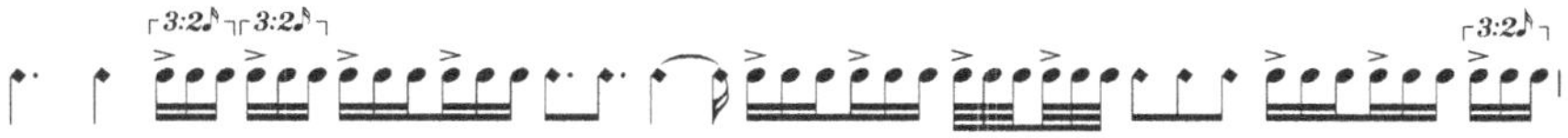

It is interesting to observe that, although a cell of 5 matras has been chosen three times, all examples have been developed using entirely different anuloma-pratiloma material as well as different atmospheres and degrees of activity. The entire sequence is thus as follows: *(track 192)*

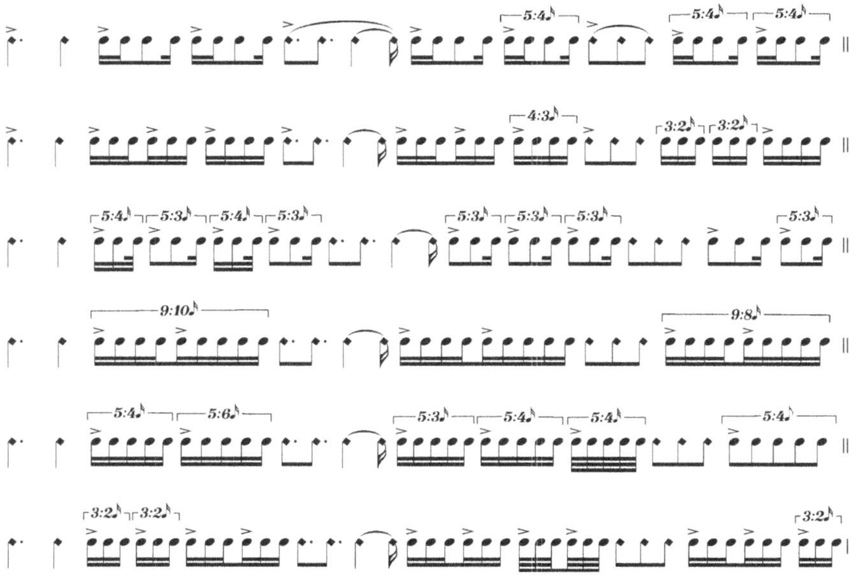

D: Recent Developments

This final section of Part I describes the most recent developments in karnatic music which, although used by only a minority of musicians, are nonetheless concepts that are likely to become mainstream in karnatic music in a few decades.

Karnatic music is continually expanding the possibilities of the 'tradition'. For its musicians, any new development is simply another way of looking at or deepening what has already existed for many centuries. Talk about 'experimental' or 'traditional' music means nothing to karnatic musicians, since everything is just an enhancement of the possibilities laid down ages before.

The concepts of the three chapters in this section are also likely to be of great interest to western musicians, since they explore new gatis; an immense variety of new talas and ways to construct them; and finally, how to use gati changes more frequently.

Chapter 22
Tala Prastara

Tala prastara means the construction or creation of new talas. As was seen in the first chapter, the concept and construction of talas in karnatic music is not merely a question of how many beats exist in a metre: many more parameters define the elaboration of a tala. This and the following two chapters will present the developments of the last century, the different ways used to create new talas and how the material seen so far is used in the new talas.

Shadanga Talas

This is the old tala system that was employed for many centuries before the prominent karnatic composer Purandaradasa elaborated and implemented the suladi tala system around the sixteenth century. Since the 1960s, however, it has been the system that has inspired musicians to produce more 'experimental' music.[1] Simultaneously, its 'rebirth' has been largely responsible for the profound and huge development of the concept of combinations anuloma-pratiloma, a concept that was studied and practised by musicians but seldom performed or used creatively (except essentially for the elements seen in Chapter 7).

Brief Historical Perspective

Comprehensive research into the history and use of this type of talas before the fourteenth century would be quite complicated, due to the extreme difficulty of obtaining any information. Moreover, it would be of exclusively historical/ethnomusicological value, since the way in which shadanga talas have been utilised over the last 50 years is completely different to the way they were used until the sixteenth century. The former can constitute a very interesting way of organising talas (or the concept of cycle as a whole) within a western framework. However, this line of research would have moved away from the main focus and purpose of this book. Therefore, just a few essential and well-known points will be considered here.

Shadanga talas were constructed upon the existence and combination of six angas (*shad* means six in Sanskrit). However, as opposed to the highly regulated

[1] This is to use a western term that somehow does not fit with the Indian way of thinking since, for them, everything is a result of the possibilities offered by 'tradition'.

suladi system, there were no restrictions as to the order, position or number of angas that could be used to construct a tala. The three other angas were *guru*, *pluta* and *kakapada*.

A very important characteristic was that there were two different ways of counting and calculating the number of beats in the tala: *aksharakala* (or *kala*) and *matra* methods. Every kriya ('conducting' pattern) could also vary from region to region.

The kala system was used for slow tempo pieces and, due to its construction, featured 'fractional' (as karnatic musicians say) or incomplete beats.[2] The matra system was used to play long cycles in faster tempi.

Although I approached quite a number of South Indian academics and musicians, regrettably no one seemed to really know how the different angas were conducted. The only element that appears to be clear is that in the matra system the guru, pluta and kakapada angas were rendered by movements of the hand towards and around the head. However, no one seems to really know how the angas in the kala system were reckoned. The finger-count of the laghu anga was created by Purandaradasa for the suladi system. It appears that the way of reckoning with hand movements towards and around the head was very unclear due to the length of the angas, and for the simple reason that musicians often had to perform in temples and other venues where the light was rather dim.

The number of talas (108) seems to have more of a religious-numerological significance than a musical or organisational one: namely, in India, the number 108 has a strong religious significance, crystallised for example in the fact that every major deity (Krishna, Vishnu, Ganesha etc) always has 108 different names and/or attributes.

The number of beats for every anga was as follows:

Name of Anga	**Kala System**	**Matra System**
Anudrutam (A)	¼	1
Drutam (D)	½	2
Laghu (L)	1	4
Guru (G)	2	8
Pluta (P)	3	12
Kakapada (K)	4	16

Before explaining the possible causes of dissolution of this tala system and, more importantly, its current usage, the chart of 108 shadanga talas will first be presented as taught in universities in South India (Table 22.1). The duration of the laghu in the first three talas is of 5 matras or 1+¼ kalas. In the other 105 talas it

2 Beats that would be shorter or longer than 4 matras in chatusra. As can be seen in the chart below, they could be thought of as western metres of 1/16, 1/8 or 3/16.

is of 4 matras or 1 kala. Once again, no one seems to know the reason behind this difference in the first three talas.

Table 22.1 Chart of 108 shadanga talas

Name of Tala	Angas	Kalas	Matras
1) Chachchatputa	G G L P	8+ ¼	3
2) Chachaputa	G G L G	6+ ½	26
3) Shatpitaputrika	P L G G L P	12+ ½	50
4) Sampadveshtaka	P G G G P	12	48
5) Udghatta	G G G	6	24
6) Adi	L	1	4
7) Darpana	D D G	3	12
8) Charchari	D D A L D D A L D D A L D D A L D D A L D D A L D D A L D D A L D D A L	18	72
9) Shimhalila	L D D D L	3+ ½	14
10) Kandarpa	D D L G G	6	24
11) Simhavikrama	G G G L P L G L	16	64
12) Sriranga	L L G L P	8	32
13) Ratilila	L G G L	6	24
14) Ranga	D D D D G	4	16
15) Parikrama	L L L G G	7	28
16) Pratyanga	G G G L L	8	32
17) Gajalila	L L L L A	4+ ¼	17
18) Tribhinna	L G P	6	24
19) Viravikrama	L D D G	4	16
20) Hamsalila	L L A	2+ ¼	9
21) Varnabhinna	D D L G	4	16
22) Rangadyotana	G G G L P	10	40
23) Rajachudamani	D D L L L D D L G	8	32
24) Raja	G P D D G L P	12	48
25) Simhavikridita	L L P G L G P L P	17	68
26) Vanamali	D D D D L D D G	6	24
27) Chatusra varna	G G L D D G	8	32
28) Traysra varna	L D D L L G	6	24
29) Misra varna	D D D D A D D D D A D D D D A	6+ ¾	27
30) Rangrapadipa	G G L G P	10	40
31) Hamsanada	L L P D D G	8	32
32) Simbanada	L G G L G	8	32
33) Malikamoda	L L D D D D	4	16
34) Sarabhalila	L L D D D L L	5+ ½	22
35) Rangabharana	G G L L P	9	36

36) Turangalila	D D L	2	8
37) Simhanandana	G G L P L G D D G G L P L P G L L K G G L L G	32	128
38) Jayasri	G G L L G	8	32
39) Vijayananda	L L G G G	8	32
40) Prati	L D D	2	8
41) Duitiya	D L D	2	8
42) Makaranda	D D L L L G	6	24
43) Kirti	G L P G L P	12	48
44) Vijaya	G G G L G	9	36
45) Jayamangala	L G P L G P	12	48
46) Rajavidyadhara	L G D D	4	16
47) Matya	L L G L L L L	8	32
48) Jaya	L G L L D D	6	24
49) Kudukka	D D L L	3	12
50) Nissaruka	L G G	5	20
51) Krida	D D A	1+ ¼	5
52) Tribhangi	L G L G	6	24
53) Kokilapriya	G L P	6	24
54) Srikirti	G G L L	6	24
55) Bindumali	G D D D D G	6	24
56) Sama	L L D D A	3+ ¼	13
57) Nandana	L D D P	5	20
58) Udikshana	L L G	4	16
59) Mattika	G D P	5+ ½	22
60) Dhenkika	G L G	5	20
61) Varnamattika	D D L D D	3	12
62) Abhinandana	L L D D G	5	20
63) Antarakrida	D D D A	1+ ¾	7
64) Malla	L L L L D D A	5+ ¼	21
65) Dipaka	D D L L G G	7	28
66) Ananga	L P L L G	8	32
67) Vishama	D D D D A D D D D A	4+ ½	18
68) Nandi	L D D L L G	6	24
69) Mukunda	L D D L G	5	20
70) Kanduka	L L L L G	6	24
71) Eka	D	½	2
72) Ata	L D D L	3	12
73) Purna kankala	D D D D G L	5	20
74) Khanda kankala	D D G G	5	20
75) Sama kankala	G G L	5	20
76) Vishama kankala	L G G	5	20
77) Chatus	G D D D	3+ ½	14
78) Dombuli	L A L A	2+ ½	10
79) Abhanga	L P	4	16
80) Raya vankola	G L G D D	6	24
81) Laghu sekhara	L A	1+ ¼	5

82) Pratapa sekhara	P D D A	4+ ¼	17
83) Jagajhampa	G D D D A	3+ ¾	15
84) Chaturmuka	L G L P	7	28
85) Jhampa	D D A L	2+ ½	9
86) Pratimaya	L L G G L L	8	32
87) Garugi	D D D D D A	3+ ¾	15
88) Vasanta	L L L G G G	9	36
89) Lalita	D D L G	4	16
90) Rati	L G	3	12
91) Karana yati	D D D D	2	8
92) Yati	G L L L	5	20
93) Shat	D D D D D D	3	12
94) Varhana	D D L P	5	20
95) Varna yati	L L P P	8	32
96) Rajanarayana	D D L G L G	7	28
97) Madana	D D P	4	16
98) Karika	D D D D A	2+ ¼	9
99) Parvati lochana	D D L D D G G L L L L G L L	15	60
100) Srinandana	G L L P	7	28
101) Lila	D L P	4+ ½	18
102) Vilokita	L G D D P	7	28
103) Lalitapriya	L L G L L	6	24
104) Jhallaka	G L L	4	16
105) Janaka	L L L L G G L L G	12	48
106) Lakshmisa	D D L L P	6	24
107) Ragavarhana	D D A D P	4+ ¾	19
108) Utsava	P L	4	16

Two talas from Table 22.1 will serve to illustrate how to count in the shadanga system:

59) Mattika	G D P	5+ ½	22

In the kala system, guru (G) is 2 beats long, drutam (D) is ½ beat long and pluta (P) is 3 beats long; adding up the three angas will result in 5+½ beats. Now simply multiply by four to give the number of beats in the matra system (22 beats). Taking the second example:

107) Ragavarhana	D D A D P	4+ ¾	19

In the kala system, once again a drutam is ½ beat long (there are 3 in this tala), the anudrutam (A) is ¼ beat and the pluta is 3 beats; added up, the total of 4+¾ is achieved. Similarly, multiplied by 4, the 19 beats of the matra system is arrived at.

Musical Developments that Contributed to the Disappearance of Shadanga Talas

As explained above, every method had a sort of 'function' in terms of tempo. However, as the result of a possibly slow process occurring over a long time span, on many occasions these functions were interchanged. Additionally, if talas of 48, 60 or, the longest, 128 beats were used in slow tempo, the feeling of cycle would most likely disappear. On the other hand, if pieces of 2+½ or 4+¾ beats were performed in fast tempi, angas as anchor points for the music would simply vanish.

The concept of jati laghu, the cornerstone of the suladi system construction, made its appearance at some point between the tenth and eleventh centuries. It expanded from the length of 1 beat (kala method) or 4 beats (matra method) to the following:

Laghu	**Kala**	**Matra**
Tisra	¾	3
Chatusra	1	4
Khanda	1+ ¼	5
Misra	1+ ¾	7
Sankirna	2+ ¼	9

Except for the first three talas, which already had a laghu of 1+¼ or 5 beats, every tala in Table 22.1 that used a laghu could choose from additional possibilities to replace the 4 matras or 1 kala. There were 84 talas with laghu; if multiplied by the five options, the chart expanded to 420 talas, plus the first 3 talas with no jati laghu and 21 talas with no laghu. Thus, added up, the original chart of 108 talas expanded into a chart of 444 talas in each method of reckoning, which for all practical purposes produced 888 talas.

Although quite a number of talas shared the same number of beats, their inner construction differed. For instance, the following talas always produced 5 beats in the kala system and 20 in the matra system. However, their inner construction differed, having 1 or 2 laghus respectively:

60) Dhenkika	G L G	5	20
62) Abhinandana	L L D D G	5	20

The different talas that the use of jati laghu could create would have been:

Dhenkika:		
Tisra laghu	4+ ¾	19
Chatusra laghu	5	20
Khanda laghu	5+ ¼	21
Misra laghu	5+ ¾	23
Sankirna laghu	6+ ¼	25

Abhinandana

Tisra laghu	4+ ½	18
Chatusra laghu	5	20
Khanda laghu	5+ ½	22
Misra laghu	6+ ½	26
Sankirna laghu	7+ ½	30

Consequently, the more than probable religious factor behind the creation of a chart with 108 possibilities was superseded at some point by musical needs, and the jati laghu concept was born.[3]

Shoshadanga Tala System

The appearance of the jati laghu at some point gave way to a more far-reaching system of 16 angas. However, in reality it was not the case that karnatic music went from a 6-anga system to another system with 16 angas where all of them could be freely combined. It was simply an expansion of the jati laghu concept applied to drutam, guru and pluta as well. Therefore, the chart of 108 talas (Table 22.1) served as a starting point, and the length of every anga was susceptible to being replaced by another anga of the same name but with a different suffix and duration.

Name of Anga	Kala	Matra
Anudrutam	¼	1
Drutam	½	2
Drutam virama	¾	3
Laghu	1	4
Laghu virama	1+ ¼	5
Laghudrutam	1+ ½	6
Laghudrutam virama	1+ ¾	7
Guru	2	8
Guru virama	2+ ¼	9
Gurudrutam	2+ ½	10
Gurudrutam virama	2+ ¾	11
Pluta	3	12
Pluta virama	3+ ¼	13
Plutadrutam	3+ ½	14
Plutadrutam virama	3+ ¾	15
Kakapada	4	16

[3] It is actually quite surprising to realise that one of the elements that contributed to the dissolution of the shadanga talas became one of the cornerstones in the construction and thought behind the creation of the suladi system.

It does not take many calculations to appreciate the enormous number of talas that could (and were) created with this system: for every laghu, guru and pluta the musician could choose from four different options plus two for the drutam. One example is given here to illustrate all the possibilities within one tala:

96) Rajanarayana	D D L G L G	7	28

If drutam virama is applied and laghu and guru remain as in the original, then the length will be:

	DV DV L G L G	7+ ½	30
Laghu virama	D D LV G LV G	7+ ½	30
Laghudrutam	D D LD G LD G	8	32
Laghudrutam virama	D D LDV G LDV G	8+ ½	34
Guruvirama	D D L GV L GV	7+ ½	30
Gurudrutam	D D L GD L GD	8	32
Gurudrutam virama	D D L GDV L GDV	8+ ½	34

This shows that when only one of the angas is replaced, the same number of beats is obtained. But drutam virama could also be combined with any of the three additional laghus and/or guru options, which results in 21 different combinations. Added to the previous seven options, this tala can give rise to 28 different talas with each counting method; thus for all practical purposes 56.

With the aforementioned problem of lack of clarity while reckoning the talas, and the almost 'exuberant' number of new talas that could be created upon a single tala – together with the poor communication infrastructure of India in the eleventh to fifteenth centuries – the seed of limitless creativity that the jati laghu and shoshadanga systems gave to the 'container' of karnatic music (the tala system), simultaneously became the seed of its own destruction. There was no agreement on how to conduct all the new talas: some became popular in some regions while being completely ignored in others. Consequently, every region or centre would eventually have created completely different talas, and it seems likely that karnatic music fractured into many different styles. Fortunately, or unfortunately (we will never know), someone with the reputation that Purandaradasa seemed to have enjoyed during his lifetime decided that something needed to be regulated and compromises made. He therefore reorganised the whole system into one much simpler and easier to transmit – that of the suladi talas. Possibly the biggest loss was the complete disappearance of the talas with 'fractional' or incomplete beats.

Current Use of Shadanga Talas: Mukhy System

Although several attempts were made over the last five centuries to re-establish the shadanga talas, it was not until the 1960s that this system, with numerous and far-reaching variations on the original, saw another dawn within the karnatic music system.

Dr M. Balamuralikrishna (b. 1930), one of the most prestigious karnatic singers and composers of the twentieth century, was largely responsible for the rebirth of this system. Unlike any previous attempt, this time a 'best of both worlds' approach was taken and made fruitful in a new fashion whereby new talas (*tala prastara*) could be created by using certain premises of both suladi and shadanga talas.

Balamuralikrishna's main and more 'revolutionary' contribution was the invention of what he coined the *mukhy* system. He felt that karnatic music needed to recover some of the structural possibilities that the shadanga talas could offer, namely, the use of incomplete beats (using the kala method) and longer talas that could be performed with a more 'chapu tala' feel and tempo (using the matra method).

What interested Balamuralikrishna about the shadanga talas was thus the multitude of talas that the original chart of shadanga talas and the application of the jati laghu and shoshadanga systems on this chart could generate. He therefore concluded that, since all karnatic musicians were familiar with the kriya (conducting pattern) of all suladi talas, this kriya should somehow remain, while simultaneously making systematic variations to it in order to accommodate the shadanga talas. Consequently, and *purposely ignoring the inner construction of the shadanga talas*, he took *exclusively the resulting number of beats of a particular tala* and distributed them using the kriya of a suladi tala but adding or subtracting beats to certain points of the tala. This is one of the principles of the mukhy system.

The very first step towards the implementation of the mukhy system was to add beats to the tala and anga sams of a suladi tala in a systematic manner. Balamuralikrishna coined the following terms:

Trimukhy:	3 beats on every sam
Panchamukhy:	5 beats on every sam
Saptamukhy:	7 beats on every sam
Navamukhy:	9 beats on every sam

The rest of beats in the tala would have either 2 or 4 beats. The three-step procedure he decided to use to translate the shadanga tala into a new tala was as follows:

1) Choose a shadanga tala, for example:

107) Ragavarhana	D D A D P	4+¾	19

2) Ignore the construction of D D A D P and work exclusively with the 4+¾ or the 19 beats.

3) Choose a kriya of any suladi tala and figure out how to distribute the number of beats. For reasons that will become clearer later, Balamuralikrishna and most his followers favoured the matra over the kala system.

If the 19 beats of the tala Ragavarhana is chosen, different methods and suladi tala kriyas could be applied. Here are a few examples using the trimukhy system (3 beats per sam).

a. The adi tala pattern (L4 D D): If 3 beats are applied to every sam (there are 3 in this tala), the number 19 is reached. Therefore, the pattern for this 'shadanga' tala would be *(track 193)*

   3 2 2 2|3 2|3 2

b. The tisra matya pattern (L3 D L3): This has the same number of beats as the previous example. However, the distribution of beats and the choice of pattern of the suladi tala will have a tremendous effect on many techniques. Once again, 3 beats are applied to every sam and the result is *(track 194)*

   3 2 2|3 2|3 2 2

c. The khanda eka pattern (L5). If 4 beats are used for every finger-count of the laghu and 3 beats for the tala sam (3 4 4 4 4), the result will be 19 beats. *(track 195)*

The following example is the transcription of a rehearsal of a piece in this tala in its matra form (19 beats, or 19/8 in western notation), composed by Jahnavi Jayaprakash and B.C. Manjunath. Pattern (a) shown above was chosen to conduct the piece, using adi tala (L4 D D), with the resulting inner division of 3 2 2 2|3 2|3 2. Besides the phrasing around the tala construction, different phrasing with crossing accents in a sort of short sequence of jathi or gati bhedam can be heard, next to yati mukthays of the A and C types along with a 6-note tirmana. This simply shows that most of the techniques seen in the book so far can and are used in this context as well.

Combinations anuloma-pratiloma and moharas need a separate explanation. The use of the former in particular experienced a formidable increase due to the characteristics of the mukhy system and the concept of regrouping the inner construction of the tala, which will be explained in Chapter 23. *(track 196)*

Soram kattu in Shadanga tala (19 beats: 3+2+2+2 / 3+2 / 3+2)

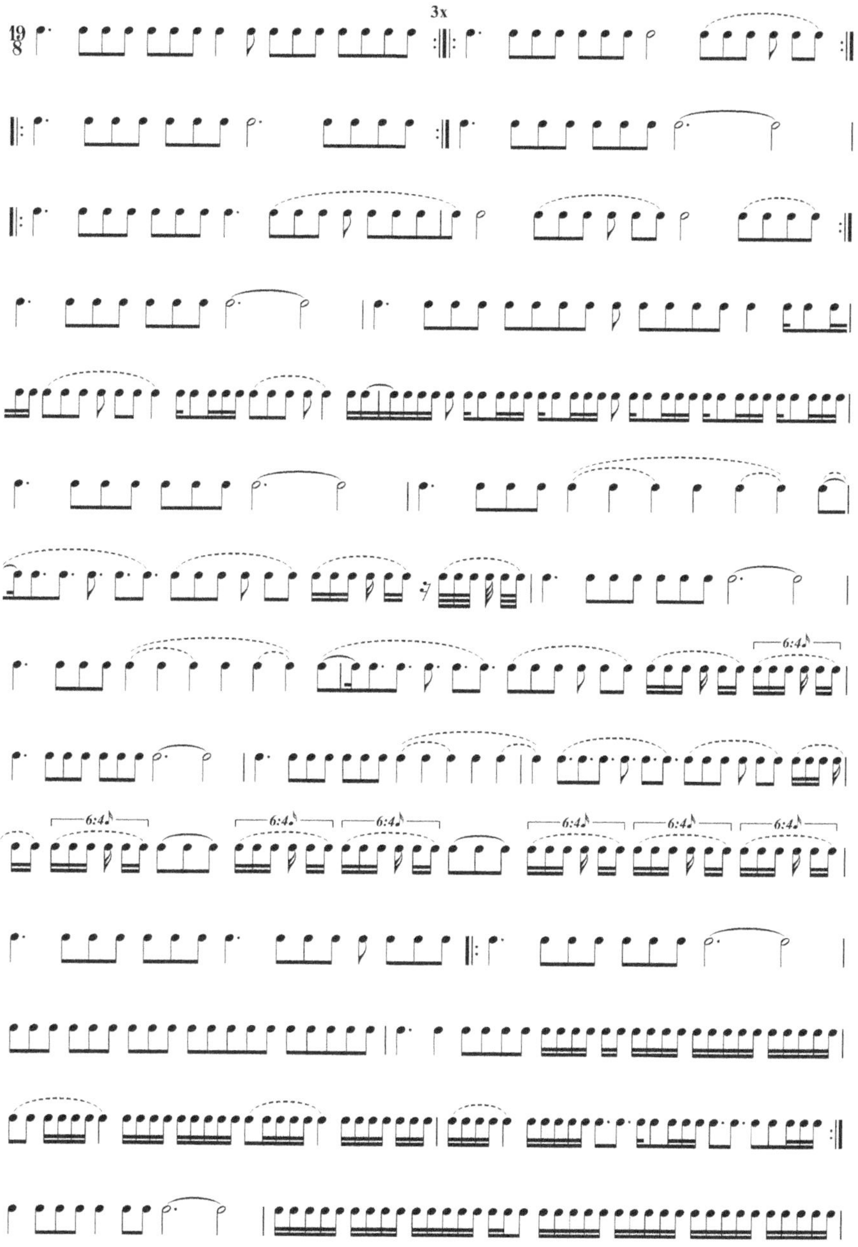

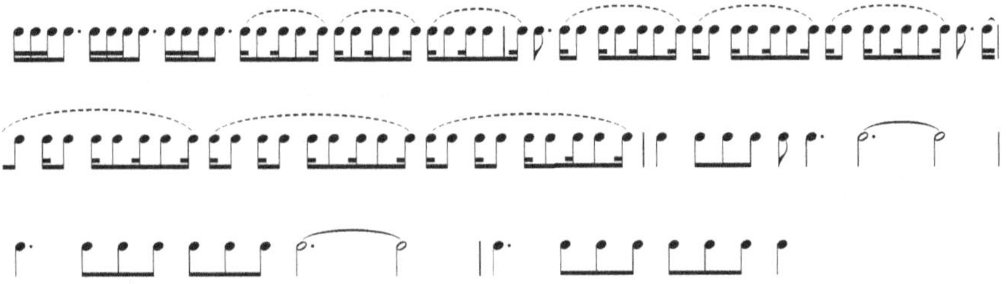

Kala Method with the Mukhy System

The following kriya process has been used:

- *Talas with x number of beats + ¼*: If using, for instance, a tala of 5+¼, the choice will be any suladi tala of 5 beats (the inner division is of no importance in this context). Each of the first 4 beats is counted as a 4/16 and the last beat becomes a 5/16. The 'extra' ¼ of the original shadanga tala becomes a 5/16 by adding the 𝅘𝅥𝅯 to the previous beat.
- *Talas with x number of beats + ½*: If the tala 7+½ is taken into account, any suladi tala of 7 beats would be chosen and conducted as a 6/4 followed by a 3/8. Once again, the 'extra' ½ is added to the previous beat to create another metre.
- *Talas with x number of beats + ¾*: For the tala of 4+¾ shown above, any suladi tala of 5 beats would be chosen. It will be conducted as a 4/4 followed by a 3/16. Consequently, the last beat will always be shortened by one 𝅘𝅥𝅯

The following examples are the transcriptions of the theme and the percussion duo of a piece by L. Shankar in this last tala of 4+¾. *(tracks 197 and 198)*

Theme in Shadanga tala (19 matras)

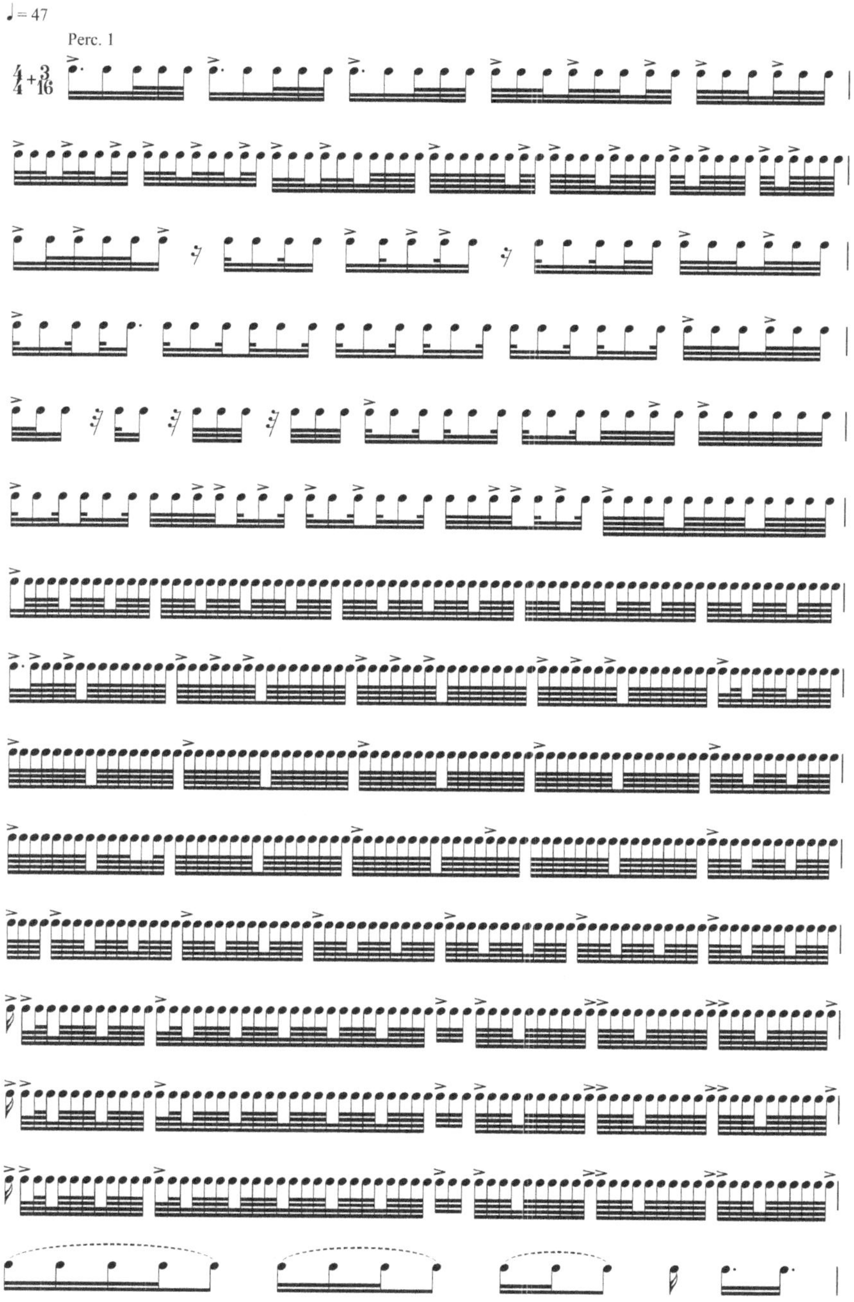
♩ = 47
Perc. 1
4/4 + 3/16

Perc. 2

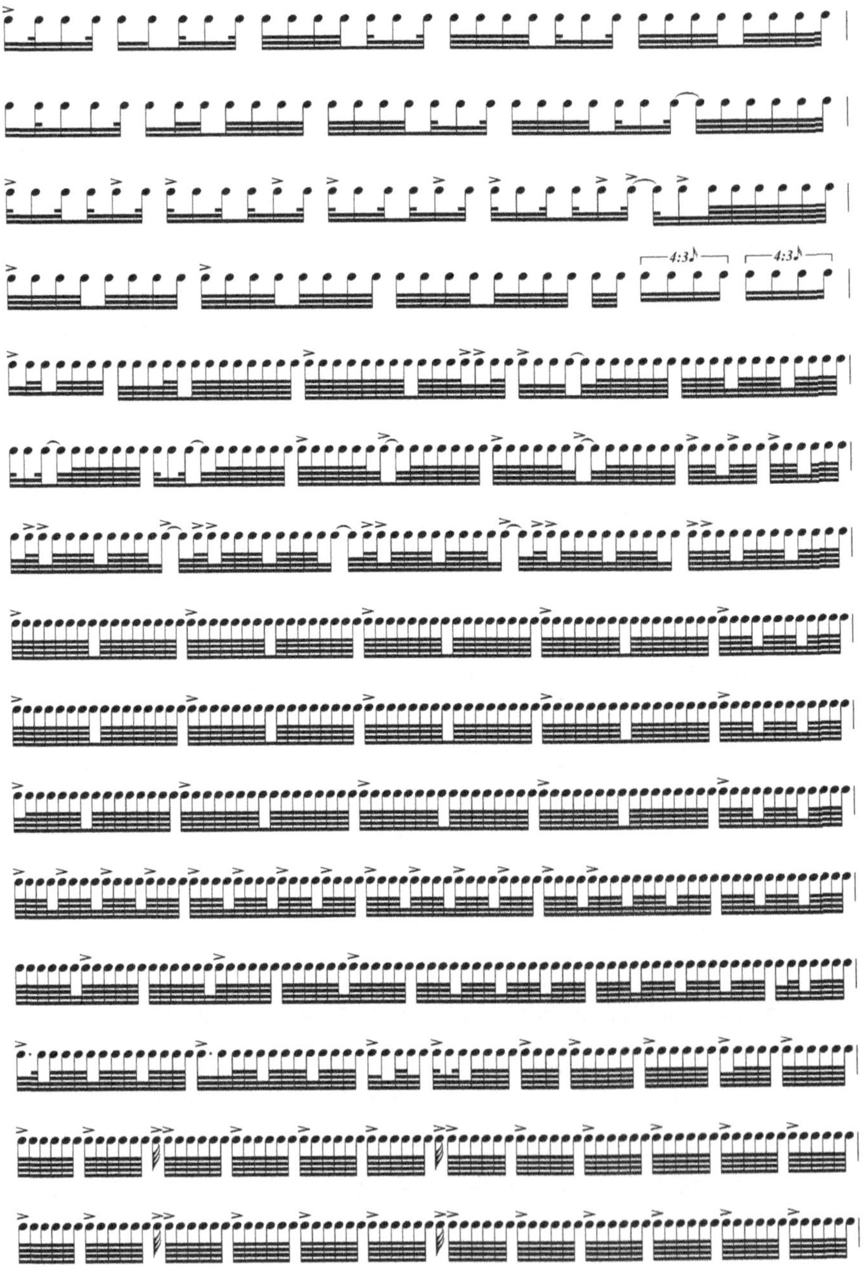

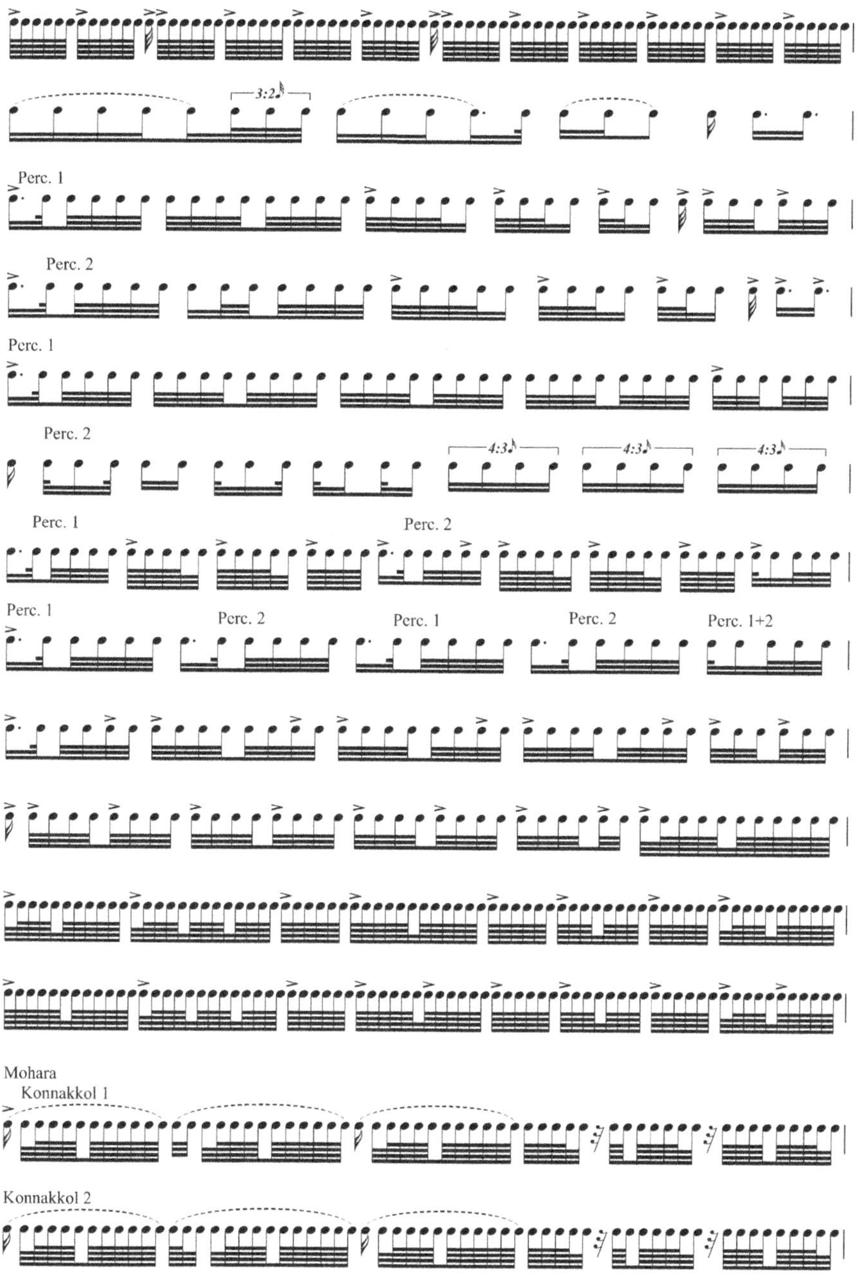
3:2
Perc. 1
Perc. 2
Perc. 1
Perc. 2
4:3
4:3
4:3
Perc. 1
Perc. 2
Perc. 1
Perc. 2
Perc. 1
Perc. 2
Perc. 1+2
Mohara
Konnakkol 1
Konnakkol 2

Konnakkol 1+2

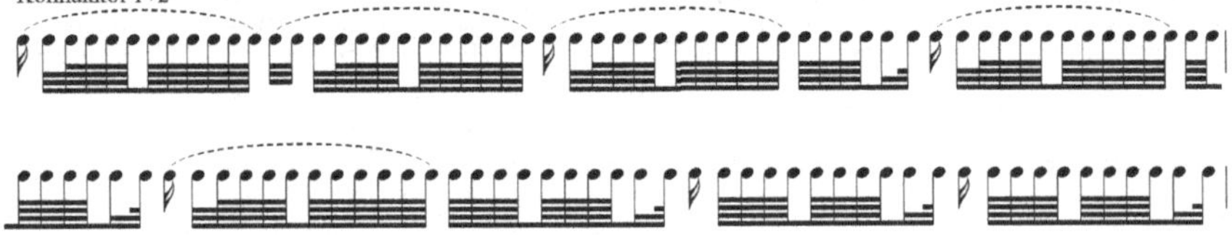

Mukthay

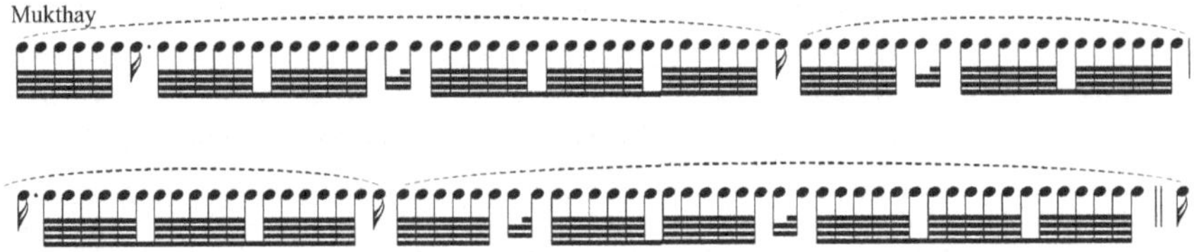

Chapter 23

Further Development of the Mukhy System

After the initial period described in the previous chapter, Dr Balamuralikrishna and many other musicians started to go beyond the self-imposed restrictions of using the tri, pancha, sapta and navamukhy exclusively on every sam of the tala. New paths of tala prastara started to take shape as long as logic and coherence in the choice of number of beats for every sam or finger-count were scrupulously observed. Different numbers started to be used in different parts of the tala, or different angas were treated differently.

Another important step was that the constructed tala would have nothing to do with the shadanga tala chart anyway, or with any of the possible ways of enhancing it (namely, the jati laghu and shoshadanga systems). Today, this phenomenon is in fact increasingly becoming the common practice.

Essentially, the 'return' of the shadanga talas provoked important changes in many aspects of karnatic music, the most important of which were the possibility of having many more, and more intricate, talas and the development of the use of combinations anuloma-pratiloma. At this point, musicians create talas without consulting the shadanga tala chart; with the aid of the jati laghu and shoshadanga systems, possibly any conceivable number could be found. However, musicians tend to create talas with one of the following objectives in mind:[1]

- A concrete number of beats, in which case they would proceed to distribute them as explained thus far, but without necessarily looking for an 'academic justification' as to how the number of beats were obtained or chosen by taking the shadanga tala as starting point.
- A concrete construction mixing a different number of mukhy beats and treating each anga with a self-constructed set of rules.

Therefore, Balamuralikrishna's great triumph was indeed to keep the suladi tala kriya patterns as the starting point to implement his invention: the mukhy system. Liberation from the initial self-imposed restrictions has enabled karnatic musicians to create new talas without having to justify them as being the result of a shadanga tala or a tala created with the aid of any of its developments (jati laghu or shoshadanga systems).

For the first option described above, the tala of 27/8 shown in Chapter 13 (yatis prastara) and poruttam 'B' is a good example.

---

[1] I reiterate the importance that karnatic musicians give to keeping a clear logic and coherence in the thought behind the construction.

Although a tala of 27 beats exists in the shadanga tala chart (tala 39, *misra varna*) the composer of this piece just wanted to have this number in order to recreate, with a shortened beat, a very well-known composition in misra chapu (7/8) whose theme was 4 cycles long. Other aims were the creation of a tala subdivision that would enable him to experiment with two types of moharas that could be constructed within this system and, ultimately, interesting frame possibilities for anuloma-pratiloma.

The suladi tala chosen for kriya purposes was tisra dhruva (L3 D L3 L3). A trimukhy is applied to every sam while every finger-count of the laghus takes 2 beats. The sole innovation here is that the number of beats assigned to the second 'beat' of the drutam is also 3 beats long, therefore differentiating the drutam from the laghu construction. The subdivision is thus *(track 199)*

3 2 2|3 3|3 2 2|3 2 2

The second option (a concrete construction mixing different numbers of 'mukhy beats') is becoming more of a 'trend' nowadays: the goal is not so much how many beats the tala will have, but rather how to organise the number of beats provided by the mukhy system within a particular suladi tala structure, and how to treat every type of anga differently while keeping a coherence in its construction.

An example for this second option is the *pallavi* and subsequent development with rhythmical sangatis in a tala of 44/16. The composer was interested in exploring all the possible mukhy numbers in one anga and keeping 4 beats per finger-count in the other angas.

The choice of suladi tala kriya was khanda triputa (L5 D D). On every 'beat' of the L5 all the available numbers were used, in increased order as follows – 3 4 5 7 9 – whereas in every 'beat' of each drutam the number 4 remained. Therefore the tala has the following inner division: *(track 200)*

3 4 5 7 9|4 4 4 4

The composition is by A.R.A.K Sharma. *(track 201)*

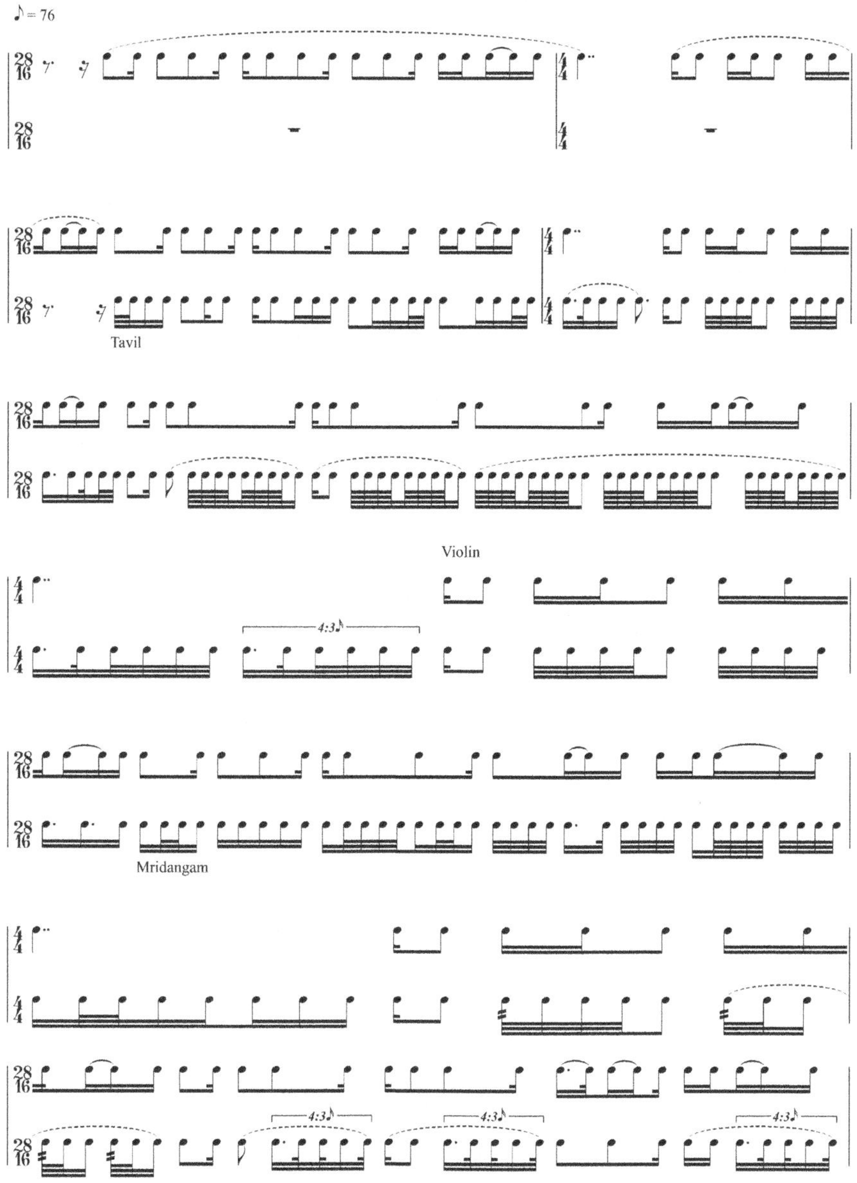
♪ = 76
Tavil
Violin
Mridangam
4:3♪

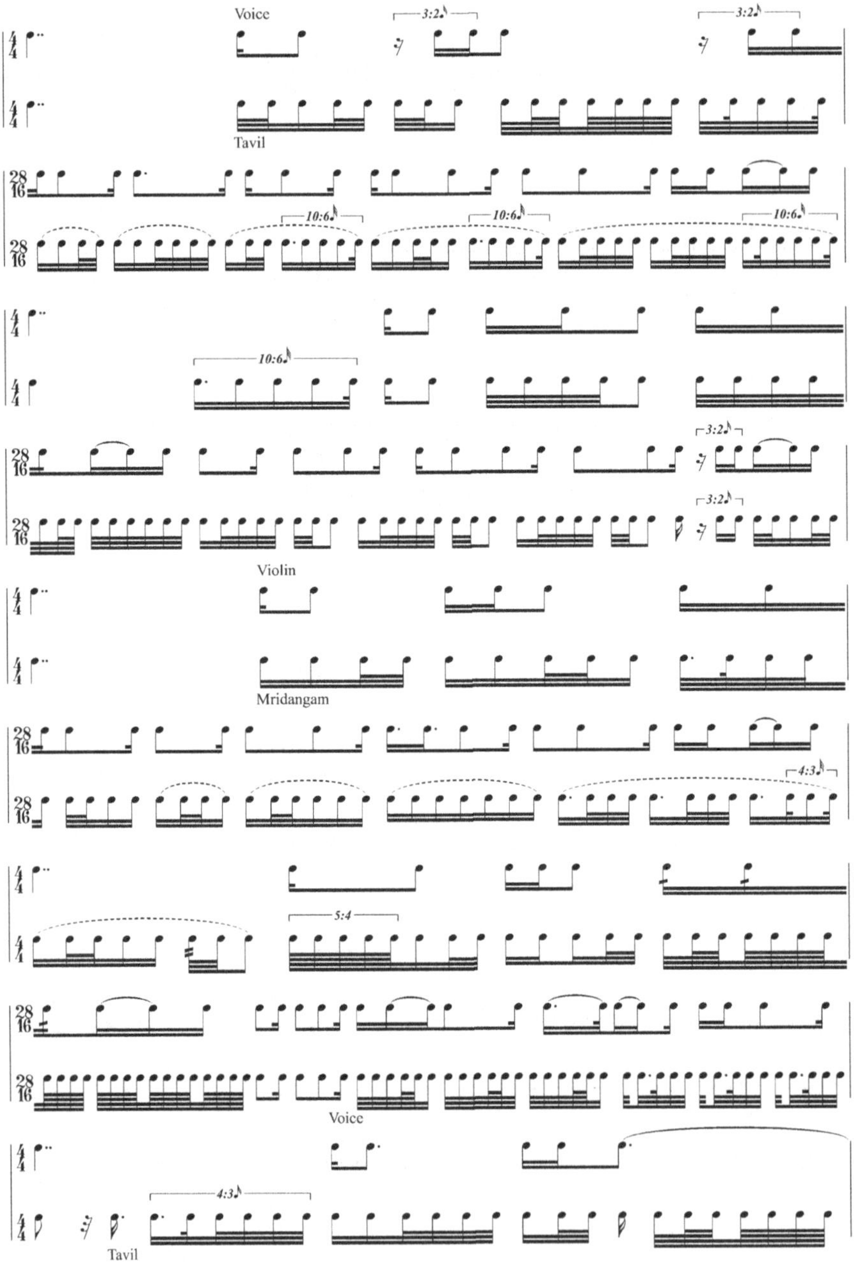
Voice
3:2
3:2
Tavil
10:6
10:6
10:6
10:6
3:2
3:2
Violin
Mridangam
4:3
5:4
Voice
4:3
Tavil

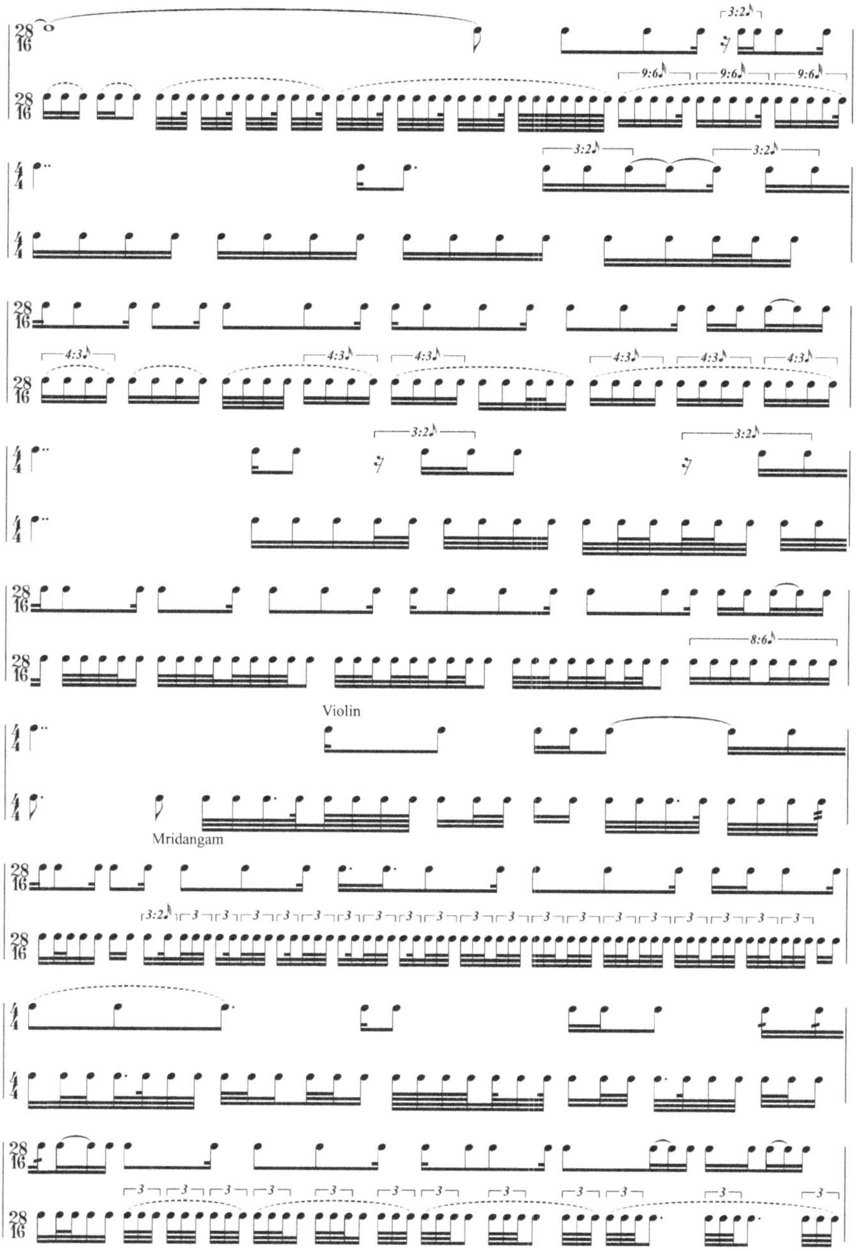
Violin
Mridangam

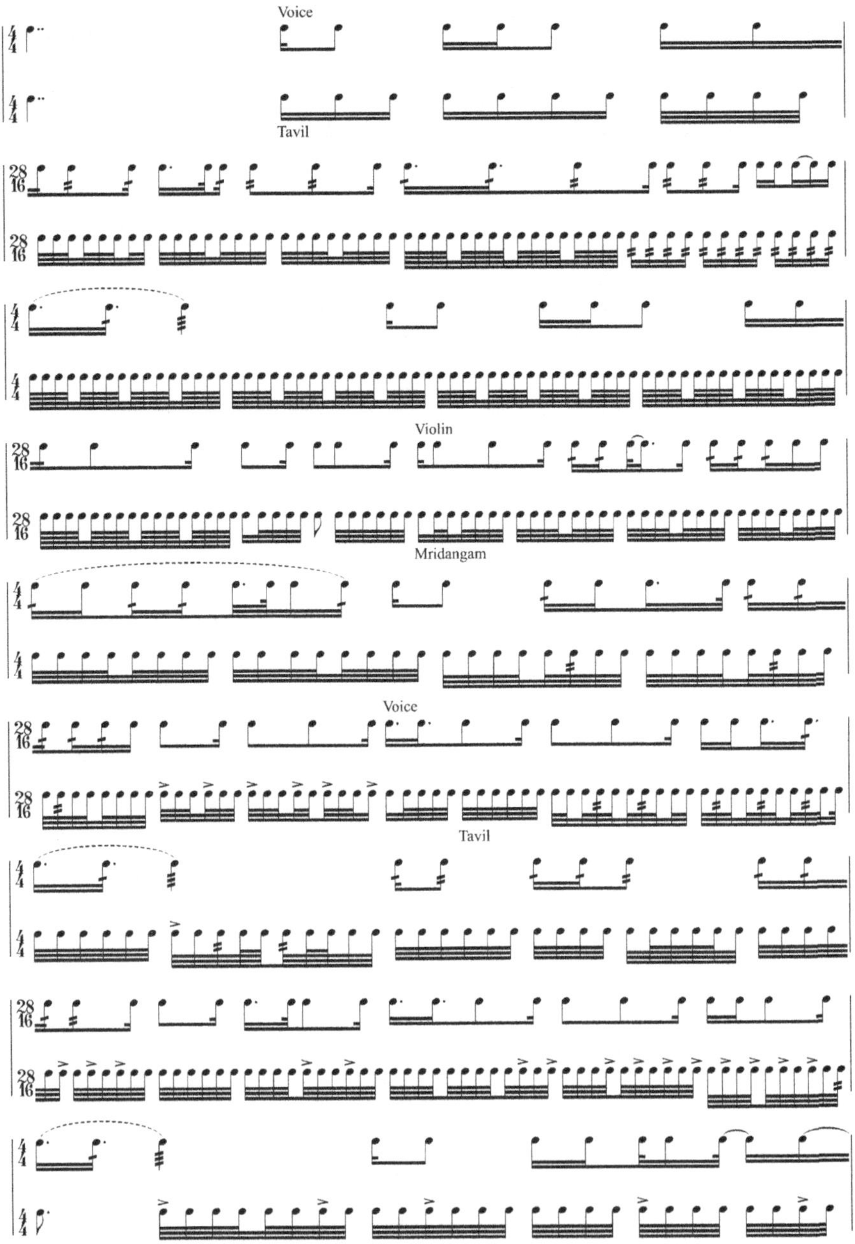
Voice
Tavil
Violin
Mridangam
Voice
Tavil

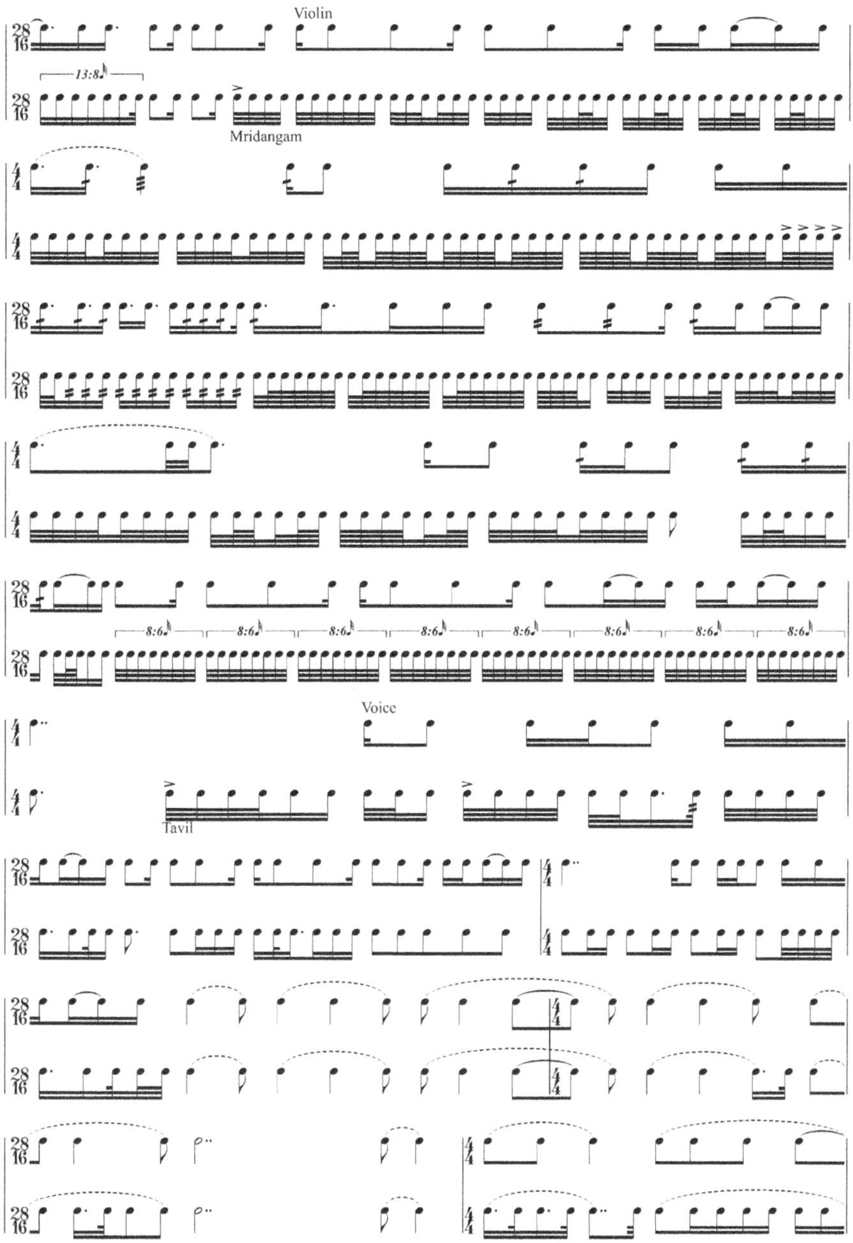
Violin
13:8
Mridangam
8:6
8:6
8:6
8:6
8:6
8:6
8:6
8:6
Voice
Tavil

The reader may wonder whether this proliferation of new talas can succeed when the birth of new talas in the eleventh to the fourteenth centuries was one cause of the total dissolution of the shadanga system. The answer comes from karnatic musicians:

> Since the 1990s, everything can be recorded in audio or video format, and either we can explain it to other musicians, record click tracks for them, or simply rely on the fact that video recordings of concerts and even rehearsals circulate in the market.

In other words, the evolution of infrastructure, communications and technology has made possible what six centuries ago endangered the unity of karnatic music.[2]

Tala Combinations

Tala combinations are talas constructed upon two suladi talas of different duration used one after the other in a cyclic manner. The real karnatic term for tala combinations is *dhruvarupaka* talas, a name which is derived from the first ever creation of a new tala by combining two different suladi talas. This occurred at the beginning of the twentieth century in order to expand the possibilities of the 35 suladi talas.

Therefore, any two talas can be taken and used alternately, thereby constantly forming a new tala. Once the two talas are presented, they form a new 'unit' and are treated as any other existing tala. In other words, the two talas would never be used randomly (for example, three cycles of one tala followed by one of the other tala, and afterwards two cycles of the first tala followed by three of the second etc). There are three anchor points in these new talas:

1. tala sam of the first tala as the strongest point;
2. tala sam of the second tala as the second strong point of resolution;
3. anga sams of both talas.

After a couple of decades, combining a suladi tala with a chapu tala became another option. Due to the short duration of the chapu talas, musicians could choose to use 1–5 cycles of the tala (a choice that remains unaltered for the whole piece), thus creating a new cyclic metre. Generally, the choice of cycles of the chapu tala would be an uneven number (1, 3 or 5) to create a more interesting tala structure (repeating a chapu tala two or four times could be felt as a suladi tala performed once or twice). Since all chapu talas have an odd number of beats, their repetition 1, 3 or 5 times avoids the feeling that the whole structure can be 'conducted' in ♩

A transcription of a theme in 37 beats can be found below. The structure of the tala combination takes an adi tala (L4 D D) of 8♩ or 16♪ followed by three times misra chapu (7/8 repeated three times gives 21♪). Thus, 16/8 plus 21/8 results in

[2] Also, we must not forget the rigorous training undertaken by most karnatic musicians. I have seen how this piece in 44/16 was taught to a singer in two days to be performed at a concert the following day, while keeping tala throughout the whole piece and improvising a long section.

37/8, which constitutes a new cyclic metre that is repeated throughout the entire piece. *(track 202)*

Previous Techniques in the New Talas

Every technique explained so far can be used within the new talas without any problem, except for nadai bhedam. Nadai bhedam needs the regularity that the suladi talas provide. The irregularity in the beating of all new talas makes the performance of nadai bhedam an almost impossible task. Therefore, this technique to create polypulses can be used exclusively within a suladi tala context.

The concept that has benefited most from the advent and development of the new talas is combinations anuloma-pratiloma. In fact, it can be said that, in general, this technique is easier to perform (or karnatic musicians have adapted this technique better) in the context and peculiarities of the new talas – especially those using the matra counting with the mukhy system – than within the suladi tala system.

Regrouping of the Inner Division

The mukhy system is not exclusively the concept of redistributing a given number of beats within the framework of a suladi tala: it also created the notion of *regrouping these beats into larger frames*. This regrouping implies that two or more contiguous 'numbers' in which the tala is subdivided can become one frame against which a gati (using an anuloma-pratiloma developmental technique) can be superimposed. It *does not* mean that the total number of beats of the tala is redistributed in an entirely different way: the original distribution of beats for every sam or finger-count and their order within the tala remain the same throughout the piece.

If the previous example of 19/8 with the pattern of tisra matya (L3 D L3) is taken, the concept of regrouping the inner division would probably become clearer. The inner division is

3 2 2   3 2   3 2 2

The bigger structure, the large 'conducting' gesture resulting from this distribution of beats is

7   5   7

A few examples of regrouping are shown below. *(track 203)*

1) 3 4 3 2 3 4

This is the result of adding up the numbers 2 2 of the first and third parts of the tala.

2) 3 2 5 2 3 4

In this example, the third and fourth numbers (2 and 3) are added, producing a 5♪ frame. The last 4 is, once again, the result of adding up the last two digits.

3) 5 5 5 4

This example breaks the boundaries of the initial subdivision even further. The first 5 is the result of adding the first and second numbers (3 and 2); the second 5 of adding the third and fourth numbers (2 and 3); the third 5 of adding the fifth and sixth numbers (3 and 2); and the last 4 is once again the result of adding up the last two numbers.

4) 3 7 5 4

The last example uses the option of adding three contiguous numbers: this is the case of 7, which is the result of adding up the second, third and fourth numbers (2, 2 and 3); 5 is again arrived at by adding together the fifth and sixth numbers (3 and 2).

There are two important points to take into consideration while regrouping the existing division of the tala:

a. The kriya or conducting pattern will always remain the same and will not change to adapt to the different regroupings. This notion is common to the general idea in karnatic music of not tampering with the tala: any technique creating crossing accents or polypulses never modifies the tala or tempo.
b. A regrouping can occur exclusively with the existing numbers, and a new frame can never be the result of using a weak beat as part of the additions. For instance, in the previous tala a regrouping resulting in the numbers 4 or 6 for the first frame is never possible. Only adding 3+2 or 3+2+2 (giving thus 5 or 7) is possible as a first frame.

Similarly, if 5 is taken as the first frame, the second frame must be either 2 or the result of adding 2+3 or 2+3+2. Therefore, a frame of 3, 4 or 6 can never be the second frame if 5 was the first frame.

A few musical examples are presented below, using the 3rd developmental technique of combinations anuloma-pratiloma as the source for the phrasing.

1) Original inner division 3 2 2 3 2 3 2 2 with khanda 1st speed *(track 204)*

⌐ *5:3♪* ¬ ⌐ *5:2♪* ¬ ⌐ *5:2♪* ¬ ⌐ *5:3♪* ¬ ⌐ *5:2♪* ¬ ⌐ *5:3♪* ¬ ⌐ *5:2♪* ¬ ⌐ *5:2♪* ¬
⌐ *5:3♪* ¬ ⌐ *5:2♪* ¬ ⌐ *5:2♪* ¬ ⌐ *5:3♪* ¬ ⌐ *5:2♪* ¬ ⌐ *5:3♪* ¬ ⌐ *5:2♪* ¬ ⌐ *5:2♪* ¬

2) First regrouping 3 4 3 2 3 4 with misra 1st speed *(track 205)*

⌐ *7:3♪* ¬ ⌐ *7:4♪* ¬ ⌐ *7:3♪* ¬ ⌐ *7:2♪* ¬ ⌐ *7:3♪* ¬ ⌐ *7:4♪* ¬
⌐ *7:3♪* ¬ ⌐ *7:4♪* ¬ ⌐ *7:3♪* ¬ ⌐ *7:2♪* ¬ ⌐ *7:3♪* ¬ ⌐ *7:4♪* ¬

3) Second regrouping 3 2 5 2 3 4 with tisra 2nd speed *(track 206)*

⌐ *6:3♪* ¬ ⌐ *6:2♪* ¬ ⌐ *6:5♪* ¬ ⌐ *6:2♪* ¬ ⌐ *6:3♪* ¬ ⌐ *6:4♪* ¬
⌐ *6:3♪* ¬ ⌐ *6:2♪* ¬ ⌐ *6:5♪* ¬ ⌐ *6:2♪* ¬ ⌐ *6:3♪* ¬ ⌐ *6:4♪* ¬

4) Third regrouping 5 5 5 4 with chatusra 2nd speed *(track 207)*

⌐ *8:5♪* ¬ ⌐ *8:5♪* ¬ ⌐ *8:5♪* ¬ ⌐ *8:4♪* ¬
⌐ *8:5♪* ¬ ⌐ *8:5♪* ¬ ⌐ *8:5♪* ¬ ⌐ *8:4♪* ¬

5) Fourth regrouping 3 7 5 4 with misra 2nd speed *(track 208)*

⌐ *14:3♪* ¬ ⌐ *14:7♪* ¬ ⌐ *14:5♪* ¬ ⌐ *14:4♪* ¬
⌐ *14:3♪* ¬ ⌐ *14:7♪* ¬ ⌐ *14:5♪* ¬ ⌐ *14:4♪* ¬

6) Overall structure 7 5 7 with khanda 2nd speed *(track 209)*

⌐ *10:7♪* ¬ ⌐ *10:5♪* ¬ ⌐ *10:7♪* ¬
⌐ *10:7♪* ¬ ⌐ *10:5♪* ¬ ⌐ *10:7♪* ¬

Combinations Anuloma-Pratiloma with the Kala System

The kala system resembles more a suladi tala with the last beat lengthened or shortened. The concept of regrouping numbers to create different frames is applied only to the matra system. The quality or 'novelty' of the kala method is the cyclic irregularity that the lengthened or shortened beat provides.

Below are a few examples with the tala 6+¾. During the 'regular' beat, performers use different inner frames of ♩ or ♪as they would within a suladi tala. The last, shortened beat of ¾ or 3/16 breaks the regularity.

1) Misra 1st speed *(track 210)*

⌐ *7:6♪* ¬ ⌐ *7:6♪* ¬ ⌐ *7:3♬* ¬ | ⌐ *7:6♪* ¬ ⌐ *7:6♪* ¬ ⌐ *7:3♬* ¬

2) Khanda 1st speed *(track 211)*

┌─5:6♪─┐ ┌─5:4♪─┐ ┌─5:4𝅘𝅥𝅯─┐ ┌─5:3𝅘𝅥𝅯─┐ | ┌─5:6♪─┐ ┌─5:4♪─┐ ┌─5:4𝅘𝅥𝅯─┐ ┌─5:3𝅘𝅥𝅯─┐

3) Tisra 1st speed *(track 212)*

┌─3:2♩─┐ ┌─3:2♩─┐ ┌─3:2♩─┐ ┌─3:3𝅘𝅥𝅯─┐ | ┌─3:2♩─┐ ┌─3:2♩─┐ ┌─3:2♩─┐ ┌─3:3𝅘𝅥𝅯─┐

4) Chatusra 1st speed *(track 213)*

┌─4:3♪─┐ ┌─4:4♪─┐ ┌─4:5♪─┐ ┌─4:3𝅘𝅥𝅯─┐ | ┌─4:3♪─┐ ┌─4:4♪─┐ ┌─4:5♪─┐ ┌─4:3𝅘𝅥𝅯─┐

5) Tisra 1st speed *(track 214)*

┌─3:5♪─┐ ┌─3:3♪─┐ ┌─3:4♪─┐ ┌─3:3𝅘𝅥𝅯─┐ | ┌─3:5♪─┐ ┌─3:3♪─┐ ┌─3:4♪─┐ ┌─3:3𝅘𝅥𝅯─┐

Combinations Anuloma-Pratiloma with Jathi Bhedam

A step further in the level of complexity occurs when these two concepts are combined. Jathi bhedam sequences are developed in the new talas very much in the same fashion as they are with suladi talas. However, when an anuloma-pratiloma technique is to be superimposed over a jathi bhedam sequence the latter cannot trespass the boundaries of the large inner structure of the tala: the jathi bhedam cells need to resolve on the strong points of the tala.

The next two examples utilise the tala of 27/8 explained previously. The inner division is

3 2 2 | 3 3 | 3 2 2 | 3 2 2

giving the overall large structure of 7 6 7 7. Consequently, the jathi bhedam sequences will start and resolve within the boundaries of every large fragment, and anuloma-pratiloma phrasing will be superimposed in a manner similar to that presented in Chapter 20. The difference in this context is that, instead of using the same number of notes per cell (the concept that enabled anuloma-pratiloma to be used on a jathi bhedam sequence), 3rd and 4th developmental techniques can be added:

1) Chatusra 1st and 2nd speeds *(track 215)*

┌──── 7♪ ────┐ ┌─── 6♪ ───┐ ┌─── 7♪ ───┐ ┌────── 7♪ ──────┐

┌ 4:5𝅘𝅥𝅯 ┐ ┌ 4:6𝅘𝅥𝅯 ┐ ┌ 4:3𝅘𝅥𝅯 ┐ ┌ 4:7𝅘𝅥𝅯 ┐ ┌ 4:5𝅘𝅥𝅯 ┐ ┌ 8:4♪ ┐ ┌ 8:3♪ ┐ ┌ 4:4𝅘𝅥𝅯 ┐ ┌ 4:5𝅘𝅥𝅯 ┐ ┌ 4:3𝅘𝅥𝅯 ┐ ┌ 4:2𝅘𝅥𝅯 ┐

2) Khanda 1st, 2nd and 3rd speeds *(track 216)*

┌——— *7♪* ———┐ ┌——— *6♪* ———┐ ┌——— *7♪* ———┐ ┌——— *7♪* ———┐

┌ *5:5𝅘𝅥𝅯* ┐┌ *5:6𝅘𝅥𝅯* ┐┌ *5:3𝅘𝅥𝅯* ┐ ┌ *5:7𝅘𝅥𝅯* ┐┌ *5:5𝅘𝅥𝅯* ┐ ┌ *15:4♪* ┐┌ *10:3♪* ┐ ┌ *5:4𝅘𝅥𝅯* ┐┌ *5:5𝅘𝅥𝅯* ┐┌ *5:3𝅘𝅥𝅯* ┐┌ *5:2𝅘𝅥𝅯* ┐

To conclude the section dedicated to anuloma-pratiloma combinations within the new talas, it is relevant to note which developmental techniques could be used.

- The 1st technique can be utilised exclusively if the chosen gati and speed ignore any possibility of regrouping. It is difficult to perform due to the regularity required for this technique, but if the chosen frame is in ♪ or 𝅘𝅥𝅯 this becomes easier.
- The 2nd technique is practically impossible to perform because it is based on keeping the same number of beats while the different speeds of a gati succeed one another. This is essentially the same problem that nadai bhedam has with the new talas.
- The 3rd and 4th techniques can be used because both are based on the change of the frame while keeping gati and speed (3rd technique) or only gati (4th technique).
- Techniques five and six, where the gati could change, are for all practical purposes impossible, in great part for the same reasons as the 2nd technique, but also because of the already mentioned reticence of karnatic musicians to change the gati in the middle of a tala.

Therefore, as was the case with nadai bhedam, any technique that would demand regularity in the beating is discarded.

Moharas

Mohara is one of the few techniques where a regularity of the beat is required, due to its characteristics of division of the tala into four equal phrases. However, and contradicting the previous paragraph, moharas is the only technique for which karnatic musicians have found solutions.

1) Phrases with different frame: The first solution is derived from the possibility provided by the mukhy system of regrouping the inner division of the tala. Through this option, a regrouping is sought by which

- the resulting number of frames should be four;
- at least two frames (preferably three) should be of the same length.

In the tala of 19 beats, with the inner division 322 32 322, one of the regrouping options was 5 5 5 4. This regrouping fulfils both requirements just mentioned. Consequently, a mohara in which the same gati would be performed against the two different resulting frames (5 and 4) could be constructed. Therefore, if for instance misra gati is chosen, the four phrases would follow the frames:

⌐ *7:5♪*¬ ⌐ *7:5♪*¬ ⌐ *7:5♪*¬ ⌐ *7:4♪*¬

On this frame, any of the possible mohara phrasing constructions could be used, along with the whole structure of the end of the 3rd cycle and the entire 4th cycle of ½ D A ½ D C mukthay.

The transcription below is of a mohara in 27/8, with the large structure of 7 6 7 7 used as the frames for the four phrases of the mohara. The gati is chatusra and the phrase division is 4+4 in all phrases. *(track 217)*

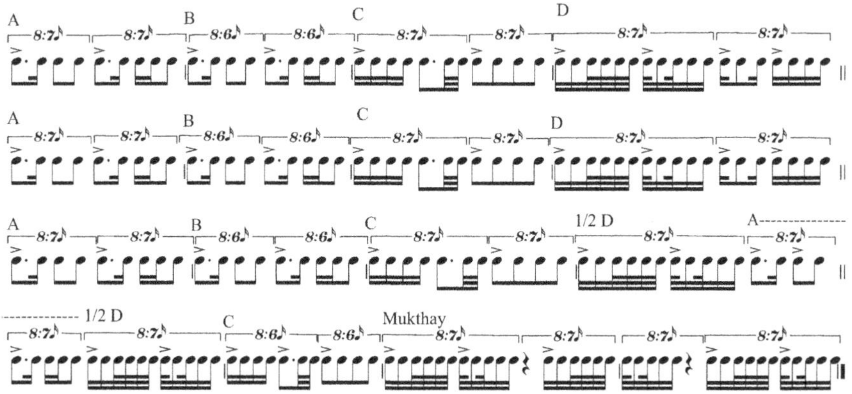

2) Phrases with different duration: The same principle applies here – four frames as a result of regrouping the inner division of the tala; and at least two of them (preferably three, *especially* with this type of mohara) of the same duration.

As opposed to the first 'solution', in which ultimately every phrase has the same number of matras, in this second possibility at least one phrase would be shorter or longer than the rest. This second option, while being generally much easier to perform than the first, is used less frequently than the first option because it goes against one of the basic pillars of moharas: the equal length of every phrase.

The following example is once again constructed on the 27/8 tala with the inner division of 7 6 7 7. Therefore, the B phrase is a ♪ shorter than the rest of phrases. *(track 218)*

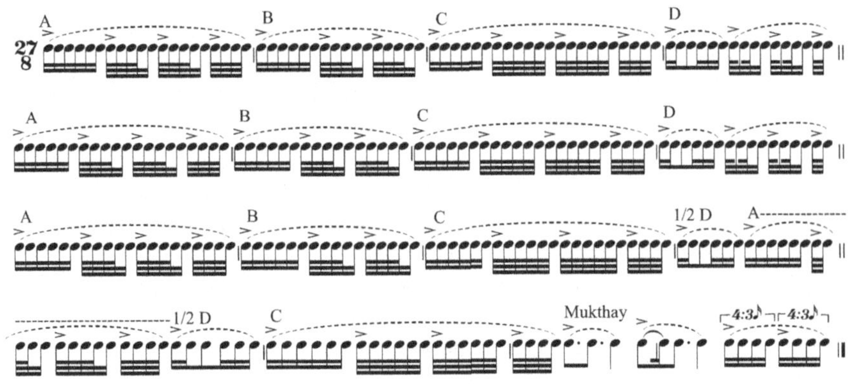

Practice Method

The majority of the techniques here are, in most cases, more difficult to perform due to the lack of regularity of the counting or beating, but this can be solved by creating click tracks for different talas in their matra and kala forms, and creating sequences of:

- phrasing with gatis
- gati and jathi bhedam (including tree of gati bhedam)
- all sorts of mukthays (except for 3-fold mukthays)
- yati phrases and yatis prastara
- tirmanas and compound-related mukthays
- poruttam A and B
- mixed jathi nadai bhedam
- phrasing through gati changes
- combinations anuloma-pratiloma.

Since it is the latter technique that benefited most from the development of the tala prastara, a few exercises are presented that can be taken as examples in order to produce individual pieces in a variety of talas. All gatis in at least two speeds should be used for every exercise against the written numbers/frames.

1) Regrouping with the Matra System

Since there are a few recorded examples in the tala of 19/8, to use the same regroupings as B.C. Manjunath's recordings in the chapter could be a good starting point to superimpose combinations anuloma-pratiloma. Two different tempi are suggested for the same frames.

♪= 80 / 120

19/8			
	7	5	7
	3 2 2	3 2	3 2 2
	3 4	3 2	3 4
	3 2 5	2	3 4
	5 5	5	4
	3 7	5	4
	7	5	7

2) Kala System Talas

Practising the alternation between a regular beat and a final incomplete beat is also recommended. Once again, the sample recordings could be a good starting point.

♩ = 46 / 56

$\frac{6}{4}+\frac{3}{16}$

⌐ *x:3*♩ ¬ ⌐ *x:3*♩ ¬ ⌐ *x:3*𝅘𝅥𝅯 ¬
⌐ *x:3*♩ ¬ ⌐ *x:2*♩ ¬ ⌐ *x:1*♩ ¬ ⌐ *x:3*𝅘𝅥𝅯 ¬
⌐ *x:2*♩ ¬ ⌐ *x:2*♩ ¬ ⌐ *x:2*♩ ¬ ⌐ *x:3*𝅘𝅥𝅯 ¬

⌐ *x:3*♪ ¬ ⌐ *x:4*♪ ¬ ⌐ *x:5*♪ ¬ ⌐ *x:3*𝅘𝅥𝅯 ¬
⌐ *x:5*♪ ¬ ⌐ *x:3*♪ ¬ ⌐ *x:4*♪ ¬ ⌐ *x:3*𝅘𝅥𝅯 ¬

3) Tala Combination Suladi-Chapu

♪= 140

$\frac{37}{8}$

⌐ *x:3*♩ ¬ ⌐ *x:3*♩ ¬ ⌐ *x:2*♩ ¬
⌐ *x:3*♪ ¬ ⌐ *x:4*♪ ¬ (x 3)
⌐ *x:5*♩ ¬ ⌐ *x:3*♩ ¬
⌐ *x:5*♪ ¬ ⌐ *x:2*♪ ¬ (x 3)
⌐ *x:7*♪ ¬ ⌐ *x:5*♪ ¬ ⌐ *x:4*♪ ¬
⌐ *x:3*♪ ¬ ⌐ *x:2*♪ ¬ ⌐ *x:2*♪ ¬ (x 3)

4) Short Jathi Bhedam Sequences within the Larger Subdivision of Talas

Once again, a good starting point for a performer is to use the sample recordings.

⌐—— 7♪ ——¬ ⌐—— 6♪ ——¬ ⌐—— 7♪ ——¬ ⌐—— 7♪ ——¬
⌐ *x:5*𝅘𝅥𝅯 ¬ ⌐ *x:6*𝅘𝅥𝅯 ¬ ⌐ *x:3*𝅘𝅥𝅯 ¬ ⌐ *x:7*𝅘𝅥𝅯 ¬ ⌐ *x:5*𝅘𝅥𝅯 ¬ ⌐ *x:4*♪ ¬ ⌐ *x:3*♪ ¬ ⌐ *x:4*♪ ¬ ⌐ *x:5*𝅘𝅥𝅯 ¬ ⌐ *x:3*𝅘𝅥𝅯 ¬ ⌐ *x:2*𝅘𝅥𝅯 ¬

Chapter 24
Latest Developments of Gatis

Gatis 9, 11 and 13

Gati 9 (or sankirna) has been referred to several times throughout the book. Although used rather sparingly, it has been in existence for at least 200 years. Gatis 11 and 13 are much more recent. Some percussionists started using them in solos in the 1980s and, since then, other musicians have also started to incorporate them into their music. As opposed to what many people may think, these three gatis are far from being complex – I would daresay that they can even 'groove' more than tisra or khanda, and all of them can be used as nadais in any frame.

Sankirna

Phrasing in this gati must always be constructed with an internal division of 4+5 or 5+4. Any other inner division is discarded. Also, except when a long passage in this gati is performed, techniques such as gati bhedam, jathi bhedam, mukthays, yati phrases etc. are never applied. However, 9 (as 3rd speed anuloma of tisra) can utilise any technique seen thus far. Consequently, it can be inferred that sankirna is essentially used as a gati that develops exclusively through phrasing and, eventually, some short mukthays. Only where it is employed for more than a few cycles can some simple and short structures of gati or jathi bhedam be found.

The first example presents a phrase exclusively using the inner division 4+5.[1] *(track 219)*

Sankirna 4+5

The second example presents a phrase exclusively using the inner division 5+4. *(track 220)*

Sankirna 5+4

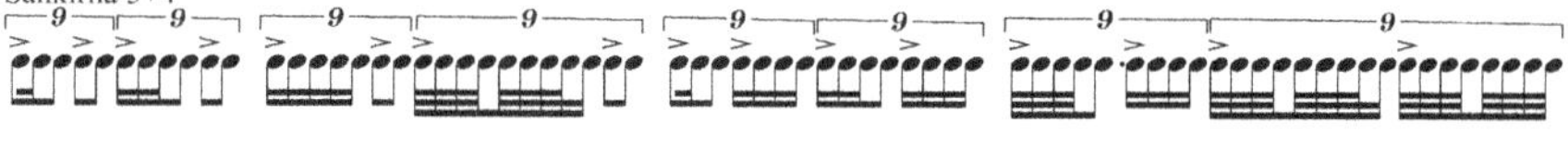

The third example presents a phrase using a combination of both possibilities of inner division: this is the most common way to develop sankirna. *(track 221)*

---

1 I preferred using ♪ as the fastest note instead of 𝅘𝅥𝅯 to avoid too many 64th notes.

Sankirna combining accents

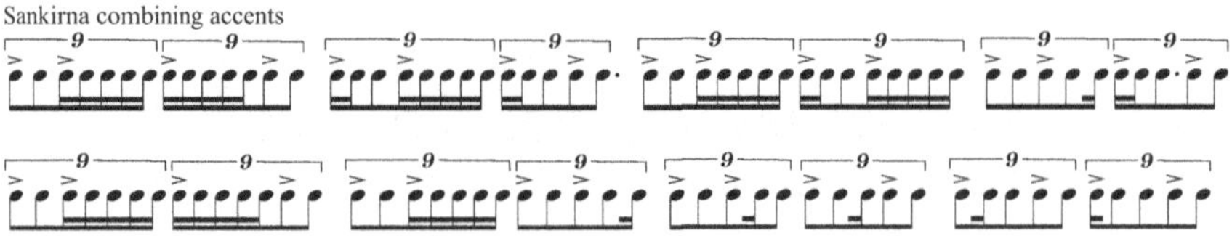

Finally, a fourth and more intricate example is presented; on this occasion the phrase is performed against two beats. *(track 222)*

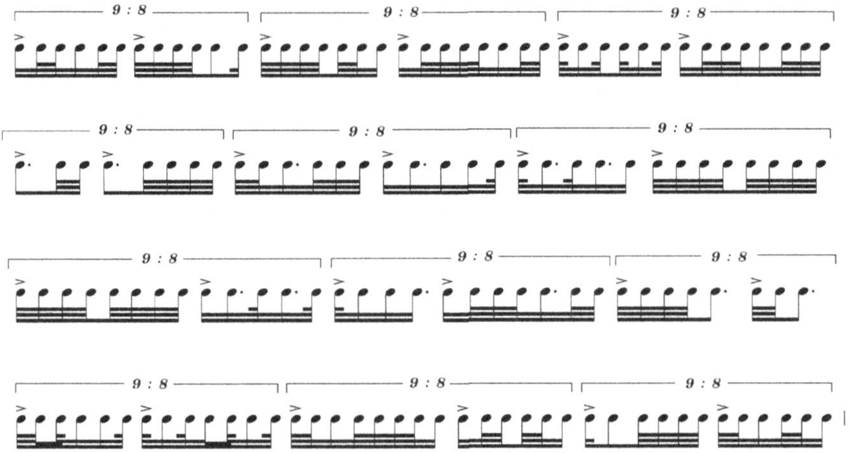

Gati 11

Until now, this gati has not been given a name. It could be called *ekadesha*, meaning 11 in Sanskrit. However, no musician describes this gati as such: rather it is simply referred to as gati 11. This gati also uses an inner division of 5+6 or 6+5 *(tracks 223 and 224)*[2]

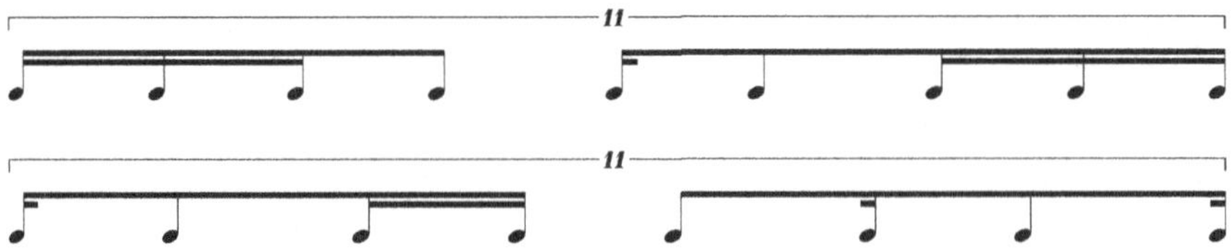

However, as opposed to sankirna, these divisions are used solely in the learning process of the gati. In reality, gati 11 does not share any of the problems of sankirna; and, consequently, any inner division for phrasing purposes, or any

[2] All recorded examples in gatis 11 and 13, except for the more elaborate and longer phrases, are performed against 2, 3 and 4 beats.

technique seen so far, can be used. The following examples use an inner division of 4+4+3. *(tracks 225 and 226)*

The next example features more phrasing possibilities, intricate 𝅘𝅥𝅯 as well as rests and tie-overs. *(track 227)*

Gati 13

As with gati 11, gati 13 has no name as yet; *trayodasha* means 13 in Sanskrit. In a similar way to gati 11, the initial step to devise this gati is to use the inner division 6+7 or 7+6. However, complete freedom of inner division, as well as the use of all techniques seen so far, is a common feature while developing this gati. The first example is a simple phrase around the inner division 7+6, whilst the second presents three accents (4+4+5). *(tracks 228 and 229)*

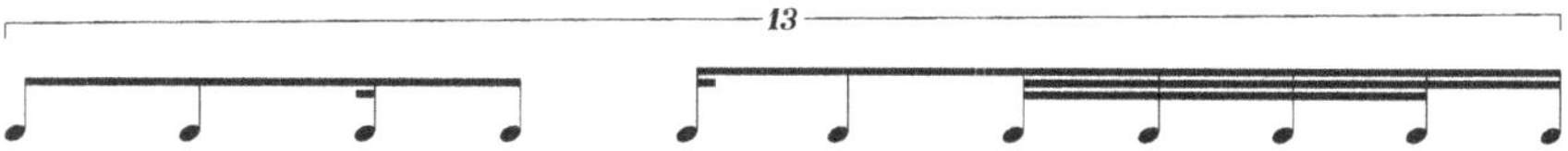

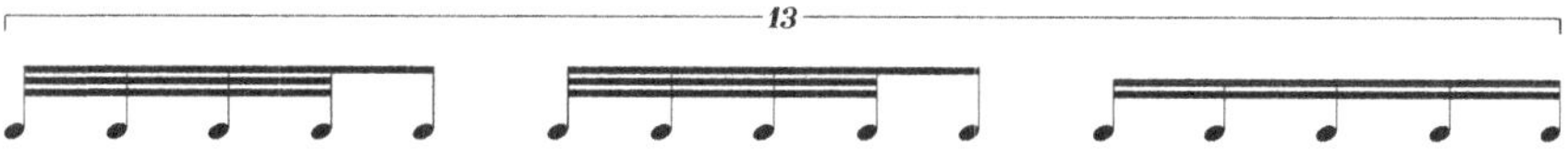

To complete this section of the chapter, a more intricate phrase in gati 13 is presented. *(track 230)*

Practice Method

1. Practise all the matras in sankirna with an inner division of 4+5 or 5+4, gati 11 with 5+6 or 6+5 and gati 13 with 6+7 or 7+6. In sankirna use the frames of 1, 2 and 4 beats; and in gatis 11 and 13 the frames of 2, 3 and 4 beats. Use the examples presented here as a starting point to elaborate your own phrases.
2. Make sequences in all gatis combining the two possible inner divisions and all frames.
3. Construct simple phrases on all gatis emphasising the accents of the inner divisions.
4. Work with different inner divisions in gatis 11 and 13 and construct phrases around them.
5. Gradually, start introducing rests and tie-overs in all gatis and frames following the procedure of phrasing with gatis from Chapter 2.

Phrasing through Gati Changes

The final subject of this part dedicated to the most important karnatic rhythmical techniques and concepts presents the latest developments taking place in South India: phrasing through gati changes.

This concept was already glimpsed in the development of mixed gati moharas, in the section on ½ D A ½ D C mukthay. Due to the shortening of the 'D' phrase and the pattern established by this type of mohara after this shortening, the 'A' and 'C' phrases (as well as the mukthay) are always performed in two different gatis, while the phrase is never interrupted or modified by this change of gati. Except for this technique, all gati changes presented thus far have resulted in a new phrase starting in a gati or speed change.

However, a transformation is rapidly taking place in karnatic music today. An increasing number of musicians are starting to break the limits of the gati changes and their subsequent phrase development by combining two or more gatis in a tala, as well as constructing phrases in which a number of matras are part of one gati and the remaining matras are part of a different gati without interruption in the flow of the phrase or the application of any accent where the gati change occurs.

Much has been said in the previous chapters not only about the reticence but also almost the pride shown by karnatic musicians in the notion of changing gatis only on tala or anga sam (the latter even in a quite restricted fashion). Only if a very clear set of parameters were present (as listed in Chapter 20) could this gati change occur somewhere else in the tala. Undoubtedly, this strict approach has enabled karnatic music to develop a highly sophisticated rhythmical system where the creation and performance of intricate and complex material go hand in hand.

The new approach is not far removed from this ingrained idea. The difference is that gati changes occur more often and phrases are not confined to the length of a particular gati; but whether using 'regular phrasing' or gati/jathi bhedam, the phrases trespass the boundaries of the gati change. However, the placement of the gati change will generally take place on the tala or anga sams of the tala (if the phrase is completely new); or eventually, and always using the notion of rhythmical sangati, on some other beat, provided that the phrase has a clear resemblance to the original (the latter being a more subjective matter and, therefore, somewhat polemic amongst musicians).

Nonetheless, these are the two parameters that enable musicians to change gatis as often as they would like:

- Gati changes occur only on the sams of the tala.
- Gati changes can be placed on a different beat, provided that the change is the result of a rhythmical sangati on a previous phrase, and that in one way or another the placement of the gati resembles the original placement of a cell of the original phrase.

A few examples will be analysed to show some of the possibilities that this new concept allows or calls for.[3]

1) The first example is set to adi tala (L4 D D) and takes the gatis khanda and tisra 2nd speed. The gati changes in the first drutam sam, thus obeying the first 'rule'. *(track 231)*

Analysis of the phrase itself shows that it consists of a combination of regular phrasing with a short jathi bhedam sequence. The numbers would be 5 5 3 5 4 10 (6+4) 6 6. The total number of matras is 20 in khanda and 24 in tisra, resulting in

[3] Due to the very recent appearance of this technique, many more possibilities are likely to develop in the next few years.

44 matras. The 3rd accent starts the short jathi bhedam sequence, and it is on the 5th accent that the 4-matra phrase goes through the gati change.

From this particular example it can be deduced that as long as the number of matras is the result of adding up the length of each gati (and it is known beforehand where the gati change/s can happen) any combination of gatis is possible in any tala. Due to the fact that there are three sams in this tala, a hypothetical 3rd gati could have been used starting on the 2nd drutam sam; alternatively, a return to the original khanda would have been possible.

Once the number of matras is obtained and the placement of the gati changes is clear, the musician is free to elaborate a phrase, making sure that the gati change does not coincide with a new cell of the phrase, but rather that a cell is created that deliberately crosses the boundary of the gati change.

2) The second example is also based on a phrase in chatusra in adi tala.

In the first rhythmical sangati version (combining tisra and khanda) there are a few elements that move away from the 'clean' approach shown in Chapter 5; also, the gati change occurs on a weak beat of the tala, and an extra note that was not part of the original phrase is added before the change to khanda.

The first 4 beats in tisra scrupulously follow the transformation of the first 12 matras of the original phrase into tisra 1st speed. However (and still as part of the same cell), in the 5th beat the tisra unit is 2nd speed anuloma. In order to complete the beat, a new note is added before proceeding to play the last 15 matras of the original phrase (chatusra jathi 5) in 3 beats of khanda. The latter probably explains why the gati change takes place on a weak beat, namely in order to resemble the idea of a phrase of 5 matras within the remaining length of the tala.

The second version on the same phrase is done exclusively in tisra but combining both speeds. Also, the last note before tisra 2nd speed jathi 5 starts is elongated in order for the feature of 5 notes to fit neatly into the tala.

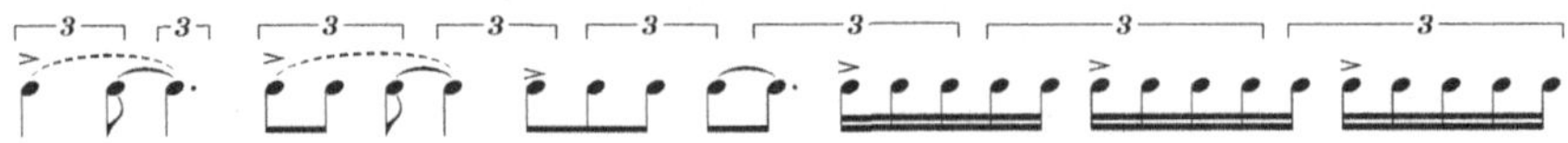

The whole phrase, thought out as a complete development of the initial idea, looks like this *(track 232)*

3) The third example takes as its starting point a phrase of 14 beats in chatusra (56 matras), to later develop it in two different ways combining tisra and chatusra within 2 cycles of adi tala.

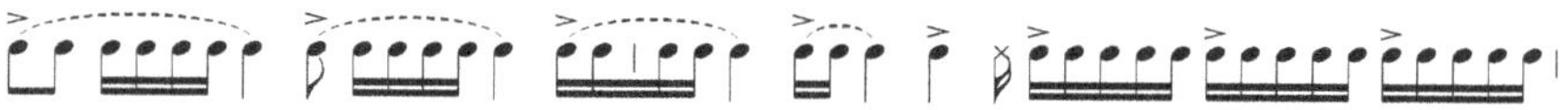

Both versions scrupulously follow the rules as to when the gati changes can take place. In the first case, the change occurs in the 1st drutam sam, and the return to chatusra also takes place in the same position.

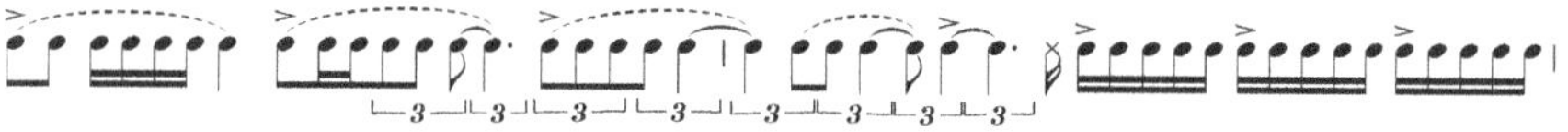

In the second version, the only alteration as far as phrasing through gati changes is concerned occurs with the jathi 5 cells when the phrase goes into tisra from the 4th matra of the jathi.

Once again, the whole sequence performed as a unit looks thus:[4] *(track 233)*

[4] The fact that the three examples have been played as a unit does not imply that this is the only way to work with the concept expounded in this chapter. Whether as a new phrase or as a rhythmical sangati, the concept can be applied anywhere in the development of a piece.

4) The fourth example is the transcription of a solo by B.C. Manjunath in a tala of 37/8, described in the previous chapter. It is a tala combination made up of adi tala (8/4 or 16/8) followed by 3 times misra chapu (7/8 × 3=21/8). An in-depth analysis of this solo would probably take too much space, so suffice it to say that it comprises the following main elements:

- Similar notion as in mixed gati mohara, most of the time dividing the 8/4 in equal halves and applying two different gatis to every tala fragment. Similarly, the 7/8 is continuously subdivided in 3+4, taking different gatis or speeds for every part.
- The length of phrases varies continuously: musicians always look for the surprise factor that the gati change or a different anuloma-pratiloma speed may provide.
- The notion behind the phrase development is similar to the way mixed jathi nadai bhedam develops phrases: through repetition of cells in both frames. However, the varying length of phrases and greater freedom in their development, together with the irregularity of the tala, avoids any feeling of predictability. *(track 234)*

Percussion solo by B.C. Manjunath

Tala: Adi tala (8/4) + Misra chapu (7/8) x 3 = 37 beats (37/8)

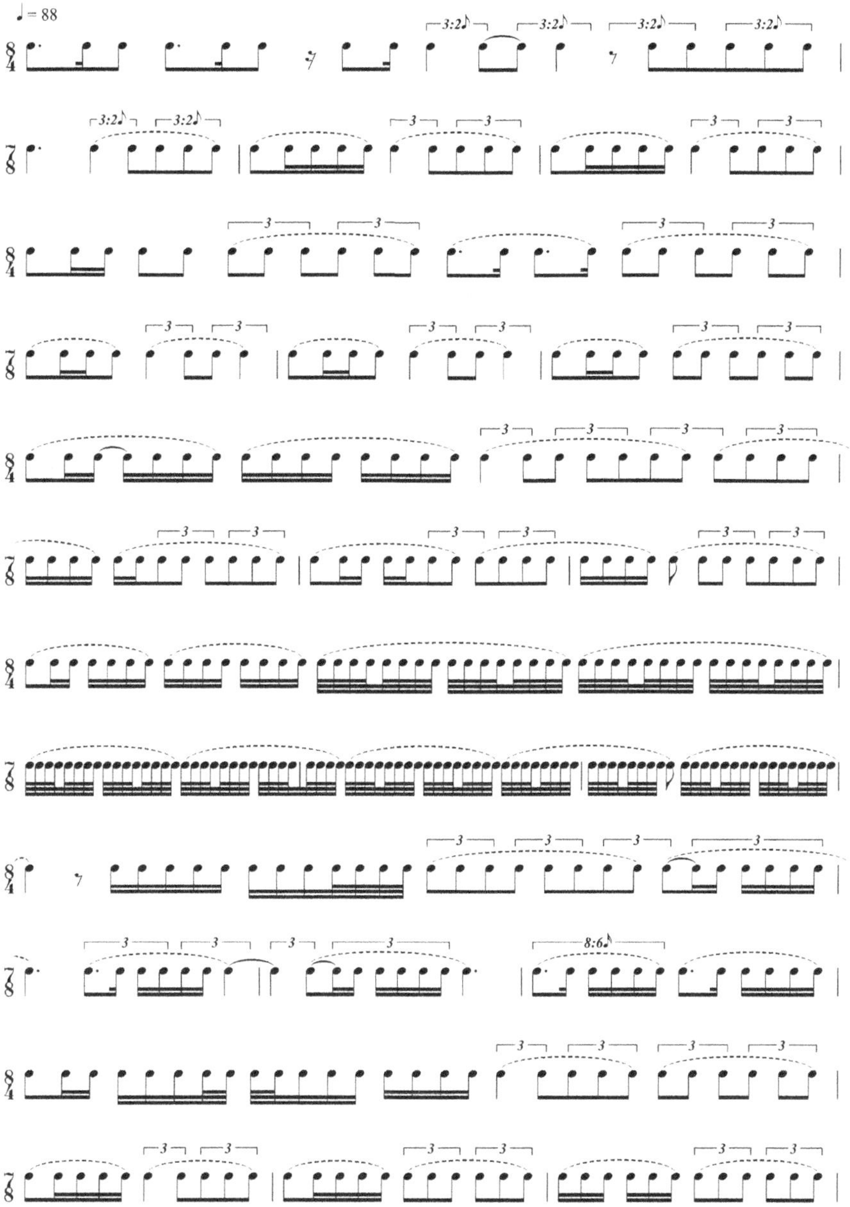

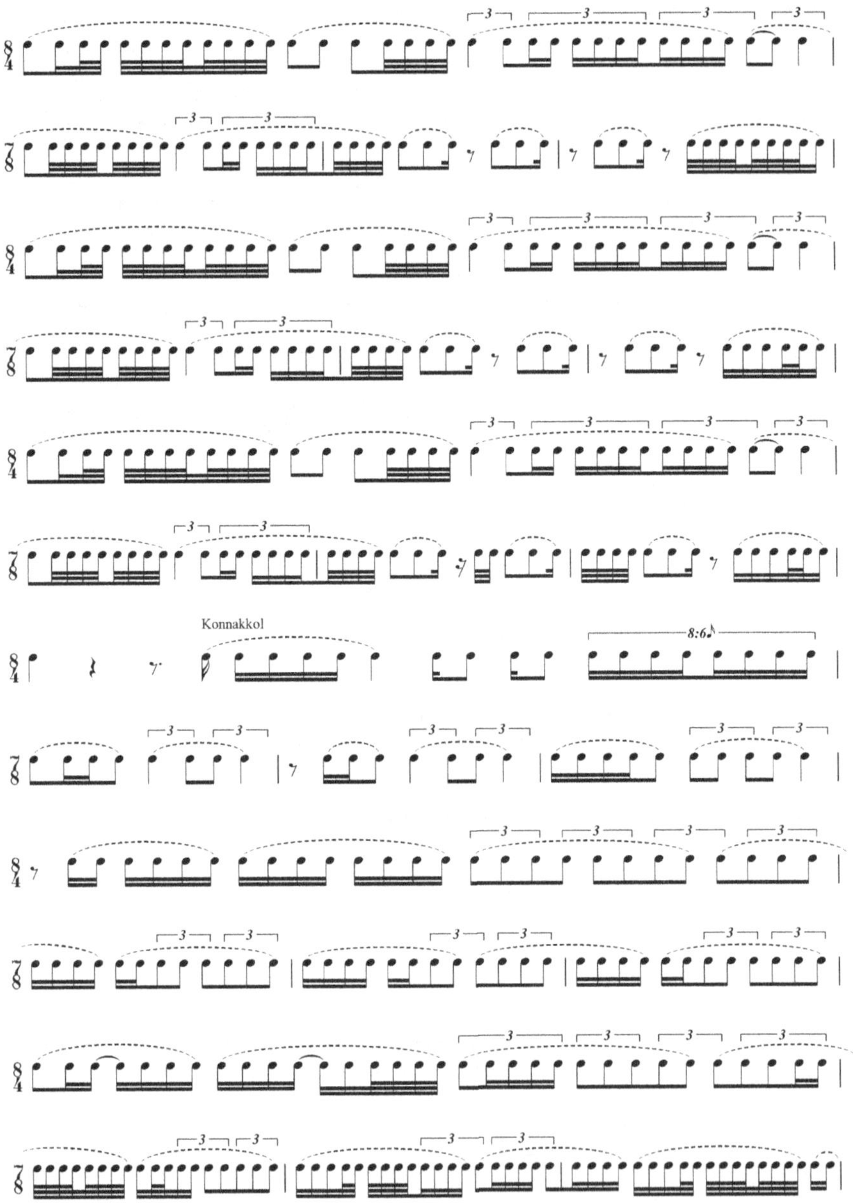
Konnakkol
8:6

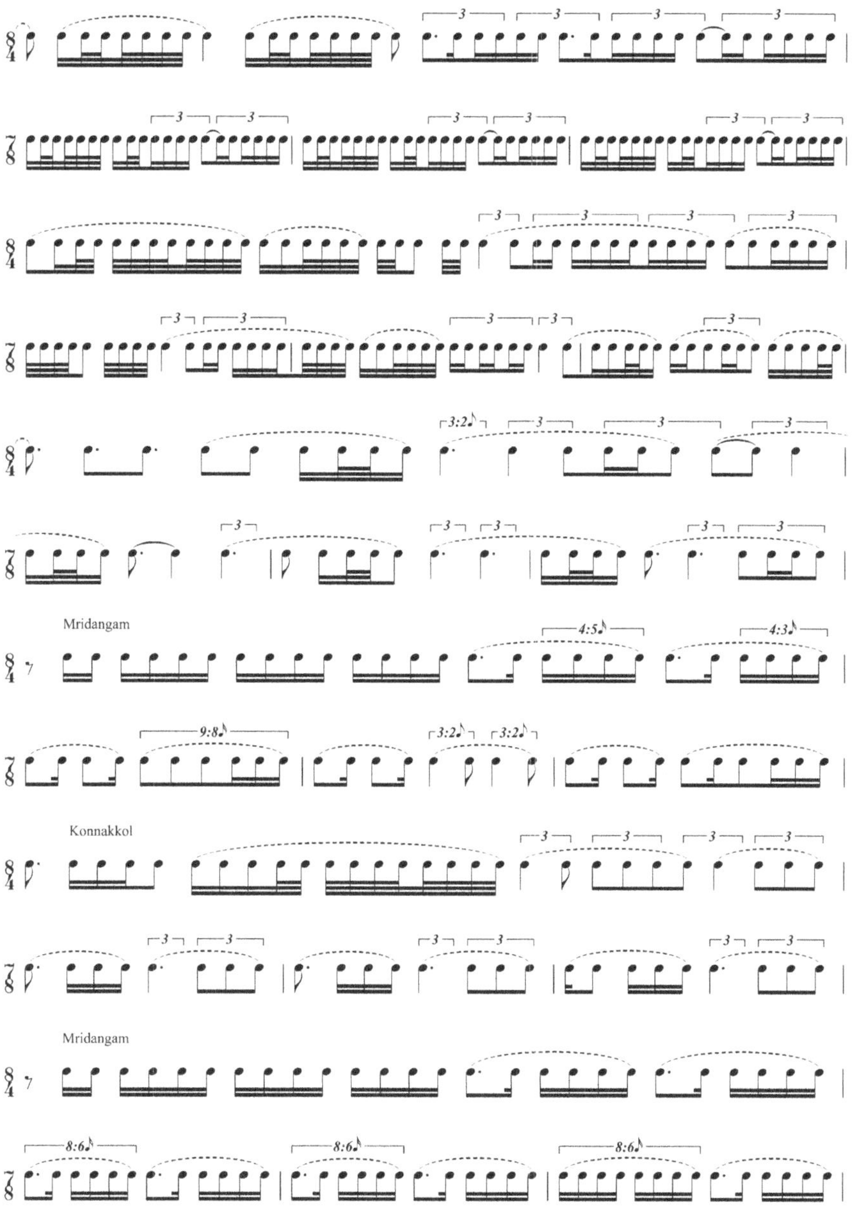
Mridangam
Konnakkol
Mridangam

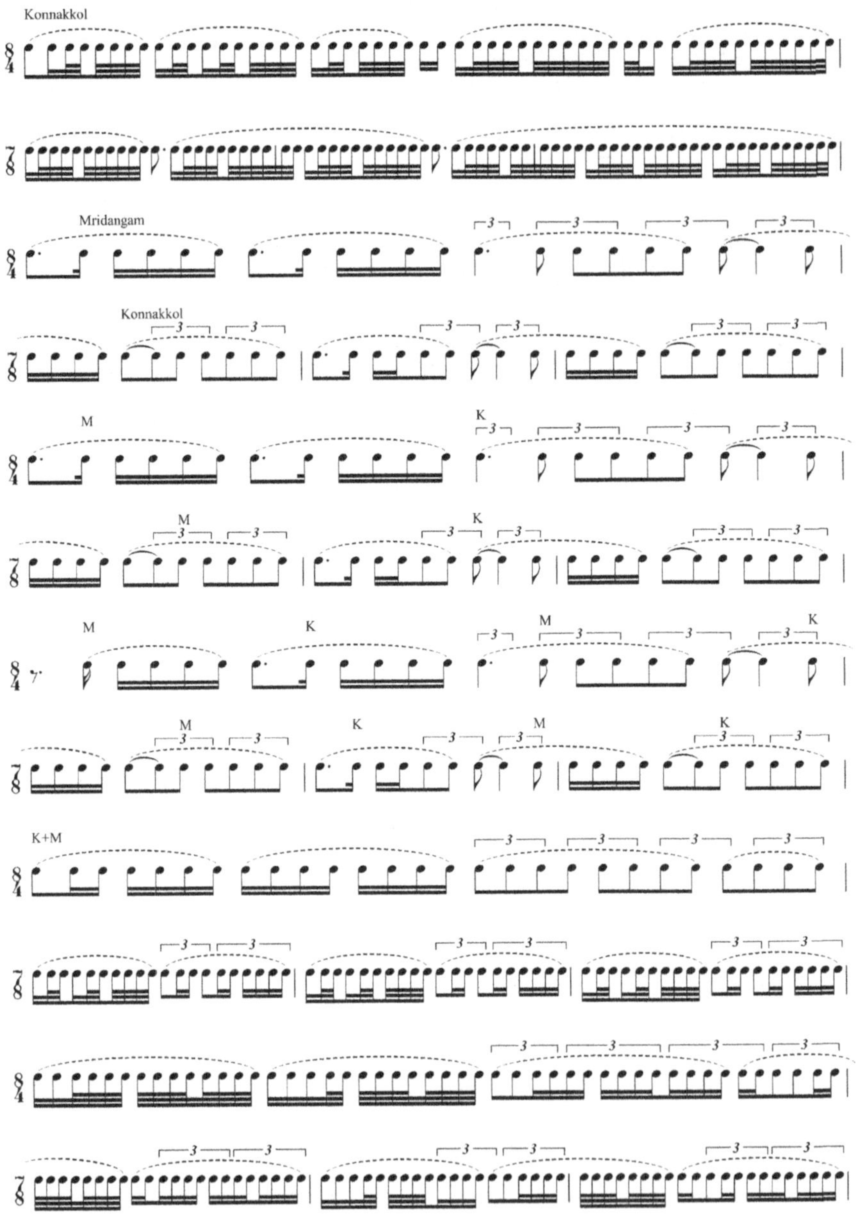
Konnakkol
Mridangam
Konnakkol
M
K
M
K
M
K
M
K
M
K
M
K
K+M

5) The last example presents the concept explained in this chapter a few times. However, I have transcribed it as a sort of final recapitulation of all techniques described in the book so far. As with the previous example, a deep analysis of this 27-minute percussion duet is not possible here; suffice to say that most techniques presented in the volume are used in some way or another. A.R.A.K. Sharma is

responsible for the tala construction and main ideas developed in this duet. Since it is written with an almost continuous metre change, I have included a double line at the end of the second 4/4 of the cycle so that the reader can see the cycles as conceived by the composer. *(track 235)*

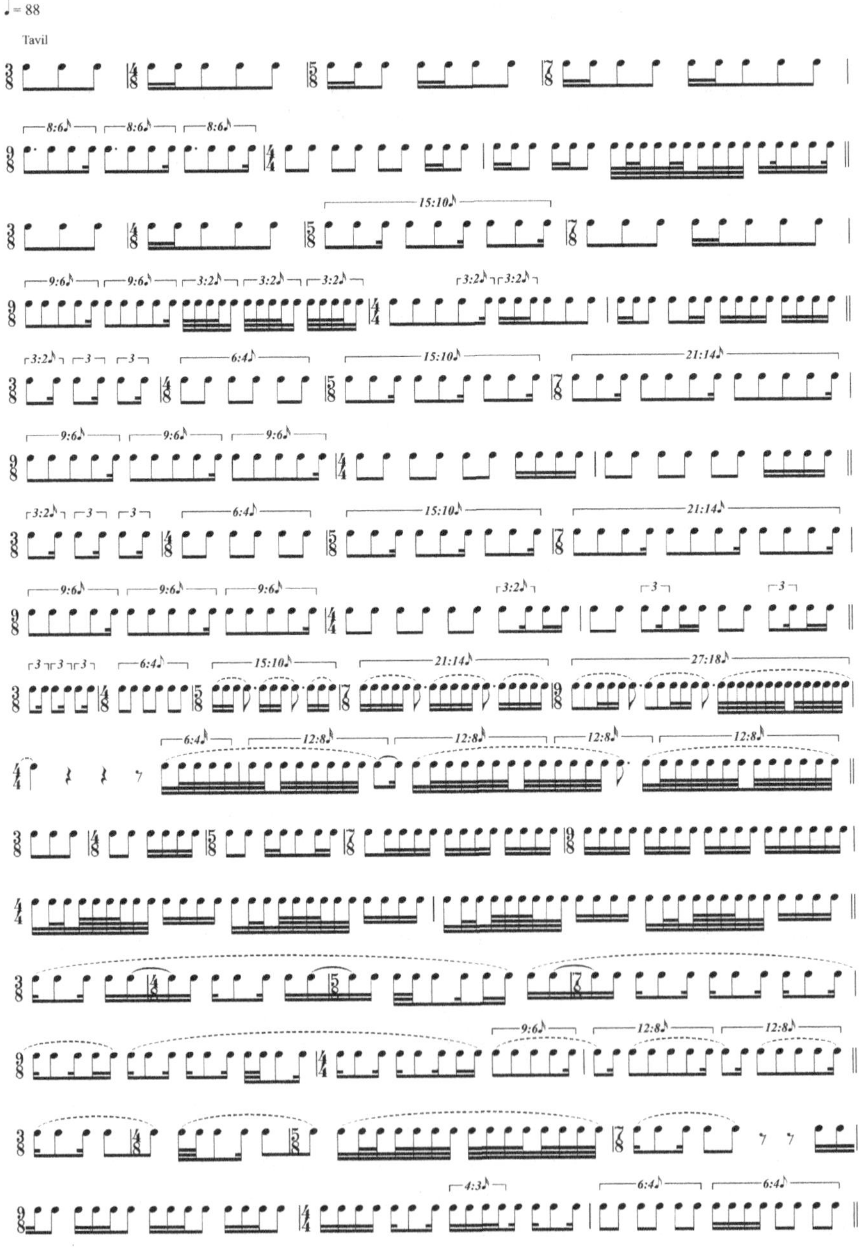

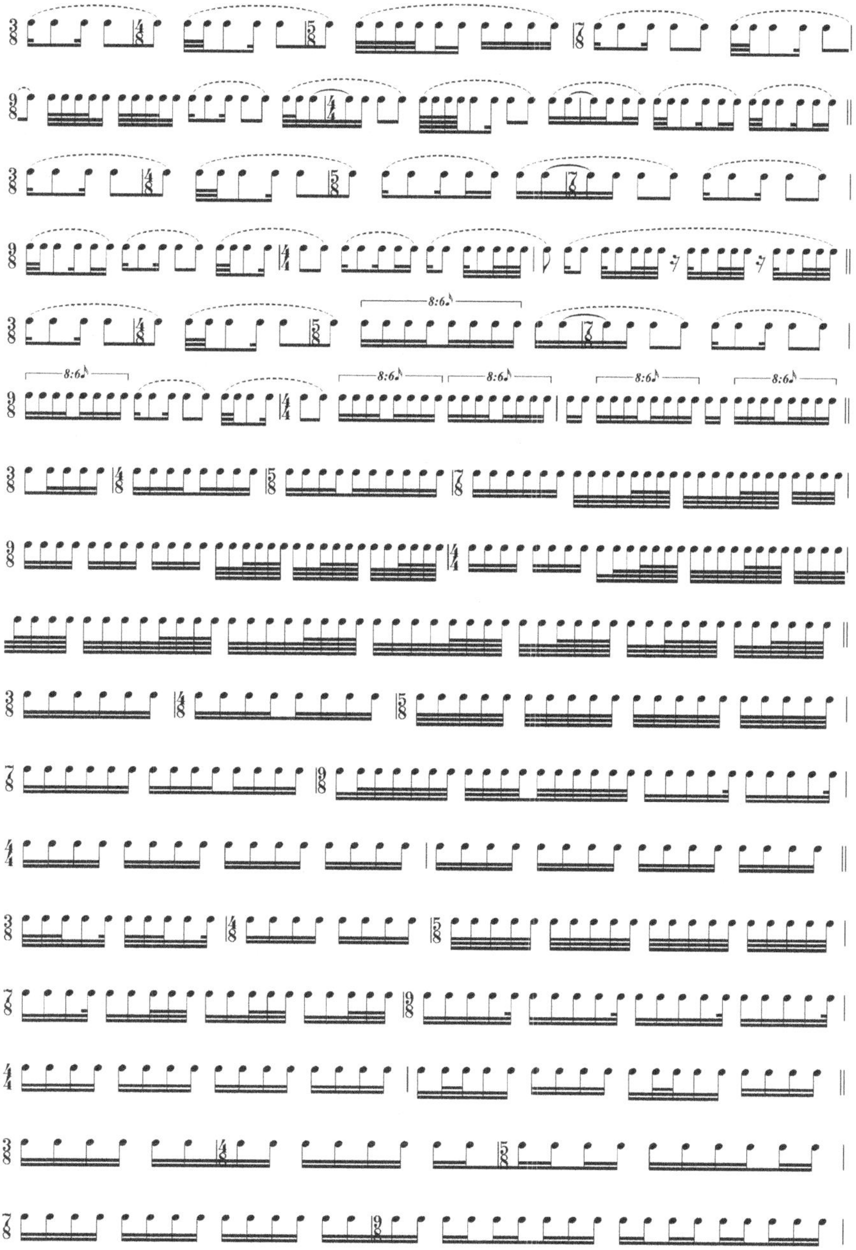

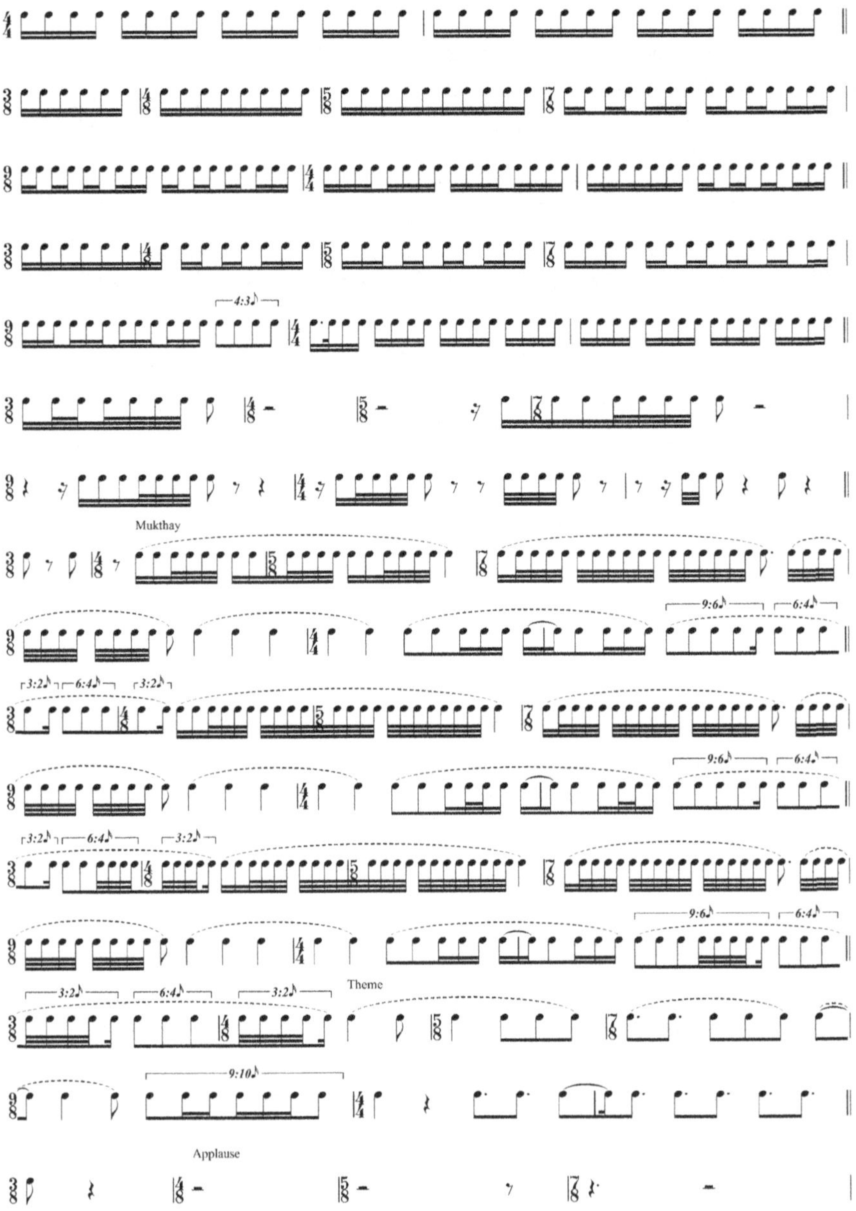
Mukthay
Theme
Applause

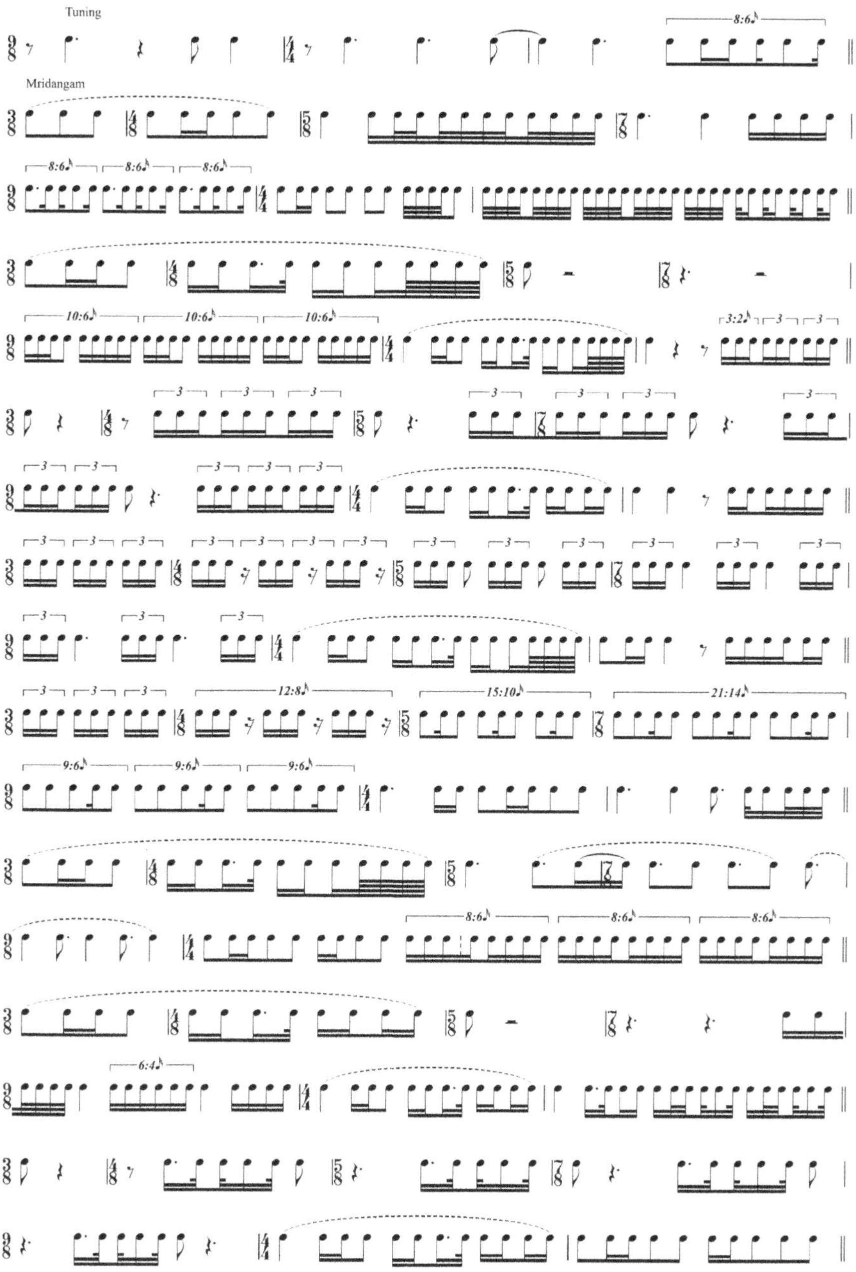
Tuning
Mridangam

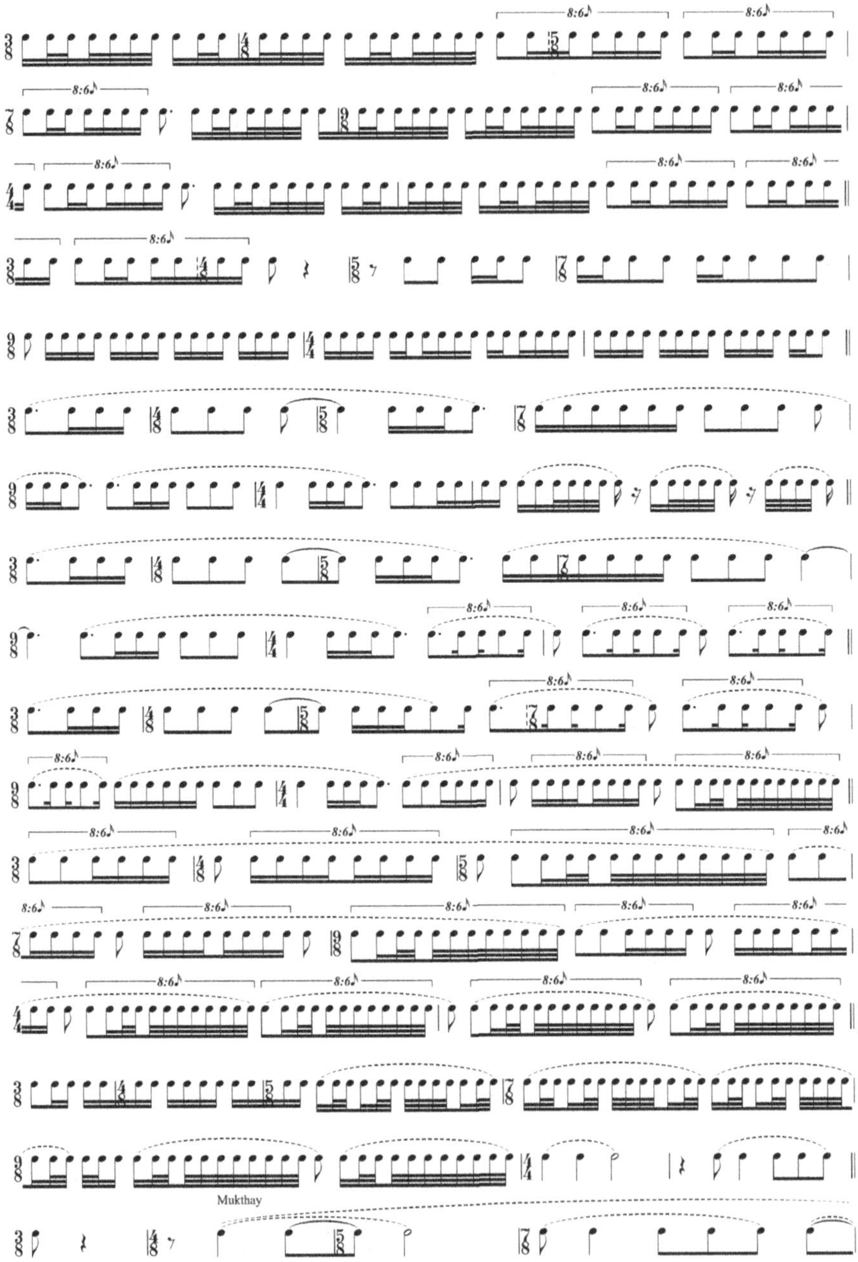
Mukthay

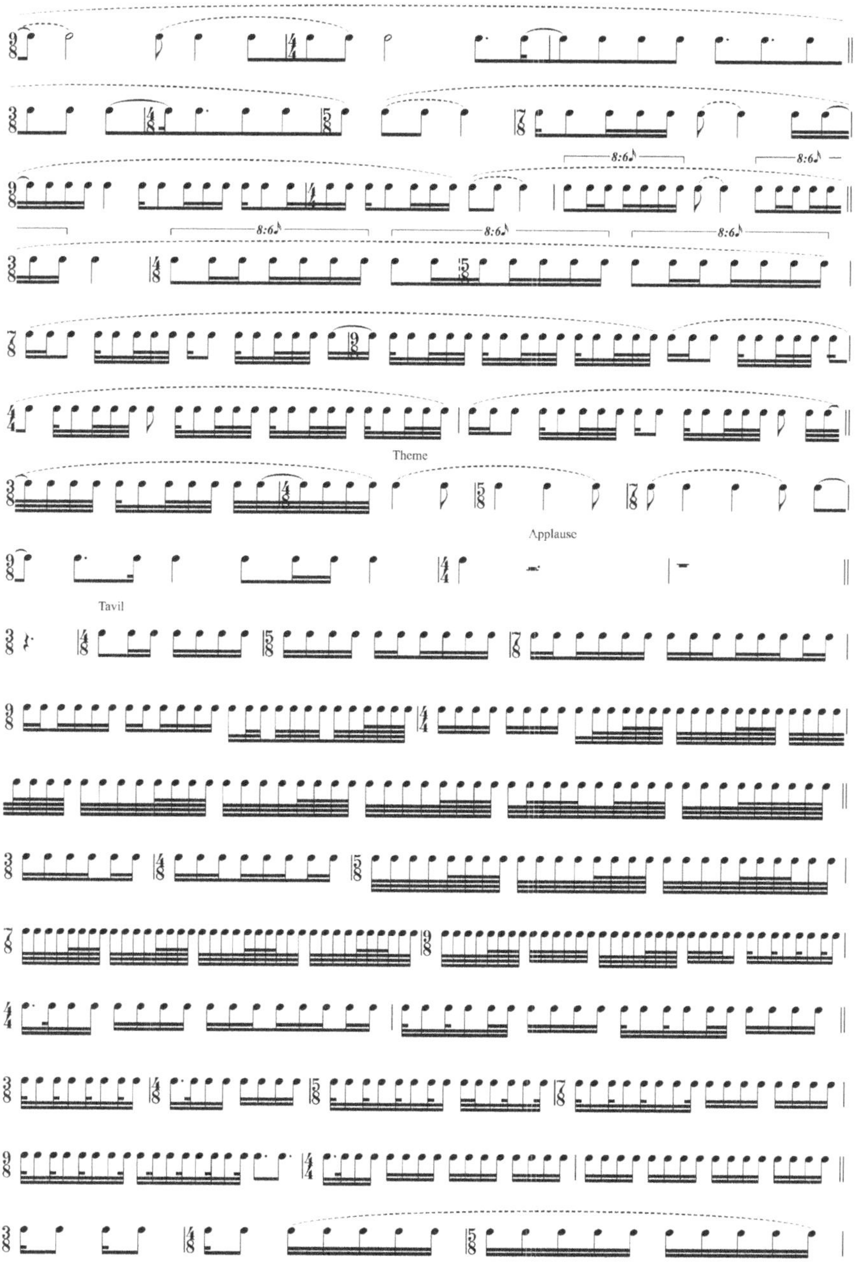
8:6
8:6
8:6
8:6
8:6
Theme
Applause
Tavil

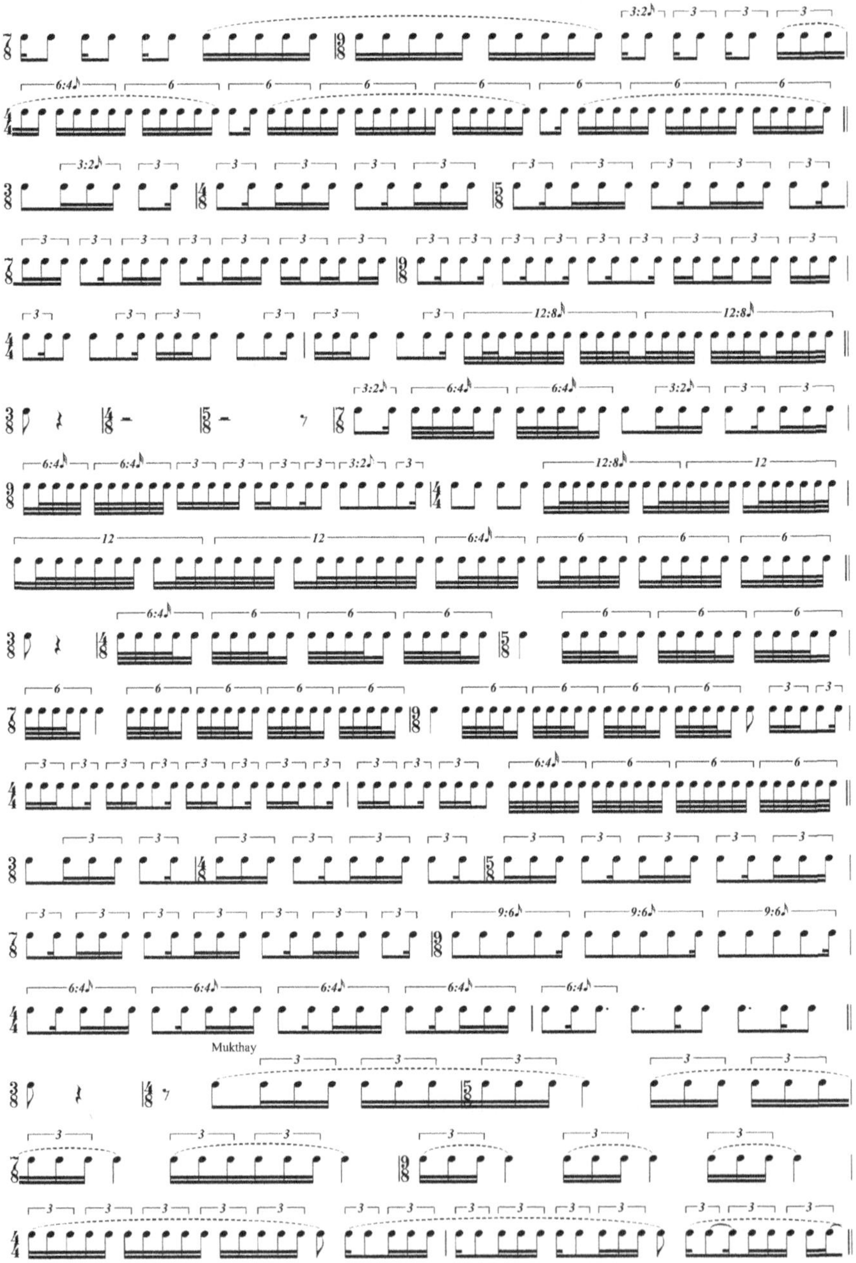
Mukthay

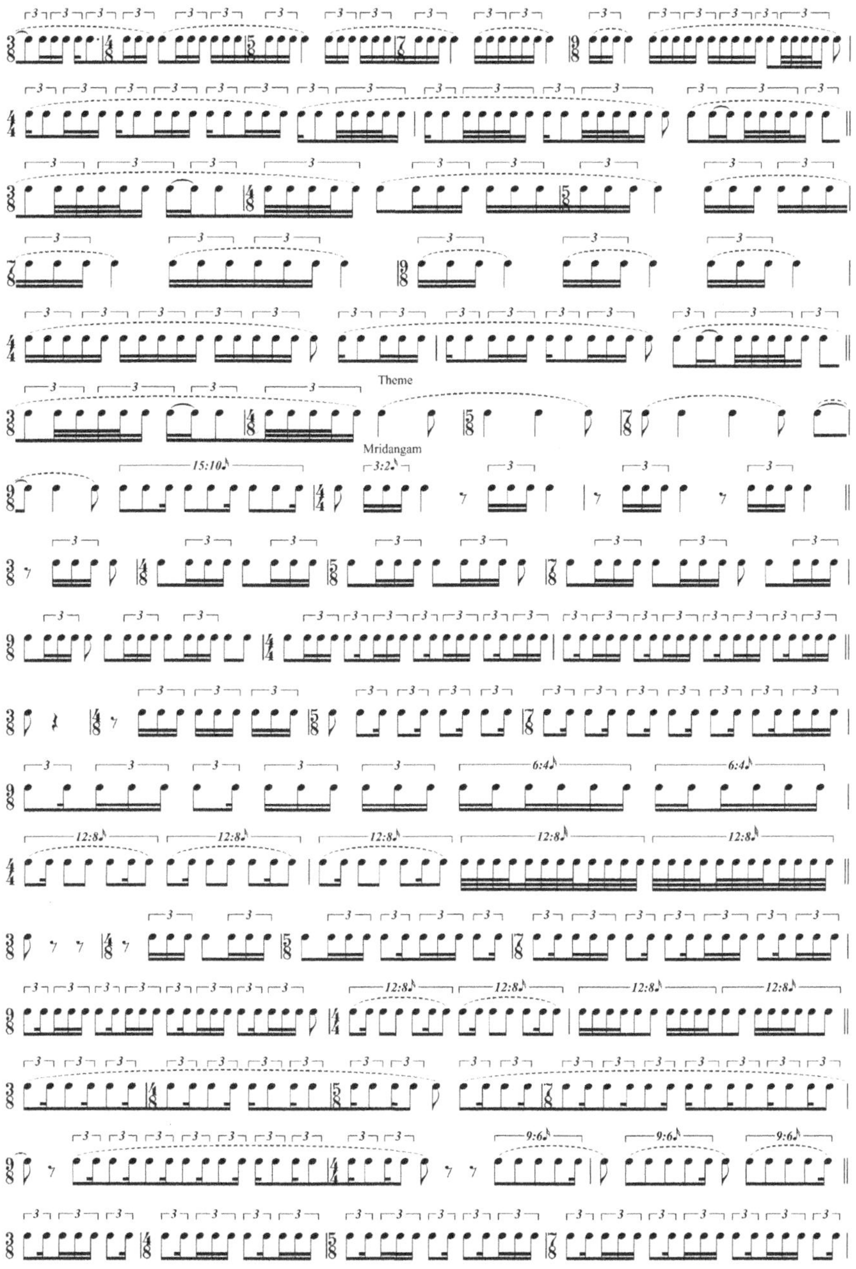
Theme
Mridangam

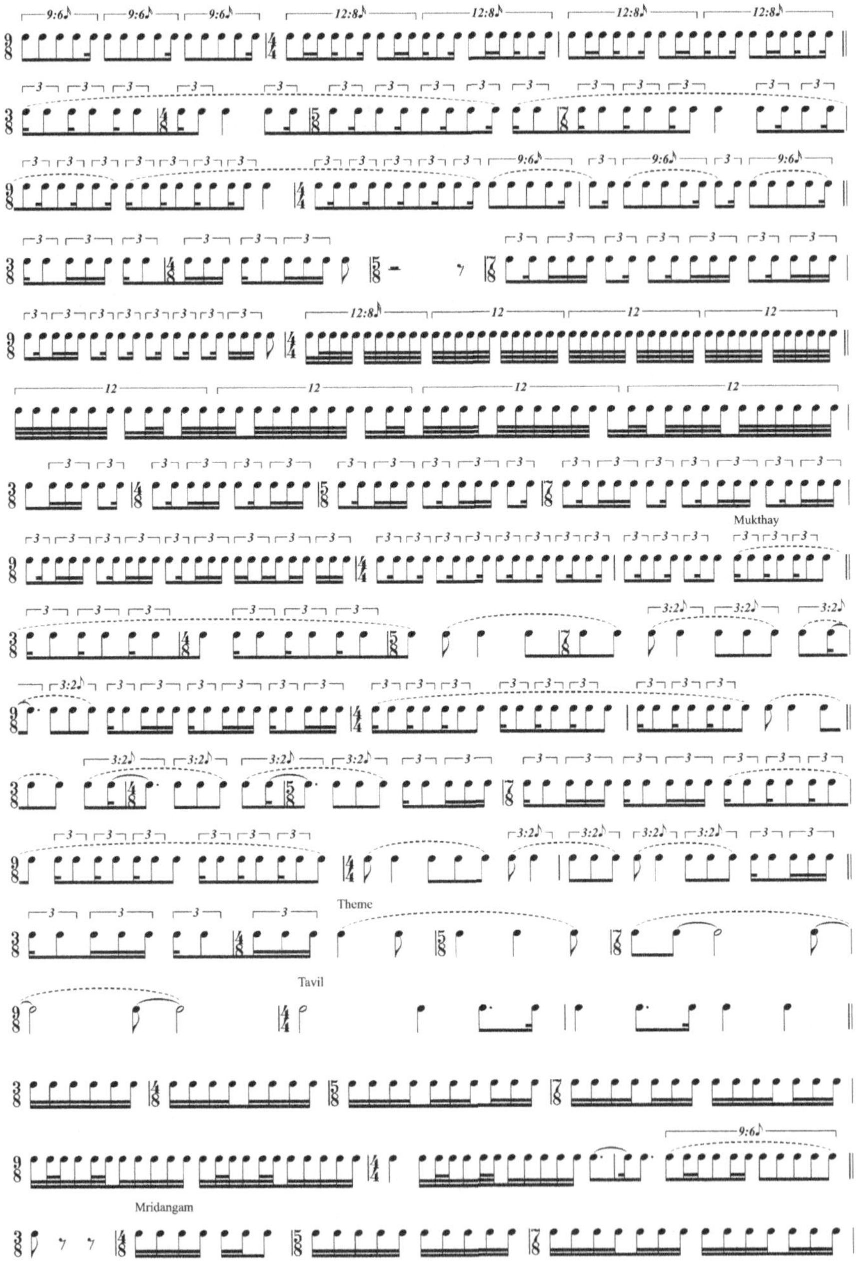
Mukthay
Theme
Tavil
Mridangam

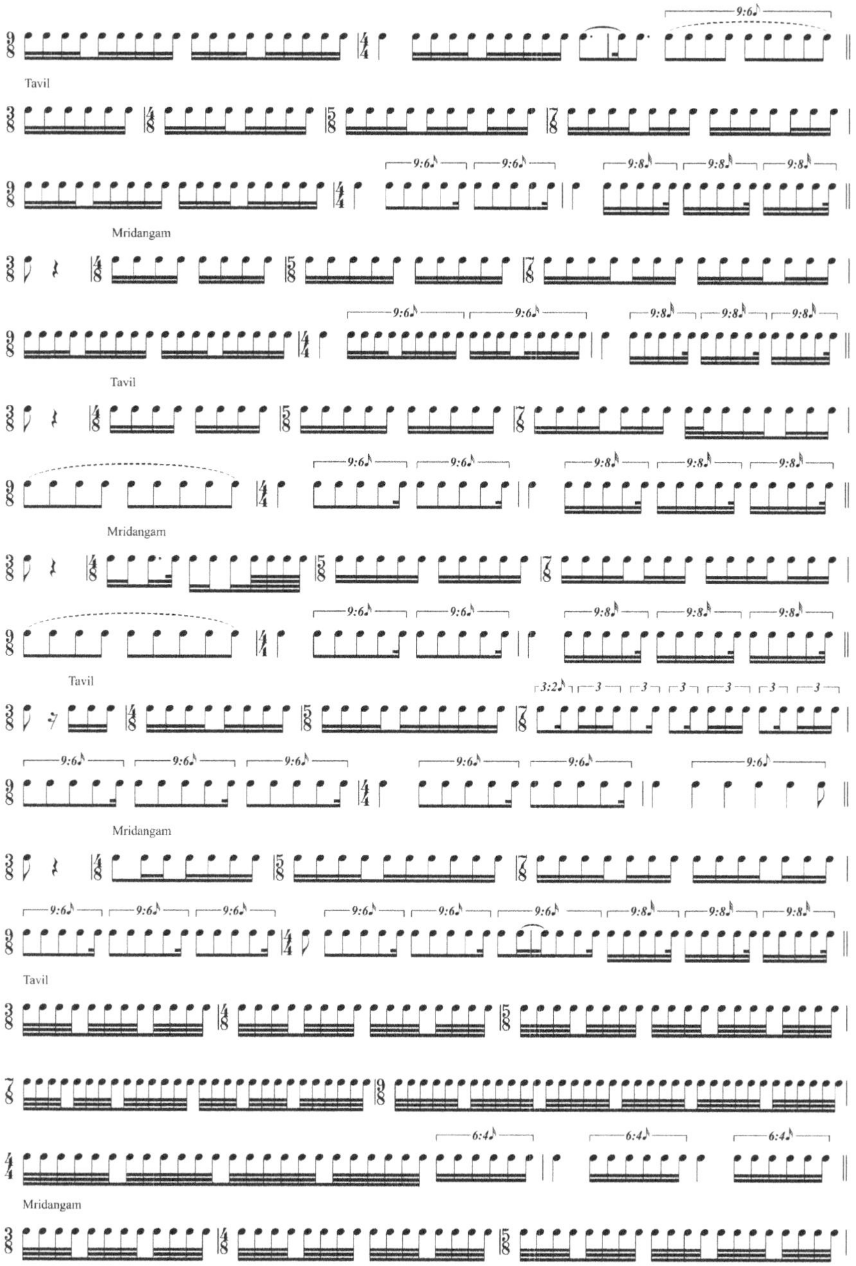
Tavil
Mridangam
Tavil
Mridangam
Tavil
Mridangam
Tavil
Mridangam

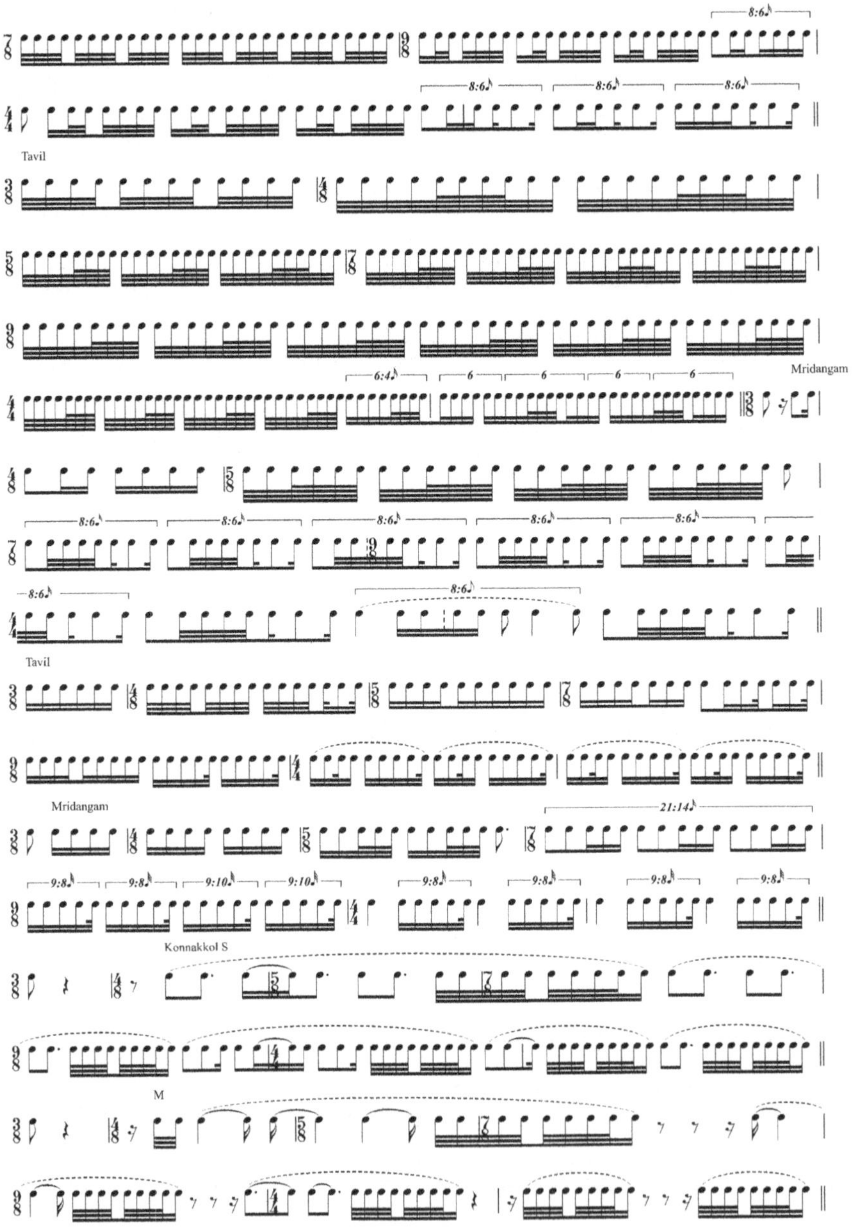
8:6
8:6 8:6 8:6
Tavil
6:4 6 6 6 6
Mridangam
8:6 8:6 8:6 8:6 8:6
8:6 8:6
Tavil
Mridangam
21:14
9:8 9:8 9:10 9:10 9:8 9:8 9:8 9:8
Konnakkol S
M

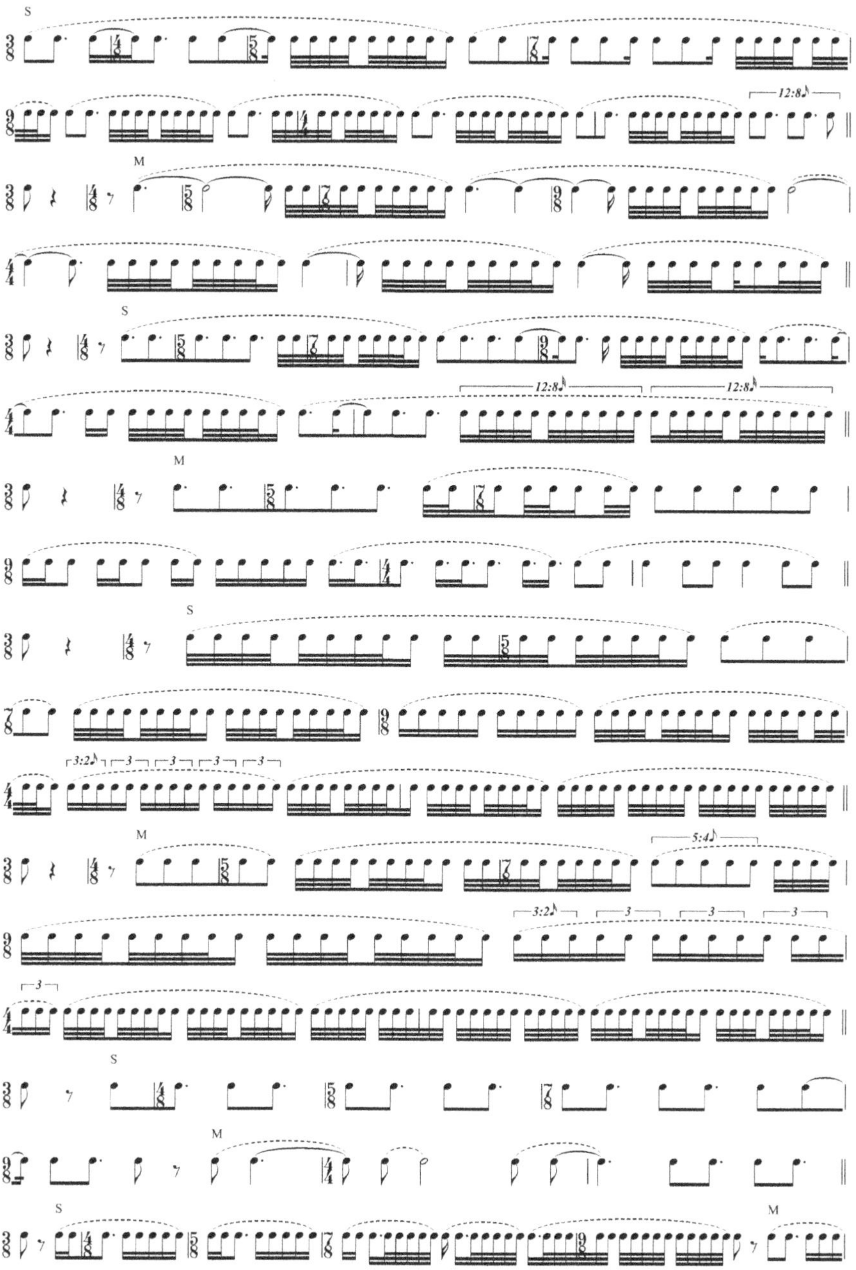
S
12:8
M
S
12:8
12:8
M
S
3:2
3
M
5:4
3:2
3
3
S
M
S
M

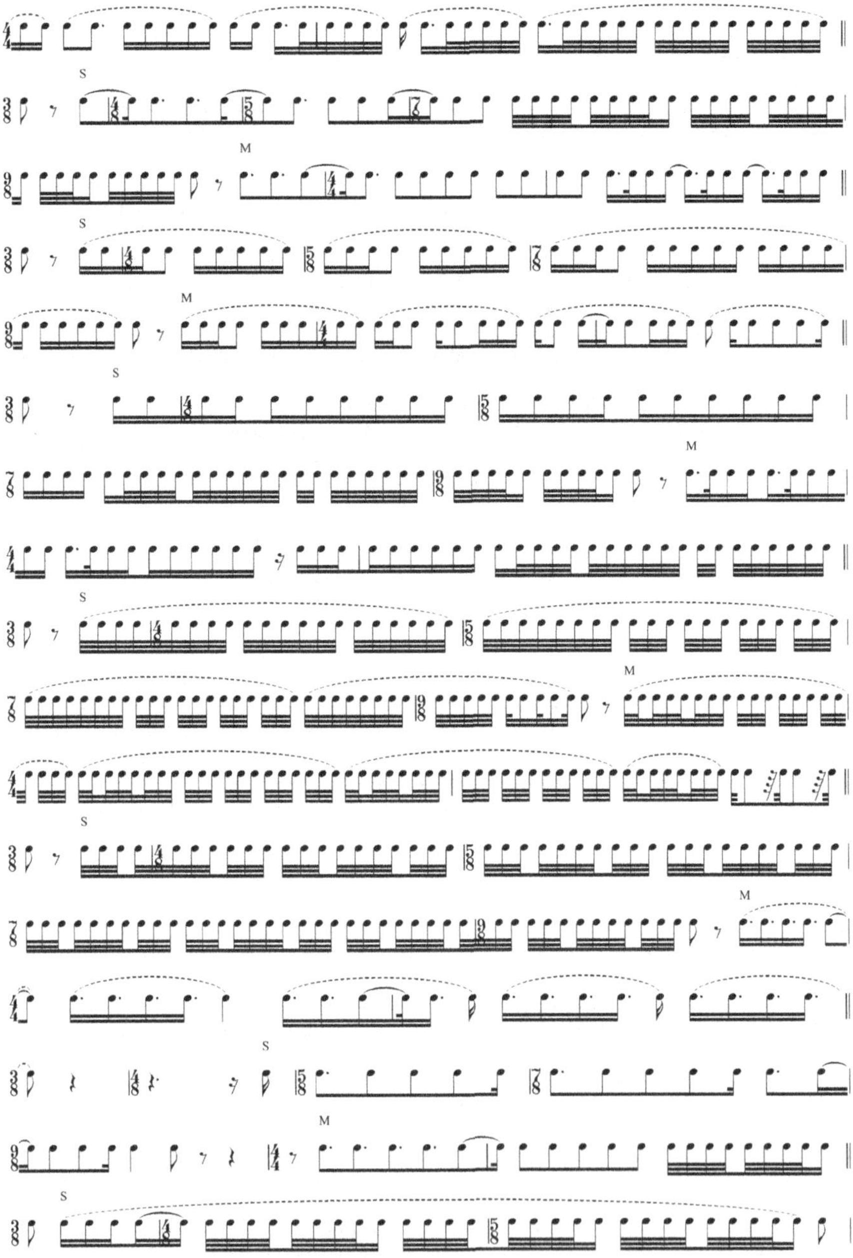
S
M
S
M
S
M
S
M
S
M
S
M
S

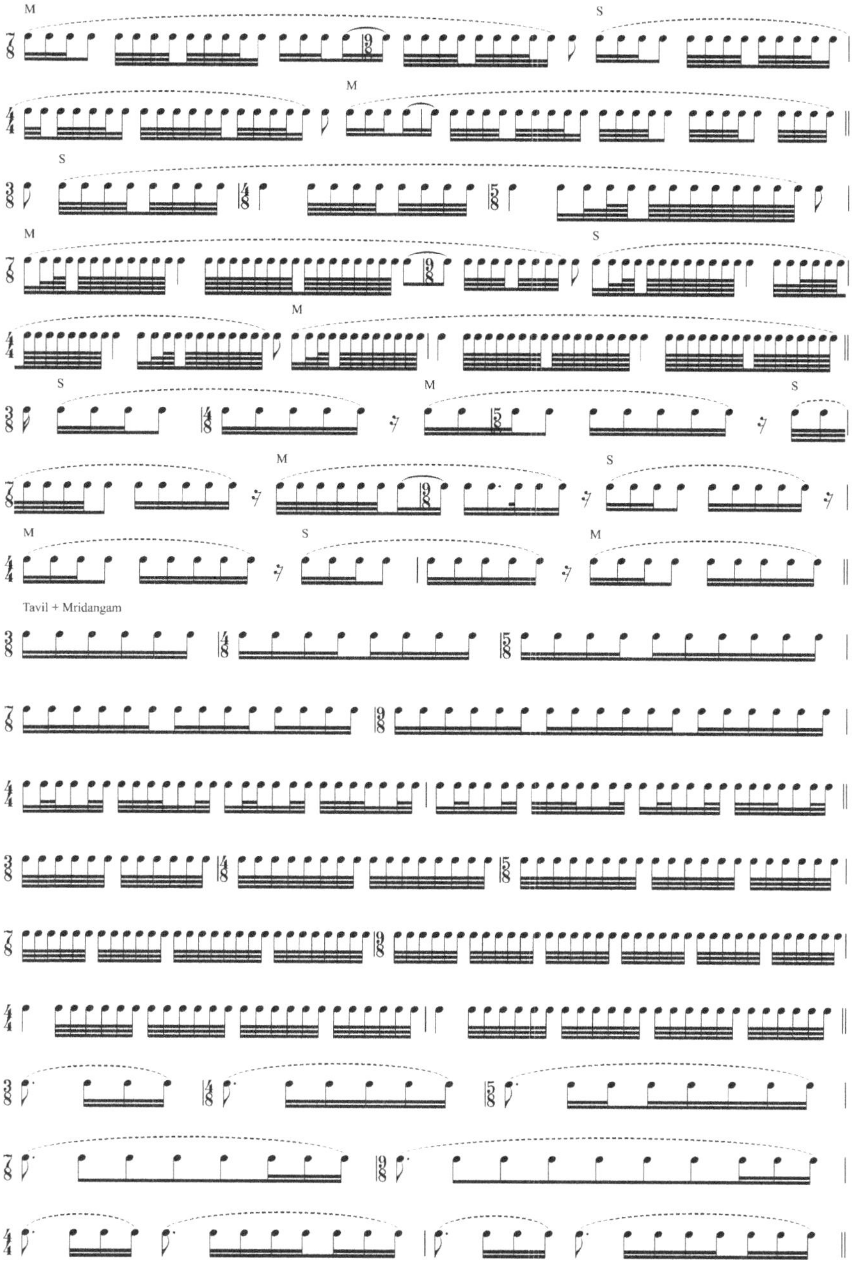
M
S
Tavil + Mridangam

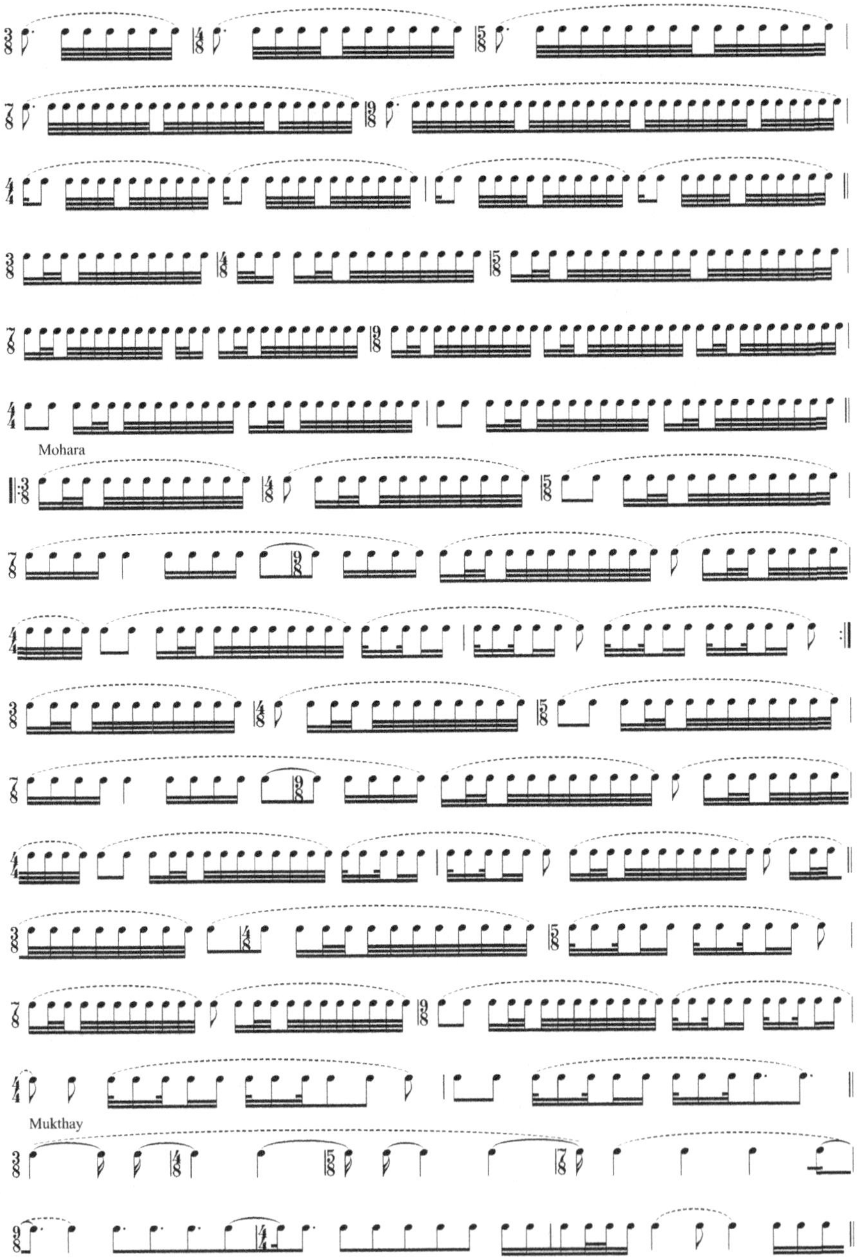
Mohara
Mukthay

Practice Method

In order to master the latest development in karnatic music, a concept that is often used in western contemporary music (with none of the self-imposed restrictions existing in karnatic music), working separately on the different elements would be the best approach initially.

1) Sing all the matras and gati changes of a sequence to become acquainted with the proportionalities provided by the gati changes. First, it would be convenient to start with sequences with only one change – for instance chatusra-tisra, chatusra-khanda, tisra-khanda and so forth. Then proceed to construct sequences with two gati changes, then three changes etc. Also, the frequency of changes should increase with every exercise. The following example presents all four gatis.

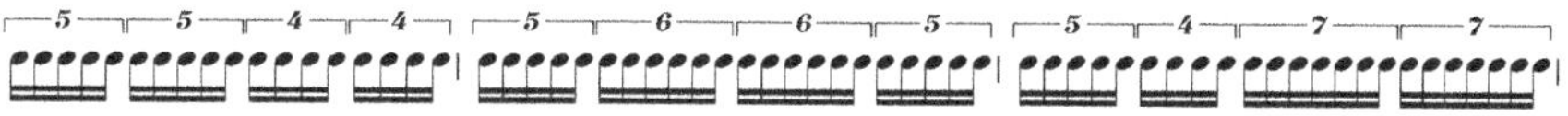

2) Perform only the matras of each cell of the phrase (i.e. with the internal division, displaced accents, different lengths of each cell etc.), so that the two different elements – the gati changes and the phrase – start getting closer to one another. Emphasise solely the accents and never the beat where a change occurs. In the example below, the whole sequence is 63 matras long, divided

7 5 3 5 6 5 3 4 3 6 5 6 5 *(track 236)*

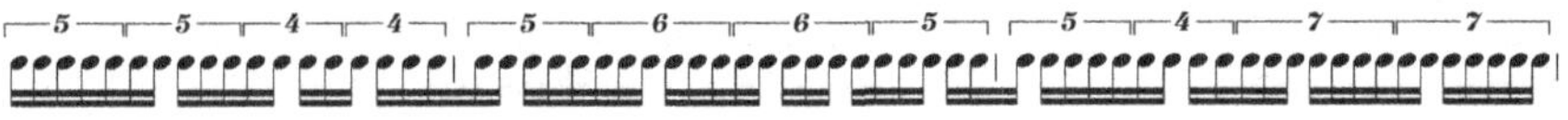

3) Rewrite the phrase in just one gati (preferably chatusra), regardless of whether or not the rewritten phrase finishes neatly on a beat. This approach will help the musician achieve a better feeling for the phrase as such, without the difficulties that the gati changes produce.

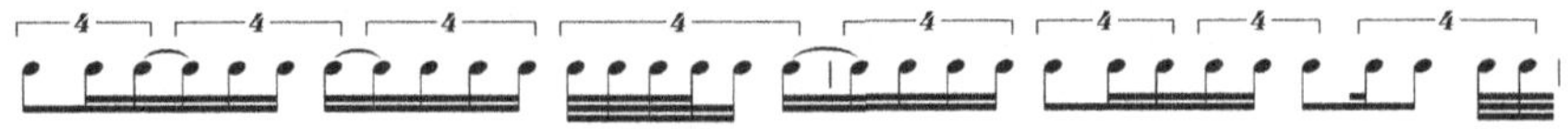

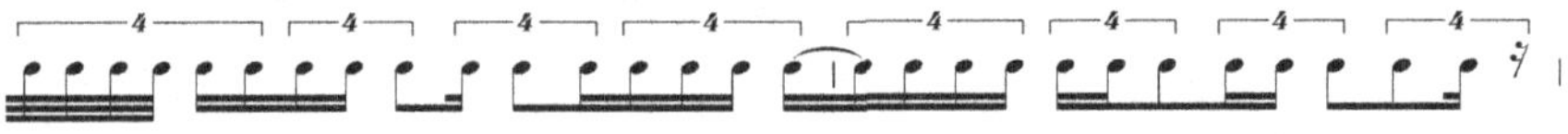

4) Proceed to perform the phrase as written once the previous three steps have been independently and sufficiently rehearsed. You could take the first three examples in this chapter as a starting point to then proceed to elaborate your own phrases. Similarly, working on the transcribed solo and duet presented here will add a considerable amount of *intuition* to the whole process. Even if these solos are eminently karnatic, listening to them and trying to reproduce them as accurately as possible will deepen the intuitive (feeling) side of the working process. *(track 237)*

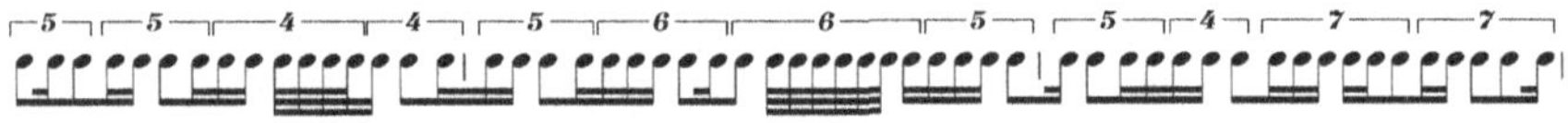

PART II
Pedagogical and Creative Applications to Western Music

Chapter 25

Application of Karnatic Techniques to Existing Western Pieces

The first of the two goals enunciated in the introduction to be explored in Part II is to analyse existing pieces of western classical contemporary and jazz repertoire in order to:

a. *Apply karnatic techniques to existing pieces from the twentieth and twenty-first centuries* in order to improve the rhythmical awareness and accuracy of performers (or any musician for that matter). This is possibly one of the most important aims of the whole book. This research and its application to western music that was created without using any karnatic concept can become a much-needed tool. Next to studying the karnatic techniques as such, many musicians can see how these techniques can be used to dissect and, subsequently, how they can be applied to rhythmically complex western pieces.
b. *Find unintentional parallels between western and karnatic concepts.* The word unintentional is used deliberately since, although most western composers or improvisers (except, perhaps, for a handful of creators exposed to karnatic music in the last few decades) have no knowledge of the karnatic rhythmical system, fragments of their music may, somehow, resemble karnatic structures. My research has gone more in the line of how a number of creators have found ways to express ideas that clearly resemble a variety of aspects of karnatic concepts.

I have limited myself to providing one or two examples per main topic. Nonetheless, I have found it necessary to try to be as detailed as possible in explaining how more complex pieces can be dissected and approached from a performer's point of view. The explanation given in Examples 8–13 should suffice in understanding how subjects like nadai bhedam or anuloma-pratiloma combinations can be applied in order to obtain the desired result of complete accuracy and understanding of the rhythmical processes.

The way of organising and developing 'complex irregular groupings' as established by nadai bhedam and anuloma-pratiloma combinations in karnatic music simply does not exist in western music. The way western 'irregular groupings' are conceived deviates widely from these highly regulated developmental techniques and the different use and purpose of both concepts in karnatic music. What prevails in the West seems to be something more along the lines of 'numbers against numbers', with no conceptual resemblance to what is proposed by karnatic music. Therefore, it is practically impossible to establish a creative parallel between karnatic and western music in this particular issue.

> However, applying nadai bhedam and combinations anuloma-pratiloma to a variety of rhythmically complex western pieces can contribute greatly to performing the music with the accuracy demanded by the notation that many composers use.

1) *Movimento* (Franco Donatoni)

This short fragment of Donatoni's piece is fairly representative of the composition as a whole, and it shows a clear parallel with the notion of using different gatis with the same jathi as explained in Chapter 3. However, Donatoni uses the same element in different ways, essentially by combining notes and rests complementing layers that use the same gati/jathi combination. Similarly, khanda, tisra and chatusra are used in different layers while various accents, in addition to the notion of mixed jathi, are presented systematically.

Layer 1

Tisra jathi 4, with 2 attacked notes and a silence of 2 matras

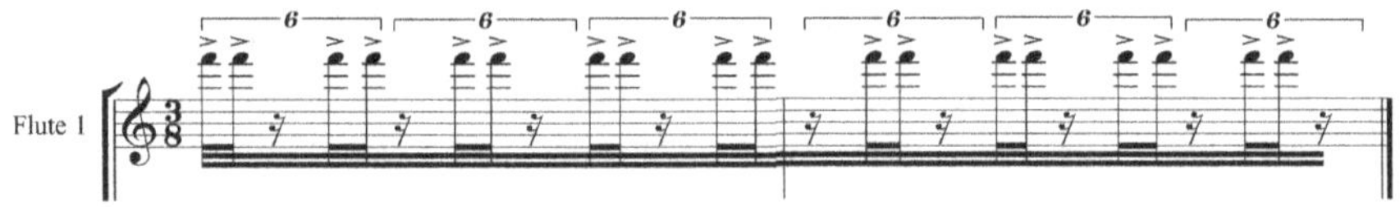

Layer 2

Khanda jathi 3, with 2 attacked notes and a silence of 1 matra

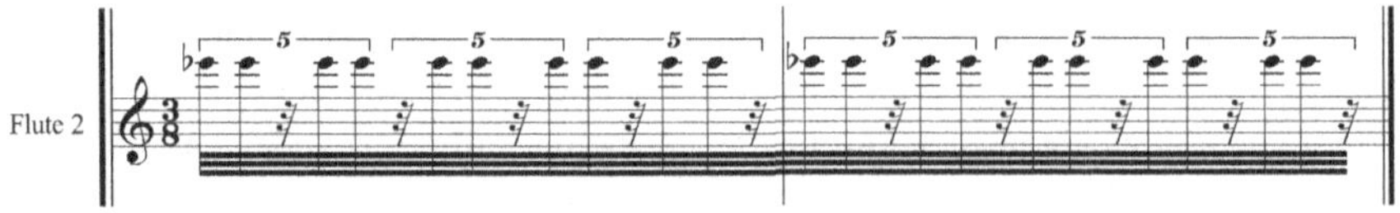

Layer 3

Chatusra jathi 3, also with 2 attacked notes and a silence of 1 matra

Layer 4

Tisra, with mixed accents of 4+3; the jathi 4 is performed as in layer 1, and the jathi 3 is realised by attacking one note and keep the other two silenced.

Layer 5

Written in khanda, it also utilises the notion of mixed jathi, 2+3 in this case. Jathi 2 is achieved by attacking the first note followed by a silence, whereas the jathi 3 responds to the pattern established in layer 2.

Layer 6

The same idea as in the previous layer but in chatusra; mixed jathi 2+3 with the same combination of attacked notes and silences.

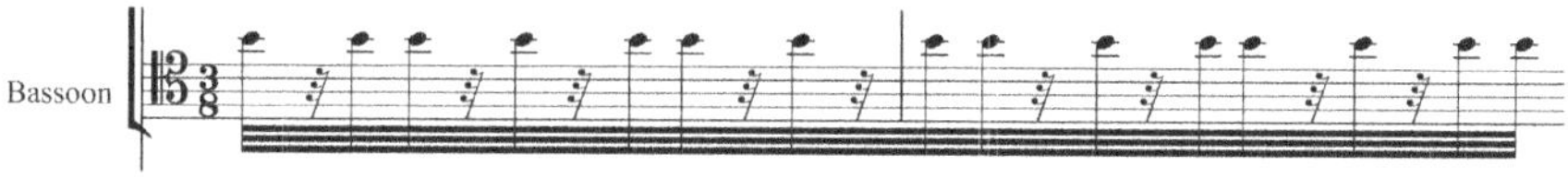

Layer 7

In tisra, using the idea of a triple accent of 3+3+4. In jathi 3 only the accent is attacked while the other 2 matras are silenced, whereas the jathi 4 responds again to the pattern of layer 1 – 2 attacked notes followed by a silence of 2 matras.

Layer 8

This instrument performs the idea of a triple jathi of 2+2+3 in khanda. The sequence of attacked and silenced notes responds to the pattern established by the previous layer.

Layer 9

Same idea as in the previous layer but in chatusra gati: 2+2+3.

The overall result is a texture of different attacks and silences in different gatis, but all of them thought out systematically. It can be observed that every layer plays only one pitch, therefore the focus seems to be on the rhythmical texture.

In order to perform this fragment without making it sound chaotic, I find it of extreme importance that the performer applies the principle of independence provided by the different two-layered exercises of gati/jathi combinations explained in Chapter 3. The short fragment looks like this:

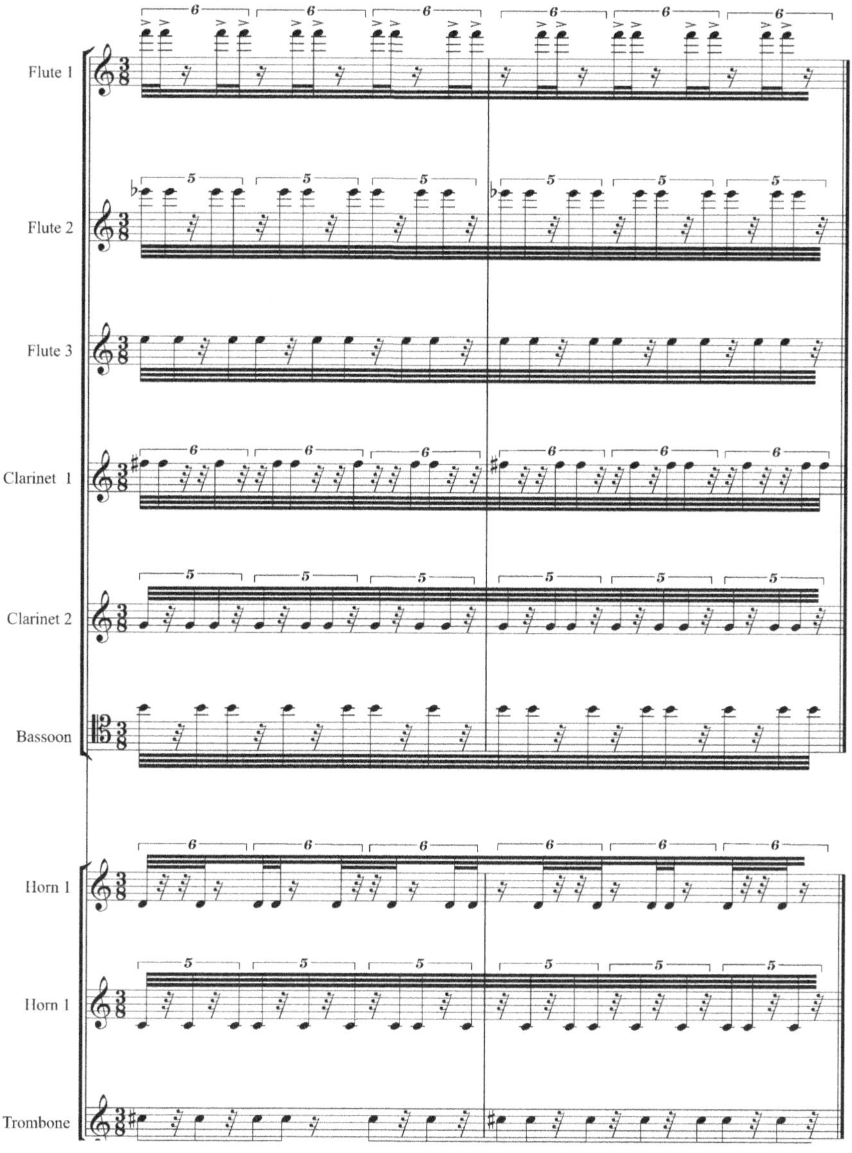

2) *Quatuor pour la fin du temps* (Olivier Messiaen)

The following fragment of this composition is a clear western parallel of the concept of jathi bhedam. Although Messiaen wrote bar lines and every measure is of a different length, no time signatures are specified. This section uses the following jathi bhedam sequence or succession of phrases of different length beamed together, as proposed in Chapter 4:

4 5 4 4 4 5 8 4 5 5 4 6 4 8 4 4 3 6 4 6 4 4 6 7 4 4 4 5 4 4 4
6 8 4 4 3 6 4

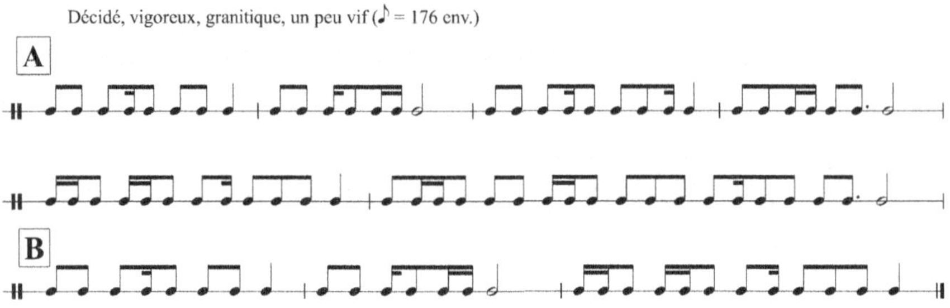

3) *Piano Concerto* (György Ligeti)

This composition is another clear example of jathi bhedam, this time in tisra, since the time signature is 12/8. The composer plays solely with accents every 2, 3 and 4 matras, conveying a sequence that, from the very first measure, breaks the regularity of 3 matras per beat, with the first beat of the measure quite often being ignored. For the purposes of illustrating the technique for this section of the book, only the following two systems have been selected. The sequence of numbers in this short fragment is

3 3 3 2 3 3 3 4| 2 2 2 3 3 3 2 3 3 3 4 2 4 2| 3 3 3 2 3 3 3 4 2
2 2 3 3

The example below shows the idea of chatusra jathi 3: the longer note in the upper stem provides the accents while the lower stem performs all the matras of the gati/jathi combination. The left hand attacks some of the accents of the jathi 3.

This regular jathi of 3 matras becomes doubled to 6 in the subsequent passage to immediately combine the numbers 4, 6 and 8 (essentially the same numbers as in the tisra passage). However, each hand performs a different combination of these numbers.

4) *Concerto in Re* (Igor Stravinsky)

Stravinsky is well known for his use of outer and inner amalgamation, as mentioned in Chapter 6. While the clearest example of the former is to be found in *Le Sacre du Printemps*, the latter (jathi bhedam in karnatic parlance) is a constant in much of his music. Notwithstanding the fact that he does not beam the phrase as proposed in Chapter 4 (or as Messiaen does), but rather keeps the imaginary beat-line characteristic of western notation, may make it look as if regular phrasing in any given gati is sought for.

The concept of inner amalgamation is used quite loosely in the following example, a violin solo from this concerto; it does not follow any sequence, as was the case in Messiaen's piece. However, the solo is permeated with the notion of crossing accents in an irregular fashion. Stravinsky's manner of asking for this technique is usually represented by the bowing that, on many occasions, embraces phrases of different lengths. Measure 3 is a good example: the first bowing takes the last two 𝅘𝅥𝅯 of the first beat, going all the way to the second note of the third beat; this long gesture is followed by three short bowings that last 3, 5 and 3 matras respectively (taking the 𝅘𝅥𝅯 as the matra).

Throughout the whole selected passage there are many occasions where he uses bowings that do not follow the western imaginary beat-line. It can be argued, because of the notation, that the bowings have only a technical application. However, knowing Stravinsky's music, I would argue in favour of a jathi bhedam approach to the phrasing, regardless of whether or not this one is pre-structured. In my view, to perform this passage with a downbeat feeling on every beat, ignoring the bowing and its structural significance, would quite drastically change his musical intention. Approaching it with a jathi bhedam notion (every first note of a bowing being attacked with a downbeat feel) would provide a much more accurate account of his phrasing.

5) *Vesalii Icones* (Peter Maxwell Davies)

For the last example of jathi bhedam, I have reserved a fragment of this composition in which every measure changes its time signature – a feature that has become a key characteristic of music of the twentieth and twenty-first centuries. In spite of the fact that this contradicts the karnatic notion of irregularly distributed accents from the creative viewpoint (that is, as a sequence contained in x number of cycles of a tala), jathi bhedam is ultimately a technique that can greatly help performers to gain accuracy while facing pieces where a continuous change of metres occurs.

The following fragment could be approached with the following number sequence in mind (if the ♪ is taken as the matra).

6 6 7 4 2 3 2 3 2 2 3 2 5. At this point the feeling should switch to an underlying pulse of 𝅘𝅥𝅯 and count the sequence as 5 6 7 7. Again, switch the feeling to ♪ and continue with 5 6 4 4 3.

6) *16_1/64_1* (Toru Nakatani)

The well-established (and predominantly) western concept of metrical modulation, a notion utilised abundantly since the 1950s, is the main feature of this piece. Although tempo changes occur sporadically in karnatic music, many elements explained so far can be of great help when trying to establish new tempi accurately.

There are two ways of expressing metrical modulations: the first is when there is some rhythmical element that produces a clear equivalence between the old and new tempi (Elliot Carter and Ligeti are clear exponents of this method); the second is when solely the new tempo is indicated, without giving any clues as to how a performer or conductor should move from one tempo to another.

Often, the two elements (equivalence and tempo) are indicated, but the musical object that provokes the new tempo may not be as practical as a performer or conductor would like. For the next two examples I asked the conductor and flautist Jos Zwaanenburg how he thought out the metrical modulations, considering that the equivalences proposed by the composer seemed to be rather cumbersome and more theoretical than practical.

The equivalence of 5 matras of tisra becoming the new beat in the new tempo 𝅘𝅥-♩♩ (♩=171) caused problems while rehearsing, since no layer was performing that particular figure. Zwaanenburg therefore resorted to using a karnatic frame that would help the transition from a 3/4 metre in ♩=102 to a 5/4 metre in ♩=171.

Using the pratiloma frame of 5:3♩. helped crystallise the new tempo accurately: 102×5:3=170, which is a number very close to the one indicated by the composer. Zwaanenburg told me that he was already thinking of this frame for a few measures prior to the tempo change in order to assure the clarity and feeling when the music changed metre and tempo. Consequently, every ♩ of the 5:3♩. frame became the new beat.

For the next example Zwaanenburg similarly ignored the equivalence proposed by the composer (the same as in the example above) and decided to use the notion of 'gati becoming jathi', explained as a creative tool for the 'tree of gati bhedam'. Consequently, a unit of tisra becomes a unit of khanda (3)♪ = ♪(5), although he was feeling all the matras in tisra prior to the metrical modulation (thus feeling the laya), to subsequently take these 3 matras as the first matras of a khanda in the new tempo. All that was then needed was to add the 2 remaining matras of the gati to obtain the new tempo/beat in a practical manner. The calculations for arriving at the new tempo are the reverse of the first one: 170×3:5=102.

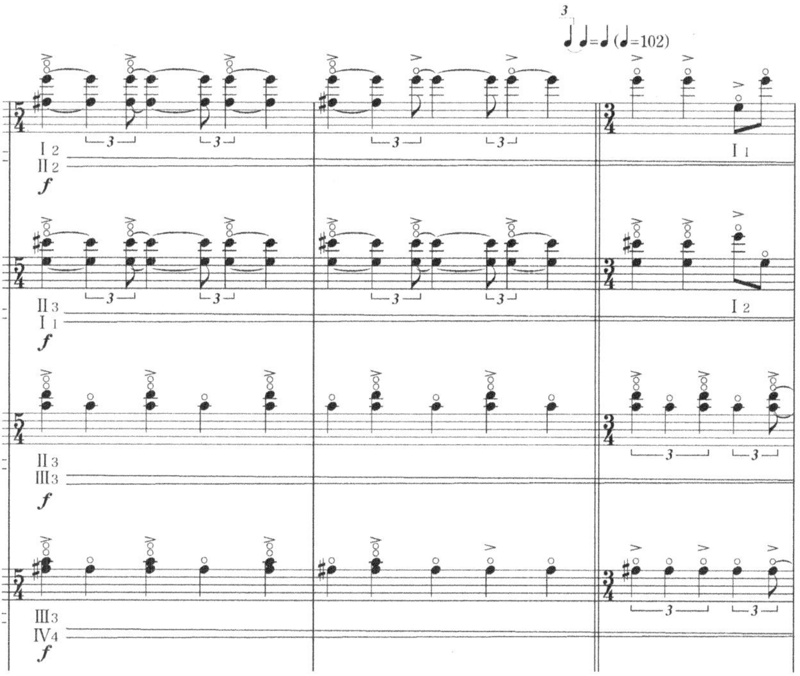

7) *Athena Keramitis* (Jan Vriend)

The following passage by this Dutch composer is an extreme example of the concept of phrasing through gati changes –as explained in Chapter 24: gati changes occur in almost every beat and phrases are mostly written starting in one gati and continuing into the next one. The phrasing exclusively uses the matras of every gati and does not use different note values, as was the case with the karnatic examples presented in Chapter 24. In order to perform this fragment accurately, the musician would need to apply the four steps explained previously in Chapter 24:

1. Sing the solkattu syllables of every gati, without any phrasing, until the changes are internalised.
2. Rewrite all the phrases in one gati (chatusra always seems to be a better choice) to obtain a good feeling for the phrasing as such (and, in this case, the rests in between phrases) without the hindrance that the gati change may represent to start with.
3. Perform only the matras of each cell of the phrase (i.e. with the internal division, displaced accents, different lengths of each cell etc.), so that the two different elements – the gati changes and the phrase – start getting

closer to one another. Emphasise solely the accents and never the beat where a change occurs.

4. Proceed to perform the passage as written, always keeping in mind the changes of speed provided by the gati changes, and treating the phrase as a unit that should not be broken by any gati change. In this way, the score will sound as the composer has written it.

8) *Symphony No. 4* (Charles Ives)

With one measure of this symphony I would like to introduce two clear examples of nadai bhedam that use the same notation as proposed in Chapter 18 with the double bracket (or nested tuplet). The origin of the first bracket can be traced back to any gati/jathi combination, and the second bracket works essentially as the nadai did in karnatic music.

This measure of the piccolo takes as the first bracket a 3:4♩ (which, from a performance viewpoint, would be the result of applying tisra jathi 4 and isolating the accents), and on every ♩ of the first bracket superimposes tisra nadai.

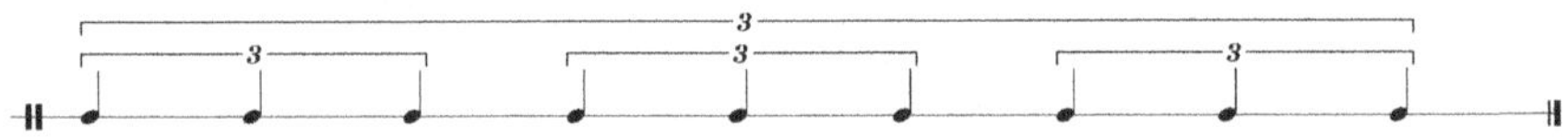

9) *Black Page* (Frank Zappa)

In this well-known composition Zappa uses the notation proposed in Chapter 18 on several occasions: first in measure 5, where in the last two beats a 3:2♩ is used as a first bracket, which is again the result of thinking of tisra jathi 2 and isolating the accents.

However, as opposed to karnatic musicians, for whom nadai bhedam is exclusively a concept to produce polypulses – and therefore a constant nadai is used throughout a whole frame – on the first two ♩. of the first bracket a khanda is superimposed, followed in the last ♩. by a superimposed tisra.

From a performer's viewpoint, this change of nadai (or superimposed tuplet) should not represent a major obstacle if, during the practice of this karnatic technique, a performer has consolidated one of the most important set of exercises, namely keeping the same number of accents and beats and changing the nadai. In this fashion, all one needs to do is to apply this concept on the bracket. *(track 238)*

Later on Zappa writes a 3:2𝅗𝅥., which, in my opinion, can create certain confusion to begin with. Possibly, a 6:4♩. would have been more transparent, since there are six different groupings, although one of them (7:8♪.) takes the time-span of two accents. *(track 239)*

Similarly to the previous example, applying the change of nadai on the same frame can produce the desired result and clarity in the performance. The only added difficulty is the 7:8♪. since it takes two of the six accents. In order to perform this particular element, the performer could start practising regular misra on every accent, and then proceed to apply a jathi 2 to misra (as seen in Chapter 7) and isolate the accents. In this way, the 7:2♩. (in karnatic thinking) is obtained and the 7:8♪. can be played accurately.

The last segment of this piece presents the same nadai bhedam as in measure 5 (3:2♩. as the first bracket with two groupings of khanda nadai and a third one of tisra nadai) followed by two beats of 11. This gati is seldom used in western music. When utilised, it is usually without any phrasing, and in most cases more as a sort of fast group of 'grace notes' or arpeggio to a main note. This example does not propose any phrasing, although in my opinion and estimation of Zappa's intention regarding the creation and performance of rhythmical complexities these two beats are written with the aim of being performed as a gati and not with the arpeggio or grace notes notion. *(track 240)*

10) *Dmaathen* (Iannis Xenakis)

As already mentioned in the general introduction to this section, the significant differences in organising and developing ‘complex irregular groupings’ as established by nadai bhedam and combinations anuloma-pratiloma in karnatic music simply do not exist in western music. Therefore, the difference between the two previous examples by Ives and Zappa and the following examples by Xenakis and Castiglioni are based exclusively on the different notations proposed by the composers rather than real conceptual differences.

In the two previous examples, it was seen that the direct use of nadai bhedam could help the musician perform the passages as written. In the next two Xenakis passages, as explained in the practice method section of combinations anuloma-pratiloma (Chapter 20), the musician would need to resort to several techniques in order to perform the passage with absolute accuracy. *(track 241)*

In the first two measures of this example (in 4/4) the following process is suggested:

a. Take the frame of each irregular grouping and make a short jathi bhedam sequence so that the performer knows exactly where every starting point of each irregular grouping falls within the beat. The sequence of this example would be 9 7 7 4 4 1, which gives 32 matras in chatusra (two measures of 4/4).
b. The first 9 matras are simply a phrase in chatusra jathi 9.
c. The first 6:7♪ starts on the 2nd matra of the beat; this would be the initial point of the 4th accent of the nadai bhedam frame

┌———— *4:7* ————┐
┌*6*┐┌*6*┐┌*6*┐┌*6*┐

All one need do is to review this particular combination and get the feeling for how the matras of a superimposed tisra are distributed in the last 7 matras of the frame.

d. The second 6:7♪ starts on the downbeat; this would therefore be the initial point of the same nadai bhedam frame and, consequently, would finish on the 4th matra of the 2nd beat.
e. What follows is a 4-matras phrase, starting and finishing on the last matra of the beat. Therefore, using a gati bhedam principle should suffice to perform this phrase.

In the next two measures of the same composition by Xenakis, a similar process is suggested. *(track 242)*

a. Construct a sequence of jathi bhedam with the frames of the irregular groupings in order to establish where each of them starts and finishes within the beat. The sequence for these two measures would be 3 7 4 5 6 7
b. Establish which accent of a nadai bhedam frame corresponds to the beginning point of every irregular grouping:

4:3♪ would be the first accent of a ┌——***4:3***——┐
┌***4***┐┌***4***┐┌***4***┐┌***4***┐

First 9:7♪, since it starts on the 4th matra, would be the 2nd accent of a
┌——***4:7***——┐
┌***9***┐┌***9***┐┌***9***┐┌***9***┐

c. 5:4♪ is a regular khanda that starts and finishes in the second half of the beat. For this, practising a regular khanda starting on the second half of the beat – or working on exercise set 'C' of combinations anuloma-pratiloma (regarding performing all regular speeds starting on every point of the beat) – could give the desired result.
d. 7:5♪ consequently starts in the second half of the beat as well; the best way to perform it would be to use the distribution of matras of the 3rd accent of a ┌——***4:5***——┐
┌***7***┐┌***7***┐┌***7***┐┌***7***┐
e. A phrase of chatusra jathi 6 follows suit, starting on the 4th matra of the beat. The last ♪ of the phrase does actually fall on the beat, but since the beaming suggests a chatusra jathi 6 phrase, this ♪ should not be emphasised because of its placement.
f. Since the last 9:7♪ starts on the 2nd matra, it would be the 4th accent of a
┌——***4:7***——┐
┌***9***┐┌***9***┐┌***9***┐┌***9***┐

11) *Quodlibet* (Niccolò Castiglioni)

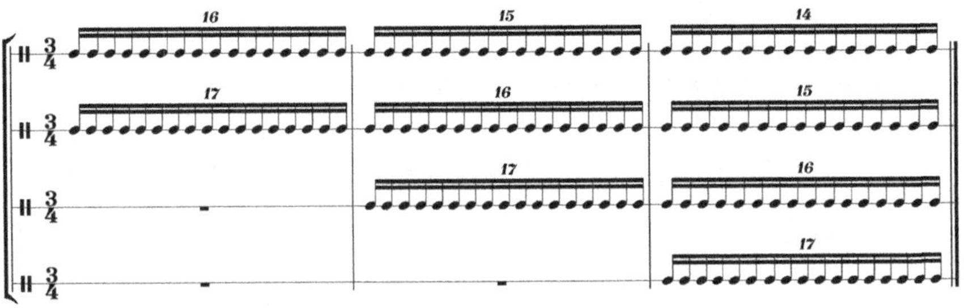

(track 243 performing 17, 16, 15 and 14)

I chose this fragment of this piece because I thought that despite the fact that the composer's intention was most likely to create a spider's web of intricate irregular groupings in a sort of canon shape in which every layer slows down by 1 matra per measure, it could be a good opportunity to show how every 'complex number' could be approached using nadai bhedam or combinations anuloma-pratiloma to assure complete accuracy while performing.

In every measure, each layer omits 1 matra, and this omission produces a different irregular grouping. Simultaneously, since it keeps a metre of 3 beats throughout the passage, it could be argued that there is a parallel with the 6th developmental technique of combinations anuloma-pratiloma (keeping the same frame, changing gati and speed). How every number can be analysed and approached from a performer's viewpoint will now be explained.

a) 17:12♪ would probably have been the most correct notation, although the notation Castiglioni employs is sufficiently clear.

17, 19 or 23 (and any other prime number after 23) are the only numbers for which no frame of nadai bhedam or combinations anuloma-pratiloma can provide a direct answer as to how to perform them. However, I remember asking B.C. Manjunath if he could play 17 and 19 against 2, 3 or 4 beats as he had done with 11 and 13, even though karnatic musicians do not use any of them. To my great surprise, he sang for me 17 and 19 against these three frames without thinking twice, and with complete accuracy.

I deduced from this that, once a musician has achieved a high degree of rhythmical precision and has a complete overview and understanding of the karnatic system, they are able to face elements which, while conceptually outside the scope of this system, they can nonetheless perform with complete naturalness and accuracy. The way Manjunath subdivided the 17 was 9+8, with the following syllables:

Ta ka di na/ta di ghi na to – ta ke di mi/ta ka jha nu

Consequently, any western musician who, in turn, gains a good aptitude for rhythmical intricacies through studying the method proposed in this volume should be capable of working out this number 17 and treating it as an independent gati when necessary.

b) 16:12𝅘𝅥𝅯 is the result of superimposing a chatusra on the frame of 4:3♩; or, using karnatic notation, it would be the nadai bhedam frame

┌——— ***4:3***♩ ———┐
┌***4***┐┌***4***┐┌***4***┐┌***4***┐

c) 15:12𝅘𝅥𝅯 is actually 3 times a regular khanda, since the measure is 3/4.

d) 14:12𝅘𝅥𝅯 was a combination already studied in Chapter 7 (introduction to anuloma-pratiloma). It is the result of superimposing misra 2nd speed anuloma within the 3rd speed pratiloma. The process of achieving it was also explained in the practice method section relevant to that topic (performing 7:6𝅘𝅥𝅯 twice).

What makes this passage especially difficult, from a linear point of view, is the extreme proximity of each number to the following one. However, if every number or irregular grouping is first practised separately until complete precision is obtained, the next step is to put the whole sequence together whilst keeping the independence from the other layers.

As mentioned before, although the construction of the passage may lead one to think that ultimately the composer does not pursue complete precision, practising this passage and performing it with absolute precision will greatly help any musician to analyse, practise and perform passages of similar complexity where the intention is absolute precision.

12) *Persephassa* (Iannis Xenakis)

If there is one rhythmical structure in western music that seems to create quite a few problems for performers and conductors it is the concept of polytempi or polypulses. Xenakis has used this concept in many of his compositions, varying the notation from piece to piece. However, the one he seemed to favour the most, especially in his later pieces, was to give different tempi to each player.

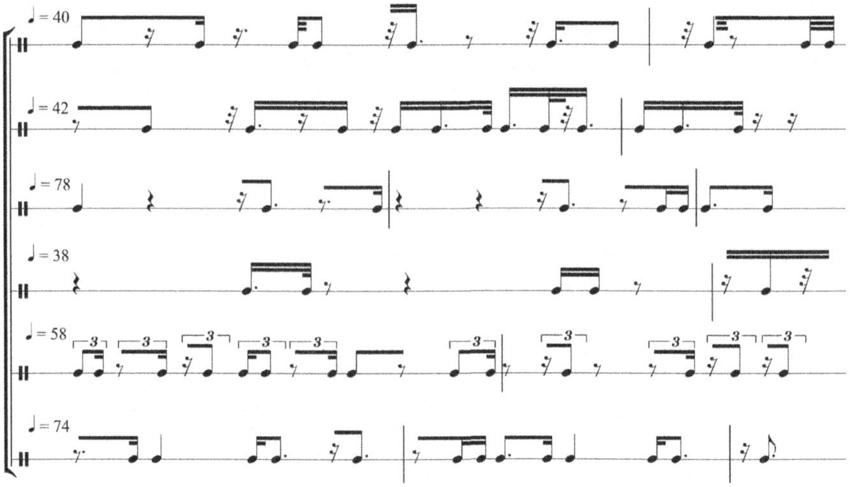

Through my work with many percussion ensembles and percussion students on my programme, I came to realise what I had suspected long before: this notation usually brings forth a few major problems, the following being the most significant:

- Changing tempo without any reference or equivalence while, simultaneously, other players are also changing to different tempi.
- Not having a common reference of some sort means the musician has to 'guess' rather than knowing his relation to other players.
- In conducted pieces (such as Persephassa), the conductor is obliged to stop conducting during the entire passage, his sole role being to cue the performers when the next section arrives. Consequently, the unifying element that a conductor provides in western music disappears altogether.

A few years ago I had the chance to collaborate with percussionists on some Xenakis pieces that used the same concept and notation as Persephassa. Although all the musicians were very experienced with contemporary music, they were all rather frustrated with the passages of polytempi because they felt directionless.

I proceeded to try to find ways with karnatic concepts that would enable them to have what karnatic music has at all times: a common reference in terms of tala and, more importantly in this context, tempo. Therefore, by keeping the previous tempo to the polytempi section in all players, and giving each performer a frame of nadai bhedam (or, alternatively, a rhythmical equivalence), they could practise and perform with a common tempo. This 'trick' subsequently enabled them to keep track of where they were and how they related to one another – which provided, as a final result, a better sense of directionality and intentionality to their playing.

While I do not know if Xenakis had some equivalences in mind when he wrote the different tempi or whether they conformed to other creative parameters, the reality is that it was not always possible to find an exact nadai bhedam frame or equivalence that would suit the tempo written by Xenakis. Sometimes it was necessary to deviate a couple of numbers from the written tempo so that the performer could use one of the devices. However, this deviation did not seem to affect the performance of that particular part, and the player felt at ease and related to the whole structure. By giving these musicians a rigorous system, I enabled them to deal with these minor 'mathematical' inconsistencies.

This is the case with Persephassa, where in two of the six tempi I had to deviate by two numbers from the written tempo. However, the passage could be conducted, and every performer could relate to the conductor's tempo while keeping in mind a nadai bhedam frame – or, in the case of this composition, other devices I created derived from related karnatic concepts.

The previous tempo to this passage is ♩=40. Therefore, I tried to relate all the parts to the old tempo so that the conductor would not need to change it, which would make the leap into nadai bhedam frames of many of the other parts easier.

- First percussionist stays in ♩=40, therefore no calculations or changes are required here.
- The indication for the third percussionist is that he should go to ♩=78. After many calculations failed to bear fruit I decided that this percussionist should simply double his tempo and go to ♩=80.
- The fifth percussionist should go to ♩=58; once again, I could not find an exact equivalence but felt that the closest (and easiest) equivalence would be in a ratio of 3:2. This would produce a tempo of ♩=60, but would enable the musician to fall every two beats with the conductor whilst feeling a simple 3:2♩ and superimpose tisra on every accent of the frame.
- The sixth percussionist needs to go to ♩=74; between 40 and 74 there is a ratio of 9:5. Consequently, the performer needs to think of a 9:5♩ (the result of a gati/jathi combination of sankirna jathi 5) and superimpose chatusra. In this way, he would meet the conductor every five beats. *(track 244)*
- The second and fourth percussionists had the task of slightly speeding up and slowing down. Unfortunately, I could not find a frame that they could keep consistently. Rather, I found metrical equivalences for both that facilitated the transition to a new tempo, although they had no meeting points with the conductor. Nonetheless, these metrical equivalences proved beneficial, and the performers could manage to realise the device and keep their tempi afterwards.
- The fourth player goes to ♩=38. I found that if the performer thought of a 15:16𝅘𝅥𝅯 (or, expressed in nadai bhedam terms, a 3:4♩ with khanda superimposed) the value of the new 𝅘𝅥𝅯 when grouped every 4 matras would produce a tempo of ♩=37,5. Consequently, the performer creates a metrical modulation in his head by using a relatively easy nadai bhedam frame, and the 𝅘𝅥𝅯 of this 15:16𝅘𝅥𝅯 becomes his new chatusra matra that he needs to keep

throughout the entire passage. The musician felt he had a tool to make the transition to the new tempo with relative ease and confidence. *(track 245)*

- For the second player the equivalence was slightly more complicated. This percussionist needed to go to ♩=42 but I could not find a known nadai bhedam frame that would allow him to do so. Finally, I thought that the matra or ♪ of a 17:16♪ would give the tempo ♩=42,5. Subsequently I instructed the player how to think of this rather difficult equivalence. The procedure would be the same as with the fourth percussionist: turn the ♪ of a 17:16♪ as a matra of chatusra and keep the new tempo throughout the whole passage. *(track 246)*

Although not easy to practise and perform, the different frames and equivalences finally enabled the ensemble to put the whole passage together within a few hours, after having spent several days working on it without any tangible result.

13) *Mort Subite (Rhythmical Grid)* (Brian Ferneyhough)

In this piece by Ferneyhough, I selected the rhythmical grid he provided to the Dutch Nieuw Ensemble as a guide. I thought that analysing this grid would help considerably to better understand the thinking behind it. In this rhythmical grid the composer uses different ways to express complex polyrhythms and polypulses, to each of which a karnatic technique can always be applied. Ironically, despite the highly complex material, the underlying notion is that of a cycle: every fragment is constructed around 10 beats, although both layers are using different gatis. Ferneyhough divides this grid into what he calls 'phases'.

Phase I

This first system uses a gati/jathi combination in the upper layer (chatusra jathi 5) which, as in karnatic music, is repeated 4 times to meet the beat (although, because he uses ♪, the third grouping already falls on the beat). In the second layer, he uses a notation in which the denominator is expressed in matras of khanda (5/10), or 5:2♩ using the karnatic way of thinking (10 is the number of matras that 5:2♩ will give in a 4/4 metre).

However, in this context, the 5 matras of khanda are actually going with the pulse every two beats. The effect is the same as explained in Chapter 3: two different layers performing a phrase of 5 notes in different gatis, in this case chatusra and khanda. *(track 247)*

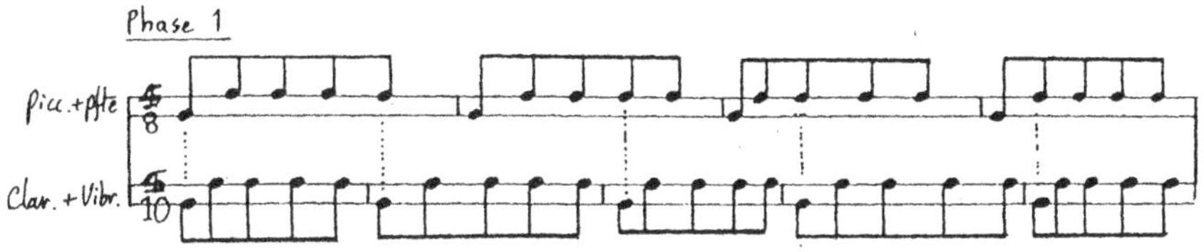

Phase II

In the first layer there is a repetition of the same element (chatusra jathi 5). In the second layer, the khanda realises a short jathi bhedam with the numbers 5 4 3 2 1, which ultimately gives 15 matras of khanda 2nd speed pratiloma (or 3 times 5:2♩.) and resolves on the 7th beat.

This is followed by a short jathi bhedam sequence in tisra (the denominator changes to 12, which is the number of matras that a regular tisra would give in 4/4). This sequence is 1 2 3 4 2, totalling 12 matras or 4 beats. Consequently, the two layers meet after 10 beats, although each of them has used different gatis, and, in the case of the second layer, an incomplete number of matras turned into differentiated time signatures. *(track 248)*

Phase III

In this section the first layer remains in chatusra, although it uses a short jathi bhedam sequence of the same length as the two previous phases (10 beats). The number sequence is 5 4 3 2 3 3. The 2nd layer is constructed in identical fashion to the previous segment. *(track 249)*

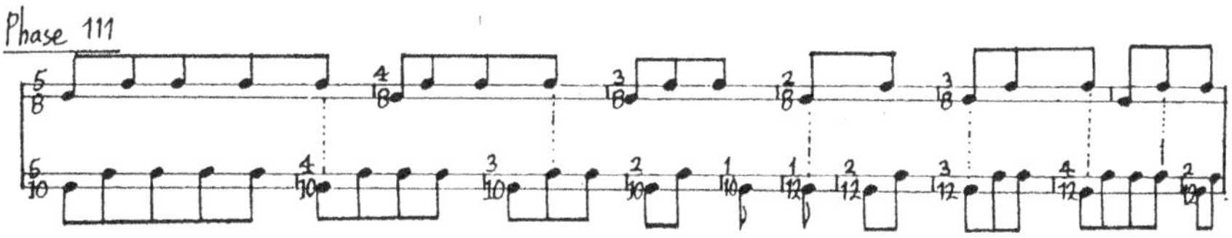

Phase IV (track 250)

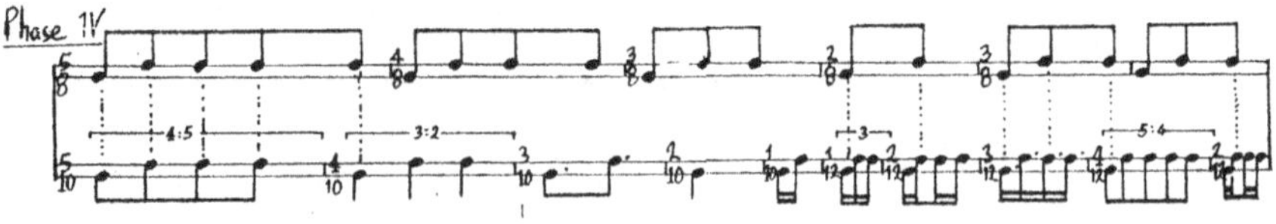

It is from this moment that the composer starts using superimpositions on the metres created by the previous jathi bhedam sequence. The first layer is identical and on the 2nd layer he uses four superimpositions. These superimpositions, within this context, can be approached as follows:

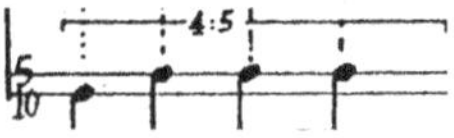

Although it looks quite complicated, this figure is actually the easiest one, since four ♪ in the place of five ♪of khanda is actually four straight ♪in chatusra.[1] I can see the need to keep the notation as written because of the whole construction in khanda so that the consistency of the notation is kept throughout the whole passage.

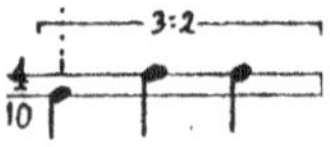

In order to perform this superimposition the musician could approach it with the following steps:

a. Think of a nadai bhedam frame of 5:4♩ but using the ♪as the unit since the 4/10 metre is constructed on khanda 2nd speed pratiloma.
b. Superimpose a tisra on the resulting frame.

This irregular grouping on a metre with a khanda denominator is no different from the nadai bhedam frame:

┌——— ***5:4♩*** ———┐ but creates groups of 4♪ of chatusra in order to
┌*3*┐┌*3*┐┌*3*┐┌*3*┐┌*3*┐ produce the 5:4♩

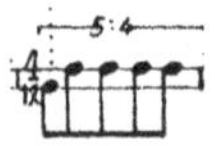

This superimposition should be approached in exactly the same fashion as the previous one, but replacing the superimposed tisra for khanda, with the frame being 3:4♩. The nadai bhedam construction should thus be:

┌——— ***3:4♩*** ———┐
┌*5*┐┌*5*┐┌*5*┐

[1] Ferneyhough does write a connecting dotted line between the two layers to help the performer realise that this is ultimately what it is.

Phase V

Both layers keep the same inner construction of different jathi bhedam sequences and almost the same superimpositions. The only novelty is that the first layer performs a 3:2♩. on the 4/8. If felt as part of a regular pulse, the 3:2♩. begins and ends on the second half of the beat. In order to perform this, instructions on how to approach a gati in regular speed displaced within the beat have been given for Xenakis' Dmaathen. *(track 251)*

Phase VI

In this segment the level of complexity of both metric changes in the second layer and superimpositions is increased significantly. I daresay that, possibly, this level of complexity is one of the highest that any performer would have to face in western music. The karnatic system can provide a solid method of approaching the performance. However, as will be seen below, the shuffling of the different metres in different gatis in the second layer renders this passage extremely difficult. *(track 252)*

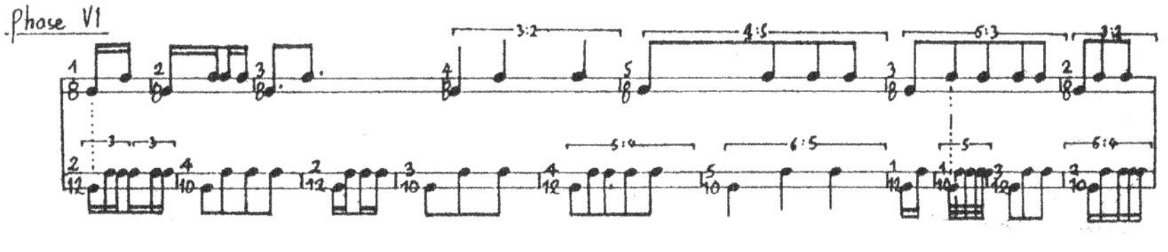

Indeed, the numbers used in both layers are the same that have been used in all previous fragments, but the composer combines them in a different order; and, in the case of the second layer, he mixes metres that are derived from different jathis in two different gatis, alternating them systematically. The second layer's metric construction becomes 2/12, 4/10, 3/12, 3/10, 4/12, 5/10, 1/12, 1/10, 3/12 and 2/10.

This is the first level of complexity that those performing the second layer would have to face. In order to perform this first element of complexity, the musician needs to have a very strong sense of the matra speed of regular tisra as well as 5:2♩., and then proceed to perform the incomplete metres derived from the jathi bhedam sequence while constantly changing the feeling between tisra and khanda.

In addition to this continuous change of metres and gatis, the composer has written superimpositions in a few measures. I will try to provide the necessary resources as far as the karnatic system can theoretically go, so that a performer could attempt an accurate performance of this passage.

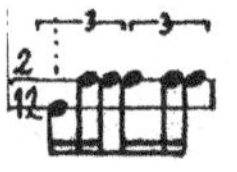

These are two groups of tisra superimposed on every matra of a regular tisra speed. This is no different from the way the 3rd speed anuloma (9) was approached while practising the different speeds of tisra in combinations anuloma-pratiloma.

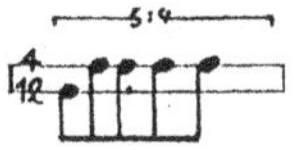

This figure was explained in Phase IV.

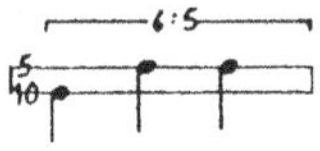

This rhythmical figure – as was the case with the 4:5♪in the 5/10 of Phase IV – is far easier than its notation might imply. In reality this is a regular 3:2♩ since the 5/10 actually takes 2 entire beats.

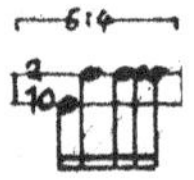

In order to perform this khanda on a 2/10 one should think of a superimposed khanda on the 1st accent of a 5:4♩ frame.

Consequently, the nadai bhedam frame ┌———— ***5:4♩*** ————┐ would greatly help in playing this figure ┌*5*┐┌*5*┐┌*5*┐┌*5*┐┌*5*┐

Once the previous figure is clearly felt, the performer needs to play this khanda on a 1/10 (twice as fast as the previous element).

Needless to say, any performer needs to practise every figure separately, while practising the metre sequence as well, before any attempt is made to combine both levels of complexity.

Here the whole grid is presented:

Jazz Pieces

1) The Dance of Maya (John McLaughlin)

With this ‘classic’ of the jazz-fusion era, I begin the analysis of parallels between karnatic music and jazz pieces of the last 50 years. The emphasis in the analysis of these pieces lies more in the creative parallels between both worlds than in giving instructions as to how the pieces could be performed.

The chosen fragment of this piece is set to a metre of 10/8, divided 3 3 4 (parallel to the notion of using a constant tala), which the electric guitar and bass articulate. Against this framework the drum pattern plays 6 groups of chatusra jathi 3 and a figure of 2 matras closing every measure. The violin’s melody is constructed within the boundaries of every ‘cycle’ of 10/8. *(track 253)*

The Dance of Maya

Composition based on E Symmetrical and E Super Locrian
Ad lib solos: E Symmetrical or E Super Locrian or E Dorian

by JOHN McLAUGHLIN

Gtr.
Vln.
Elec. Pno.
Bass
Dr.

Gtr.
Vln.
Elec. Pno.
Bass
Dr.

2) Sightseeing (Russell Ferrante and Jimmy Haslip)

This composition revolves around two layers: one in 6/4 and the other in 12/8. Although both metres contain the same number of beats, the layer in 6/4 maintains a chatusra feeling while the layer in 12/8 stays in a tisra feeling. This is manifested from the very beginning when two 'metronomes' (performed by two synthesised sounds) outline both metres, providing the impression of polyrhythm or even polytempi.

The percussion and drums have a key function in outlining both pulses. After this exposition of the two metronomes, the percussion performs a clear 12/8 (or tisra feeling), marking every downbeat of the measure. This 12/8 feeling is kept throughout.

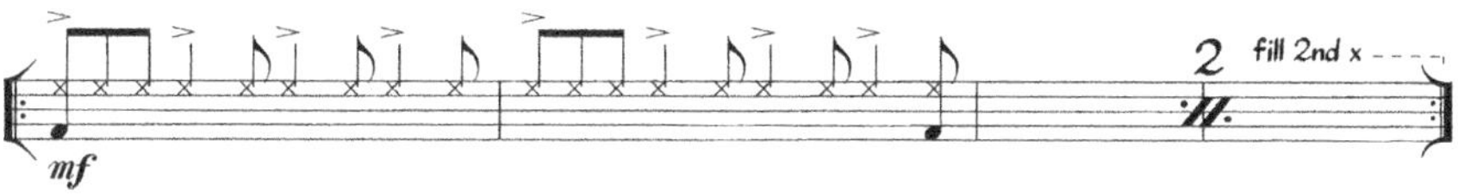

After the introduction, the drums play a clear 6/4 pattern, with an off-beat stroke on the snare on the sixth ♪ of the measure, while the bass drum articulates the 1st, 4th and 5th ♪ of the 6/4 bar. This pattern adds to the general feeling of ambiguity that, in my opinion, is one of the main elements sought after in the piece.

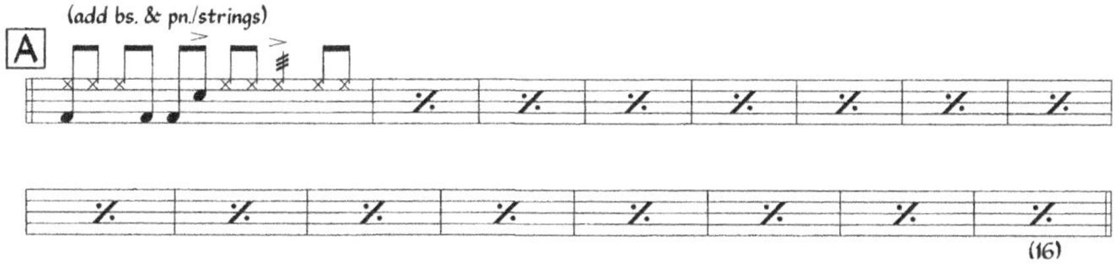

This pattern clearly creates a counterpoint with the vamp performed by another synthesised sound in the introduction, featuring a highly syncopated phrase that is even notated ambiguously (it can be read as either of the two metres).

All these five different elements comprise the backdrop against which the other instruments (sax, piano and bass) continuously move from one feeling to the other. The parallel I find with karnatic music is that there is often a similar idea here of two gatis continuously playing against each other (usually chatusra and tisra, as in this example) and creating the impression of being in two different talas or tempi. The lead sheet of the piece looks like this: *(track 254)*

3) Falling in Between (Toto)

This piece with a clear (hard) rock feel uses quite a few elements that resemble some of the karnatic concepts seen in the first part of the book.

- The introduction is written as a compound metre of 12/8, 2/4, 9/8 and 4/4. This pattern is performed four times, although the fourth time the last 4/4 is shortened by a ♪ to produce a 7/8 measure.

This idea strikes a parallel with the shadanga talas constructions seen in Chapter 22 (tala prastara), resulting in a metre of 33/8. Another way of looking at it would be as a sequence of gati/jathi bhedam within the metre: the phrase is built around the numbers 3 3 3 3 2 2 3 3 3 4 4 with the last number being replaced by a 3 in the fourth repetition of the entire construction.

- This introduction is followed by a 5-measure verse in 4/4 (quite an unusual length in this style of music where blocks of 4 or 8 measures seem to be the norm), in which the melody and drums articulate the measure and the electric guitar and bass play a pattern in chatusra jathi 5 (possibly the reason why the fragment is 5 measures long) . The same pattern can be seen displaced one beat at a time in every cycle (2nd, 3rd and 4th beats in measures 2, 3 and 4). The entire fragment of the guitar and bass looks thus:

- Finally, the chorus follows the construction of the karnatic tala dhruva tisra (11 beats in L3 D L3 L3) or, expressed in western time signatures, 3/4, 2/4, 3/4, 3/4.

The entire fragment of this composition is thus: *(track 255)*

4) Matter of time (Stormvogel)

This composition includes a few concepts that remind me greatly of recent developments in karnatic music.

- The first is the metre structure that it is repeated with a cycle feeling. The construction is 6/4, 5/4, 4/4, 3/4, 2/4, 3/4, 4/4 and 5/4. In a way, this structure is similar to the manner in which many talas are being constructed nowadays in South India after the shadanga talas were reintroduced in the 1960s.
- The other element is the use of one of the developmental techniques of combinations anuloma-pratiloma (same gati and speed, different frame). It

is interesting to see in this piece how the rhythm section always plays 4 notes against every frame – thus creating a 4:6♩., 4:5♩., 4:4♩., 4:3♩., 4:2♩., 4:3♩., 4:4♩., 4:5♩. – and also how this continuous change of frame and, somehow, tempo feeling does not affect an element considered important in much of jazz music: the 'groove'. On top of the rhythm section (including piano) there are different solos. Here I show only one of the fragments with a sax solo over it. *(track 256)*

5) Spiral (Miles Okazaki)

In this piece there are several elements that hold a clear parallel with karnatic concepts.

- Use of controlled *accelerando* and *rallentando* by going through contiguous gatis in several segments: the drums intro, during the theme development and its resolution. All instruments go through all main gatis seen in the karnatic part of the text.

- While the guitar plays all the matras of every gati without accents, the drum-set is continuously using gati/jathi combinations and using all possible combinations in every gati.
- The drum part contains the information as to which accents are used. It is quite interesting to note that the ending of every gati is closed with a combination of accents that greatly resemble the concept of mukthay. Also, the end of the theme sounds quite similar to a 3-fold mukthay.

The development of the drum part is presented first in order to show how it is structured, followed by the first fragment of the piece. *(track 257)*

SPIRAL, DRUMSET

SPIRAL

♩ = 64
INTRO
Drums + Kanjira
Guitar
(sim.)
(sim.)
TO 1
=
1
♩ = 80 (= 100, 2nd x)
Guitar + Soprano Sax
Guitars + Bass
Drums + Kanjira

II
Guitar + Soprano Sax
Guitars + Bass + Horns
Drums + Kanjira
A5
B5
C5
A6
B6

6) Three Oceans (Fabrizio Cassol/Aka Moon)

This piece plays with the notion of rhythmical sangati as its main creative source. A melody of 30 matras is performed simultaneously in three different gatis and the three layers meet every 30 beats.

The first layer, in khanda, is performed in 6 beats, thus repeated five times. The second layer, in tisra, needs 10 beats to complete the same melody and therefore is played three times. Lastly, the third layer is performed in chatusra, each repetition lasting 7+½ beats; consequently it is played four times. The bass improvises freely over these three layers. *(track 258)*[2]

THREE OCEANS

FABRIZIO CASSOL

7) Accelerando (Vijay Iyer)

This composition by the New York-based South Indian musician Vijay Iyer features some of the concepts explained in the last chapters of the karnatic section. Firstly, he employs a metre that has a clear parallel with the kala system of the shadanga talas. It is a time signature made up of a 5/16 followed by a 4/4, and this frame is used quite explicitly throughout the fragment presented here.

The second element actually combines several features: the start point is the overall concept of using chatusra as a constant gati whilst the frame changes continuously, as seen in combinations anuloma-pratiloma. A 4:5♪ is systematically used on the 5/16 part of the metre and the next beat uses a regular chatusra.

This is followed by a 4:3♩ with chatusra nadai as second layer of the bracket. The 16 matras are further divided into a short jathi bhedam structure of 4 3 3 2 4. These numbers are subsequently used as frames to superimpose a third layer of chatusra, subtly hinted at by the drums at the beginning of the piece. *(track 259)*

[2] The feeling that the sound at the beginning of the piece is of bad quality is actually a decision taken by the group while recording. After approximately 30 seconds the sound is what anyone would expect from a CD recording.

Accelerando

Vijay Iyer

E
9
3
4:5
4:3
Pno.
B.
Dr.

F
11
4:5
4:3
Pno.
B.
Dr.

4
G
13
4:5
4:3
Pno.
B.
Dr.

H
15
4:5
4:3
Pno.
B.
Dr.

I
Pno.
B.
Dr.
J
K
L

Chapter 26
Analysis of Students' Pieces

This final chapter presents three compositions written by students who have followed the programme I teach at the Amsterdam Conservatoire. These creators use the techniques and concepts in their own way and combine them with their own background, aesthetics etc. Two of the pieces can be classified as 'contemporary classical music', whilst the third has a very clear jazz influence. The musicians on these pieces are exclusively students who have studied at least two years of the performers' programme.

This section tackles how to use the concepts and techniques described in Part I in creative ways. It should be reiterated again that the goal of using these karnatic concepts is always the expansion of possibilities within a western framework, and never as a way of creating karnatic music as such.

Firstly, the composers explain how they conceived the pieces, how their previous musical knowledge and background have interacted with karnatic techniques and, vice versa, how these concepts have influenced their music. The main techniques used are then analysed, punctuated by some comments I find pertinent.

1) *Sorry to interfere ... anyone cares?* (Andys Skordis)

For clarinet, percussion, piano, violin, viola and cello

> I tried to use the instrumentation in two groups. The first group (clarinet, piano and percussion) and the second group (string instruments) work somehow like a double trio. Interfering means in this context that one group 'clashes' with the other one by using contrasting elements.
>
> Even though I used the techniques in a polyphonic manner, where every technique might not be audible as a technique itself due to the created texture, I felt that the whole piece always had something holding it together. As karnatic musicians see it, the whole development is somehow like a tree, where a seed brings forth branches, sub-branches etc. I feel the same way about this piece – that every section or even single voice is just another branch of a tree.
>
> I personally relate these techniques with literary writing. Words are like cells, sentences are like short phrases (yati phrases, jathi bhedam, anuloma-pratiloma), paragraphs are like organised techniques (mukthay combination, moharas, jathis

> kalpana) and, finally, the 'book' is the mosaic produced by all these concepts together.
>
> This piece has been the starting point of a musical journey. Previously I tried various ways to create polyrhythmic structures, but I always had the sensation that an organic part was missing. By using karnatic techniques, I felt that the result was very different, more harmonious. The relationship that every rhythmical cell has with the following or the preceding one is like a spider's web and I tend to believe that this relationship is something you may even feel at an unconscious level. Everything is related to everything else and therefore there is an organic essence in the entire piece.
>
> Besides the polyrhythmic structures, karnatic techniques helped me to develop a better sense of phrasing. I realised how many more possibilities I had to create phrases with a specific rhythmical concept or technique in mind, rather than mixing everything, as I used to (in the past, I composed phrases that would start with ♬ then a quintuplet, and then perhaps an 11♪:4♪). This ultimately frustrated me because not only could I never feel the phrase, but I also 'knew' that it would be very difficult to perform. With nadai bhedam I can create many more complex phrases, but because of the way they are constructed become much easier to feel and perform. So, ultimately, not only the result is something I find more interesting than the phrasing ideas I used before, but it is also much easier to perform and understand.

This piece is composed in a tala of 10 beats. However, because the inner structures for tala 10 in the suladi tala system (L4 D L4 or L7 A D) were not suitable for the composer's structures, he decided to make up a tala 10 divided L5 L5. Skordis used the karnatic notion of resolving techniques and phrases on tala and anga sam in order to provide a feeling of cycle. The following karnatic techniques have been used.

Yati Phrases

1) Measures 29–30 (violin): a mridangamyati following the palindrome construction. This yati phrase does not add any cells to a previous phrase, but rather uses the numbers of the sequence to increase and decrease the *length of each of its notes*. The duration of the gap is used for a 3 matras long note.

Chatusra: **5** (3) **8** (3) **11** (3) **14** (3) **11** (3) **8** (3) **5**

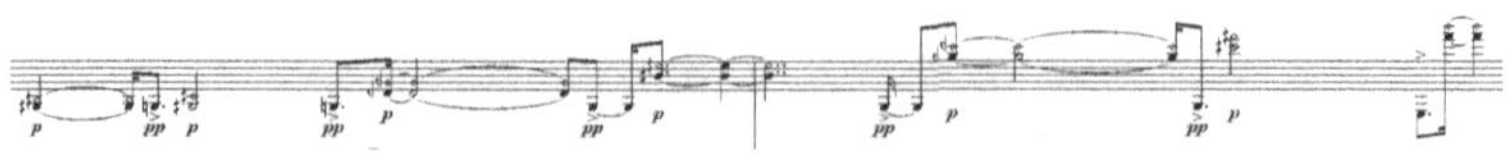

2) Measure 32 (viola): a srotovahayati, omitting 1 matra per pala and a silent gap.

Chatusra: 7 (2) **6** (2) **5** (2) **4** (2) **3** (2) **2** (2) **1**

3) Measure 23 (violin): a gopuchayati in tisra 2nd speed: **11** (5) **9** (5) **7** (5) **5** (5) **3** (5)

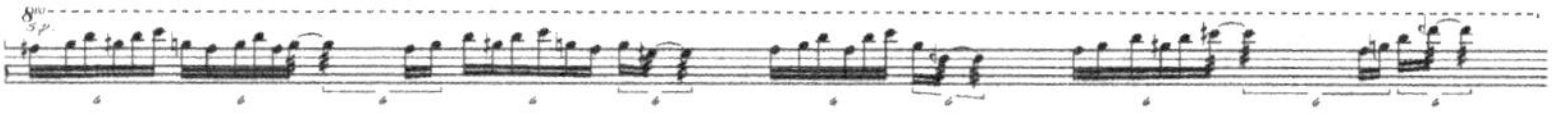

The gap is emphasised by using a tremolo on the 5 matras long note. Also, this yati phrase could be interpreted as a yatis prastara; because of the last 'gap' placed at the end of the sequence, this gap could be analysed as a samayati instead, yielding thus a gopuchayati interspersed with a samayati.

4) Measures 29–30 (cello): a srotovahayati that combines adding notes from the middle with elongating note values. The gap is an attacked note.

Chatusra: **3** (9) **5** (9) **7** (9) **9** (9) **11**

Tirmana

Measure 31 (viola): calculations are 5×3, 5×2 and 5×1. It is constructed in tisra. The first five ♩ are thought out as a ♩. in tisra 1st speed.

Nadai Bhedam

1) Measures 16–18 (piano): the frame is 4:5♩ with chatusra nadai.

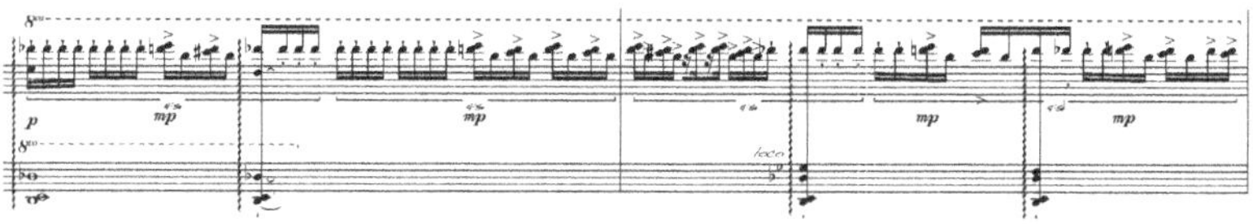

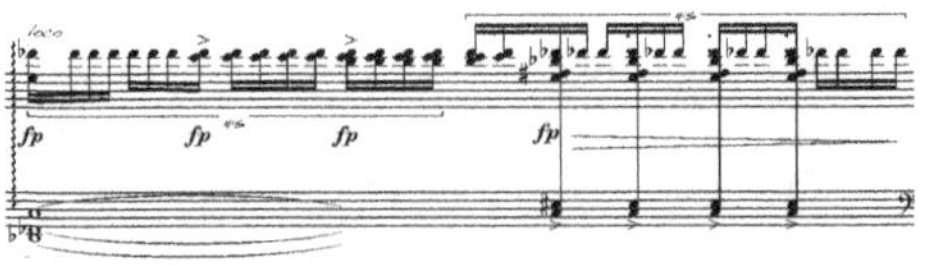

2) Measures 60–63 (percussion): in this segment the composer uses an uncommon frame based on misra. He switches between 7:5♩ and 6:5♩ and the nadai is always chatusra.

Mixed Gati Mohara

Measures 35–42 (clarinet): this technique is developed in eight cycles.

A +B + C + D (twice)
A + B + C + 1/2D + 1/2A
1/2A +1/2D + C + mukthay

The inner construction of the phrases is

A: Chatusra 8, 4, 8 B: Khanda 8, 9, 8

C: Chatusra 8, 4, 8 D: Khanda 7, 5, 5, 8

In the last three cycles, following the characteristic pattern of moharas, phrases get shortened, displaced and rhythmical sangatis take place. At the end (starting on the last beat of the second cycle below) there is a mukthay that begins in khanda, changes into chatusra and returns to khanda once again. The calculations are 11 (9) 11 (9) 10+|1.

The construction follows scrupulously the rules given in Chapter 17 (moharas). However, as it seems to be a pattern throughout the piece, a few numbers are used for long notes rather than for phrasing.

Mixed Jathi Nadai Bhedam

1) Measure 24 (viola): the composer took the double accent 4+5 and superimposed tisra nadai (6:4♪. + 6:5♪). This combination needs 9 beats to resolve. In order to resolve on tala sam, the device starts on the second beat of the cycle.

2) Measures 55–6 (piano): the second time the technique spreads over 2 cycles, starting and finishing on tala sam. There are two sequences, one of 4+5 followed by a frame of 4+7. This combination (9+11 beats, the result of 4+5 and 4+7) fits into the 2 cycles of the tala 10. The first frame takes tisra nadai, whereas the second one utilises misra nadai.

Mukthay Combination

Measures 38–42 (piano): this elaborated mukthay is based on a triple mukthay made up of a srotovahayati, a sub-mukthay and a tirmana. The calculations are:

1st pala: Srotovahayati 7 (1) 10 (1) 13

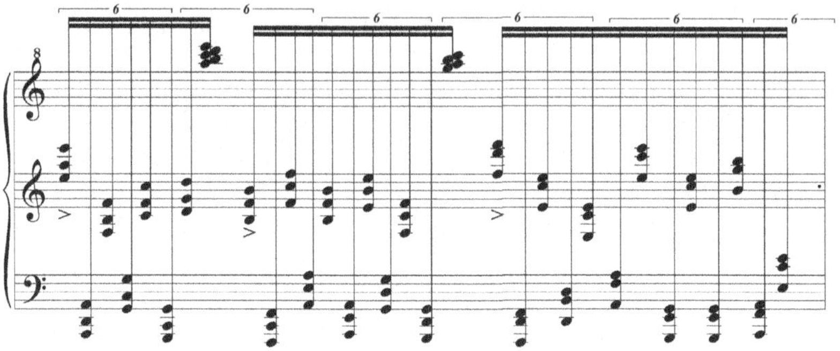

Sub-mukthay: 5, 6 (2) 5, 6 (2) 6 (2) 6

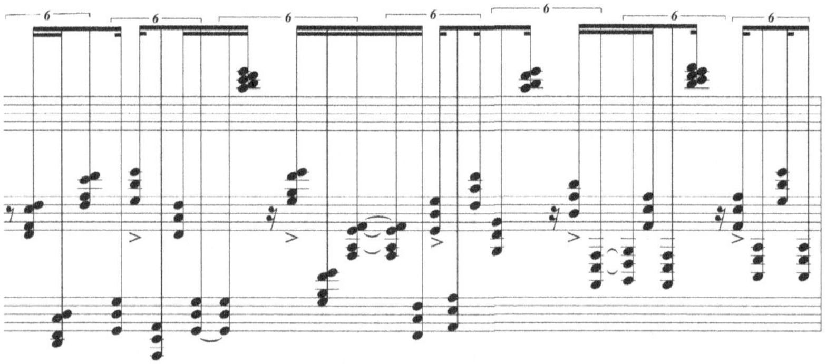

Tirmana (in tisra): 5×1, 5×2, 5×3

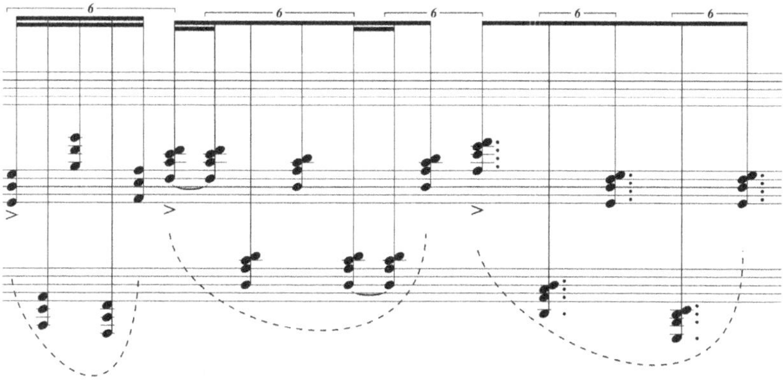

The matra for the gap in the srotovahayati and sub-mukthay is attacked in a very high register of the piano: rather than giving the impression of silence or resolution, the gap produces small climactic points at irregular intervals.

The tirmana is actually a viloma version of the regular construction, since it starts with the shortest distance between notes.

2nd pala: Srotovahayati that has decreased its length by two matras: 5 (1) 8 (1) 11

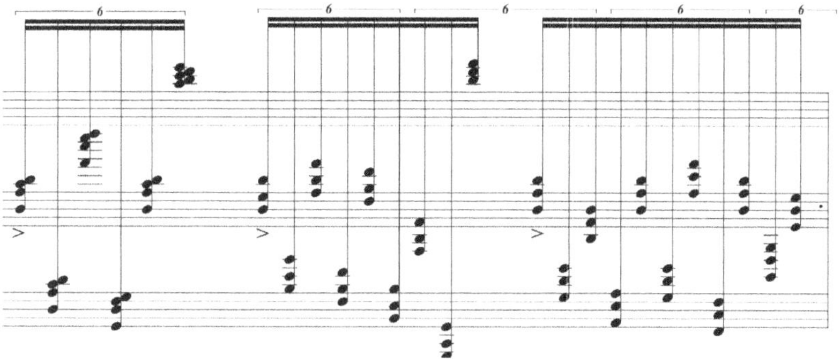

Sub-mukthay that, similarly, has decreased by one matra. There is also an overlapping of mukthays, as the last pala of the sub-mukthay is simultaneously the first pala of the tirmana compound that follows.

4, 5 (2) 4, 5 (2) 5 (2) <u>5</u>

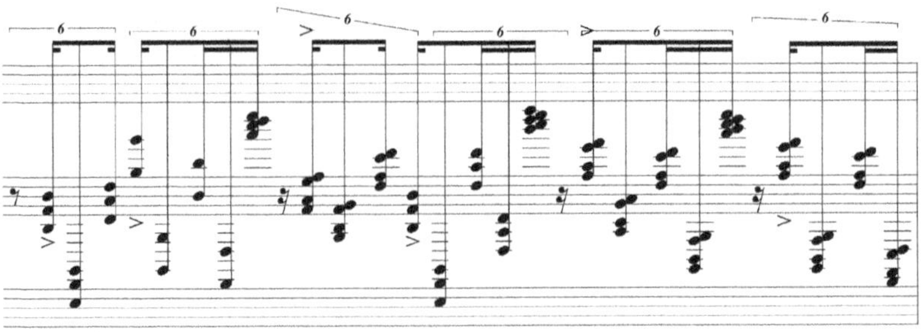

Tirmana: 5×1 5×2 5×3. The first pala is simultaneously the last pala of the previous mukthay. The original tirmana of 5 matras gives way to a tirmana compound mukthay concept: the second note is twice as long as the rest. Calculations are kept as in the first pala, but the phrase construction modifies the notion of tirmana.

3rd pala: Srotovahayati that has decreased its length once again by two matras: 3 (2) 6 (2) 9.

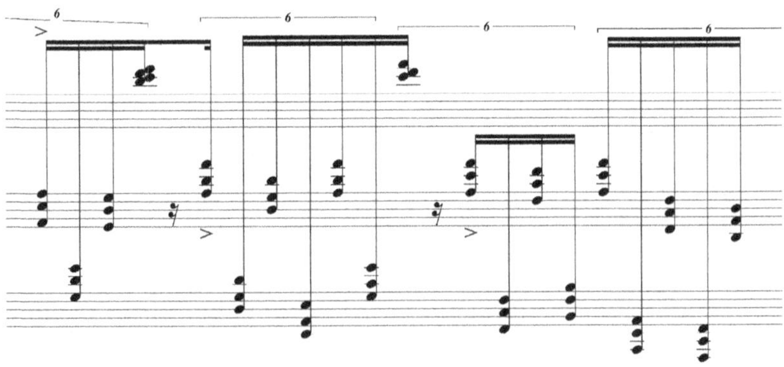

Sub-mukthay is an increased version of the first pala: 6, 7 (3) 6, 7 (3) 7 (3) 7.

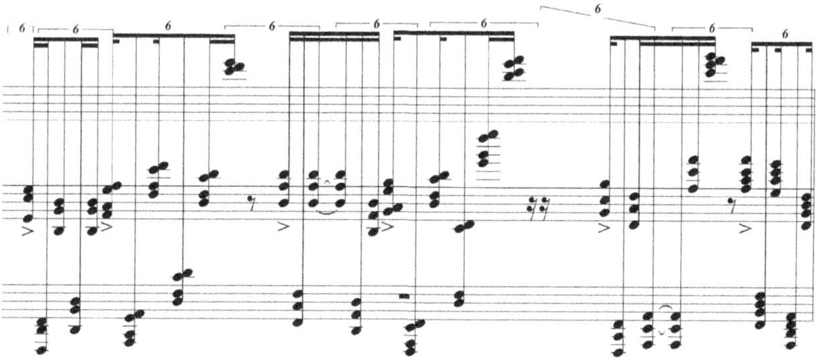

The composer has deliberately chosen to avoid a linear development and decided in favour of a vakra concept. Therefore, instead of increasing or decreasing systematically in every pala, his 'root' calculations are placed in the 1st block, distributing the decreased and increased version in the 2nd and 3rd blocks respectively.

Tirmana: 7×1, 7×2, 7×3

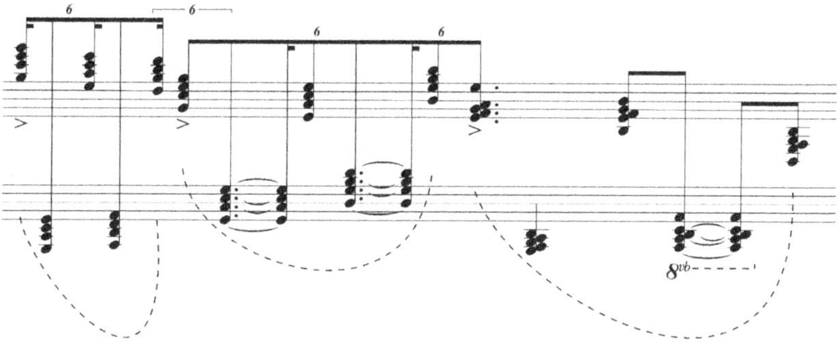

The final tirmana mukthay plays with the idea of keeping the same number of notes as in the previous pala, but increasing the length of every step. Whereas in the 2nd pala the idea of increasing one note whilst keeping the original duration was introduced, in this pala both ideas are employed. *(track 260)*

" Sorry to Interfere...anyone cares?"
Andys Skordis
Amsterdam, June 2010
Score in Concert Pitch
Immobile ♩= 56 - 62
Clarinet in B♭
Percussion
Piano
Violin
Viola
Cello
Crotales
Big Gong
arco
Woodblocks + Temple Blocks
plastic mallets
Big Gong
with brushes
with open palm, inside piano
approx. pitches, very low!
L.V.
con sord., molto s.t.
flaut., non vibrato
Sempre senza crescendo
Cl.
Perc.
Pno.
Vln.
Vla.
Vlc.
WB + TB
©Andreas Skordis 2010

2
"Sorry to interfere...anyone cares?"
Clr.
Perc
Tam Tam with mallet
Pno.
Vln
Vla.
Vlc.
fast bow
Flz (throat)
Bass Drum with hands
Glock. soft mallets
Celesta
touch string lightly
loure
ord.

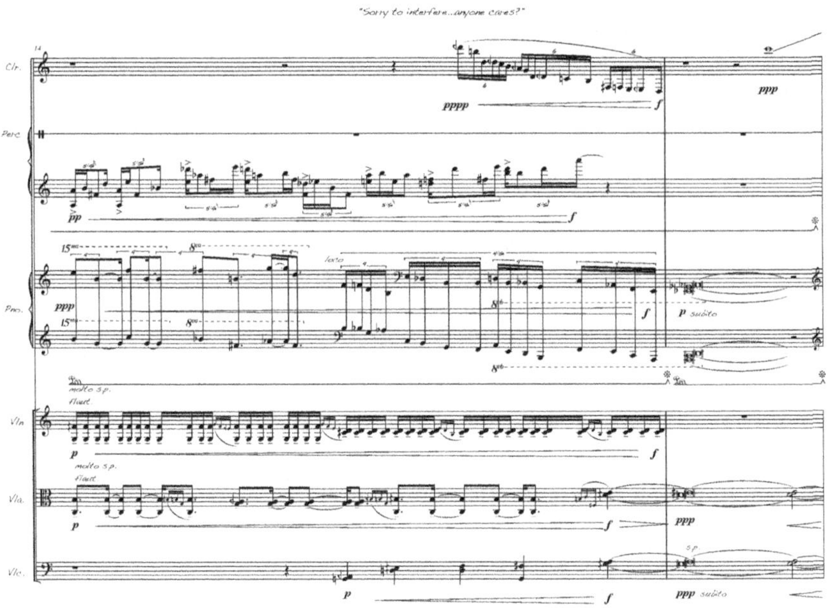
"Sorry to interfere...anyone cares?"
Clr.
Perc.
Pno.
Vln
Vla.
Vlc.
molto s.p.
flaut.
loco
p subito
ppp subito

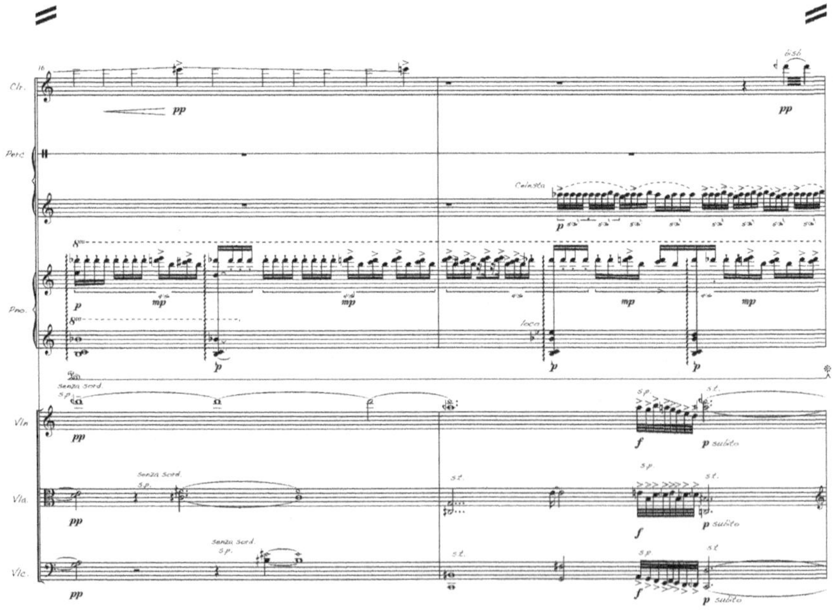
Clr.
Perc.
Pno.
Vln
Vla.
Vlc.
bisb.
Celesta
loco
senza sord.
s.p.
s.t.
p subito

4
"Sorry to interfere...anyone cares?"
Cl.
Perc
Pno
Vln
Vla.
Vlc.
loco
Crotales
with soft mallet
inside piano
Big Gong
Bass Drum
with hands
+ Big Gong
with fist
Subtones
Bass Drum
Super Ball Mallet
touch skin with hands
creating hish sound
Crotales
arco
hit with palm inside piano
st.
sp.
Al. Punt.
ord.

"Sorry to interfere...anyone cares?"
Cl.
Perc.
Glock. soft mallets
Pno.
Vln
Vla.
Vlc.
ord. bow
(on the string)

6
"Sorry to interfere...anyone cares?"
Cl.
Woodblocks + Temple Blocks
Perc
Pno.
ord.
Vln
Vla.
Vlc.
Big Gong
non vib.
Al. Punt.

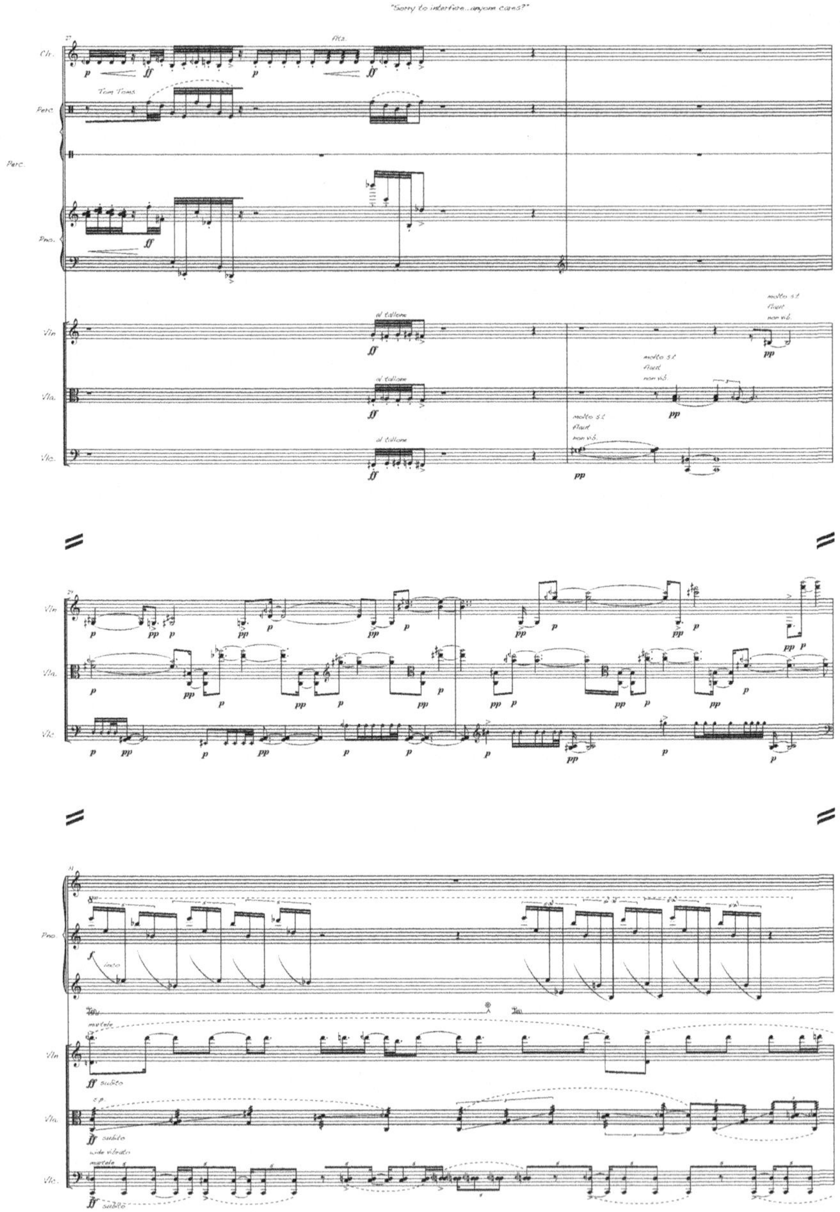
"Sorry to interfere...anyone cares?"
Cl.
Perc.
Tom Toms
Pno.
Vln.
Vla.
Vlc.
al tallone
molto st.
flaut.
non vib.
f
laisse
marcato
subito
sp.

"Sorry to interfere...anyone cares?"
Pno
Vln
Vla
Vlc
Cl
Perc
Tam Tam
ppp
pp subito
ff
mp
fp
p
f

"Sorry to interfere...anyone cares?"
9
Vln
Vla.
Vlc.
Woodblocks + Temple Blocks
Perc
Pno.

10
"Sorry to interfere...anyone cares?"
Clr.
Perc.
Pno.
Vln
Vla.
Vlc.
sopra s.p.
ord.
s.p.
al tallone
pp
p
f
ff

"Sorry to interfere...anyone cares?"
any loud and ugly motif, starting from given pitch
Clr.
Perc
Bass Drum + Tam Tam
Pno.
With fist up to Elbow
both hands
as low as possible
black and white clusters!
Vln
Vla.
Vlc.
Crotales
l.v.
arco
s.p.

12
"Sorry to interfere...anyone cares?"
Cl.
Perc.
Glock
marcato sempre
Pno.
Senza Ped.
pizz.
Vln
Vla.
Vlc.

"Sorry to interfere...anyone cares?"
13
49
Clr.
Perc
Pno.
arco
Vla.
ff
arco
Vlc.
ff
50
Clr.
ff
Perc
p
Pno.
ff
f
Vln
ff
arco
spiccato
Vla.
ff
Vlc.

14
"Sorry to interfere...anyone cares?"
Clr.
Woodblocks + Temple Blocks
Perc
Bass Drum
Pno.
Vla.
Vlc.
Tam Tam
Vln
pizz

"Sorry to interfere...anyone cares?"
15
Clr.
Perc.
con forza!
Pno.
arco
Vln
Vla.
Vlc.
martele

16
"Sorry to interfere...anyone cares?"
Clr.
Perc
Pno.
Vln
Vla.
Vlc.
Bass Drum
con forza!
+ Floor Tom

"Sorry to interfere...anyone cares?"
Clr.
Woodblocks + Temple Blocks
Perc
Pno.
loco
Vln
Vla.
Vlc.
Bass Drum

"Sorry to interfere...anyone cares?"
Clr.
Perc
Pno.
Vln
Vla.
Vlc.

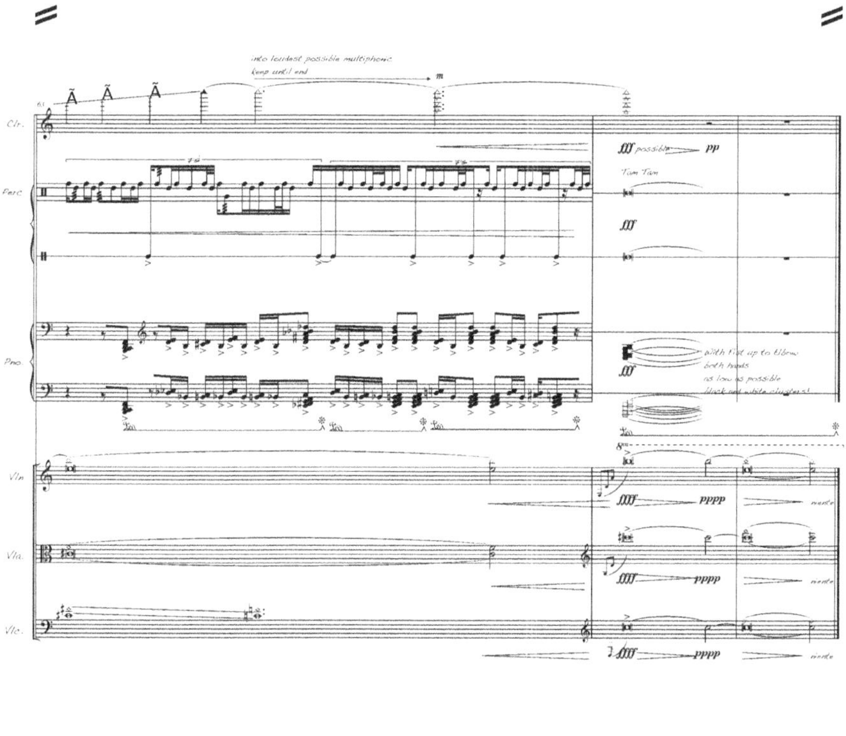
into loudest possible multiphonic
keep until end
Clr.
Perc
Pno.
Vln
Vla.
Vlc.
fff possible
pp
Tam Tam
with fist up to elbow
both hands
as low as possible
(black and white clusters)
pppp

2) *Shape Shifting* (Hans Leeuw)

For flute, alto sax, trumpet, tenor recorder (with effects), electric piano, electric bass and drums

> The programme 'Contemporary music through non-western techniques' has been of significant influence for my musical development. I had always been searching for a way into jazz composition that would be both structured and free, a way of composing that would enable me to use grooves and rhythms of the more complex kind but that would still sound organic.
>
> The content of the programme is a constant source for generating material. I am not completely strict with it, but I do create rules on a piece-to-piece basis that are derived from the way of thinking I learnt during the studies. Devices that I often use in my work are mukthays, yati phrases, jathi bhedam, tirmana, mukthay combinations and mohara. I would like to use more elements like nadai bhedam or anuloma-pratiloma (as I did in 'Shape Shifting'), but according to my experience, such devices require players who either studied the programme or have been researching the same concepts of their own accord. In my own ensemble, I have been able to educate musicians through pieces, but only to a certain extent.
>
> As the base for my compositions, I mostly use some sort of algorithmic phrase (usually much shorter than a theme on one tala) and I build from there. I do not use the tala as such, but rather the concept of a fixed length, similar somehow to the concept of cycle. One piece I wrote for my band uses a fixed length of 363 matras ($3 \times 11 \times 11$) for each of its seven parts. Using the material in this way I can use the logic of karnatic music as a starting point whilst adapting it to my own whims.
>
> I also discovered that teaching the basics of karnatic music to musicians of different degrees of proficiency can be very rewarding. Most students – ranging from amateur to (semi)professional – are very enthusiastic because they become much stronger rhythmically.
>
> Lastly, I am also programming karnatic rhythms in a computer program called MAXMSP. The algorithmic possibilities of karnatic music are endless and can deliver as well more interesting groovy and 'accessible' music than much of the looped based electronic music that has become mainstream.

'Shape Shifting' is a piece in which karnatic principles and jazz aesthetics are intertwined. It is based on three shadanga talas of the composer's own creation (as well as three ragas) using a form called *ragatalamalika*, which usually calls for metrical modulations.

All talas are used in a cyclic fashion, and in most of them the composer constructs several outer amalgamation sequences. Since this is a crucial part of the creative process, I think it important to specify the manner in which the cycles have been developed.

Structure

First section (cycle of 52 beats) ♩=184

Cycles 1–5:	9/8, 4/8, 9/8, 4/8, 9/8, 4/8, 9/8, 4/8
Cycle 6:	7/8, 5/8, 3/8, 3/8, 7/8, 5/8, 3/8, 3/8, 7/8, 5/8, 4/8
Cycle 7:	Only ½ tala (26 beats) 4/4, 1/8, 4/4, 1/8, 4/4
Cycles 8–16:	7/8, 5/8, 3/8, 3/8, 7/8, 5/8, 3/8, 3/8, 7/8, 5/8, 4/8
Cycle 17:	Only ½ tala (26 beats) 9/8, 4/4, 1/8, 4/4
Cycles 18–19:	7/8, 5/8, 3/8, 3/8, 7/8, 5/8, 3/8, 3/8, 7/8, 5/8, 4/8
Cycle 20:	Only ½ tala (26 beats) 4/4, 1/8, 4/4, 1/8, 4/4
Cycle 21:	¾ of a tala (39 beats): 6/8, 4/8, 6/8, 4/8, 6/8, 4/4, 5/8

Metrical modulation: the ♩ of a 4:5♪becomes the new ♪

Second section (cycle of 17 matras), ♪=74

Cycle 22:	4/8, 4/8, 3/8, 4/8, 2/8
Cycles 23–9:	4/16, 3/16, 2/16, 3/16, 4/16, 3/16, 2/16, 3/16, 4/16, 3/16, 3/16
Cycles 30–31:	3/8, 4/8, 3/8, 4/8, 3/8
Cycle 32:	7/8, 7/7, 3/8

Metrical modulation: ← 

→

Third section (cycle of 27 matras), ♪=105

Cycles 33–44: 7/8, 6/8, 7/8, 7/8

Metrical modulation: 105×10:7=150 (10𝅘𝅥𝅯:7♪). So the tempo of each 𝅘𝅥𝅯 of this irregular grouping is 150. The tempo of the 𝅘𝅥𝅯 is the same as the ♩ of the 6:7♪in the new tala. To finally establish the new tempo the following calculation is required 150:6×7=175.

Last section (52 matras), ♩=175

Cycles 45–7:	7/8, 5/8, 3/8, 3/8, 7/8, 5/8, 3/8, 3/8, 7/8, 5/8, 4/8
Cycles 48–53:	13/8 (× 4)

Analysis

I find it important to explain the entire structure, since from the very beginning of my studies in India and my teaching in Amsterdam, the question of what a cycle is has been a recurrent question and generated much discussion.

For a karnatic musician, any structure conforming to a number of beats (tala) is synonymous of cycle, be it 3 or 128 beats. When working with karnatic musicians in my own music, I sometimes used similar manners of constructing cycles as in this piece. I found that for them it was very difficult to even conceive that different amalgamated metres that share the same number of beats could be the equivalent of a cycle.

Hans Leeuw's way of thinking regarding cycle is, from my point of view, a very creative manner of developing this eastern concept, but adapted to the needs of western creation. Whilst I find the concept of cycle one of the most important findings of eastern music in general, I always found that a complete respect for eastern musicians' way of constructing could be somewhat constrictive for westerners.

However, having said that, I do not agree with the decision not to be completely faithful to a chosen number of beats, as is the case in the first section of 52 beats. Whereas I can fully understand that in specific moments only ½ cycle could be utilised, I think this should always be done (not necessarily consecutively) twice or four times etc, so that the total number of beats is ultimately achieved. In this sense, I share the view of karnatic musicians that the music has to adapt to the tala (or cycles or fixed lengths), and not the other way around. Therefore, I feel that cycle 21, in which ¾ of the tala is used, destroys the otherwise well-thought out changing metres structure. This would be my sole objection to the construction of the whole piece.

As explained in Chapter 1 (suladi talas), the concept of cycle is something that really belongs to the realm of feeling, and I find (and have found) it very difficult to rationalise this concept. Consequently, and probably because I somehow feel I live in between two worlds, my assessment or criticism of Hans's constructing manner is very personal. Whereas for a karnatic musician this piece would have nothing to do with the tala system, for many westerners the use of ¾ of a cycle is something they would never have a problem with. As said in the first chapter, one has to 'experience' the concept of cycle, and this experience can be completely different depending on cultural and musical background. The more one is exposed to the sources, the more one is bound to understand and 'feel' the concept of cycle as conceived in karnatic music.

Techniques

The entire composition is based on all sorts of yati phrases and yati mukthays (some of them of the composer's own creation) in almost every single instrument and musical parameter. Every layer constantly uses these notions to construct phrases, note values or grooves. The other element abundantly employed is combinations anuloma-pratiloma. Since every single cycle utilises the aforementioned yati concept in one way or another, to proceed to explain every cycle would possibly be superfluous. Therefore, I have chosen the most representative ones.

Yati Phrases and Mukthays

1) Measures 1–16 (piano): 1 (10) 2 (10) 3 3 (10) 2 (10) 1. Mridangamyati with viloma structure.

2) Measures 17–24 (piano): 1 (7) 4 (7) 7, 1 (2) 3 (2) 5, 2 (2) 3 (2) 4. Three successive srotovahayatis

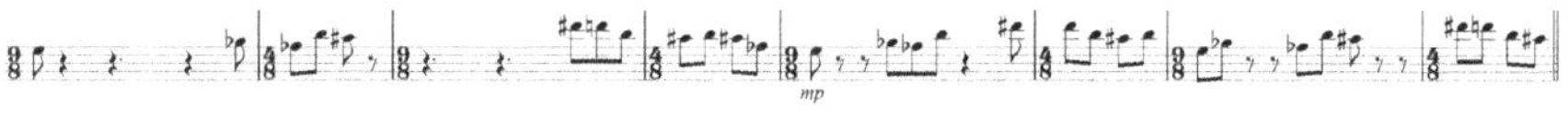

3) Measures 33–40 (piano): 2 (1) 2 (1) 2 (1) 2, 3 (1) 3 (1) 3 (1) 3. Two samayatis followed by another mridangamyati with viloma structure 1 (1) 2 (1) 3 (1) 4 4 (1) 3 (1) 2 (1) 1

The second and third examples epitomise how most of the material is drawn: the use of all sorts of yati phrases succeeding one another. Most instruments throughout the composition respond to this notion.

4) Measures 41–52 (piano): 7 5 3 1 (2) 7 5 3 1 (2) 7 5 3 1. A sama mukthay with an internal division following a gopuchayati concept.

5) Measures 207–72 (drums and bass): 4 3 2 1 (2) 4 3 2 1 (2) 4 3 2 1. Same as the previous example.

The fourth and fifth examples are the other main ideas of the composition: whether as a groove or as a source for melodic development, mukthays with an inner division following a yati concept are present in much of the piece.

Anuloma-Pratiloma

1) Measures 101–55 (horns): 7 5 3 1, 7 5 3 1, 7 5 3 1. The starting point is the same mukthay as in measures 41–56, but Leeuw uses it to superimpose different gatis on the frame, employing the third developmental technique of combination anuloma-pratiloma (keeping the same gati and speed, changing the frame). The composer also follows the phrasing idea of using the same number of notes per cell, together with the notion of systematically increasing the number of matras. In this manner, each cycle takes a different gati or speed.

1:7♪, 1:5♪, 1:3♪, 1 (2) 1:7♪, 1:5♪, 1:3♪, 1 (2) 1:7♪, 1:5♪, 1:3♪, 1

2:7♪, 2:5♪, 2:3♪, 1 (2) 2:7♪, 2:5♪, 2:3♪, 1 (2) 2:7♪, 2:5♪, 2:3♪, 1

3:7♪ 3:5♪ 3:3♪ 1 (2) 3:7♪ 3:5♪ 3:3♪ 1 (2) 3:7♪ 3:5♪ 3:3♪ 1

x 3 times

4:7♪, 4:5♪, 4:3♪, 1 (2) 4:7♪, 4:5♪, 4:3♪, 1 (2) 4:7♪, 4:5♪, 4:3♪, 1

x 3 times

5:7♪, 5:5♪, 5:3♪, 1 (2) 5:7♪, 5:5♪, 5:3♪, 1 (2) 5:7♪, 5:5♪, 5:3♪, 1

x 3 times

2) Measures 218–72 (horns):

1:2♪, 1:3♪, 1:2♪ 1 (2) 1:2♪, 1:3♪, 1:2♪ 1 (2) 1:2♪, 1:3♪, 1:2♪ 1.

Exactly the same elements as the previous sequence, except that the utilised frames do not follow a yati pattern:

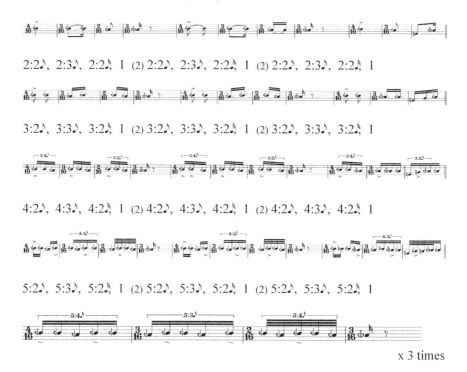

2:2♪, 2:3♪, 2:2𝅘𝅥𝅯 1 (2) 2:2♪, 2:3♪, 2:2𝅘𝅥𝅯 1 (2) 2:2♪, 2:3♪, 2:2𝅘𝅥𝅯 1

3:2♪, 3:3♪, 3:2𝅘𝅥𝅯 1 (2) 3:2♪, 3:3♪, 3:2𝅘𝅥𝅯 1 (2) 3:2♪, 3:3♪, 3:2𝅘𝅥𝅯 1

4:2♪, 4:3♪, 4:2𝅘𝅥𝅯 1 (2) 4:2♪, 4:3♪, 4:2𝅘𝅥𝅯 1 (2) 4:2♪, 4:3♪, 4:2𝅘𝅥𝅯 1

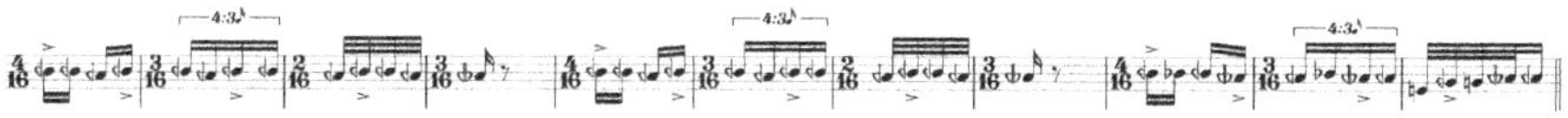

5:2♪, 5:3♪, 5:2𝅘𝅥𝅯 1 (2) 5:2♪, 5:3♪, 5:2𝅘𝅥𝅯 1 (2) 5:2♪, 5:3♪, 5:2𝅘𝅥𝅯 1

x 3 times

3) Measures 273–7 (horns): 10:6𝅘𝅥𝅯 10:8𝅘𝅥𝅯, 10:6𝅘𝅥𝅯 10:8𝅘𝅥𝅯 10:6𝅘𝅥𝅯 (the last 10:6𝅘𝅥𝅯 subdivided into 4 3 2 1). Another example of the third developmental technique of anuloma-pratiloma combinations, constructed this time around the changing metres sequence.

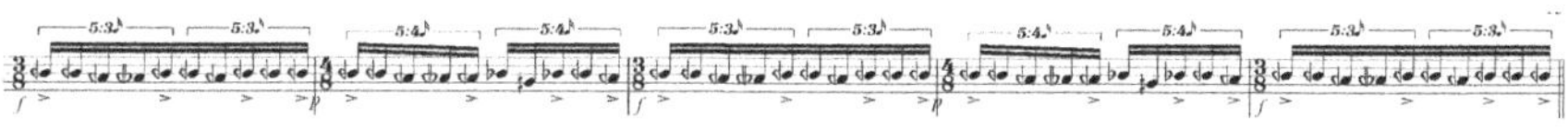

4) Measures 273–7 (piano and bass):

10 [4321]:6𝅘𝅥𝅯 10 [4321]:8𝅘𝅥𝅯 10 [4321]:6𝅘𝅥𝅯 10 [4321]:8𝅘𝅥𝅯 10 [4321]:6♪

The subdivision of 4 3 2 1 used by the horns for the last 10:6𝅘𝅥𝅯 is applied to every frame in this layer. By doing so, the composer also enters the territory of phrasing through gati changes (speeds in this case).

In all previous examples, although the main idea is the use of anuloma-pratiloma, this concept is developed once again using a yati notion of increasing or decreasing systematically.

5) Measures 310–13 (horns):

6:3♪, 3:2♪, 3:2♪, 10:3♪, 10:3♪, 6:3♪, 3:2♪, 3:2♪, 10:3♪, 10:4♪

There are several elements converging in this section:

- The structure provided by the mukhy system for the tala of 27 beats is 3 2 2|3 3|3 2 2|3 2 2. The composer uses tisra in the first and third parts and khanda in the second and fourth.
- An overall sama mukthay construction: 20 (2) 20 (2) 20.
- Phrasing through gati changes: since the total number of matras in 1 cycle (by using the previous gatis) is 64, the mukthay goes through gati and speed changes. It is ultimately a similar idea to moharas within shadanga talas, as seen in Chapter 23 (further developments of the mukhy system).
- There is a slow build-up to the mukthay/melody of measures 310–13 by using four previous mukthays that increase their length in a gopuchayati fashion: every mukthay increases by 4 matras in every pala and decreases by 6 matras in the gap.

Measures 294–309: development towards final mukthay following a yati pattern.
4 (26) 4 (26) 4

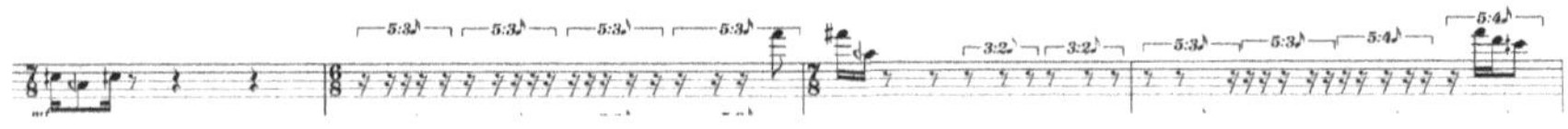

8 (20) 8 (20) 8

12 (14) 12 (14) 12

16 (8) 16 (8) 16

Mohara

Measures 314–29 (horns): This device is developed in 4 cycles of the tala of 27 beats and uses the same anuloma-pratiloma frames as in the previous example. Since the bigger gesture of 7 6 7 7 employed in this tala produces four frames, the four phrases of a mohara are structured around them.

6:3♪, 3:2♪, 3:2♪
A

5:3♪, 5:3♪
B

6:3♪, 3:2♪, 3:2♪
C

10:3♪, 10:4♪
D

½ D–A

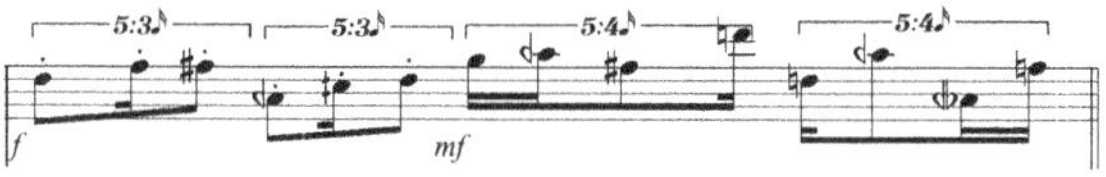

A (end), 2nd cell ½ D

B

Final mukthay: 8 (4) 8 (4) 8

In this mohara the composer combines various elements presented in Chapter 17, as well as their use within shadanga talas. On one hand he employs two different gatis, tisra for phrases A and C and khanda for phrases B and C, and on the other he makes use of the mukhy system of regrouping the inner cells of the shadanga tala. The anuloma-pratiloma frames remain unaltered throughout the mohara. *(track 261)*

Compositie: Hans Leeuw s

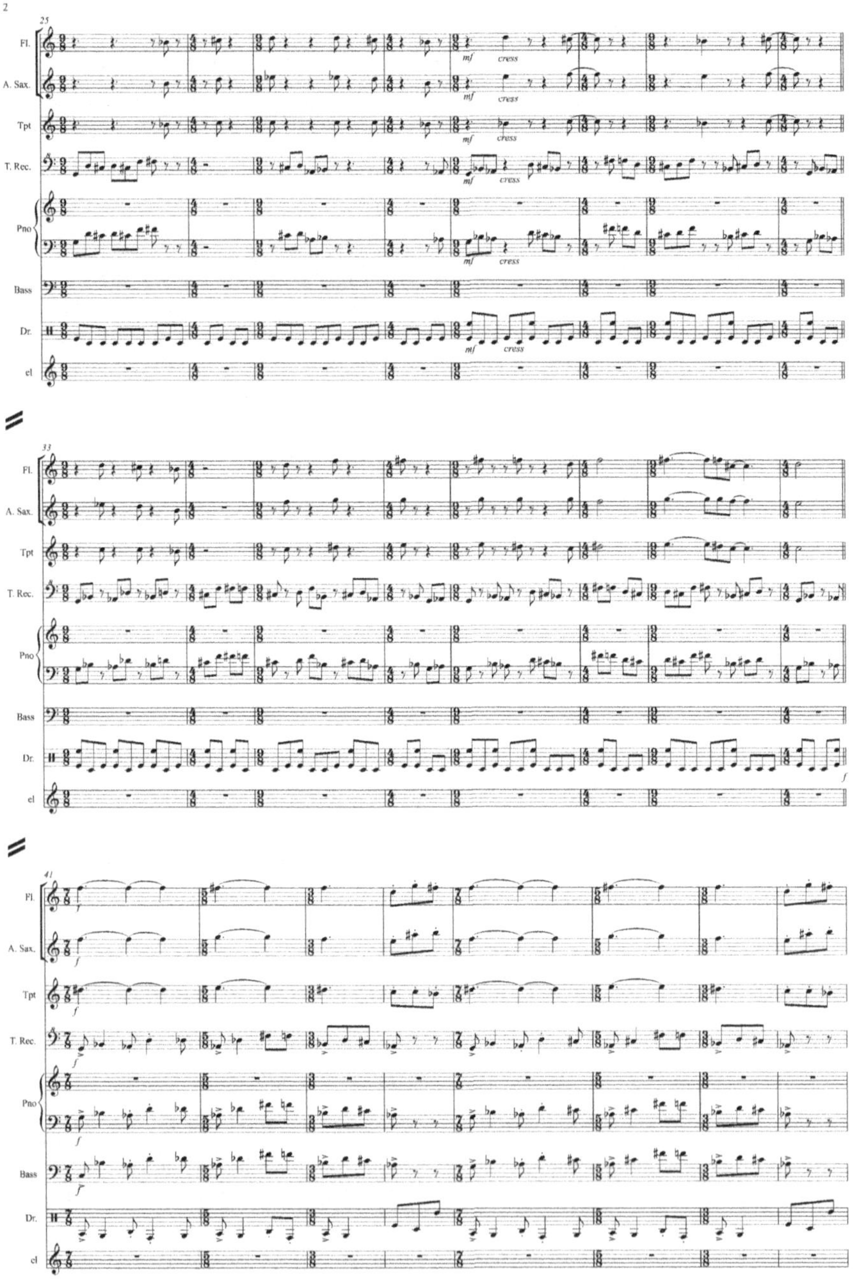
2
25
Fl.
A. Sax.
Tpt
T. Rec.
Pno
Bass
Dr.
el
mf
cress
33
41
f

3
49
Fl.
A. Sax.
Tpt
T. Rec.
Pno
Bass
Dr.
el
ff
f
57
62

4
68
Fl.
A. Sax.
Tpt
T. Rec.
Pno
Bass
Dr.
el
73
79

5
84
Fl.
A. Sax.
Tpt
T. Rec.
Pno
Bass
Dr.
el
90
101

6
112
Fl.
A. Sax.
Tpt
T. Rec.
Pno
Bass
Dr.
el
8:7
4:5
4:3
123
6:7
6:5
128

7
134
139
145
Fl.
A. Sax.
Tpt
T. Rec.
Pno
Bass
Dr.
el

8
150
Fl.
A. Sax.
Tpt
T. Rec.
Pno
Bass
Dr.
el
5:3
10:7
156
play
3
ff
f
mf
162

9
168
Fl.
A. Sax.
Tpt
T. Rec.
Pno
Bass
Dr.
el
179
185

10
Fl.
A. Sax.
Tpt
T. Rec.
Pno
Bass
Dr.
el
Soundscape from part 1

11
218
Fl.
A. Sax.
very slow gradual cressendo till 71
Tpt
T. Rec.
Pno
Bass
vrij tempo fills, met grote gaten, veel verschillende geluiden
Dr.
el
229
Fl.
A. Sax.
Tpt
T. Rec.
Pno
Bass
Dr.
el
240
Fl.
A. Sax
Tpt
T. Rec.
Pno
Bass
Dr.
el

12
251
Fl.
A. Sax.
Tpt
T. Rec.
Pno
Bass
Dr.
el
262
268

13
273
Fl.
A. Sax.
Tpt
T. Rec.
Pno
Bass
Dr.
el

278
Fl.
A. Sax.
Tpt
T. Rec.
Pno
Bass
Dr.

283
Fl.
A. Sax.
Tpt
T. Rec.
Pedaal 9 (heavy bas)
Pno
Bass
Dr.

14
286
♪= 105
290
294
Fl.
A. Sax.
Tpt
T. Rec.
Pno
Bass
Dr.
mf

15
298
Fl.
A. Sax.
Tpt
T. Rec.
Pno
Bass
Dr.
302
306

16
310
Fl.
A. Sax.
Tpt
T. Rec.
Pno
Bass
Dr.
314
Fl.
A. Sax.
Tpt
T. Rec.
Pno
Bass
Dr.
318
Fl.
A. Sax.
Tpt
T. Rec.
Pno
Bass
Dr.

17
322
Fl.
A. Sax.
Tpt
T. Rec.
Pno
Bass
Dr.
mf
f
326
330

18

334
♩ = 175
Fl.
A. Sax.
f and gradual crescendo
Tpt
f and gradual crescendo
T. Rec.
Pno
f and gradual crescendo
Bass
f and gradual crescendo
Dr.
f and gradual crescendo

345
Fl.
A. Sax.
Tpt
T. Rec.
Pno
Bass
Dr.

350
Fl.
A. Sax.
Tpt
T. Rec.
Pno
Bass
Dr.

19
356
Fl.
A. Sax.
Tpt
T. Rec.
Pno
Bass
Dr.
10:7♪
5:3♪
361
367
Pedaal 5 (RAGA 2 and bas 1)

20
368
Fl.
A. Sax.
Tpt
T. Rec.
Pno
Bass
Dr.
369
Pedaal 6 (RAGA 1 and bas 1)
370

21

371
Fl.
A. Sax.
Tpt
T. Rec.
Pno
Bass
Dr.
ff

372
Fl.
A. Sax.
Tpt
T. Rec.
Pno
Bass
Dr.
fff

3) *Oshún Olodí* (Louis Aguirre)

For flute and clarinet

> Oru is a sequence of chants and percussive strokes dedicated to the Orishas (the pantheon of African gods who rule and represent all aspects of our world and life). My music is nourished by Santería ceremonies, where music forms an integral part of making contact with 'other worlds': gods, ancestors and with 'another reality' – trance, possession, divination. In most of my music, sound is the vehicle of catharsis and sacred meaning. It was, indeed, my spiritual beliefs that made me realise I needed a sound that would reflect the atmosphere of these rituals. A sound capable of transmitting the frantic and complex sonorities of the ceremony.
>
> I was educated as a violin player within the old Soviet school (transplanted to Cuba) and within the most conservative western traditions. But the fact of being Cuban made me understand the importance of knowing different cultures as a way to enrich my own creative process and my own life. It is exactly this idea of global integration between different components of different cultures that has become one of my main characteristics as a composer. To this end, I came to Amsterdam to study the programme 'Contemporary music through non-western techniques'. I somehow knew that the complexity of karnatic rhythms could be an answer to my search.
>
> Whilst at the beginning I composed scrupulously following the rules learnt in this programme, shortly after my graduation I began to use the techniques in a much more intuitive way. I let myself be inspired by the 'spirit' of a technique even if I had to break the rules or adapt it to the musical needs of the moment. Cycles become shortened or stretched; techniques such as mukthays, yati phrases or mixed jathi nadai bhedam were more like brush strokes on a canvas that rarely finished as they do in karnatic music. What interested me of karnatic music was the unfolding of rhythmical richness that this system has created and how I could use it for my own aims.
>
> Nonetheless, in this piece cycles and techniques are still broken, but it oozes karnatic techniques even if these are often difficult to perceive or even analyse.

The analysis of this piece necessarily has to differ from the two previous compositions; as the composer mentions in his own description, his work with karnatic material is more 'intuitive'. The 'brushes on the canvas', as the composer describes his use of karnatic material, will somehow influence the manner in which his piece is analysed. The whole composition revolves exclusively around a few elements.

1) Firstly, on a macro-structural level, the piece is loosely constructed on the tala of 11 beats, dhruva tisra (L3 D L3 L3). The beginning cycles of the piece respond to this pattern, although this quite rapidly gives way to freer combinations of the 4 angas that do not always follow any intention of creating a cycle. Nonetheless, scattered throughout the piece, and as a contrasting element to the main micro-structural idea (explained below), the composer uses the same numbers as in measures 27–30.

2) Secondly, the numbers used to configure the main micro-structural idea are 3+5. This combination is the main leitmotif throughout the entire composition. However, the composer uses different extended techniques (as, for instance, in measures 16–18) to disguise this almost 'obsessive' element.

Nonetheless, the main technique that permeates the composition is a 'loose' interpretation and creative development of mixed jathi nadai bhedam (Chapter 19). There are several ways in which the composer uses the underlying 3+5 to superimpose nadais.

a) 'Regular' way: the same nadai is superimposed on both numbers, as in measures 17 and 52 in khanda and 53 in misra.

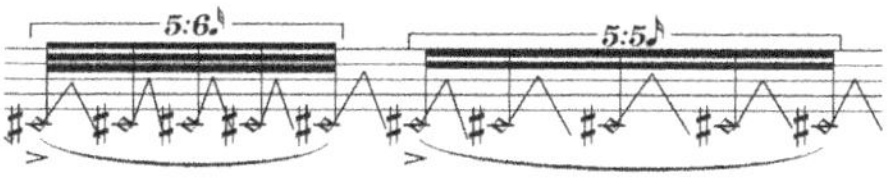

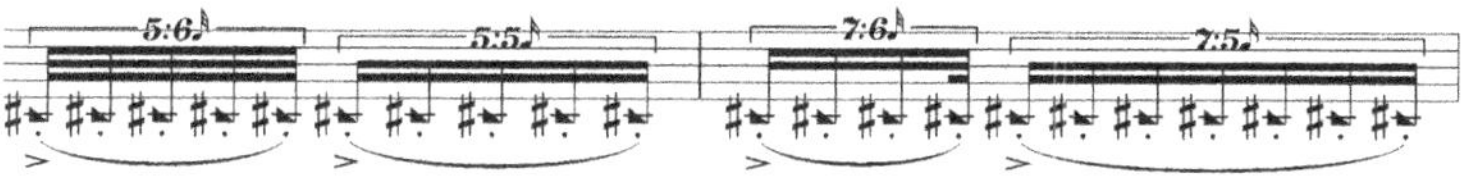

b) Leaving one cell without superimposition and using misra on either the cell of 3 or 5, as in measures 18, 25 and 26.

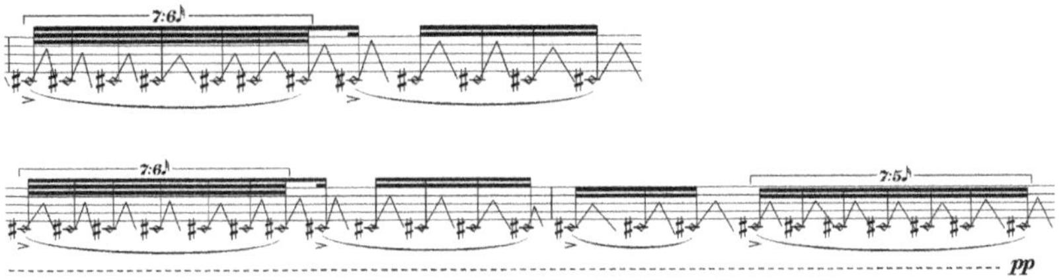

c) Fragmenting the nadai between the two instruments. In measure 19 the flute plays the cell of 3 matras followed by a 7:5♪, whereas the clarinet performs a 7:3♪ and then the cell of 5 matras.

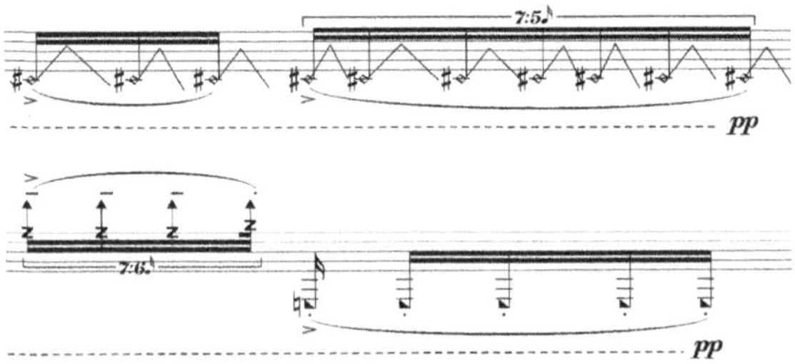

d) Combination of all previous ideas: in measures 102–3 khanda and misra are mixed, superimposed on the frame of 3+5.

In measures 57–8 Aguirre goes a step further. By using a metre of 3/4 and having 4 extra matras added to the 3+5 combination, he plays with the idea of 3+1, as in the 3rd beat of measure 57 and the 2nd beat of measure 58. He then goes on to superimpose misra on the 3 matras cell whilst either leaving 1 matra on its own (measure 57) or adding it to the 4 finishing matras of the fragment to create another 5 matras cell (measure 58).

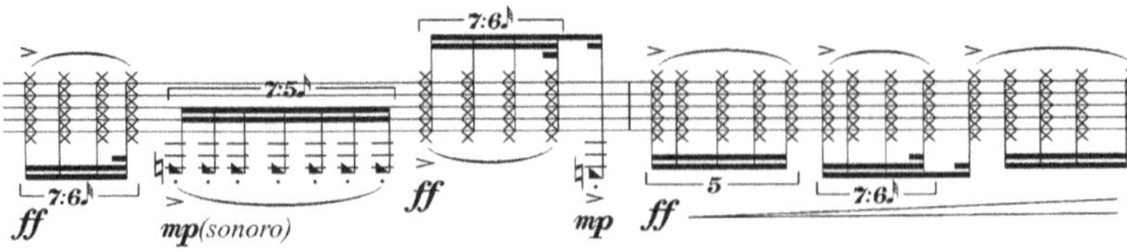

A similar idea is explored in measure 55, superimposing khanda and chatusra at the beginning and the end of the measure.

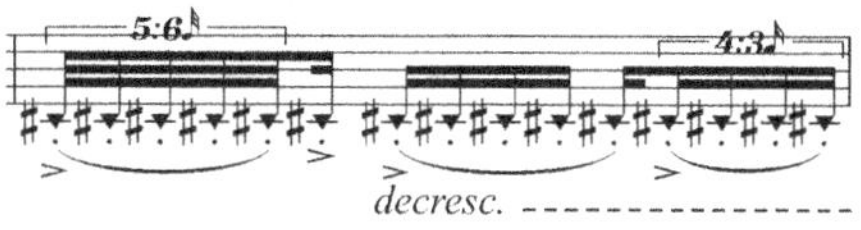

e) Using tisra with accents 5+7: The same idea of using a combination of numbers that would complete 2 beats is used in tisra; the 12 matras of 2 beats of tisra 2nd speed are split in the same way that 3+5 were used in chatusra. However, the composer does not use any superimposition on the frames. This idea can be seen several times, as presented in measures 82 and 101.

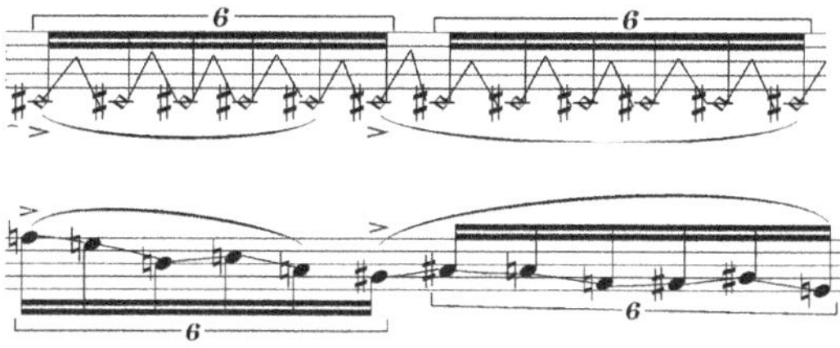

Besides the predominant use of mixed jathi nadai bhedam, on several occasions Aguirre plays with sequences of 3+5 in which repetitions or displacements occur. This is the case in the following passage that starts on the last matra of measure 69 and creates the numerical sequence 3 5 3 5 3 3 5 3 5 3.

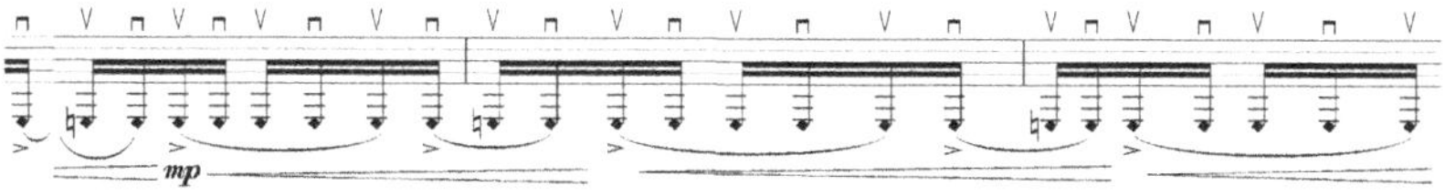

Another combination is given by repeating the numbers 3 and 5 twice at the beginning and the end of measures 97–8 and provoking displacement of the accents (3 3 5 3 5 5).

The last element used in 'Oshún Olodí' presents the notation of nadai bhedam, as explained in Chapter 18; however, not with the idea of producing a polypulse but rather in the way combinations anuloma-pratiloma develop material.

The initial frame is a 4:3♩ which is prepared by using chatusra jathi 3, but with the double bracket notation, giving the performer a clear indication of the composer's intention with this frame (measure 104). This leads to 3 measures with continuous changes of frames and nadais inside these frames.

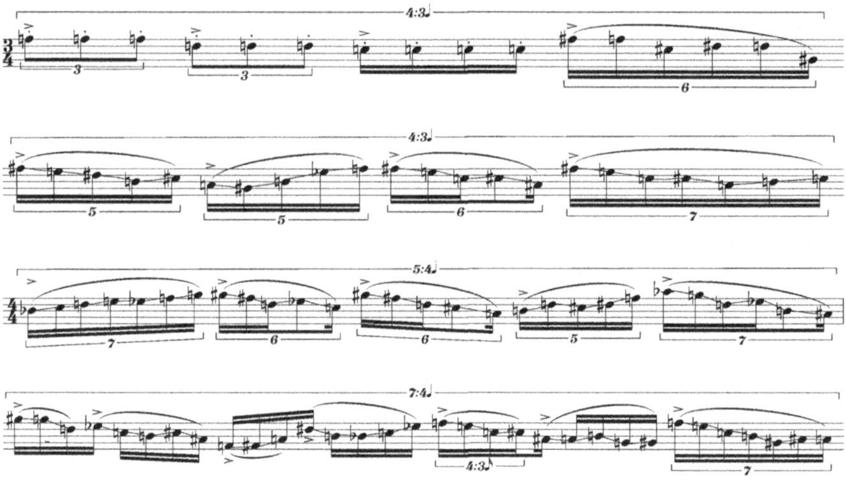

Although this use of nadai bhedam does not conform to the karnatic notion of creating polypulses, the composer needs to resort to the nested tuplet notation of nadai bhedam to convey his rhythmical idea of producing the feeling of tempo changes and mixing gatis within these tempo changes.

When I started this project, I knew I had to ask this Cuban composer to write a piece. Not only was I interested in his 'brutality' and 'massiveness', but I also wanted to present a composition in which the intuitive side of karnatic techniques would play a central role.

As the reader will find in the conclusion, I have strong doubts as to how karnatic techniques, except for combinations anuloma-pratiloma, can be integrated if creators do not give up a continuous or random metre change. However, the 'brush stroke on the canvas' Aguirre refers to is, from my point of view, yet another valid path to creation using karnatic techniques.

My intention in presenting three composers was not only to show different aesthetics or influencing backgrounds, but also how every piece is conceived in a completely different manner. Some composers use almost exclusively karnatic techniques in every parameter; others have personalised them and used them with almost complete disregard for the original architecture of the concepts, while others use a combination of both approaches. *(track 262)*

OSHÚN OLODÍ

♩= 50
(Jet Whistle)
Flute
Voice in C
Clarinet in B♭
Voice in Bb
pp
fff
p
Fl.
Voice in C
Cl.
Voice in Bb
mp
molto
(T.R)
(Toneless)
(Slap)
ff

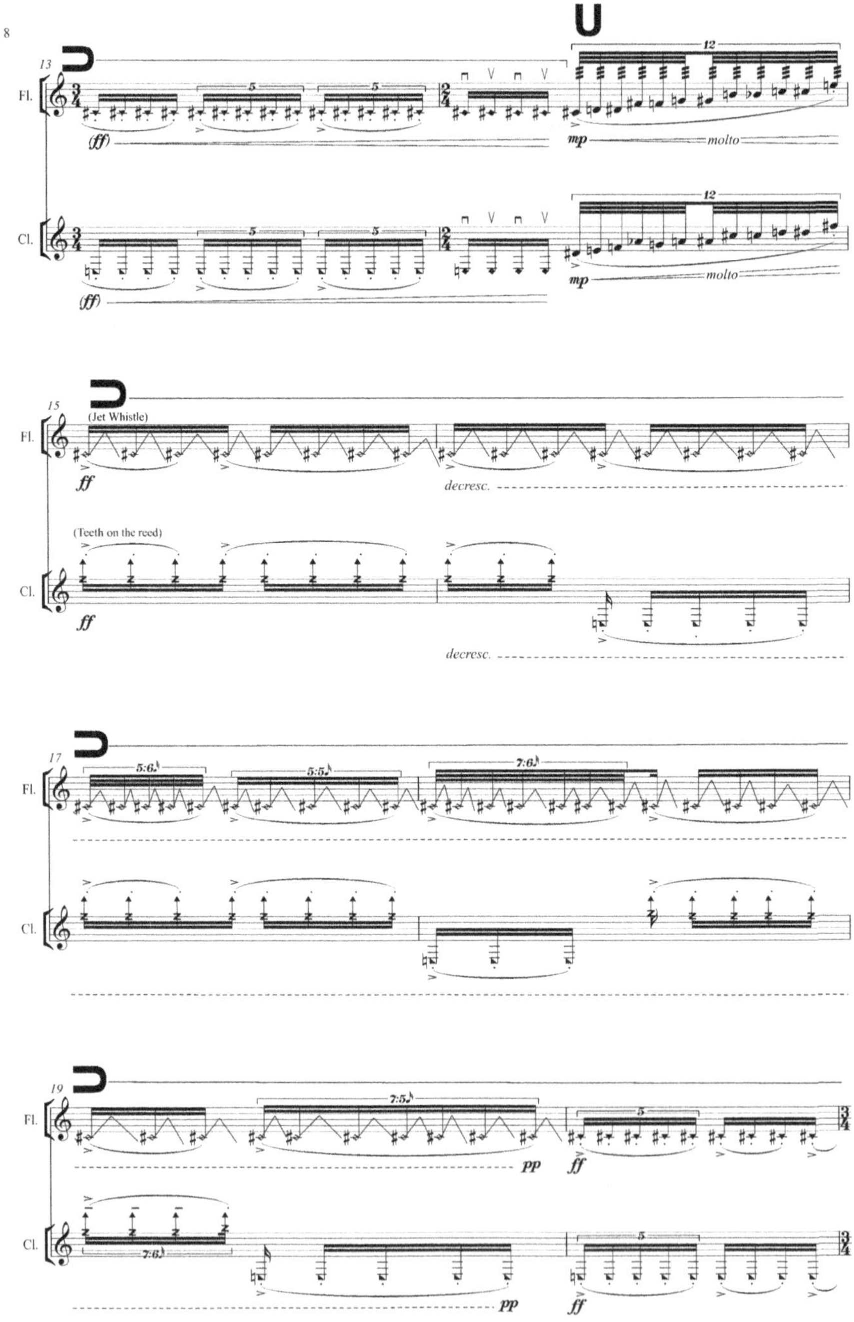
8
Fl.
Cl.
mp
molto
(ff)
(Jet Whistle)
(Teeth on the reed)
ff
decresc.
pp

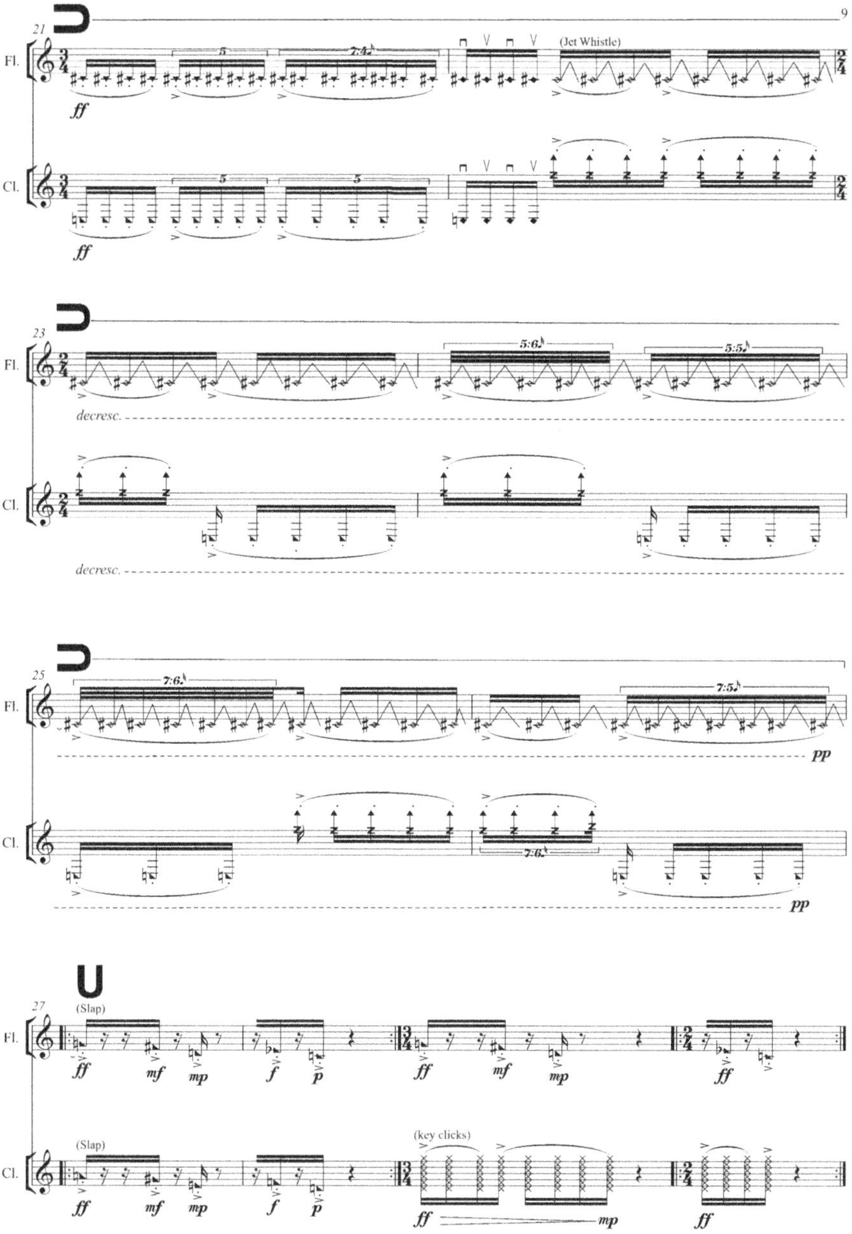
21
Fl.
Cl.
(Jet Whistle)
ff
23
decresc.
25
pp
27
(Slap)
(key clicks)
ff
mf
mp
f
p

10

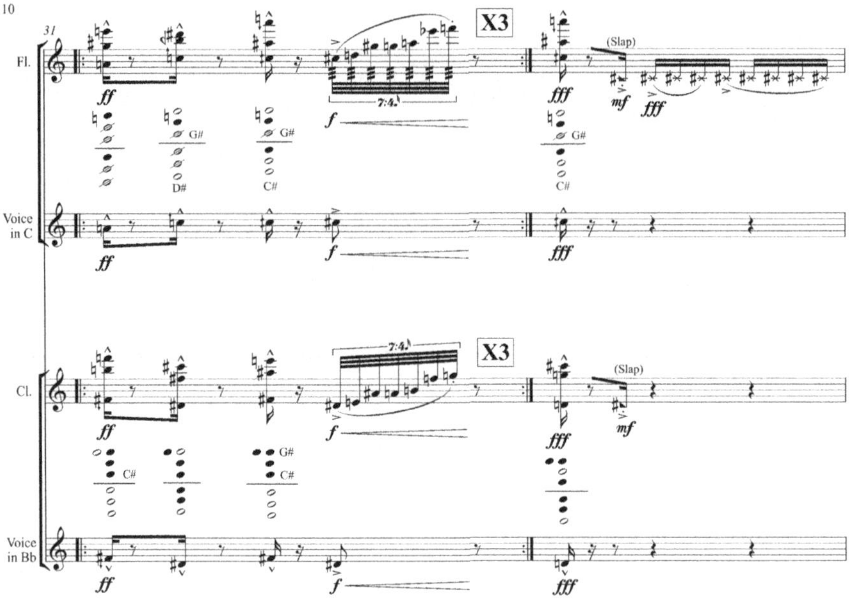
31
Fl.
X3
(Slap)
Voice in C
Cl.
X3
(Slap)
Voice in Bb

33
Fl.
X3
Voice in C
Cl.
X3
Voice in Bb

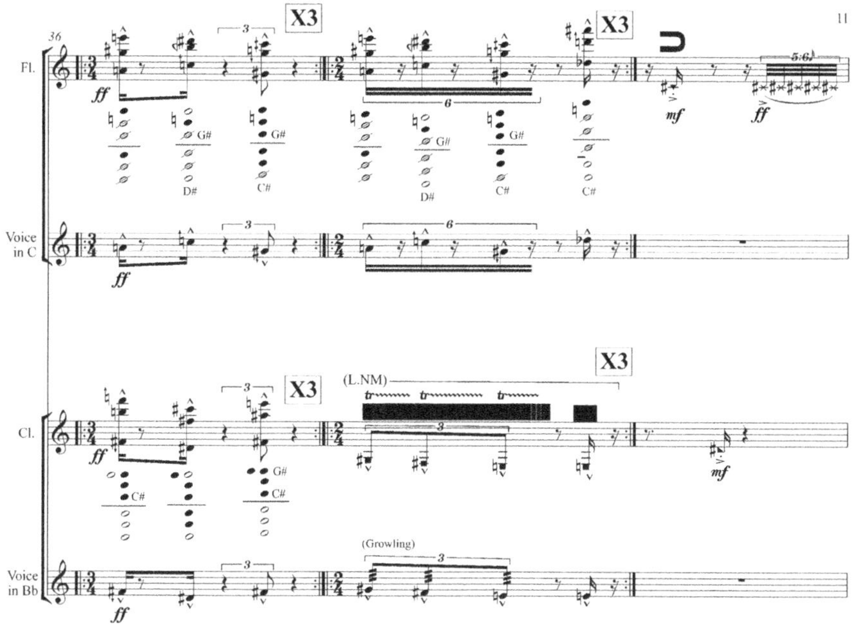
11
36
Fl.
Voice in C
Cl.
Voice in Bb
X3
(L.NM)
(Growling)

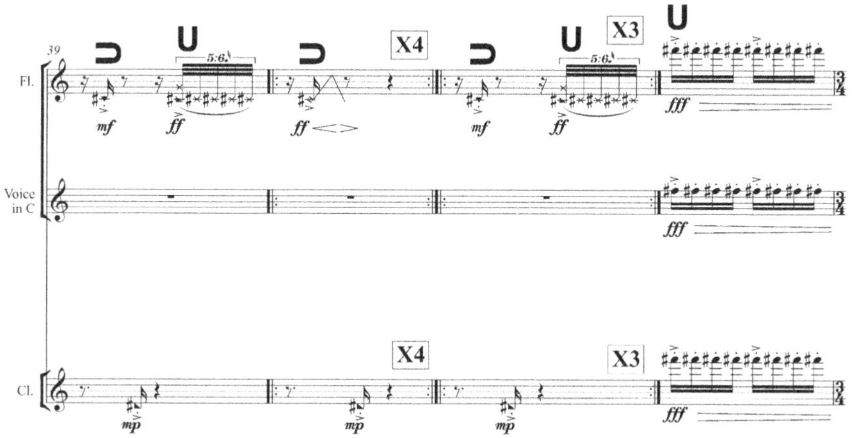
39
Fl.
Voice in C
Cl.
X4
X3

12
Fl.
Voice in C
Cl.
Voice in Bb
mf
fff
pp
ff
mp
molto
ppp
(T.R)
(Slap)
p
mf
f

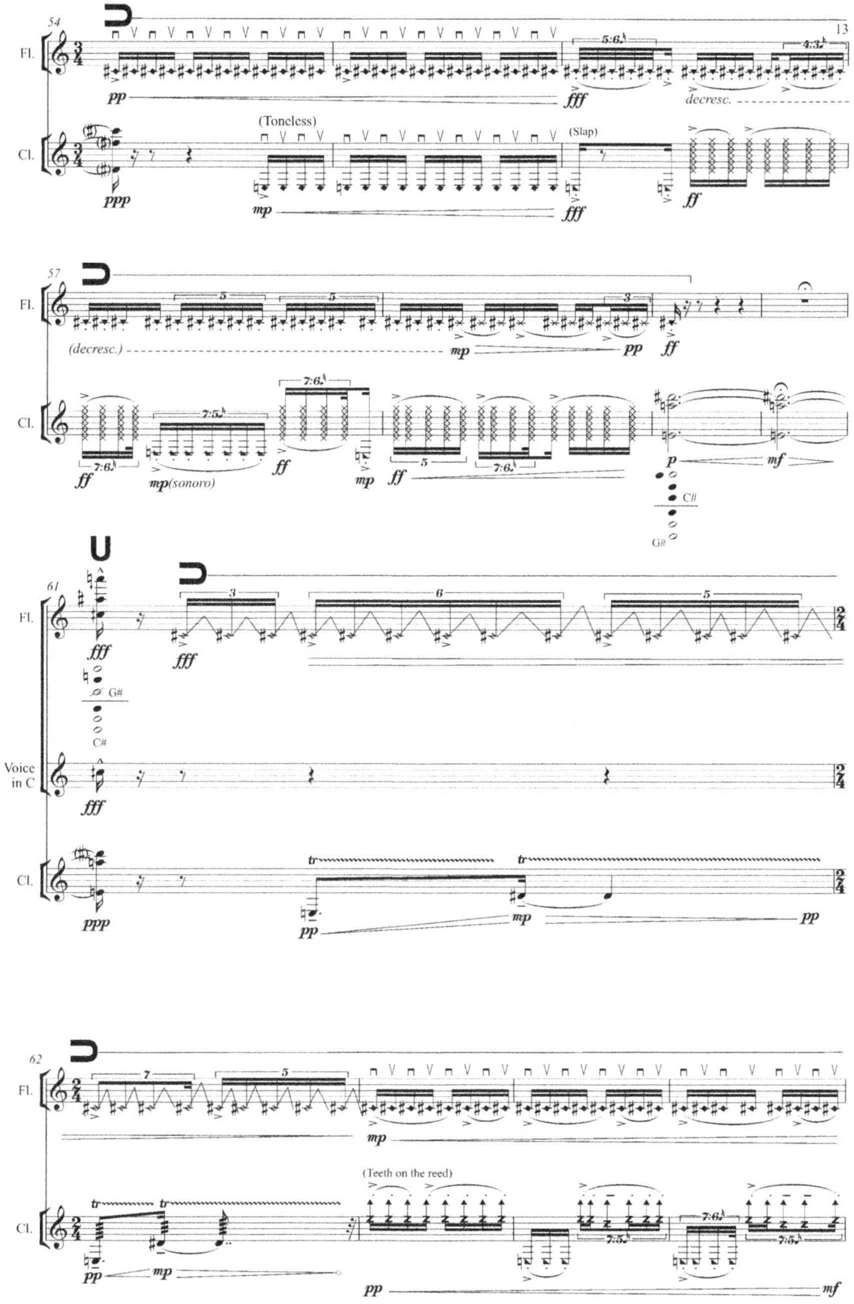
Fl.
Cl.
(Toneless)
(Slap)
decresc.
(decresc.)
mp(sonoro)
C#
G#
Voice in C
tr
(Teeth on the reed)

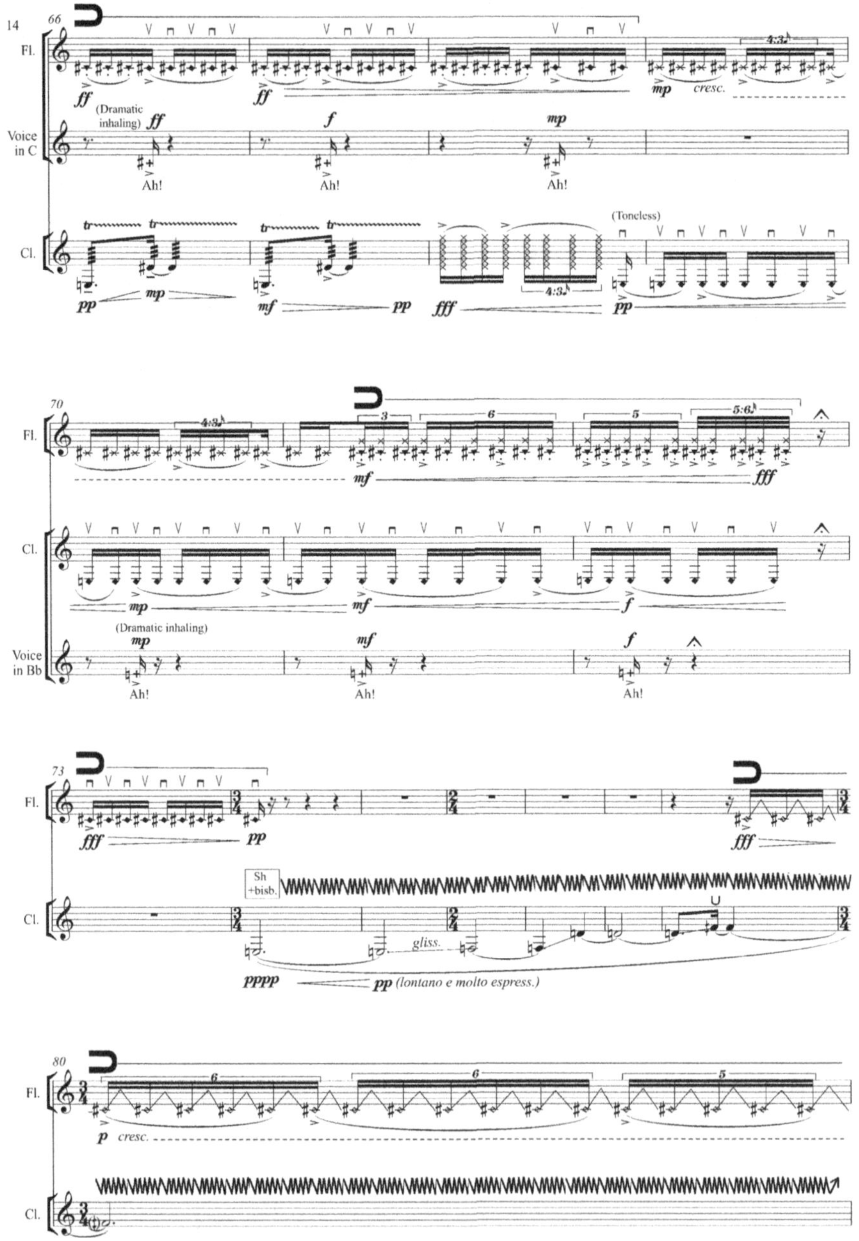
14
Fl.
Voice in C
Cl.
(Dramatic inhaling)
Ah!
(Toneless)
cresc.
Voice in Bb
(Dramatic inhaling)
Sh +bisb.
gliss.
pp (lontano e molto espress.)
p cresc.

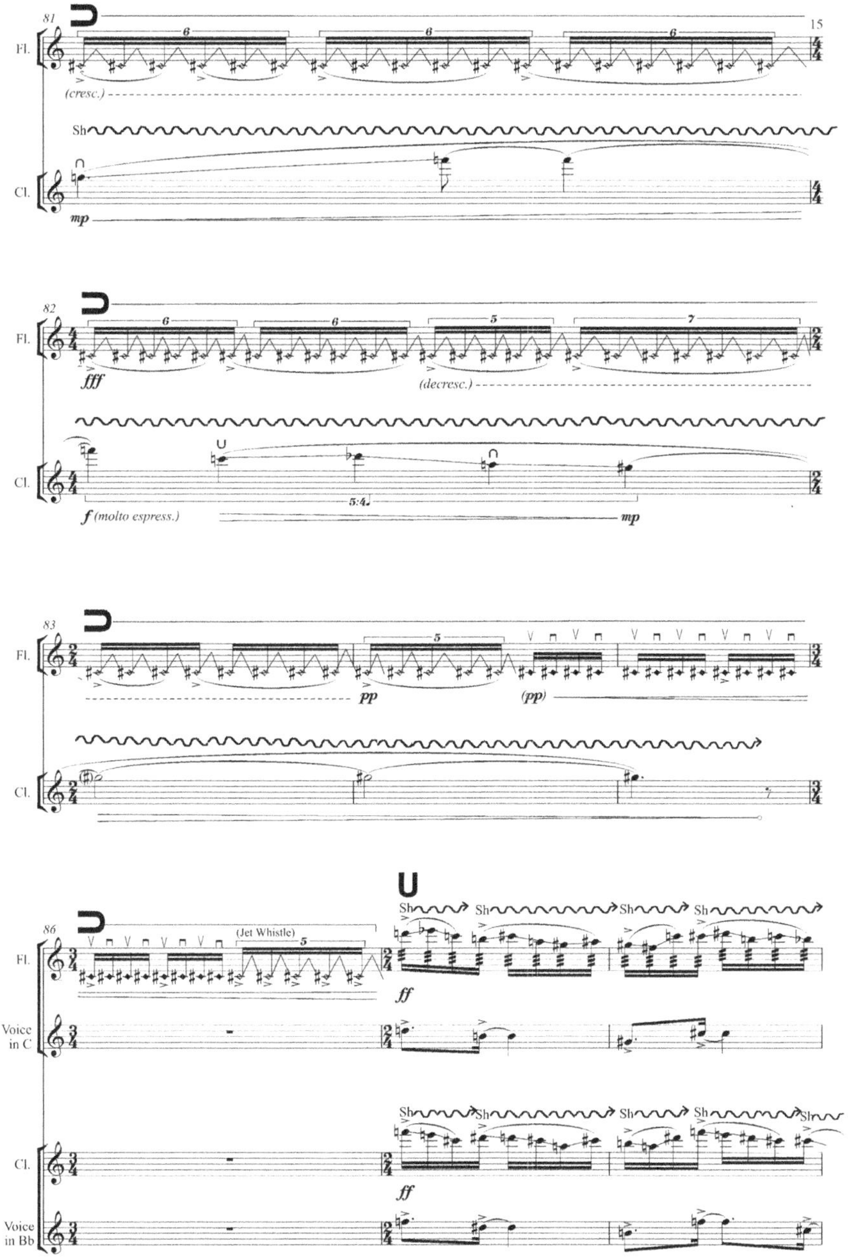
81
Fl.
(cresc.)
Sh
Cl.
mp
15
82
Fl.
fff
(decresc.)
Cl.
f (molto espress.)
5:4
mp
83
Fl.
pp
(pp)
Cl.
86
Fl.
(Jet Whistle)
Sh
ff
Voice in C
Cl.
Voice in Bb

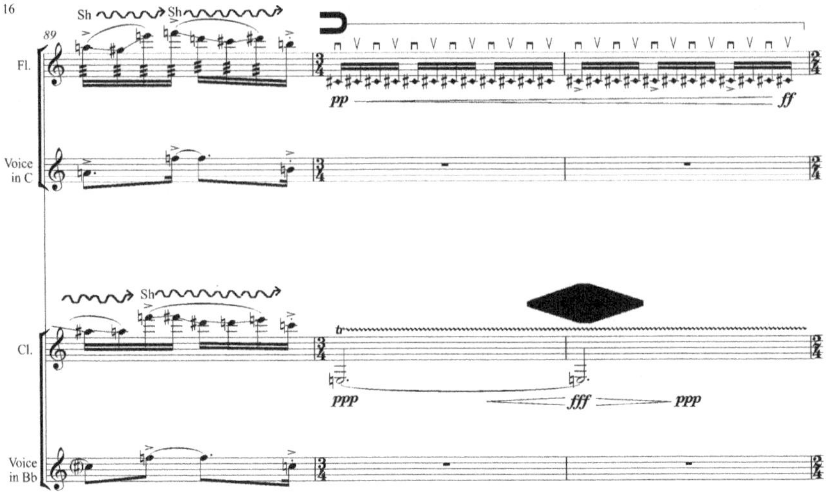
16
89
Sh
Sh
Fl.
pp
ff
Voice in C
Sh
Cl.
tr
ppp
fff
ppp
Voice in Bb

U
92
Sh
Sh
Sh
Sh
Sh
Sh
Fl.
ff
p
ff
p
Voice in C
Sh
Sh
Sh
Sh
Sh
Sh
Flzg.
Sh
Cl.
ff
p
ff
p
ff
Voice in Bb

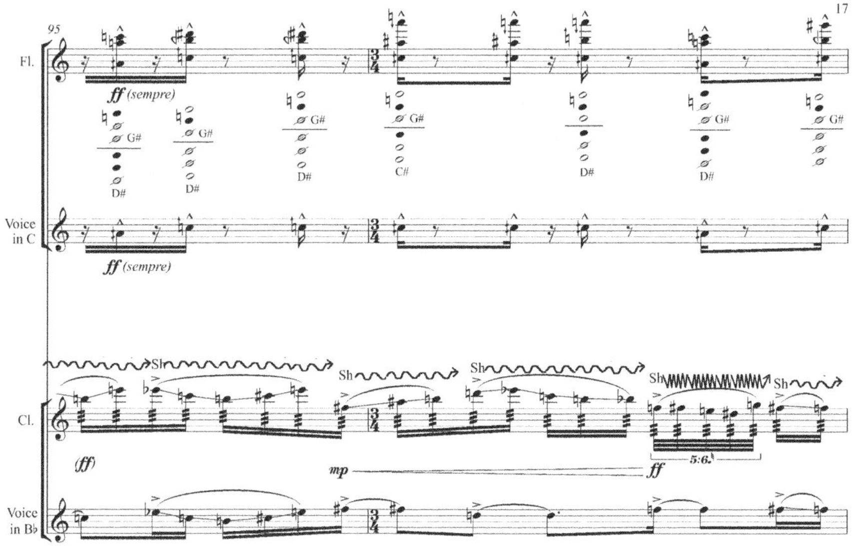
95
17
Fl.
ff (sempre)
Voice in C
ff (sempre)
Cl.
Sh
(ff)
mp
ff
5:6
Voice in B♭

97
Fl.
(ff)
Voice in C
(ff)
Cl.
Sh
ff
mp
ff
mp
ff
mp
Voice in B♭

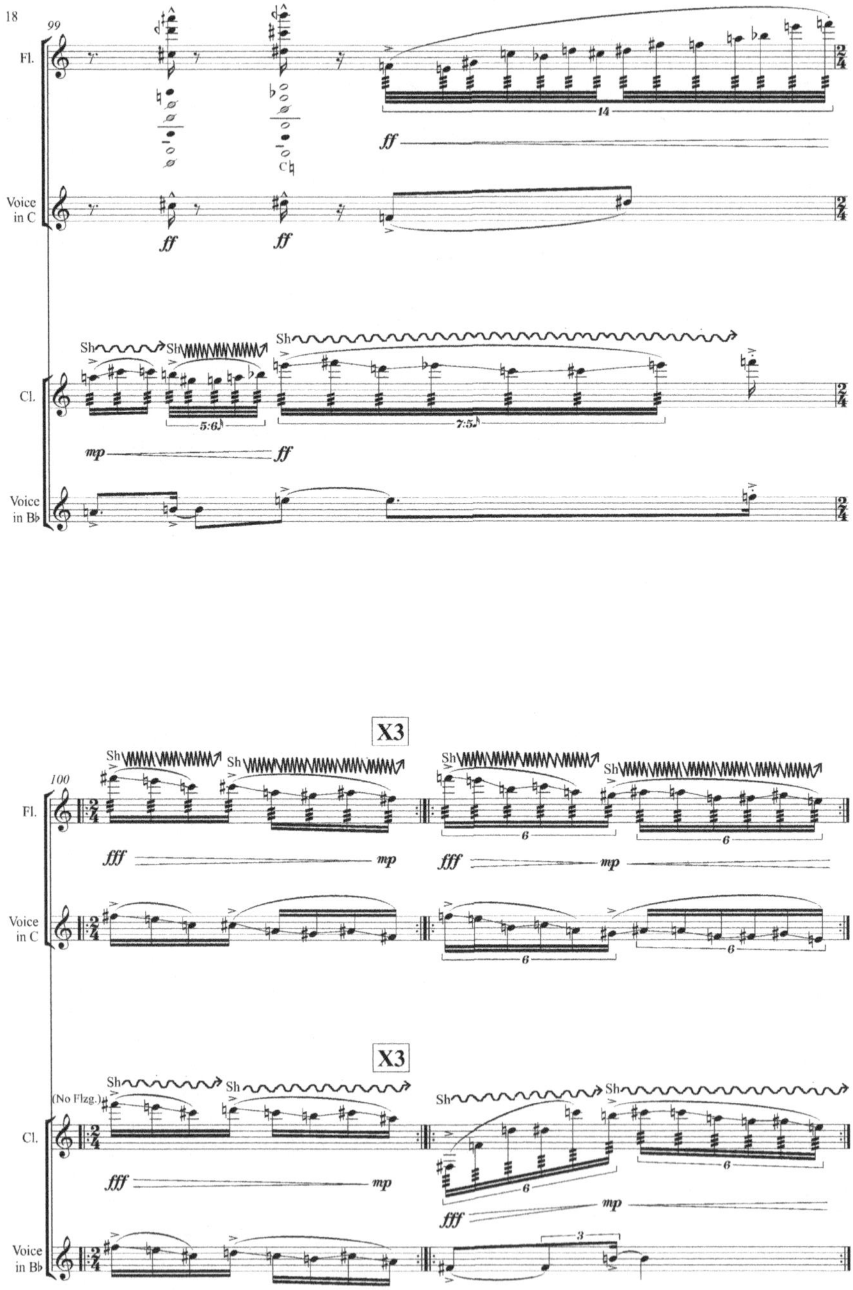
18
99
Fl.
Voice in C
Cl.
Voice in B♭
ff
Sh
5:6
7:5
14
mp
100
X3
(No Flzg.)
fff
6
3

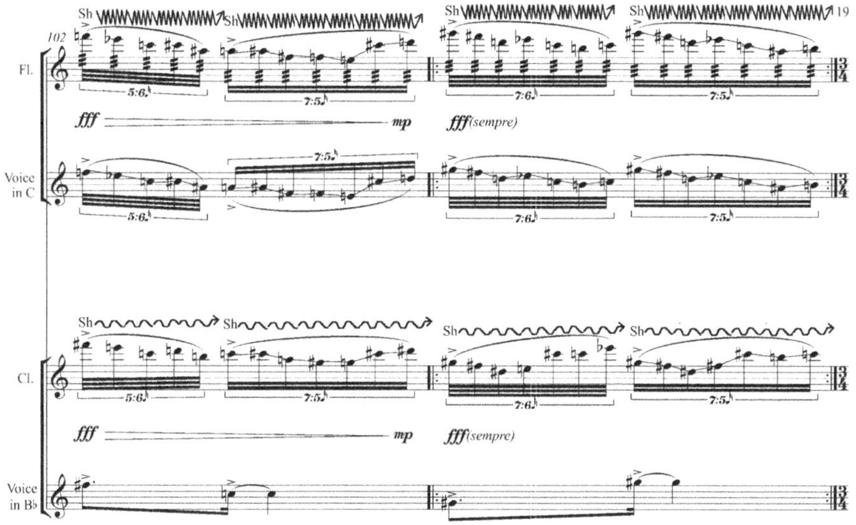
102
Fl.
Voice in C
Cl.
Voice in B♭
Sh
19
5:6
7:5
7:6
fff
mp
fff (sempre)

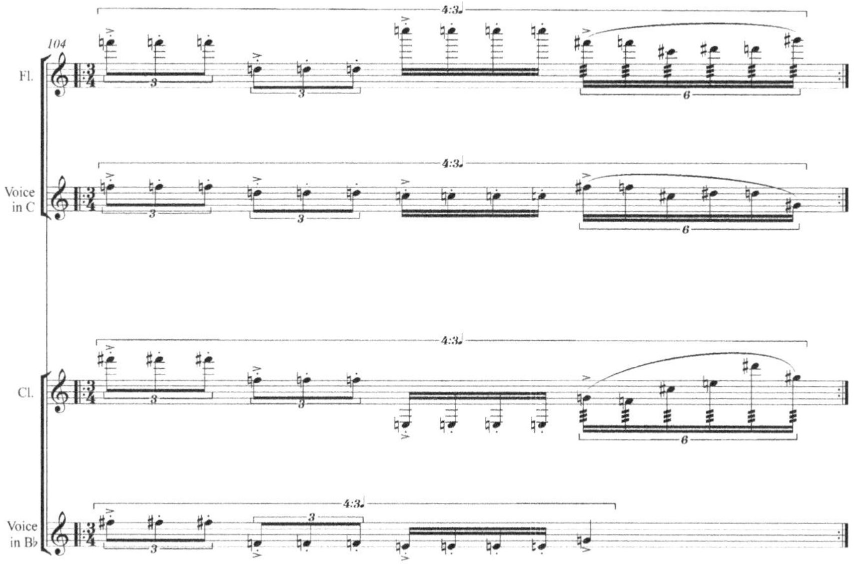
104
Fl.
Voice in C
Cl.
Voice in B♭
4:3
3
6

20

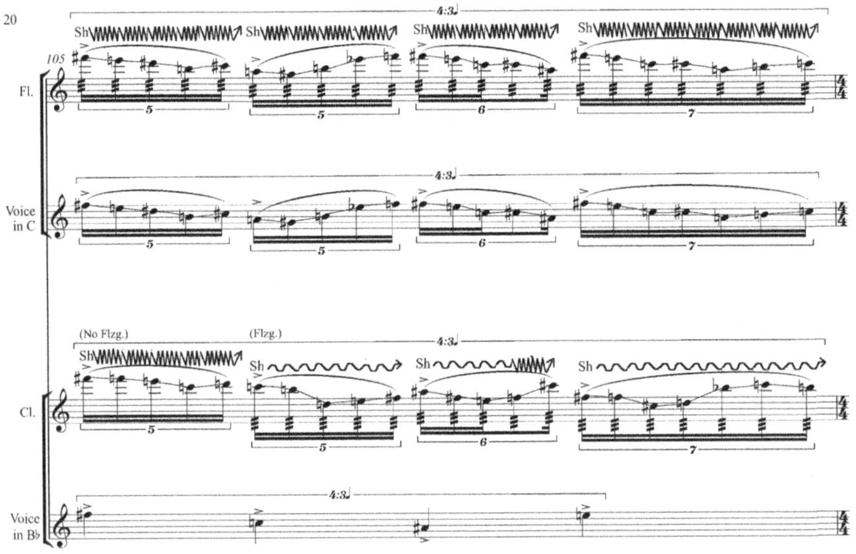
4:3
Sh
105
Fl.
5
6
7
Voice
in C
(No Flzg.)
(Flzg.)
Cl.
Voice
in B♭

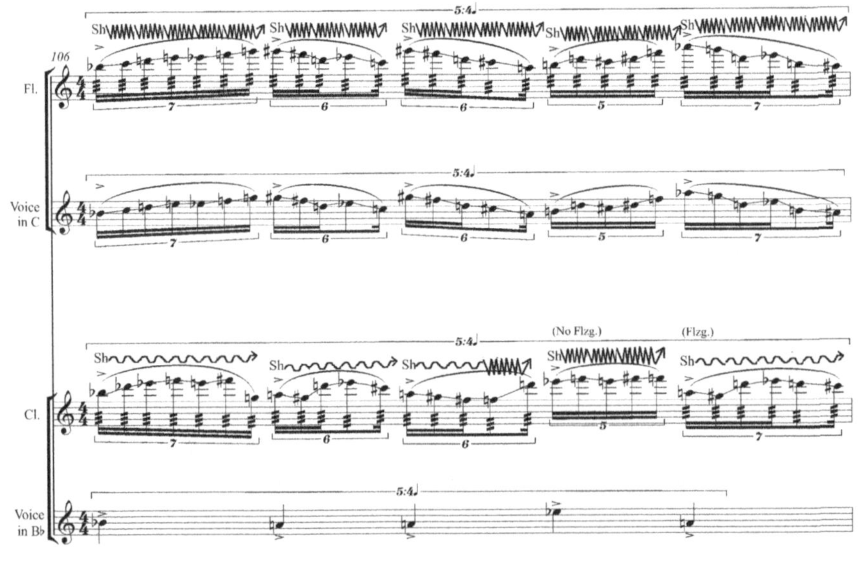
5:4
Sh
106
Fl.
7
6
5
Voice
in C
(No Flzg.)
(Flzg.)
Cl.
Voice
in B♭

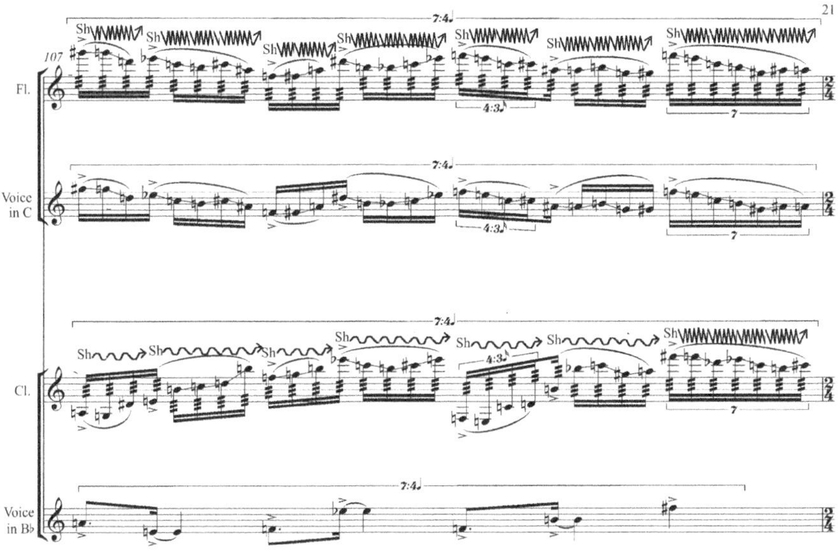
21
107
Fl.
Voice
in C
Cl.
Voice
in B♭
Sh
7:4
4:3
7

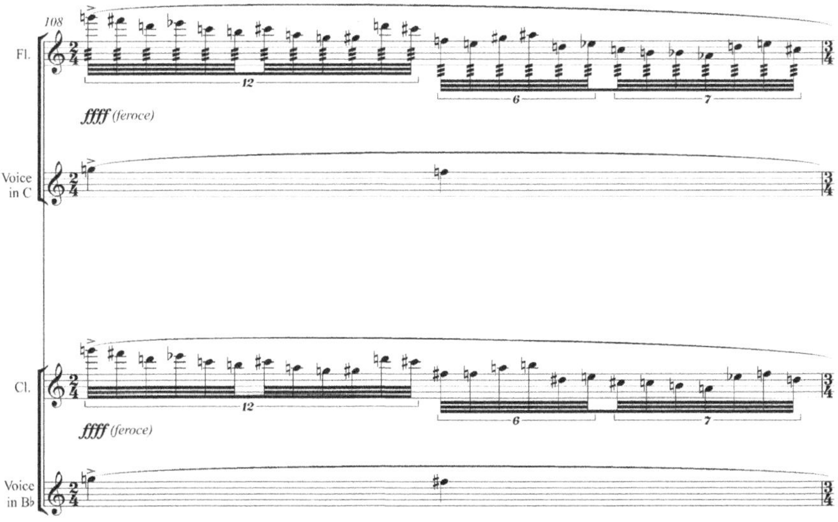
108
Fl.
ffff (feroce)
Voice
in C
Cl.
ffff (feroce)
Voice
in B♭
12
6
7

22

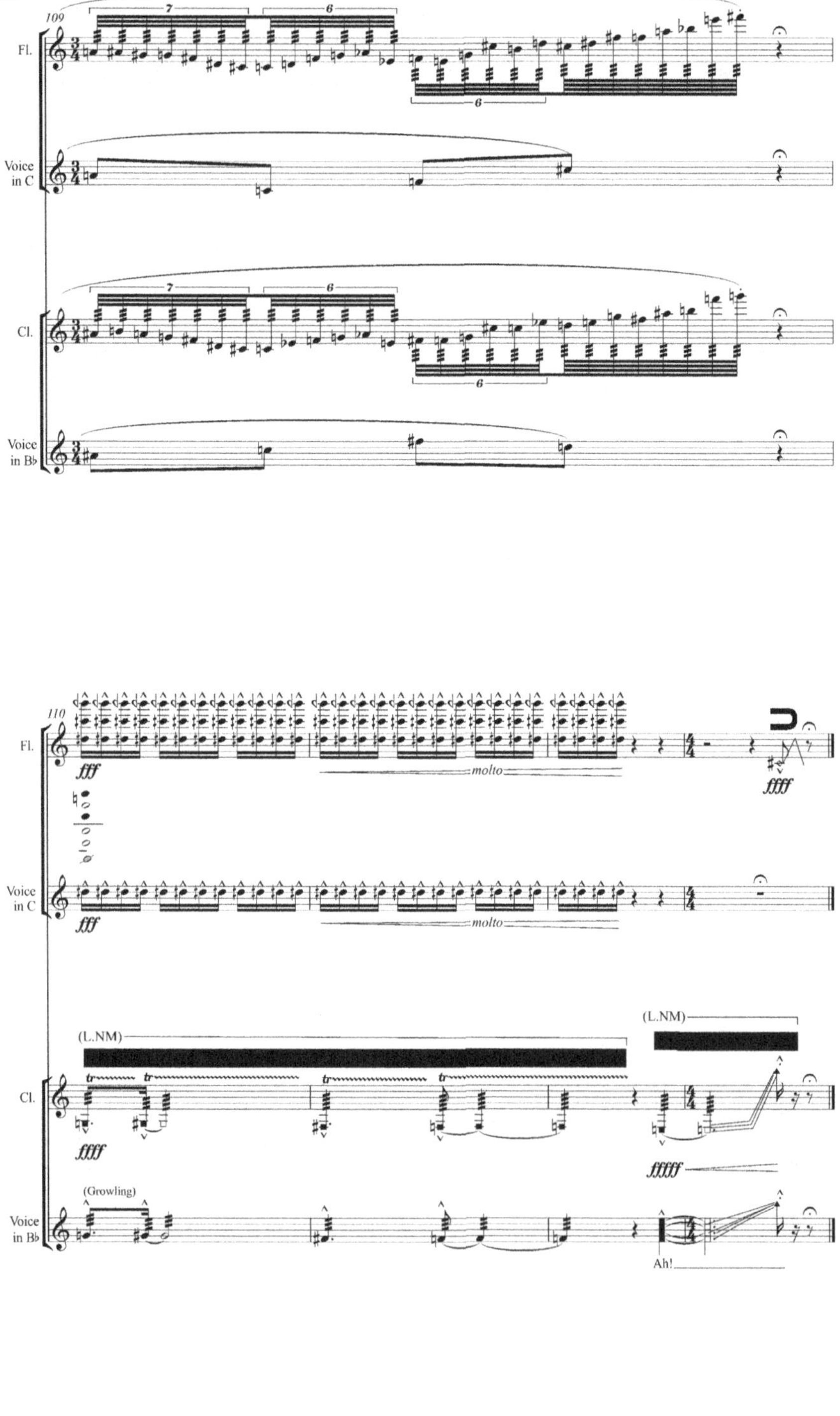
109
Fl.
Voice in C
Cl.
Voice in B♭
7
6
110
fff
molto
ffff
(L.NM)
(Growling)
fffff
Ah!

Conclusion

To conclude, I would like to begin with the last paragraph of the interview with Pierre Boulez that was quoted in the introduction:

> If the rhythms and phrasing that are peculiar to contemporary music would be taught in the best conservatories in an intensive way, the future of contemporary music would certainly change and performers and [the] general public would really start enjoying pieces by Berio, Xenakis or myself. The lack of accuracy in orchestras is the biggest obstacle for communication between composers and [the] public.

The ultimate intention behind my whole research, and the construction of a programme for performers at the Amsterdam Conservatoire, has precisely been to lay a bridge to restore the communication referred to by Boulez in the measure that I can contribute to this end through my knowledge of karnatic rhythm. I would argue that the only way for this to happen would be to implement the material presented in this volume within a western educational framework. My proposal involves replacing the current rhythmical teaching methodology in western conservatoires and music academies with the methodical, transparent, effective and far-reaching techniques and concepts seen in karnatic music. *The main issue here is to what extent the mentality of learning rhythm and the importance given to this issue in the West (at an educational stage as well as at a professional level) needs to be deeply reviewed or even changed entirely.*

In fact, many pieces from the 1950s onwards and by composers born in the third decade of the twentieth century are bound to become 'classics' in no more than 20 or 30 years from now; but, unless the curriculum for classical performers adopts a radical transformation of the current methodology, today's state of affairs will be likely to perpetuate itself.

In addition to this pedagogical and performance-oriented goal, I find it very important to reiterate the great palette of creative possibilities that the karnatic rhythmical system can provide to westerners (furthered by creative and imaginative use). This is, I believe, illustrated in the students' pieces presented in the last chapter.

At this point, it should be clear that my research and the teaching of this material has a double aim: a pedagogical one, catering to classical and jazz performers, as well as a creative one for composers and improvisers.

This final section has to necessarily be empirical in nature: all the conclusions I arrived at are the direct result of the research, teaching and development of this material for over 18 years; 21 years of composing and experimenting with karnatic concepts; and the experiences of my students (performers and creators alike) during their studies and when employed in their professional careers.

Performers

From a performance and pedagogical point of view all the karnatic material can be divided into two large conceptual corpuses: one dealing with *superimpositions* (nadai bhedam, anuloma-pratiloma and derived notions); and techniques that work with *crossing accents phrasing* (gati and jathi bhedam and all their subsequent concepts).

Performers today are confronted with pieces that have not been composed with any knowledge of karnatic rhythmical structures but that utilise rhythmical complexities in various ways, and increasingly encounter works by composers who have studied karnatic music either through the programme at the Amsterdam Conservatoire or with Indian musicians. Below are some reflections on these points.

Superimpositions

Apart from some preferences for either the notation proposed here or the notation employed by many composers of the twentieth century, I do not think there should be any doubt about the efficiency that the karnatic system can provide in the performance of this sort of material (in general, all 'irregular groupings'). In fact, as stated several times, it is only the creative approach by karnatic musicians regarding these techniques that differentiates western and karnatic music as far as this concept is concerned.[1]

Crossing Accents Phrasing

In the section on applications to western music, except for Stravinsky's example, I chose fragments of pieces that use the same notation as the one proposed in the chapters on gati and jathi bhedam. However, my experience as a teacher working with student ensembles performing twentieth-century pieces – together with my observation of various experiences of students in a professional setting (where the students applied these karnatic techniques even if the notation did not clearly call for it) – led me to reflect upon how much more frequently performers could use these techniques than when called for by the notation.

I am well aware of the reluctance that applying these techniques to traditionally notated phrases can arouse in many musicians. I do not advocate for a radical change to phrasing in the performance of twentieth-century music. However, I

[1] Later on I would like to expand upon the karnatic approach to creation with this sort of material.

would suggest that some composers, at least in some of their pieces, did indeed have in mind (in one way or another) a phrasing closer to an inner amalgamation concept than to the traditional 'imaginary beat-line' interpretation.

Bowing and breathing slurs (as in Ligeti or Messiaen), dotted slurs (as used by Xenakis) or other similar articulation techniques can be clues from which to extract shorter or longer passages that may resemble gati or jathi bhedam; in other words, a simple form of polyrhythm (gati bhedam) or inner amalgamation (jathi bhedam).

My work with students, and the experience of former students performing in professional ensembles, has aroused the interest of colleagues who perceive this approach to phrasing as less rigid than the traditional one. I would therefore suggest that some compositions, or fragments of certain pieces by some composers, can be approached with karnatic techniques in mind. Thus the final result may be more in line with what they may have intended, even if they did not take the step of using (or consider it necessary to use) the notation found in, for instance, Ligeti's 'Piano Concerto' or Messiaen's 'Quatuor pour la fin du temps'.

Compositions with Non-Karnatic Concepts

The manner in which the karnatic concepts are presented in this text (and taught at the Amsterdam Conservatoire) and the way in which contemporary music has developed rhythmical complexities may not appear to bear any relationship to one another. Nevertheless, any rhythmical device found in western music can be analysed and performed by using one or more karnatic techniques, as I think I have proved in the section on applications to western music. However, it is absolutely essential that the student possess an analytical mind to establish a parallel between a karnatic technique and its use in a concrete passage of contemporary music. Studying and mastering all karnatic techniques without having the ability to translate them into an existing piece of music makes the study of karnatic rhythm less valuable for a classical performer.

Compositions with Karnatic Concepts

Although these pieces should, in principle, be more 'straightforward' for a student of karnatic techniques, and the performer should be able to perceive which techniques have been used or could be applied, the reality is that in general western creators want to be innovative. The tendency is to bend rules, mix techniques or, as I myself encourage my students to do, find new paths to use karnatic concepts while respecting the bare minimum set of rules (or, as I prefer to call it, the 'architecture') for each technique. All this – without mentioning the immense possibilities that western concepts such as 'counterpoint-oriented' notions, orchestration, background versus foreground, fragmentation of techniques among different instruments (to mention just a few) – can add to the way karnatic rhythmical structures can be developed and notated in the West.

Subsequently, performers are bound to use a similar approach when performing compositions with karnatic concepts, as with any other piece of contemporary music – with the sole difference that, notation-wise, the concomitances between what they studied and the notation will likely tend to be much closer. Therefore, my conclusion as to how performers should approach rhythmically complex pieces is that they need to apply an analytical mind and view karnatic techniques as tools to be adapted to specific circumstances. By analysing contemporary pieces and contemplating ways of implementing these techniques at almost every step of the process, these studies can become a powerful performance tool.

Creators

The combination of karnatic techniques with the arsenal of possibilities provided by a western musical background can produce completely new paths in western creation (whether improvised or composed).

As a lover of karnatic music (and aesthetics), and simultaneously a teacher of these techniques, I have always walked a fine line between respecting the minimum architecture I consider necessary to make a technique what it is and respecting the imaginative approach of my students.

Paradoxically, those more prone to break rules and bend the use of techniques are usually in their first year of the programme, while those who 'see beyond' the techniques and respect their rules tend to be in the third or fourth year. I find the most plausible explanation for this attitude lies in the fact that the more karnatic concepts students learn and the more time spent working with the material, the more 'meaning' they find in trying to respect the architecture of the techniques while creating and starting to conceive how to blend both worlds. It is as though, as students progress in the understanding and variety of concepts, they begin to gain an 'aerial' view and to see the puzzle in its entirety.

I am not advocating erecting fences to innovation and imagination aimed at anyone studying karnatic rhythmical structures (especially if they are the result of combining them with western concepts of orchestration that do not exist in karnatic music). However, there are two quintessential karnatic concepts that I consider important to reflect upon: cycle and common denominator.

Cycle

Most karnatic techniques seem to work exclusively with this concept, however it may be called or conceived. New cyclic structures as seen in Chapters 22 and 23 (tala prastara) or Hans Leeuw's 'repetitive time units' are both paths that significantly expand the possibilities provided by the first tala system explained, the suladi talas.

For many years, quite a number of students (myself included) tried to create music using karnatic elements whilst changing metres without any 'cyclical thinking' behind it. The result was that we could seldom use techniques like tirmana, mohara, gati bhedam, nadai bhedam, complex mukthays, rhythmical sangatis or mixed jathi nadai bhedam (just to mention a few options). Only combinations anuloma-pratiloma seemed feasible in any context.

I am well aware that a lot of rhythmical complexities can and have been used in the West with continuous metre changes. However, in my experience, this approach of continuous or random metre changes clashes with quite a large number of karnatic possibilities; or at least makes the use of karnatic devices a highly laborious process requiring very elaborate calculations and making performance extremely difficult.

Essentially, my conclusion is that in order to utilise the aforementioned techniques (and not exclusively anuloma-pratiloma), creators would most likely have to 'sacrifice' the use of continuous or random metric changes unless they create a unit that would closely resemble the concept of cycle. This does not mean that I would advocate discarding the use of continuous or random metric changes in western music. Nevertheless, after years of attempting to use karnatic techniques with random metre changes, I realised that the 'sacrificed' element has always been the karnatic rhythmical structures. Both rhythmical approaches seem to simply exclude each other. My experience as a composer, and that of many (former) students, has been that the more the notion of cycle is used (in one way or another), the easier it becomes to integrate karnatic techniques.

Common Denominator

This concept permeates the whole corpus of concepts and techniques of karnatic music from a creative viewpoint. It is the element that has enabled karnatic musicians to elaborate both a highly complex rhythmical system and a methodology of study of rhythm to a high level of sophistication. To illustrate the concept of common denominator I would like to concentrate on the aspects furthest removed from our use of 'irregular groupings', namely nadai bhedam and combinations anuloma-pratiloma.

I would argue that these concepts are two of the greatest achievements of the whole karnatic system. As mentioned in the section on applications to western music, the West has essentially developed a 'numbers against numbers' approach. In contrast, karnatic music has been able to organise these 'numbers' into two completely differentiated and highly elaborate systems: one is exclusively used as a method to establish polypulses (nadai bhedam), whereas the other introduces rather complex irregular groupings and displacements within the beat 'constrained' into six different developmental techniques (combinations anuloma-pratiloma). It is precisely this notion – the fact that two consecutive 'numbers' need to have a common element – that I find fascinating, both as a body of theory in itself and as a method to create with.

For a number of years I have wondered: what can we gain from the karnatic approach materialised in nadai bhedam and anuloma-pratiloma? Why does the gap between composers and performers in the West seem to be much wider than in South India? Could their approach be a solution to bridge the gap between composers and performers, and, ultimately, audiences in the West?

I would argue that a system in which the *practice methodology* and the *developmental possibilities* of the same concept are *inextricably linked*, as is the case in nadai bhedam and anuloma-pratiloma techniques, could very well be a solution to the gap mentioned by Pierre Boulez.

Once again, I would like to refer to my experience as a teacher to illustrate the latter. The continuous change of gatis or irregular groupings common in western music from the 1950s onwards is again completely ingrained in our system. On the other hand it is precisely the fact that two consecutive steps in karnatic music need a common denominator that has enabled karnatic music to construct a highly sophisticated creative and practice methodology.

I have advocated for a change in the current rhythmical solfege imparted in music centres so that musicians begin to better perform existing contemporary music. Most creators who have studied karnatic rhythm for at least two years have acknowledged that using the common denominator approach provided by nadai bhedam and combinations anuloma-pratiloma is the best way if they want their music to be performed as intended, and simultaneously to achieve more rhythmical cohesiveness. The main conclusions that many of my students and I have reached are:

- Unless there is a much closer relationship between what performers study and what creators compose or improvise, the gap between both worlds will most likely be perpetuated.
- It may not only fall to the performers to close this gap by improving their rhythmical accuracy. It may also fall on creators' shoulders to create complexity that can on one hand be studied methodically by performers, and that on the other hand could have a rhythmical coherence departing from the 'numbers against numbers' approach.

Therefore, I do not question the musical value of random metre changes or a lack of the use of a common denominator. I have reservations regarding the feasibility of blending karnatic techniques simultaneously with these notions without sacrificing the enrichment possibilities that the karnatic rhythmical system can provide.

As a way of summarising my research and its aims I would like to conclude with the following. The study of karnatic rhythm, as presented in this volume, does not have as a goal the performance of karnatic music, but rather its *integration within a western framework*. The ultimate aims, after a process of internalising all rhythmical techniques, are:

- a rapid translation and application of these techniques to existing western music (performers);
- a clear understanding of the architecture of the techniques, followed by an imaginative and innovative integration of these techniques into the creator's music vocabulary (composers and improvisers).

To study these techniques as an 'exotic' curiosity of another culture, or as an interesting collection of concepts totally unrelated to us, falls far short of these aims. The complete assimilation of these techniques can only occur when they become part of our culture via an ample revision of how rhythm is taught (and I would daresay conceived) in the West.

Appendix
Sources of Information

Classes

My main sources of information have been the daily classes with Jahnavi Jayaprakash during the period 1993–97 at her home in Bangalore or when she gave seminars at the Conservatorium van Amsterdam (1998–2002). Besides these lessons, I also took many classes from the percussionists N.G. Ravi (1993–97) and B.C. Manjunath (2002–12). A few very valuable sessions were held with percussionists A.R.A.K Sharma, Rajakeishari, Karaikkuddi Mani and Chander Shaker. I also had the fortune of meeting Dr Balamuralikrishna twice, which helped me to better understand his innovative ideas in the fields of tala prastara and how he conceived his mukhy system that has come to be the trigger for many new developments in karnatic music, as explained in Chapters 22–3.

While staying in India I attended innumerable rehearsals and concerts, where I was always asked to analyse the content of the rhythmical as well as the melodic structures. Attending rehearsals – whether for concerts, dance programmes or operas, or to make recordings (in Bangalore or the Netherlands) – was very inspiring. I was able to observe how the musicians were creating on the spot and discuss developmental possibilities and a wide array of creative issues.

Written Sources

Although my research has been essentially in the field, I consider it important in the context of this volume to provide examples of the literature available and the books that have helped me obtain a better understanding of the world of karnatic rhythm.

Sangeetha Akshara Hridaya: A New Approach to Tala Calculations by Vidwan S.R. Iyer (Bangalore: Gaana Rasika Mandali, 1988, revised 2000).

This book opened a big window to understanding the world of *motta kannakku*, as covered in Chapters 18–21. It explained the world of superimpositions, and the importance of the common denominator as a guiding tool for performance and practice is exposed with enough clarity to make me wonder about the ideas it expounded and enquire more of my main teachers. For reasons I will never understand, karnatic musicians are quite reluctant to provide westerners with information about this huge body of concepts (as my students found out when they went to India). Fortunately, Iyer's book provides sufficient information on this issue, once one has been able to assimilate the 'jungle' of terms and the non-Cartesian mode of explanation that characterises karnatic musicians and academics.

Permutative Genius in Tala (-Prastara) in South Indian Music by Akella Mallikarjuna (Hyderabad: Telugu University Press, 1992).

This highly complex book (I needed to read it three times before I began to really understand the implications and theories exposed in it) opened the path to comprehending the full potential of what Dr Balamuralikrishna initiated in the 1960s: the construction of new talas with logic and a system, and how techniques that have been born and developed within the *tala* system explained in Chapter 1 (*suladi talas*) have been adapted to the new possibilities presented by the ideas he conceived and developed (as explained in Chapters 22–3).

The Theory and Practice of Mridangam by Dharmala Ramamurty. Published by the author in 1973, revised 1987 and with a final revision by his son Ramamurty Rao in 2001.

This is the most 'practical' book available in English. Although with many explanations addressed at *mridangists* (the *mridangam* is the most important percussion instrument in South India) regarding fingering and other technical issues, this book includes a wealth of phrases in a variety of techniques described in the first 17 chapters of the current volume. Notwithstanding the lack of theoretical explanation of any technique and that all phrases are written using highly sophisticated karnatic notation, once I overcame these difficulties I found a fountain of phrases and an underlying logic, exposition of exceptions and combinations between techniques (as explained in Chapters 13–16) that were certainly of great help. However, I should mention that unless one has knowledge of how these techniques are constructed, the book would only provide the westerner with hundreds of phrases/structures, without any background to clarify the reasons behind their existence (besides the already mentioned difficulty of having to learn the karnatic notational system to a very high level).

Tala Sangraha: Compendium of Talas in Karnatak Music by B.M. Sundaram (Bangalore: Percussive Arts Centre, 1987).

This book in a clever compilation of theoretical possibilities of *tala prastara* based on the premises invented and developed by Dr Balamuralikrishna, as explained in Chapter 22. It provides thousands of talas by working out combinations and permutations derived from the *mukhy* system (see Chapter 23). I doubt that many karnatic musicians would use this book for any practical purposes, and it would be of no use to westerners unfamiliar with the system Balamuralikrishna produced in the 1960s–1990s. This is information I only learnt in a more or less clear form in 2010, after more than 17 years of research and 14 of teaching.

These are the only four books I could find of real help, and then only after struggling with many handicaps such as terminology, roundabout ways of explaining concepts and a lack of background information.

The following books provided some rather superficial comment on some of the techniques covered in this volume.

South Indian Music by P. Sambamurty (6 vols, Madras: Indian Music Publishing House, 1947).

This has gone through multiple revisions since the first edition and is considered the most important book on karnatic music covering the basics. With chapters such as 'Music and Health' and similar matters not directly concerning pure karnatic theory and practice, this book is compulsory reading in all music universities in South India, possibly more because it was the first attempt to establish some written material on karnatic music than for its actual musical value. Dedicated mostly to ragas and a superficial explanation of forms, Professor Sambamurty only superficially mentions the topics covered in Chapters 1–3 and Chapter 9 of the present text. For example, he refers several times to *mukthays* without offering any explanation regarding the many different types or providing any instructions as to how to construct them. Nonetheless, this source was quite useful at the very beginning of my studies.

A Rational Approach to Manodharma Sangitam by Radha Venkatachalam (Music Education Trust, 2001).

Manodharma means improvisation. Due to the importance of improvisation in karnatic music and the vast number of rules of construction, proportionalities and techniques that can and cannot be used in an improvised section, I found this book interesting in order to see how the rhythmical concepts are interwoven with other rules pertaining to a particular section of improvisation. Possibly a great help for Indian (or western) students who have started working on improvisation, it has provided more help to me as a musician and as a teacher of improvisers than is reflected here.

Recorded Material

I would like to distinguish between two different sources. Firstly, self-made recordings of concerts and rehearsals (live or in the studio) not commercially available, as well as many selected recordings of live performances provided by Bhanu Prakash (the son of my main teacher) and B.C. Manjunath; secondly, commercial CDs and tapes acquired in India (some without credits except for the name of the main artist).

Recordings Not Commercially Available

Studio recordings with Jahnavi Jayaprakash, Hemanth Kumar and Shri Hari, Bangalore, August 1995.

Studio recordings with Jahnavi Jayaprakash, Rajakeishari, Shri Hari and Shridart, Bangalore, August 1997.

Live recordings with Jahnavi Jayaprakash, Rajakeishari, Shri Hari and Hemanth Kumar at the Conservatorium van Amsterdam, April 1998.

Live recordings with Jahnavi Jayaprakash, Rajakeishari, A.P. Sarvothama and Shridart at the Conservatorium van Amsterdam, January 2000.

Studio recordings with Jahnavi Jayaprakash and B.C. Manjunath. Preparation of material for my piece 'Sranang Tongo' for the Amsterdam Percussion Group and these two musicians. Bangalore, December 2000.

Live recordings with Jahnavi Jayaprakash and B.C. Manjunath at the Bimhuis, Amsterdam, May 2001.

Studio recording of the soundtrack of a Madras film (completely unrelated to the Bollywood trend), composed by Jahnavi Jayaprakash for 8 singers, 4 violinists, 4 flautists, 4 nagaswaram players and 8 percussionists (possibly one of the most complex pieces of music I have ever heard). Madras, December 2001.

Live recording with Jahnavi Jayaprakash, B.C. Manjunath and Shridart with Turkish musicians at the Felix Meritis Theatre (Amsterdam), April 2002.

Mp3 collection of more than 100 examples provided by Bhanu Prakash of what he would describe as 'the best of', with live performances by Dr Balamuralikrishna, Mysore Brothers, T.N. Seshagopalan, B.N.S. Praveen, Hyderabad Brothers, Lalgudi Jayaram and D.K. Pattamal.

Mp3 compilation provided by B.C. Manjunath of more than 40 pieces in the form called *ragam-tanam-pallavi* (considered the pinnacle of complexity in karnatic music; each piece lasts 45–90 minutes).

Compilation of mridagam, kanjeera and tavil solos and duets made by Bhanu Prakash, featuring solos between 1997 and 2005 by Palghat T.S. Mani Iyer, Sivaraman, Palghat R. Raghu, Karaikkuddi Mani, N.G. Ravi, Pravesh Tani and Trichy Sankaran.

Video of a live concert by Karaikkuddi Mani (mridangam) and Harakrishna (kanjeera) in a temple in Madras, 2001.

Live recording of a concert by Kalavathy group with compositions by A.R.AK. Sharma and B.C. Manjunath at the Tropen Museum (Amsterdam, Netherlands, 2005).

Commercially Available Recordings

Here I would again like to distinguish between sources of *information* and of *inspiration*. The following were sources of information:

'Bharatanatyam', by Jahnavi Jayaprakash, released by the Italian CD label Stradivarius in 1999.
Live recording at the Reformist Church of Haarlem (Netherlands) in May 1997. Jahnavi Jayaprakash is the main artist. Released by VPRO classics.
CD 'Legacy', released by Karnatic Lab records in 2007 on the 5th anniversary of Jahnavi Jayaprakash's death.

The following were sources of inspiration:

Latangi, by N. Ravikiran (Digital Work Station, 2000).
Live recording by Mallikarjun Mansur (label and year unknown).
CD 'Live Music Academy' with T.N. Seshagopalan and Karaikkuddi Mani (Madras, 2003, Sony Music).
Series of tapes by Trichy Sankaran featuring various percussion instruments recorded to a metronome. Recorded in Toronto (Canada) between 1993 and 1995 (label unknown).
CD 'Raga Aberi' by L. Shankar (ECM Records, 1995).
Tape of an LP by L. Subramanian (label and year unknown).
Tape of 'Varnam Bhairavi' by L. Subramanian, L. Shankar and Vidjanathavi (violin) (label and year unknown).
CD 'Live at the Music Academy' by T.N. Seshagopalan (Madras, 1992, Sony Nad).
CD 'Live at the Music Academy', by D.K. Pattamal (Madras, 1989, Sony Nad).
CD 'Kiravani', by P. Unnikrishnanan (Digital Work Station, 1999).
CD 'Live at the Music Academy' by Alathur Srinivasa Iyer, L.Subramanian and T.S. Mani Iyer (Madras, 2001, Sony Nad).

Index

adi tala 16, 174, 264, 279, 293–6
amalgamation, inner 69, 71, 327, 445
amalgamation, outer 73, 393
Amsterdam conservatoire vii, 1, 3–4, 29, 365, 443–45
angas xi, xii, 13, 14, 19, 255–7, 259–62, 271–2, 423
anudrutam xi, 14, 19, 256, 259, 261
anuloma xi, 25, 72, 81–4, 86, 89, 101–3, 144, 168–70, 183, 213–6, 219, 221–2, 224, 226–7, 233–5, 240, 245–6, 250–1, 272, 280, 283, 289, 294, 296, 337, 344, 353, 365, 392, 396–7, 399, 400, 444, 447–8

Balamuralikrishna, Dr. ix, xi, xii, 228, 263–4, 271, 451–4
Bhedam xi, 45 (*see* gati *bhedam,* jathi *bhedam,* nadai *bhedam* and mixed jathi nadai *bhedam)*
Boulez, Pierre 2, 443, 448

Carter, Elliot 2, 329
Castiglioni, Niccoló 334, 336
chapu talas xi, 13, 17, 19, 20, 149, 228, 263, 272, 279, 287, 296
chatusra xi, 14–6, 21–2, 35, 38–41, 43–4, 47–9, 51–4, 56–7, 61–5, 69–71, 73–6, 78, 8103, 86, 93, 102, 109, 113, 123, 137, 144, 153, 155, 163, 166–70, 173–5, 177–8, 180, 183–90, 192–3, 195, 198, 206–9, 213–4, 217, 220, 222, 226, 232, 236–8, 240–3, 248, 256, 260–1, 282–3, 285, 294–5, 317–8, 322–4, 326, 331, 334–5, 447, 339–42, 345, 348, 350–1, 360, 366–9, 425
combinations anuloma-pratiloma xi, 82–4, 181, 200, 205, 213, 215, 219, 223–5, 228, 232, 240, 245, 249, 256, 264, 271, 280–4, 286, 321, 322, 334–6, 344, 353, 360, 395, 397, 425–6, 447–8
common denominator 4, 6, 13, 38, 51–2, 57, 89, 93, 133, 224–8, 446–8, 451
common reference 13, 338
compound mukthay xi, 129, 130–2, 141, 145–6, 153–5, 164, 170, 372
compound-related 164, 169, 286
cycle xiii, 13, 17–9, 26, 41–2, 54, 69–71, 74–6, 86, 93, 100, 106, 108–9, 113, 115–6, 118, 123, 126–7, 129, 132, 135–7, 139, 142–5, 147, 149, 151, 155–6, 159, 161–5, 171, 173–6, 180, 194, 228, 245, 247, 249, 250–1, 255–6, 260, 271, 279, 285, 289, 295, 302, 328, 340, 345, 351, 353, 366, 368, 369, 392–6, 398–9, 422–3, 446–7

damaruyati xi, 110, 227
drutam xi, 14, 16, 19, 41–2, 256, 259, 261–2, 272, 293–5

eduppu 163

gati xi, xii, xii, xiv, 17–8, 22, 29–34, 36, 55, 59–60, 67–8, 70, 73, 75, 79–80, 83, 106, 112, 117, 125–9, 131, 133, 140–52, 154–7, 160–3, 165–7, 169–72, 179, 182, 186, 195–7, 204–5, 207–8, 211–2, 214, 218, 229–31, 236, 238–9, 242, 252, 254–79, 281–3, 287–8, 297–316, 319–21, 323, 325–6, 328–9, 335, 338–9, 342, 435–9, 351–2, 354, 357–8, 361–7, 369–95, 401–25, 427–47
gati 11 290–2

gati 13 291–2
gati bhedam xii, 7–8, 45–9, 51–5, 57, 65, 69–71, 78, 86, 88, 93, 99, 100, 163, 183, 189, 190, 193, 195, 203, 209, 222, 2267, 246, 248–9, 264, 286, 289, 330, 334, 445, 447
gati bhedam, tree 51–5, 65–6, 86, 195, 209, 226–7, 286, 230
gati/jathi combination xiii, 35, 37–9, 41–6, 51, 53–4, 56–7, 65, 88, 183–5, 189–90, 195, 200, 216, 233–3, 322, 324, 326, 332, 339–40, 356
gopuchayati xii, 107–10, 135–9, 144–5, 149

inner pulse 7
irregular groupings 72, 83, 185, 189, 214–5, 232, 250, 321, 334, 335, 336, 444, 447–8
Ives, Charles 69, 332

jathi xii, 35–49, 51–4, 56–7, 61–6, 70–8, 88, 100–3, 137, , 144, 153–5, 183–5, 188–90, 192–5, 201, 203, 207–9, 216, 222, 226–7, 234, 240, 248, 294–5, 322–3, 326–7, 330, 332–5, 339–41, 343, 345, 351, 425
jathi bhedam 8, 70–8, 86, 93, 95–7, 121, 163, 190–1, 193, 197, 225–6, 228, 264, 283, 286–7, 289, 293–4, 325–8, 334–5, 341–3, 351, 360, 365, 392, 444–5
jati laghu xii, 14, 260–3, 271
Jayaprakash, Jahanavi ix, 3, 116, 228, 264, 451, 454–5

kala xii, 256–7, 259–60, 263–4, 266, 282, 286–7, 360
Kalavathy ix, 454
Karaikkudi Mani ix, 228
Khanda xii, 14–6, 19–21, 23, 26–6, 28, 35, 38–41, 43, 45–7, 49–54, 56–7, 61–4, 70–3, 76, 78, 81–3, 86, 88–9, 97–103, 109, 123–4, 132, 144, 151, 153–4, 156, 158, 168–70, 173, 175, 178, 180, 183, 185–9, 192–3, 195, 198–9, 206, 208, 214–6, 218–20, 222, 226, 228, 233–4, 236–7, 239, 241–3, 246, 248, 260–1, 264, 272, 282,-4, 289, 293–4, 217, 322–3, 330, 333, 335, 337, 339–44, 360, 368–9, 398, 400, 423–5
konnakkol xii, xiv, 21–2
krama xii, 115, 117, 125–6, 137–9, 143
kriya xii, 19, 256, 263–4, 266, 271–2, 281

laghu xii, 14–6, 19, 256, 260–4, 271–2
laya xii, 17, 38, 43, 45–6, 84, 183–4, 188, 190, 193–4, 197–9, 206, 330
Le Sacre du Printemps 69, 327
Ligeti, György 2, 326, 329, 445

Manjunath, B.C. ix, 3, 54, 86, 165, 240, 264, 286, 296, 336, 451, 453–4
matra xi-xv, 21–3, 27, 35, 43, 45–8, 57, 61–5, 69–73, 75–8, 81–5, 88–90, 93–5, 97–102, 105–11, 113–24, 126–37, 139, 141–6, 148, 150–1, 153–7, 159, 163–71, 173, 175, 179–80, 185, 199–4, 198, 200–1, 203, 206, 208–10, 213, 226, 228, 234–5, 237, 239–40, 245–51, 256–7, 259–61, 263–4, 280, 282, 285–6, 292–5, 317, 322–3, 326–31, 334–6, 339–41, 343–5, 356, 359, 360, 366–7, 371–2, 392–3, 396, 398, 424–5
Messiaen, Oliver 246, 325, 327, 445
metrical modulation 329–30, 339, 392–3
misra xii, 14, 19, 21, 24, 26, 28, 38–41, 43–4, 47, 51–4, 56–7, 81–2, 84, 88–90, 99, 100, 102, 132, 137, 151, 155–6, 158, 183, 185–8, 198–200, 208, 213, 215, 218, 221, 223, 226, 228, 233, 236–7, 239, 241–3, 247, 260–1, 272, 282, 285, 296, 333, 337, 368–9, 423–4
mixed gati mohara xiii, 176, 227, 292, 296, 368
mixed jathi nadai bhedam xii, 137, 205–7, 209, 215, 222, 240, 286, 296, 369, 422–3, 425, 447
mohara xii, 173–6, 264, 272, 284–5, 292, 365, 369, 392, 398–400, 447
motta kannakku xiii, 6, 181, 451
mridangam 22, 452, 454
mridangamyati 107–10, 227, 366, 395

mukhy system xiii, 263–4, 266, 271–2, 280, 284, 398, 400, 451–2
mukthay xi, xiii, xiv, xv, 7, 8, 75–7, 93–103, 105–11, 125–6, 133–4, 141–6,163–4, 169–71, 174–8, 180–1, 190–1, 1934, 226–7, 285–6, 289, 292, 356, 368–9, 372, 392, 395–6, 398, 400, 422, 447, 453
mukthay combination xiii, 133, 145–59, 164, 168, 227, 365, 370, 392

nadai xiii, 183–5, 189–95, 197–201, 203, 332–3, 360, 368–9, 423–4, 426
nadai bhedam xii, xiii, 181, 183–5, 187–94, 197–203, 213, 215–7, 222–3, 232–5, 239–40, 280, 284, 286, 290, 321–2, 332–40, 342, 344, 366–7, 392, 425–6, 444, 447–8
'numbers against numbers' 81, 322, 447–8

pala xiii, xiv, xv, 93–103, 105–59, 164, 166–70, 191, 226–7, 367, 370–73, 398
palindrome 109–10, 336
permutations xiv, 122, 130, 236–8, 240, 452
phrasing through gati changes 176, 286, 292, 295, 331, 397–8
phrasing with gatis 22, 25, 28, 286, 292
polypulse xiii, 3, 17, 39, 43, 49, 53, 183–4, 189–91, 198, 280–1, 322, 337, 340, 425–6, 447
polyrhythm 3, 17, 38–43, 53–4, 62, 65, 195, 340, 349, 366, 445
polytempi 49, 205, 337–8, 349
poruttam A xiii, 161–5, 168, 171, 227, 286
poruttam B 161, 249
pratiloma xi, xiii, 25, 81–4, 86, 88–9, 183, 213–6, 219–22, 226–7, 233–5, 240–1, 245–6, 250–1, 272, 280, 283, 296, 330, 337, 341–2, 365, 392, 396–7, 399, 400, 444, 447–8
Purandaradasa xiii, xiv, 15, 255–6, 262
Purvanga xiii, 123–4, 126, 245–8

Quatuor pour la fin du temps 325, 445

Raga xiii, 4, 15, 392, 453–5
Rajakeishari ix, 451, 455
Ravi, N.G. ix, 228, 451, 454
rhythmical sangati xiii, 55, 61, 63–6, 86, 96–7, 129, 168, 176, 209, 226–7, 272, 293–5, 359, 369, 447

sam xiii, xiv, 16–7, 19, 26, 41–2, 54, 69–70, 75–7, 86, 93–5, 97–8, 100, 105, 107, 109, 113, 116, 121, 123, 126, 135–7, 144, 149, 161, 163–4, 171, 192–4, 197, 209, 219, 226–7, 263–4, 271–2, 279–80, 293–4, 366, 369
sama mukthay 93–100, 105, 107, 114–5, 121, 134, 136, 141–2, 147–9, 151–6, 159, 164, 226, 395, 398
samayati 105, 135–9, 227, 367, 395
Sankaran, Trichy 454–5
sankirna xii, 14–16, 19, 21, 260–1, 289–90, 292, 339
seed phrase xi, 129–33, 141, 146, 151, 153–5, 164, 166, 169–70, 227
Seshagopalan, T.N. ix, 228, 454–5
shadanga tala xii, 15, 255–7, 260–1, 263, 271, 351, 353, 360, 392, 398, 400
Shankar, L. 266, 455
Sharma, A.R.A.K ix, 272, 301, 451, 454
solkattu xii, xiv, 4, 21–2, 25, 27, 37–8, 116, 331
srotovahayati xiv, 105, 107–11, 135, 139, 143, 150–1, 157–8, 164, 166–9, 367, 370–2, 395
Stravinsky, Igor 69, 327–8, 444
sub-mukthay xiv, 133, 141, 149–50, 164, 169–70, 370–1, 373
suladi talas xiii, xiv, 13, 15, 17, 51, 255–6, 260–4, 266, 271–2, 279–80, 282–3, 287, 366, 394, 446, 452
superimposed xii, xiii, 136–8, 183–4, 188–9, 193, 200, 205–8, 210, 215, 219, 227–8, 237, 245–5, 280, 283, 333–4, 339, 342, 344, 369, 423
superimpositions 138, 342–4, 444, 451

tala xi-xiv, 3–5, 13–20, 26, 41–3, 52–4, 69–71, 74–7, 86, 93–104, 105, 107, 109, 111, 113, 115–6, 118–9, 121, 123, 126–7, 129–37, 139, 141–5,

147–9, 151, 155–6, 159, 161–4, 171, 173–8, 192–5, 197, 199, 209, 219, 226–8, 245, 247, 250, 253, 255–7, 259–60, 262–4, 266, 271–2, 278, 280–7, 292–4, 296, 302, 328, 338, 345, 350, 351, 353, 366, 369, 392–4, 398–9, 423, 446, 451–2
tala combination 279, 287, 296
tala prastara 13, 255, 263, 271, 286, 351, 446, 451–2
three-fold mukthays 93, 99, 100, 115, 164, 199, 286
tirmana xiii, xiv, 123–8, 131–3, 137, 141–2, 145–7, 149, 153–5, 164, 287, 245–9, 264, 286, 367, 370, 373, 392, 447
tisra xiv, 14–6, 19, 21–4, 26, 28, 37–41, 43–7, 51–4, 63–4, 71, 73, 78, 81–3, 88, 101–3, 116, 118, 129–31, 151, 153–6, 158, 177–8, 183, 185–9, 192, 195, 198–9, 201, 206–8, 211–1, 216–7, 221–2, 225–6228, 232, 234, 235–8, 241–3, 246, 248, 260–1, 264, 272, 280, 282–3, 289, 293–5, 317, 322–3, 326–7, 329–30, 332–4, 339, 341–4, 348–51, 360, 367, 371, 398, 400, 423, 425

uttaranga xiv, 123–6, 227, 245–9

vakra xiv, 115–7, 125–6, 137, 168, 170, 373
viloma xiv, 108–10, 115–7, 125–6, 137–9, 143, 168, 371, 395

Xenakis, Iannis 2, 46, 334–5, 337–9; 343, 443, 445

yati mukthays 113–22, 135, 137, 148, 159, 164, 168, 264, 394
yati phrases ix, xv, 7, 105–114, 120–1, 135, 137, 141, 158, 164, 190–1, 286, 289, 365–6, 392, 394–5, 422
yatis prastara xv, 105, 136–9, 141, 143–4, 164, 227, 272, 286, 367

Zappa, Frank 332–4
Zwaanenburg, Jos vii, ix, 329–30

Made in the USA
Monee, IL
12 October 2021

79864705R00262